REAL ECONOMICS FOR REAL People

Charles L. Ballard

Addison Wesley Longman

Pearson Custom Publishing

Please visit our web site at www.pearsoncustom.com

ISBN 0–536–61334–6

BA 992373

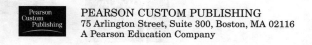

PEARSON CUSTOM PUBLISHING
75 Arlington Street, Suite 300, Boston, MA 02116
A Pearson Education Company

ACKNOWLEDGEMENTS

This book has had a complicated history. As such, it could not have been produced without the involvement of a large number of people. I would first like to thank Jack Greenman of Harper Collins College Publishers, who provided the original inspiration for a new textbook. It was my pleasure to work with the editorial staff at Harper Collins, which also included Bruce Kaplan, Arlene Bessenoff, and Sharon Balbos. The editors at Harper Collins worked with me, and with my former co-authors, Jim Breece and Dominick Salvatore, to give the book its initial shape. I would also like to thank Cara Warne for providing encouragement and fostering communication.

In 1996, Addison Wesley Longman acquired the college division of Harper Collins. Although I was sad that the relationship with Harper Collins had to be severed, I enjoyed my association with the editorial staff at Addison Wesley, including Lena Buonanno, Rebecca Ferris, and Sylvia Mallory. However, when the management of Addison Wesley decided to terminate the contract in 1998, I found myself with an advanced draft of a textbook, but with no publisher. Fortunately, in 1999, I came into contact with Allen Kozlowski of Pearson Custom Publishing. I would like to thank Allen, and also Dave Gehan, for helping to bring this book over its final hurdle.

Of course, this book has also benefited tremendously from my experiences in the classroom at Michigan State University. I would like to thank all of the students and Teaching Assistants who have contributed to the process over the years. And I would like to thank my colleagues, who have provided so many valuable ideas about teaching. Special thanks to Byron Brown, Dan Hamermesh, Carl Liedholm, Larry Martin, and Steve Woodbury.

And finally, I would like to thank the people who are most important of all: Anne and Mark and Scott, Mary Fran and Don, and, most especially, Michael, Andy, Jonathan, Mark, and Shirley.

East Lansing, Michigan
July 13, 2000

Contents

Chapter 1

What Is Economics, Anyway?

ECONOMICS AND YOU: DECISIONS, DECISIONS, DECISIONS

The alarm clock just went off. Amy Neyland is lying in bed, struggling to decide whether to get up. She can stay in bed, or she can get up and get ready for work. If she stays in bed, she'll get a little more rest, but she won't have time for a shower and a cup of coffee. On the other hand, if she gets up, she'll be able to take the shower, drink the coffee, have some toast, and maybe even read the paper. But she will be a little more tired than she would have been, if she had stayed in bed.

Amy has only a limited amount of time. If she decides to spend the time in bed, she won't be able to have breakfast. If she decides to have breakfast, she won't be able to spend the time in bed. So, she will have to make a decision. She doesn't know it, but Amy's about to make an *economic* decision. Economics is fundamentally concerned with making decisions. We only have a limited amount of resources, and we have to make choices about how to use those resources, in an attempt to do our best in life. That is what economics is all about.

In fact, Amy will be making economic decisions all day long. At work, she'll have to decide whether to get a task done "in house",

or to contract with another company. On her lunch hour, she will have to decide whether to have a burger and fries, or a burrito, or fish and chips. After work, she'll go to the grocery store, and she will have to decide whether to buy more, or less, of each of a thousand items.

And so it goes all through the day. We all make decisions. Whether we know it or not, those decisions are central to the discipline called economics. In this book, you will have the opportunity to learn a lot about one important branch of economics, called microeconomics. Of course, whether you learn will depend on the decisions you make. No one is holding a gun to your head, forcing you to learn economics. You can choose to do nothing but eat, sleep, and watch TV. If so, you won't learn much economics. On the other hand, you can choose to read the book, and work the questions and problems. If so, you might not get to watch as much TV. It's your choice. And choice is one of the most important topics of economics.

Before this book is over, we will study the ways in which consumers make choices, about how much to buy, how much to save, how much to work. We'll also study the ways in which business firms make choices, about how much to produce, how many workers to hire, how many machines to use, and what prices to charge.

Important Issues Covered by This Book

Our study of decision making will prepare us to confront many of the most important policy issues of our time. For example, in Chapters 2 and 5, we will study international economics. *International economics* deals with why we import some goods from other countries, and export different goods to other countries. What will happen if the government levies a tariff, which is a tax on imports?

In Chapters 9–12, we will study the economics of industrial organization. For example, the *economics of industrial organization* deals with how the behavior of the firms in an industry would change, if they were to merge into one giant firm. What happens when the government regulates the firms in an industry? What types of industry are best for consumers?

Another important field of study is labor economics, which we will consider in Chapter 13. *Labor economics* is concerned with what happens in labor markets. For example, why do some people make high wages, while others make less? What are the effects of unions? What happens as a result of a minimum-wage law?

Toward the end of this book, in Chapter 16, we will take a look at public economics. *Public economics* deals with the causes and effects of government spending, and the taxes that are used to pay for government operations. Would it be better to rely more on taxes on labor income, or on corporate taxes, or on some other revenue sources?

The final chapter of the book, Chapter 17, deals with environmental economics. Using the tools of *environmental economics*, we will discuss how economic principles can be used to find ways to clean up pollution in the most efficient way.

How to Read This Book

Many of the people who read this book will be reading about economics for the first time. When you're exploring a new subject, it's important to have some idea of what approach to take. It is important for you to know that *it won't make sense to read this book like a novel*. Most novels can be read fast. If you try to go too fast in this book, everything will be a jumbled blur, and your understanding will be mushy, at best.

Some people think it's OK to settle for a superficial understanding. For a subject like economics, however, understanding the material at a superficial level is often the same as not understanding it at all. You will have to stop from time to time, to make sure that you *really* understand what you have read. For this reason, each chapter has "Interim Review Questions". (IR) It may be tempting to skip over these questions, but you'll be better off if you tackle them. The only way to be sure that you understand is to see whether you can answer the questions. At the end of each chapter, you will find more Questions and Problems (QP). You are urged to do these, too. As in most activities, the more you practice, the better you will be.

Often, the concepts introduced in one chapter will build upon the concepts that were developed in earlier chapters. Thus, it is really important to have a solid understanding, before moving on to the next chapter. Going forward in a steady, methodical way is the best way to master the material.

The last few paragraphs have stressed the importance of being slow and steady and careful. We hope that it has been possible to stress these things, without making it seem that economics is extremely difficult. Almost everyone who is serious about studying this material will be able to learn it. Introductory microeconomics is not rocket science.

Quantitative Skills

Since introductory microeconomics is not rocket science, it does not require sophisticated mathematics. This book does not have any calculus, or matrix algebra, or differential equations. However, we will use some basic algebra. We will also use *lots* of graphs.

Most people who read a book like this are college students. Almost all of these students have had a few years of algebra and geometry in middle school and high school. In most cases, students find that their mathematical background is more than enough to do well in an introductory microeconomics course.

However, a few of you may have been the kind of person who limped through high-school algebra. Then, at the end of your sophomore year of high school, you closed the algebra book and said "Hallelujah! I'll never have to do that again!". Now, it's three or four or five years later, and your quantitative skills are very rusty. If that's you, then it will be really important for you to brush up on your quantitative skills. The appendix to this chapter is designed to help you with that task. Even if you are pretty strong with algebra and graphs, it might not be a bad idea to look at the appendix. If you are weak with algebra and graphs, then it is essential that you study the appendix.

WHAT IS ECONOMICS?

Economics can be defined in several different ways. Here's one: *Economics* is the study of how people use their limited resources to satisfy unlimited wants. Here's another definition: Economics is the study of how a society chooses to use its scarce resources to produce, exchange, and consume goods and services.

The two definitions are not identical. However, they do have a lot in common. At the center of each definition is the idea that our resources are *scarce*, or *limited*. However, our desires are unlimited. The human imagination has an infinite capacity to dream. Wouldn't it be great to be sunning yourself on the beach in Hawaii, and eating a gourmet meal at a famous New York restaurant, and circling Saturn in a spaceship, all at the same time? Yes, it would be great. But, for better or worse, it can't be done. We are *constrained* by the limits on our resources. Therefore, we have to *choose*.

Three Fundamental Choices

In the chapters to come, we will discuss all sorts of choices. However, all of these choices can be considered as special cases of three *fundamental* choices. The three fundamental choices are (1) what to produce, (2) how to produce, and (3) for whom to produce.

What to Produce. Every society has to make choices about what to produce. Since our resources are scarce, we can't have everything that we would like. We can build more airliners, but devoting more resources to airliners may mean that we won't be able to build as many automobiles. So, the question is whether we shall build more airliners or more automobiles. Similarly, we can raise more chickens, but devoting more resources to raising chickens may mean that we won't be able to produce as much asparagus. Do we produce more chickens or more asparagus? Different societies make these choices in different ways. In simple tribal societies, many economic decisions are made by a chief, or by a council of tribal elders. In some countries, such as North Korea, most economic decisions are made by government officials. However, in the United States, most decisions are the result of interactions between buyers and sellers. Much of this book will be devoted to describing the process by which a modern industrial nation, such as the United States, makes its decisions about what to produce.

How to Produce. If a new highway were to be built in the United States, it would be built by a relatively small number of workers. Each worker would have a tremendous amount of equipment to work with, including graders, bulldozers, and trucks. On the other hand, if a new highway were to be built in a country like India, which has less heavy equipment but a very large population, it would probably be built with a relatively large number of workers. The workers would be more likely to use shovels and wheelbarrows, instead of gigantic earthmoving machines. This example illustrates the fact that it's possible to produce goods and services in a wide variety of ways. Therefore, it is necessary to make choices about how to produce.

Once again, different societies may make these choices in different ways. In this book, we will focus primarily on the way in which a modern industrial economy chooses how to produce. Usually, these choices are made by business firms, in a process that involves interactions with workers, and with the owners of machinery, equipment, energy, and materials.

For Whom to Produce. In parts of medieval Europe, the local lord was very wealthy, and the serfs had very little. In most countries today, the gap between rich and poor is not as great as it was then, but there are still huge differences between those at the top and those at the bottom. The distribution of income is largely determined by the interaction between employers and workers. Highly skilled workers can earn a lot of money, while less skilled workers earn less. The distribution of income is also determined by other interactions in the private economy, and by governments. When a government raises taxes from some people, and makes payments of Social Security, Medicare, Medicaid, and food stamps to other people, the government has an effect on the distribution of income.

There is no way to escape these three fundamental choices. *Every* society must decide what to produce, how to produce, and for whom to produce.

Microeconomics

Economics is divided into two broad branches—*micro*economics and *macro*economics. This book focuses on microeconomics. **Microeconomics** is concerned with the behavior of households and business firms, and the way in which they interact with each other in markets. The phrase "micro" means "very small". Microeconomics is concerned with households and business firms, because these are usually the smallest units that make decisions in the economy.

Just because microeconomics is concerned with the smallest decision-making units in the economy, it does *not* follow that microeconomics is somehow trivial or unimportant. In this chapter, we have already mentioned some of the issues that can be studied, using the tools of microeconomic analysis. These issues include taxes, policy toward international trade, government spending, regulation of businesses, environmental pollution, and the wage differences among workers. These are *not* small issues. These are issues that often find their way to the front page of the newspaper.

In addition, even though microeconomics deals with the smallest decision-making units in the economy, some of the units are very large indeed. Companies like General Motors, Exxon, General Electric, and AT&T have hundreds of thousands of employees, and they generate hundreds of *billions* of dollars of sales every year.

Macroeconomics

The other big branch of economics is macroeconomics. **Macroeconomics** is concerned with the aggregates for the economy as a whole, such as the overall rate of economic growth, the overall rate of unemployment, and the overall rate of inflation. "Macro" means very large, and it's appropriate that macroeconomics would deal with the totals for the economy. However, even when we study macroeconomics, microeconomics is never far away. After all, what are the totals? They are the sum of all of the little pieces. We get the overall rate of economic growth by putting together the rates of growth for all of the sectors of the economy. It would be wrong to think that microeconomics is completely different from macroeconomics. In many cases, microeconomics and macroeconomics use very similar tools.

Reality Check:
Interim Review Questions

IR1-1. What is economics?

IR1-2. Describe the difference between micro-economics and macroeconomics.

IR1-3. What are the three fundamental choices that every society must make?

THE ANALYTICAL PERSPECTIVE OF ECONOMICS

Before we go any further, it will be useful to give you a few ideas about how economists approach the world.

Positive Economics and Normative Economics

In most of this book, we are concerned with understanding how the economy works. When we think about the *actual workings* of the economy, we are concerned with *positive economics.* Here is an example of a prediction that could come from positive economics: "If the minimum wage is raised, there will be an increase in unemployment among teenagers." This statement is a *statement of fact.* If we can gather enough data, and analyze the data properly, we can show the statement to be right or wrong.

Positive economics deals with what *is.* In other words, positive economics deals with the *actual* workings of the economy. On the other hand, **normative economics** deals with what ought to be. Here is a statement that could come from normative economics: "It would be immoral for the minimum wage to be anything less than $7 per hour." Clearly, this normative statement involves a value judgment. As such, this statement cannot be

shown to be right or wrong. Some people may agree with it, and some may disagree. However, if one person insists that the "just" wage is $7 per hour, and another person disagrees, there is no way for one of them to prove that the other is wrong. It is merely a matter of opinion.

Economists have value judgments, like everyone else. Thus, economists can reach normative conclusions, just like everyone else. However, normative statements are not the economist's strong suit: Our normative opinions aren't any better than anyone else's normative opinions. Instead, our strength is in the area of positive economics. Economists' views about positive economics should be given special weight. Over the years, economists have developed a very useful framework for thinking about the actual, positive workings of the economy.

Since economists are on stronger ground when they talk about positive economics than when they offer normative opinions, and since this book is written by an economist, it is not surprising that this book will concentrate mostly on positive economics. Of course, value judgments will inevitably creep into the book. However, we will spend most of this book thinking about why prices are what they are. We won't spend as much time thinking about whether a price is "just" or "unjust", or "fair" or "unfair".

The Role of Models and Assumptions

The economy of the United States has more than 270 million people, divided into more than 100 million households. Each of these households makes dozens of economic decisions every day: Do we pay cash, or use the credit card? Do we buy hamburger or steak? Do we fill the tank with regular gasoline, or with premium? Do we buy another pair of jeans, or save the money for the future? Do we make a sandwich and take it to work, or do we buy lunch at a fast-food joint?

The economy that we observe is the result of *billions* of decisions that are made every day. There is no way to describe every one of these decisions in complete detail, or with complete accuracy. Because the economy is so large and so complex, we will have to rely on *models* of the economy.

Before we describe *economic* models, let's think about other kinds of model. If you go to a hobby store, you can buy a kit for a model automobile, such as a model version of a Porsche sports car. If you follow the instructions, and glue the pieces of the model together carefully, you will end up with a stylized representation of a Porsche sports car. It won't be a *real* Porsche. (For example, it won't be able to drive 140 miles per hour.) However, it will look a lot like a real Porsche. It will have two wheels on the front axle, and two wheels on the rear axle. The model will have the sleek styling that Porsche is famous for. Some models will be designed in such a way that you can turn the steering wheel, and get the model's wheels to turn. So, even though the model Porsche is not a real Porsche, it can still give a fairly decent idea of what a real Porsche is like.

Just as a model sports car is not a real sports car, an economic model is not a real economy. And yet, just as a model sports car can give some idea of what a real sports car is like, an economic model can give some idea of what a real economy is like. An *economic model* is a stylized representation of some aspect of the real economy.

When we construct an economic model, we know that we cannot hope to predict every single detail of what happens in the real economy. Thus, an economic model can be a good economic model, even if it doesn't get every single detail correct. Instead, we say that an economic model does a good job if it gives us a useful guide to thinking about an economic issue. If the model makes predictions that are pretty close to the mark, much of the time, it is a good model.

To decide whether a model is doing a good job, we have to see whether it is consistent with the facts. If we were physicists, or chemists, we would test our theoretical models in the laboratory. In a laboratory setting, it is possible to hold everything else constant, so that we can focus on one particular relationship. Physicists can perform laboratory experiments, because they are dealing with photons, or neutrons, or other particles and forces from the natural world. Chemists are able to perform laboratory experiments, because they are dealing with chemical compounds. However, for better or worse, economists are trying to understand the behavior of *people*. Therefore, economists are usually unable to perform laboratory experiments. Instead, we have to rely on statistical techniques to test our theoretical models. Economists gather data, from a wide variety of sources, and analyze the data. Often, the data reveal facts that aren't consistent with the theories. Then, it is necessary to refine our models, and test the new models against the data.

Thus, as economic science develops, there is a constant interplay between economic models and economic data. We develop models, and test them against data. Then, based on new insights from the data, we develop new models. Then, we test the new models against data. And so the process continues.

An Example of the Relationship Between Model and Data. Here is a story that illustrates the interplay between a model and the data that can be used to test the model. An economist tells the story of his younger daughter, Meredith, from the time when she was three years old. Meredith learned that she was soon going to see her grandmother. She didn't remember ever having seen Grandma before. Meredith began to ask questions of her father, in an attempt to get a better understanding of what Grandma might be like.

First, Meredith verifies her own age: Meredith is three years old. Then, she asks about her older sister, Stephanie, and learns that Stephanie is 10 years old. Then, she asks, "How old is Mommy?", and learns that her mother is 35. Then, she asks "How old are you, Daddy?", and learns that her father is 38. Finally, she asks "How old is Grandma?", and learns that her grandmother is 63.

Meredith thinks about all of this information, and says "Wow. Grandma must be VERY tall."

Let's think about Meredith's thought process. (1) She had probably developed her theory before she started to ask questions. Roughly speaking, her theory was that people continue to grow taller throughout their lives, so that older people are always taller than younger people. (2) With a theory in mind, Meredith collected data. She already knew that her father was the tallest member of her immediate family, followed by her mother, followed by her older sister, and she knew that she was the shortest member of the family. Then, she got the data on the ages of the individuals. (3) Next, Meredith tested her model against the data. In fact, the data provided support for her model: For these four people,

an increase in age was always accompanied by an increase in height. (4) On the basis of her model, Meredith formed a prediction about her grandmother's height. Since her model predicts that older people are taller, and since her grandmother is older, the model predicts that Grandma must be very tall.

Now, it turns out that Meredith's model is incomplete. But that doesn't mean that it was a bad model. In fact, it was a very good starting point. For one thing, Meredith's theoretical model has implications that are easy to test against data. For another thing, her model *is* consistent with much of the data on the heights and ages of people. Sooner or later, however, Meredith would observe data that do not fit well with her simple model. For one thing, she would find that her Grandma was *not* as tall as her father, even though her model would predict that Grandma would be much taller than Daddy. In order to explain these data, it would be necessary to develop a more refined model. A more complete model would need to account for a variety of facts, such as (1) most people stop growing taller in their late teens or early 20s, (2) on average, men reach an adult height that is taller than women, and (3) at any age, and for either gender, there is considerable variation in heights.

We have just described a process of scientific thought. The scientist begins by observing some facts, and develops a model to explain those facts. Then, the scientist tests the model against data. Often, the scientist will find that the model is consistent with some aspects of the data, but that some aspects of the data do not correspond very well to the model. Then, the scientist must go back and refine the model, and the process repeats itself.

Another Example. A similar process is followed in the economic literature. For example, since 1938, the United States has had minimum-wage laws, and economists have long been interested in the effects of these laws. The most popular theory *(which will be developed in Chapter 4 of this book) goes like this: Lots of people won't be affected by the minimum wage at all. If the minimum wage is $5.15 per hour, and if your employer is already paying you $10 per hour, then the law won't have any effect. However, if the wage that you would be paid (in the absence of the minimum-wage law) is $4 per hour, then the minimum-wage law might lead to unemployment.*

Over the years, dozens of research studies have attempted to get an idea of the size of the employment losses. These research studies have used all sorts of data. A few studies have even reached the absurd conclusion that the minimum wage *increases* employment. However, most studies have found that the minimum wage does reduce employment. In fact, some of the best of the recent studies suggest that the employment losses may be fairly substantial. When the minimum wage is increased, some workers do keep their jobs, and their wages go up. However, many workers lose their jobs, so that the total amount of wages paid to low-wage workers may not increase at all.

Each time a new study comes out, it gives us new evidence, and it forces economists to refine their models. The economic models of the minimum wage have been refined over the years, to consider (1) the fact that the law is sometimes ignored, (2) the fact that not all workers are covered by the minimum-wage law, (3) the fact that some States have higher minimum-wage laws than other States. The economy is very complex, and we can never hope to have a model that will explain every single effect of the minimum-wage laws. However, as we continue to gather more information, we can continue to gain a stronger understanding of the effects.

The Assumption of "All Else Equal"

When a natural scientist performs a laboratory experiment, the goal is to look at one relationship in isolation, while holding everything else constant. However, as we said earlier, it is usually impossible for economists to make controlled laboratory experiments. But we still want to concentrate on one influence at a time. Instead of holding everything else constant in a laboratory setting, we have to hold other things constant in other ways.

In this book, we will develop a number of economic models. In virtually every case, we will employ the *assumption* that all other things are equal. This is called the *ceteris paribus* assumption. **Ceteris paribus** is the Latin phrase that means "all other things equal".

In fact, all sorts of things are changing every day. If we did not employ the assumption of *ceteris paribus*, the world would be a blur, and it would be extremely difficult to make sense of things. Here is an example. In Chapter 13, we will see that people who work at dirty, dangerous jobs tend to earn higher wages, *all else equal.* However, this does *not* mean that people who work at dirty, dangerous jobs always earn more than people who work in clean, safe jobs. The reason is that wages are determined by *many* influences, including the skill level that is required on the job. Many of the most unpleasant jobs are also jobs that don't require a lot of skill. So, if we compare a worker in a poultry-processing plant (whose work is very unpleasant) with an accountant (whose work is clean and safe), we find that the accountant earns a higher wage. This is because it takes a lot more education, training, and skill to be an accountant than to be a poultry-plant worker.

Therefore, if we want to test the idea that people who work at dirty, dangerous jobs tend to earn higher wages, *all else equal,* we need to hold constant the skill level of the job. In statistical studies, this is done by including data on a whole host of variables, so that we can assess the influence of each variable, while holding constant all of the other influences.

Reality Check:
Interim Review Questions

IR1-4. Which of the following is a normative statement, and which is a positive statement? (a) If it gets too hot in the chicken-growing regions of Arkansas this summer, some chickens will die from the heat, and the price of chicken will increase. (b) Everyone should eat two pounds of chicken per week.

IR1-5. What does *ceteris paribus* mean?

IR1-6. Why is the *ceteris-paribus* assumption important?

ECONOMICS AND YOU:
DECISIONS, DECISIONS, DECISIONS

This chapter began by emphasizing that economics is concerned with how people make decisions, and with how those decisions interact with one another. Then, we surveyed some of the questions that can be addressed, using the tools of microeconomics. These include the behavior of large and small businesses, the buying behavior of consumers, the determination of wages and prices, the effects of taxes, tariffs, minimum-wage laws, and much, much more.

The next decision is up to you, the reader. You have to decide whether to read the rest of this book, or whether to devote your time to other activities. It is hoped that this chapter has stimulated your interest. Reading this book is like taking a journey. You'll find lots of interesting things along the way. Here's an invitation: Let's take this journey together.

Chapter Summary

1. Economics is the study of how people use their limited resources to satisfy unlimited wants. Similarly, economics can be defined as the study of how a society chooses to use its scarce resources to produce, exchange, and consume goods and services.

2. Microeconomics is the study of the decisions of households and business firms, and the interactions of those decisions.

3. The tools of microeconomic analysis can be used to study international economics (which deals with international trade, and the effects of policies that interfere with international trade), the economics of industrial organization (which deals with the way in which firms interact with one another and with their customers, and with government policies to control businesses), and labor economics (which deals with wage rates, participation in the labor force, labor unions, and policies such as minimum-wage laws). The tools of microeconomic analysis can also be used to study public economics (which deals with taxes and government spending) and environmental economics.

4. Macroeconomics is the study of the economy-wide aggregates, such as the overall rate of economic growth, or the overall rate of unemployment, or the overall rate of inflation.

5. Every society must make three fundamental choices: (a) What to produce, (b) How to produce, and (c) For whom to produce.

6. Positive economics is concerned with understanding the actual workings of the economy. In principle, positive statements can be proven to be right or wrong.

7. Normative economics is concerned with what ought to be. Therefore, normative statements involve value judgments. People can disagree about normative judgments, but it is not possible to prove normative statements wrong.

8. Because the economy is very complex, economists use models to represent some the workings of the economy. These models are tested against data, using statistical techniques. Then, the models are refined, and tested again.

9. In economics, it is usually impossible to perform controlled laboratory experiments. Therefore, it is especially important to perform thought experiments in which one variable is changed, while holding everything else constant. The assumption that all other things are the same is called the *ceteris-paribus* assumption.

Key Terms

Economics

Microeconomics

Macroeconomics

International Economics

Economics of Industrial Organization

Labor Economics

Public Economics

Environmental Economics

Positive Economics

Normative Economics

The Ceteris-Paribus Assumption

Questions and Problems

QP1-1. Which of these is a subject of microeconomics? Which is a subject of macroeconomics?

a. The overall rate of inflation.

b. The choice made by an individual household, regarding how many tacos to buy.
c. The overall rate of economic growth.
d. The wages paid by high-tech firms.

QP1-2. What is the difference between positive analysis and normative analysis?

QP1-3. What kinds of question are addressed by international economics? What about labor economics? How about the economics of industrial organization?

Appendix to Chapter 1:
A Brief Review of Graphs and Algebra

A few pages ago, we discussed the quantitative skills that are important for success in understanding introductory microeconomics. Here is part of what was said: "Since introductory microeconomics is not rocket science, it does not require sophisticated mathematics. This book does not have any calculus, or matrix algebra, or differential equations. However, we will use some basic algebra. We will also use *lots* of graphs."

Many readers of this book are very well-prepared in basic algebra, and are able to understand graphs. However, some readers may be rusty in their skills with algebra, and others may have trouble digesting information that is presented in the form of a graph. This appendix is designed to help anyone who wants to use this book, but it is especially aimed at those who may need to brush up on their quantitative skills. We begin with fractions, proportions, and percentages, and we review how to multiply and divide fractions. Then, we discuss the techniques for solving equations. Finally, we consider graphs. If you are strong in these areas, then you may want to go through this appendix fairly quickly. However, if your skills are out of shape, it will definitely be worthwhile to go through this appendix in detail.

FRACTIONS, PROPORTIONS, AND PERCENTAGES

In economics, we often relate the size of one quantity to the size of some other quantity. This can be done in different ways. In this book, we will use fractions, proportions, and percentages.

A *fraction* is one number divided by another number. For example, 1/2 and 3/4 are fractions.

A *proportion* expresses a fraction in decimal terms. For example, if we were to express 1/2 as a proportion, it would be 0.5. If we were to express 3/4 as a proportion, it would be 0.75.

A *percentage* is a proportion multiplied by 100. For example, if we were to express 0.5 as a percentage, it would be 50 percent, or 50%.

If we were to express 0.75 as a percentage, it would be 75 percent, or 75%.

In the preceding paragraphs, we have seen that 1/2 = 0.5 = 50%, and that 3/4 = 0.75 = 75%. Here are some other relationships:

$$1/20 = 0.05 = 5\%$$
$$1/10 = 0.1 = 10\%$$
$$1/5 = 0.2 = 20\%$$
$$1/4 = 0.25 = 25\%$$
$$1/3 = 0.3333 = 33.33\% \text{ (approximately)}$$
$$2/5 = 0.4 = 40\%$$
$$3/5 = 0.6 = 60\%$$
$$2/3 = 0.6666 = 66.66\% \text{ (approximately)}$$
$$4/5 = 0.8 = 80\%$$

MULTIPLICATION AND DIVISION OF FRACTIONS

To multiply one fraction by another, we multiply the two numerators by each other, and multiply the two denominators by each other, and then divide the product of the numerators by the product of the denominators. For example, $(1/3)x(1/2) = 1/6$, and $(2/5)x(3/4) = 6/20 = 3/10$.

To divide one fraction by another, it is useful to understand the concept of the reciprocal. The *reciprocal* of a fraction is the number which, when multiplied by the fraction, gives one. Thus, since $(1/2)x2 = 1$, we say that two is the reciprocal of one-half. Since $(2/3)x(3/2) = 1$, we say that 3/2 is the reciprocal of 2/3.

Now, let's divide by a fraction. Let's say that we want to divide one by one-half: $1 ÷ (1/2)$. We have seen that 2 is the reciprocal of 1/2. What would happen if we were to multiply both the numerator and the denominator of our expression by 2? This would preserve the value of the expression, because multiplying both the numerator and the denominator by 2 is the same as multiplying the entire expression by $(2/2) = 1$, and multiplying an expression by 1 will preserve its value.

So, our goal is to take $[1 ÷ 1/2]$, and multiply both the numerator and the denominator by 2. After multiplying by 2, the numerator would be $(1)x(2) = 2$. The denominator would be $(1/2)x(2) = 1$. This simplifies things greatly! When we multiply the denominator by its reciprocal, we get 1. Therefore, the value of the entire expression is equal to the numerator multiplied by the reciprocal of the denominator: $[1 ÷ 1/2] = 2$.

Sometimes, this procedure is called "invert and multiply". The more correct way to say it is "multiply by the reciprocal". Regardless of what we call it, the easiest way to divide by a fraction is to multiply by the reciprocal of the fraction. For example, $(1/2) ÷ (3/4) = (1/2)x(4/3) = 4/6 = 2/3$.

Reality Check:
Interim Review Questions

IR1A-3. What is the reciprocal of 3/7? What is the reciprocal of 9/4?

IR1A-4. What is $(2/3) ÷ (3/4)$?

SOLVING EQUATIONS

An Example

In this book, we will sometimes have occasion to solve a simple equation. For example, what if we want to solve the following equation for x:

$$z = x/2.$$

To solve for x, we need to get the x all by itself, so that it is no longer divided by 2. The way to do this is to multiply both sides of the equation by 2:

$2z = x(2/2) = x$. Therefore, $x = 2z$.

Example No. 2

Here is another type of equation that we will want to solve on occasion. Let's solve the following for y:

$$z = 3/y.$$

In this case, it will take two steps to solve for y. First, we need to get y out of the denominator of the right-hand side of the equation. To do this, we multiply both sides of the equation by y:

$$zy = 3.$$

Now, to finish the job of solving for y, we divide both sides of the equation by z:

$$y = 3/z.$$

Example No. 3

Finally, it will sometimes be useful to solve more than one equation at the same time. For example, let's say that we have the following two equations:

(1) $y = 100 - x$

and

(2) $y = 3x$.

In order to solve this system of two equations, we need to recognize that (100–x) and 3x are both equal to y. Therefore, we can form a new equation by substituting equation (2) into equation (1):

$$3x = 100 - x.$$

To solve this equation, the first step is to get all of the "x" terms on the same side of the equation. This can be done by adding x to both sides of the equation:

$$3x + x = 100 - x + x.$$

This can be simplified to say that $4x = 100$. Now, to solve for x, we divide both sides of the equation by 4:

$$x = 100/4 = 25.$$

So, x = 25 is the value of x that satisfies both equation (1) and equation (2). To check our work, we can substitute x = 25 into equation (1) and equation (2). In equation (1), we have:

$$y = 100 - x = 100 - 25 = 75.$$

In equation (2), we have

$$y = 3x = (3)(25) = 75.$$

This verifies that we have done the arithmetic properly. There is only one combination of values of x and y that satisfy both equation (1) and equation (2) at the same time. These values are x = 25 and y = 75.

Reality Check:
Interim Review Questions

IR1A-5. $y = (x/2) + 3$. Solve for x.

IR1A-6. $y = 10/x$. Solve for x.

IR1A-7. (a) $y = 10 - x$

    (b) $y = x$

Using (a) and (b), solve for the values of x and y that satisfy the two equations.

GRAPHS

Often, a picture is worth a thousand words. Economists find it useful to represent the relationships between variables in graphs, and we will use a large number of graphs in this book. For example, we will draw graphs of the relationship between the price of a good and the quantity of that good that buyers are willing and able to buy. We will also draw graphs of the relationship between the quantity of a good that is produced and the total cost of production. And these are just two of the many relationships that we will draw.

It is possible to draw a graph in more than two dimensions. However, all of the graphs in this book will be in two dimensions. In a two-dimensional graph, we represent the value of one variable on the *horizontal axis*, or *x-axis*, and we represent the value of another variable on the *vertical axis*, or *y-axis*. (Some people have trouble remembering the difference between horizontal and vertical. A good memory aid involves seeing that "horizontal" has the same root as "horizon". The horizon is flat, and the horizontal axis is flat, whereas the vertical axis goes straight up.)

Let's begin by writing down the values of two variables in a table, and then representing those values with a simple graph. In order to keep our focus on graphing techniques, we will use a (ridiculously) simple example. Table 1.1 shows the relationship between the number of people in a room and the number of hands in a room. If zero people are in the room, then zero hands are in the room. If one person is in the room, then two hands are in the room. If two people are in the room, then four hands are in the room. And so on.

Now, let's graph the information from Table 1.1. We put the number of people on the horizontal axis, or x-axis. We put the number of hands on the vertical axis, or y-axis. The first point that we graph is the point that corresponds to zero people and zero hands. This point is labeled as (0,0) in Figure 1.1. The first number in parentheses stands for the value of the variable on the x-axis, and the second number in parentheses stands for the value of the variable on the y-axis.

Next, we graph the point that corresponds to one person and two hands. This point is labeled as (1,2) in Figure 1.1. The rest of the

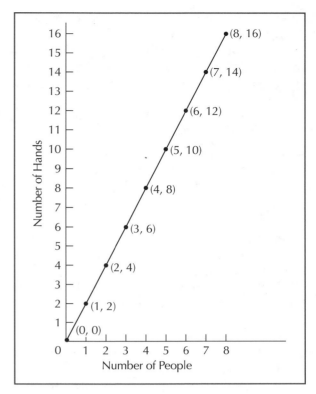

Figure 1.1 A Straight-Line Graph with Positive Slope

The number of people in a room is on the horizontal axis, and the number of hands is on the vertical axis. Because each person has two hands, the value on the vertical axis always increases by two, whenever the value on the horizontal axis increases by one. Therefore, the slope of the line is (2 ÷ 1) = 2.

points in Figure 1.1 are graphed in a similar manner.

The Slope of a Line

Every time the number of people in the room increases by one, the number of hands in the room increases by two. In other words, the ratio of the change in the number of hands to the change in the number of people is always two. This is an example of an important concept in graphing. When we interpret graphs, we are often interested in comparing the rate

Table 1.1 The Relationship Between the Number of People and the Number of Hands

Number of People	Number of Hands
0	0
1	2
2	4
3	6
4	8
5	10
6	12
7	14
8	16

of change of one variable with the rate of change in another variable.

The *slope of a line* is equal to the change in the value of the y variable, divided by the change in the value of the x variable. In other words,

slope = $\Delta y / \Delta x$,

where Δ (the Greek letter delta) stands for the change in the value of a variable. Another popular way to define the slope is to say that

slope = rise/run,

where the "rise" is the change in the value of the y variable, and the "run" is the change in the value of the x variable.

Let's calculate the slope for the graph in Figure 1.1. One point on the graph is (0,0), and another point is (1,2). Between these two points, the rise (the change in the value of the y variable) is (2 – 0) = 2. The run (the change in the value of the x variable) is (1 – 0) = 1. If we divide the rise by the run, we see that the slope of the line in Figure 1.1 is 2 ÷ 1 = 2.

In the case of a straight line, such as the one in Figure 1.1, the slope is constant. The slope of this line is 2, regardless of where we look along the line.

The Equation for a Line

We have used a graph to represent the relationship between the number of people and the number of hands. We can also represent the same information with an equation. In this case, the equation is

y = 2x,

where y is the y-variable (the number of hands), and x is the x variable (the number of people).

Table 1.2 has a set of numbers that are similar to those in Table 1.1. The only difference is that, if we use the same x value that was used in Table 1.1, the value of the y-variable is always greater in Table 1.2. The difference is always three.

Table 1.2	
x value	y value
0	3
1	5
2	7
3	9
4	11
5	13
6	15
7	17
8	19

Figure 1.2 is a graph of the numbers in Table 1.2. Once again, we have a straight line, with a slope of 2. However, the y values in Figure 1.2 are always three greater than the corresponding values in Figure 1.1.

It's especially important to focus on the value of y that occurs when the value of x is zero. In Figure 1.2, when x = 0, y = 3. When x = 0, the value of the y variable is called the *y intercept*, or *vertical intercept*.

We can express the line in Figure 1.2 using an equation. In this case, the equation is

y = 2x + 3.

In fact, any straight line can be expressed by an equation of this form. The general form for the equation for a straight line is

y = mx + b,

where y is the value of the variable on the vertical axis, m is the slope of the line, x is the value of the variable on the horizontal axis, and b is the vertical intercept. This equation can be used to describe *any* straight line.

A Straight Line with Negative Slope

In Tables 1.1 and 1.2, when the x value increases, the y value also increases. As a result, the graphs in Figures 1.1 and 1.2 slope upward as we move to the right. However, Table 1.3 shows the relationship between two other vari-

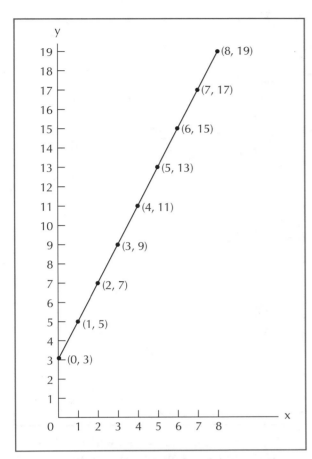

**Figure 1.2 Another Straight-Line Graph
with Positive Slope**

This graph is similar to the graph in Figure 1.1. In each of these graphs, the slope of the line is 2. The difference is that the vertical intercept is zero in Figure 1.1, while the vertical intercept is three in Figure 1.2.

ables, in which an increase in the x variable is accompanied by a decrease in the y variable.

The numbers in Table 1.3 are graphed in Figure 1.3. Since there is an inverse relationship between the x variable and the y variable in Table 1.3, the graph in Figure 1.3 slopes downward as we move to the right. In Table 1.3, whenever the x variable increases by one, the y variable decreases by 4. Therefore, the slope of the line is $\Delta y / \Delta x = -4/1 = -4$. The equation for this line is

$$y = -4x + 40.$$

Table 1.3	
x value	**y value**
0	40
1	36
2	32
3	28
4	24
5	20
6	16
7	12
8	8

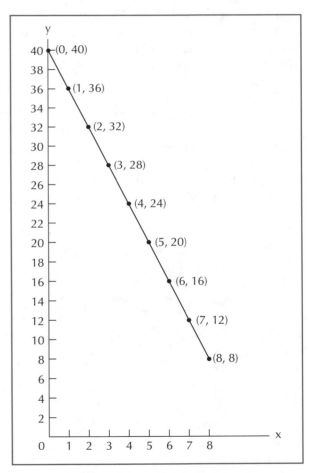

**Figure 1.3 A Straight-Line Graph
with Negative Slope**

In this graph, whenever the variable on the horizontal axis *increases* by one, the variable on the vertical axis *decreases* by four. Therefore, the slope of the line is $(-4 \div 1) = -4$.

Curved Lines

So far, all of our graphs have been straight lines. However, many relationships cannot be graphed as straight lines. An example can be found in Table 1.4 and Figure 1.4. Earlier in this chapter, we discussed the relationship between age and height. Table 1.4 shows this relationship for Kelly Morrison, who grows in fairly typical fashion. At birth, Kelly's height is 21 inches. She grows rapidly during childhood. However, the rate of growth is not constant. Therefore, the slope of the graph in Figure 1.4 is not constant. Kelly has one last major growth spurt in her early teenage years. After that, she experiences only a little more growth before she reaches her adult height of 67 inches (five feet, 7 inches).

Figures 1.5 and 1.6 show two other lines, of kinds that we will often see in this book. Figure 1.5 shows what we might call a "U-shaped" curve. At first, at low values of the x variable, the slope of the line in Figure 1.5 is negative. But then the curve flattens out. At point A, the curve reaches its minimum point.

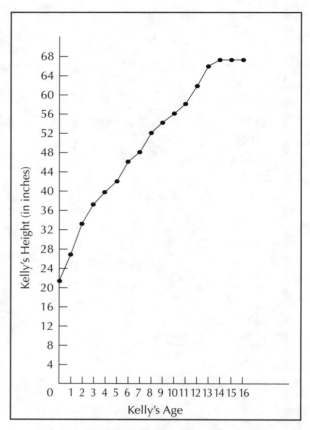

Figure 1.4 The Relationship Between Age and Height for Kelly Morrison

The graphs in Figures 1.1 through 1.3 have all been straight lines. However, this graph of the age-height relationship is not a straight line, since Kelly does not grow at a constant rate. Kelly eventually stops growing, so that the slope is zero after the age of 14.

At that point, the slope of the line is zero. As we move to the right of point A, the slope of the line is positive.

Figure 1.6 is what we might call an "inverse-U-shaped" curve. At low values of the x variable, the slope of the line in Figure 1.6 is positive. But then the curve flattens out, and reaches its maximum point at point B. At point B in Figure 1.6, the slope of the line is zero, just as it was zero at point A in Figure 1.5. As we move to the right of point B, the slope of the line is negative.

Table 1.4 The Relationship Between Age and Height for Kelly Morrison

Age	Height (in inches)
0 (birth)	21
1	27
2	33
3	37
4	40
5	43
6	46
7	48
8	52
9	54
10	56
11	58
12	62
13	66
14	67
15	67
16	67

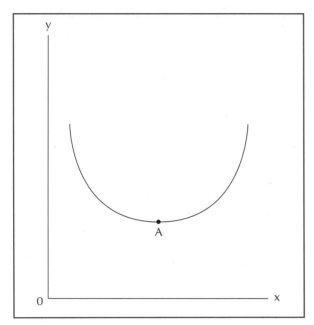

Figure 1.5 A Graph of a "U-Shaped" Curve

At low values of the variable on the horizontal axis, this curve has negative slope. (In other words, the curve slopes downward as we move to the right.) By point A, however, the curve flattens out, and has slope of zero. To the right of point A, the curve has positive slope.

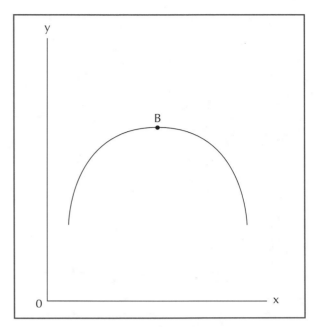

Figure 1.6 A Graph of an "Inverse-U-Shaped" Curve

At low values of the variable on the horizontal axis, this curve has positive slope. (In other words, the curve slopes upward as we move to the right.) By point B, however, the curve flattens out, and has slope of zero. To the right of point B, the curve has negative slope.

Two Intersecting Lines

Earlier in this appendix, we solved two equations simultaneously. The two equations were

(1) $y = 100 - x$

and

(2) $y = 3x$.

We used algebra to find that $x = 25$ and $y = 75$ are the values that satisfy both equation (1) and equation (2). We can also use graphs to find these values of x and y.

In Figure 1.7, we draw graphs of equations (1) and (2). Since equation (1) has negative slope and equation (2) has positive slope, it is not surprising that the lines cross. They cross at the point (25,75). Thus, the two lines cross at the values of x and y that satisfy the two equa-

tions. In other words, we can solve the system of two equations in two ways—we can either use algebra, or we can draw graphs and find the point at which the two lines cross.

Finding the Areas of Rectangles and Triangles

On several occasions in this book, we will represent economic information by the area of a rectangle or a triangle. Figure 1.8 shows a rectangle whose vertices are A, B, C, and D. The coordinates of these vertices are A: (2,2), B: (2,6), C: (7,6), D: (7,2). Figure 1.8 is drawn with a grid of small squares. The area of each small square is one square unit. Since the rectangle ABCD consists of 20 small squares, it must be that the area of ABCD is 20 square units.

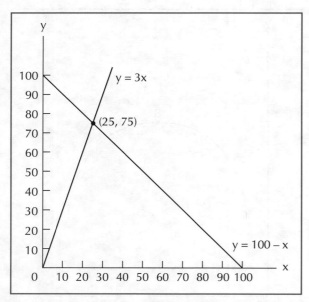

Figure 1.7 Graphs of Two Intersecting Lines

The equation for the upward-sloping line is y = 3x. The equation for the downward-sloping line is y = 100 − 3x. We can use algebra to find that x = 25 and y = 75 are the values of x and y that satisfy both equations at the same time. By drawing the graphs carefully, we can see that the two lines cross where x = 25 and y = 75. Therefore, the intersection of two lines gives us a graphical representation of the values of x and y that satisfy both equations at the same time.

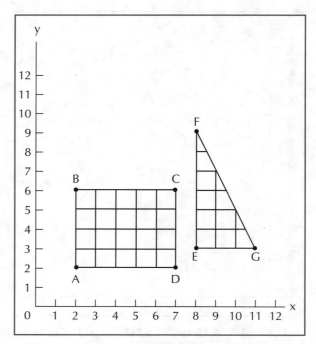

Figure 1.8 Graphs of the Area of a Rectangle and the Area of a Triangle

The height of the rectangle ABCD is 4, and the base of the rectangle is 5. The area of the rectangle is equal to the base multiplied by the height. Therefore, the area of the rectangle is (4)(5) = 20. The height of the triangle EFG is 6, and the base of the triangle is 3. The area of the triangle is one-half times the base times the height. Therefore, the area of the triangle is 0.5(3)(6) = 0.5(18) = 9.

However, we don't have to count squares to calculate the area of a rectangle. *The easier way to calculate the area of the rectangle is to multiply the base of the rectangle by its height:*

Area of Rectangle = bh,

where b = base of the rectangle, and h = height of the rectangle.

The base of the rectangle is (7−2) = 5, and the height is (6−2) = 4. Therefore, the area of the rectangle is (5)x(4) = 20.

Figure 1.8 also includes a triangle, which is defined by the vertices E, F, and G. The coordinates of these vertices are E: (8,3), F: (8,9), G: (11,3). Once again, it's possible to determine the area by counting squares. By counting

squares (and half squares), we can determine that the area of the triangle is nine square units. However, there is once again an easier way to find the area of the triangle. The easier way to calculate the area of the triangle is to multiply the base by the height, and then divide by two:

Area of Triangle = 1/2 bh,

where b = base of the triangle, and h = height of the triangle. The base of the triangle is (11 − 8) = 3, and the height of the triangle is (9 − 3) = 6. The area of the the triangle is (1/2)(3)(6) = 9.

IR1A-8. Find the slope of the line that is defined by the points (1,3) and (2,7).

IR1A-9. Find the slope of the line that is defined by the points (3,6) and (5,4).

IR1A-10. A rectangle has height of 10 and base of 8. What is the area of the rectangle?

IR1A-11. A triangle has height of 9 and base of 4. What is the area of the triangle?

Chapter 2

Opportunity Cost
and Comparative Advantage

ECONOMICS AND YOU:
SHOULD YOU BUILD YOUR OWN HOUSE?

About two-thirds of American households own their own homes. You may not own a home now, but there is probably a good chance that you will own one, sooner or later. Most of the time, when a family acquires a home for the first time, they either buy an existing home, or they buy a newly built home from a builder. Some people do build their own homes, but this doesn't happen often.

Why? Why don't most people build their own homes? The reason is that, for most people, it is cheaper to let someone else build the home than to build it yourself. Consider Anthony Varelli, who is a marketing manager for a consumer-products company. Anthony knows just about everything there is to know about toothpaste. He can quote you all of the latest sales figures for his company's five brands of toothpaste, for every region of the country, for the past five years. He knows which brands of toothpaste appeal to women, which to men, and which to teenagers. He makes $90,000 per year.

Now, Anthony is a smart guy, and he probably *could* build his own house. If he were to spend several years at it, he could probably develop his skills in carpentry, and plumbing, and masonry, and electrical wiring, and roofing, to the point where he could build a house. But what would it cost him to do so? To build his own house, Anthony would have to quit his job for several years. Let's say that he could build a nice house in three years. If so, then he would have to give up salary in the amount of ($90,000 per year)x(3 years) = $270,000. And that's before he even buys the land and materials for the house. Let's say that the materials cost $30,000, and the land costs $50,000. Then, the total cost of the house would be $30,000 for materials, plus $50,000 for land, plus $270,000 for the cost of Anthony's time. This comes to a total of $350,000.

On the other hand, if Anthony were to buy his home from a builder, he could get it for $200,000, and the workmanship would be better than he could have done by himself. It makes sense for Anthony to buy the house, rather than build it himself, because it's cheaper to do so. It's cheaper for Anthony to specialize in marketing toothpaste, and to let other people specialize in carpentry, plumbing, and roofing.

And that's the way it is for most people. Most people specialize in one profession. For example, the author of this book specializes in teaching and research in economics. Relatively speaking, I am much better at economics teaching and research than at growing food, or making clothes, or producing automobiles. Instead of growing my own food, and making my own clothes, and building my own car, I let other people specialize in those activities. The farmers who grow the food that ends up on my table are relatively good at growing food, so they specialize in that activity. The auto workers who built my car are relatively good at making cars, so they specialize in that activity.

All over the world, we see people specializing in the activities at which they are relatively highly skilled. Shaquille O'Neal and Grant Hill specialize in playing basketball.

Mel Gibson and Julia Roberts specialize in acting in motion pictures. Christina Aguilera specializes in one kind of music, and the New York Philharmonic Orchestra specializes in another kind. If it weren't for this specialization, the world would be a much poorer place, because everyone would have to provide everything for himself or herself.

Specialization is extremely important to the modern economy. When people specialize a lot, it's necessary for them to exchange goods and services with each other. The exchanges that are made between people who specialize in different activities are also extremely important. In this chapter, we will begin to develop an understanding of the workings of specialization and exchange. Before this chapter is over, you will have an idea of why specialization and exchange are so beneficial to the economy, and you will have developed a language for thinking about these concepts.

OPPORTUNITY COST

In the introduction to this chapter, we discussed what it would cost for Anthony to build his own home. The biggest part of the cost was associated with the fact that he could not build a house without quitting his job. As a result, if he were to build the house himself, he would have to give up his salary for three years. In order to do one thing, he would have to give up something else.

In order to do one thing, we all have to give up something else. If you spend an hour reading this book, then you won't be able to spend the hour playing football. If you stay up late watching TV, you won't have as much time for sleep. If you spend $4 on a burger, fries, and a drink, you won't have those four dollars to spend on a movie ticket, or a pair of underwear, or the lunch special at a Chinese

restaurant. If you spend $10,000 on college tuition, you won't have those ten thousand dollars to spend on something else.

Again and again, we bump into the same idea. Our resources are scarce. If we devote a portion of our resources to one activity, or one purchase, then those resources will not be available for another activity, or another purchase. The poet Robert Frost had it right: "Two roads diverged in a yellow wood, And sorry I could not travel both . . . ". The narrator of that poem could take one road, or he could take the other, but he could not take both. Consequently, it is necessary to make choices. We must make choices because our resources are scarce. This idea is so fundamental to economics that we put it in our definition of economics, in Chapter 1.

Economists have a phrase that captures the idea that, by doing one thing, we give up another thing. The phrase is "opportunity cost". The *opportunity cost* of one activity is the value of the next-best alternative. If you spend one extra hour watching TV, you will have one less hour for other activities. Thus, the opportunity cost of spending an extra hour watching TV is the value of the next-best activity to which you could have devoted that hour. If the next-best alternative to an hour of TV is an hour of playing volleyball, then the opportunity cost of spending the hour in front of the TV set is that you give up the possibility of spending that hour on the volleyball court.

Often, it is easy to measure opportunity cost in dollars. What is the opportunity of spending $27 on a pair of jeans? The opportunity cost is that those $27 will not be available to be spent on something else. However, the $27 can be spent on so many things. Twenty-seven dollars can buy four movie tickets, or eight burger-&-fries combos at a hamburger place, or any number of other things. Therefore, it probably doesn't make sense to try to figure out the next-best way to spend the $27. Instead, we just say that the opportunity cost of spending $27 on a pair of jeans is $27.

However, there are some circumstances under which it is not so easy to measure opportunity cost in dollars. For instance, let's say that you decide to go to a concert by the Dave Mathews Band. (If you don't like the Dave Mathews Band, substitute Gloria Estefan, or the Dixie Chicks, or Whitney Houston, or whoever.) Certainly, one big part of the cost will be the price of the ticket. However, it is often the case that tickets for popular musical groups sell out very quickly. Because of this, the really devoted fans often spend a long time waiting in line for tickets. For example, let's say that you decide to spend the night outside the box office, waiting for the office to open.

This long wait is certainly a part of the opportunity cost of going to the concert. (Pre-sumably, if you did not go to the concert, you would not have spent the night sleeping on the sidewalk next to the box office.) But it will not be easy to put a dollar value on spending the night sleeping on the sidewalk. In fact, the opportunity cost may vary greatly from person to person. If you have to be at work the next morning, then spending the night on the sidewalk might be very costly, because it might affect your performance on the job. If you fall asleep at your desk and get fired from your job, then the concert is very expensive indeed. In addition, sleeping on the sidewalk isn't the most comfortable thing to do. You will probably be a little bit stiff when you wake up. The older you are, the more likely you are to have sore muscles the next day.

Based on the preceding paragraph, we can develop an understanding of one important fact about the people who spend the night waiting in line for concert tickets: Most of these people are young. Young people are less likely to have a steady job, and they won't be as sore in the morning. Therefore, we can say that the opportunity cost of spending the night in line for tickets is likely to be smaller for a young person than for a middle-aged or elderly person.

So far, we have identified two opportunity costs of the concert. You have to spend time waiting in line for tickets, and, when you get to the front of the line, you have to spend money to buy the tickets. There are other opportunity costs, as well. If the concert is a long way from your home, you will have to drive there, or perhaps take a train or bus. Either way, it will take money (for gasoline, or train fare, or bus fare), and it will take time. Once you get to the concert site, you may need to pay for parking. And, of course, when you are actually at the concert, there is an opportunity cost of your time. You could have done something else.

In *Real Economics for Real People 2.1*, we discuss the opportunity cost of going to college.

Real Economics for Real People 2.1:
How Much Does It Cost to Go to College?

Erin Van Nuys is trying to decide whether to go to college. She's been accepted at a publicly supported college that offers her in-state tuition. She gets a letter saying that the estimated cost of tuition, books, room, and board is $10,000 for the year.

But Erin wonders whether these figures really represent the true opportunity cost of spending a year at college. The answer is that some of the "costs" are true costs of college, and some are not. In addition, there is at least one important opportunity cost that is *not* included in the numbers that are reported.

It is reasonable to include tuition as a cost of going to college. After all, Erin's family would not choose to write a big check to the college every semester, unless she were registered for classes. The same is true for most of the books that Erin will have to buy. Of course, she might have bought a few books, even if she weren't attending college. But it's likely that she would not have bought many of the books, except for the fact that they are required for one of her college courses.

The official numbers also include expenses for room and board, but it's highly questionable whether these expenses should be included among the true opportunity costs of college. Let's begin by thinking about the food expenses. Very few people can function effectively for more than a few days, without eating some food. Regardless of whether she goes to college, Erin will have to eat. Consequently, for the most part, it is *not* appropriate to think of food expenses as a true opportunity cost of going to college. For one reason or another, it's possible that food expenses could be a little higher at college. In this case, the true opportunity cost of college should include the *difference* between the cost of food at college

and the cost of the food that Erin would have eaten if she had not gone to college. On the other hand, it's possible that the cost of food at college will be a little *less* than the food costs that Erin would have incurred, if she had not gone to college. In this case, the difference between the two costs would be a *negative* opportunity cost of going to college.

Similar reasoning applies to Erin's room expenses. Regardless of whether she goes to college, she will want to have a roof over her head. If the monthly cost of renting an apartment at college is the same as the cost of renting an apartment in Erin's hometown, then room should not be included as a true opportunity cost of college. If it costs a little more to rent an apartment at college, then the *difference* between the college rental and the hometown rental would be a true opportunity cost.

Finally, we come to the most important cost of all, even though it is *not* included in the estimate of $10,000. If Erin doesn't go to college, she can get a full-time job for $9 per hour. At 40 hours per week, and 50 weeks per year, this job will pay $18,000 for the year. If Erin goes to college, she will only be able to work part time for most of the year. Her earnings for the year will be $6000, if she goes to college. Therefore, if Erin goes to college, her *foregone earnings* will be $(18,000–6000) = $12,000. ***Foregone earnings*** are the additional wages and salaries that could be earned, if a person were to go to work right after high school, instead of going to college. The foregone earnings are a true opportunity cost of going to college. If Erin doesn't go to college, she will definitely earn more during the years when she would have been enrolled.

The remarkable thing about foregone earnings is that they are the largest cost of all, in spite of the fact that they aren't included in the official numbers on college costs. The problem is that the official numbers are not based on the idea of opportunity cost. Instead, they are just an accounting of the explicit, out-of-pocket costs of going to college. For students at the more expensive private colleges, the out-of-pocket costs of college can be more than foregone earnings.

However, a majority of students attend publicly supported colleges and universities. These institutions are able to keep tuition down because of their reliance on government funds. For students at many of these institutions, foregone earnings are the biggest cost of all.

Reality Check:
Interim Review Questions

IR2-1. What is the opportunity cost of going to a professional baseball game?

IR2-2. What is the opportunity cost of spending $15 on a compact disc?

THE PRODUCTION-POSSIBILITIES FRONTIER

Economists have a graphical tool for representing scarcity, choice, and opportunity cost. The *production-possibilities frontier* is a graphical representation of the combinations of outputs that can be produced, if all of the available resources are used as well as possible.

A Straight-Line Production-Possibilities Frontier

We will start with a very simple production-possibilities frontier (or p.p.f. for short). Figure 2.1 shows the p.p.f. for red flannel shirts and green flannel shirts, which are produced at a factory owned by the Red Green Company. In this graph, we put red shirts on the horizontal axis, and green shirts on the vertical axis. (However, this is not an important assumption. We could have put green shirts on the horizontal axis, and red shirts on the vertical, and we would still be able to develop the same ideas.)

This is an especially simple example, because red shirts and green shirts use virtually identical resources. They both use cotton cloth. They both require that the cloth must be cut and sewn, and buttons must be added. The only difference is that red shirts use red dye,

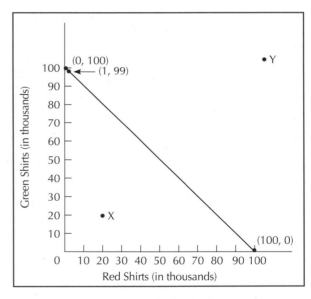

Figure 2.1 A Straight-Line Production-Possibilities Frontier

Green shirts and red shirts use the same resources and technology. As a result, the trade-off between red shirts and green shirts is always at the same rate, and the production-possibilities frontier is a straight line. The slope of the frontier is –1, which means that the opportunity cost of one red shirt is one green shirt. Point X is below the frontier, which means that producing at X involves waste, or inefficiency. Point Y is above the frontier. This means that, given the current resources and technology, point Y is unattainable, or infeasible.

while green shirts use green dye. If the shirt factory is to change from producing red shirts to producing green shirts, it's only necessary to flip a switch.

If the factory devotes all of its resources to producing red shirts, it can produce 100,000 red shirts per year. Of course, if it devotes all of its resources to producing red shirts, it won't produce any green shirts. Thus, if we use 1000 shirts as our unit of measurement, one of the points on the production-possibilities frontier is (100,0). At the other extreme, the factory could devote all of its resources to producing green shirts. In this case, it would produce 100,000 green shirts and no red shirts. Therefore, another point on the p.p.f. is (0,100). Let's say that the Red Green Company is currently producing only green shirts. If it wants to produce 1000 red shirts, it can do so, but it will have to give up production of 1000 green shirts. Thus, another point on the p.p.f. is the point (1,99), representing 1000 red shirts and 99,000 green shirts. Every time the company wants to produce more red shirts, it can do so, but it has to give up green shirts.

In fact, every time the company increases its output of red shirts by one shirt, it must reduce its output of green shirts by one shirt. In other words, the opportunity cost of one additional red shirt is one green shirt. The reverse is also true: The opportunity cost of one additional green shirt is one red shirt.

Opportunity Cost and the Slope of the P.P.F. The p.p.f. for red shirts and green shirts is a downward-sloping line. This illustrates the concept of scarcity. The available resources are limited. The only way to get more of one good is to give up some of another good.

The p.p.f. doesn't just slope downward; its slope is exactly –1. This is not a coincidence. The slope of any line is the change in the quantity on the vertical axis, divided by the change in the quantity on the horizontal axis. In this case, the slope of the p.p.f. is the change in the number of green shirts, divided by the change

in the number of red shirts. Whenever the number of red shirts increases by one, the number of green shirts must decrease by one. Therefore, the slope must be –1.

There is a close connection between the slope of the p.p.f. and the opportunity costs. For any production-possibilities frontier, the slope of the p.p.f. is the negative of the opportunity cost of the good on the horizontal axis.

Waste. By definition, every point on the p.p.f. represents a combination of outputs that can be produced, *if all of the available resources are used as well as possible.* Of course, any point *under* the p.p.f. can also be produced, but a point under the p.p.f involves waste, or inefficiency. For example, in Figure 2.1, point X involves only 20,000 green shirts and 20,000 red shirts. Thus, at point X, some 40,000 shirts are produced, whereas 100,000 shirts are produced at any of the points on the p.p.f. How could we end up at a point like X? It might happen because the factory manager makes lots of mistakes. Or it might happen because some of the workers go out on strike. In any event, a point below the p.p.f. involves incomplete or inefficient use of the available resources.

Figure 2.1 also includes point Y, which is *above* the p.p.f. With today's resources and technology, point Y simply cannot be produced. A point like Y may be available at some time in the future, but for today it is unattainable, or infeasible.

A Curved Production-Possibilities Frontier

We started with the simple case of a straight-line p.p.f., because it is easy to show some important concepts with a straight p.p.f. But you should understand that the straight-line p.p.f. is a very special case. A straight-line p.p.f occurs when the two goods use the same resources and technology. It is much more common to consider goods that do *not* use the same resources and technology. When the production processes are different, we will get a curved p.p.f.

To illustrate a curved p.p.f., we use an example in which the two goods are wine and wool. These two goods definitely *don't* use the same resources and technology. Some resources are better suited for producing wine, while other resources are better suited for producing wool. People with nimble fingers are better suited for producing wine, because they can pick grapes quickly, without doing a lot of damage to the grapes. On the other hand, big, strong guys are better suited for producing wool, because they can wrestle a sheep to the floor at shearing time. Some soils and climates are better for growing grapes, while other soils and climates are better for raising sheep.

Figure 2.2 is a p.p.f. for wine and wool. We have put wine on the horizontal axis and wool on the vertical axis. Once again, however, these choices are arbitrary. We could show the same information with wool on the horizontal axis and wine on the vertical. If all of the available resources are devoted to producing wool, 100 million pounds per year can be produced. Of course, if all of the available resources are devoted to producing wool, then no wine can be produced. Thus, one of the points on the p.p.f. in Figure 2.2 is (0,100). (We are using one million pounds as our unit of measurement for wool.) If all of the available resources are devoted to producing wool, it would be necessary to produce wool with many resources that are really much better suited to producing wine. If we produce only wool, that means that we would use nimble-fingered grape pickers to wrestle with sheep. We would take hillsides that are well suited for growing grapes, and use them for raising sheep. Consequently, if we decide to produce the first few units of wine, we would use the resources that are relatively best for producing wine. Therefore, in order to produce the first few units of wine, we won't have to give up a relatively

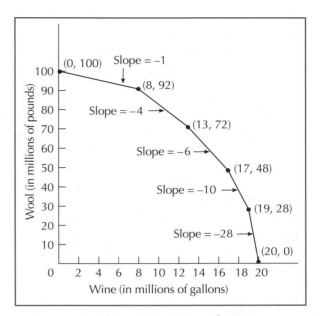

Figure 2.2 A Curved Production-Possibilities Frontier

Since wine and wool use different resources and technologies, the production-possibilities frontier is bowed outward, or concave with respect to the origin. The absolute value of the slope of the frontier increases as we move downward and to the right. This means that the production-possibilities frontier exhibits the Law of Increasing Opportunity Cost: As we increase the amount of wine, the opportunity cost of further increases in wine production will become greater and greater.

large amount of wool. Figure 2.1 shows that, if we give up eight million pounds of wool (so that production of wool is now 92 million pounds, instead of 100 million pounds), we get 8 million gallons of wine.

What is the opportunity cost of these first units of wine? To get 8 million gallons of wine, we have to give up 8 million pounds of wool. Therefore, the opportunity cost of an additional 8 million gallons of wine is 8 million pounds of wool. We can express this in the form of an equation:

8WI = 8WO,

where WI represents wine, and WO represents wool. In this equation, wine is measured in millions of gallons, and wool is measured in millions of pounds, so we can say that 8 units of wine are equivalent to 8 units of wool.

The equation shows us the opportunity cost of *eight* units of wine. If we divide both sides of this equation by 8, we can get the opportunity cost of *one* unit of wine:

$$(8/8)WI = (8/8)WO \Rightarrow 1WI = 1WO$$

Note that the opportunity cost of one additional unit of wine is one unit of wool, and the opportunity cost of one additional unit of wool is one unit of wine. This isn't an accident. In fact, for any two goods, *the opportunity cost of good A in terms of good B is the reciprocal of the opportunity cost of good B in terms of good A.*

So far, we have seen the movement from the point (0,100) to the point (8,92) in Figure 2.2. Now, what happens if we want to produce *even more* wine? In producing the first 8 million gallons of wine, we have already used the resources that are best suited for wine production. The people with the nimblest fingers, and the land with the best climate and soil, and the best chemists, have all been pulled from wool production into wine production. If we want even more wine, we will have to begin using resources that aren't quite so well suited for wine production. The next point that is identified in Figure 2.2 is (13,72). We get an additional (13 – 8) = 5 units of wine. To get those units of wine, we have to give up an additional (92 – 72) = 20 units of wool. The opportunity cost of an additional five units of wine is 20 units of wool. Therefore, the opportunity cost of an additional one (=5/5) unit of wine is (20/5) = 4 units of wool.

Let's recap what we have seen so far: For the first few units of wine, the opportunity cost was one unit of wool per unit of wine. For the next few units of wine, the opportunity cost was four units of wool per unit of wine. The opportunity cost of an additional unit of wine increases as we produce more and more wine. As we go to other points on the p.p.f. in Figure 2.2, we see that this trend continues. The opportunity cost of an additional unit of wine increases to six units of wool, and then to 10 units of wool, and finally to 28 units of wool.

The p.p.f. in Figure 2.2 has the usual shape for a production-possibilities frontier. In most cases, p.p.f.'s are bowed outward, or "concave with respect to the origin". This shape is a result of the fact that wine and wool use different resources and different technologies. When the p.p.f. has this shape, we say that it obeys the *Law of Increasing Opportunity Cost.* The **Law of Increasing Opportunity Cost** says that the opportunity cost of producing one additional unit of a good will increase, as we produce more and more of the good.

Reality Check: Interim Review Questions

IR2-3. Why are some production-possibilities frontiers straight, whereas others are bowed outward?

IR2-4. What is the relationship between opportunity cost and the slope of the production-possibilities frontier?

IR2-5. Define the Law of Increasing Opportunity Cost.

IR2-6. What is happening when a country produces below its p.p.f.?

CHANGES IN THE PRODUCTION-POSSIBILITIES FRONTIER

So far, we have shown two production-possibilities frontiers, in Figures 2.1 and 2.2. These p.p.f.'s, like all p.p.f.'s, are defined at a particular moment in time. They show the maximum amount that can be produced, given the resources that are available at one time. However, p.p.f.'s can shift over time. In fact, the productive capacity of the economy has improved tremendously over the last few hundred years.

Figure 2.3 shows an outward shift in the production-possibilities frontier for the United States economy. The p.p.f. is defined over manufactured goods and services, which are two broad categories of production. Over the years, our ability to produce either goods or services has increased dramatically.

The productive capacity of the economy can increase over time, as a result of any of several influences. The first of these is technological improvements. *Technological improvements* include new inventions, as well as new techniques that allow us to produce more or better goods from a given amount of resources. A century ago, there were no airplanes, no television, no radio, no computers, no antibiotics, no microwave ovens, and no videocassette recorders. Far more inventions were made in the 20th century than in all the rest of the history of the world. As technology improves, the p.p.f. shifts outward.

The second source of improved production is *capital investment*. When economists use the phrase "capital investment", their meaning is somewhat different from one of the common meanings of the word. In ordinary conversation, people often talk about "capital investments" in purely financial terms. They refer to stocks, bonds, checking accounts, savings accounts, cash, etc. However, when an economist refers to *capital investment*, he or she refers to the real man-made inputs into the production process, such as factories, pieces of equipment, computers, and office buildings. In the economist's dictionary, "capital" includes *machinery and equipment*, such as computers, drill presses, drop forges, and circular saws. "Capital" also includes *structures*, such as office buildings, factory buildings, and warehouses. And capital also refers to moving capital, such as delivery vans and railroad cars.

Each year, most people in most countries save a small percentage of their output. These savings are put into financial institutions, which then lend the money to businesses. The businesses, in turn, acquire new capital and replace old capital. When the amount of

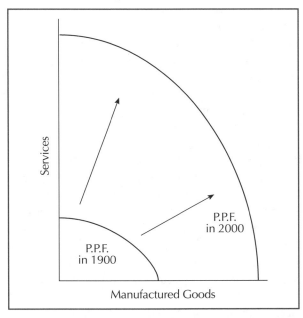

Figure 2.3 The Expansion of the Production-Possibilities Frontier in the United States

Over time, the productive capacity of the United States economy has expanded greatly. This is represented as an outward shift of the production-possibilities frontier. This outward shift has occurred as a result of improved technologies, capital investment, and increases in the size and quality of the labor force.

capital increases, there is an improvement in the productive capacity of the economy, and the p.p.f. will shift outward.

So far, we have mentioned two sources of improved production—technological improvement and capital investment. Although these two sources of improved production are not the same thing, they are often closely related. This is because many technological improvements are embodied in new capital. Thus, when a team of chemists and engineers comes up with a new process for making propylene oxide, they demonstrate the new technology by getting a chemical company to build a new plant.

The last (but not least) of our three sources of improved productivity is increases in the size and quality of the work force. Nothing can be produced in the economy, unless someone does some work. Therefore, if the size of the labor force grows, we can expect that the production-possibilities frontier will shift outward. In fact, in the United States, the labor force has grown enormously over the years. For example, the population has more than doubled since 1940. In addition, the proportion of the population that is working has also increased, as women have increased their labor-force participation.

Not only has the size of the labor force increased, but its quality has also increased. As recently as 1910, only a little more than 10 percent of Americans completed high school. The figure reached about 60 percent by 1940, and today nearly 90 percent are able to get a high-school diploma. The proportion of the work force with a college education has also increased dramatically. Nowadays, almost one-fourth of American workers have a college degree. Because of these increases in education, the work force is much more highly skilled than it was before.

Thus, we have identified several sources of increased productivity: technological advances, capital investment, increases in the size of the labor force, and increases in the quality of the labor force.

Of course, it is also possible for the productive capacity of an economy to *decrease*. As an example, let's consider the change in the size of the German economy from 1942 to 1945. In 1942, German armies controlled an empire that stretched from Norway to Tunisia to Greece, and on through much of western Russia. The German economy was in high gear, producing huge quantities of war materials, as well as consumer goods. Three years later, at the end of World War II, the German economy lay in ruins. Many of its factories had been bombed to rubble. Five million Germans were killed, along with millions of farm ani-

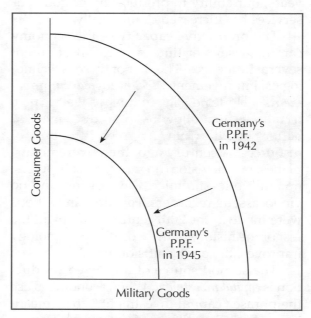

Figure 2.4 The Shrinkage of the German Production-Possibilities Frontier, 1942–1945

Between 1942 and 1945, millions of Germans were killed in the Second World War. Factories, cities, and farms were devastated by the war. As a result, the productive capacity of the German economy decreased. This is represented by an inward shift of the production-possibilities frontier.

Real Economics for Real People 2.2: The Expanding American Economy

We have identified several ways in which production-possibilities frontiers can expand. The economy can grow as a result of technological improvements, capital investments, and increases in the quantity and quality of the labor force. The United States economy has been fortunate to have an abundance of all of these sources of growth. Let's get an idea of the magnitude of the changes over the last four decades.

First of all, the labor force has expanded greatly. In 1960, the U.S. population was nearly 181 million. By 1997, population had grown to nearly 268 million, for an increase of about 48.3%. The labor force has grown even more rapidly than the population. In 1960, the civilian labor force was just under 70 million. By 1997, the labor force had grown to a little more than 136 million, for an increase of about 95.8%. The labor force grew faster than the population, because there was an increase in the proportion of the population that is in the labor force. This period saw an exceptional increase in the labor-force participation of women.

Not only did the number of workers increase, but their productivity increased, as well. Productivity increased for a variety of reasons. Education levels increased, so work-ers had better skills. Worker productivity was also enhanced by technological improvements and growth of the capital stock. Output per hour in the business sector is estimated to have increased by about 105% from 1960 to 1997! (For the entire economy, the rate of growth of output per hour is not quite this fast because output tends to grow faster in the business sector than in the government sector. Still, the economy has experienced major productivity improvements.)

Since the labor force nearly doubled over this period, and since output per worker also increased substantially, it should not come as a surprise that workers were able to make more money. In 1960, employee compensation was about $297 billion. By 1997, employee compensation had grown to about $4.687 *trillion*. This represents an increase by a factor of more than 15! However, much of the increase is more of an illusion than a reality, because of inflation. But even if we adjust for inflation, we still find that real employee compensation increased by a factor of about 3.3.

The overall picture is one of strong economic growth, driven by a variety of sources. Expansion of production possibilities is the key to prosperity.

mals. Millions of others were injured. These losses can be represented by an inward shift in the production-possibilities frontier, as shown in Figure 2.4.

Earlier in this section, we saw that an economy's p.p.f. can *grow,* as a result of improved technology, capital investment, and growth of the labor force. From 1942 to 1945, the German economy *shrank,* because of the destruction of much of its capital stock and population.

On a happier note, *Real Economics for Real People 2.2* discusses the expansion of the p.p.f. in the United States.

Reality Check: Interim Review Question

IR2-7. What are the main ways in which an economy's production-possibilities frontier can expand outward?

COMPARATIVE ADVANTAGE AND TRADE

At the beginning of this chapter, we asked whether a man should build his own house, or get other people to build it for him. More recently, we have introduced the idea of the production-possibilities frontier. Now, it's time to put these two thoughts together. We can do this by asking the following question: What happens if two people, or two nations, have p.p.f.'s that are shaped differently? As it turns out, it will make sense for them to specialize in the activities in which they are relatively more productive, and then trade with each other.

We begin by defining two important terms, "absolute advantage" and "comparative advantage".

Absolute Advantage

Mark and Jason run a 100-yard dash. Mark wins. In other words, Mark can produce an output (traveling 100 yards) using fewer resources (less time) than Jason. We say that Mark has absolute advantage over Jason, in terms of running the 100-yard dash. In general, one person has *absolute advantage* over another person, if he or she can produce a given output using fewer resources than the other person.

Absolute advantage can be defined with reference to only one activity. A calculation of absolute advantage only looks at one activity at a time.

Let's consider a further example. Gwen and Cecil are both cooks in a diner. Gwen can make one stack of pancakes per minute. When it comes to making pancakes, Cecil isn't as quick as Gwen. It takes him one minute and 15 seconds (or 75 seconds) to make a stack of pancakes. Therefore, Gwen has absolute advantage over Cecil in the production of pancakes, because it takes her less time to produce the same amount of pancakes.

Gwen can also make one hamburger in one minute. Just as Cecil was slower in making pancakes, he is also slower when it comes to making hamburgers. It takes him one minute and 40 seconds (100 seconds) to make a hamburger. Gwen has absolute advantage over Cecil in the production of hamburgers, because it takes her less time to produce the same amount of hamburgers.

Comparative Advantage

Even though Gwen is better than Cecil at both activities, the *proportion* by which she is better is different in the two activities. The next step in our analysis involves determining the activity in which Gwen is *relatively* better, and the activity in which Cecil is *relatively* better. The way to do this is by comparing the opportunity cost of each activity for the two people.

Remember that Gwen can produce one hamburger per minute, and she can produce one stack of pancakes per minute. Therefore, *for Gwen, the opportunity cost of one hamburger is one stack of pancakes*. Our next step is to calculate the opportunity cost for Cecil. Recall that Cecil takes 75 seconds to make a stack of pancakes. If we divide 60 seconds by 75 seconds, we find that Cecil can make $(60/75) = 0.8$ stacks of pancakes per minute. In addition, Cecil takes 100 seconds to make a hamburger. Dividing 60 seconds by 100 seconds, we see that Cecil can make $(60/100) = 0.6$ hamburgers in a minute. Thus, Cecil can produce 0.6 hamburgers per minute, and he can produce 0.8 stacks of pancakes per minute. We can express this relationship as

$$0.6\,H = 0.8\,P,$$

where H stands for hamburgers, and P stands for pancakes. Thus, for Cecil, the opportunity cost of 0.6 hamburgers is 0.8 stacks of pancakes. Now, let's find the opportunity cost of *one* hamburger. To do this, we divide both sides of the equation by 0.6:

$$(0.6/0.6)H = 1H = (0.8/0.6)P = 1.3333\,P.$$

For Cecil, the opportunity cost of one hamburger is one and one-third stacks of pancakes.

We can now determine the activities in which Gwen and Cecil are *relatively* better. For Gwen, the opportunity cost of one hamburger is one stack of pancakes. For Cecil, the opportunity cost of one hamburger is one and one-third stacks of pancakes. The opportunity cost of a hamburger is lower for Gwen. We say that Gwen has "comparative advantage" in the production of hamburgers, because she has the lower opportunity cost of producing hamburgers. Following similar reasoning, we find that Cecil has comparative advantage in the production of pancakes. Generally, an individual has *comparative advantage* in an activity if his or her opportunity cost of that activity is lower than the opportunity cost of that activity for anyone else.

Notice that, although Gwen has *absolute* advantage in both activities, she only has *comparative* advantage in hamburger production. It's possible to be better than another person in every single activity, but it is not possible to be *relatively* better at everything.

Comparative Advantage and Opportunities for Beneficial Trade

If you were the owner of the diner where Gwen and Cecil work, you would notice that Gwen is relatively better at hamburger production, and Cecil is relatively better at pancake production. Consequently, the diner could operate more efficiently by having Gwen specialize (as much as possible) in hamburgers, and by having Cecil specialize (as much as possible) in pancakes.

This is basically the same as the idea that we introduced at the very beginning of this chapter. Anthony Varelli's comparative advantage is as a marketing manager for toothpaste. He does *not* have comparative advantage in building houses. Instead of attempting to build his own house, Anthony should spe-cialize in being a marketing manager, and he should let other people specialize in building houses. The people who should build houses are the ones who have comparative advantage in building houses.

An Example of Comparative Advantage and Trade, with Production-Possibilities Frontiers

Now, we are ready to demonstrate the gains that can occur, when people specialize in the activity in which they have comparative advantage, and then trade with each other. To develop this idea, we'll use another numerical example, and we will draw production-possibilities frontiers, based on the numbers.

Kenny lives alone on a desert island. On this island, the only two things to do are to catch fish, or gather coconuts. Kenny is great at catching fish. If he devotes all of his energies to fishing, he can catch 60 fish per month. On the other hand, Kenny can only gather 12 coconuts per month. We graph Kenny's production-possibilities frontier in Figure 2.5. (Note that, to keep the analysis simple, we assume that Kenny's p.p.f. is a straight line.)

For Kenny, the opportunity cost of 12 coconuts is 60 fish. Another way to put this is as follows:

$$12\ C = 60\ F,$$

where C stands for coconuts, and F stands for fish.

To calculate the opportunity cost of *one* coconut, divide both sides of the equation by 12. This gives us $(12/12)\ C = 1C = (60/12)\ F = 5F$. For Kenny, the opportunity cost of one coconut is five fish.

Let's assume that Kenny always likes to consume fish and coconuts in equal proportions. In other words, every time Kenny eats one fish, he prefers to eat exactly one coconut. There is only one point on his p.p.f. that has equal proportions, and that is the point (10,10).

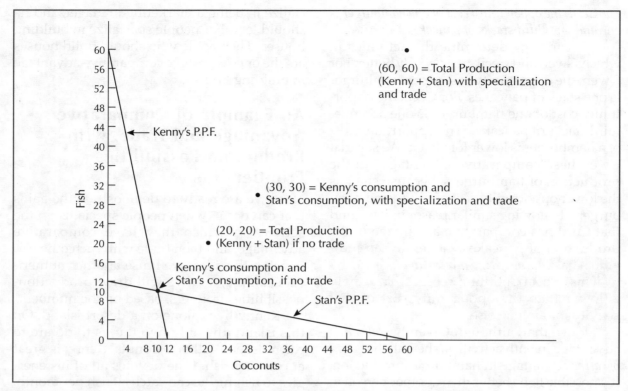

Figure 2.5 The Gains from Specialization and Trade

If Kenny and Stan do not cooperate, each of them will produce 10 coconuts and 10 fish, and each will consume what he produces. Therefore, if they do not cooperate, the total production of the two people is 20 coconuts and 20 fish. However, Kenny has comparative advantage in production of fish, and Stan has comparative advantage in production of coconuts. If they specialize in the activity in which they have comparative advantage, Kenny will produce 60 fish and Stan will produce 60 coconuts. This would allow each of them to consume 30 coconuts and 30 fish. Thus, as a result of specialization and trade, the two people are able to increase production and consumption by a factor of three.

Therefore, Kenny will catch and eat 10 fish, and he will gather and eat 10 coconuts. Since Kenny lives alone, his only choice is to consume some combination of outputs that he can produce himself.

Now, Stan washes up on the same desert island. However, Stan's productive capacities are very different from Kenny's. Kenny could produce either 12 coconuts or 60 fish, but Stan can produce either 60 coconuts of 12 fish. Earlier, we found that Kenny's opportunity cost of one coconut is five fish. By following the same procedure, we find that Stan's opportunity cost of one coconut is one-fifth of a fish. Kenny has lower opportunity cost in fish production, and Stan has lower opportunity cost in coconut production. Therefore, Kenny has comparative advantage in fish production, and Stan has comparative advantage in coconut production. Stan's p.p.f. is also graphed in Figure 2.5.

By coincidence, Stan has the same preferences as Kenny. Stan also likes to eat fish and coconuts in equal proportions. This means that Stan will also choose the point (10,10). If Kenny and Stan don't communicate with each other, then Stan, like Kenny, will catch and eat 10 fish, and he will gather and eat 10 coconuts.

However, if one of these guys is smart, he will notice that their productive capacities are different. Let's say that Kenny is the first to raise the issue. He says "Hey, Stan, why don't we specialize in the activities in which we have comparative advantage, and then trade with each other?" (You see, Kenny has already had an economics course, so he knows the lingo.)

The two shake hands. From that moment on, Kenny specializes in fish production, and Stan specializes in the production of coconuts. Kenny produces 60 fish, and Stan produces 60 coconuts. Since both of them like to consume fish and coconuts in equal proportions, it makes sense that they will divide the food equally. Kenny ends up with 30 fish and 30 coconuts, and so does Stan.

By specializing and trading, each man is able to *triple* his consumption!

If everyone had the same production possibilities, then the kind of gains shown in this example could not occur. However, people and nations do have very different production possibilities. The message of this example is that it is possible to improve living standards dramatically, by specializing in the activities in which we have comparative advantage, and then trading.

Obviously, this has been a simplified example. Nevertheless, it captures many of the most important ideas in all of economics. First of all, our resources are scarce, which means that we have to make choices. (We will return to this idea repeatedly, throughout this book.) Second, specialization and trade can make everyone better off. (We will return to this idea again, especially in Chapter 5.)

Reality Check: Interim Review Questions

IR2-8. Arnold can produce 5 units of good A, if he devotes all of his time and energy to producing good A. He can produce 10 units of good B, if he devotes all of his time and energy to producing good B. Between these two end-points, Arnold's p.p.f. is a straight line. What is the opportunity cost of one additional unit of good A for Arnold? What is the opportunity cost of one additional unit of good B for Arnold?

IR2-9. Lynnette can produce 15 units of good A, if she devotes all of her time and energy to producing good A. She can produce 20 units of good B, if she devotes all of her time and energy to producing good B. Between these two end-points, Lynnette's p.p.f. is a straight line. What is the opportunity cost of one additional unit of good A for Lynnette? What is the opportunity cost of one additional unit of good B for Lynnette?

IR2-10. If we refer to the preceding two questions, does Arnold or Lynnette have *absolute* advantage in the production of good A? Who has *absolute* advantage in the production of good B? Who has *comparative* advantage in the production of good A? Who has *comparative* advantage in the production of good B?

ECONOMICS AND YOU: LET SOMEBODY ELSE BUILD THE HOUSE FOR YOU

At the beginning of this chapter, we posed the question of whether Anthony Varelli should build his own home. The answer is that he should not do so, because the opportunity cost of building it himself is bigger than the opportunity cost of letting someone else do it for him.

The same principle pervades every aspect of our lives. If you are a lawyer, you have comparative advantage in the production of legal services. It makes sense to specialize in that activity, and to let others specialize in other activities. The lawyer will make money from providing legal expertise, and he or she will then be able to use that money to buy groceries, hardware, appliances, housewares, and all manner of other things, from people who have comparative advantage in those activities. If you're a loan officer at a bank, it makes sense to specialize in that activity, and to let other people provide the food that you eat, and the clothes that you wear. Of course, you might keep a small garden, because it's nice to have fresh vegetables in the summer. However, when compared with a bank loan officer, a farmer will have comparative advantage in providing most food items.

Here's the bottom line: We can get more out of our resources by taking advantage of specialization. People should specialize in the activities in which they have comparative advantage, and then they should trade with each other. Comparative advantage, specialization, and trade are at the very heart of the success of the modern world economy.

Chapter Summary

1. The opportunity cost of one activity is the value of the next-best alternative. Often, opportunity cost can be measured easily, as the dollar price of a good. However, it is important to define opportunity cost broadly. For example, the opportunity cost of going to a concert includes the value of time spent waiting in line for tickets. Another example is that the opportunity cost of going to college includes the "foregone earnings", which are the wages and salaries that could have been earned if the person had gone to work right after high school.

2. The production-possibilities frontier (p.p.f.) is a graphical representation of the combinations of outputs that can be produced, if all of the available resources are used as well as possible. The p.p.f. slopes downward as we go to the right. This illustrates the concept of scarcity—as we increase production of one good, we must decrease production of another good.

3. The slope of the p.p.f. is the negative of the opportunity cost of the good on the horizontal axis.

4. If two goods use the same resources and technology, then the p.p.f. for those two goods will be a straight line. In the more common case, in which two goods use different resources and technology, the p.p.f. will be bowed outward. In other words, when two goods use different resources and technology, the p.p.f. will be concave with respect to the origin. When the p.p.f. has this shape, we say that it obeys the "Law of Increasing Opportunity Cost": As we increase production of one good, the opportunity cost of producing additional amounts of that good will increase.

5. A combination of outputs that is below and to the left of the p.p.f. is associated with wasteful or inefficient use of the available resources. A combination of outputs that is above and to the right of the p.p.f. is infeasible.

6. The p.p.f. describes the production possibilities that are available at a particular moment in time. However, over time, the p.p.f. can shift. The production-possibilities frontier can shift outward, due to technological improvements, or capital investment, or increases in the size of the labor force, or improvements in the quality of the labor force.

7. One person has absolute advantage over another person in the production of some output, if he or she can produce a given amount of output using fewer resources than the other person. Absolute advantage can be defined with respect to only one good or activity.

8. One person has comparative advantage over another person in the production of some output, if he or she has lower opportunity cost for that output. In order to define comparative advantage, it is necessary to consider at least two goods or activities.

9. If people specialize in the activities in which they have comparative advantage, and then trade with each other, total production can be increased.

Key Terms

Opportunity Cost

Foregone Earnings

Production-Possibilities Frontier

Law of Increasing Opportunity Cost

Technological Improvements

Capital Investment

Machinery and Equipment

Structures

Absolute Advantage

Comparative Advantage

Questions and Problems

QP2-1. Taco Town and The Taco Joint are right next door to each other. You've been to both places before, and you consider the tacos to be just as good at either place. However, you were planning to get your lunch at Taco Town, because their tacos are only 79 cents, whereas the tacos are 99 cents at The Taco Joint. When you arrive, you notice that there is a long line at Taco Town, but no line at The Taco Joint. Use the idea of opportunity cost to discuss the circumstances under which it would make sense to change your mind and go to The Taco Joint, as well as the circumstances under which it would make sense to wait in line at Taco Town.

QP2-2. Use the idea of opportunity cost to explain why a highly paid business executive should not mow his own lawn.

QP2-3. Draw a production-possibilities frontier, for any two goods of your choosing. Now, put point A above and to the right of the p.p.f. What can be said about the production possibilities depicted at point A?

QP2-4. Once again, use the p.p.f. that you drew for the previous question. This time, put point B below and to the left of the frontier. What can be said about the production possibilities depicted at point B?

QP2-5. Now, put point C on the production-possibilities frontier, so that point C has more of both goods than point B. In moving from point B (below the frontier) to point C (on the frontier), would it be necessary for the total available supply of resources to increase?

QP2-6. If Jane devotes all of her time to making gazpacho, she can produce 8 gallons of gazpacho in a day. If she devotes all of her time to making blintzes, Jane can produce 16 dozen blintzes in a day. Between these endpoints, Jane's production-possibilities frontier is a straight line.

a. Draw a graph of Jane's production-possibilities frontier, with gazpacho on the hor-

izontal axis and blintzes on the vertical axis. (In making the axes, you can assume that a gallon is the unit of measurement for gazpacho, and one dozen is the unit of measurement for blintzes.)

b. What is the slope of Jane's production-possibilities frontier?

c. What is the opportunity cost of one additional gallon of gazpacho for Jane?

d. If Jane were producing six gallons of gazpacho per day, what is the maximum number of dozens of blintzes that she could produce?

e. If Jane were producing 12 dozen blintzes per day, would it be possible for her to produce four gallons of gazpacho per day?

QP2-7. If Samantha devotes all of her time to making gazpacho, she can produce 6 gallons of gazpacho in a day. If she devotes all of her time to making blintzes, Samantha can produce 8 dozen blintzes in a day. Between these endpoints, Samantha's production-possibilities frontier is a straight line.

a. Draw a graph of Samantha's production-possibilities frontier, with gazpacho on the horizontal axis and blintzes on the vertical axis. (You can use the same units of measurement that were used in the previous question.)

b. What is the slope of Samantha's production-possibilities frontier?

c. What is the opportunity cost of one additional gallon of gazpacho for Samantha?

d. If Samantha were producing three gallons of gazpacho per day, what is the maximum number of dozens of blintzes that she could produce?

e. If Samantha were producing six dozen blintzes per day, would it be possible for her to produce four gallons of gazpacho per day?

QP2-8. Based on the information in the previous two questions, who has comparative advantage in gazpacho production? Who has comparative advantage in the production of blintzes?

Chapter 3

Supply and Demand: The Basics

ECONOMICS AND YOU: WHERE DO CAR PRICES COME FROM?

When you shop for a car, you are faced with a tremendous variety of models and prices. In 1997, you could buy a Chevrolet Geo Prizm for about $13,000, a Ford Taurus GL for $19,000, or a BMW 528i for about $38,000. A Ferrari or a Lamborghini will cost you a whole lot more.

Why do some cars sell for so much more than others? One reason is that some cars are more expensive to build: A high-performance luxury car uses costly materials, and requires more workmanship. Other things also influence prices. For example, a car may become popular because of an exciting design, or because it gets great reviews in magazines such as *Road and Track* or *Consumer Reports.* When a car is very popular, dealers may be able to charge higher prices. However, if a particular model isn't selling very well, the sellers may have to cut prices in order to stimulate sales.

The number of sellers can also have an effect: If you live in an area with lots of auto dealerships, the dealers may be willing to cut prices in an attempt to win your business. On the other hand, if there's only one dealership within 100 miles, the dealer may not feel much pressure to keep prices down.

Price determination is one of the most important topics in economics. Whether you're buying a car, a cheeseburger, a T-shirt, or a house, it's important to think clearly about how prices are determined. In this chapter, we will begin to learn how prices are determined by the interaction of buyers and sellers in markets. We will see:

- how the behavior of buyers is affected by prices, incomes, and other factors,

- how the behavior of sellers is affected by prices, technologies, and other factors, and

- how buyers and sellers come together to determine the price of a good, and the quantity that will be bought and sold.

MARKETS

In everyday language, we use the word "market" to refer to a particular place, where groceries and other items are bought and sold. But economists define markets in a broader way. A *market* is defined as *any organized exchange of a good or service between buyers and sellers.* Another way to say this is that a market is *any institution or mechanism that allows people to interact, for the purpose of buying and selling some good or service.*

Each good or service has its own market. There is a market for decaffeinated coffee, and a market for concert tickets, and a market for computer spreadsheet programs. There's one market for the services of emergency-room doctors, and another for the services of welders. There is a market for Iowa farmland, and another for California farmland. The market for hairstyling services in the Cincinnati area is a local market, in the sense that it isn't greatly affected by the hairstyling markets in other cities. On the other hand, the market for automobiles is a global market. The sellers come from the United States, Japan, Germany, Korea, and other countries, and they sell their products all around the world.

The details differ from one market to another, but all markets have one thing in common: In every case, there is regular communication between buyers and sellers, for the purpose of buying and selling some good or service.

In order to have an economic transaction in a market, we need both a buyer and a seller. We look at the behavior of buyers in the next section. After that, we look at the behavior of sellers. Finally, we put them together, to see how market outcomes are determined by the *interaction* between buyers and sellers.

DEMAND

We use the term *demand* to describe the actions of buyers. The *quantity demanded* is the amount of some good or service that buyers are willing to buy, at a specific price, in a given period of time. It's important to be specific about the time period that we are considering. For example, there is a vast difference between the quantity of gasoline demanded per week and the quantity of gasoline demanded per year.

The Law of Demand

Red-delicious apples often sell for about one dollar per pound. What would happen if the price were to rise to $1.50 per pound, while everything else stays the same? Most likely, the quantity demanded would decrease. Some people would switch to pears or bananas, and others would just eat less fruit. On the other hand, if the price of apples were to drop to 50 cents per pound, consumers would buy more apples. In other words, when price decreases, quantity demanded will rise.

This type of relationship occurs so frequently that we call it the *Law of Demand*.

The Law of Demand states that:

When the price of a good or service increases, the quantity demanded will decrease, all else equal. Conversely, when the price decreases, the quantity demanded will increase, all else equal.

In other words, the Law of Demand states that price and quantity demanded are *inversely related,* all else equal. The phrase "all else equal" is extremely important. The Law of Demand describes the relationship between price and quantity demanded, *when all variables other than the price of the good are unchanged.* If the price of apples goes up while all other variables remain the same, then the Law of Demand says that the quantity of apples demanded will go down. However, if the price of apples goes up while incomes or tastes or other variables are changing, there's no guarantee that people would want to buy fewer apples.

The Demand Schedule and the Demand Curve

There are several ways to illustrate the relationship between quantity demanded and price. Two of these are the demand schedule and the demand curve. A *demand schedule* is a table showing the quantity of a good or service that would be demanded, at a number of different prices. When constructing a demand schedule, we assume that *all other influences on consumers are held constant.* Thus, when we go from one entry in a demand schedule to the next entry, we assume that there are no changes in incomes, or in the prices of other products, or in any of the other variables that might have an influence on demand.

Table 3.1 is Rhonda's demand schedule for red-delicious apples. Since it is a demand schedule for a single person, it is called an *individual demand schedule*. (Later in this chapter, we will look at a *market demand schedule*, which describes the quantities demanded for all of the buyers in the market.)

At the store where Rhonda shops, red-delicious apples have been selling for $1 per pound. Table 3.1 tells us that, if the price were to stay at $1 per pound, Rhonda would buy 20 pounds of red-delicious apples per year.

However, if the price were to change, Rhonda would change her quantity demanded. In the top row of Table 3.1, we see that she would buy only 16 pounds per year if the price were to rise to $1.50 per pound. On the other hand, if the price were to fall to $0.50 per pound, she would buy 24 pounds per year. Rhonda obeys the Law of Demand: When there is an increase in the price of red-delicious apples, she demands a smaller quantity.

A *demand curve* is a graph of the information in a demand schedule. Figure 3.1 is Rhonda's demand curve for red-delicious

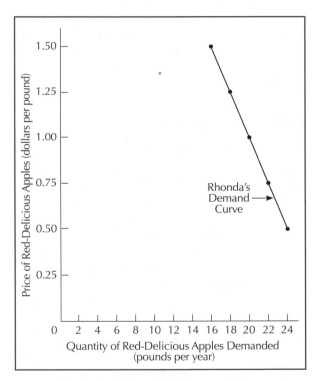

Figure 3.1 Rhonda's Demand Curve for Red-Delicious Apples

This demand curve shows the relationship between the price of red-delicious apples and the quantity of these apples that Rhonda is willing to buy. For example, when the price of apples is $1 per pound, Rhonda will buy 20 pounds per year. If the price drops to $0.50 per pound, she is willing to buy 24 pounds per year. The demand curve slopes downward as we move to the right, which indicates that Rhonda obeys the Law of Demand.

Table 3.1 Rhonda's Demand Schedule for Red-Delicious Apples

Price per pound	Quantity Demanded (pounds per year)
$1.50	16
1.25	18
1.00	20
0.75	22
0.50	24

apples. Figure 3.1 represents the same information that was shown in Table 3.1. Because Rhonda obeys the Law of Demand, *the demand curve slopes downward as we move to the right*. In this particular case, the demand curve is a straight line. However, the demand curve doesn't have to be straight in order to obey the Law of Demand. It can be curved in almost any way, as long as it slopes downward to the right.

Note that, in Figure 3.1, quantity demanded is on the horizontal axis and price is on the vertical axis. In the natural sciences, it's standard to put the independent variable on the horizontal axis. However, for better or worse, economists traditionally put price, which is the independent variable, on the vertical axis. Quantity demanded goes on the horizontal axis.

Individual Demand and Market Demand

Figure 3.1 deals with the demands of a single consumer. However, we are usually more interested in *market* demand. In order to get market demand, we add up the individual demands for all of the individuals in the market, as shown in Figure 3.2.

In Figure 3.2, we assume that Rhonda and Brian are the only two people in the market. To determine the market demand curve, we add Rhonda's demand and Brian's demand. When the price of red-delicious apples is $1.50 per pound, Brian doesn't buy any, so that the entire quantity demanded by the two people is Rhonda's 16 pounds per year. When the price is $1.25, Brian is willing to buy four pounds and Rhonda is willing to buy 18 pounds, so that the total quantity demanded by the two people is (4 + 18) = 22 pounds. We follow this same method in calculating all of the other points shown in Figure 3.2.

In order to plot a point on the market demand curve, we first locate the relevant price on the vertical axis. Then we move across

the graph horizontally, and add up the quantities demanded by all by the consumers. In other words, we add the individual demand curves *horizontally* to get the market demand curve.

We use the same techniques, regardless of how many consumers are in the market. In Figure 3.2, we add the demands of two people. If there were three people, we would add the demands of all three, and if there were 100 million people, we would add the demands of them all.

For the rest of this chapter, we will emphasize *market* demand. We show a market demand schedule and a market demand curve for red-delicious apples in Figure 3.3.

Movements Along the Demand Curve vs. Shifts in the Demand Curve

When we construct a demand curve for red-delicious apples, the price of red-delicious apples is the *only* thing that is allowed to change. Everything else is held constant. If there is a change in the price of red-delicious apples, the price change causes a movement along the existing demand curve for these apples. The same holds true for any demand curve: *If there is a change in the price of a good, the change in price will cause a movement along the existing demand curve for that good.*

The market demand curve shows the *willingness to pay* of the consumers in the market. At point A in Figure 3.3, if the price is $1.00 per pound, people are willing to buy 800 million pounds of red-delicious apples per year. If the price of red-delicious apples were to decrease from $1.00 per pound to $0.75 per pound, some consumers would react by increasing their quantity demanded. Figure 3.3 shows that, when the price drops from $1.00 per pound to $0.75 per pound, quantity demanded increases from 800 million pounds per year to 1000 million pounds per year. This is graphed as a movement downward and to

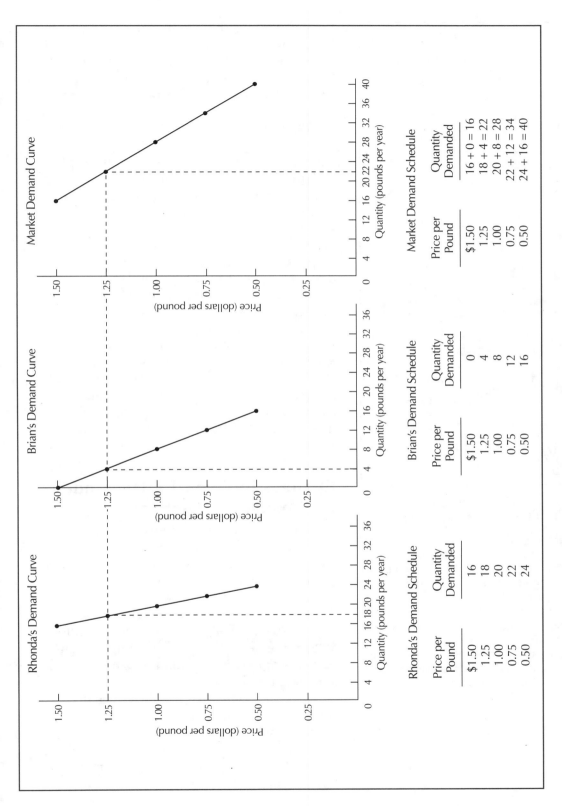

Figure 3.2 Combining Rhonda's Demand and Brian's Demand to Get Market Demand

This figure shows how we combine individual demand curves to get a market demand curve. For example, if the price of red-delicious apples is $1.25 per pound, we add Rhonda's quantity demanded of 18 pounds to Brian's quantity demanded of 4 pounds, and this gives us a total quantity demanded of 22 pounds. In a more realistic setting, with millions of buyers, we would still follow the same basic procedure, except that we would add over millions of buyers, instead of only two. Each point on the market demand curve is found by holding constant the price, and then moving horizontally across the demand curves for the individuals. Thus, we say that we form market demand curves by adding horizontally. Since Rhonda's demand curve slopes downward as we move to the right, and Brian's demand curve does the same, the market demand curve will also slope downward as we move to the right. This indicates that the market demand curve obeys the Law of Demand.

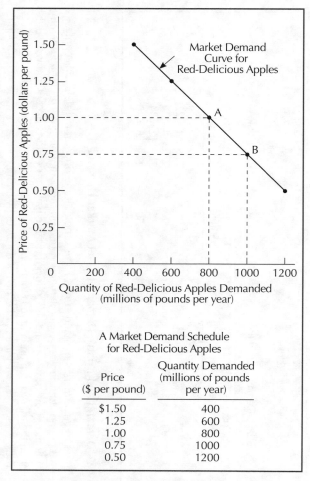

A Market Demand Schedule for Red-Delicious Apples	
Price ($ per pound)	Quantity Demanded (millions of pounds per year)
$1.50	400
1.25	600
1.00	800
0.75	1000
0.50	1200

Figure 3.3 A Market Demand Curve for Red-Delicious Apples

If we add together the quantities demanded for everyone in the market, we find a market demand curve. For example, at point A, the price is $1.00 per pound, and consumers are willing to buy 800 million pounds per year. If the price were to fall to $0.75 per pound, consumers would increase their quantity demanded from 800 million pounds per year to 1000 million pounds per year. This is shown by the movement from point A to point B. The market demand curve slopes downward as we move to the right, which indicates that the apple market obeys the Law of Demand.

the right along the existing demand curve, from point A to point B. The entire demand curve shown in Figure 3.3 slopes downward to the right. This indicates that the Law of Demand is obeyed by consumers in the market for red-delicious apples.

When we constructed the demand curve in Figure 3.3, we held everything constant, except for the price of red-delicious apples. What if there is a change in something other than the price of red-delicious apples? If a change occurs in something else, such as consumer incomes, or the prices of bananas and pears, we no longer move along the existing demand curve. Instead, we shift to a different demand curve. *If anything other than the price of the good changes, the change will cause a shift to an entirely new demand curve.*

This is a very important distinction. It's crucial to understand the difference between *moving along* an existing demand curve and *shifting* to a new demand curve. Movements along an existing demand curve are caused by changes in the price of the good; shifts to a new demand curve are caused by changes in something else.

Changes in Quantity Demanded vs. Changes in Demand

We have distinguished between (1) movements along an existing demand curve, which are caused by changes in price, and (2) shifts to a new demand curve, which are caused by changes in other variables. We can also use a different terminology to describe these two events. A *change in quantity demanded* refers to a movement along an existing demand curve. A *change in demand* refers to a shift to a new demand curve.

Thus, if the price of gasoline goes up, we could refer to a movement along the existing demand curve for gasoline, or we could refer to a change in the quantity of gasoline demanded. Each phrase has the same meaning. On the other hand, if incomes go up, we could refer to a shift to a new demand curve for gasoline, or we could refer to a change in demand for gasoline. Once again, each of these phrases has the same meaning.

Some of the forces that can lead to shifts in demand curves are:

- changes in the incomes of consumers,

- changes in the "tastes" or "preferences" of consumers,

- changes in the prices of other goods,

- changes in expectations of future prices,

- changes in expectations of future incomes, and

- changes in the size and composition of the population.

We now take a more detailed look at these influences.

The Effect of a Change in Incomes: Normal Goods and Inferior Goods

If you're like most people, you will respond to an increase in your income by spending more on a wide variety of goods. For example, if there is an increase in consumer incomes, many buyers will increase their demand for red-delicious apples. In other words, when consumer incomes go up, the market demand curve for red-delicious apples will shift *to the right*. This is shown in Figure 3.4(a). The original demand curve is D_0. When incomes rise, the result is a new demand curve, D_1. This

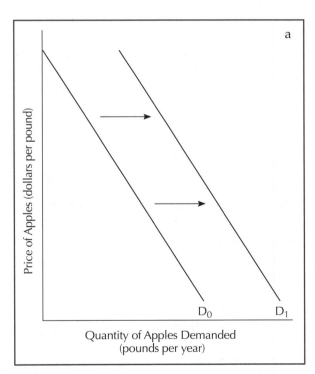

Figure 3.4 Shifts in the Demand Curve, Caused by Changes in Income

Red-delicious apples are normal goods. This means that an increase in incomes will lead to an increase in the demand for such apples. This is shown as a rightward shift in the demand curve for apples.

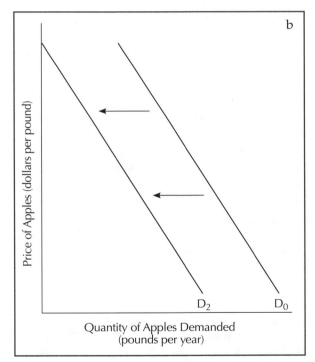

For a normal good such as red-delicious apples, a decrease in incomes will lead to a decrease in demand. This is shown as a leftward shift in the demand curve for apples.

shift can be interpreted in two ways. First, at any given price, the quantity that consumers are willing to buy has increased. Second, at any given quantity, the amount that consumers are willing to pay has increased.

Normal Goods. If demand for a good increases when incomes increase, we call the good a *normal good*. Apples are normal goods, as are concert tickets, new cars, and most other goods. For all of these goods, an increase in income leads to an increase in demand. In Figure 3.4(a), when incomes rise, the demand curve shifts *to the right,* because we are dealing with a normal good. It follows that, if incomes were to fall, the demand curve would shift *to the left* for a normal good. This is shown as a shift from D_0 to D_2 in Figure 3.4(b). This leftward shift can be interpreted in two ways. First, at any given price, the quantity that consumers are willing to buy has decreased. Second, at any given quantity, the amount that consumers are willing to pay has decreased.

Inferior Goods. Most goods are normal goods, but the demand for some goods responds to income changes in a different way. If you want to buy a car and your income is very low, you may feel that you can only afford an old used car. If your income increases, you'll probably decide to buy a better car. If there is a general increase in incomes, the demand for old used cars will fall; that is, the market demand curve for old used cars will shift *to the left.* Similarly, if there is a general *decrease* in incomes, we expect the market demand curve for old used cars to shift *to the right.* If demand for a good decreases when incomes increase, we call the good an *inferior good.* Some types of used clothes may be inferior goods, while higher-quality new clothes are normal goods. One study indicates that butter is a normal good, but margarine is an inferior good. Can you think of any good that might be an inferior good for you?

The Effect of a Change in Tastes or Preferences

Once again, it's important to remember that a demand curve is constructed by allowing the price to vary, while everything else remains constant. If there is a change in another influence, such as consumer tastes or preferences, then the demand curve will shift.

In recent years, the American public has become much more aware of the need for a healthy diet. Doctors urge their patients to eat five servings of fruits or vegetables per day, as a way to reduce the risk of cancer. Because of this, consumer preferences have changed, and consumers have increased their demand for many fruits and vegetables, including red-delicious apples. This would be represented by a rightward shift in the demand curve for red-delicious apples, as with the shift from D_0 to D_1 in Figure 3.4(a). Some changes in preferences can lead to increased demand for some goods, but other changes in preferences can lead to decreased demand for certain goods. In *Real Economics for Real People 3.1*, we discuss several cases of changes in tastes.

The Effect of a Change in the Price of Another Good: Substitutes and Complements

If there is a change in the price of red-delicious apples, we move along the existing demand curve for these apples. However, if the price of any *other* good changes, the demand curve for red-delicious apples may shift.

Substitutes. If there is an increase in the price of Granny Smith apples, then some people may increase their demand for red-delicious apples. In a case like this, where the demand for one good increases when the price of a different good increases, we say that the two goods are *substitutes*. In other words, two goods are substitutes if the demand curve for one good shifts to the right when the price of

Real Economics for Real People 3.1:
Oprah Winfrey and the Book Market

Jacquelyn Mitchard is the author of a novel called *The Deep End of the Ocean.* Some 100,000 copies of this book were in print by September, 1996. Then, however, the book was recommended on "Oprah's Book Show", a monthly feature of Oprah Winfrey's television talk show. Within a few months, 850,000 copies were in print. Economists would say that the publicity from the Oprah Winfrey Show caused the demand curve for *The Deep End of the Ocean* to shift to the right.

The shift in demand for Jacquelyn Mitchard's book was caused by a change in "preferences" or "tastes". Preferences can change for many reasons. For example, since the 1960s, medical reports have suggested that smoking cigarettes is unhealthy, and this has caused many people to decrease their demand for cigarettes. In other words, the demand curves for many brands of cigarettes have shifted to the left. However, there has been some increase in the demand for cigarettes that are low in "tar", because these are perceived as less unhealthy than other cigarettes. The demand curves for some low-tar brands of cigarette have shifted to the right.

There is nothing new about changes in preferences. In 1934, "It Happened One Night" was a very popular movie. Audiences were amazed by one scene in which the actor Clark Gable took off his shirt. In so doing, he revealed that he wasn't wearing an undershirt. This was considered very unusual and daring, because most men wore undershirts at that time. As a result of Gable's dressing habits, undershirts suddenly became much less popular than they had been before. Sales of undershirts decreased dramatically. Economists would say that the demand for undershirts decreased; that is, the demand curve for undershirts shifted to the left.

Toy manufacturers are especially aware of shifts in demand. Every year, some new product will capture the imagination of buyers. Teenage Mutant Ninja Turtles were a hot item in the early 1990s. In 1996, the big fad was Beanie Babies. In each case, the preferences of consumers changed, leading to large shifts in the demand curves for particular products.

These examples have shown just a few of the ways in which tastes or preferences can change. When preferences change, demand curves will shift.

the other good rises. Similarly, we say that two goods are substitutes if the demand curve for one good will shift to the left when the price of the other good falls. The word "substitutes" comes from the fact that consumers will *substitute* away from the good that has become relatively more expensive, when there is a change in the price of one of the goods. Consumers will then substitute toward the good that has become relatively cheaper. *When two goods are substitutes, the price of one good and the demand for the other good will move in the same direction.*

The increase in the demand for red-delicious apples, brought about by the increase in the price of Granny Smith apples, is represented as a rightward shift in the demand curve for red-delicious apples, as in Figure 3.4(a). On the other hand, if the price of Granny Smith apples had *fallen*, the demand curve for red-delicious apples would have shifted to the *left*, as in Figure 3.4(b).

Coffee and tea are substitutes. Vacations at the beach and vacations in the mountains are substitutes. Similarly, vacations in Europe are a substitute for vacations in the United States. Other pairs of substitutes include butter and margarine, and oranges and grapefruit. In every case, consumers are likely to use one or the other, but not both at the same time. Therefore, consumers will tend to substitute from one good to the other when the prices change. In *Real Economics for Real People 3.2*, we take a look at another example of substitutes.

Complements. Many people like to consume bread and butter together. If the price of butter goes up substantially, these people will probably decide to buy less bread. We say that bread and butter are ***complements.*** Two goods are complements if the demand for one good decreases when the price of another good increases. Here's another way to say the same thing: Two goods are complements if the demand curve for one good shifts to the left when the price of the other good increases. Similarly, two goods are complements if the demand curve for one good shifts to the right when the price of the other good decreases. *When two goods are complements, the price of one good and the demand for the other good will move in* opposite *directions.*

The decrease in demand for bread that is caused by the increase in the price of butter is represented as a leftward shift in the demand curve for bread. This is similar to the leftward shift shown in Figure 3.4(b). On the other hand, if the price of butter had *fallen,* the demand curve for bread would have shifted to the *right*. This is similar to the rightward shift shown in Figure 3.4(a).

There are many examples of goods that are complements. Coffee beans are complementary with several goods, including donuts, cream, sugar, coffee filters, and coffee makers. Automobiles and gasoline are complements, as are computers and printers.

Of course, many pairs of goods are neither substitutes nor complements. When the price of milk goes up, there is probably no effect on the demand for umbrellas. When the demand for one good is unaffected by the price of another good, we say that the two goods are *independent in demand*.

Other Influences on Demand

So far, we have identified three variables that can lead to shifts in demand curves. These are (1) incomes, (2) tastes or preferences, and (3) the prices of other goods. In this section, we'll look at a few other influences.

Expectations of Future Prices. Suppose that you're thinking of buying airline tickets for a vacation. If you believe that today's ticket prices will continue for the foreseeable future, you may as well buy some today. However, if you believe that the airlines will begin to offer discounted airfares in a few weeks, it might make sense for you *not* to buy today. Since you expect that prices will decrease in the future, your demand curve for *today's* purchases will shift to the left.

If you think that prices are about to go *down,* you may delay your purchases, in order to take advantage of the lower prices in the future. On the other hand, if you think that prices are about to go *up,* you may hurry to buy now. Another way to think of this is that buying now is usually a fairly close substitute with buying in the near future. *The expected future demand for a good and the current price of that good move in the* same *direction.*

Expectations of Future Incomes. If you believe that your income will be higher in the future, you may consume more now. For example, a woman who is just finishing medical school may be poor right now, but she can reasonably expect to have a much higher income in the future. She may be willing to borrow money in order to consume more now.

Real Economics for Real People 3.2:
Going South of the Border in Search of Cheap Gas

Drivers in the San Diego area usually buy their gasoline in the San Diego area, and pay little attention to the prices in Los Angeles, or across the border in Tijuana, Mexico. However, in 1996, gasoline prices increased substantially in the San Diego area. Eventually, the price of regular gasoline was 22 cents per gallon higher in San Diego than in Tijuana. For diesel fuel, the price difference was 64 cents per gallon! When the price differences got this large, some San Diegans began to drive across the border to buy their gasoline.

We can analyze this example, along with some similar examples, to get a better idea of how consumers make their buying decisions. Let's say that an Exxon station and a Texaco station are right across the street from each other. Furthermore, let's say that each sells regular gasoline for $1.30 per gallon. Some people go to the Texaco station, and some go to the Exxon station, and each station sells a large volume of gasoline.

What will happen if the Exxon station keeps its price at $1.30, and the Texaco station lowers its price to $1.25 per gallon? In all likelihood, many more people will buy from the Texaco station, because it is now selling gasoline for a lower price. If the two stations are very close to each other, and if they sell gasoline that is of similar quality, why pay more? This example indicates that Texaco gasoline and Exxon gasoline are substitutes: When the price of Texaco gasoline falls, the demand for Exxon gasoline falls. In fact, an economist would say that the Texaco gasoline is a *very close* substitute for the Exxon gasoline, because the two stations are so close to each other, and they sell similar products.

The situation is a little different if the two stations are farther apart from each other. The true opportunity cost of buying gasoline includes the price charged at the pump, but it also includes the time and trouble that it takes to get there. If the Exxon station is right around the corner, and the Texaco station is miles away, you still might be willing to buy from the Exxon station, even if it sells for a few cents more per gallon. When the two stations are farther apart, economists would say that their products are substitutes, but not necessarily very close substitutes.

If two stations are quite far apart, it will take a large price difference before the prices can have an effect on each other. If Tijuana gasoline is only cheaper than San Diego gasoline by one cent per gallon, no one will take the trouble to cross the border to buy gasoline. However, as we have seen, people will cross the border to buy gasoline if the price difference is large enough. San Diego gasoline and Tijuana gasoline are substitutes, although not very close substitutes: When the price of San Diego gasoline increases by a sufficiently large amount, the demand for Tijuana gasoline increases.

This example reminds us that consumers are always on the lookout for a bargain. If they can buy one product for a lower opportunity cost than a substitute product, they will shift their demand from one product to the other, even if it's necessary to cross international borders.

On the other hand, if you believe that your income will be lower in the future, you may want to consume less now. For instance, as people approach retirement, they know that their income is about to decrease. In response, they will typically spend less than their current income. That is, they will save. By saving, people increase the amount that they can spend during retirement. *For most goods, current demand will move in the same direction as expected future income.*

Size and Composition of the Population. All else equal, market demands are affected by the size of the population. When there are more consumers, we would expect more demand. Populations around the world have been rising steadily for centuries, and the demand curves for many goods have shifted to the right over the years.

Market demands are also affected by the *composition* of the population. For example, the elderly population has grown very rapidly in

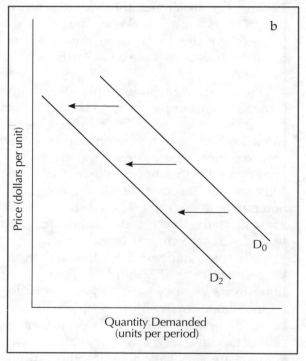

Figure 3.5 Summary of the Influences That Can Shift Demand Curves

An increase in demand (that is, a rightward shift in the demand curve) can be caused by:
- An increase in incomes, if the good is a normal good.
- A decrease in incomes, if the good is an inferior good.
- A change in consumer tastes or preferences.
- An increase in the price of a substitute good.
- A decrease in the price of a complement good.
- Expectations of higher prices in the future.
- Expectations of higher incomes in the future.
- An increase in the size of the population.
- A change in the composition of the population.

A decrease in demand (that is, a leftward shift in the demand curve) can be caused by:
- A decrease in incomes, if the good is a normal good.
- An increase in incomes, if the good is an inferior good.
- A change in consumer tastes or preferences.
- A decrease in the price of a substitute good.
- An increase in the price of a complement good.
- Expectations of lower prices in the future.
- Expectations of lower incomes in the future.
- A decrease in the size of the population.
- A change in the composition of the population.

recent years. This has led to increases in the demand for retirement communities, nursing-home care, and so on.

The various influences on demand are summarized in Figure 3.5.

Reality Check:
Interim Review Questions

IR3-1. Let's say that photographic film is a normal good, and that incomes increase. What will happen to the demand curve for photographic film?

IR3-2. Let's say that the price of photographic film increases, because of a government price control. Would we represent this as a shift in the demand curve for photographic film, or a movement along the existing demand curve?

IR3-3. Consumers learn that a local furniture store is having a sale next week. That is, next week's prices will be lower than this week's prices. What will happen to *this week's* demand curve for furniture?

SUPPLY

When we talk about the actions of sellers, we use the term *supply*. Boeing is a supplier of commercial aircraft, Sony is a supplier of consumer electronics, and Volkswagen is a supplier of automobiles. In the market for the services of accountants, the suppliers are individual people who have been trained to provide such services.

The *quantity supplied* is the amount of some good or service that sellers are willing to sell, at a specific price, in a given period of time.

The Law of Supply

Economists think about supply and demand in similar ways. Many things can affect supply, but economists single out the price of the good for special attention. We will focus on the price of the good when we think about supply, just as we focused on price when thinking about demand.

The *Law of Supply* states that:
When the price of a good or service increases, the quantity supplied will increase, all else equal. Conversely, when the price decreases, the quantity supplied will decrease, all else equal.

In other words, the Law of Supply states that sellers have a *direct, positive relationship* between price and quantity supplied, all else equal.

We have two main reasons to expect sellers to obey the Law of Supply. First, *when production of a good increases, the costs of additional production will often increase*. If apple growers try to increase their production, they will have to use more intensive methods of cultivation. For example, they may use more pesticides and fertilizer. These may succeed in increasing the size of the apple crop, but they will also increase costs.

The second reason for suppliers to obey the Law of Supply is that *price is a powerful signal of opportunities for profit*. Consider a business firm that makes contact lenses and plastic packaging. What happens if the price of contact lenses goes up, while the price of plastic packaging stays the same? The firm will see that it can increase profits by putting more of its production into contact lenses.

The Supply Schedule and the Supply Curve

A *supply schedule* is a table that lists different prices for a good or service, and shows the quantity that would be supplied at each price. When we construct a supply schedule, we allow the price of a good to change, but we assume that *all other influences on suppliers are held constant.* Thus, the technology of production is assumed to be unchanged. The prices of the materials used in the production process are also assumed to be unchanged, as are all other influences. In a supply schedule, the *only* thing that we allow to vary is the price of the good.

A *supply curve* is a graph of the information in a supply schedule. Figure 3.6 shows a market supply schedule for red-delicious apples, as well as the corresponding market supply curve. *Because of the Law of Supply, the supply curve slopes upward as we move to the right.*

We construct a market supply curve, such as the one in Figure 3.6, by adding together the supply curves of the individual business firms. We won't actually show any supply curves for individual firms here, although we will study firm supply curves in a later chapter. For the rest of this chapter, we focus on market supply curves.

Movements Along the Supply Curve vs. Shifts in the Supply Curve

When we construct a supply curve, the *only* thing that changes is the price of the good. Everything else is held constant. If there is a change in the price of red-delicious apples, we move along the existing supply curve for red-delicious apples. The same holds true for any other good. *A change in the price of a good will cause a movement along the existing supply curve for that good.*

This can be seen in Figure 3.6. At point C, the price is $0.75 per pound of apples, and the quantity supplied is 750 million pounds per year. When the price goes up to $1.00 per pound, sellers respond by increasing their quantity supplied. In this example, the sellers of red-delicious apples increase their quantity supplied to 800 million pounds per year, as a result of the increase in price. In Figure 3.6,

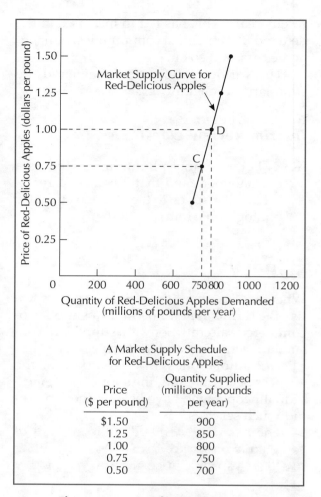

A Market Supply Schedule
for Red-Delicious Apples

Price ($ per pound)	Quantity Supplied (millions of pounds per year)
$1.50	900
1.25	850
1.00	800
0.75	750
0.50	700

Figure 3.6 A Market Supply Curve for Red-Delicious Apples

If we add together the quantities supplied by all of the sellers in the market, we find a market supply curve. For example, at point C, the price of red-delicious apples is $0.75 per pound, and sellers are willing to supply 750 million pounds per year. If the price were to increase to $1.00 per pound, sellers would increase their quantity supplied from 750 million pounds per year to 800 million pounds per year. This is shown by the movement from point C to point D. The market supply curve slopes upward as we move to the right, which indicates that apple sellers obey the Law of Supply.

this is seen as a movement from point C to point D. The entire supply curve shown in Figure 3.6 slopes upward to the right. This indicates that the Law of Supply is obeyed by firms in the market for red-delicious apples.

When we constructed the supply curve in Figure 3.6, we held everything constant, except for the price of red-delicious apples. What if there is a change in something other than the price of red-delicious apples? If a change occurs in something else, such as the price of pesticides, we no longer move along the existing supply curve. Instead, we shift to a different supply curve. *If anything other than the price of the good changes, the change will cause a shift to an entirely new supply curve.*

This is a crucial distinction. *Movements along* an existing supply curve are caused by changes in the price of the good; *shifts* to a new supply curve are caused by changes in something else.

Changes in Quantity Supplied vs. Changes in Supply

In the last few paragraphs, we have distinguished between (1) movements along an existing supply curve, which are caused by changes in price, and (2) shifts to a new supply curve, which are caused by changes in other variables. We can also use a different terminology. A *change in quantity supplied* refers to a movement along an existing supply curve. A *change in supply* refers to a shift to a new supply curve.

Thus, if the price of 3.5-inch computer diskettes were to go up, we could refer to a movement along the existing supply curve for these diskettes, or we could refer to a change in the quantity of diskettes supplied. Each phrase has the same meaning. On the other hand, consider what would happen if there were an increase in the price of the plastics that are necessary to produce computer diskettes. This would make it more costly to produce diskettes, and it would cause a shift to a new

supply curve for diskettes. Alternatively, instead of referring to a shift to a new supply curve, we could refer to a change in the supply of diskettes. Once again, each of these phrases has the same meaning.

We will now discuss some of the forces that can lead to shifts in supply curves, including:

- changes in input prices,
- changes in technology,
- changes in the prices of other goods,
- changes in taxes or regulations, and
- changes in the number of sellers.

We will now take a more detailed look at some of these influences.

The Effect of a Change in Input Prices

Fertilizer is used in the production of apples. In Figure 3.7(a), we show what happens to the supply curve for red-delicious apples, when there is an increase in the price of fertilizer. When the price of fertilizer goes up, it becomes more expensive to produce apples. After an increase in the price of an important input, such as fertilizer, the cost of bringing any given quantity of apples to market will be greater than before. Therefore, the supply curve for red-delicious apples will shift *to the left* when there is an increase in the price of fertilizer. In Figure 3.7(a), this is shown as a shift from the old supply curve, S_0, to the new supply curve, S_1. We can interpret this shift in two ways. First, at any given price, the quantity that sellers are willing to bring to market has decreased. Second, for any given quantity, there has been an increase in the price that firms need to receive, in order to be willing to supply that quantity to the market.

When an office building is built, the construction firm uses bulldozers, welding equipment, steel, and lumber, as well as the labor of engineers and construction workers. If any of these inputs were to become cheaper, the

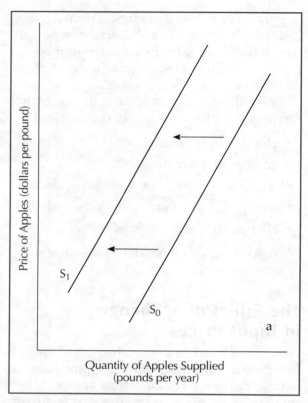

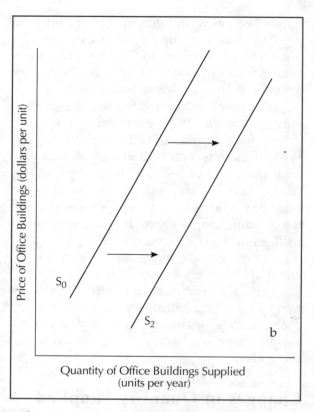

Figure 3.7 Shifts in the Supply Curve, Caused by Changes in the Price of an Input

An increase in the price of any input will cause a decrease in supply. In this case, the price of fertilizer increases, and the supply of red-delicious apples decreases. This is shown as a leftward shift of the supply curve for apples.

A decrease in the price of any input will cause an increase in supply. In this case, the price of steel goes down, and the supply of office buildings increases. This is shown as a rightward shift of the supply curve for office buildings.

supply curve for office buildings would shift to the right. This is shown in Figure 3.7(b). When the price of steel goes down, the supply curve for office buildings shifts to the right, from S_0 to S_2.

The Effect of a Change in Technology

The *technology* of production is society's pool of knowledge about how to produce. In the last hundred years, many industries have experienced rapid improvements in technology. For example, agriculture has gone from using horse-drawn plows to using massive

tractors. The accounting profession has changed with the introduction of hardware and software for high-speed data processing, such as computer spreadsheet programs.

When there is an improvement in production technology, producers are able to supply products more cheaply, without having to reduce the quality of their products. Thus, most technological changes will shift supply curves *to the right*. Consider a new production process that allows firms to produce more apples, without increasing the amount of inputs that must be used. This would cause a rightward shift in the supply curve, much like the shift from S_0 to S_2 in Figure 3.7(b). At any given price, the quantity that firms will supply has gone up. Alternatively, for any given quantity, there has been a decrease in the price that firms need to receive, in order to be willing to supply that quantity to the market.

Other Influences on Supply

We've highlighted the effects of input prices and technology on supply. These are certainly among the most important influences on supply. However, there are several other important influences, and we discuss them briefly here.

Prices of Other Goods. Consider a publishing house that produces a variety of books and magazines. If the price of magazines goes up, the publisher may reduce its output of books, in order to devote more resources to the production of magazines. This would be shown as a leftward shift of the supply curve for books. On the other hand, if the price of magazines were to fall, there may be a rightward shift in the supply curve for books.

In some cases, one good is a by-product of the production of another good. For example, the main product of a sawmill is finished lumber. However, sawmills also create by-products such as sawdust and wood chips. These by-products can be used to make packaging, cat litter, and other products. Consequently, when the price of lumber goes up, the quantity of lumber supplied will increase. At the same time, the supply curve of wood chips will shift to the right.

Taxes and Regulations. From the point of view of the business firm, a tax is just like any other cost of doing business. Thus an increase in a property tax, or a corporation income tax, or a business license fee is much like an increase in the price of an input, which we discussed above. If a tax goes up, supply will decrease, so that the supply curve will shift to the left. If a tax goes down, the supply curve will shift to the right. (In later chapters, we will discuss the effects of taxes in more detail.)

Regulations also affect supply. Firms face a number of regulations relating to product safety, occupational health and safety, employee benefits, and the environment. For example, firms that process meat or poultry are required to follow a number of government regulations, in an attempt to ensure that the nation's food supply is safe. The Federal government requires car manufacturers to meet a standard, in terms of the number of miles per gallon that can be achieved by the average car. Dental hygienists, barbers, psychologists, and doctors are all required to obtain government licenses before they can practice their professions. Many of these regulations may produce benefits, but it's also important to realize that they are not free. The regulations raise costs, and lead to reductions in supply.

The Number of Sellers. If we hold constant the amount that each firm in a market produces, then the market supply curve will shift to the right when more firms enter the market (all else equal). Similarly, when firms exit from the industry, the market supply curve will shift to the left (all else equal). In *Real Economics for Real People 3.3,* we discuss the increase in the number of sellers in the commercial airlines industry.

We summarize some of the influences on supply curves in Figure 3.8.

Reality Check: Interim Review Questions

IR3-4. One type of plastic is an important input in the production of compact discs. There is an increase in the price of this type of plastic. What effect will this have on the supply curve for compact discs?

IR3-5. Scientists come up with a new invention, which makes it possible to produce steel with fewer inputs than were necessary before. What will happen to the supply curve for steel?

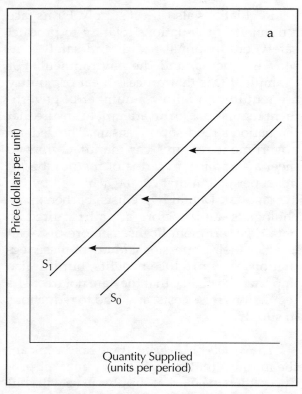

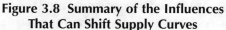

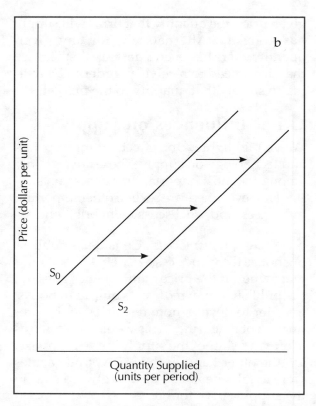

Figure 3.8 Summary of the Influences That Can Shift Supply Curves

A decrease in supply (that is, a leftward shift in the supply curve) can be caused by:
- An increase in the price of an input.
- A deterioration of technology. (Fortunately, this doesn't happen very often.)
- Certain types of change in the price of another good.
- An increase in a tax.
- An increase in a regulation.
- A decrease in the number of sellers.

An increase in supply (that is, a rightward shift in the supply curve) can be caused by:
- A decrease in the price of an input.
- A technological advance.
- Certain other types of change in the price of another good.
- A decrease in a tax.
- A decrease in a regulation.
- An increase in the number of sellers.

MARKET EQUILIBRIUM: THE INTERACTION OF SUPPLY AND DEMAND

So far, we've looked at demand and supply separately. We can now put them together. Our goal is to learn how the market determines the price and the quantity that will be bought and sold.

In Figure 3.9, we combine the market demand curve from Figure 3.3 and the market supply curve from Figure 3.6.

Surpluses

We can see the interaction between supply and demand, by examining three situations that can occur in markets. The quantity demanded can be *less than* the quantity supplied, or the quantity demanded can be *greater than* the quantity supplied, or the quantity demanded

Real Economics for Real People 3.3:
How Southwest Airlines Got More People to Fly

From the late 1930s until the late 1970s, if a company wanted to enter the commercial airlines industry, it had to get the approval of a government agency called the Civil Aeronautics Board (CAB). Since the CAB turned down every application, it was effectively impossible for new firms to enter the industry. As a result, the supply of airline flights was restricted. In other words, the supply curve of airline flights was kept farther to the left than it would have been. We would expect that this restriction of supply would keep the quantity of airline trips down, relative to what it might have been.

During the 1970s, there was more and more dissatisfaction with the CAB and its policy of keeping new airlines out of the business. Finally, in 1978, Congress passed a law that allowed new airlines to offer their services. One of the biggest success stories has been that of Southwest Airlines, which had a dramatic effect on air travel in the western United States in the early 1990s. Southwest tended to concentrate on smaller airports, such as the ones at Burbank and San Jose, California, instead of larger ones, such as those at Los Angeles and San Fran-

cisco. By offering more flights, Southwest Airlines pushed the supply curve to the right. One study of the West Coast airlines market indicates that the amount of traffic increased by 60 percent, while prices fell by an average of one-third. Southwest may not have been responsible for all of these changes in price and quantity, but it certainly had an important effect.

In 1996 and 1997, Southwest Airlines began to pursue the same kind of strategy on the East Coast. Once again, Southwest prefers to focus on smaller airports, such as Providence, Rhode Island, instead of bigger ones like Boston's Logan Airport. If the experience in California is any guide, Southwest should be able to increase the supply of flights on the East Coast.

In almost every market, the entry of new firms can bring benefits. When supply curves are pushed to the right, consumers will be able to enjoy a higher quantity. Thus, economists tend to be very skeptical about artificial restrictions on entry into an industry, such as those that were once enforced by the Civil Aeronautics Board.

can be *equal to* the quantity supplied. We begin with the situation in which quantity demanded is *less* than quantity supplied.

What would happen if the price of red-delicious apples were $1.50 per pound? At this price, Figure 3.9 shows that the quantity supplied is 900 million pounds per year, but the quantity demanded is only 400 million pounds per year. When quantity demanded is less than quantity supplied, we have a *surplus*. The amount of the surplus is the difference between the quantity supplied and the quantity demanded. In this case, there is a surplus

of (900 million − 400 million) = 500 million pounds of red-delicious apples per year.

The surplus means that crates of unsold apples will accumulate. At a price of $1.50 per pound, the surpluses would pile up, week after week after week. Pretty soon, stores and warehouses would be bursting with surplus apples that can't be sold.

This creates an expensive problem for the sellers, because it costs a lot to carry large inventories. Very quickly, sellers will have a bright idea: "If we charge a lower price, we can sell some of that stuff in the warehouse."

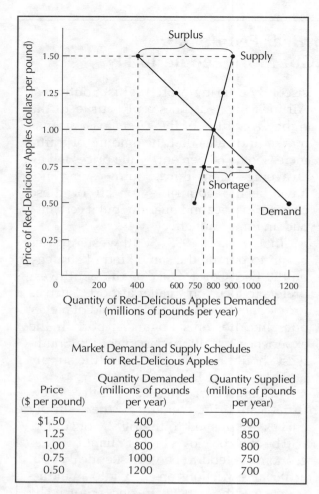

Market Demand and Supply Schedules
for Red-Delicious Apples

Price ($ per pound)	Quantity Demanded (millions of pounds per year)	Quantity Supplied (millions of pounds per year)
$1.50	400	900
1.25	600	850
1.00	800	800
0.75	1000	750
0.50	1200	700

Figure 3.9 Equilibrium in the Market for Red-Delicious Apples

If the price of red-delicious apples is $1.50 per pound, the quantity supplied is 900 million pounds per year, but the quantity demanded is only 400 million pounds per year. This means that we have a surplus of (900 million – 400 million) = 500 million pounds per year. The surplus will create pressure for the price to fall. If the price of apples is $0.75 per pound, the quantity demanded is 1000 million pounds per year, but the quantity supplied is only 750 million pounds per year. This means that we have a shortage of (1000 million – 750 million) = 250 million pounds per year. The shortage will create pressure for the price to rise. If the price of red-delicious apples is $1.00 per pound, the quantity demanded will be 800 million pounds and the quantity supplied will also be 800 million. This is an equilibrium. When the quantity demanded is equal to the quantity supplied, there is no reason for the price to change, because both buyers and sellers are satisfied.

A surplus creates pressure for the price to fall. As the price falls, the quantity supplied will decrease, and the quantity demanded will increase. Because of this, surpluses don't usually last for very long.

Shortages

What would happen if the price of red-delicious apples were only $0.75 per pound? At this price, Figure 3.9 shows that the quantity demanded is 1000 million pounds per year (that is, one billion pounds per year). However, the quantity supplied is only 750 million pounds per year. When the quantity demanded is greater than the quantity supplied, we have a *shortage.* The amount of the shortage is the difference between the quantity demanded and the quantity supplied. When the price is $0.75 per pound, the shortage is (1000 million – 750 million) = 250 million pounds of apples per year. In this situation, some buyers will be unable to find any apples at all.

A shortage is a difficult situation. Before long, buyers will begin to offer more money for apples. Since many people are willing to pay more than $0.75 per pound, sellers will guess that they can increase their profits by raising the selling price. *A shortage creates pressure for the price to rise.* As the price increases, the quantity supplied will increase, and the quantity demanded will fall. Because of this, shortages can't usually last for very long.

Equilibrium

An interesting thing happens when the price of red-delicious apples is $1.00 per pound. At this price, the quantity demanded is 800 million pounds per year, and the quantity supplied is also 800 million pounds per year! We have neither a surplus nor a shortage. Instead, quantity demanded and quantity supplied are equal. When quantity demanded equals quantity supplied, economists say that the market is in *equilibrium.* When the market is in equilibrium, there is no incentive for buyers or sellers to change their behavior. Both buyers and sellers are satisfied.

The equilibrium has two parts—a price and a quantity. The *equilibrium price* is the price at which quantity supplied equals quantity demanded. The phrase *equilibrium quantity* can be used to refer to either the quantity supplied or the quantity demanded, since they are equal when the market is in equilibrium.

Clearly, an equilibrium has some big advantages, but these advantages can only be realized if the market is able to find the equilibrium price. Fortunately, *powerful market forces lead toward equilibrium.* When the market price is higher than the equilibrium price, there is a surplus, and we have seen that surpluses lead to downward pressure on price. When the market price is lower than the equilibrium price, there is a shortage, which leads to upward pressure on price. Thus, the price will tend to fall when it is above equilibrium, and it will tend to rise when it is below equilibrium. Most markets move toward equilibrium very quickly.

Remember that the demand curve shows the relationship between price and quantity demanded, while the supply curve shows the relationship between price and quantity supplied. In Figure 3.9, we have plotted a supply curve and a demand curve on the same graph. The equilibrium price is $1.00 per pound of apples. If you find $1.00 per pound on the vertical axis in Figure 3.9, and then follow the dashed line to the right, you will go to the place where the supply curve crosses the demand curve. *Graphically, the equilibrium can be found at the intersection of the demand curve and the supply curve.*

Whenever you see a supply-demand diagram, such as Figure 3.9, you can easily find the equilibrium price and quantity by locating the place where the supply curve intersects the demand curve. From that point, if you go straight to the left, you will find the equilibrium price. If you go straight down, you'll find the equilibrium quantity.

The Beauty of Market Equilibrium

No one sets out with the goal of achieving market equilibrium. Buyers just want to get the most for their money, and sellers just want to make a profit. And yet, the interaction of buyers and sellers leads the market to equilibrium. This is a remarkable fact, and it is one of the most important concepts in all of economics. In equilibrium, both buyers and sellers are satisfied. This is a very good outcome, and markets achieve it without government intervention. There is no need for a dictator or a bureaucracy to tell people what to do. Instead, the market achieves a desirable outcome on its own.

The Scottish economist Adam Smith used the phrase *invisible hand* to describe the beauty of market equilibrium. Even though no one sets out with the goal of achieving market equilibrium, it is as if an invisible hand leads the market in that direction.

The invisible hand is extremely powerful. Markets usually move quickly and strongly toward equilibrium. Consequently, if there is an attempt to keep a market away from its equilibrium price and quantity, lots of problems can occur. In the next chapter, we will learn about some of the problems that happen when governments try to keep prices away from their equilibrium levels.

Reality Check: Interim Review Questions

IR3-6. The equilibrium price of one type of spiral-bound notebook is $2.50. If the price were $1, would there be a shortage or a surplus? What would happen if the price were $4?

IR3-7. In a supply-demand diagram, what is special about the point at which the demand curve crosses the supply curve?

ECONOMICS AND YOU: SUPPLY, DEMAND, AND AUTOMOBILE PRICES

At the beginning of this chapter, we asked why different automobile models are sold for different prices. The ideas developed in this chapter should help us to answer the question. *Prices are determined by the* interaction *of supply and demand.*

Supply is clearly important to the determination of prices. One reason that a Ferrari is more expensive than an Oldsmobile Cutlass Ciera is that the Ferrari is costlier to build. The Ferrari uses more expensive materials, and more labor is required.

Taxes also have an effect on supply. Any tax will effectively raise the costs of production. All else equal, a car buyer will have to pay a greater total price if the car is taxed than if it is not taxed. One form of tax is a tariff, which is a tax on items that are imported from one country to another. Since cars are subject to tariffs, the price of an imported car will be higher than the price of a domestically produced car, as long as all other influences on price are the same.

In the determination of prices, demand is just as important as supply. Some Mercedes-Benz models are sold at higher prices in the United States than in Germany. In some cases, the price in the U.S. is more than twice as high!

Shipping costs and tariffs aren't large enough to explain such a big difference in prices. The reason for the difference is that some Americans are willing to pay more than some Germans, for the same car. In other words, demand for some Mercedes cars is relatively greater in the U.S. than in Germany.

Supply and demand are both essential for understanding prices and quantities. A British economist, Alfred Marshall, popularized a way of thinking about the interaction of supply and demand. Marshall compared supply and demand to a pair of scissors. For one thing, an intersecting supply curve and demand curve look a little like a pair of scissors. Moreover, you can't cut a piece of paper very easily unless you have *both* blades of the pair of scissors. And you can't explain prices and quantities unless you have *both* supply and demand.

In this chapter, we've set out the basics of supply and demand. In the next chapter, we will apply the supply-demand framework in a variety of ways. We'll look closely at what happens when the supply and demand curves shift, and we will study the effects of price controls.

Chapter Summary

1. A market is an organized exchange of a good or service between buyers and sellers. Markets can be local, national, or international.

2. Demand refers to the actions of buyers in a market. The Law of Demand states that when the price of a good or service increases, the quantity demanded will decrease, all else equal. A demand curve is constructed by allowing the price of a good to change, while holding everything else constant. The Law of Demand means that the graph of a demand curve will slope downward as we move to the right.

3. If there is a change in the price of a good, then we move along the existing demand curve. If any other influence changes, we shift to a new demand curve. Many influences can shift demand curves; the most important of these are consumer incomes, the prices of other goods, tastes or preferences, expectations, and the size and composition of the population.

4. Supply refers to the actions of sellers in a market. The Law of Supply states that, all else equal, the quantity supplied will increase when the price of a good or service increases. The supply curve is constructed by allowing the price of the good to change, while holding everything else constant. The Law of Supply means that the graph of a supply curve will slope upward as we move to the right.

5. If there is a change in the price of a good, then we move along the existing supply curve. If any other influence changes, we shift to a new supply curve. The most important influences that shift supply curves are the prices of inputs, the technology of production, the prices of other goods, taxes, subsidies, regulations, and the number of sellers in the market.

6. If the quantity demanded is greater than the quantity supplied, we have a shortage. If the quantity supplied is greater than the quantity demanded, we have a surplus. Equilibrium is achieved when the quantity supplied equals the quantity demanded. Graphically, equilibrium is found at the point where the supply curve intersects the demand curve.

7. If the price is below its equilibrium level, the resulting shortages will put upward pressure on price. If the price is above its equilibrium level, the resulting surpluses will put downward pressure on price. Thus, the market will tend to move toward equilibrium.

Key Terms

Market

Demand

Quantity Demanded

Law of Demand

Demand Schedule

Individual Demand Schedule

Market Demand Schedule

Demand Curve

Change in Quantity Demanded

Change in Demand

Normal Good

Inferior Good

Substitutes

Complements

Independent in Demand

Supply

Quantity Supplied

Law of Supply

Supply Schedule

Supply Curve

Change in Quantity Supplied

Change in Supply

Technology

Surplus

Shortage

Market Equilibrium

Equilibrium Price

Equilibrium Quantity

Invisible Hand

Key Figure

The key figure for this chapter is Figure 3.9, showing the equilibrium of supply and demand.

Questions and Problems

QP3-1. Throughout much of the 20th century, practicing Catholics were prohibited from eating meat on Fridays, but they were allowed to eat fish. In the 1960s, this requirement was removed. As a result of this change, what do you expect happened to the demand for codfish?

QP3-2

a. Explain the Law of Demand.

b. Explain the difference between a change in demand (or a shift in the demand curve) and a change in the quantity demanded (or a movement along an existing demand curve).

QP3-3. In 1998, the price of corn increased. Corn is an important input into the production of fatted hogs. As a result of the change in the price of corn, what do you expect happened to the supply curve of fatted hogs?

QP3-4

a. Explain the Law of Supply.

b. Explain the difference between a change

in supply (or a shift in the supply curve) and a change in the quantity supplied (or a movement along an existing supply curve).

QP3-5. Japanese automobile companies raise the prices of the cars that they are selling in North America. What would this do to the demand for American-produced cars? Why?

QP3-6. Analyze the following statement: "The worldwide reserves of oil are fixed, but the size of the economy keeps increasing. Sooner or later, demand will just outrun supply."

QP3-7. Which of the following will shift the *supply curve* for blue jeans? If the supply curve will be shifted, will it shift to the left or to the right?

a. A decrease in the price of cotton, which is an input into the production of blue jeans.

b. A government price control that mandates that the price of blue jeans must be above its equilibrium level.

c. A technological improvement which allows manufacturers to dye blue jeans with less blue dye than before.

d. An increase in the price of blue dye.

e. An increase in the price of cowboy boots, which are a complement of blue jeans.

f. An increase in the number of firms that produce blue jeans. You may assume that the technology of production of blue jeans is unchanged, so that each individual firm has the same costs as before.

QP3-8. Which of the following will shift the *demand curve* for raisins? If the demand curve will be shifted, will it shift to the left or to the right?

a. A government price control that mandates that the price of raisins must be below its equilibrium level.

b. An increase in consumer incomes, assuming that raisins are a normal good.

c. An increase in consumer incomes, assuming that raisins are an inferior good.

d. An increase in the price of grapes, which are an important input to the production of raisins.

e. A decrease in the price of prunes, which are a substitute for raisins.

f. A climate forecast, which suggests that *next* year will be a poor year for raisins. As a result of the forecast, people come to believe that raisin prices will be higher next year.

g. A decrease in the price of bran flakes, which are a complement of raisins.

h. An increase in the wages of workers at the raisin factory.

QP3-9. Each of the following changes can be expected to have an effect on the market for disposable diapers. Predict the direction of the shift in supply or demand.

a. A campaign by environmentalists causes parents to feel uncomfortable about using diapers that will eventually end up in landfill.

b. An increase in the number of babies being born each year.

c. A new technology that allows producers to use fewer workers in making diapers.

d. A decrease in the price of pulp. (Pulp is used in the production of disposable diapers.)

QP3-10. Each of the following changes can be expected to have an effect on the market for newly built houses. Predict the direction of the shift in supply or demand.

a. The price of lumber goes down.

b. There is a decrease in interest rates. (You may assume that most people borrow most of the money that is necessary to buy new homes.)

c. The number of new households being formed decreases.

d. New regulations on land development reduce the amount of land available for new home construction.

QP3-11. The supply schedule and demand schedule for Pittsburgh Pirate baseball caps are given below.

a. Fill in the blanks. If you subtract the number of caps demanded from the number of caps supplied, a positive number will correspond to a surplus, and a negative number will correspond to a shortage.

b. What is the equilibrium price? What is the equilibrium quantity?

Price	Caps Demanded	Caps Supplied	Surplus or Shortage
$26/cap	70,000	130,000	
24	80,000	120,000	
22	90,000	110,000	
20	100,000	100,000	
18	110,000	90,000	
16	120,000	80,000	
14	130,000	70,000	

QP3-12. In the previous problem, we could express the supply schedule by an equation: $Q_s = 5000P$, where Q_s is the quantity supplied and P is the price in dollars. The demand schedule can be expressed as $Q_d = 200{,}000 - 5000P$, where Q_d is the quantity demanded. Equilibrium can also be expressed by an equation: $Q_s = Q_d$.

a. Substitute the equation for Q_s and the equation for Q_d into the equilibrium equation. Solve the equation to find the equilibrium price.

b. Now, take the equilibrium price that you found in (a), and substitute it into the equation for Q_d. Solve for the equilibrium quantity.

c. Now, take the equilibrium price that you found in (a), and substitute it into the equation for Q_s. Solve for the equilibrium quantity. Your answer should match with the answer that you found in (b).

d. If the price is $16 per cap, how many people will have unsatisfied demand for caps?

Chapter 4

Applications of Supply and Demand

ECONOMICS AND YOU:
THE ECONOMICS OF FINDING A PARKING SPACE

At age 32, Jeanette Cogan has returned to her studies at a college in the Southeastern United States. Once every year, she pays $50 to buy a parking sticker, which allows her to park her car in the college's parking lots for the next 12 months. However, Jeanette's sticker doesn't allow her to park in some of the lots that are closest to the center of the campus. And unless she arrives very early in the morning, some of the other lots are already full. She often has to drive around for 10 minutes before finding a parking space, and she still has to settle for a space that's far from her classes. As she lugs her books from the distant parking lot to her classroom, Jeanette thinks to herself that there must be a better way.

There may indeed be a better way to allocate parking spaces at Jeanette's campus, and it has to do with the pricing structure used by the college. In the previous chapter, we saw that the forces of supply and demand in the marketplace will usually move quickly to establish equilibrium. In other words, markets usually do a good job of eliminating shortages or surpluses. However, the parking situation at Jeanette's college is one of chronic shortages. Day after day, the quantity of good parking spaces demanded is greater than the quantity supplied. So, it must be that the college's pricing structure is preventing the parking lots from achieving equilibrium. In this chapter, we will develop an understanding of how chronic parking shortages can occur, and of what might be done about them.

In this chapter, you will learn a great deal about how markets work:

- You will begin by looking at what happens to the equilibrium price and quantity, when something causes the demand curve or the supply curve to shift.

- Then, you will look at what happens when a market is not able to achieve equilibrium, because of a law, or for some other reason.

After reading this chapter, you will know how markets respond to changes in supply or demand. You will also have an understanding of the public policy issues that arise when prices aren't allowed to find their equilibrium level. In Chapter 3, we saw that markets have an exceptionally strong tendency to move toward equilibrium. Because the invisible hand is so strong, a government will usually run into serious problems if it tries to keep a market away from its equilibrium price and quantity.

We begin our study of applications of the supply-demand framework in the next sec- tion. We will look closely at examples in which something changes, so that there is a shift in the supply curve or the demand curve.

SHIFTS IN THE DEMAND CURVE

If the supply curve and the demand curve in a market are unchanged, the equilibrium price and quantity will also be unchanged. But what if something causes one of the curves to shift? In that case, the supply and demand curves will intersect each other at a new point, and the market will have a new equilibrium price and quantity.

We begin by looking at shifts in the demand curve. Supply-curve shifts will come later in the chapter.

An Increase in Demand: The Demand Curve Shifts to the Right

In the previous chapter, we discussed the mar- ket for red-delicious apples. We'll continue with the apple example here, although this chapter also contains examples from several other markets. Before trying to understand the effects of a shift in the demand curve for apples, it's best to figure out the *original* equi- librium price and quantity, *before* the shift takes place. The original situation is shown in Figure 4.1. The original supply curve for red-delicious apples is S_0, and the original demand curve is D_0. We find the equilibrium by looking for the intersection of the supply curve and the demand curve. The original equilibrium price of red-delicious apples is P_0, and the original equilibrium quantity is Q_0.

Now that we have established the original equilibrium in the apple market, let's consider what will happen if the demand curve shifts. What would happen if medical researchers were to discover that cancer is completely pre-

vented by eating red-delicious apples? After hearing this dramatic news, millions of peo- ple would want to eat more of these apples. People would stand shoulder to shoulder in the produce sections of grocery stores, eagerly shopping for red-delicious apples. At any given price, the quantity of apples demanded would be greater than it had been before. This increase in demand is represented by a right- ward shift in the demand curve, as shown in Figure 4.1. Because of the news about the health effects of red-delicious apples, the mar- ket demand curve will shift from D_0 to D_1.

After the shift, P_0 can't continue to be the equilibrium price, and Q_0 can't continue to be the equilibrium quantity. At a price of P_0, some consumers won't be able to find the apples that they want to buy. In other words, if P_0 were still the price, there would be a shortage of red- delicious apples. The amount of the shortage would be $(Q_d–Q_0)$. In this situation, some con- sumers will offer to pay a higher price. There- fore, the shortage will create pressure for the price to rise. The price will continue to rise until the apple shortage is eliminated, and the market reaches a new equilibrium. At the new equilibrium, quantity supplied will again be equal to quantity demanded. Graphically, the new equilibrium is given by the intersection of the old supply curve, S_0, with the new demand curve, D_1. In Figure 4.1, the new equilibrium price of red-delicious apples is P_1, which is *greater* than P_0. The new equilibrium quantity is Q_1, which is *greater* than Q_0.

Thus, when the demand curve shifts to the right, the equilibrium price will increase, and the equilibrium quantity will also rise. This

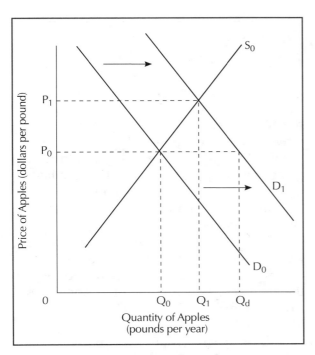

Figure 4.1 The Effects of an Increase in the Demand for Red-Delicious Apples

The original demand curve for red-delicious apples is D_0, and the original supply curve is S_0. The intersection of these curves gives us the original equilibrium price of red-delicious apples, P_0, and the original equilibrium quantity, Q_0. Then, buyers get new information about the health benefits of eating red-delicious apples, and this increases the demand for the apples. The demand curve shifts to the right, to D_1. If P_0 were to remain the price, there would be a shortage of (Q_d – Q_0). The apple market will move to a new equilibrium, in which the price is P_1 and the quantity is Q_1. As a result of the increase in demand, there is an increase in the equilibrium price and the equilibrium quantity.

will occur for *any* rightward shift of the demand curve in *any* market, as long as the supply curve slopes upward to the right. When the demand curve shifts to the right, the equilibrium point slides upward and to the right along the existing supply curve. This leads to a higher equilibrium price and quantity.

In this example, the news about the effect of apples on health leads to a rightward shift in the demand curve for red-delicious apples. Many other changes could also lead to an increase in demand. One such change is a decrease in the price of a complement. Let's say that red-delicious apples and cheddar cheese are complements. Then, if the price of cheddar cheese were to fall, the demand curve for red-delicious apples would shift to the right. An increase in the price of a substitute would also cause an increase in demand. For example, let's assume that pears are a substitute for apples. Then, if the price of pears were to rise, the demand curve for apples would shift to the right. Also, if red-delicious apples are a normal good, an increase in the incomes of consumers would shift the demand curve for apples to the right. In each of these cases, the increase in demand would cause increases in the equilibrium price and quantity, as shown in Figure 4.1.

We have concentrated on rightward shifts in the demand curve for red-delicious apples, but similar influences could increase the demand for any good. In general, the demand curve for any good could be shifted to the right by

- certain changes in tastes and preferences, or

- a decrease in the price of a complement, or

- an increase in the price of a substitute, or

- an increase in incomes (if the good is a normal good), or

- a decrease in incomes (if the good is an inferior good).

If demand increases, for any reason, the equilibrium price and quantity will both increase.

In *Real Economics for Real People 4.1*, you will read about another example of a rightward shift in a demand curve. Then we will move on to learn about what happens when the demand curve shifts to the left.

By the middle of the 1980s, the American public was becoming aware of the health hazard posed by Acquired Immune Deficiency Syndrome (AIDS). In August, 1987, the Centers for Disease Control in Atlanta urged health-care workers "to treat blood and other body fluids from all patients as potentially infective." This announcement led to dramatic increases in the demand for latex examination gloves and surgical gloves, on the part of dental hygienists, doctors, and other health-care professionals. Many surgeons began to wear two pairs of gloves at a time. Over a six-month period, St. Mary's Hospital in Richmond, Virginia, doubled its orders for gloves, to 80,000 gloves per month. UCLA Medical Center in Los Angeles increased its orders by 60% in a year.

The increases in demand led to increases in price, as well as increases in quantity. Prices of latex gloves rose by as much as 40% in some cases.

The increase in demand for gloves was exceptionally fast. As a result, temporary shortages sometimes occurred, even though there were large price increases. Faced with possible shortages of latex gloves, some health-care professionals began to buy more vinyl gloves, even though these are of lower quality than the latex gloves. In addition, some medical personnel are allergic to latex gloves, which are made from natural rubber. This led to an expansion of the market for synthetic gloves.

Since supplies of domestically produced gloves were extremely tight, more buyers began to look overseas. In 1987 and 1988, there were big increases in imports of gloves from Taiwan, China, Thailand, and Malaysia.

All of these changes occurred because the fear of AIDS caused an increase in demand for goods that could help protect against infection, such as latex gloves. In terms of the supply-demand diagram, this means that the demand curve for latex gloves shifted to the right. As with any increase in demand, this led to an increase in the equilibrium price, and an increase in the equilibrium quantity.

A Decrease in Demand: The Demand Curve Shifts to the Left

In much of the United States, the spring and summer of 1997 were unusually cloudy and cool. When the weather is cool and wet, most people don't like to engage in outdoor activities. Thus, the cool weather caused big decreases in the demand for swimming pools, swimming-pool chemicals, patio furniture, sunglasses, pleasure boats, mountain bikes, and many other goods.

We can use the tools of supply and demand to analyze the effects of the cool weather on the market for sunscreen. Once again, we start by looking for the original situation, which occurs before there is any shift in either the supply curve or the demand curve. This original situation is shown in Figure 4.2. The original supply curve for sunscreen is S_0, and the original demand curve is D_0. The intersection of D_0 and S_0 gives us the original equilibrium price and quantity of sunscreen, which are P_0 and Q_0.

Now, the summer of 1997 arrives, bringing temperatures that are cooler than had been anticipated. The weather means that, at any given price, consumers won't be willing to buy as much sunscreen as they had been willing to buy before. In other words, the strange

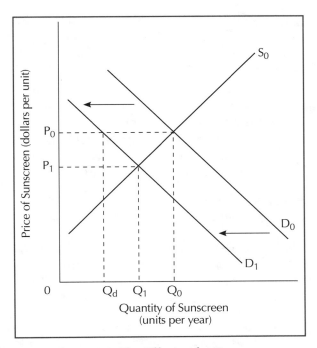

Figure 4.2 The Effects of a Decrease in the Demand for Sunscreen

The original demand curve for sunscreen is D_0, and the original supply curve is S_0. The intersection of these curves gives us the original equilibrium price of sunscreen, P_0, and the original equilibrium quantity of sunscreen, Q_0. Then, buyers experience unusually cool and cloudy summer weather, and this decreases the demand for sunscreen. The demand curve shifts to the left, to D_1. If P_0 were to remain the price, there would be a surplus of $(Q_0 - Q_d)$. The market for sunscreen will move to a new equilibrium, in which the price is P_1 and the quantity is Q_1. As a result of the decrease in demand, there is a decrease in both the equilibrium price and the equilibrium quantity.

weather causes the demand for sunscreen to decrease, so that the demand curve shifts to the left. This is shown in Figure 4.2 as a shift from D_0 to D_1. In Figure 4.2, as in the other figures in this chapter, the shift from D_0 to D_1 is a parallel shift. The shifts are drawn in this way in order to make them easy to read. However, shifts don't *have* to be parallel.

After the shift of the demand curve, P_0 can't be the equilibrium price of sunscreen any more, and Q_0 can't continue to be the equilibrium quantity. If P_0 were still the price, there would be a surplus of $(Q_0 - Q_d)$. As a result of the surplus, there will be pressure for the price to fall. The price will continue to fall until the sunscreen market reaches a new equilibrium. When the market reaches its new equilibrium, quantity supplied will be equal to quantity demanded, which means that the surplus will be gone. The new equilibrium in the market for sunscreen is given by the intersection of the new demand curve, D_1, with the old supply curve, S_0. The new equilibrium price is P_1, which is *lower* than P_0. The new equilibrium quantity is Q_1, which is *lower* than Q_0.

Thus, when the demand curve shifts to the left, the equilibrium price will decrease, and the equilibrium quantity will also fall. This will happen for *any* leftward shift in the demand curve in *any* market, as long as the supply curve slopes upward to the right. When the demand curve shifts to the left, the equilibrium point slides downward and to the left along the existing supply curve. This reduces both the equilibrium price and the equilibrium quantity.

When both the price and quantity fall, revenues for sellers have to fall. Thus, the suppliers of sunscreen were hurt by the cool weather. Companies that sell equipment and chemicals for swimming pools also suffered, and so did the sellers of ice cream.

Of course, cool weather isn't the only thing that could reduce the demand for sunscreen. If sunscreen is a normal good, then a decrease in incomes would also lead to a leftward shift in the demand curve for sunscreen.

An increase in the price of a complementary good would have a similar effect. For example, let's assume that swimsuits are a complement of sunscreen. If the price of swimsuits were to increase, the demand for sunscreen would decrease.

A decrease in the price of a substitute good would also cause the demand curve to shift to the left. For example, let's assume that cable-television services are a substitute for sunscreen. (If you're watching a lot of TV, you are probably staying indoors, so that you won't be buying sunscreen.) If the price of cable-TV services were to fall, then the demand curve for sunscreen would shift to the left. As a result of any of these decreases in demand, the equilibrium price of sunscreen would fall, and so would the equilibrium quantity.

Similar influences could decrease the demand for any good. In general, the demand curve for any good could be shifted to the left by

- certain changes in tastes and preferences, or

- an increase in the price of a complement, or

- a decrease in the price of a substitute, or

- a decrease in incomes (if the good is a normal good), or

- an increase in incomes (if the good is an inferior good).

SHIFTS IN THE SUPPLY CURVE

When there is a change in demand, the equilibrium price and quantity will both move in the *same* direction. That is, when the demand curve shifts, either the equilibrium price and equilibrium quantity will both rise, or they will both fall. However, we will see that a supply-curve shift will cause price and quantity to move in *opposite* directions. In other words, when supply changes, either the price will rise and the quantity will fall, or the price will fall and the quantity will rise.

A Decrease in Supply: The Supply Curve Shifts to the Left

Let's return to our example of the market for red-delicious apples, and consider what would

If any demand curve shifts to the left, for any reason, the equilibrium price and quantity will both decrease.

In this section, we've concentrated on shifts in the demand curve: When demand increases, the equilibrium price and quantity will both rise; when demand decreases, the equilibrium price and quantity will both fall. In the next section, we'll think about what happens when a supply curve shifts.

Reality Check: Interim Review Questions

IR4-1. The demand for peanuts increases. In other words, the demand curve for peanuts shifts to the right. What will happen to the equilibrium price and quantity of peanuts?

IR4-2. Silk socks and cotton socks are substitutes. The price of silk socks goes down. As a result, the demand for cotton socks decreases; that is, the demand curve for cotton socks shifts to the left. What will happen to the equilibrium price and quantity of cotton socks?

happen if the supply curve were to shift to the left. As usual, we begin by finding the *original* equilibrium price and quantity, which would exist before any shifts occur. The original situation is shown in Figure 4.3. The original supply curve for red-delicious apples is S_0, and the original demand curve is D_0. The intersection of these two curves gives us the original equilibrium price of red-delicious apples, P_0, and the original equilibrium quantity, Q_0.

The supply curve for apples could be shifted to the left as a result of a variety of influences. One such influence would be an event that disrupts supply, such as a drought in apple-growing regions. At any given price, the drought means that the quantity of red-

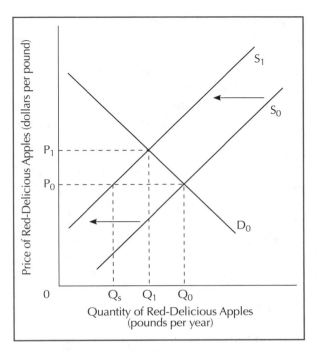

Figure 4.3 The Effects of a Decrease in the Supply of Red-Delicious Apples

The original demand curve for red-delicious apples is D_0, and the original supply curve is S_0. The intersection of these curves gives us the original equilibrium price of red-delicious apples, P_0, and the original equilibrium quantity, Q_0. Then, there is a drought in the apple-growing regions, and this decreases the supply of red-delicious apples. The supply curve shifts to the left, to S_1. If P_0 were to remain the price, there would be a shortage of $(Q_0 - Q_s)$. The apple market will move to a new equilibrium, in which the price is P_1 and the quantity is Q_1. As a result of the decrease in supply, the equilibrium price increases and the equilibrium quantity decreases.

delicious apples supplied would be less than it had been before. Another way to think of the shift in the supply curve is that the drought makes it more costly to produce apples. The price that's necessary to get sellers to supply apples is higher than it had been before, because of the increased need for irrigation and the increased possibility of diseases in the apple trees. This decrease in supply is represented in Figure 4.3 by a leftward shift in

the supply curve for red-delicious apples, from S_0 to S_1.

After the supply-curve shift, P_0 can no longer be the equilibrium price, and Q_0 can't remain the equilibrium quantity. If P_0 were still the price, there would be a shortage of $(Q_0 - Q_s)$. A shortage will lead to upward pressure on the price of red-delicious apples. The price will continue to rise until the apple market reaches a new equilibrium. When the market reaches its new equilibrium, quantity supplied will be equal to quantity demanded, which means that the shortage will end. The new equilibrium will be given by the intersection of the new supply curve, S_1, and the old demand curve, D_0. The new equilibrium quantity will be Q_1, which is *lower* than Q_0. The new equilibrium price of red-delicious apples will be P_1, which is *higher* than P_0.

Thus, when the supply curve shifts to the left, the equilibrium price will increase, but the equilibrium quantity will fall. This will happen for *any* leftward shift of the supply curve in *any* market, as long as the demand curve slopes downward to the right. When the supply curve shifts to the left, the equilibrium point slides upward and to the left along the existing demand curve. This causes the equilibrium price to rise and the equilibrium quantity to fall.

There are many examples of how a disruption of production can cause a leftward shift in the supply curve. For instance, vegetable crops in Florida were damaged by an unexpectedly hard freeze in January of 1997. We would expect prices to rise as a result of the leftward shift in supply, and that is exactly what happened. The price of cucumbers rose quickly from $8 per bushel to $25 per bushel. A similar story occurred in June, 1994, when coffee trees in Brazil were damaged by freezing temperatures. As a result of the freeze, coffee prices rose by 26 percent in one day.

Other changes can also lead to a leftward shift in the supply curve. Suppose that the United States government imposes a new set of regulations governing the use of pesticides, and that these regulations increase costs in the apple-growing industry. This will effectively shift the supply curve to the left. It would cause a decrease in quantity, and an increase in the price paid by consumers, as shown in Figure 4.3.

An increase in the price of an input will also cause a decrease in supply. When an input becomes more expensive, there is an increase in the price that is necessary to get sellers to bring a given quantity to market. For example, if the price of steel were to rise, the supply curve for automobiles would shift to the left, since steel is an input into the production of steel. This leftward shift in the supply curve would lead to an increase in the equilibrium price of automobiles, and a decrease in the equilibrium quantity.

You have now read about several influences that could cause supply to decrease. The supply curve for a good could be shifted to the left by

- an increase in the price of an input, or
- the imposition of a regulation that increases costs, or
- a disruption in production, such as might be caused by bad weather in agricultural regions, or
- a deterioration in technology.

If supply decreases, for any reason, the equilibrium price will increase and the equilibrium quantity will decrease.

Next, we will learn about what happens when supply increases, and the supply curve shifts to the right.

An Increase in Supply: The Supply Curve Shifts to the Right

Many families would like to recycle their bottles, cans, and newspapers, in order to reduce the amount of solid waste that gets buried in landfill. However, recycling is difficult for people who live far away from a recycling center. In order to make it easier to recycle, many towns and cities established programs of curbside recycling in the late 1980s and early 1990s. In effect, the curbside recycling programs improved the technology of recycling. These programs made it cheaper and easier for people to recycle, and they responded by recycling huge amounts of material.

At any price, the quantity of recycled material that is supplied will be higher, when curbside recycling programs are in place. In the language of supply and demand, curbside recycling programs cause rightward shifts in the supply curves for recycled newsprint, scrap paper, tin, glass, and so on. In other words, curbside recycling programs lead to an increase in the supply of these materials.

We can study the effects of curbside recycling on the market for scrap paper, using the tools of supply and demand. As usual, we begin by finding the original equilibrium that exists before any shifts take place. As shown in Figure 4.4, the original demand curve for scrap paper is D_0, and the original supply curve is S_0. In order to find the original equilibrium, we go to the intersection of D_0 and S_0. This tells us that the original equilibrium price of scrap paper is P_0, and the original equilibrium quantity is Q_0.

Now, because of the increased availability of curbside recycling programs, the supply of scrap paper increases. This increase in supply is shown in Figure 4.4 as a shift in the supply curve for scrap paper, from S_0 to S_1.

After the shift in the supply curve, P_0 and Q_0 can no longer be the equilibrium price and quantity of scrap paper. If P_0 were still the price of scrap paper, there would be a surplus of $(Q_s - Q_0)$. The surplus will create pressure for the price to fall. The price of scrap paper will continue to fall until the scrap-paper market reaches a new equilibrium. When the market reaches its new equilibrium, quantity supplied will be equal to quantity demanded, which means that the surplus will be gone.

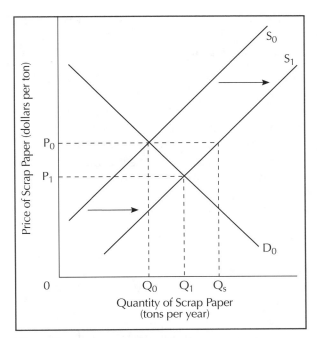

Figure 4.4 The Effects of an Increase in the Supply of Scrap Paper

The original demand curve for scrap paper is D_0, and the original supply curve is S_0. The intersection of these curves gives us the original equilibrium price of scrap paper, P_0, and the original equilibrium quantity, Q_0. Then, communities institute curbside recycling programs, which make it easier to recycle. This increases the supply of scrap paper. The supply curve shifts to the right, to S_1. If P_0 were to remain the price, there would be a surplus of $(Q_s - Q_0)$. The market for scrap paper will move to a new equilibrium, in which the price is P_1 and the quantity is Q_1. As a result of the increase in supply, the equilibrium price goes down, but the equilibrium quantity rises.

The new equilibrium will be given by the intersection of the new supply curve, S_1, and the old demand curve, D_0. The new equilibrium price of scrap paper will be P_1, which is *lower* than P_0. The new equilibrium quantity will be Q_1, which is *higher* than Q_0.

Thus, when the supply curve shifts to the right, the equilibrium price will decrease, but the equilibrium quantity will rise. This will happen for *any* rightward shift of the supply curve in *any* market, as long as the demand curve slopes downward to the right. When the supply curve shifts to the right, the equilibrium point slides downward and to the right along the existing demand curve. As a result, the equilibrium quantity rises and the equilibrium price falls.

The increase in curbside recycling caused major reductions in the prices of recyclable materials. Scrap paper sold for $120 per ton in 1988, but the price fell to $30 per ton by 1993. The price of recycled glass went down from $160 per ton to $90 per ton.

Many local governments have encouraged recycling, in order to cut down on the expense of burying garbage in landfill. However, the success of the recycling programs has caused new problems. When the amount of recycling increased, it became necessary to dispose of a tremendous amount of recycled material. As a result, governments have tried to find new ways to use recycled materials. In other words, they are trying to push the *demand curve* for recycled materials to the right. For example, some governments use recycled paper for letterheads, forms, and envelopes, and in copying machines, and they are encouraging private businesses to do the same. The city government of Newark, New Jersey, requires firms to use recycled products if they want to do business with the city.

A supply curve for a good could be shifted to the right by a variety of changes, including

- a decrease in the price of an input, or

- relaxation in government regulations, so that it becomes less costly to produce, or

- an improvement in the conditions of production, such as might be caused by unusually good weather in agricultural regions, or

- an improvement in technology.

If supply increases for any reason, the equilibrium price will fall and the equilibrium quantity will rise.

Technological improvements are associated with rightward shifts in supply curves. We discuss another example of a technological improvement in *Real Economics for Real People 4.2*.

Reality Check:
Interim Review Questions

IR4-3. Because of technological improvements, the supply of electric pianos increases. In other words, the supply curve for electric pianos shifts to the right. What will happen to the equilibrium price and quantity of electric pianos?

IR4-4. Electricity is used in the production of aluminum. The price of electricity increases. As a result, the supply of aluminum decreases. In other words, the supply curve for aluminum shifts to the left. What will happen to the equilibrium price and quantity of aluminum?

PRICE CONTROLS

In Chapter 3, we saw that market forces normally work to eliminate shortages and surpluses very quickly. Also, in all of the examples given so far in this chapter, we have assumed that the market will find its new equilibrium. However, in some situations, markets are unable to achieve equilibrium. We will look at some of these situations now.

Sometimes, a government will pass a *price-control law*, which makes it illegal to buy and sell at some prices. If a price-control law is enforced, it may prevent the market from finding equilibrium. As a result, shortages or surpluses may stay around for a long time. There are two basic types of price-control law. Some laws establish a *price floor*, which is a *minimum* price that must be paid. In other words, a price floor makes it illegal to buy and sell at less than a certain price. On the other hand, a *price ceiling* sets a *maximum* legal price: A price ceiling makes it illegal to buy and sell at more than a certain price.

In this section, we'll consider each of these types of price control, beginning with price floors. Later in the chapter, we'll discuss other situations in which markets can't easily get to equilibrium.

Price Floors

A price floor is a minimum legal price. This kind of law is especially common in agriculture. In this section, we'll focus on the price floors in the markets for sugar.

Effects of the Sugar Price Floor. In the United States, the legally-mandated price of raw cane sugar is 18 cents per pound. In the rest of the world, the price of sugar rises and falls from time to time, depending on the conditions of supply and demand. However, the price in the rest of the world has most often been far below the price in the United States. On occasion, the world price has been as low as five cents per pound.

It's possible that the equilibrium price of sugar might actually be *above* the price floor. In this case, the price floor would have no effect. If the equilibrium price were higher than the price floor, then consumers and producers would voluntarily obey the law, simply by buying and selling at the equilibrium price. A more interesting situation occurs when the equilibrium price is *below* the price floor, which has usually been the case in the sugar market. Figure 4.5 shows what will happen in a case like this. As usual, we begin by finding the original equilibrium price and quantity. The demand curve is D_0, and the supply curve is S_0. The intersection of these two curves tells us that the equilibrium price is P_0, and the equilibrium quantity is Q_0. But with the price floor at P_{floor}, the prices in the shaded area

Real Economics for Real People 4.2:
Changing Technology and the Price of Personal Computers

In April, 1982, the first issue of *PC Magazine* advertised the new IBM Personal Computer. For $1600, you could buy a machine with 256 kilobytes of memory, no hard disk drive, and a one-color monitor.

Because of inflation, the $1600 that you spent in 1982 would be equivalent to about $2800 in 2000. What kind of computer could you buy in 2000 for that amount of money? Typically, you could get a computer with a Pentium III processor and a high-resolution color monitor. This machine would come with at least 256 times as much memory as the PC from 1982. It would process information hundreds of times faster. It would have a hard disk capable of storing several billion bytes of information, whereas the 1982 computer had none. The 2000 version would have an internal modem for data or fax transmissions, and it would have a built-in CD-ROM Drive. Neither of these devices was even available in 1982. Finally, the 2000 version would come loaded with all sorts of software that was not available in 1982.

Technological change is the explanation for these phenomenal developments. In the last several years, the design of personal computers has been improved repeatedly. These improvements can be seen as increases in the supply of personal computers and computer accessories. At any given price, the computer makers are now willing and able to produce more (and better) computers. If we combine a rightward shift in the supply curve with a demand curve that slopes downward and to the right, we get increases in quantity and decreases in price. That is exactly what we have observed in the computer industry in the last two decades.

The personal-computer hard drive is one of the best examples of the effects of technological change. As mentioned above, when the IBM PC was first introduced, it didn't even have a hard drive as standard equipment. However, by 1983, Corvus Systems was offering a 20-megabyte hard drive for $3495. In 2000, a 3.2-gigabyte (3200-megabyte) hard drive could be bought for $220.

Thus, in 17 years, the price per megabyte went down from ($3495/20 megabytes) = $174.75 per megabyte, to ($220/3200 megabytes) = about $0.07 per megabyte. Price fell by a factor of ($174.75/$0.07), which is about 2500! Even this doesn't quite give the full indication of the real price decrease, since inflation pushed up the overall price level by about 80 percent during that 17-year period. If we were to correct for inflation, the price per megabyte has fallen by a factor of more than 4000!

Today's hard drives are far superior to the hard drives of 1983, in every way. They're faster, more reliable, more durable, lighter, and more compact. All of these changes are the result of technological improvements. Technological improvements push supply curves to the right. These increases in supply lead to decreases in price and increases in quantity.

are illegal! Most importantly, the price-floor law means that the equilibrium price of P_0 is illegal.

If the equilibrium price is illegal, and if the price-floor law is obeyed, then it will be impossible for the market to find its equilibrium. This will force the market into a *disequilibrium* situation, in which the quantity supplied is different from the quantity demanded. When the price is P_{floor}, the quantity supplied

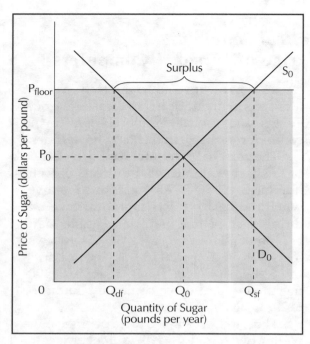

Figure 4.5 The Effects of a Price Floor in the Sugar Market

The supply curve in the sugar market is S_0, and the demand curve is D_0. This means that the equilibrium price of sugar is P_0, and the equilibrium quantity is Q_0. However, the United States government imposes a price floor on sugar, at P_{floor}. This means that all of the prices in the shaded region are illegal. Since the equilibrium price, P_0, is now illegal, the sugar market cannot reach equilibrium. If the price floor is enforced, the quantity supplied will be Q_{sf}, and the quantity demanded will be Q_{df}. The sugar market will have a surplus of $(Q_{sf} - Q_{df})$.

is Q_{sf}, but the quantity demanded is Q_{df}. Thus, the price-floor law causes a surplus of $(Q_{sf} - Q_{df})$.

Because a surplus is created, you might predict that we would have more consumption than we had before the price-control law was imposed. However, the amount actually consumed is Q_{df}. Buyers can't be forced to buy more than an amount that is on their demand curves. Consequently, the price floor reduces the amount of sugar that is actually consumed by consumers. Here, the consumption of sugar goes down from Q_0 to Q_{df}.

If there were no price-control law, the market would quickly drive the price down to its equilibrium level, P_0. When the price floor is in effect, however, surpluses could pile up indefinitely, and this causes a problem. We would soon have miles and miles of warehouses full of surplus sugar. Thus, our next task is to think about what to do with the surpluses.

How to Deal with the Surpluses That Are Caused By Price Floors. Governments create the potential for surpluses by imposing price-floor laws. This leads to political pressure for the same governments to do something to prevent the surpluses from building up. For example, price floors on dairy products have led to surpluses, and the government has responded by buying tons of surplus cheese, and storing it in warehouses.

In the case of sugar, the U.S. government uses a system of *import quotas* to control the surpluses. An import quota is a restriction on the quantity that can be imported from another country. Because of these sugar import quotas, there is a great reduction in the amount of sugar imported from Caribbean and Latin American countries, such as Jamaica.

Figure 4.6 shows the effect of the import quotas on the sugar market. If there were no import quotas, the supply curve would be S_0, and the price in the United States would be the same as the price in the rest of the world, P_{world}. The import quotas reduce the quantity of sugar that can be supplied in the United States. In Figure 4.6, because of the import quotas, the supply curve of sugar in the United States is driven leftward, to S_1. In the figure, S_1 is far enough to the left that the price of sugar goes all the way up to P_{floor}. In this case, the import quotas eliminate the surpluses that would otherwise occur.

If the import quotas were removed, sugar would be imported into the United States in much greater amounts. This would drive the price of sugar in the U.S. down to P_{world}. In short, the import quotas raise the price at

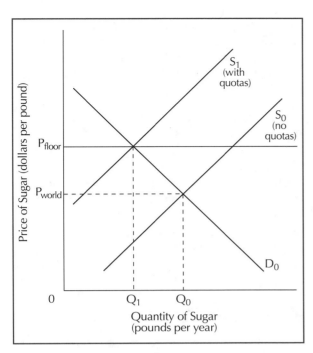

Figure 4.6 The Effects of a System of Import Quotas on the Sugar Market

In the absence of import quotas, the supply curve in the sugar market in the United States is S_0, and the demand curve is D_0. This means that the equilibrium price of sugar is P_{world}, and the equilibrium quantity is Q_0. However, the United States government imposes a price floor on sugar, at P_{floor}. In order to keep the price above its equilibrium level without creating surpluses, the government imposes an import-quota law. This restricts the quantity of sugar that can be brought into the country from abroad, and it pushes the supply curve of sugar to the left, to S_1. In this case, the reduction in supply is so great that the price is driven all the way up to P_{floor}.

which sugar is sold in the United States, and they reduce the quantity of sugar that is bought and sold in the U.S.

One side effect of the sugar laws is that it can be profitable to go to great lengths to get around the import quota. When the difference between the U.S. price and the world price is large enough, the following sequence of events has occurred: (1) Sugar from Jamaica is sold to buyers in Germany. (There's a quota on sugar sent from Jamaica to the United States, but there is no quota on sugar sent from Jamaica to Germany.) (2) In Germany, the sugar is put into pancake mixes, iced-tea mixes, and other such products. (3) The mixes are then sold to buyers in the United States. (There is no quota on imports of pancake mix from Germany into the U.S.) (4) Once the pancake mixes are in the United States, producers extract the sugar from the mix, and throw the rest of the mix away. (5) After two trips across the Atlantic Ocean, the sugar can still be sold for a profit, because the price of sugar is so much higher in the United States than in the rest of the world!

Winners and Losers from the Sugar Price Floor. The sugar price floor may cost American consumers as much as $3 billion per year. It also has side effects. Domestically, the high price of sugar can make it very profitable to grow sugar beets. This raises the price of the land that can be used for growing sugar beets. Of course, the land that can be used for growing sugar beets can also be used to grow other crops, especially grains. This puts a financial squeeze on the grain farmers: They have to pay higher prices for land, but they don't receive as much government help as is received by the sugar-beet farmers. This has caused conflicts in Minnesota and North Dakota, where sugar-beet farmers are pitted against grain farmers.

The price floor also hurts sugar growers in the rest of the world, because it reduces their ability to sell in the United States. In addition, sugar is an important input in the production of candy, baked goods, and processed foods. Since the price of sugar is above its equilibrium level, the supply curves for candy and related goods are farther to the left than they would otherwise be. Therefore, the prices of candy and other goods are higher than they would be if there were no quotas on sugar. This hurts the consumers of candy and baked goods.

So far, we have discussed a number of problems and distortions caused by the sugar price floor. However, if *everyone* were to be harmed by the price floor, we would not expect that it would continue to receive support in Congress. In fact, some people do benefit from the sugar price floor. The main winners are the farmers who grow sugar cane and sugar beets. The high price of sugar also stimulates demand for corn syrup, artificial sweeteners, and other substitutes for sugar. Thus, the sugar price floor also provides benefits for corn farmers, corn processors, and the producers of artificial sweeteners.

So, it's true that some groups do benefit from the price-floor law. However, these groups are small in number. Even the most optimistic assessment would say that the sugar price floor gives benefits for a few million Americans, out of a population of about 275 million. How does a law stay on the books, when the number of people harmed by the law is so much greater than the number of people who are helped? The reason is that the benefits are highly concentrated and visible, whereas the costs are dispersed and hard to see. Sugar-cane growers have the potential to gain huge sums of money every year from the price supports. The growers organize themselves politically, and give generously to political campaigns. On the other hand, each individual family loses only a relatively small amount every year, so that consumers haven't been well-organized in opposing the price controls.

In summary, a price floor can lead to three possible outcomes:

- If the price floor is below the equilibrium price, it has no effect.

- If the floor is above the equilibrium price but is not enforced by the government, it has no effect.

- If the price floor is above the equilibrium price and is enforced, it will lead to surpluses. In order to avoid having surpluses

pile up, the government will often take some additional steps, such as instituting a sugar quota. Of course, the problem of surpluses could also be solved by repealing the price floor.

In recent years, the public has become more and more aware of the problems associated with price floors in agriculture. Eventually, this led to political pressure to reform the agricultural pricing system. In 1996, Congress passed a law to phase out the price controls for many crops. If Congress doesn't change its mind, the system of price supports will be phased out by 2002, for feed grains, wheat, cotton, and rice, although the sugar price floors were left in place.

Price Ceilings

A price *floor* sets a legal *minimum* price. We have seen that price floors can lead to surpluses. On the other hand, a price *ceiling* sets a legal *maximum* price. In many ways, price ceilings are a mirror image of price floors: Whereas price floors can lead to surpluses, price ceilings can lead to shortages.

Rent Controls. **Rent-control laws** are a type of price ceiling. Rent controls on apartment rentals are in effect in New York City, Washington, D.C., and about 200 other cities in the United States.

As usual, we begin the analysis by finding the equilibrium price and quantity. In Figure 4.7, the supply curve of rental apartments is S_0, and the demand curve is D_0. Therefore, the equilibrium rental price is P_0, and the equilibrium quantity is Q_0. Now, let's consider a price ceiling at $P_{ceiling}$, which is below the equilibrium price. When this price ceiling is in place, all prices in the shaded area (including the equilibrium price) are illegal. At this price, the quantity demanded is Q_{dc}, and the quantity supplied is Q_{sc}. The quantity demanded is greater than the quantity supplied, so we have a shortage of $(Q_{dc} - Q_{sc})$. Thus, there is a

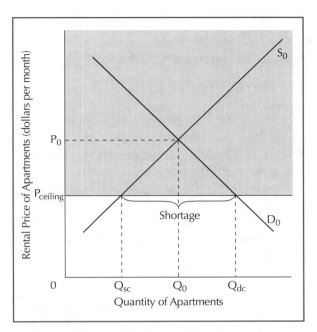

Figure 4.7 The Effects of a Rent-Control Law

The supply curve of rental apartments is S_0, the demand curve is D_0, the equilibrium price is P_0, and the equilibrium quantity of apartments rented is Q_0. However, the local government imposes a rent-control law, under which it is illegal to rent apartments for more than $P_{ceiling}$. If the law is enforced, the quantity demanded will be Q_{dc}, but the quantity supplied will only be Q_{sc}. As a result of the rent-control law, there is a shortage of $(Q_{dc} - Q_{sc})$.

decrease in the quantity of rental housing that is actually consumed, from Q_0 to Q_{sc}. *As a result of the rent-control law, there is a decrease in the total amount of rental housing actually consumed.*

In most cases, one of the first effects of rent-control laws is that the quality of housing deteriorates. If landlords are prevented from charging a rent that covers their costs adequately, they may respond by reducing maintenance and postponing repairs. Many properties are eventually abandoned. In New York City, the local government has spent billions of dollars to buy abandoned properties. This is ironic, since the properties would not have been abandoned at all, if it weren't for the government's rent-control policy.

Rent-control laws lead to some surprising uses of resources. For example, in Santa Monica, California, a young professional was renting a rent-controlled apartment near the ocean, at a price far below its equillibrium price. When she got a new job on the East Coast, she decided to keep her California apartment, since she was able to rent it for such a low rate. She could then use the rent-controlled apartment for a couple of weeks per year, when she was back in California on vacation. Thus, due to the rent-control law, a valuable apartment was idle for 50 or 51 weeks of the year.

As shortages appear in a rent-controlled city, some people may become homeless, but most will probably look for housing in nearby cities that don't have rent controls. This means that the demand curve for housing in the non-controlled cities will shift to the right. As a result, the equilibrium rental price of housing will rise in the cities without rent control. For example, the rent controls in New York City will lead to increases in the price of rental housing in Fort Lee, New Jersey, and other nearby communities.

Fortunately, price ceilings aren't used very widely in the United States, but there are other examples. In the 1970s, price controls on gasoline led to severe shortages. Service stations often had to turn customers away, because their supplies were sold out. Moreover, drivers began to form long lines, because they were afraid of running out of gas. (When there's a shortage, it's important to be first in line.) About a billion gallons of gasoline were wasted, as cars sat in long lines with their engines idling.

Fortunately, price ceilings are not very common in the United States. They are much more common in socialist countries, and in the poor countries of Africa and Asia. In some cases, the price ceilings can have devastating effects, as described in *Real Economics for Real People 4.3.*

Black Markets. When a price ceiling is below the equilibrium price, we see shortages,

Real Economics for Real People 4.3:
Food Price Controls and Starvation in China

In the mid-1950s, the communist government in China forced millions of small farmers to become part of large communes. In most of the communes, *food was given away free of charge.* When food is being given away for free, there's no incentive to use it wisely. Tremendous amounts of food were wasted. In many parts of China, food supplies were exhausted before the harvest could be collected in 1959, even though the 1958 harvest had been a good one.

The three years from 1959 to 1961 are known as the Great Famine. In terms of the number of people who starved to death, it was the worst famine in the history of the world. It is estimated that at least 20 million people died from the famine, and the death toll may have been as high as 30 million. In addition, there was a dramatic decline in the birth rate, since so many women suffered from malnutrition. It's estimated that there were about 30 million fewer births during this period than there would have been without the food crisis.

The Great Famine was one of history's worst tragedies, but it is not actually very surprising. The Chinese authorities set the price of food at zero. From our analysis of price controls, we know that a price ceiling below the equilibrium price will cause shortages. Certainly, a price of zero is below the equilibrium price of food, so it's not surprising that China suffered food shortages.

The price ceiling on food wasn't the only factor that contributed to the Great Famine. For example, when food began to run out, the government underestimated the size of the problem. If the authorities had allowed the market to work, the scarcity of food would have sent prices soaring. This might have helped to alert the government to the true dimensions of the problem. However, since prices were controlled, the government relied on crop forecasts, which turned out to be highly inaccurate. This reminds us that market prices are extremely good at conveying information.

Even when the food shortages became severe, it might have been possible to reduce the suffering by importing more food, but this did not happen. In fact, China continued to export food, and the Chinese government rejected an offer of food aid from the International Red Cross.

Weather conditions were not at their best during the years of the Great Famine, but they weren't extremely bad, either. When the famine ended in 1962, it was because of a change in government policies, rather than a change in the weather. The worst famine in history was primarily man-made, and the price ceiling on food played an important role in the disaster.

where the demands of buyers are not satisfied. Some buyers would be willing to pay more than the ceiling price, if only they could find someone who is willing to sell. In a situation like this, *black markets* may develop. A black market involves illegal sales, for the purpose of getting around a price control.

If the government enforces the price ceilings actively, black-market sales will have to occur in secret. The supply curves of sellers on the black market will be pushed to the left, since sellers will be afraid of being thrown in jail. This may raise the black-market price to a level that is higher than the equilibrium price.

Since black-market sales are illegal, buyers will be uncertain about the quality of the goods that they are buying: It's hard for a seller to maintain a reputation for quality merchandise when the buying and selling have to occur in darkened doorways.

Summary of the Effects of Price Controls

We have seen that price floors can lead to surpluses, while price ceilings can lead to shortages and black markets. We summarize some of these effects in Table 4.1.

Reality Check: Interim Review Questions

IR4-5. Assume that the equilibrium price of pencils is 10 cents each. What would hap-

pen to the price at which pencils are sold if the government were to impose a price floor, stating that it is illegal to sell pencils for less than 5 cents each? How would the price floor affect the quantity of pencils bought and sold? What would happen to the price and quantity if the price floor were at 20 cents per pencil?

IR4-6. Assume that the equilibrium price of pajamas is $10 per pair. What would happen to the price at which pajamas are sold if the government were to impose a price ceiling, stating that it is illegal to sell pajamas for more than $20 per pair? How would the price ceiling affect the quantity of pajamas bought and sold? What would happen to the price and quantity if the price ceiling were at $5 per pair?

Table 4.1 Summary of Effects of Price Controls

Type of Price Control	Relationship to Equilibrium Price	Effects
1. Price Floor (Legal minimum, such as dairy price support)	Below equilibrium	No Effect
2. Price Floor	Above equilibrium	Surpluses; Illegal sales may occur
3. Price Ceiling (Legal maximum, such as rent-control law)	Above equilibrium	No Effect
4. Price Ceiling	Below equilibrium	Shortages; Black markets may develop

PRICES THAT AREN'T SET AT THEIR EQUILIBRIUM LEVEL

A price control is a deliberate attempt to outlaw some prices. Consequently, the shortages and surpluses that are brought about by price controls are the result of deliberate policy decisions. On the other hand, shortages and surpluses are common in some other markets, even though these markets don't have price ceilings or price floors in the usual sense. We will take a look at some of these markets now. If a price isn't at its equilibrium level, then the market will be out of equilibrium, regardless of whether the disequilibrium is caused by an explicit price-control law, or by something else.

Concert Pricing

Peppermint Sponge is a rock group. The band is giving a concert in a basketball arena, and exactly 12,000 tickets are available. Panel (a) of Figure 4.8 shows that the supply curve is a vertical line, S_0, at a quantity of 12,000. The demand curve is D_0. The equilibrium quantity is 12,000, and the equilibrium price is $50 per ticket. In other words, if the concert by Peppermint Sponge is in equilibrium, the people who go to the concert will pay a price of $50, and the arena will be full.

However, if the tickets are printed up a year ahead of time, the concert promoters may not know for certain whether the equilibrium price is $50 per ticket. If the promoters set the price at only $35 per ticket, the quantity demanded will be 18,000. There will be a shortage of (18,000 – 12,000) = 6000 tickets, even though the concert promoters did not set out intentionally to create a shortage.

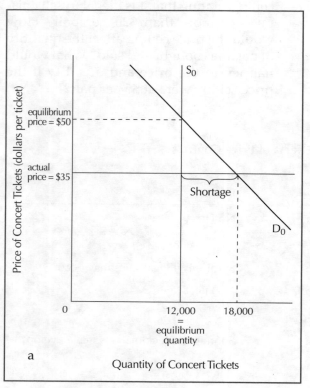 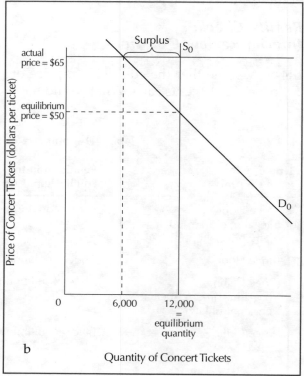

Figure 4.8 What Happens When the Price of Concert Tickets Cannot Easily Be Adjusted to its Equilibrium Level

In both panel (a) and panel (b), the supply of concert tickets if fixed at S_0, which says that the equilibrium quantity of tickets bought and sold is 12,000. Also, the demand curve for concert tickets is D_0 in both panels (a) and (b), so that the equilibrium price is $50 per ticket in each case. In panel (a), the concert promoters set the price at $35. If this price can't be adjusted, the quantity demanded will be 18,000 tickets, and there will be a shortage of (18,000 – 12,000) = 6000 tickets. In this situation, we might expect "scalpers" to try to re-sell tickets. In panel (b), the concert promoters set the price at $65. If this price can't be adjusted, the quantity demanded will be 6000 tickets, which means that there will be a surplus of (12,000 – 6000) = 6000 tickets. In this situation, the concert promoters might cut prices for the unsold tickets, shortly before the concert.

Since there is unsatisfied demand for tickets to the concert, it would not be surprising if a black market were to arise. When there is a black market for tickets to a concert or sporting event, the sellers in the black market are often called "scalpers". Ticket "scalping" is restricted by law in 26 states, and in most cities with professional sports franchises. Some of the laws set a maximum re-sale price for tickets. Others make it illegal to sell near the site of the event. Still other laws require sellers to obtain a costly license. However, it's reasonable to ask whether scalpers are really doing a bad thing. After all, they serve the valuable function of moving the market closer to equilibrium. The scalpers help to allocate tickets to those who are willing to pay the most for tickets.

Panel (b) of Figure 4.8 shows a different possibility for the concert by Peppermint Sponge. Again, let's say that the equilibrium price is $50. This time, however, we assume that the promoters set the price at $65 per ticket. This time, there will be a surplus; that is, some of the tickets will go unsold. In Figure 8(b), the amount of the surplus is (12,000 − 6000) = 6000 tickets.

As the date of the concert draws near, the concert promoters will see that they have chosen a price that's higher than the equilibrium price. On the day of the performance, they may offer to sell the unsold tickets at a discount. After all, the sellers will make more money if they can sell the remaining tickets at a reduced price, instead of not selling them at all. Many concert halls and theaters have a system of selling tickets at a reduced price, if some tickets remain unsold on the day of the performance. Similarly, if a commercial airline is committed to offering a particular flight, it will make more money by flying a full aircraft, rather than flying with empty seats. If airline tickets are still unsold within a few days of the flight, the airlines and ticket brokers will try to sell reduced-price tickets, through channels such as the Internet.

In short, tickets for rock concerts, Broadway plays, and similar events are often sold far in advance, so sellers must decide on ticket prices long before the event actually occurs. This means that it's relatively difficult to adjust prices in these markets, so that shortages or surpluses can occur.

Illegal Drugs and Other Illegal Activities

The market for cocaine doesn't have a price ceiling in the usual sense. Instead, it's illegal to buy cocaine. Thus, for all practical purposes, it's as if the market for cocaine has a price ceiling, at a price of zero. Not surprisingly, there is a shortage of cocaine, and a huge black market.

Similar things can be said about the market for babies for adoption. Once again, there is not a price ceiling, as such. However, it's illegal to buy and sell babies. Effectively, this means that the market for babies has a price ceiling of zero. It's no surprise, therefore, that there is a shortage of babies. Families who wish to go through an agency in order to adopt a baby must often spend five years or more on waiting lists. It is extremely rare to see outright purchases of babies, but it is now common for families seeking a private adoption to pay some of the expenses of the natural mother during her pregnancy. These payments can amount to several thousand dollars. Payments to lawyers and other intermediaries often run to tens of thousands of dollars. In effect, there is an indirect black market.

We can think of the market for organs for transplant in a similar way. It's illegal to buy and sell livers, kidneys, or other organs. As we might expect, there is a shortage: Thousands of people die while waiting for a transplant. It might be possible to solve this problem by allowing payments to the estates of people who donate their organs when they die. In this way, the supply of transplantable organs could be increased, and the shortage could be relieved.

In this chapter, we have studied several examples of price ceilings. These include the price ceilings on food in China, as well as rent controls, and price ceilings on gasoline. Now, we have seen that we can think about the markets for cocaine, babies, and organs for transplant in a similar way. However, there is a crucial difference between these two sets of markets: The restrictions on the markets for drugs, babies, and human organs are based on *ethical* concerns, rather than narrowly economic concerns.

The case against price ceilings in the market for gasoline is extremely strong. However, it's more difficult to build a convincing case against restrictions on selling cocaine or babies, because of ethical concerns about such sales. Of course, there may be benefits from removing the restrictions on the markets for cocaine and babies. If cocaine were legalized, there might be a reduction in drug-related violence. If adoptive parents were allowed to pay for children, it would probably help those children who would otherwise be harmed by long waits for a home. On the other hand, reasonable people can reach the ethical judgment that buying and selling drugs and babies is morally wrong. If so, society may have an interest in restricting such buying and selling, even though it will lead to shortages.

Thus, economic analysis can be an important tool for thinking about policy problems, but it shouldn't be viewed as the *only* tool. In order to solve society's most difficult problems, we need to rely on our moral compass, as well as on the tools of supply and demand.

ECONOMICS AND YOU: HOW TO FIX THE SHORTAGE OF PARKING SPACES

We began this chapter with a discussion of the parking problem that can be found on many college campuses. At Jeanette's college, students have to pay a fixed fee to get a parking sticker. However, they aren't required to pay anything at the time when they actually park their cars. Jeanette has to pay a parking fee of $50 per year, regardless of whether she uses the college parking lots for one hour per year, or for 1000 hours. Effectively, this means that the price of each additional hour of parking in the college lots is zero.

At two o'clock in the morning, a price of zero may not lead to shortages of parking spaces. However, at the times of peak usage during the day, a price of zero may not be high enough to achieve equilibrium. In other words, if the price is zero, we should not be surprised to see shortages, where the quantity of parking spaces demanded is greater than the quantity supplied. As a result, people will have to waste time and gasoline, looking for a parking space. If the price were at its equilibrium level, the parking lots would be just about full, but it wouldn't be necessary to wait a long time to find a spot.

The solution is to charge a positive price for parking (as is done at private parking garages). The price that would achieve equilibrium would be higher during the peak times of day, and it would be higher for the parking lots that are in more central locations. If people are faced with a schedule of prices, they can make sensible decisions about where to park. For instance, if Jeanette has plenty of time, she may be willing to pay a low price for a space in a far-away parking lot. However, if she is rushing to turn in a term paper by a five-o'clock deadline, she will probably be willing to pay something extra, in order to find a parking space that's close to her destination. In this way, prices could be used to allocate parking spaces to those who need them most.

Shortages will occur whenever a price is

below its equilibrium level, and surpluses will occur whenever a price is above its equilibrium level. In this chapter, you have learned about several situations in which markets aren't allowed to find their equilibrium prices. In most cases, it would probably be much better to let prices go to their equilibrium level. This will eliminate the shortages or surpluses.

When markets are allowed to work properly, prices usually do a very effective job of allocating resources. The beauty of the price system is that its "invisible hand" matches buyers and sellers in a quick and efficient way. It does so without needing a vast government bureaucracy, and without forcing people to waste a lot of time waiting in line.

Chapter Summary

1. When demand increases, the demand curve shifts to the right. This leads to a new equilibrium, in which both the equilibrium price and the equilibrium quantity are higher than they were before the shift. If demand decreases, so that the demand curve shifts to the left, we get the opposite effects: Both the equilibrium price and the equilibrium quantity are lower than they were before the shift.

2. When supply increases, the supply curve shifts to the right. This leads to a new equilibrium, in which the equilibrium price is lower and the equilibrium quantity is higher than before the shift. If supply decreases, the supply curve shifts to the left, and we get a higher equilibrium price and a lower equilibrium quantity than before.

3. A price floor is a legal minimum price. (Examples include the price supports for sugar and milk.) If the floor is not enforced, or if it is below the equilibrium price, it will have no effect. If the floor is above the equilibrium price, it will lead to surpluses. In order to deal with the surpluses, governments often pass additional laws, designed to buy up the surpluses or to decrease supply.

4. A price ceiling is a legal maximum price. (Examples include gasoline price controls and rent controls.) If the ceiling is not enforced, or if it is above the equilibrium price, it will have no effect. If the ceiling is below the equilibrium price, it will lead to shortages. Black markets often arise in response to the shortages.

Key Terms

Price-Control Law

Price Floor

Price Ceiling

Disequilibrium

Import Quota

Rent-Control Law

Black Market

Questions and Problems

QP4-1. The equilibrium price for a videotape rental differs from one part of the country to another, and from one part of the week to another. Nevertheless, it is common to see rental prices of $2 or $3 per day. Suppose that the government passes a price ceiling law, so that it is illegal to rent videotapes for more than 25 cents per day. What do you expect would happen as a result? Would your answer change if the ceiling were set at $6 per day? If so, how?

QP4-2. For each of the following changes, what will happen to the equilibrium price of lumber? What will happen to the equilibrium quantity?

a. An increase in incomes. (You may assume that lumber is a normal good.)
b. A decrease in the price of brick, which is a substitute for lumber.
c. A drought in the Pacific Northwest, which makes trees more susceptible to disease and insects.
d. A technological innovation which allows sawmills to cut trees into boards more quickly, and with less labor.

QP4-3. Explain why the price will go up when the demand curve shifts to the right. Explain why the price will go down when the supply curve shifts to the right.

QP4-4. For each of the following changes, what will happen to the equilibrium price of cotton sweaters? What will happen to the equilibrium quantity?

a. Good growing conditions in the South, in Arizona, and in California lead to a record cotton crop, and this leads to lower prices for cotton, which is an important input into the production of cotton sweaters.

b. An increase in the price of wool sweaters, which are a substitute for cotton sweaters.

c. Large numbers of people decide that they don't like the feel of cotton, and that they want to increase their use of polyester.

d. An improvement in technology, which allows textile mills to produce cotton sweaters more rapidly than before.

QP4-5. In the early 1990s, some studies indicated that red wine could reduce the risk of heart disease. As a result of this news, what do you expect would happen to the equilibrium price and quantity of red wine?

QP4-6. The equilibrium price of a particular type of portable radio is $30. A price ceiling is passed into law, so that the legal maximum price is $40. Do you expect that this will lead to black-market activity? Would your answer change if the price ceiling were set at $20? If so, how?

QP4-7. A highly prized type of mineral water comes from a spring in the Alps. There is nothing that producers can do to speed up the flow of water. As a result, the supply of this water is completely unresponsive to price. No matter what happens to price, the quantity supplied is always the same. If a price floor is set above the equilibrium price for this type of water, what will happen to the quantity that is actually bought and sold? What about the case of a price ceiling below the equilibrium price? (Hint: In answering this question, it may be especially useful to draw a supply-demand diagram for yourself.)

QP4-8. Explain why shortages arise when the government enforces a price ceiling below the equilibrium price. Explain why surpluses arise when the government enforces a price floor above the equilibrium price.

QP4-9. The Transplant Act of 1984 makes it a felony to buy and sell body organs (such as livers and kidneys) for transplant. It is illegal to offer any financial compensation to the families of organ donors. Do you expect that this would lead to shortages or surpluses, or do you think that the market for transplant organs will be in equilibrium?

QP4-10. For each of the following changes, what will happen to the equilibrium price of audiocassette tapes?

a. A change in tastes, such that many more music lovers prefer to attend live performances, instead of listening to recorded music.

b. An increase in the price of the plastic components that are used in manufacturing audiocassettes.

c. A technological improvement that allows manufacturers to produce more audiocassette tapes without increasing the number of workers.

d. An increase in income. (You may assume that audiocassette tapes are normal goods.)

QP4-11. In the table on the following page, we have the demand schedule and supply schedule for imports from Belgium of a particular type of cut-glass vase.

a. What are the equilibrium price and quantity?

b. The government sets a price floor at $70. Will there be any effect? If so, will there be a shortage or a surplus? What will be the amount of the shortage or surplus?

c. How do your answers to (b) change if the price floor is set at $30?

d. The government sets a price ceiling at $80. Will there be any effect? If so, will there be a shortage or a surplus? What will be the amount of the shortage or surplus?

e. How do your answers to (d) change if the price ceiling is set at $20?

Price	Quantity Demanded per week	Quantity Supplied per week
$100	0	100
90	10	90
80	20	80
70	30	70
60	40	60
50	50	50
40	60	40
30	70	30
20	80	20
10	90	10
0	100	0

QP4-12. The demand curve for a particular type of mountain bike is given by $Q_d = 100,000 - 250P$, where P is the price of the bike. The supply curve is given by $Q_s = 250P$. At the equilibrium price, the quantity demanded and the quantity supplied are equal, so that $Q_d = Q_s$.

a. Substitute the equation for the demand curve and the equation for the supply curve into the equation for equilibrium, and solve for the equilibrium price.

b. Once you have solved for the equilibrium price, substitute it into either the supply equation or the demand equation, to get the equilibrium quantity.

c. Senator Puffinstuff says that mountain bikes are too expensive, and he suggests that a price ceiling be instituted in the market for mountain bikes. If the price ceiling is set at $500, what will be the effect on the market? What quantity will be demanded? What quantity will be supplied? Will there be a surplus? Will there be a shortage? If there will be either a surplus or a shortage, how great will it be (that is, what will be the difference between quantity supplied and quantity demanded)?

d. If the price ceiling is set at $100, what will be the effect on the market? What quantity will be demanded? What quantity will be supplied? Will there be a surplus? Will there be a shortage? If there will be either a surplus or a shortage, how great will it be (that is, what will be the difference between quantity supplied and quantity demanded)?

Chapter 5

International Trade

ECONOMICS AND YOU:
IS THERE A GIANT SUCKING SOUND?

In 1992, the Texas billionaire Ross Perot ran for President of the United States. His opponents were the incumbent Republican President, George Bush, and Bill Clinton, the Democratic Party candidate, who won the election. Both Bush and Clinton were generally supportive of free international trade. In particular, both Bush and Clinton were in favor of the North American Free Trade Agreement (NAFTA), which would reduce barriers to international trade between Canada, Mexico, and the United States.

But Perot opposed NAFTA. He said that reduced barriers to trade with Mexico would create a "giant sucking sound", as American industries re-located to Mexico. Some of his campaign literature suggested that Americans might lose a truly staggering six million jobs.

No serious economist believed Perot's numbers. If the United States was to lose six million jobs as a result of NAFTA, the following things would have been necessary: (1) First, the Mexican economy would have had to double in size overnight. (2) Second, all of the growth of the Mexican economy would have had to be in the form of exports to the United States. (3) Third, there would have had to be no increase in exports from the United States to Mexico, even though U.S. exports of machinery and equipment had been a very important source of Mexico's economic growth in the past.

The ultimate test of Perot's prediction would come from looking at what actually happened to employment in the United States. In 1992, when Perot made his prediction about the giant sucking sound, about 118 million Americans had jobs. NAFTA was enacted the following year. By 2000, the number of American jobs had risen to about 136 million. Whereas Perot predicted that there would be a huge Depression, the 1990s were actually the scene of one of the most remarkable economic expansions in history. Of course, international trade was not the only source of growth in the American economy, or in the economy of the rest of the world. However, there is no doubt that international trade was an important part of the economic expansion.

In spite of this evidence that jobs and trade can happen at the same time, Ross Perot's ideas remain stubbornly popular. In this chapter, we will study international trade more closely, with an eye toward understanding the arguments for and against free trade. In most cases, we will find that the pro-trade arguments are the stronger ones.

SOME FACTS ABOUT INTERNATIONAL TRADE

When a country *sells* goods or services to another country, we say that the selling country has made an ***export***. When a country *buys* goods or services from another country, we say that the buying country has made an ***import***. In 1999, the United States exported just barely less than $1 trillion ($996 billion, to be exact). This was about 10.8 percent of gross domestic product (GDP). In the same year, imports into the United States were about $1.25 trillion, or about 13.5 percent of GDP.

Figure 5.1 shows that, over time, international trade has accounted for an increasing fraction of GDP for the United States. In most years in the 1960s, exports accounted for about five percent of GDP, and imports were at about the same level. In most years in the 1970s, both

exports and imports were around eight to ten percent of GDP. In the early 1980s, exports fell back slightly, and imports continued to grow as a percentage of GDP. As a result, the United States experienced unusually large *trade deficits*. A ***trade deficit*** occurs when imports are greater than exports. A ***trade surplus*** occurs when exports are greater than imports. In 1986 and 1987, the trade deficit was about three percent of GDP. However, exports surged in the late 1980s, and continued to grow rapidly in the 1990s. Imports grew, too, so that trade deficits continued, but they were not as large as they had been in the middle 1980s.

Thus, if we look at the last 40 years of the 20th century, we see a period in which international trade was growing more rapidly than purely domestic transactions. As a result, we can say that international trade was a major "engine of growth" for the United States. (The same is true for many other countries, as well.)

Figure 5.1 presents the time trend of the overall level of exports and imports, for goods and services combined. Table 5.1 gives a country-by-country breakdown of exports and imports, for 1998. Table 5.1 includes only goods, so that the numbers are not completely comparable with the data in Figure 5.1. However, goods exports are more than 70 percent of total exports, and goods imports are more than 80 percent of total imports, so that Table 5.1 can give a fairly accurate impression of what is going on. The world has well over 150 countries, and tables that include the trade data for all of them are pretty messy. Therefore, Table 5.1 includes only those countries for which U.S. exports and/or imports were greater than $10 billion in 1998. In this table, the countries are listed in order of the amounts of U.S. exports.

Table 5.1 reveals a number of things. First of all, trade is very dispersed. Although some countries clearly have more trade with the

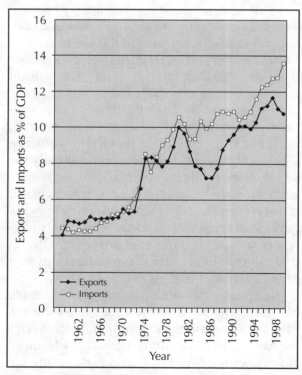

Figure 5.1 United States Exports and Imports as Percentage of Gross Domestic Product, 1959–1999

Table 5.1 United States Exports and Imports of Merchandise Goods, for Selected Countries, 1998*

Country	Exports from U.S. (in Billions of Dollars)	Imports to U.S. (in Billions)	Trade Surplus (Positive) or Trade Deficit (Negative) (in Billions)
Canada	$156.3	$174.8	− $18.5
Mexico	79.0	94.7	− 15.7
Japan	57.9	122.0	− 64.1
United Kingdom	39.1	34.8	+ 4.3
China (including Hong Kong)	27.2	81.7	− 54.5
Germany	26.6	49.8	− 23.2
Netherlands	19.0	7.6	+ 11.4
Taiwan	18.2	33.1	− 15.0
France	17.7	24.1	− 6.3
South Korea	16.5	23.9	− 7.4
Singapore	15.7	18.4	− 2.7
Brazil	15.2	10.1	+ 5.0
Belgium	13.9	8.4	+ 5.5
Australia	11.9	5.4	+ 6.5
Saudi Arabia	10.5	6.3	+ 4.2
Italy	9.0	21.0	− 12.0
Malaysia	9.0	19.0	− 10.0
Philippines	6.7	11.9	− 5.2
Thailand	5.2	13.4	− 8.2

* Surpluses or deficits may not agree exactly with export and import levels, because of rounding.

United States than do other countries, it is not as if one or two countries were dominating the picture completely. Second, the table shows that many of our biggest trading partners are other affluent countries, such as Australia, Belgium, Canada, France, Germany, Italy, Japan, the Netherlands, and the United Kingdom. A lot of our trade is with other rich countries, because that's where a lot of the money is. Third, although the United States has an overall trade deficit, it does not have a deficit with every single country. As shown in Table 5.1, the U.S. had substantial surpluses in 1998 with Australia, Belgium, Brazil, the Netherlands, Saudi Arabia, and the United Kingdom.

One of the most interesting features of Table 5.1 is that the United States has large surpluses with some countries, and very large deficits with some other countries. We are not even close to "bilateral trade balance", which is a situation in which the exports to each country are exactly equal to the imports to that country. In *Real Economics for Real People 5.1*, we explore the question of whether trade balance is a good thing.

Reality Check: Interim Review Questions

IR5-1. Over the last few decades, have exports and imports become more important, or less important, as a fraction of gross domestic product?

IR5-2. In what regions of the world are the most important trading partners of the United States located?

Real Economics for Real People 5.1:
Are Trade Deficits Good or Bad?

If you listen to some commentators and politicians, it would be easy to think that there is nothing worse in the entire world than a trade deficit. The idea is a fairly simplistic one. Exports are "good", because they create American jobs. Imports are "bad", because they create jobs for people in other countries. If exports are "good", and imports are "bad", then it must be that trade surpluses are good, and trade deficits are bad.

This sort of thinking can be very misleading. First of all, it is important to remember that the United States was running substantial trade deficits in the year 2000, even though employment was at an all-time record high. Clearly, it is simplistic to think that trade deficits inevitably lead to unemployment.

Second, although employment considerations are worth worrying about, they are not the only important thing. Consumption is also important. Americans import goods from other countries because they find that those goods provide a good level of satisfaction for the dollar. Part of the trade deficit is caused by imports of coffee from Brazil, and wooden bowls from Thailand, and radios from South Korea, and cheese from Denmark. It is very difficult to argue that consumers in the United States would be better off if we were to cut off these imports. Part of the trade deficit is caused by imports of oil. In recent years, the United States has been importing about 9 million barrels per day. (We get the oil from all over the world, but our four biggest suppliers are Canada, Mexico, Saudi Arabia, and Venezuela.) We could "solve" a part of the trade deficit by prohibiting imports of oil, but would that make us better off? Instead of making us better off, a prohibition on oil imports would

just make us cold in the winter, because it would be difficult to find enough energy to heat our homes.

A third important point is that there is no way for the world as a whole to run a trade surplus. By definition, one country's surplus is another country's deficit. This means that the world as a whole has a trade balance of exactly zero: For the world as a whole, total imports have to be exactly equal to total exports. Thus, there is no way for all countries to reduce deficits (or increase surpluses) simultaneously. If lots of countries were to try to increase their surpluses (or reduce their deficits) at the same time, the results could be disastrous. In the 1930s, a number of countries increased their barriers against imports. This led to a downward spiral, as economic activity decreased around the globe. The Great Depression of the 1930s had many causes, and trade restrictions weren't the most important one. But trade restrictions certainly contributed to the Great Depression.

When a country runs an overall trade deficit, as the United States is doing now, the country is consuming more than it produces. In other words, the country is borrowing. If we really want to address the trade deficit, the best way to do it would be to save more. This has more to do with policies toward Social Security and pensions than with trade policies.

It is true that, if a country runs huge trade deficits, year after year after year, it can accumulate a lot of debt. In the long run, this can cause big problems. In fact, several of the poorer countries of the world have encountered major difficulties, because of persistently large trade deficits. But trade deficits like those being run today by the United

States are not large enough, relative to the overall economy, to cause major headaches.

In the last few paragraphs, we have tried to make the point that today's trade deficits really aren't something to worry about very much. Another way to see this is to use an analogy between a country and a household. Most households have at least one worker. The workers earn money by working for an employer. Thus, we could say that most households have a big "trade surplus" with their employers. On the other hand, households spend money in all sorts of places, including the grocery store, the hardware store, the gasoline station, and so on. We could say that most households have "trade deficits" with all of these retailers.

In the aggregate, it would be good if the sum of the household's "trade surpluses" with employers is about as big as the sum of all of the "trade deficits" with the various retailers. If the household's "deficits" are extremely large in comparison with its "surpluses", then the household will go deeply into debt. But it's not a big problem if the household runs a more moderate aggregate deficit: Households borrow all the time, and most do so without bad consequences.

Similarly, it would be good if the sum of a country's trade surpluses with some countries were roughly as big as the sum of its trade deficits with other countries. If the overall trade deficits are too large, the country will fall deeply into debt. But it's not a big problem if a country runs a modest aggregate deficit. It happens all the time, without severe repercussions.

It's *even more* important to avoid worrying about trade deficits with any one country. As shown in Table 5.1, we run surpluses with some countries, and deficits with others. This is very common. Even when the United States has had an overall trade balance of zero, with total exports equal to total imports, we have always run deficits with some countries, and surpluses with other countries. Once again, we can reinforce our ideas by using an analogy with the household. It simply would not make sense for a household to try to have bilateral trade balance with the grocery store, the clothing store, the book store, and so on. And it would be extremely counterproductive for a country to try to have exact bilateral trade balance with every other country.

COMPARATIVE ADVANTAGE REVISITED

In Chapter 2, we introduced the idea of comparative advantage. We showed that it would be beneficial for people and countries to specialize in the activities in which they have comparative advantage, and then to trade with each other. In Figure 2.5, we illustrated the case for trade between Kenny, who has comparative advantage in the production of fish, and Stan, who has comparative advantage in the production of coconuts.

But some readers might object to that example in Chapter 2. Not only did Kenny have *comparative* advantage in the production of fish, but he also had *absolute* advantage in fish production. Not only did Stan have *comparative* advantage in the production of coconuts, but he also had *absolute* advantage in coconut production.

Some readers might say that the example in Chapter 2 was too easy. Some might ask what would happen in a case in which one side has absolute advantage in *all* activities. In this section, however, we will show that it is still possible to enjoy gains from trade, even when one side has absolute advantage in every activity. This is not merely a sterile academic exercise. It has relevance to many of the most important debates in the international economy today. Often, the most heated opposition to free trade comes in the form of opposition to free trade with relatively poor countries, most notably Mexico and China. Although the debate is usually not carried on using the language that we have developed in this book, we could still characterize the opponents of trade with Mexico or China as saying something like this: "Workers from poorer countries are less productive than workers in the United States. Therefore, there is nothing to be gained from trading with these countries."

But that simply is not true. Even though American workers may have *absolute* advantage in every activity, when compared with workers in Mexico or China, it is impossible for American workers to have *comparative* advantage in every activity.

We'll illustrate this idea with another example from a desert island. Once again, there are two commodities, fish and coconuts. This time, the two workers are Al and Zeke. Al isn't as quick or clever as Zeke, and Zeke has absolute advantage, both in catching fish *and* in gathering coconuts.

The production-possibilities frontiers for Al and Zeke are shown in Figure 5.2. If Al devotes all of his energies and resources to fishing, he can catch 15 fish. If he devotes all of his energies and resources to gathering coconuts, Al can gather 5 coconuts. Between those two endpoints, Al's production-possibilities frontier is a straight line.

If Zeke devotes all of *his* energies and resources to fishing, he can catch 16 fish. If Zeke devotes all of his energies and resources to gathering coconuts, he can gather 16 coconuts. Between these two endpoints, Zeke's production-possibilities frontier is also a straight line.

Zeke has *absolute* advantage in both activities. However, in order to determine *comparative* advantage, we must calculate the opportunity costs for each man. Let's begin by calculating opportunity cost for Al. Al can produce either 15 fish or 5 coconuts. Therefore, for Al, the opportunity cost of 5 coconuts is 15 fish. We can write this as an equation, as follows:

$$5C = 15F \text{ (for Al)},$$

where C stands for coconuts and F stands for fish. If we divide both sides of this equation by 5, we can find the opportunity cost of *one* coconut for Al:

$$(5/5)C = 1C = (15/5)F = 3F \text{ (for Al)}.$$

We now know that, for Al, the opportunity cost of one coconut is three fish.

Next, let's calculate the opportunity cost for Zeke. Zeke can produce either 16 fish or 16 coconuts. This can be expressed in equation form, as follows:

$$16C = 16F \text{ (for Zeke)}.$$

If we divide both sides of this equation by 16, we find that, for Zeke, the opportunity cost of one coconut is one fish.

To recap, the opportunity cost of one coconut is three fish for Al, whereas the opportunity cost of one coconut is only one coconut for Zeke. Therefore, Zeke has comparative advantage in coconut production, because the opportunity cost of a coconut is lower for Zeke than it is for Al. In other words, coconuts are "cheap" for Zeke. On the other hand, Al has comparative advantage in fish production. Thus, even though Zeke has *absolute* advantage in both activities, Al does have *comparative* advantage in the production of fish.

To illustrate the gains from trade, we have to figure out what each of these gentlemen would do, in the absence of trade. It is possible to develop an elaborate mathematical structure, to specify the consumer's prefer-

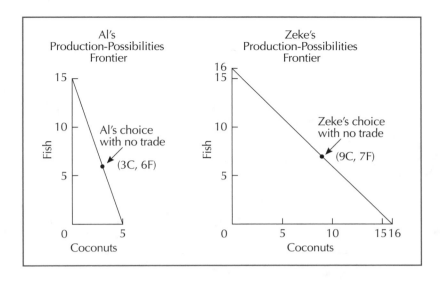

Figure 5.2 The Production-Possibilities Frontiers for Al and Zeke, in the Absence of Trade

Zeke has *absolute* advantage in the production of both fish and coconuts. However, Al has comparative advantage in the production of fish.

ences. But doing that would take us off on a distant tangent. So, for now, we will simply make assumptions about the consumption choices of Al and Zeke. If the two men do not trade, Al will have to consume one of the combinations of output that is given by his production-possibilities frontier. Let's assume that Al would choose to consume three coconuts and six fish. (This point is indeed on Al's production-possibilities frontier, as shown in Figure 5.2.)

Let's assume that, if there is no trade, Zeke will choose to consume nine coconuts and seven fish. (This point is on Zeke's production-possibilities frontier, as shown in Figure 5.2.)

So, if there were no trade, Al would consume three coconuts and six fish, while Zeke would consume nine coconuts and seven fish. This means that the total production of this two-person society is (6 + 7) = 13 fish, and (3 + 9) = 12 coconuts.

Sooner or later, one of these guys is going to get an idea. What if Al specializes in fish production (which is his comparative advantage), while Zeke specializes in coconut production (which is his comparative advantage)? Al will then catch 15 fish, while Zeke will gather 16 coconuts. Note that *total production of*

each commodity has gone up, as a result of exploiting comparative advantage! The two men used to have a total of 13 fish, and they now have 15 fish. In addition, they used to have a total of 12 coconuts, and they now have a total of 16 coconuts. This increase in total production is the thing that allows the two men to make themselves better off, by specializing and trading.

After they specialize, Al and Zeke will have to figure out how to trade with each other. In effect, they will have to determine the price at which they can buy and sell coconuts and fish. In a more advanced course, it would be possible to spell out the process of price determination in more detail. Here, however, we will just make an arbitrary assumption about the price of fish in terms of coconuts. In the absence of trade, Al's production-possibilities frontier told him that he could trade *three* fish for one coconut. In the absence of trade, Zeke's production-possibilities frontier told him that he could trade *one* fish for one coconut. Let's assume that they trade at a rate that is in between three-to-one and one-to-one. Let's assume that they trade at a rate of *two* fish for one coconut.

In Figure 5.3, we trace out the consumption possibilities that are available to each

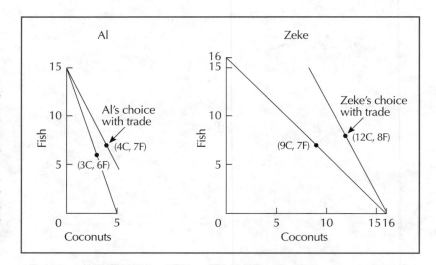

Figure 5.3 The Gains from Specialization and Trade

Al has comparative advantage in the production of fish, and Zeke has comparative advantage in the production of coconuts. If each of them specializes in the activity in which he has comparative advantage, the total amount of production will increase. We assume that, after specializing, they trade with each other at the rate of two fish for one coconut. Trading in this manner allows each of the men to increase his consumption of both goods.

man, given that they trade at a rate of two fish for one coconut. These "consumption-possibilities frontiers" are farther out than the individual production-possibilities frontiers. This tells us that the two men should be able to improve their lot by specialization and trade, even though Zeke has *absolute* advantage in each activity.

The exact consumption choices will depend on the preferences of the two men. One possibility would be for Al to trade eight of his 15 fish to Zeke. Since the rate at which they trade is two fish for one coconut, Al will get four coconuts in return for the eight fish that he gives up. As a result, Al ends up with

four coconuts and (15 – 8) = seven fish. Zeke ends up with eight fish and (16 – 4) = 12 coconuts.

Table 5.2 makes a "before-and-after" comparison for each of the two men. We see that, as a result of specialization and trade, Al increases his consumption by one coconut and one fish. Zeke increases his consumption by three coconuts and one fish. Each man is unambiguously better off.

Some readers might object that this example was rigged. Well, of course it was rigged. As with so many other examples and problems in this book, the details have been chosen so that the numbers come out nicely. In this

Table 5.2 The Gains from Trade for Al and Zeke

	Al's Consumption				Zeke's Consumption	
	No Trade	With Trade			No Trade	With Trade
Coconuts	3	4		Coconuts	9	12
Fish	6	7		Fish	7	8

case, the numbers were chosen so that we didn't have to deal with any cumbersome fractions. Nevertheless, it is still true that this example tells us a lot. Even though the details have been streamlined and simplified, the underlying ideas can be applied in an extremely wide variety of real-world situations. Yes, it is true that American workers have absolute advantage over Mexican workers in virtually every activity. But we can't possibly have comparative advantage in every activity. Therefore, the United States exports machinery and equipment and computers to Mexico, and imports petroleum, fruits and vegetables, and textiles.

In *Real Economics for Real People 5.2*, we take a look at another issue that is associated with trade with low-income countries.

Reality Check: Interim Review Question

IR5-3. Is there any hope that a high-income country (such as the United States) can gain anything from trading with a low-income country (such as China)?

Real Economics for Real People 5.2:
Trade, the Environment, and Human Rights

In November, 1999, the World Trade Organization tried to hold a meeting in Seattle, Washington. The meeting was disrupted by a series of protests. Some of the protestors were merely engaged in vandalism, and they trashed a large portion of downtown Seattle. However, other protestors were more peaceful. They brought forth a wide variety of complaints about free trade. Many of the same arguments were repeated a few months later, in protests in Washington, D.C., at the meetings of the International Monetary Fund and the World Bank. Some of the protestors suggested that international trade is harming human rights and the environment. Most of the criticism was aimed at international trade with poorer countries, since many of the poorer countries do not have especially good records on environment or human rights.

The question is whether a reduction in international trade is likely to lead to any improvement in human rights or the environment. Of course, unless one is able to read the future in a crystal ball, it is not possible to make any absolutely certain predictions. However, there are good reasons to think that cutting off trade with poor countries will *not* cause them to improve their records on human rights or the environment.

First of all, it is important to remember that trade barriers are viewed as unfriendly, hostile actions. If the United States were to impose trade restrictions on some other country, because the other country has a poor human-rights record, it is possible that the other country would say "Oh, yes, USA, you are so right! We have been bad, but now that you have imposed trade restrictions on us, we will mend our ways!" However, it seems more likely that the other country will respond angrily, and say "None of your business."

Cuba is an important example of the problems of using trade restrictions, in an attempt to punish other countries. The United States has now had an embargo in place against the regime of Fidel Castro in Cuba for 40 years, and yet Castro is still in power. It certainly appears that the embargo has strengthened Castro's grip on Cuban

---

society. The embargo has given Castro the opportunity to blame his country's problems on the United States. If there were no embargo, it would be more difficult for Castro to deflect the blame from his own mismanagement of the Cuban economy. Moreover, if there had been no embargo, it would have been much easier for private businesses to thrive in Cuba. This could have created an economically powerful middle class, which might have been much more successful in pushing for changes in Castro's policies.

Another problem with using trade restrictions to punish other countries is that people in glass houses should not necessarily be throwing stones. If the United States had a spotless record on human rights and the environment, it might make more sense for us to lecture others on the errors of their ways. However, American society is far from perfect. Even though the situation is not as bad as it once was, it is well known that racial minorities have often been treated very badly in the United States. (In Chapters 13 and 15, we will look at the gap between the races in earnings and income.) And, even though some improvements have been made, the United States is still the world's biggest polluter. (We will study the economics of the environment in Chapter 17.) So, when the United States lectures other countries on their human-rights records, or their environmental records, it is hard to avoid the conclusion that we are being a little bit hypocritical.

In many countries, capital punishment is prohibited. This is not the place to debate the merits of the death penalty, but it is fair to say that many Europeans consider it barbaric that there are executions in the United States. What would happen if the Europeans decided to use trade restrictions, as a means of convincing us that we should stop capital punishment? Most likely, the trade restrictions would reduce the rate of economic growth, and they would reduce the choices available to consumers, but they would do little to change the laws on capital punishment.

As mentioned above, the United States creates a lot of pollution. And yet, our environmental record is significantly better than it was before environmental laws were passed in the 1960s and 1970s. Why were those laws passed then? There are many reasons, of course, but one reason is that the United States had reached a level of economic development at which many Americans felt comfortable about turning their attention to environmental improvements. When people are very poor, they tend to worry much more about where their next meal is coming from, than about the environment. As the United States became more and more affluent, it was possible for environmental concerns to reach the top of the list. (In other words, environmental quality is a normal good.) It's no surprise that the richest countries are the ones with the strictest environmental laws. Therefore, there is reason to believe that other countries will improve their environmental records as their levels of income rise. One way to help their incomes to rise is to allow them to benefit from participation in the world economy, through international trade. Thus, if we punish poor countries with trade restrictions, we will help to keep them poor, and this may actually slow down their progress toward a cleaner environment.

Politics and economics on the world stage are very complicated. It is impossible to prove a mathematical theorem that trade restrictions will always fail to achieve their intended goals. Nevertheless, it is hoped that this discussion has made clear that the case for trade restrictions is a very difficult one to make.

BARRIERS TO INTERNATIONAL TRADE

In Chapter 2, and again in this chapter, we have emphasized the idea that trade is mutually beneficial. If people specialize in the activities in which they have comparative advantage, and then trade with each other, then everyone can be made better off. In spite of this, nearly all countries engage in at least some restrictions on international trade. Later in this chapter, we will discuss why this might occur. For now, however, our goal is to analyze the economic effects of the barriers to trade.

There are all sorts of barriers to international trade. Customs officials can put many obstacles in the way of firms that want to engage in international trade. Some countries require excessive amounts of paperwork, or impose complicated regulations. In this chapter, however, we will focus our attention on three types of barrier to free trade:

- *Tariffs*, which are taxes on imports,

- *Import Quotas*, which are restrictions on the quantity of a good that can be sold from one country to another, administered by the importing country, and

- *Voluntary Export Restraints* (VERs), which are also restrictions on the quantity of a good that can be sold from one country to another, except that VERs are administered by the exporting country.

The Economic Effects of a Tariff

To understand the effects of a tariff, we need to begin by looking at the equilibrium that would exist in the absence of any tariff. Then, we introduce a tariff, and see how the market is affected.

Let's consider the exports of computer chips from the United States to France. Figure 5.4 shows the supply and demand curves in the market for sales of U.S. computer chips to France. The import-demand curve in Figure

5.4, D_0, represents the behavior of the French who would like to import computer chips from the United States. The demand curve slopes downward as we move to the right, because of the Law of Demand. The export-supply curve in Figure 5.4, S_0, represents the behavior of Americans who would like to export computer chips to France. The supply curve slopes upward as we move to the right, because of the Law of Supply.

The equilibrium quantity of computer-chip sales from the U.S. to France is determined by the intersection of the export-supply curve and the import-demand curve. The

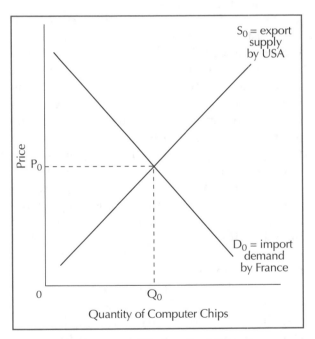

Figure 5.4 Equilibrium in the Market for Exports of Computer Chips from the United States to France

The behavior of sellers in the United States is represented by the export-supply curve, S_0. The behavior of buyers in France is represented by the import-demand curve, D_0. The equilibrium quantity of exports from the United States to France is Q_0, and the equilibrium price is P_0.

equilibrium quantity is Q_0, and the equilibrium price is P_0.

Now, what will happen if the French government imposes a tariff on imports of computer chips from the United States? As a result of the tariff, the price paid by French buyers of U.S. computer chips will be greater than the price received by U.S. sellers. The difference between the buyers' price and the sellers' price is the amount of tariff per unit. We represent the tariff as creating a shift in the supply curve. However, this supply-curve shift is different from any other shift that we have seen so far. In Chapter 4, when something caused a shift in one of the curves, the old curve no longer existed. In our model of the tariff, on the other hand, the net-of-tariff supply curve is still there, and it still plays a role.

Figure 5.5 shows two supply curves in the market for sales of computer chips from the U.S. to France. The lower supply curve is the same as S_0 from Figure 5.4. In other words, the lower supply curve in Figure 5.5 is the same as the supply curve that existed when there was no tariff. In Figure 5.5, we refer to this old supply curve as S_{net}, to indicate that it represents the relationship between the *net-of-tariff* price and the quantity supplied. S_{net} is the supply curve as perceived by the sellers, who are the American exporters of computer chips. Ultimately, the sellers are only concerned with the price that they will receive, *excluding* any tariffs, so S_{net} is the supply curve that is relevant from the point of view of the exporters.

Figure 5.5 also shows a second, higher supply curve, S_{gross}. This is called S_{gross} to indicate that it represents the relationship between the gross-of-tariff price, or tariff-inclusive price, and the quantity supplied. S_{gross} is the supply curve as perceived by the buyers, who are the French importers of computer chips. Ultimately, the buyers are only concerned with the price that they will have to pay, *including* any tariffs, so S_{gross} is the supply curve that is relevant from the point of view of the importers. The vertical distance between S_{gross}

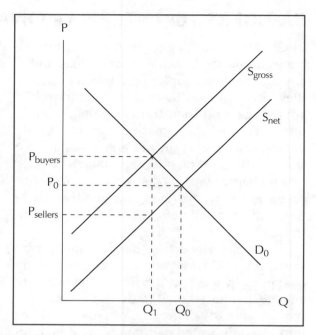

Figure 5.5 The Effects of a Tariff on Imports of Computer Chips from the United States into France

S_{net} is the supply curve that existed in the absence of the tariff. S_{net} represents the behavior of sellers, because sellers are interested in the net-of-tax price. S_{gross} is the supply curve perceived by the buyers, because it includes all taxes. (S_{gross} is "gross of taxes".) The new equilibrium is given by the intersection between D_0, the original demand curve, and S_{gross}, the new supply curve. The equilibrium quantity is reduced from Q_0 to Q_1. The price paid by buyers in the importing country rises to P_{buyers}, and the price received by sellers in the exporting country falls to $P_{sellers}$. The tariff revenue for the French government is represented by the area of the rectangle, $(P_{buyers} - P_{sellers}) \times Q_1$.

and S_{net} is the amount of tariff per computer chip.

After the tariff is imposed, the new equilibrium is determined by the intersection of the demand curve (which has not changed) with the new, gross-of-tariff supply curve, S_{gross}. The new supply curve is the one that is relevant from the buyers' point of view, because the new curve includes the tariff. The demand curve represents the buyers' behavior. In looking for the equilibrium after the tariff is imposed, it's appropriate to search for the intersection of the demand curve and the *gross-of-tariff* supply curve.

The new equilibrium quantity is Q_1, which is lower than Q_0. One of the effects of the tariff is to reduce the quantity of goods that are sold from one country to another.

The tariff also has an effect on prices. In fact, as a result of the tariff, there are now *two* prices. The price paid by the buyers is P_{buyers}, while the price received by the sellers is $P_{sellers}$. The difference between the two prices is the tariff per unit. Thus, in addition to reducing the quantity of international sales, the tariff will also raise prices for consumers in the importing country, and it will reduce the prices that are received by the sellers in the exporting country.

If we know Q_1 (the quantity bought and sold after the tariff is imposed), and if we know the amount of tariff per unit, we can figure out the amount of tariff revenue that is raised. The tariff revenue is collected by the government of the importing country. In this case, the tariff revenue is collected by the French government. The tariff revenue is equal to the amount of tariff per unit, multiplied by the number of units that are bought and sold. The number of units bought and sold is Q_1, and the amount of tariff per unit is $(P_{buyers} - P_{sellers})$. Thus, the French government's tariff revenue is $(P_{buyers} - P_{sellers}) \times (Q_1)$.

In Figure 5.5, this tariff revenue is represented by the area of a rectangle. The base of the rectangle is the quantity, Q_1. The height of the rectangle is the amount of tariff per unit, $P_{buyers} - P_{sellers}$.

In summary, the tariff will raise the prices paid by buyers in the importing country, and it will reduce quantities. Who wins and who loses as a result of the tariff? The biggest losers are the consumers in the importing country (in this case, the French buyers of computer chips). They face higher prices, and they end up paying more for every unit they buy. The

producers in the exporting country (in this case, the American sellers of computer chips) are also worse off as a result of the tariff.

Of course, if *everyone* were made worse off by the tariff, it would be very difficult to understand why the tariff exists. But two groups gain as a result of the tariff. One of these is the government of the importing country, which gets tariff revenue. The others who gain are the producers of the importing country. Without having to work harder or produce a better product, the sellers in the importing country are able to sell for a higher price than before. The tariff makes it more difficult for foreign firms to compete, so that some of the sales may be diverted from the foreign producers to the producers in the importing country. As a result, the producers in the importing country often have a lot to gain from tariffs. These companies often lobby very hard for tariffs (or for other trade barriers), and they often give big contributions to political campaigns, in the hope of influencing public officials.

Import Quotas

A tariff raises the *price* of imports. This causes a reduction in the quantity of imports, as the buyers move upward and to the left, along their demand curves. The exact amount of the quantity reduction depends on the shape of the demand curve for the imported goods.

Another way to reduce imports is to clamp down directly on the quantity of imports. A direct control on the quantity of imports can occur as a result of an import quota. Let's return to the example of U.S. sales of computer chips to France. In Figure 5.5, we have seen what would happen if a tariff were imposed in that market. Figure 5.6 shows what would happen if an import quota were imposed.

Figure 5.6 has S_0 and D_0, which are the same as the net-of-tariff supply curve and the demand curve in Figures 5.4 and 5.5. As before, the original equilibrium (before any policy to restrict imports) is determined by the

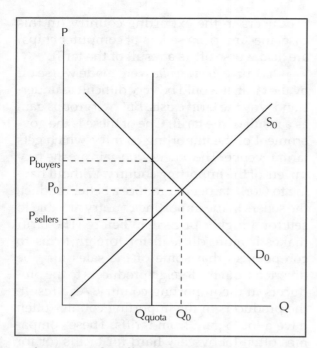

Figure 5.6 The Effects of a Quota on Imports of Computer Chips into France from the United States

Another way of restricting imports is to control the quantity of imports directly, through a quota. In this case, the quota is set at Q_{quota}. The price paid by the buyers will increase, and the price received by the sellers will decrease. The difference will be pocketed by the holder of the import license.

intersection of S_0 and D_0. The original equilibrium price is P_0, and the original equilibrium quantity is Q_0.

Now, the French government decides to impose a quota on imports of computer chips from the United States. In Figure 5.6, Q_{quota} is the level at which the quota is set. If Q_{quota} were higher than Q_0, the quota would have no effect. (It is possible to draw an analogy between a quota and a price ceiling. In Chapter 4, we saw that, if a price ceiling is above the equilibrium *price*, it will have no effect. Here, if a quota is above the equilibrium *quantity*, it will have no effect. Thus, you can think of a quota as a quantity ceiling.) The more interesting case is the case in which the quota

is below the equilibrium quantity. This case is illustrated in Figure 5.6. If the quota is below the equilibrium quantity, and if the authorities enforce the quota, then the quota will have an effect.

With the quota at Q_{quota}, the demand curve tells us that the buyers in the importing country are willing to pay a higher price than P_0. In this case, they will pay P_{buyers}.

In Figure 5.5, we saw that the government of the importing country gets revenue from a tariff. The tariff revenue is associated with the fact that the tariff drives a wedge between the price that buyers pay and the price that sellers receive. Something very similar happens in the case of an import quota. After the quota is imposed, there is a gap between the buyers' price and the sellers' price. The only real difference between the tariff and the quota has to do with who grabs the difference between the buyers' price and the sellers' price. In the case of the import quota, this money is taken by the organization that is given a license to import, by the government of the importing country. In many countries, the import licenses are given to the dictator, or the dictator's brother-in-law, or to other people with powerful connections.

Voluntary Export Restraints

In the early 1980s, the American automobile industry was in bad shape. At that time, it was widely perceived that the quality of compact and midsize American cars was inferior to the quality of comparable Japanese cars. The American car companies wanted the U.S. government to do something, to slow down the flow of imports from Japan. We have seen that a tariff or a quota would have accomplished this purpose. However, what occurred was a set of "voluntary export restraints" or VERs. (In fact, it is a bit misleading to use the word "voluntary" to describe these restraints. If the Japanese had not "voluntarily" imposed a system of export restraints, it is likely that the U.S. government would have imposed an import quota.)

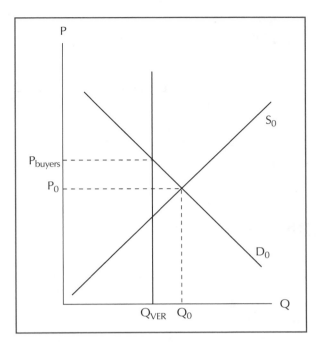

Figure 5.7 The Effects of a Voluntary Export Restraint

A voluntary export restraint (VER) is an explicit restriction on quantity. Thus, it is similar to an import quota. The difference is that a quota generates an advantage for the person or persons who holds the import license. A VER generates an advantage for the exporters.

The effects of the VER are shown in Figure 5.7. This figure should look very familiar. It is virtually identical to Figure 5.6, which showed the effects of an import quota. The only important difference between an import quota and a VER is that the exporters get to receive the full buyers' price with a VER, while the holder of the import license is the one to benefit from an import quota. Thus, in the case of the VERs on exports of Japanese automobiles to the United States, the Japanese auto companies received higher profits.

Comparison of the Different Ways of Restricting Trade

We have studied three ways of restricting international trade: tariffs, import quotas, and voluntary export restraints. In many ways, these mechanisms are very similar to each other. First of all, each hurts the consumers in the importing country. These consumers are forced to pay higher prices, and they consume a reduced quantity.

Second, each of these mechanisms gives an advantage to the producers in the importing country. These producers are able to charge higher prices. They don't have to compete as vigorously as they would have, if the trade restrictions were not in place. Therefore, it is not surprising that the producers in the importing country are almost always at the heart of efforts to restrict trade.

The big differences among the three mechanisms for restricting trade have to do with who gets the pot of money, represented by the rectangle $(P_{buyers} - P_{sellers}) \times Q_1$ in Figure 5.5. In the case of a tariff, the money goes to the government of the importing country. In the case of an import quota, the money goes to the holder of the import license. (Of course, if the government of the importing country were to auction the import license to the highest bidder, then the government would share in the pot of money, and the ultimate effect of the quota would be even more similar to the ultimate effect of the tariff. However, the auction method is rarely used.) In the case of a VER, the money goes to the producers in the exporting country.

Because of the damage done to the consumers in the importing country, none of these restrictions on trade would be favored by economists. However, if the political pressure to impose trade restrictions becomes overwhelming, so that some sort of trade restriction is unavoidable, then there may be an argument in favor of a VER. The reason is that the VER is the only one of the three mechanisms that provides any benefit to the exporting country. Consequently, the exporting country is probably less likely to retaliate against a VER than against some other sort of trade restriction. This is important, because one of the biggest potential dangers of trade restrictions is that they might lead to a vicious cycle of one restriction after another, as politicians in each country scramble to look tough by retaliating against the other country. If the restrictions were to escalate into a full-scale "trade war", with a major increase in barriers to trade, it could be catastrophic for the entire world.

Reality Check:
Interim Review Questions

IR5-4. What happens when an import quota is imposed at a level that is higher than the equilibrium quantity?

IR5-5. What are the similarities between a tariff, an import quota, and a voluntary export restraint? What are the differences?

ECONOMICS AND YOU:
DON'T BE AFRAID OF A SUCKING SOUND

Economists disagree about many things, but international trade is one thing about which virtually all economists are agreed. The arguments in favor of free trade are so compelling, and the arguments against free trade are so weak, that economists are virtually unanimous in their support of free trade.

Of course, there are some situations in which free trade is not appropriate. For example, national-security concerns may make it sensible to restrict trade in some commodities. There are good reasons to have restrictions on trade in nuclear warheads and intercontinental ballistic missiles.

It is also possible to argue against free trade when an industry is just getting started in a country. This is the *infant-industry argument*. According to the infant-industry argument, it may be beneficial to give trade protection to a domestic industry during the first few years of its existence. This will give the domestic industry the opportunity to get on its feet, and not be run out of business by foreign firms that are already well established. However, if the infant-industry argument makes any sense at all, it would require that the trade restrictions must be removed, soon after the domestic industry establishes itself.

Except in these few cases, however, the arguments against free trade are not strong at all. We will close this chapter by thinking about how the United States became such a prosperous country. Certainly, one reason is that we have an abundance of natural resources: good harbors, navigable rivers, a temperate climate, fertile soil, and a wealth of minerals below ground. Another reason is that Americans tend to place a lot of value on education and hard work. But one other reason is that the United States has been dedicated to free trade from the very beginning.

The war for independence from Great Britain, from 1775 to 1783, was fought by 13 loosely federated colonies. Immediately after the 13 colonies achieved their independence, they continued to have only loose connections. Under the Articles of Confederation, the authority of the central government was very limited, and the 13 States were free to levy tariffs. Tariffs could be applied to goods traveling from New York to Massachusetts, or from Maryland to Pennsylvania, or from North Carolina to Virginia, or from Georgia to South Carolina.

When the Constitutional Convention met at Philadelphia in 1787, the Founding Fathers recognized that this system was harming the economies of all 13 States. The Constitution prohibited the States from interfering with interstate commerce. The new nation abolished its internal tariffs. Eventually, the United States of America became the world's largest free-trade area. As much as anything else, this dedication to free trade explains the nation's prosperity.

Chapter Summary

1. During the last several decades, both exports and imports have increased dramatically. In the early 1960s, exports accounted for a little more than 4 percent of gross domestic product, and imports were of about the same size. By the late 1990s, both exports and imports accounted for more than 10 percent of gross domestic product. Thus, international trade has been an important engine for economic growth.

2. When exports are greater than imports, we say that a country has a trade surplus. When imports are greater than exports, we say that a country has a trade deficit. In recent years, the United States has run deficits. If a country sustains large trade deficits for a long period of time, it may run up a very large external debt, which can cause problems. However, modest trade deficits are not a cause for concern.

3. Even if a country's overall level of imports were the same as its overall level of exports, it would still probably have deficits with some of its trading partners, and surpluses with some others. There is no reason to desire to have bilateral trade balance with every country.

4. It is beneficial for countries to specialize in the activities in which they have comparative advantage, and then to engage in international trade. This is even true in the case in which one country has absolute advantage in all activities.

5. A tariff is a tax on imports. An import quota is an explicit restriction on the quantity of imports. A voluntary export restraint is a quantity restriction, similar to an import quota. The difference is that an import quota is organized and administered by the importing country, whereas a voluntary export restraint is organized and administered by the exporters.

6. Tariffs, quotas, and voluntary export restraints all lead to higher prices for consumers in the importing country. They all reduce the quantity of imports. They all reduce the competition faced by producers in the importing country, so that those producers will usually increase their profits. However, a tariff collects revenue for the government of the importing country, while an import quota gives an advantage to the holder of the import license, and a voluntary export restraint gives an advantage to the exporting companies.

Key Terms

Export

Import

Trade Deficit

Trade Surplus

Tariff

Import Quota

Voluntary Export Restraint

Infant-Industry Argument

Questions and Problems

QP5-1. The export supply curve for brupkas is given by $Q_s = 2P$. The import demand curve for brupkas is given by $Q_d = 100-2P$.

a. What is the equilibrium price of internationally traded brupkas?

b. What is the equilibrium quantity of internationally traded brupkas?

c. Now, the government of the importing country imposes a tariff of $10 per brupka. The old, net-of-tariff export supply curve, which is perceived by the exporters, stays the same as it was before: $Q_s = 2P$. It turns out that the new, gross-of-tariff export supply curve, which is perceived by the importers, is given by $Q_s = -20 + 2P$. What is the new equilibrium price of brupkas, gross of tariff (that is, including the tariff)?

d. What is the new equilibrium quantity of brupkas?

e. What is the new equilibrium price of brupkas, net of tariff (that is, not including the tariff)? You can find the answer to this question in one of two ways. You can take the quantity (from (d)) and substitute it into the net-of-tariff supply curve. Or, you can take the gross-of-tariff price (from (c)) and subtract from it the tariff of 10.

f. How much revenue is raised by the tariff?

QP5-2. Assume that the export-supply curve for brupkas (net of tariff) and the import-demand curve for brupkas are the same as in the previous question. However, this time there is no tariff. Instead, the government imposes a quota, such that only 40 brupkas can be imported into the country. Assume that the quota is enforced.

a. What price will be paid by buyers in the importing country? (Insert a quantity of 40 into the demand curve.)

b. What price will be received by sellers in the exporting country? (Insert a quantity of 40 into the supply curve.)

c. If the quota were set at 60 brupkas, what price would be paid by the buyers? What price would be received by the sellers? What quantity would be bought and sold?

d. If the quota were set at 20 brupkas, what price would be paid by the buyers? What price would be received by the sellers? What quantity would be bought and sold?

QP5-3. If a government decides that it must restrict imports from another country, is there any reason to prefer a tariff, or a quota, or a VER?

QP5-4. U.S. exports to Mexico are much higher than U.S. exports to any other low-income country. Why?

QP5-5. Evaluate the following statement: Exports are good, because exports create jobs in the domestic economy. Imports are bad, because imports create jobs somewhere else. Therefore, a trade surplus is better than a trade deficit. Therefore, the best outcome for the world as a whole is for every country to have a trade surplus.

Chapter 6

Elasticity of Demand and Supply

ECONOMICS AND YOU: IF YOU *REALLY* WANT TO GO TO A PARTICULAR COLLEGE, YOU MAY HAVE TO PAY MORE

Ryan Flynn has always dreamed of going to Pastoria College, which has an attractive campus and good business programs. By his senior year in high school, Ryan has decided that Pastoria College is his top choice, and he applies for admission on an "early-admission" basis.

Unfortunately, Ryan's decision to apply for early admission may cost him several thousand dollars. Pastoria's Admissions and Awards Committee knows that early-admission applicants are especially enthusiastic about Pastoria. Because of this, the Committee believes that early-admission applicants are very likely to attend, even if they receive less financial aid than other students. Therefore, the Committee has decided to offer less financial aid to early-admission applicants. If the College can get students like Ryan to attend, without giving them much financial aid, it will have more money left over for other purposes.

In recent years, more and more colleges have adopted this type of policy. In fact, it has been estimated that 60 percent of American colleges are adjusting their financial-aid offers, in order to offer more aid to those students who are most sensitive to price. In other words, if a student is likely to go somewhere else unless he or she gets a good deal, a college will offer more financial aid. But if a student is likely to attend, even if the price is higher, that student will get less financial aid. The college is saying, "Why should we offer more financial aid to applicants like Ryan, since they will probably come here anyway?"

In Chapter 3, you learned that demand curves slope downward to the right. In some cases, that's all that we need to know about demand curves. However, in cases such as this example of college financial-aid policies, it's important to know *how rapidly* the demand curve slopes downward. An economist would say that Ryan's demand curve for attending Pastoria is *unresponsive* to changes in price. Even if the price were to increase substantially, Ryan would still attend Pastoria. On the other hand, Stacey is less certain that she wants to attend Pastoria, but she might be convinced to come if she is offered a good financial-aid package. An economist would say that Stacey's demand curve for attending Pastoria is *responsive* to changes in price.

In this chapter, you will learn about how to measure the responsiveness of demand and supply. You will learn:

- how to calculate the *elasticity*, which is the economist's way of measuring the degree of responsiveness,

- how sellers (such as colleges, airlines, and others) can use information about the elasticity of demand to increase their revenues, and

- which factors have an effect on the elasticity of demand or supply.

PRICE ELASTICITY OF DEMAND

In Chapter 4, we saw that a drought in the apple-growing regions will cause the supply curve of apples to shift to the left. This will lead to an increase in the equilibrium price of apples, and a decrease in the equilibrium quantity of apples that are bought and sold.

In Figure 6.1, we show two examples of a leftward shift in the supply curve for apples.

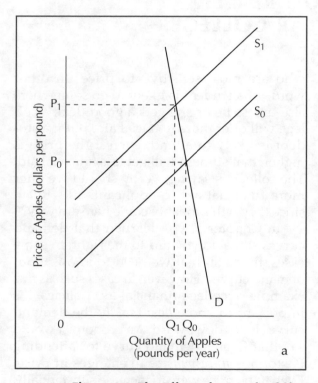
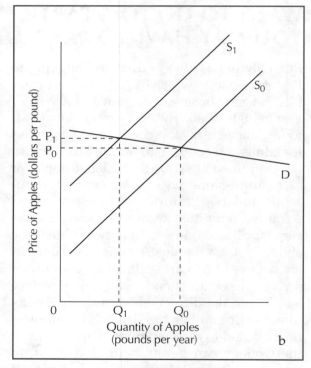

Figure 6.1 The Effect of a Supply Shift Depends on the Shape of the Demand Curve

Panel (a) and panel (b) both have the same original supply curve, S_0, and the same new supply curve, S_1. Both panels also have the same original equilibrium quantity of apples, Q_0, and the same original equilibrium price of apples, P_0. However, in the demand curve in panel (a), quantity demanded is very unresponsive to changes in price, while quantity demanded is very responsive to changes in price in panel (b). Because of the difference between the two demand curves, the supply shift has very different effects in the two panels. In panel (a), where quantity demanded is unresponsive, the supply shift leads to a relatively large increase in equilibrium price, and a relatively small decrease in equilibrium quantity. In panel (b), where quantity demanded is responsive, the supply shift leads to a relatively small increase in equilibrium price, and a relatively large decrease in equilibrium quantity.

The two panels of Figure 6.1 have the same original supply curve, S_0, and the same new supply curve, S_1. They both have the same original equilibrium price, P_0, and the same original equilibrium quantity, Q_0. The only difference between the two diagrams is in the shape of their demand curves.

In the demand curve shown in panel (a) of Figure 6.1, the quantity demanded is very unresponsive to changes in price. Even when the price increases by a large amount, there isn't much of a decrease in the quantity of apples demanded. Effectively, the buyers in panel (a) of Figure 6.1 are saying "We've gotta have our apples!" In this case, the supply-curve shift leads to a large increase in the equilibrium price, and a relatively small decrease in the equilibrium quantity. The buyers are willing to pay substantially more, and they end up doing just that.

On the other hand, the demand curve in panel (b) of Figure 6.1 is very responsive to changes in price. When the price increases, even by a small amount, there is a relatively large decrease in quantity demanded. The buyers in panel (b) are saying "If you raise the price on us, we'll spend our money on something else." In this case, the shift in the supply curve leads to a relatively small increase in the equilibrium price, along with a relatively large decrease in the equilibrium quantity. The buyers aren't willing to accept a very large price increase, and, indeed, they don't end up paying a lot more.

Slope Is Not a Good Measure of Responsiveness

By comparing the two panels of Figure 6.1, you can see that the responsiveness of quantity demanded to changes in price is crucial for understanding the outcomes in the market. In this chapter, one of our most important goals is to develop a precise method for measuring responsiveness.

At first, it might seem sensible to measure the responsiveness of demand by calculating the slope of the demand curve. Unfortunately, this causes problems. For example, gasoline is sold by the gallon in the United States, but it's sold by the liter in Canada. If we were to draw a Canadian demand curve for gasoline and an American demand curve for gasoline, the slopes would differ by about a factor of four (since there are almost four liters in a gallon), even if the responses of consumers were *exactly* the same in the two countries. Here is a related problem: How do we compare the demand for chewing gum (which is measured in packs) with the demand for apples (which is measured in pounds or bushels)?

The problem is that *slope depends on the units of measurement.* Instead of using slope, we would like to use a measure that is unit-free. Economists use a unit-free measure of responsiveness called elasticity. Elasticity doesn't depend on the units of measurement, because it compares *percentage* changes or *proportional* changes, instead of absolute changes.

The Definition of Elasticity

Most of this chapter is concerned with the elasticities of supply and demand, since these are so important for our study of economics. However, the elasticity concept can be applied in many situations, some of which don't sound like economic examples. In every case, **elasticity** *is defined as the percentage change in one variable, divided by the percentage change in another variable.* For example, medical researchers collected information on the cholesterol levels of a sample of people. Over a period of many years, the researchers observed whether the people had heart attacks. They concluded that a 10-percent increase in cholesterol is associated with a 20-percent increase in the chance of having a heart attack. The elasticity of heart attacks with respect to the cholesterol level is the percentage change in the chance of a heart attack, divided by the percentage change in cholesterol level. This is (20% / 10%) = 2. Since the elasticity is based on percentage changes, the units in which we measure cholesterol are irrelevant.

Here's another example of an elasticity: An economics professor took attendance at every class, so that he was able to calculate the effect of class attendance on exam scores. He found that a ten-percent increase in attendance was associated with a 15-percent increase in exam scores. The elasticity of exam scores with respect to class attendance is the percentage change in exam scores, divided by the percentage change in class attendance. This is (15% / 10%) = 1.5.

Now that you've seen that the elasticity concept can be used in all sorts of situations, it's time to look at elasticities of demand and supply.

We define the *price elasticity of demand* for jogging shorts as:

$$\text{elasticity} = \frac{\text{percentage change in quantity of jogging shorts demanded}}{\text{percentage change in price of jogging shorts}}.$$

This is also called the *own-price elasticity of demand*. The phrase *"own-price"* indicates that we are looking at the change in the quantity demanded for a good, caused by a change in its *own* price. (Later in this chapter, we'll look at the change in demand for one good, caused by a change in the price of a *different* good.)

In this chapter, we will sometimes use the phrase "price elasticity of demand", and we'll sometimes use the phrase "own-price elasticity of demand". Both phrases have the same meaning.

Another way to define the price elasticity of demand is to use proportional changes, instead of percentage changes:

$$\text{elasticity} = \frac{\dfrac{\Delta Q_d}{Q_d}}{\dfrac{\Delta P}{P}},$$

where ΔQ_d is the change in quantity demanded, Q_d is the reference level of quantity demanded, ΔP is the change in price, and P is the reference level of price. In this equation, $(\Delta Q_d / Q_d)$ is the proportional change in quantity demanded, and $(\Delta P / P)$ is the proportional change in price.

In summary, we have two ways of calculating the own-price elasticity of demand. We can divide the *percentage* change in quantity demanded by the *percentage* change in price, or we can divide the *proportional* change in quantity demanded by the *proportional* change in price. Either way, we will get the same answer, since a percentage is equal to a proportion multiplied by 100.

Let's say that the price of jogging shorts goes down from $13 per pair to $11 per pair. The change in price, ΔP, is ($13 – $11), or $2 per pair. As a result of the price change, the quantity demanded increases from 70,000 pairs of shorts per week to 90,000 pairs per week. The change in quantity demanded, ΔQ_d, is (90,000 – 70,000), or 20,000 pairs per week.

The elasticity formula has four parts: ΔQ_d, ΔP, Q, and P. We have now calculated ΔP and ΔQ_d. However, in order to complete the elasticity calculation, we need to decide what to use for the reference level of price, P, and the reference level of quantity demanded, Q. Do we use 70,000 pairs of jogging shorts for the reference level of quantity demanded, or do we use 90,000, or some number in between? And do we use $13 for the reference level of price, or $11, or something else? The elasticity that we calculate will change somewhat, depending on the values that we use for the reference level of price and the reference level of quantity demanded.

Calculating Elasticity

Economists make a standard assumption in calculating the elasticity. The standard assumption is to use the *midpoint* between the beginning quantity demanded and the ending quantity demanded as our reference level of quantity demanded. Similarly, we use the midpoint between the beginning price and the ending price as our reference level of price. The midpoint can be calculated by adding the two numbers together, and dividing by two. The midpoint between $11 and $13 is ($11 + $13) / 2 = $12. The midpoint between 70,000 and 90,000 is (70,000 + 90,000) / 2 = 80,000.

One advantage of using the midpoint is that it allows us to get the same answer for an increase or a decrease in price or quantity. If we were to use the starting point, we would get a different percentage change, depending on whether we move from $11 to $13 or from $13 to $11. By using the midpoint, we find the same percentage change, regardless of whether the price is going up or down.

Before we actually calculate the own-price elasticity of demand, we need to establish one more rule. Along any demand curve, the price and the quantity demanded will move in opposite directions; that is, if the change in price is greater than zero, the change in quantity demanded will be less than zero, and *vice versa*. However, in order to simplify the calculation of the price elasticity of demand, economists traditionally *drop the minus sign*. In other words, we use the absolute value. This means that the own-price elasticity of demand is never less than zero.

We now have three rules for calculating the price elasticity of demand:

- We use percentage changes, or proportional changes.

- We use the midpoint between the beginning quantity demanded and the ending quantity demanded as our reference level of the quantity demanded. We use the midpoint between the beginning price and the ending price as our reference level of price.

- We drop the minus sign, so that the elasticity is never a negative number.

With these three rules in mind, the next step is to calculate an elasticity.

Let's calculate the own-price elasticity of demand for the example described above, where the price of jogging shorts goes down from $13 per pair to $11 per pair. As a result of this price change, the quantity demanded goes up from 70,000 pairs per week to 90,000 pairs per week. Here is the elasticity calculation:

elasticity

$$= \frac{\dfrac{\Delta Q_d}{Q_d}}{\dfrac{\Delta P}{P}}$$

$$= \frac{\dfrac{(90,000 - 70,000)}{\text{midpoint between 70,000 and 90,000}}}{\dfrac{(\$13 - \$11)}{\text{midpoint between \$11 and \$13}}}$$

$$= \frac{\dfrac{20,000}{80,000}}{\dfrac{\$2}{\$12}}$$

$$= (2/8) / (2/12) = 12/8 = 1.50.$$

In this case, the price elasticity of demand for jogging shorts is 1.50.

Figure 6.2 contains a demand schedule for jogging shorts, as well as the corresponding demand curve. The demand schedule and demand curve include prices of $13 and $11, and quantities demanded of 70,000 and 90,000, which we used above, plus some other combinations of price and quantity demanded.

Next, let's calculate the elasticity of demand along a different part of the demand curve, where price falls from $11 to $9, and quantity demanded rises from 90,000 pairs to 110,000 pairs. The basic formula is the same, but the numbers are different.

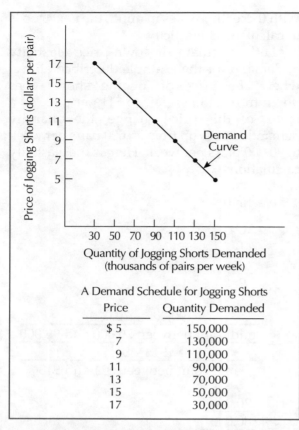

A Demand Schedule for Jogging Shorts

Price	Quantity Demanded
$ 5	150,000
7	130,000
9	110,000
11	90,000
13	70,000
15	50,000
17	30,000

Figure 6.2 A Demand Schedule for Jogging Shorts, and the Corresponding Demand Curve

elasticity

$$= \frac{\dfrac{\Delta Q_d}{Q_d}}{\dfrac{\Delta P}{P}}$$

$$= \frac{\dfrac{(110,000 - 90,000)}{\text{midpoint between 90,000 and 110,000}}}{\dfrac{(\$11 - \$9)}{\text{midpoint between \$9 and \$11}}}$$

$$= \frac{\dfrac{20,000}{100,000}}{\dfrac{\$2}{\$10}}$$

$= (2/10) \, / \, (2/10) = 1.$

In this case, the price elasticity of demand for jogging shorts is 1.0.

Price (P)	Quantity Demanded (Q_d)	Total Revenue (P)x(Q_d)	Price Elasticity of Demand
$ 5	150,000	$750,000	
			0.4286
$ 7	130,000	$910,000	
			0.6666
$ 9	110,000	$990,000	
			1.0
$11	90,000	$990,000	
			1.5
$13	70,000	$910,000	
			2.3333
$15	50,000	$750,000	
			4.0
$17	30,000	$510,000	

Table for Figure 6.2 Calculating Total Revenue and the Price Elasticity of Demand from a Demand Schedule for Jogging Shorts

These two examples show that the price elasticity of demand can take on different values. In fact, as we move along a straight-line demand curve, such as the one in Figure 6.2, there is a regular pattern to the changes in elasticity. *As we move downward and to the right along a straight-line demand curve, the price elasticity of demand becomes smaller. As we move upward and to the left, the elasticity increases.*

We've now seen the basics of how to calculate the elasticity. This is an important step, but it's only a beginning. The real purpose of this chapter is to learn how to *apply* the elasticity concept. We'll see several applications in this chapter, and many more later in the book. The own-price elasticity of demand is one of the most useful concepts in all of economics.

Reality Check: Interim Review Questions

IR6-1. There is an increase in the price of red-delicious apples, from $0.95 per pound to $1.05 per pound. As a result, there is a decrease in the quantity demanded, from 4200 million pounds per year to 3800 million pounds per year. What is the own-price elasticity of demand for red-delicious apples?

IR6-2. There is a 10-percent increase in the price of renting the most popular movies from the video store. The price elasticity of demand for videos is 0.5, and price is the *only* thing that has changed. What will happen to the quantity of videos that is demanded?

ELASTICITY AND TOTAL REVENUE

The *total revenue* that a business firm gets from selling a product is the amount of money that the firm receives from its sales. Business firms want to know what will happen to their total revenue if they raise prices, and what will happen if they cut prices. If you're a financial analyst for a firm, and you can figure out a way to increase total revenue, you will be very popular with your boss. In this section, you will learn how the relationship between price and total revenue depends on the own-price elasticity of demand.

Price, Quantity, and Total Revenue

The total revenue that is received by a business firm is equal to the price multiplied by the number of units sold:

Total Revenue = TR = (P)(Q).

Let's calculate total revenue for some of the points on the demand schedule that we used earlier. In our first example, the price of jogging shorts decreases from $13 per pair to $11 per pair. As a result, the quantity demanded increases from 70,000 pairs per week to 90,000 pairs per week. Before the change, total revenue is ($13/pair)(70,000 pairs) = $910,000. After the change, total revenue is ($11/pair)(90,000 pairs) = $990,000. Price went down, but total revenue went up! Even though each pair of shorts is sold for a lower price, the increase in quantity demanded is large enough that there is also an increase in total revenue!

Over the years, economists have calculated the own-price elasticity of demand for thousands of markets. They have found that it's useful to distinguish between demand curves that have a price elasticity greater than one, and those that have an elasticity equal to one, and those that have an elasticity less than one.

- When the own-price elasticity is greater than one, we say that demand is *elastic*. When demand is elastic, quantity demanded is relatively responsive to changes in price. The term "elastic" reminds us of things that respond a lot when a force is applied to them, such as a very stretchy fabric or a rubber band.

- When the elasticity equals one, demand is *unit-elastic*.

- Demand is *inelastic* when the elasticity is less than one.

We'll look at each of these cases in turn.

Elastic Demand. Let's return to the example that we considered above: The price of jogging shorts decreases from $13 per pair to $11 per pair. As a result, the quantity demanded increases from 70,000 pairs per week to 90,000 pairs. Thus, there are two offsetting influences on total revenue. Taken by itself, the decrease in price would *decrease* total revenue. However, the drop in price also leads to an increase in quantity demanded. Taken by itself, this increase in quantity demanded would *increase* total revenue. The reason that total revenue goes up in this example is that the effect of quantity demanded is *relatively* stronger than the effect of price.

Here's another way to say the same thing: When the price went down, total revenue went up, because the proportional change in quantity demanded was greater than the proportional change in price. But remember that the own-price elasticity of demand is equal to the proportional change in quantity demanded, divided by the proportional change in price! Thus, the price elasticity of demand tells us what we need to know, in order to assess what will happen to total revenue.

When the proportional change in quantity demanded is greater than the proportional change in price, the elasticity is greater than one, so that demand is elastic. In this case, a decrease in price will lead to an increase in total revenue, and an increase in price will lead to a decrease in total revenue.

A special case of elastic demand is the case where the demand curve is completely horizontal. In this case, we say that demand is *per-*

fectly elastic. This may seem like a strange case, because it's hard to think of any examples where the *market* demand curve would be perfectly elastic. However, in some cases, the demand for the product of an *individual firm* may be perfectly elastic. For example, the demand for the Anderson Farm's apples may be perfectly elastic, even though the market demand for apples isn't perfectly elastic. We will discuss this possibility in Chapter 9.

Real Economics for Real People 6.1 on p. 118, deals with the airline industry and its response to elastic demand.

We can use graphs to increase our understanding of the relationship between elasticity and total revenue. Total revenue is equal to price multiplied by quantity. Therefore, total revenue is shown graphically by the area of a rectangle. The quantity demanded is the base of the rectangle, and the price is the height of the rectangle.

In Panel (a) of Figure 6.3, we show an elastic demand curve. When the price is P_0, total revenue is the rectangle $0P_0AQ_0$. When the price is P_1, total revenue is the rectangle $0P_1BQ_1$. You can see that the second rectangle is larger than the first. When demand is elastic, quantity demanded changes relatively more than price, and a price decrease means that total revenue will rise.

Unit-Elastic Demand. Now, let's consider another example from Figure 6.2: The price of jogging shorts drops from $11 to $9, and the quantity demanded rises from 90,000 pairs to 110,000 pairs. We have already calculated that the elasticity for this change is 1.0. This means that the proportional change in quantity demanded is exactly the same as the proportional change in price. What happens to total revenue? At the price of $11 per pair, total revenue is ($11)(90,000) = $990,000. At the new price of $9 per pair, total revenue is ($9)(110,000) = $990,000. Total revenue is unchanged!

When the proportional change in quantity demanded is equal to the proportional change in

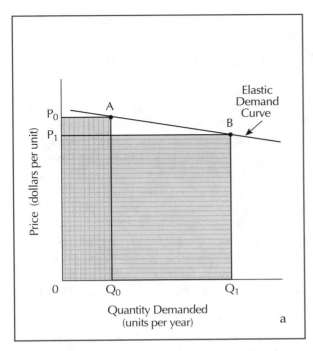

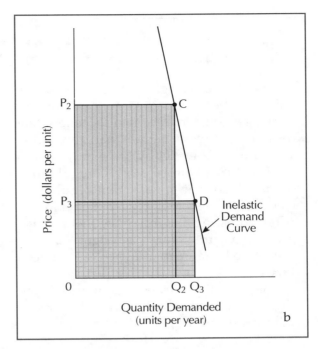

Figure 6.3 The Effect of a Price Change on Total Revenue Depends on the Elasticity of Demand

In panel (a), the original price is P_0, the original quantity demanded is Q_0, and the original total revenue is represented by the area of the rectangle, $0P_0AQ_0$. When price falls to P_1, there is a relatively large increase in quantity demanded, to Q_1. The new total revenue is the area of the rectangle, $0P_1BQ_1$. Demand is elastic, because the increase in quantity demanded is large relative to the decrease in price. Therefore, the new total revenue, $0P_1BQ_1$, is larger than the old total revenue, $0P_0AQ_0$. In panel (b), the original price is P_2, the original quantity demanded is Q_2, and the original total revenue is represented by the area of the rectangle, $0P_2CQ_2$. When price falls to P_3, there is a relatively small increase in quantity demanded, to Q_3. The new total revenue is the area of the rectangle, $0P_3DQ_3$. Demand is inelastic, because the increase in quantity demanded is small relative to the decrease in price. Therefore, the new total revenue, $0P_3DQ_3$, is smaller than the old total revenue, $0P_2CQ_2$.

price, the own-price elasticity of demand is 1.0, so that demand is unit-elastic. In this case, a change in price will not have any effect on total revenue.

When demand is unit elastic, it doesn't matter whether the price goes up or down—total revenue will remain the same.

Inelastic Demand. Finally, let's consider one more example from Figure 6.2: When there is a decrease in the price of jogging shorts from $9 to $7, the quantity demanded increases from 110,000 pairs of shorts to 130,000 pairs. The elasticity is two-thirds, or 0.6666. (See if you can do the calculation.) The proportional change in quantity demanded is *smaller* than

the proportional change in price. At the price of $9 per pair, total revenue is ($9)(110,000) = $990,000. At the new price of $7, total revenue is ($7)(130,000) = $910,000. In this case, total revenue goes *down* as a result of the decrease in price.

When the proportional change in quantity demanded is less than the proportional change in price, the own-price elasticity of demand is less than one, and demand is inelastic. In this case, an increase in price will lead to an increase in total revenue, and a decrease in price will lead to a decrease in total revenue.

In Panel (b) of Figure 6.3, we show an *inelastic* demand curve. When the price is P_2, total revenue is the rectangle $0P_2CQ_2$. When the price is P_3, total revenue is the rectangle $0P_3DQ_3$. The second rectangle is smaller than the first. When demand is inelastic, the change in quantity demanded is relatively less than the change in price, and a price decrease means that total revenue will fall.

Here is an example of the importance of inelastic demand: Some retailers use "everyday low prices", while others have advertised specials on a few items, with higher prices on

other goods. A marketing research team compared stores using the two pricing strategies. They found that the stores featuring everyday low prices did get more sales. (We would expect this, because of the Law of Demand.) However, their profits were significantly lower. This suggests that the increases in quantity were relatively small, when compared with the decreases in price. In other words, demand was inelastic for many of the goods that sold for lower prices. These calculations

For many years, there has been a heated debate about how to reduce the use of marijuana, cocaine, and other drugs. For a long time, the dominant approach has involved what is called "supply interdiction". Under this approach, law-enforcement officers attempt to reduce the *supply* of drugs by capturing shipments and arresting dealers. An alternative approach might be called "demand control". Under this approach, we would increase our use of counseling and drug-treatment programs, in order to get drug users to reduce their *demand.*

Even though supply-interdiction efforts have not been completely successful, they have reduced supply somewhat. As a result, what has happened to total revenue from sales of marijuana? If the supply curve shifts to the left, the price will increase. The effect on total revenue will depend on the price elasticity of demand. Assuming that the demand for marijuana is inelastic, the increase in price will be relatively larger than the decrease in quantity demanded. This means that *successful supply interdiction will lead to increased total revenue for marijuana sellers.* Some individual sellers will lose their revenue if they get caught. However, if demand is inelastic, the sellers who don't

get caught will receive a greatly increased amount of revenue, so that the overall amount of revenue will increase.

To many observers, it seems unfortunate that the reduced supply of marijuana will lead to higher revenues for marijuana sellers. This may be one reason why there has been more emphasis on demand control in recent years. If demand control is successful in pushing the demand curve for drugs to the left, the equilibrium price will fall, and the equilibrium quantity will also decrease. Therefore, total revenue *must* decrease, regardless of the elasticities.

Some estimates suggest that the demand for cocaine may be significantly more elastic than the demand for marijuana. If the demand for cocaine is unit-elastic, then a leftward shift in the supply curve will not change total revenues for cocaine sellers. Thus, the policy of supply interdiction may be more sensible for cocaine than for marijuana. However, it is still true that a policy of demand control would definitely reduce revenue for sellers. The effect on total revenue of a leftward shift in the supply curve will depend on the elasticity of demand, but a leftward shift in the demand curve will *always* reduce total revenue.

mean that these stores may want to re-think their pricing strategy.

A special case of inelastic demand is the case where quantity demanded does not change at all when price changes. The demand curve would be graphed as a vertical line. In this case, we say that demand is *perfectly inelastic*. The elasticity is zero. The demand for addictive drugs might be perfectly inelastic, at least over some ranges of price increases. Even if the demands for cocaine and heroin

aren't *perfectly* inelastic, they are almost certainly inelastic. In *Real Economics for Real People 6.2*, we look at the markets for cocaine and marijuana.

We have now looked at elastic demand, unit-elastic demand, and inelastic demand. In each case, there is a unique relationship between the price elasticity of demand and the effect on total revenue of a change in price. These important relationships are summarized in Figure 6.4.

Price Elasticity	Name	Effect of Price Increase on Total Revenue	Effect of Price Decrease on Total Revenue	Graph
0	Perfectly Inelastic	P↑TR↑	P↓TR↓	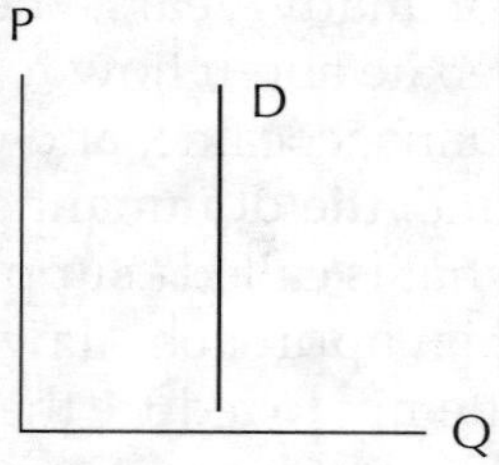
0<e<1	Inelastic	P↑TR↑	P↓TR↓	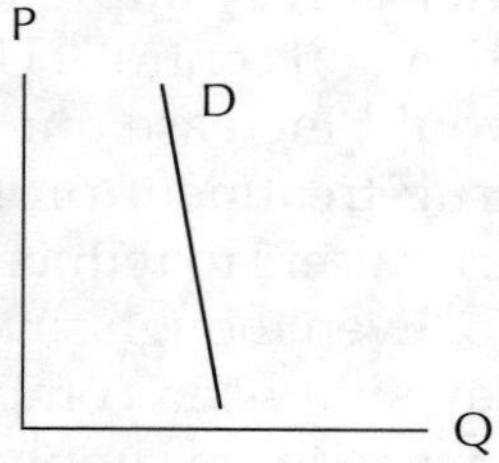
1	Unit Elastic	TR constant	TR constant	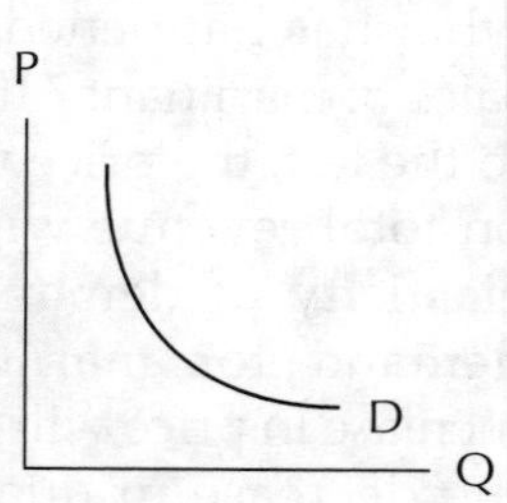
1<e<∞	Elastic	P↑TR↓	P↓TR↑	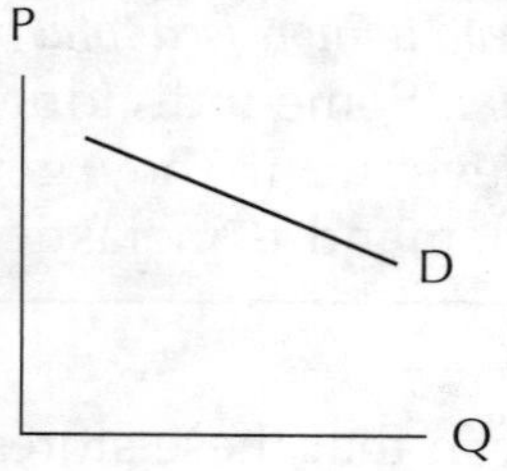
∞	Perfectly Elastic	Price does not change	Price does not change	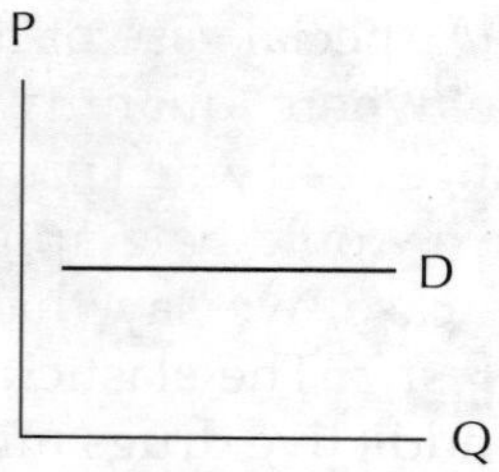

Figure 6.4 Summary of Relationships Between Price Elasticity and Total Revenue

IR6-3. Assume that the own-price elasticity of demand for red-delicious apples is 1.0. Is this elastic, unit elastic, or inelastic? Given that the elasticity is 1.0, if there is an increase in the price of red-delicious apples, what will happen to total revenue? How will your answer be different if the elasticity is greater than one?

IR6-4. The price of a videocassette recorder falls by 10 percent. As a result of the decrease in price, there is a 7-percent increase in the quantity of videocassette recorders demanded. What is the price elasticity of demand for videocassette recorders? Is demand inelastic, unit elastic, or elastic? Will total revenue increase or decrease?

FACTORS THAT INFLUENCE THE PRICE ELASTICITY OF DEMAND

Economists have used statistical methods to estimate the price elasticity of demand for many goods. Table 6.1 contains some of these estimates. You can see that different goods can have very different elasticities. In Table 6.1, the estimated own-price elasticity of demand for milk is 0.14. This is highly inelastic: If the price of milk were to increase by 10 percent, consumers would reduce their quantity demanded by only $(10)(0.14) = 1.4$ percent. On the other hand, a number of goods are approximately unit-elastic. For example, Table 6.1 indicates that the price elasticity of demand for furniture is estimated to be 1.01. Other goods are elastic. These include automobiles, for which the elasticity is estimated to be 1.35.

We can identify a number of forces that cause demand to be elastic for some goods, but inelastic for others. These include

- the availability of substitutes,

- the importance of the good in the consumer's budget, and

- the amount of time during which consumers can adjust to the price change.

We'll discuss each of these in this section.

Table 6.1 Estimates of the Own-Price Elasticity of Demand for Selected Goods

Good	Elasticity	
Fresh tomatoes	4.60	Elastic Demand
Fresh green peas	2.80	
Restaurant meals	1.63	
Automobiles	1.35	
Cable television	1.20	
Furniture	1.01	
Movies	0.87	Inelastic Demand
Shoes	0.70	
Water	0.52	
Toilet articles	0.44	
Medical insurance	0.31	
Eggs	0.23	
Milk	0.14	

Sources: C.B. Blankart, "Towards an Economic Theory of Advice and its Application to the Deregulation Issue", *Kyklos*, 1981; G.E. Brandow, "Interrelations Among Demands for Farm Products and Implications for Control of Market Supply", Bulletin 680, Pennsylvania State University Agricultural Experiment Station, 1961; H.S. Foster, Jr., and B.R. Beattie, "Urban Residential Demand for Water in the United States", *Land Economics*, 1979; H.S. Houthakker and L.D. Taylor, *Consumer Demand in the United States: Analyses and Projections*, Harvard University Press, 1970.

The Availability of Substitutes

Why would the demand for milk be so inelastic? One reason is that parents believe that there is no good substitute for milk for their children. Since milk provides so many important nutrients, many buyers feel that they really must have it. In other words, families find it difficult to substitute away from milk when its price increases. If it's hard to find a good substitute for milk, then the quantity of milk that families buy will not change very much, even when the price changes. If a family is currently buying two gallons of milk per week, they won't suddenly drop to one gallon when the price goes up. *Generally speaking, demand will be less elastic when it is hard to substitute away from the good whose price goes up, and more elastic when it is easy to substitute.*

It's important to understand that we have been referring to the *market* elasticity of demand for milk. This is different from the elasticity of demand for any *one brand* of milk. Consumers may find it difficult to substitute away from milk, in general, and yet they may find it very easy to substitute away from one particular brand of milk. If Golden Dairies raises the price of its milk, it may find that it faces a very elastic demand curve for *its* milk. People will substitute away from Golden Dairies milk, and buy Happy Cow milk instead.

While Table 6.1 indicates that the demand for milk is inelastic, it also indicates that the demand for restaurant meals is fairly elastic. If restaurants raise their prices, it's easy for most people to substitute away from restaurant meals, by eating more at home.

The Importance of the Good in the Consumer's Budget

If the price of toothpaste were to rise by 10 percent, many consumers would hardly notice the difference. However, if the price of a new car were to increase by 10 percent, it would mean an increase of $1000 or $2000 or even more. Consumers would definitely notice this. If consumers pay close attention to the price of a good, their demand is likely to be relatively more elastic. *Other things equal, consumers will have more elastic demand for items that make up a larger portion of their budgets.*

Given the importance of items such as cars and houses, it isn't surprising that people shop around a great deal when they are about to buy these items. In fact, consumers try to get help in making decisions about these big purchases. This is why there are jobs for realtors and automobile salespersons.

Time for the Consumer to Adjust

In 1973 and 1979, and again in 1999–2000, American consumers faced large increases in the prices of gasoline, heating oil, and other petroleum products. What happens to the quantity demanded, if the price of gasoline goes up by a large amount?

In the very short run, not much will happen. It may take days or weeks for workers to make carpooling arrangements. It will take even more time for people to trade in their old gas guzzlers for new, fuel-efficient cars. It will take months to acquire more buses, and years to build more mass-transit facilities.

The same is true for the demand for heating oil and natural gas. In the short run, it may be possible to turn down the thermostat a few degrees. It will take a much longer time for people to insulate their homes better, or to install newer, more efficient furnaces.

These examples suggest that *demand will be more elastic when consumers have a longer time to adjust to the change in price.* One study found that the short-run elasticity of demand for sports equipment is 0.88, while the long-run elasticity is 2.39. In other words, if there were a 10-percent decrease in sports-equipment prices, the quantity demanded would only increase by (10)(0.88) = 8.8 percent, at first. However, if consumers were given enough time to adjust, their quantity demanded would eventually increase by (10)(2.39) = 23.9 percent.

In the case of gasoline and oil, one estimate is that the short-run elasticity is 0.14, while the long-run elasticity is 0.48. This is important for policy. In Chapter 4, we discussed the gasoline price ceilings that were in effect during the 1970s. At that time, some people argued that the price controls would not lead to serious shortages, because they believed that demand was extremely inelastic. In fact, however, fairly serious shortages occurred almost immediately, with long lines of cars waiting to fill up with gasoline. In addition, we should expect the shortages to become even more severe over time, because demand is more elastic when we consider a longer period of time. Fortunately, the price ceilings were eventually removed, and this eliminated the shortages.

Reality Check:
Interim Review Questions

IR6-5. In the eyes of many consumers of soft drinks, it's easy to substitute between Sprite, 7-Up, and Slice. If the price of Sprite were to increase substantially, while the prices of 7-Up and Slice stay the same, do you expect that the demand for Sprite would be elastic or inelastic?

IR6-6. Assume that the supply curve for eggs has exactly the same shape as the supply curve for red-delicious apples. However, the demand for red-delicious apples is more elastic than the demand for eggs. In addition, let's assume that the government institutes a price floor in both the egg market and the apple market. If the price floors are both 10 percent above the equilibrium price, which market will have a relatively larger surplus?

OTHER ELASTICITIES OF DEMAND

We have started with the own-price elasticity of demand, because it's the most important elasticity. However, the elasticity concept can also be used to describe other important relationships. In this section, we will look at the elasticity of demand with respect to income. We'll also look at the elasticity of demand for one good, with respect to the price of another good, which is called the cross-price elasticity of demand.

It's important to understand one difference between the various elasticities of demand. The own-price elasticity of demand is concerned with *movements along an existing demand curve*, whereas the income elasticity of demand and the cross-price elasticity of demand are concerned with *shifts to different demand curves*.

Income Elasticity of Demand

The income elasticity of demand tells us how consumers change their demand for a given good, when their incomes change.

The *income elasticity of demand*, e_I, is defined as:

$$e_I = \frac{\frac{\Delta Q}{Q}}{\frac{\Delta I}{I}} = \frac{\%\Delta Q}{\%\Delta I},$$

where Q is the quantity of some good, and I is income. The basic structure of the formula is identical to that of the price elasticity of demand. The only difference is that we have income in the denominator, instead of the price of the good.

In Chapter 3, we saw that most goods are *normal goods*, which means that the demand curve shifts to the right when incomes increase. In other words, if the change in income is greater than zero, the resulting change in demand will also be greater than zero for a normal good. This means that *the income elasticity of demand is greater than zero for a normal good.*

Certain poor-quality goods are *inferior goods*. If income goes up, the demand curve will shift to the left for an inferior good. Thus, when the change in income is greater than zero, the resulting change in demand will be less than zero for an inferior good. *The income elasticity of demand is less than zero for an inferior good.*

It's important to avoid one source of confusion about income elasticities of demand. When we calculate the own-price elasticity of demand, we drop the minus sign. This is an acceptable thing to do, because demand curves never slope upward to the right. Therefore, we can use the absolute value without causing a misunderstanding. However, when we deal with the income elasticity of demand, the minus signs have an important meaning. The income elasticity of demand is greater than zero for a normal good, but less than zero for an inferior good. If we were to drop the minus sign, we wouldn't be able to tell the difference between the income elasticities for normal goods and inferior goods. Therefore, we *don't* drop the minus sign when calculating the income elasticity of demand.

In Table 6.2, we show some estimates of the income elasticity of demand for selected goods. These estimates suggest that owner-occupied housing, rental housing, and butter are all normal goods, while margarine is an inferior good.

Table 6.2 Estimates of the Income Elasticity of Demand for Selected Goods

Good	Income Elasticity	
Owner-occupied housing	1.49	
Books	1.44	
Restaurant meals	1.40	
Clothing	1.02	Normal
Gasoline and oil	0.48	Goods
Rental housing	0.43	
Butter	0.42	
Residential electricity	0.20	
Margarine	−0.20	Inferior
Flour	−0.36	Goods

Sources: H.S. Houthakker and L.D. Taylor, *Consumer Demand in the United States: Analyses and Projections,* Harvard University Press, 1970; L. Taylor and R. Halvorsen, "Energy Substitution in U.S. Manufacturing", *The Review of Economics and Statistics,* 1977; H. Wold and L. Jureen, *Demand Analysis,* Wiley, 1953.

Cross-Price Elasticity of Demand

The own-price elasticity of demand tells us how the buyers of a good respond when the price of *that good* changes. The **cross-price elasticity of demand** tells us how the buyers of one good respond when the price of *some other good* changes. Here is the formula for the cross-price elasticity of demand for good X with respect to changes in the price of good Y, which we call e_{xy}:

$$e_{XY} = \frac{\dfrac{\Delta Q_X}{Q_X}}{\dfrac{\Delta P_Y}{P_Y}} = \frac{\%\Delta Q_X}{\%\Delta P_Y},$$

Once again, the basic structure of the elasticity formula is the same as we have seen before.

In Chapter 3, we discussed *substitutes*. Two goods are substitutes if an increase in the price of one good leads to an increase in demand for the other good. For example, cola drinks are substitutes for coffee, romaine lettuce is a substitute for green-leaf lettuce, and vacations in Europe are substitutes for vacations in the U.S. For any pair of substitutes, if there is an increase in the price of one good, there will also be an increase in the demand for the other good. In this case, the numerator and the denominator of the cross-price elasticity have the same sign. *The cross-price elasticity of demand is greater than zero for substitutes.*

Table 6.3 includes information on the cross-price elasticities between some pairs of goods. The table indicates that butter and margarine are substitutes. Other substitute pairs include natural gas and fuel oil, and beef and pork. We usually expect pairs of goods to be substitutes when consumers would like to use one or the other of the goods at any one time, but not both.

Two goods are independent in demand if a change in the price of one good has no effect on the demand for the other good. If two goods are independent in demand, the cross-price elasticity of demand is zero.

Two goods are *complements* if an increase in the price of one good leads to a decrease in demand for the other good. Automobiles and gasoline are complements, as are bread and butter. *The cross-price elasticity of demand is less than zero for complements.* Generally, we would expect to see complementary relationships when consumers would tend to use the two goods together.

If we were to drop the minus sign, we wouldn't be able to tell the difference between the cross-price elasticities for complements and substitutes. Therefore, we *don't* drop the minus sign when calculating the cross-price elasticity of demand.

Reality Check: Interim Review Questions

IR6-7. If incomes increase, the demand curve for sports cars will shift to the right. Does

Table 6.3 Estimates of the Cross-Price Elasticity of Demand for Selected Pairs of Goods

Good with Quantity Change	Good with Price Change	Cross-Price Elasticity	
Florida interior oranges	Florida Indian River oranges	1.56	Substitutes
Margarine	Butter	0.81	Substitutes
Natural gas	Fuel oil	0.44	Substitutes
Beef	Pork	0.28	Substitutes
California oranges	Florida interior oranges	0.14	Substitutes
Fruits	Sugar	−0.28	Complements
Cheese	Butter	−0.61	Complements

Sources: M.B. Godwin, W.F. Chapman, Jr., and W.T. Hanley, *Competition Between Florida and California Valencia Oranges in the Fruit Market,* U.S. Department of Agriculture, Economic Research Service, Bulletin 704, 1965; R. Stone, The Measurement of Consumers' Expenditure and Behavior in the United Kingdom, 1920–1938, Cambridge University Press, 1954; L. Taylor and R. Halvorsen, "Energy Substitution in U.S. Manufacturing", *The Review of Economics and Statistics,* November, 1977; H. Wold and L. Jureen, *Demand Analysis,* Wiley, 1953.

this mean that sports cars are normal or inferior? Is the income elasticity of demand greater than zero or less than zero?

IR6-8. If there is an increase in the price of vacations in France, the demand curve for vacations in the United States will shift to the right. Does this mean that vacations in France and vacations in the United States are complements or substitutes? Is the cross-price elasticity of demand for vacations in the U.S. with respect to the price of vacations in France greater than zero or less than zero?

ELASTICITY OF SUPPLY

We have concentrated on demand elasticities so far. However, it's also important to measure the responsiveness of supply.

The *price elasticity of supply, e_s, is defined as:*

$$e_s = \frac{\dfrac{\Delta Q_s}{Q_s}}{\dfrac{\Delta P}{P}} = \frac{\%\Delta Q_s}{\%\Delta P},$$

where Q_s is the quantity supplied. Suppose that there's an increase in the price of breath mints, from 45 cents per roll to 55 cents per roll. The change in price is $(55 - 45) = 10$ cents. The reference level of price is the midpoint between 45 cents and 55 cents, or 50 cents. This means that the proportional price increase is $(10/50) = 0.2$. As a result of this price change, the quantity supplied increases from 16,000 to 24,000 rolls per day. This is a change of $(24,000 - 16,000) = 8000$ rolls per day. The reference level of quantity supplied is the midpoint between 16,000 rolls per day and 24,000 rolls per day, which is 20,000 rolls per day. The proportional increase in quantity supplied is $(8000/20,000) = 0.4$. In order to calculate the elasticity of supply, we divide the proportional increase in quantity supplied by the proportional increase in price. This gives us $0.4/0.2 = 2$.

The Law of Supply tells us that quantity supplied will move in the same direction as price. *Since supply curves slope upward, the price elasticity of supply is greater than zero.*

Real Economics for Real People 6.3 discusses the hotel industry, in which the elasticity of supply is very small over a short period of time.

Supply Elasticity and Adjustment Time

What would happen if fish prices in Boston were to increase during the late afternoon? By late in the day, New England's fishing boats would either have returned to port, or they would be committed to spending the night on the water. It wouldn't be possible to bring any additional fresh fish to market that day. In order for the Law of Supply to hold, producers need some time to respond to a change in price.

If the firms in the fishing industry believe that the price will stay higher, they might be able to increase supply over a period of a few days or weeks. They might keep their boats at sea for longer periods. They might speed up the work on boats that need repairs, so as to get more boats into the water. Thus, if firms are given a certain amount of time, the elasticity of supply will be greater than zero.

But if we give the fishing firms even more time to adjust, they may be able to increase their catch a great deal. If the firms believe that the higher price will continue for a long time, they can build new boats. The conclusion is that the elasticity of supply will be higher when firms have a longer time to adjust. In the very long run, the elasticity of supply may be very large.

This relationship between adjustment time and supply elasticity occurs in virtually every industry. For example, if oil prices go up in the afternoon, oil companies won't be able to increase the quantity supplied by evening. However, the oil producers will be able to increase supply within a few weeks, by running their existing wells harder. It will take many years to increase production substantially by drilling new wells.

Supply Elasticity and the Specialization of Resources

Many industries have some special requirements. They require specialized workers, specialized machinery, and specialized equipment. For example, the grape-growing industry requires particular types of soil and climate. The land on which the best grapes can

Real Economics for Real People 6.3:
Mardi Gras and Hotel Prices in New Orleans

New Orleans is a popular tourist attraction in any season, but two special events are especially popular. These are the Sugar Bowl football game, held around New Year's Day, and the Mardi Gras Festival in February or March. At these special times of year, there is a strong rightward shift in the demand curve for hotel and motel rooms in the New Orleans area. We would expect this to increase both the equilibrium price and the equilibrium quantity.

How much will price increase as a result of the demand shift, and how much will quantity increase? The answer depends on the elasticity of supply. For any given period of three days, the elasticity of supply of rooms in New Orleans is probably very small. Some families might rent rooms in their homes during times of high demand, but the major hotels and motels won't add new rooms, just for the Sugar Bowl and Mardi Gras.

If the supply elasticity is small, then the change in quantity won't be very large. Instead, the largest effect will be on price. This is exactly what happens in the hotel business. During the two special times of year in 1998, the Riverside Hilton hotel in New Orleans charged $265 per night for a standard room for two persons. However, if you wanted to have the same room during October, you could have had it for $160. That's a big difference in price.

New Orleans isn't the only city that experiences surges in demand at certain times. Every four years, the Summer Olympic Games lead to a large rightward shift in the demand for hotel and motel rooms in the host city. Not surprisingly, prices increased dramatically in Barcelona in 1992 and Atlanta in 1996. Similarly, the Cedar Point Amusement Park in Sandusky, Ohio, has a big effect on the prices of hotels and motels in the surrounding area. Motel prices are much higher in the summer, when Cedar Point is open, than in the winter, when the park is closed.

The elasticity of supply will determine what happens when the demand curve shifts. If the supply elasticity is large, demand shifts will result in relatively large quantity changes, compared with rather small changes in price. However, if the supply elasticity is small, demand shifts will result in relatively large price changes and relatively small quantity changes.

---

be grown is very limited in supply. Thus, the elasticity of supply of the highest-quality grapes is likely to be small. The problem of specialized resources is even more severe in the entertainment and sports industries. There is only one Mark McGwire, only one Madonna, only one Mick Jagger. These artists can only give so many performances per year, regardless of how high the ticket prices go. The elasticity of supply of superstars is small. Generally speaking, the elasticity of supply will be smaller when the resources that are used in a particular industry are relatively more specialized and scarce.

In summary, supply is more elastic:

- when sellers have a longer period of time over which to respond to changes in price, and

- when the resources employed in the production process are not especially scarce or specialized.

IR6-9. The price of bicycle helmets increases by 20 percent. As a result, there is a 10-percent increase in the quantity of bicycle hel-mets supplied. What is the elasticity of supply for bicycle helmets?

IR6-10. Explain why the elasticity of supply of red-delicious apples is likely to be much larger over a period of ten years than over a period of ten weeks.

ECONOMICS AND YOU:
IF YOU WANT TO PAY LESS, DON'T LET THEM KNOW THAT YOU REALLY WANT TO BUY

We began this chapter by noting that some colleges give less-generous packages of financial aid to early-admission applicants. These colleges believe that the early-admission applicants are less likely to respond to a higher price by going elsewhere. In other words, the colleges believe that these applicants have inelastic demand. The colleges know that they can increase their revenues if they charge higher prices to those with inelastic demand. As a result, many colleges try to identify the groups of students who are more inelastic. These students are offered less-generous financial aid, while the ones with elastic demand are given more attractive aid packages.

This suggests that, if you want a good deal, you don't want to appear too eager. By applying for early admission, students give the impression that their demand is inelastic. A better strategy might be to apply for regular admission, so as to make it appear that you are thinking seriously about many different colleges.

There are many other examples in which buyers may be able to get a better deal if they appear to have elastic demand. For instance, a man was planning a trip to New York City, and he called the reservation office of a hotel in midtown Manhattan. When he asked for the rate for a standard double room, he was told that it would be $152 plus tax. If he had asked the reservation agent to book the room right then, he would have revealed that he was willing to pay the full price of $152 plus tax. Instead, however, he asked whether any discounts were available. This indicated to the hotel that his demand was more elastic. Rather than lose his business, the hotel offered him a room for $105 plus tax. By indicating that he is sensitive to price, the traveler got the price reduced by nearly one-third. Of course, discounts aren't always available, but it doesn't hurt to ask.

Elasticity is especially important for the pricing strategies of business firms, which we will study in Chapters 9 through 11. Elasticity is also crucial for understanding the effects of taxes, as we shall see in Chapter 16. Elasticity is one of the most important concepts in economics, and we will continue to use it throughout this book.

Chapter Summary

1. Elasticity is the economist's measure of the responsiveness of demand or supply. Elasticity has the advantage of being unit-free, so that it does not depend on the units in which quantity demanded, quantity supplied, and other variables are measured.

2. The price elasticity of demand, or own-price elasticity of demand, is defined as the percentage change in quantity demanded, divided by the percentage change in price. As with the other elasticities introduced in this chapter, we calculate the price elasticity of demand at the *midpoint* of the changes in price and quantity demanded. We also take the *absolute value* of the own-price elasticity, so that it will not be negative. All else equal, the price elasticity of demand will be larger: (a) if more substitutes are available, or (b) if the good makes up a larger fraction of the consumer's budget, or (c) if consumers have a longer period of time over which to adjust to the price change.

3. If the percentage change in quantity demanded is greater than the percentage change in price, then the price elasticity of demand is greater than one, and demand is said to be elastic. If demand is elastic, a price increase will lead to a decrease in total revenue, and a price decrease will lead to an increase in total revenue.

4. If the percentage change in quantity demanded is the same as the percentage change in price, then the price elasticity of demand is exactly 1.0, and demand is said to be unit-elastic. In this case, price changes will not have any effect on total revenue.

5. If the percentage change in quantity demanded is less than the percentage change in price, then the price elasticity of demand is less than one, and demand is said to be inelastic. In this case, a price increase will lead to higher total revenue, and a price decrease will lead to lower total revenue.

6. The income elasticity of demand is defined as the percentage change in quantity, divided by the percentage change in income. The income elasticity will be greater than zero for normal goods, and less than zero for inferior goods.

7. The cross-price elasticity of demand is defined as the percentage change in the quantity of one good, divided by the percentage change in the price of some other good. The cross-price elasticity will be greater than zero for substitutes, and less than zero for complements. The cross-price elasticity will be zero if the two goods are independent in demand.

8. The price elasticity of supply is defined as the percentage change in quantity supplied, divided by the percentage change in price. The Law of Supply tells us that the supply elasticity will be greater than zero. The supply elasticity will be larger when producers have a longer period of time over which to adjust to the price change. Also, if the resources necessary to produce a good are very scarce or highly specialized, the supply elasticity of that good may be fairly small.

Key Terms

Elasticity

Own-Price Elasticity of Demand

Total Revenue

Elastic Demand

Perfectly Elastic Demand

Unit-Elastic Demand

Inelastic Demand

Perfectly Inelastic Demand

Income Elasticity of Demand

Cross-Price Elasticity of Demand

Price Elasticity of Supply

Key Figure

The key figure for this chapter is Figure 6.4, which summarizes the different types of price elasticity of demand, and the relationship between price elasticity and the change in total revenue.

Questions and Problems

QP6-1. The price of lettuce goes up from 70 cents per head to 90 cents per head. As a result, the quantity of lettuce demanded goes down by 25 percent.

a. What is the price elasticity of demand for lettuce?
b. Is the demand for lettuce inelastic, unit-elastic, or elastic?
c. What will happen to total revenue for lettuce sellers?

QP6-2. Both coffee and tea contain caffeine. Many people like caffeine, but really don't care what drink gives them their caffeine. For people like this, would the cross-price elasticity of demand for coffee with respect to the price of tea be positive or negative?

QP6-3. Incomes increase. As a result, the demand for turnips goes down. On the basis of this information, what can we say about the income elasticity of demand for turnips? Are turnips a normal good or an inferior good?

QP6-4. A price ceiling is instituted on leather belts. The price ceiling is below the equilibrium price, so that it leads to shortages. Let us assume that the supply elasticity is 0.5. Will the shortages be more severe if the own-price elasticity of demand is 0.5 or 0.8?

QP6-5. The price of a type of hand-held programmable calculator goes down from $55 to $45. As a result, the quantity demanded rises from 1000 units per week to 1500 units per week.

a. What is the own-price elasticity of demand for calculators?
b. Is the demand for calculators unit-elastic, elastic, or inelastic?
c. What is the change in total revenue for calculator sellers, as a result of this change?

QP6-6. Ace Computer Equipment Company raises the price on its printer cables by 20 percent. All of the other companies in the area keep their prices unchanged. As a result, the quantity demanded for Ace printer cables goes down by 80 percent.

a. What is the own-price elasticity of demand for cables from Ace?
b. Is the demand for Ace's cables elastic, unit-elastic, or inelastic?
c. If *all* companies were to raise their prices by 20 percent, do you think that the *market* elasticity of demand would be different from the elasticity facing Ace? If so, how would the market elasticity be different from the elasticity for an individual firm?

QP6-7. Real income in Winesburg, Ohio, goes up from $80 million to $120 million. As a result, there is a 10-percent increase in the quantity of bread demanded.

a. What is the income elasticity of demand for bread?
b. Is bread a normal good or an inferior good in Winesburg, Ohio?

QP6-8. The cross-price elasticity of demand for automobiles with respect to the price of gasoline is –0.2. The cross-price elasticity of demand for chicken with respect to the price of fish is 0.7. The cross-price elasticity of demand for oranges with respect to the price of notebook paper is zero.

a. Which of these pairs of goods shows a substitute relationship?
b. Which of these pairs shows a complement relationship?
c. Which of these pairs is independent in demand?

QP6-9. A price floor is instituted for sunflower seeds. The price floor is above the equilibrium price, so that a surplus occurs. Assume that the price elasticity of demand for sunflower seeds is 1.0. Will the surpluses be greater if the price elasticity of supply is 0.6 or 1.3?

QP6-10. The own-price elasticity of demand for raisins is 0.8. An industry analyst suggests that the price will go up by 50 percent next year.

a. Is the demand for raisins elastic, unit-elastic, or inelastic?
b. What will be the percentage change in the quantity of raisins demanded?
c. Will total revenues for raisin sellers go up or down as a result of the price change and the resulting change in quantity demanded?

QP6-11. The price elasticity of demand for computer spreadsheet programs is 1.5. We observe that the quantity demanded increases by 30 percent. Assume that the change in quantity demanded was caused by a change in price.

a. What must have happened to the price of the spreadsheets?
b. Is the demand for spreadsheet programs elastic, unit-elastic, or inelastic?
c. What will have happened to total revenue for spreadsheet sellers as a result of the decrease in price and the associated increase in quantity demanded?

QP6-12. List and briefly discuss the factors that have an influence on the own-price elasticity of demand.

QP6-13. For each of the following sets of assumptions, state what will happen to total revenue.

a. Demand is inelastic; price rises.
b. Demand is elastic; price rises.
c. Demand is unit-elastic; price rises.
d. Demand is elastic; price falls.
e. Demand is unit-elastic; price falls.
f. Demand is inelastic; price falls.

Chapter 7

Consumer Choice

ECONOMICS AND YOU:
WHY ARE BASEBALL CARDS WORTH MORE THAN WATER?

Very few people can survive more than a few days without a drink of water. And yet, in spite of the extreme importance of water, most Americans pay very little for water. Residential water is often sold for much less than a penny per gallon.

In 1990, a collector paid $451,000 for a baseball card from 1910 featuring Honus Wagner, the Pittsburgh Pirates' shortstop. Another collector paid about $80,000 for a copy of the comic book in which Batman made his first appearance. In 1997, an art collector paid $48.4 *million* for a painting by Pablo Picasso.

Water is essential for life, while even the most die-hard baseball fan would probably not suggest that baseball cards are necessary for survival. Why would people pay so little for water and so much for baseball cards, comic books, and paintings?

The answer has to do with the demand behavior of consumers. We have already talked about demand curves, in Chapters 3 and 4. Now is the time to study the subject in more depth. The purpose of this chapter is to develop our ideas about consumer behavior more fully. In this chapter, you will learn:

- how to measure consumer satisfaction,

- how the consumer makes choices about how much to spend on various items, and

- how to measure the extent of the consumer's gains or losses that occur as a result of changes in price.

By the end of this chapter, you will have a clearer understanding of why consumers behave as they do. Among other things, you will learn why baseball cards sell for more than water.

THE RELATIONSHIP BETWEEN MARGINAL QUANTITIES AND TOTAL QUANTITIES

We still have one other thing to take care of, before we develop our ideas about consumer behavior. In order to understand the economic theory of the consumer (as well as many other ideas presented later in this book), it is important to understand the relationships between *marginal* quantities, *total* quantities, and *average* quantities. It's easiest to illustrate these relationships with examples. In this section, we will look at an example that involves marginal and total quantities. Then, in Chapter 8, we'll consider average quantities.

In this section, we'll use an example that involves the distances traveled by a truck driver. However, this does *not* mean that the relationships between marginal quantities and total quantities can *only* be applied to the distances traveled by truck drivers. In fact, the concepts of marginal and total can be applied in one situation after another, and they always have the same relationship to each other.

Joe Andrews is a driver for a moving and storage company. His current assignment is to drive the Leone family's household goods from Portland, Maine, to their new home in Texarkana, Texas. Here is the route that Joe takes:

- On the first day, Joe drives through New Hampshire and Massachusetts, and ends up in Syracuse, New York. On this day, he drives *400 miles*. (He might have gone farther, but he had to wait for the final items to be loaded onto the truck.)

- On day 2, Joe drives past Erie, Pennsylvania, and Cleveland, Ohio, and ends up near Cincinnati, Ohio. He covers *600 miles* on this day.

- On the third day, Joe drives past Louisville, Kentucky, and Nashville, Tennessee, and ends up near Memphis, Tennessee. On this day, he travels *500 miles*.

- On day 4, Joe drives across Arkansas. Early in the afternoon, he delivers his cargo in Texarkana. On this day, he drives *300 miles*.

The distances traveled on each day are listed in the second column of Table 7.1.

Marginal Quantities

In the next several chapters, you will learn about concepts like "marginal utility", "marginal cost", and "marginal revenue". The details differ, but they are all defined in fairly similar ways. Whenever we use the word *marginal*, we refer to the value associated with *one additional unit*. In our example of the distances traveled by Joe's truck, the marginal distance is the distance traveled on the most recent day.

Table 7.1 Marginal and Total Distances Traveled in a Journey from Portland, Maine, to Texarkana, Texas

Day	Marginal Distance Traveled (Additional Distance This Day)	Total Distance Traveled (Total Distance for All Days So Far)
1	400 miles	400 miles
2	600 miles	1000 miles (= 400 + 600)
3	500 miles	1500 miles (= 400 + 600 + 500)
4	300 miles	1800 miles (= 400 + 600 + 500 + 300)

When we consider the first day of Joe's journey, the "marginal distance traveled" is 400 miles. When we consider the second day, the marginal distance traveled is 600 miles. And so on.

Total Quantities

If we start at the beginning of Joe's trip, and add together the marginal distances traveled on each day, we can calculate the *total* distance traveled. If we consider only the first day, then the total distance traveled is 400 miles. If we consider the first two days, the total distance traveled is equal to the marginal distance traveled on the first day (400 miles) plus the marginal distance traveled on the second day (600 miles), for a total of 1000 miles. Then, if we consider the first three days, the total distance becomes 400 miles + 600 miles + 500 miles = 1500 miles. Thus, *we get the total distance by adding the marginal distances.* Finally, if we consider all four days of the journey, the total distance is equal to the sum of the marginal distances traveled on each of the four days, which is 1800 miles. The total distances, as of the end of each day on the trip, are shown in the third column of Table 7.1.

In the chapters to come, you will learn how to use concepts like "total utility", "total cost", and "total revenue". Again, the details differ, but the definitions really have a lot in common. We always find a *total* value by adding all of the relevant *marginal* values.

Notice the connection between our definition of total distance and our definition of marginal distance: *Marginal* distance is the additional distance that is traveled in one additional day, and *total* distance is calculated by adding all of the marginal distances together. Thus, *marginal distance is the* change *in total distance when we travel for one additional day.*

In summary, *marginal* is associated with one additional unit, regardless of whether we are talking about marginal distance traveled,

or marginal utility, or marginal cost, or marginal revenue. *Total* is calculated by adding up the marginals. Thus, we calculate total distance traveled by adding the marginal distances, and we calculate total utility by adding the marginal utilities, and so on.

Graphs of Marginal and Total Quantities

So far, we have defined marginal and total, and we've given a numerical example. It's also useful to represent these ideas in a graph. In later chapters, we will have many graphs of marginal and total quantities. Figure 7.1 illustrates these concepts, using the numbers from our example of Joe's trip from Maine to Texas.

In Figure 7.1, when we consider only the first two days of the journey, the total distance traveled is 1000 miles. When we then include a third day, the total distance increases to 1500 miles. In other words, when we move from considering the first two days to considering the first three days, total distance increases by 500 miles. This is because Joe drove 500 miles on the third day of his trip.

We can calculate the slope of the total distance graph in Figure 7.1. Remember that the slope of a line is the change in the variable on the vertical axis, divided by the change in the variable on the horizontal axis. In this case, the slope of the total-distance graph is equal to the change in the total distance traveled, divided by the change in the number of days. The slope of the total distance graph will change, depending on which day we are considering. If we calculate the slope of the total-distance graph for the third day, we get (500 additional miles / one additional day) = 500 additional miles per day. If we calculate the slope of the total-distance graph for the fourth day, we get (300 additional miles / one additional day) = 300 additional miles per day.

Now, take a look at the graph of *marginal* distances in Figure 7.1. When we consider the

Figure 7.1 Graph of Marginal and Total Distances Traveled on a Journey from Maine to Texas

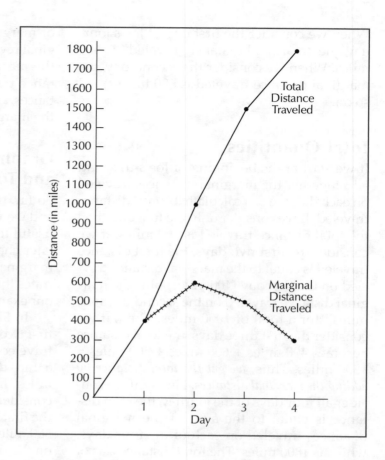

The marginal distance traveled on the first day is 400 miles. Therefore, the total distance traveled by the end of the first day is 400 miles. The marginal distance on the second day is 600 miles, so that the total distance by the end of the second day is (400 + 600) = 1000 miles. The marginal and total distances are connected in a similar manner for the third and fourth days. You can always find the total distance traveled, by adding up the marginal distances. Graphically, the marginal distance traveled is the slope of the total-distance curve.

third day of the trip, the marginal distance traveled is 500 miles. But we just showed that, when we consider the third day, the change in total distance is also 500 miles. *Graphically, the marginal distance is the slope of the total distance curve.* This is not a coincidence. This kind of relationship occurs for all sorts of marginal and total quantities. In later chapters, for example, we will see that the slope of a total-revenue curve is marginal revenue, and the slope of a total-cost curve is marginal cost. *The marginal value of a variable is the slope of the graph of the total value of that variable.*

Reality Check: Interim Review Questions

IR7-1. The Miami Dolphins football team has the ball. They make a marginal gain of six yards on their first play, followed by marginal gains of four yards on the second play and 11 yards on the third play. What is the total gain from the first two plays? What is the total gain from the first three plays?

IR7-2. A financial analyst draws a "total-revenue curve" for a corporation. What would we call the slope of the total-revenue curve?

UNDERSTANDING CONSUMER BEHAVIOR

The main purpose of this chapter is to learn how consumers make decisions regarding how much to buy. In this section, we introduce some economic ideas that can help us to understand consumer behavior. As part of this effort, we will use the marginal and total concepts that were just introduced.

The Rational Consumer

Economists do *not* believe that consumer decisions are just accidents. Instead, economists believe that consumers behave with purpose. The economic theory of consumer behavior starts from the idea that *consumers are rational, which means that they do the best they can with what they have.* However, we won't have a complete understanding of consumer behavior until we have an idea of the *exact way* in which consumers are rational. To do that, we have to be precise about the benefits that consumers get when they consume goods and services.

In the 19th century, economists developed a concept called *utility*, to describe the psychological satisfaction that consumers get from consuming goods and services. Sometimes, economists also use other words, such as "happiness" or "satisfaction", to describe the consumer's benefit from consuming. However, utility is the word that is used most commonly, and we will use it here.

In the early days, it was believed that utility could be measured precisely. Economists began to say that one unit of psychological satisfaction is one "util". So, for example, we might say that Alex gets 3.4 utils from consuming a hamburger, and Stephanie gets 6.9 utils from watching the movie *Titanic* on video.

Unfortunately, there's a problem with this approach, because it is extremely difficult to measure psychological satisfaction so precisely. Therefore, we sometimes use another

approach. Sometimes, we simply measure utility in dollars. Under this approach, it doesn't matter how much happiness Courtney gets from buying a wristwatch. The only thing that matters is the *amount of money that she is willing to pay* for the wristwatch.

Thus, there are two approaches to the theory of consumer behavior. The difference between the two approaches has to do with the way in which utility is measured.

- Under one approach, utility is measured in "utils", which are units of psychological satisfaction.

- Under the other approach, utility is measured by the number of dollars that the consumer is willing to pay.

In this chapter, we'll show how either of these approaches can be used to understand consumer demand. We begin with the case in which utility is measured in dollars, because this is somewhat easier for most students.

Marginal Utility and Total Utility, Measured in Dollars

Jason O'Donnell has a summer job with a roofing company. It's one of the hottest, sweatiest jobs around. At the end of one very steamy day, Jason sees some neighborhood children selling plastic cups of lemonade. Jason now has a decision to make: Should he buy any lemonade? If so, how many cups should he buy?

In part, Jason's decision will depend on how much pleasure he thinks he will get from drinking the lemonade. We define Jason's *marginal utility* of lemonade consumption as the maximum amount of money that he would be willing to pay, to receive one additional cup of lemonade.

Jason decides that he would be willing to pay as much as $1.25 for his first cup of lemonade. Thus, his marginal utility from the first cup is $1.25. A second cup would taste good, too, but it wouldn't quite match the first one. He decides that he would be willing to pay up to an additional $1.00 for a second cup. According to our definition, this means that his marginal utility for the second cup is $1.00.

Jason decides that he would be willing to pay an additional $0.75 for a third cup, so that the marginal utility of a third cup is $0.75. We have put these marginal utilities in Table 7.2, along with some others.

Note that the first line of Table 7.2 is for the case in which Jason doesn't drink any lemonade. It's possible to define *total* utility in this situation. The total utility is zero, because Jason would not be willing to pay anything, if he were to get nothing in return. However, for the case in which no lemonade is consumed, we have not put a number in the column for *marginal* utility. Since Jason's marginal utility is the amount that he would be willing to pay for one *additional* cup of lemonade, it isn't possible to define marginal utility until the first cup is consumed.

You should also notice that this example only has *positive* marginal utilities. That is, all of the numbers in Table 7.2 are greater than zero. However, you can imagine that marginal utility could eventually be negative. If Jason had already drunk 10 cups of lemonade in the space of a few minutes, one more cup of lemonade might actually make him worse off. His marginal utility from the 11th cup of lemonade would be less than zero.

If Jason is willing to pay as much as $1.25 for the first cup of lemonade, plus as much as another $1.00 for the second cup, it follows that the maximum total amount that he is willing to pay for two cups would be $1.25 + $1.00 = $2.25. If he's willing to pay as much as another $0.75 for a third cup, then his total willingness to pay for all three cups is $1.25 + $1.00 + $0.75 = $3.00. We define Jason's *total utility* from a given number of cups of lemonade as the maximum total amount that he is willing to pay to receive them all. *Total utility is the sum of the marginal utilities.* The total utilities are also shown in Table 7.2. This is just another example of the relationship between marginal quantities and total quantities, which we developed earlier in this chapter with our example of a trip from Maine to Texas.

The Law of Diminishing Marginal Utility

In Figure 7.2, we graph Jason's marginal utility and total utility from consuming lemonade. In other words, Figure 7.2 is a graph of the same information that was contained in Table 7.2. The total-utility curve is increasing, but at a decreasing rate. This is because marginal utility is the slope of the total-utility curve, and marginal utility is decreasing. In this example, Jason does become better off each time he drinks an additional cup of lemonade (up to the fifth cup, at least). But he becomes better off by less and less, with each additional cup. This is not just because of something unusual about lemonade. In fact, this relationship occurs so often that economists refer to the *Law of Diminishing Marginal Utility*: *For virtually every consumer good, the amount of additional utility provided by consuming one additional unit of the good will eventually go down, as the consumer increases his or her level of consumption.* The first hot dog at a picnic is really great, but the second is only OK. For most people, the marginal utility of the fifth hot dog would be small, or even negative.

Table 7.2 Jason's Marginal Utility and Total Utility from Additional Cups of Lemonade

Cup	Marginal Utility	Total Utility
0	—	$0.00
1	$1.25	1.25
2	1.00	2.25
3	0.75	3.00
4	0.50	3.50
5	0.25	3.75

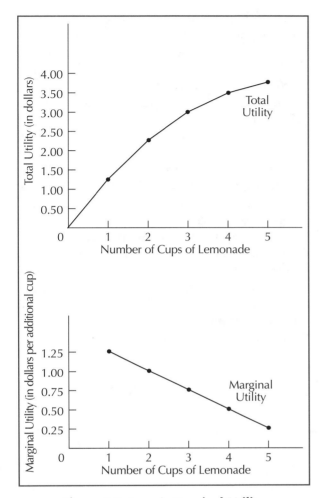

**Figure 7.2 Jason's Marginal Utility
and Total Utility from Cups of Lemonade**

We are measuring utility in dollars. Jason is willing to pay as much as $1.25 for the first cup of lemonade, so that his marginal utility is $1.25 for the first cup. His marginal utility declines to $1.00 for the second cup, $0.75 for the third cup, $0.50 for the fourth cup, and $0.25 for the fifth cup. Thus, Jason obeys the Law of Diminishing Marginal Utility. His total utility is calculated by adding up the marginal utilities. Thus, Jason's total utility from the first two cups of lemonade is $(1.25 + 1.00) = $2.25. His total utility from the first four cups is $(1.25 + 1.00 + 0.75 + 0.50) = $3.50. Marginal utility is the slope of the total-utility curve. Since marginal utility is decreasing, the slope of the total-utility curve is decreasing. In other words, when marginal utility is positive but declining, total utility will increase at a decreasing rate.

In this example, Jason's marginal utility decreases by $0.25, every time he drinks one additional cup of lemonade. This means that the marginal-utility curve in Figure 7.2 is a straight line. However, it's important to understand that marginal-utility curves do not *have* to be straight lines. They can curve in a variety of ways, and still obey the Law of Diminishing Marginal Utility. The important thing is that the marginal-utility curve should eventually slope downward as we move to the right.

The Consumer's Equilibrium: Marginal Utility Meets Price

So far, we have described the *benefits* that Jason gets from drinking lemonade, but we have said nothing about the *costs*. However, if Jason is to make an intelligent decision, he has to consider *both* the benefits and the costs. If the children operating the lemonade stand were to charge $1000 for a cup, then Jason would be foolish to buy one. In fact, if the price is set at *any* level above $1.25 per cup, Jason will decide not to buy any lemonade from the children, because he is not willing to pay any more than $1.25 for the first cup. If the children were to charge $2.00 per cup, Jason would not buy from them.

What if the price of a cup of lemonade were $0.50 (that is, 50 cents)? Jason's first cup gives him utility of $1.25, and this means that it will make sense for him to buy at least one cup, if it only costs 50 cents. Any time you can pay $0.50 to get $1.25 worth of satisfaction, you should do it. In fact, Jason should buy a second cup and a third cup, as well. The second cup provides $1.00 of utility, and the third cup provides $0.75 of utility, but each of them costs only $0.50. Finally, Jason should buy a fourth cup, for which the marginal utility of $0.50 is exactly equal to the price. However, if he were to buy a fifth cup, he would have to pay 50 cents more, but the fifth cup would only generate 25 cents worth of satisfaction.

Therefore, after Jason buys his fourth cup of lemonade, he shouldn't buy any more.

We can now state the ***consumer decision rule***, for the case in which marginal utility is measured in dollars: *Consumers should continue to buy products as long as marginal utility is equal to or greater than price. For the last unit purchased, marginal utility will be equal to price.* When the consumer buys the quantity at which marginal utility equals price, we say that ***consumer equilibrium*** has been reached. When the consumer is in equilibrium, he or she is making the best possible decision. Therefore, when the consumer is in equilibrium, there is no reason to change behavior by consuming more or less.

The consumer is in equilibrium when he or she consumes the quantity at which the marginal utility from consuming the last unit of a good is equal to the price of buying that good.

The consumer decision rule is the first of many similar rules that we will develop in this book. Again and again, we will see that people should engage in economic activities until the value of what they get from one extra unit of the activity is equal to the value of what they have to give up. In other words, people should engage in economic activities until *marginal benefit equals marginal cost*. In the case of the consumer's decision rule, the marginal benefit is called "marginal utility". The marginal cost of consuming a good is the price of the good.

The Graph of the Consumer's Decision. We graph Jason's decision in Figure 7.3. The price is graphed as a horizontal line. This is because Jason pays the same price (50 cents per cup) for every cup that he buys. In fact, most consumers face constant prices for most of the goods they buy. In other words, *consumers usually take prices as given*. This is because, in most markets, each individual consumer only accounts for a small fraction of the demand. When you go to the supermarket to buy a loaf of bread, you are only one of thousands of buyers. If the individual consumer is small relative to the market, then he or she won't have

Figure 7.3 The Consumer's Equilibrium

Jason's marginal utility is the maximum amount that he would be *willing* to pay for an additional cup of lemonade. The price is the amount that he is actually *required* to pay. If his marginal utility is equal to or greater than the price, he should buy. If his marginal utility is less than the price, he should not buy. When the price is $0.50, Jason's marginal utility is greater than price for the first three cups of lemonade, and his marginal utility is equal to price for the fourth cup of lemonade. Thus, when the price is $0.50, Jason's equilibrium decision is to buy four cups of lemonade.

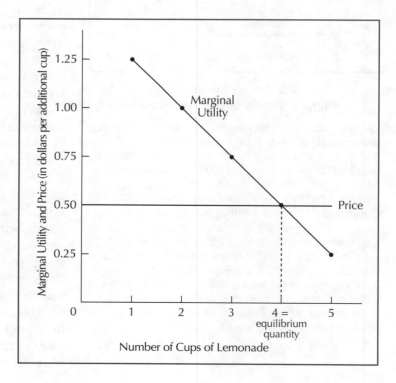

much bargaining power. Therefore, the individual will just have to take the going market price as given. The consumer faces the same price for the first unit, and the second, and the third, and the hundredth. The graph of this kind of price relationship is drawn as a horizontal line.

We have said that the consumer equilibrium occurs at the quantity at which marginal utility is equal to price. Graphically, Jason's consumer equilibrium is found at the place where the marginal-utility curve crosses the price line. In Figure 7.3, with a price of 50 cents per cup, the equilibrium quantity of lemonade is four cups.

The Individual's Demand Curve

We have illustrated Jason's decision rule by looking at the case where a cup of lemonade costs 50 cents. What would happen if the price of a cup were to increase to $1.00? When facing a different price, Jason would still want to obey the consumer decision rule, which means that he would still want to consume the quantity at which marginal utility is equal to price. But just because he follows the same *rule* in every case, it does not follow that he would choose the same *quantity* in every case. If the price were to increase to $1.00 per cup, Jason would respond by buying only two cups. This is because, when the price is $1.00 per cup, marginal utility equals price for the *second* cup. If the price of a cup of lemonade were to rise to $1.25, Jason would only buy one cup, because marginal utility would equal price for the *first* cup.

From the examples in the previous paragraph, we see that Jason's quantity demanded will decrease when the price increases. This is the Law of Demand. By changing the price and observing the changes in Jason's quantity demanded, we can derive his *individual demand curve*. The demand curve is shown in Figure 7.4. *The individual demand curve is the same as the marginal utility curve!*

In Chapter 3, we saw that market demand curves can be derived by adding the individ-

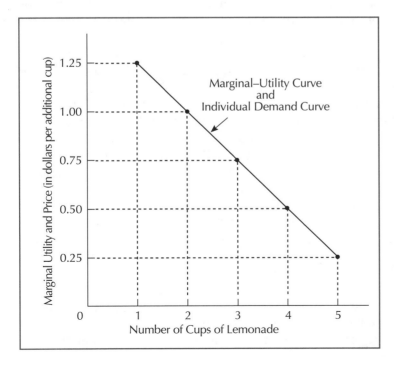

Figure 7.4 The Marginal-Utility Curve and the Individual Demand Curve

Jason's marginal utility from the first cup of lemonade is $1.25. Therefore, if the price were $1.25, he would choose to buy one cup. His marginal utility from the second cup is $1.00, so that he would choose to buy two cups if the price were $1.00. His marginal utility from the third cup is $0.75, so that, if the price were $0.75, he would choose to buy three cups. If we follow this same reasoning, we see that Jason will increase his quantity demanded to four cups, if the price is $0.50, and his quantity demanded will be five cups, if the price is $0.25. Thus, every point on the marginal-utility curve represents the quantity that would be demanded at a particular price. In other words, the marginal-utility curve is the individual's demand curve.

ual demand curves. If Jason is one of 20 people who are interested in buying lemonade in this neighborhood, we would add all of their individual demand curves together to get the market demand curve.

In Chapters 3 and 4, we looked at shifts in demand curves. In *Real Economics for Real People 7.1*, we take another look at demand-curve shifts, using the concept of marginal utility.

Consumer Surplus

Our example of Jason the lemonade drinker has an important implication. Let's say that the price of lemonade is 50 cents per cup. Jason is *willing* to pay $1.25 for the first cup, but he only *has* to pay 50 cents. He's then *willing* to pay $1.00 for the second cup, but, once again, he only *has* to pay 50 cents. He gets a bargain! This bargain is called consumer surplus. *Consumer surplus is the number of dollars by which total willingness to pay exceeds the total amount actually paid.* If we express utility in dollars, we can also say that consumer surplus is the difference between total utility and the total amount paid by the consumer.

Jason's consumer surplus is represented by the shaded area in Figure 7.5. His consumer surplus is ($1.25 − $0.50) = $0.75 for the first cup of lemonade, plus ($1.00 − $0.50) = $0.50 for the second cup, plus ($0.75 − $0.50) = $0.25 for third cup. For the fourth cup, Jason is willing to pay exactly 50 cents, and he must pay exactly 50 cents. Thus, the fourth cup doesn't generate any additional consumer surplus. Jason's total consumer surplus is $0.75 + $0.50 + $0.25 + $0.00 = $1.50. *Graphically, consumer surplus is the area between the demand curve and the horizontal line that represents the price.*

Consumer Surplus and the Consumer Decision Rule. We can use the concept of consumer surplus to gain a better understanding of the consumer decision rule. Remember that the

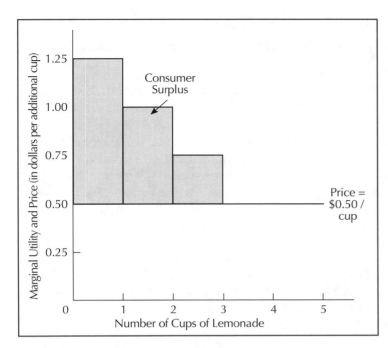

Figure 7.5 Jason's Consumer Surplus when the Price of Lemonade is $0.50 per Cup

Jason's marginal utility from the first cup of lemonade is $1.25. However, if the price is only $0.50, then $0.50 is all that he has to pay. Therefore, his consumer surplus from the first cup of lemonade is $(1.25–0.50) = $0.75. His marginal utility from the second cup of lemonade is $1.00. Using the same kind of reasoning, we can calculate his consumer surplus from the second cup of lemonade, which is $(1.00–0.50) = $0.50. Similarly, his consumer surplus from the third cup of lemonade is $(0.75–0.50) = $0.25. Jason actually consumes a fourth cup of lemonade, but he doesn't get any additional consumer surplus from the fourth cup, because marginal utility is exactly equal to price for the fourth cup. If we add together the consumer surpluses from the first three cups, we find that Jason's total consumer surplus is $(0.75 + 0.50 + 0.25) = $1.50.

consumer decision rule says that consumers should continue to buy products as long as marginal utility is equal to or greater than price. In Jason's case, the consumer decision rule dictates that he should buy four cups of lemonade when the price is 50 cents per cup. This gives him $1.50 of consumer surplus.

What if Jason were *not* to follow the consumer decision rule? For example, what if he were to buy only one cup of lemonade? The answer can be found in Figure 7.5. If Jason were to buy only one cup, his consumer surplus would be only $0.75. If he were to buy two cups of lemonade, his consumer surplus would be $0.75 from the first cup, plus $0.50 from the second cup, for a total consumer surplus of $1.25. In each of these cases, Jason's consumer surplus is less than the consumer surplus that he would have from following the consumer decision rule.

On the other hand, what if Jason had bought five cups of lemonade? The fifth cup generates marginal utility of only $0.25, but it

costs $0.50. Therefore, the additional consumer surplus from the fifth cup is –$0.25. If Jason were to buy a fifth cup of lemonade, his total consumer surplus would actually *decrease* by 25 cents. If Jason were to follow the consumer decision rule by buying four cups of lemonade, his consumer surplus would be $1.50. However, if he were to violate the consumer decision rule by buying five cups, his consumer surplus would fall to $1.25.

Jason maximizes his consumer surplus by following the consumer decision rule! There is no way for him to get more consumer surplus than he gets by following the consumer decision rule. In fact, this gives us another way to think about the consumer decision rule: If you want to maximize your consumer surplus, the way to do it is to keep buying as long as marginal utility is equal to or greater than price.

In *Real Economics for Real People 7.2*, we show how consumer surplus can be used to measure the true cost of a government policy that leads to higher prices.

Real Economics for Real People 7.2:
The Consumer's Losses from "Voluntary" Export Restrictions

In the 1970s and early 1980s, American automobile manufacturers lost a great deal of market share to their Japanese competitors. As we saw in Chapter 5, the American firms responded by putting pressure on Congress, asking for restrictions on Japanese exports. The United States government threatened to put tariffs or quotas on Japanese exports, unless the Japanese restricted those exports themselves. As a result, the Japanese began a policy of "voluntary export restrictions", or VERs.

Figure 7.6 shows what happened as a result of the VERs. The supply curve of Japanese cars was S, and the demand curve was D. Therefore, the equilibrium price was P*, the equilibrium quantity was Q*, and consumer surplus was the area ABC. However, the export restriction set Q_{VER} as the maximum number of Japanese cars that could be sent to the United States. Because of this, the Japanese firms were able to charge a higher price. The new price was P_{VER}, instead of P*. American consumers were forced to move upward and to the left, along their demand curve for Japanese cars. As a result of the VERs, consumer surplus fell to ADE. Consumer surplus decreased for two reasons: (1) fewer units were bought, and (2) for those items that were still bought, the price was higher than it had been before. The lost consumer surplus was the area EDBC.

Figure 7.6 only looks at the market for Japanese autos, but economists also believe that the VERs had spillover effects onto other markets: With higher prices for Japanese cars sold in America, the European and American manufacturers could charge higher prices, as well. This means that buyers of European and American cars also lost some of their consumer surplus.

Economists have used the concept of consumer surplus to get some idea of the losses from trade restrictions. Basically, the idea is to try to estimate the size of the area EDBC in Figure 7.6. Some estimates are in the vicinity of $10 billion per year. This could translate into a cost of about $250,000 per year, for every American job "saved". The auto industry is not the only one in which international trade has been restricted. The U.S. government also restricts trade in a wide variety of other industries, including steel, textiles, and shoes. In each of these industries, the losses to consumers are much greater than the gains for American workers.

Trade restrictions are only one of several government policies that raise prices. For example, in Chapter 4, we looked at price supports for milk and sugar. The costs of these policies can also be measured by calculating the lost consumer surplus.

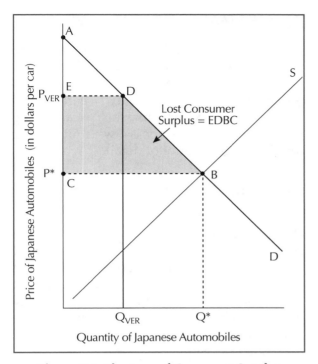

Figure 7.6 The Loss of Consumer Surplus as a Result of a Trade Restriction

The supply curve of Japanese automobiles is S, and the demand curve is D. As a result, the equilibrium quantity is Q*, and the equilibrium price is P*. Consumer surplus is the area between the demand curve and the price line. When the price is P* and the quantity is Q*, consumer surplus is the area of the triangle, ABC. When a "voluntary export restriction" is instituted, there is a limit on the number of Japanese automobiles that can be purchased. Consumer surplus decreases, for two reasons. First, the quantity is reduced. Second, the price is higher, so there is less consumer surplus from the units that are purchased. The new consumer surplus is the area of the smaller triangle, ADE. Therefore, the lost consumer surplus is the area EDBC. This loss of consumer surplus is a measure of the amount by which consumers have been made worse off by the trade restriction.

Reality Check:
Interim Review Questions

IR7-3. Vicky is considering whether to buy a scarf. Her marginal utility from the first scarf is $10, and the scarf costs $15. Should she buy?

IR7-4. For Derek, the marginal utility of the first grapefruit is $1. If Derek obeys the Law of Diminishing Marginal Utility, will the marginal utility of the second grapefruit be greater than or less than $1?

IR7-5. Catherine's marginal utility from the first movie is $10, her marginal utility from the second movie is $8, her marginal utility from the third movie is $6, and her marginal utility from the fourth movie is $4. The price of a movie ticket is $6. How many movie tickets should Catherine buy? How much consumer surplus does she get?

ANOTHER WAY TO LOOK AT CONSUMER BEHAVIOR

So far, we have measured marginal utility in dollars. This gives us a consumer decision rule, which says that the consumer should keep buying as long as marginal utility is equal to or greater than price. The advantage of this approach is that it is very simple. The disadvantage is that it only deals with one good at a time.

As mentioned earlier in the chapter, marginal utility can also be measured in "utils", which are units of psychological satisfaction. Utils are associated with another popular way to present the theory of consumer behavior, and we will outline it here. Earlier, we said that it is actually very difficult to measure satisfaction precisely. However, that doesn't mean that the ideas outlined here are not useful. The ideas presented in this section are valuable, because they help us to organize our thoughts about the way in which consumers make their choices. It's true that consumers don't actually say "My marginal utility from consuming one pair of socks is 17.4 utils." However, most consumers act *as if* they were calculating their marginal utilities. Therefore,

this theory is useful, because it can help us to understand real-world consumer decisions.

We start with a very simplified example of a woman who consumes only two goods. By using a simple example like this, we are trying to get the basic idea across, without getting lost in a huge amount of detail.

Marginal Utility and Total Utility, Measured in Utils

Rachel Locantore only consumes apples and bananas. Currently, the price of apples is $1 per pound, and the price of bananas is also $1 per pound. Rachel has to make a decision about how many apples to buy and how many bananas to buy. Table 7.3 shows some information that will be useful to Rachel, as she makes her decision.

Like any consumer, Rachel can only spend as much money as she has. In this example, let's assume that Rachel has a total of $6 to spend on apples and bananas. Therefore, even though she might *wish* to spend more than $6, it just won't be possible. The most that she can

Table 7.3 Rachel's Utility from Combinations of Apples and Bananas That Can Be Bought for $6 (The Price of Apples Is $1.00 Per Pound, and the Price of Bananas Is $1.00 Per Pound)

	APPLES				BANANAS		
Pounds Consumed	Total Utility (in Utils)	Marginal Utility From One Extra Pound (in Utils)	Marginal Utility Per Dollar Spent	Pounds Consumed	Total Utility (in Utils)	Marginal Utility From One Extra Pound (in Utils)	Marginal Utility Per Dollar Spent
0	0	—	—	0	0	—	—
1	12	12	12	1	10	10	10
2	22	10	10	2	19	9	9
3	30	8	8	3	27	8	8
4	36	6	6	4	33	6	6
5	40	4	4	5	38	5	5
6	42	2	2	6	42	4	4

spend is $6, period. On the other hand, it won't make any sense for Rachel to spend less than $6. If she were to spend only $4, and throw the other $2 in the trash, she wouldn't be as well off as she would be if she were to spend the entire $6. Thus, in searching for Rachel's best choice, we will concentrate on the combinations of apples and bananas that can be bought for *exactly* $6. Since the prices of apples and bananas are both $1 per pound, there are seven combinations of apples and bananas that cost exactly $6:

(1) no apples and six pounds of bananas,
(2) one pound of apples and five pounds of bananas,
(3) two pounds of apples and four pounds of bananas,
(4) three pounds of apples and three pounds of bananas,
(5) four pounds of apples and two pounds of bananas,
(6) five pounds of apples and one pound of bananas, and
(7) six pounds of apples and no bananas.

The third column of Table 7.3 shows Rachel's marginal utility from apples, and the seventh column shows her marginal utility from bananas. In each case, the Law of Diminishing Marginal Utility is obeyed.

Utility Maximization

Which of these combinations is best for Rachel? Since Rachel is a rational person, she will choose the combination of apples and bananas that gives her the highest level of satisfaction. In other words, Rachel will choose the combination that *maximizes her total utility*, subject to the constraint that she can only spend her budget of $6.

Let's use the information from Table 7.3 to find the combination of apples and bananas that maximizes Rachel's utility. One of Rachel's possibilities is to buy six pounds of bananas, but no apples. If she were to buy this combination, she would get no utility from

apples, and she would get 42 utils from bananas. Therefore, Rachel's total utility would be 42 utils.

Next, let's consider the case in which Rachel buys five pounds of bananas and one pound of apples. In this case, she gets 12 utils from apples and 38 utils from bananas, for a total utility of 50 utils. Continuing through Table 3, we have the following combinations:

- Two pounds of apples, four pounds of bananas: Total utility = (22 + 33) = 55 utils.

- Three pounds of apples, three pounds of bananas: Total utility = (30 + 27) = 57 utils.

- Four pounds of apples, two pounds of bananas: Total utility = (36 + 19) = 55 utils.

- Five pounds of apples, one pound of bananas: Total utility = (40 + 10) = 50 utils.

- Six pounds of apples, no bananas: Total utility = (42 + 0) = 42 utils.

Rachel maximizes utility by consuming three pounds of apples and three pounds of bananas. This gives her 30 utils from apples, and 27 utils from bananas, for a total of 57 utils. There is no way that she can re-arrange her purchases to give a total utility that is greater than 57 utils.

The Consumer's Equilibrium: Equal Marginal Utility Per Dollar Spent

We can use the concept of marginal utility to get a deeper understanding of what is going on here. Whenever Rachel gives up a pound of bananas, she makes one more dollar available to be spent on apples. If the marginal utility of spending the dollar on apples is greater than the marginal utility of spending the dollar on bananas, then it makes sense to spend it on apples. *Whenever the marginal utility of spending a dollar on one good is greater than the marginal utility of spending a dollar on another good, the consumer can improve his or her situation* by shifting consumption toward the good with the higher marginal utility per dollar. Thus, it is not just a coincidence that Rachel chooses to buy three pounds of apples and three pounds of bananas. When she buys her third pound of apples, Rachel gets 8 utils per dollar spent. When she buys her third pound of bananas, she also gets 8 utils per dollar spent. Three pounds of apples and three pounds of bananas is the *only* combination at which the marginal utility per dollar spent is the same for both goods.

We can now state the consumer decision rule, for this case in which marginal utility is measured in utils:

The utility-maximizing consumer will be in equilibrium when he or she spends all of the available money, and chooses the combination of goods that gives the same marginal utility per dollar spent, for every good.

In our example with apples and bananas, there were only two goods. But the same principle applies, regardless of whether there are two goods, or three, or 1000. The utility-maximizing consumer should have the same marginal utility per dollar spent for *every* good. We can write the consumer decision rule as follows:

$$\frac{MU_a}{P_a} = \frac{MU_b}{P_b} = \frac{MU_c}{P_c} = \ldots, \text{ for } \textit{every} \text{ good.}$$

"Marginal utility per dollar spent" expresses the same idea as the popular phrase "bang for the buck". If you can get more bang for the buck by doing more of one activity, then you should increase that activity. This means that you will do your best by equalizing your bang for the buck across all activities.

The Individual's Demand Curve

What would happen if the price of apples were to rise to $2 per pound, with everything else remaining the same? First of all, some combinations that could be bought when apples cost $1 per pound are no longer possible when apples cost $2 per pound. For example, you have seen that Rachel will choose to buy three pounds of apples and three pounds of bananas, when the price of each type of fruit is $1. However, when the price of apples is $2, it would cost a total of $9 to buy three pounds of apples and three pounds of bananas. This is greater than Rachel's budget of $6, and so it can't be one of her choices any more.

When the price of apples is $2 per pound and the price of bananas is $1 per pound, there are four combinations that can be bought for $6. These are:

(1) no apples and six pounds of bananas,
(2) one pound of apples and four pounds of bananas,
(3) two pounds of apples and two pounds of bananas, and
(4) three pounds of apples and no bananas.

Rachel's task is to choose one of these combinations. She should choose the one that gives her the highest total utility. Some of the information that is necessary for her decision is in Table 7.4, which is similar to Table 7.3. The difference between the two tables is in the fourth column, which shows the marginal utility per dollar spent on apples. The numbers in the fourth column of 7.4 are exactly half as large as the comparable numbers in Table 7.3, because the price of apples is twice as high in Table 7.4 as in Table 7.3.

If Rachel were to buy no apples and six pounds of bananas, she would get zero utils from the apples and 42 utils from the bananas. Thus, her total utility would be 42 utils. If we continue to use Table 7.4, we can find the following utility combinations:

- One pound of apples, four pounds of bananas: Total utility = (12 + 33) = 45 utils.

- Two pounds of apples, two pounds of bananas: Total utility = (22 + 19) = 41 utils.

- Three pounds of apples, no bananas: Total utility = (30 + 0) = 30 utils.

Table 7.4 Rachel's Utility from Combinations of Apples and Bananas That Can Be Bought for $6 (The Price of Apples Is $2.00 Per Pound, and the Price of Bananas Is $1.00 Per Pound)

	APPLES				BANANAS		
Pounds Consumed	Total Utility (in Utils)	Marginal Utility From One Extra Pound (in Utils)	Marginal Utility Per Dollar Spent	Pounds Consumed	Total Utility (in Utils)	Marginal Utility From One Extra Pound (in Utils)	Marginal Utility Per Dollar Spent
0	0	—	—	0	0	—	—
1	12	12	6	1	10	10	10
2	22	10	5	2	19	9	9
3	30	8	4	3	27	8	8
4	36	6	3	4	33	6	6
5	40	4	2	5	38	5	5
6	42	2	1	6	42	4	4

The combination that gives the highest total utility is the one with one pound of apples and four pounds of bananas, which gives 45 utils. If you look at Table 7.4, you can see that the first pound of apples gives six units of marginal utility per dollar spent. The fourth pound of bananas also gives six units of marginal utility per dollar spent! Once again, utility maximization involves choosing the combination for which the marginal utility per dollar spent is the same for each good.

In this section, we have gone through two examples. In the first, the price of apples was $1 per pound, and Rachel chose to buy three pounds of apples. In the second example, everything else remained the same, except that the price of apples was now $2 per pound, and Rachel chose to buy one pound of apples. Figure 7.7 is a graph of these two choices. It is a downward-sloping demand curve! Regardless of whether marginal utility is measured in dollars or in utils, we can use marginal-utility calculations to derive a downward-sloping demand curve for the individual consumer.

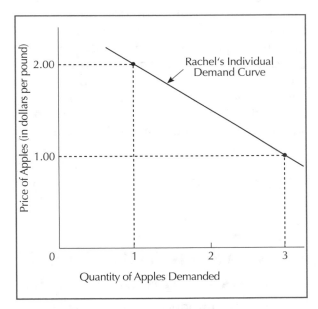

Figure 7.7 Rachel's Individual Demand Curve for Apples

When the price of a pound of apples is $1, Rachel chooses to consume three pounds of apples. However, when the price rises to $2 per pound, she reduces her quantity demanded to one pound of apples. Thus, the demand curve slopes downward as we move to the right, which means that Rachel obeys the Law of Demand.

A Comparison of the Two Ways of Understanding Consumer Behavior

Prices are measured in dollars. Therefore, when marginal utility is measured in dollars, it's possible to make a direct, immediate comparison between marginal utility and price. However, when marginal utility is measured in utils, we can't make such a direct comparison any more. Because of this, we have to state the consumer decision rule somewhat differently when marginal utility is measured in utils. Thus, in this chapter, we have two slightly different consumer decision rules. When marginal utility is measured in dollars, we say that the consumer should set marginal utility equal to price, for every good. When marginal utility is measured in utils, we say that the consumer should have the same marginal utility per dollar spent, for all goods. But this does *not* mean that one of the rules is correct, and the other is incorrect. They're *both* correct. The difference between the two consumer decision rules is just the result of a slight difference in the method of measuring marginal utility. Each of the two systems has an advantage. The advantage of measuring marginal utility in dollars is that it leads to a very simple consumer decision rule. The advantage of measuring marginal utility in utils is that gives us a consumer decision rule that compares many different goods.

Reality Check: Interim Review Questions

IR7-6. Kerry's marginal utility from consuming one more sweater is 120 utils, and her marginal utility from consuming one more blouse is 60 utils. The price of a sweater is $30, and the price of a blouse is $15. Should she consume more sweaters, or more blouses, or is she in equilibrium?

IR7-7. Lisa is studying for the final exam in her Economics course. Her goal is to maximize the total number of points that she will receive on the exam. She has divided the course material into three sections, each of which will receive equal weight on the exam. If she devotes more time to one section of the course, she can improve her score on that section. However, as she devotes more and more time to a particular section, the *marginal* improvement in her score will decrease. She has three more hours of study time before the exam. How should she divide her time between the three parts of the course?

MORE APPLICATIONS OF THE THEORY OF CONSUMER BEHAVIOR

We have now introduced some ways of thinking about consumer behavior. In fact, these ideas have proven to be very useful for many different applications. We've already seen some applications, such as the use of consumer surplus to measure the loss from restrictions on international trade. Some additional applications are discussed in this section.

The Value of Time

There are a number of ways to get from New York to Paris. You can take an ordinary commercial jetliner and get there in about seven hours and 45 minutes. If you were to fly in a coach seat to Paris on a Monday and return on Friday of the same week, the round-trip cost would be about $2000. An alternative is to take the supersonic Concorde, and get there in about three hours and 45 minutes. However, if you take the Concorde, you will have to pay more than $6000 for a round-trip ticket. Thus, in order to reduce your time in the air by four hours in each direction, it costs more than $4000. If time had no value, nobody would fly the Concorde.

But time is money. The true cost of the trip is the out-of-pocket cost of a plane ticket, *plus* the value of the time spent on the trip. If a highly paid executive considers her time to be extremely valuable, it might really make sense for her to take the Concorde. On the other hand, most people do not place such a high value on their time, so that they are willing to take an ordinary jetliner. In short, people who place a higher value on their time will be willing to pay more money to save time.

The market for trans-Atlantic air travel is not the only one where the value of time plays an important role. In domestic travel, people often have the choice of flying, driving, or riding a bus. Over short distances, the time advantage of air travel is very small, so travelers usually choose to take ground transportation. However, as the distance traveled becomes greater and greater, travelers can save more and more time by taking an airplane. Even though the airfare from Houston to St. Louis is higher than the price of a bus ticket, many people decide to fly, in order to save time.

All else equal, people may be willing to pay more to get a meal quickly, especially if they are in a hurry. Taco Bell, McDonald's, and other companies are not just selling food; they're selling *fast* food. In addition, many people want their food to be just as fast at home as it is in restaurants. In recent years, ready-to-eat preparations and microwave cuisines have been one of the most rapidly growing parts of the food industry.

Wage rates have a very important effect on the value of time. As wage rates increase, time becomes more valuable. Since wage rates have been rising for almost all of the 20th century, there are more and more people whose time is very valuable. Because of this, it's not surprising that an increasing number of business firms are focused on meeting the needs of customers who are in a hurry. You can get around the golf course more quickly if you use a golf cart than if you walk, and you can mow your lawn more quickly if you use a riding mower than if you use a push mower. For some people, time is valuable enough that they will pay extra for golf carts and riding mowers.

In this section, we have mentioned a few markets that are affected by the value of time. You can probably think of many more. In *Real Economics for Real People 7.3*, we consider another topic that has to do with consumer behavior: the value of saving a life.

Reality Check: Interim Review Question

IR7-8. Mr. A is a highly paid accountant, and Mr. B is a janitor. Each of them lives in Sacramento, and each needs to travel to Los Angeles. Which of the two is more likely to travel by air, and which is more likely to travel by bus? Why?

HOUSEHOLD EXPENDITURE: WHERE DOES THE MONEY GO?

So far in this chapter, we have developed some ideas about consumer behavior, and we have applied those ideas to some interesting cases, such as the value of time and the value of saving a life. However, we haven't discussed the amounts of money that consumers spend on different goods and services. Table 7.5 shows the amounts that were spent by U.S. consumers on different commodities in 1997.

From looking at Table 7.5, you may get an idea of the immense size and diversity of the U.S. economy. First of all, in 1997, American consumers spent nearly $5.5 *trillion* (that is, nearly $5500 billion). Another thing to notice from Table 7.5 is how little is spent on items that are absolute necessities. In the U.S. economy of the 19th century, most expenditure was on the basics of food, clothing, and shelter. The same is true for the poorest countries today. However, in the United States in 1997, less than half of the total was spent on food, clothing, housing, and household operation. Moreover, it's important to remember that even these categories include many were carried out. If you agree, then you are saying that the value of saving one life per year is less than $1 trillion.

Economists have attempted to estimate the dollar value of a life saved. One way to do this is to compare the wages of workers in dangerous jobs with the wages of workers in safe jobs. Some people are willing to work for a lower wage rate, in order to work at a safer job. In measuring the tradeoff between risk and wage rates, we are measuring the amount that workers are willing to pay for safety.

To get a meaningful estimate of the value of saving a life, we have to measure the relationship between wage rates and the risk of death, *while holding other things equal*. The other things that should be held equal would include the education, age, and experience of workers, as well as other factors. Fortunately, modern statistical techniques do allow us to control for these other factors. The estimates vary, but they tend to give us numbers in the ballpark of $1 million per life saved to $6 million per life saved. With an estimate like this, we can judge which safety projects are worthwhile, and which are not.

Many safety projects have been shown to be very beneficial, in that their marginal benefits are greater than their marginal costs. For example, the steering-column protection equipment that is installed in cars has been estimated to cost only about $100,000 per life saved. Since the estimates of the value of saving a life are all much higher than $100,000, steering-column protection is a bargain. A variety of regulations to reduce fires in automobiles are also very effective at saving lives.

However, some safety projects have been estimated to save only a very few lives, at very high cost. For example, it has been estimated that the cost of regulations to reduce arsenic in the workplace is more than $90 million per life saved. Even if we assume that the value of a life saved is $6 million, the arsenic regulations are bad for society. If the marginal costs of a safety project are high enough, then society would be better off if the project were *not* undertaken.

items that can't really be called necessities, such as restaurant meals, alcoholic beverages, designer clothing, luxury homes, and vacation homes.

In the last generation, medical care has been one of the fastest-growing parts of the economy. By 1997, medical care accounted for $957 billion, which is more than 17 percent of personal consumption expenditure. Other services have also grown very rapidly. For example, Americans spent $367 billion on financial services and life insurance, which is nearly seven percent of personal consumption expenditure. In addition, about $56 billion (or one percent of the total) were spent on legal services.

All of these expenditures were the result of the decisions of individual consumers. In this chapter, we have shown how utility maximization can be used to explain the behavior of consumers. The numbers shown in Table 7.5 give an overview of the millions of decisions that are made by consumers every day, in an effort to maximize their utility.

Table 7.5 Categories of Personal Consumption Expenditure in the United States, 1997

Category	Expenditure (in Billions of Dollars)	Percentage of Total Expenditure
Food and Tobacco	**$832.3**	**15.2%**
Food Other Than Alcohol and Tobacco	692.4	12.6
Alcoholic Beverages	88.6	1.6
Tobacco Products	51.4	0.9
Clothing, Accessories, and Jewelry	**$353.3**	**6.4%**
Toilet Articles, Barbershops, Health Clubs, and Other Personal-Care Expenditures	**$ 79.4**	**1.4%**
Housing	**$829.8**	**15.1%**
Household Operation	**$620.7**	**11.3%**
Furnishings and Appliances	207.7	3.8
Utilities and Telephone	282.7	5.1
Other Household-Operation Expenditures	130.3	2.4
Medical Care	**$957.3**	**17.4%**
Doctors and Dentists	257.8	4.7
Hospitals and Nursing Homes	408.1	7.4
Other Medical-Care Expenditures	291.4	5.3
Personal Business Services	**$459.1**	**8.4%**
Financial Services and Life Insurance	367.0	6.7
Legal Services	55.9	1.0
Other Personal Business Services	36.2	0.7
Transportation	**$636.4**	**11.6%**
New Automobiles	86.2	1.6
Gasoline and Oil	126.5	2.3
Automobile Repair, Washing, Parking, and Rental	154.9	2.8
Other Transportation	268.8	4.9
Recreation	**$462.9**	**8.4%**
Education and Research	**$129.4**	**2.4%**
Religious and Welfare Activities	**$157.6**	**2.9%**
Foreign Travel and Other Expenditures Abroad	**$ 62.9**	**1.1%**
TOTAL	**$5,493.7**	**100.0%**

Source: *Survey of Current Business,* August, 1999, Table B.4.

NOTE: Percentages of sub-categories may not add to percentages for categories, due to rounding.

NOTE: Category totals do not add to aggregate total, because aggregate total is net of expenditures in the United States by nonresidents, and personal remittances in kind to nonresidents.

ECONOMICS AND YOU: RESOLVING THE PARADOX OF BASEBALL CARDS AND WATER

At the beginning of this chapter, we raised a paradox. Why do consumers pay so little for water, which is necessary for survival, and so much for some baseball cards and comic books and paintings? Actually, this is not a new dilemma. The Scottish economist Adam Smith wondered about it more than 200 years ago. There weren't any baseball cards or comic books in Smith's time, but there were diamonds. Smith was puzzled about why diamonds could be sold for prices that were so much higher than the price of water. This puzzle has come to be called the ***Diamond-Water Paradox.***

We can resolve the paradox with the use of our ideas about marginal utility. It is true that we need water to survive. The marginal utility of the first cup of water that you consume in a given day is very great, because you might die if you don't have a little bit of water.

However, the marginal utility of the next cup is a little less, and the marginal utility of the third cup is even less than that.

Only a tiny fraction of the water that we use is absolutely necessary for survival. We use water to keep our lawns green, and to keep our cars clean. We use water in swimming pools, and we use it to take showers. If all of these uses of water were eliminated, nobody would die of thirst. Even though the *total* utility of water is very great, the *marginal* utility is really quite small. Water is so plentiful that the marginal utility of the last gallon of water is tiny.

By contrast, rare comic books, rare baseball cards, diamonds, and Picasso paintings are in short supply, and they have great *marginal* value, at least for some people. If diamonds were as plentiful as water, the price of a diamond would be much lower than it is today.

Chapter Summary

1. The marginal value for any variable is the value of one additional unit of the variable. A marginal value can also be defined as the change in the total value. A marginal value is the slope of the graph of a total value.

2. Marginal utility can be defined in either of two ways. Under one definition, marginal utility is the amount that a consumer is willing to pay (measured in dollars), in order to have one additional unit of some good. Under the other definition, marginal utility is the amount of additional psychological satisfaction (measured in "utils") that a consumer gets from consuming one additional unit of some good. The Law of Diminishing Marginal Utility states that marginal utility will eventually decrease, as more and more units of a good are consumed.

3. When marginal utility is defined in dollars, the consumer should buy additional units of a good, as long as marginal utility is equal to or greater than the price that must be paid for the additional unit. The consumer's equilibrium involves buying a good until its marginal utility equals its price.

4. If the price changes, the consumer equilibrium will change. If we change the price repeatedly, we see that the marginal-utility curve is the consumer's individual demand curve. Because of the Law of Diminishing Marginal Utility, the individual demand curve will slope downward as we move to the right.

5. Except for the last unit consumed, the consumer's marginal utility will be greater than the price. Consumer surplus is the difference between the total number of dollars that the consumer is willing to pay and the total number of dollars that is actually paid.

6. When marginal utility is measured in utils, the consumer's equilibrium will occur when each good provides the same marginal utility per dollar spent. Thus, in this case, the consumer should choose the quantities at which the ratio of marginal utility to price is the same for every good.

7. The "Diamond-Water Paradox" refers to the fact that water commands a much lower price than diamonds, in spite of the fact that water is essential for life. This paradox is resolved when we understand that the *marginal* utillity that most people get from water is small, even though the *total* utility is very great.

Key Terms

Rational

Utility

Marginal Utility

Total Utility

Law of Diminishing Marginal Utility

Consumer Decision Rule

Consumer Equilibrium

Individual Demand Curve

Consumer Surplus

Diamond-Water Paradox

Questions and Problems

QP7-1. Explain the Law of Diminishing Marginal Utility. Can you think of any goods for which the Law might not hold?

QP7-2. Stu Incinerator is a basketball player. In the first game of the season, he scores 20 points. In the next games, he scores 24, 15, 19, and 26 points respectively.

a. Construct a table showing Stu's marginal points for each game, and his total points for all games up to and including that game.

b. Draw graphs of Stu's marginal points and total points. Graphically, what is the relationship between marginal points and total points?

QP7-3. Police officers have higher rates of death and injury on the job than do file clerks. *All else equal,* what effect do you expect this will have on the relative wage rates of police officers and file clerks?

QP7-4. Convenience stores, such as 7-Eleven and Stop 'n' Shop, typically allow consumers to make quick purchases. However, they usually charge higher prices than other stores charge. Explain why buyers would be willing to pay higher prices at convenience stores.

QP7-5. The table below shows Betsy's marginal utility from different numbers of trips to the movies every month. Graph Betsy's demand curve for trips to the movie theater.

QP7-6. To answer this question, use the information from the chart in question (5).

a. Assuming that the price of a movie ticket is $4, calculate Betsy's consumer surplus.

Movie	Marginal Utility
1	$15
2	9
3	6
4	4
5	2
6	1

b. How does consumer surplus change if the price increases to $6?

QP7-7. If you travel with an airline, you can get from Chicago to San Francisco in less than four hours. The airfare will probably be more than $300. You can also get from Chicago to San Francisco by bus. It will cost less money, but it will take several days. Explain who would be more likely to take the bus, and who would be more likely to fly.

QP7-8. The daily market demand curve for kazoos in Kokomo is given by $Q_d = 10 - P$, where Q_d is the quantity demanded and P is the price. The supply curve is perfectly horizontal, and is given by P = $1. This means that sellers will sell as many units as buyers want to buy, so long as the price is $1.

a. Substitute the expression for supply (P = $1) into the expression for demand, and solve for Q_d. This is the equilibrium quantity.

b. Calculate consumer surplus.

QP7-9. Assume that the demand curve from question (8) is unchanged. However, the government levies a tax on kazoos, such that the supply relationship is changed to P = $2.

a. Substitute the new expression for supply (P = $2) into the expression for demand, and solve for the new equilibrium quantity.

b. Calculate the consumer surplus that consumers will have under the new equilibrium.

c. How much consumer surplus is lost as a result of the tax?

Chapter 8

Production and Cost

ECONOMICS AND YOU:
IF YOU'VE ALREADY PAID FOR A MEAL,
DO YOU HAVE TO EAT IT?

Allison and Zachary go to Pat's Pasta Palace for spaghetti and meatballs every Wednesday night, because Wednesday is all-you-can-eat night. After they pay $8 at the door, Allison and Zachary can have as many helpings as they want.

Unfortunately, on this particular Wednesday, the chef is out sick. The spaghetti is overcooked, the sauce is watery, and the meatballs are hard and gritty, with a taste of sawdust. Zachary says "This food is horrible, but I guess I should pig out anyway, to get my money's worth." Allison asks him whether he's hungry. He says "Not really. I ate a big lunch." She says "I'm not really hungry, either. As for getting my money's worth, I kissed my eight dollars goodbye when I paid at the door. It doesn't make sense to eat this food unless I like it, and I don't."

If Allison and Zachary are to make the right decision, they will need to think carefully about the *true cost* of eating tonight's spaghetti at Pat's Pasta Palace. In this chapter, you will learn more about how to think about costs, in a variety of situations. You have already learned about the idea of opportunity cost, in

Chapter 2. Here, we will focus on costs in much greater detail. Before this chapter is over, you will have a framework for thinking about the dilemma facing Allison and Zachary at Pat's Pasta Palace, and you will also learn a great deal more. In fact, most of this chapter is concerned with the costs that business firms have to pay when they produce goods and services. These cost concepts are important, in and of themselves. In addition, they provide the foundation for our understanding of how firms make their production decisions. We will take a close look at the firm's decision-making processes in Chapters 9, 10, and 11.

Some students find the material in this chapter to be harder than most other parts of a course in microeconomics. If this stuff is difficult for you, here is a word of advice: The best strategy is to take it one step at a time. Don't try to learn the entire chapter in one big gulp. Instead, concentrate on one concept at a time, and don't move on to the next concept until you have mastered the current one. It's true that this chapter has a lot of pieces. However, if you take the pieces one at a time, you can learn them all.

THE RELATIONSHIPS AMONG MARGINAL, AVERAGE, AND TOTAL QUANTITIES

We introduced marginal and total relationships in Chapter 7, by looking at the distances traveled on a trip from Maine to Texas. In that example, the marginal distance is the number of additional miles that is traveled in one additional day. The total distance is the total number of miles traveled, on *all* of the days up to some point in the journey. Thus, we can calculate the total distance by adding the marginal distances. Graphically, the marginal distance is the slope of the total-distance curve. The marginal distances and total distances for the trip from Maine to Texas are shown in Table 8.1, which is adapted from Table 7.1.

Now that we have information on marginal distance and total distance, our next step is to define the *average* distance. The average distance is the average number of miles traveled *per day*, for a group of days. *The average distance per day is defined as the total distance divided by the number of days traveled*. Table 8.1 shows that, at the end of the first day of the journey, the total distance is 400 miles. Therefore, the average distance per day at the end of the first day is (400 miles) / (1 day) = 400 miles per day. When we include the second

day of travel, the total distance increases to 1000 miles, while the number of days increases to two. Therefore, the average distance increases to (1000 miles) / (2 days) = 500 miles per day.

When we include the third day, the average distance is (1500 miles) / (3 days) = 500 miles per day. Finally, when we include the fourth day, the average distance is (1800 miles) / (4 days) = 450 miles per day. The average distance at the end of each day in the trip is shown in the fourth column of Table 8.1.

Later in this chapter, and in the chapters to come, we will look at several other concepts involving averages, such as average product, average cost, and average revenue. Every one of these average concepts is defined in a way that is similar to the definition of average distance that we have just used. In each case, the average is calculated by dividing a total quantity by the number of units that have occurred so far. For example, average revenue is the firm's sales revenue per unit sold. To calculate average revenue for the business firm, we start with the total revenue for all units sold, and divide by the number of units sold. If the firm's total revenue is $10 million, and if the

Table 8.1 Marginal, Total, and Average Distances Traveled in a Journey from Maine to Texas

Day	Marginal Distance = Additional Mileage on This Day	Total Distance = Total Mileage for All Days So Far	Average Distance = Total Distance / Number of Days	Comment
1	400	400	400	
2	600	1000	500	Marginal > Average => Average increases
3	500	1500	500	Marginal = Average => Average is unchanged
4	300	1800	450	Marginal < Average => Average decreases

firm sells one million units, then average revenue is (\$10 million)/(1 million units) = \$10 per unit.

The Relationship between Marginal and Average Quantities

Let's look at some of the relationships between marginal distances and average distances, beginning with the information in the first row of Table 8.1. On the first day of the trip, the marginal distance traveled is 400 miles, and the average distance is also 400 miles. If we only consider the first day of the trip, the average distance traveled must be equal to the marginal distance traveled.

Now, let's compare the first and second lines of Table 8.1. On the second day, the marginal distance traveled is 600 miles. This is *more* than the average distance as of the end of the first day, which was only 400 miles. As a result, there is an *increase* in the average distance traveled per day, from 400 miles per day to 500 miles per day. When the marginal distance is greater than the average distance, the average distance must increase.

Next, compare the second and third rows of Table 8.1. On the third day of the trip, the marginal distance traveled is 500 miles. This is *exactly equal* to the average distance as of the end of the previous day. As a result, the average distance *stays the same.* Since the average distance per day was already 500 miles per day, and the distance traveled on the third day was also 500 miles per day, the average had to remain unchanged.

Finally, compare the third and fourth rows of Table 8.1. At the end of the third day, the average distance traveled was 500 miles per day, while the marginal distance for the fourth day is only 300 miles. Therefore, the marginal distance for the fourth day is *less* than the average distance for the previous three days. As a result, the average distance

decreases, from 500 miles per day to 450 miles per day. When the marginal distance is less than the average distance, the average distance must decrease.

These relationships aren't just the result of coincidence. In fact, we will see these same relationships again and again:

- *When the marginal is* more *than the average for the preceding units, the average will* increase.

- *When the marginal is* equal *to the average for the preceding units, the average will stay the* same.

- *When the marginal is* less *than the average for the preceding units, the average will* decrease.

Now, to reinforce your understanding, let's consider another example. We measure the heights of five people in a room. We then add the heights of the five people, and divide by five. This gives us the average height for these five people. Let's say that this average is 5 feet, 8 inches. Next, we bring a sixth person into the room. At this point, this sixth person can be considered the *marginal* person.

If the marginal person is 6 feet, 2 inches tall, what will happen to the average height? The marginal person is *taller* than average, so the average height would *increase.* (In fact, the average height will increase to 5 feet, 9 inches.) On the other hand, if the sixth person is exactly 5 feet, 8 inches tall, then the marginal person is *just as tall* as the average. In this case, the average height would *stay the same.* Finally, what if the sixth person is only 5 feet, 2 inches tall? In this case, the marginal person is *shorter* than average, so that the average height would *decrease.* (In fact, the average height will drop to 5 feet, 7 inches.)

In summary: When marginal exceeds average, the average rises. When marginal is equal to average, the average is unchanged. When marginal is less than average, the average falls.

These relationships can also be written as follows:

Marginal > Average => Average ↑

Marginal = Average => Average is unchanged

Marginal < Average => Average ↓

These relationships will keep coming up. Later in this chapter, we will revisit these relationships when we look at marginal product and average product, as well as marginal cost and average cost. In later chapters, we will see the same relationships between marginal revenue and average revenue.

A Graph of Marginal and Average Distances

Figure 8.1 is a graph of the marginal and average distances from our example of a journey from Maine to Texas. This figure illustrates the points that we were just making. On the second day of the trip, the marginal distance traveled is greater than the average distance for the previous day, and the average-distance curve is pulled upward. In other words, when we go from day 1 to day 2 on the horizontal axis of Figure 8.1, the value on the average-distance curve increases on the vertical axis. On the third day, the marginal distance is equal to the average distance, and the average distance remains the same. Therefore, the graph of average distance is a flat line as we move from day 2 to day 3. Finally, on the fourth day, the marginal distance is less than the average distance, and the average-distance curve is pulled downward: The graph of the average-distance curve slopes downward as we move from day 3 to day 4.

Reality Check:
Interim Review Questions

IR8-1. A basketball team is averaging 68 points per game. How will this average be

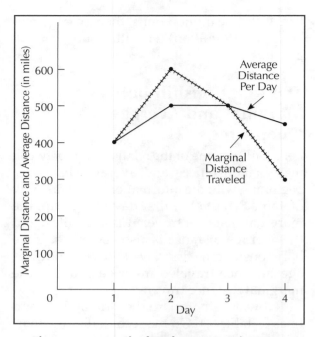

Figure 8.1 Marginal and Average Distances on a Trip from Maine to Texas

The marginal distance traveled on the first day of the journey is 400 miles. Therefore, at the end of the first day, the average distance is also 400 miles. On the second day, the marginal distance is 600 miles. Because the marginal distance is larger than the average distance, the average distance increases. At the end of the second day, the average distance is 500 miles. The marginal distance on the third day is 500 miles, which is exactly equal to the average distance from the previous days. Therefore, the average distance stays the same. On the final day, the marginal distance of 300 miles is less than the average distance. Therefore, the average distance decreases.

changed if the team scores 75 points in its next game? (In other words, if the team scores 75 points in its next game, will the average increase, or decrease, or stay the same?) What if the team scores 68 points in its next game? What if the team scores only 59 points in its next game?

IR8-2. Hot Stuff Corporation has produced 10,000 smoke detectors so far this year. On average, the cost of production has been

$20 per detector. If the marginal cost of producing the 10,001st smoke detector were $22, would the average cost go up, or go down, or stay the same? What if the marginal cost of the 10,001st smoke detector were $20? What if it were $19?

PRODUCTION: THE RELATIONSHIP BETWEEN INPUTS AND OUTPUTS

In Chapter 7, we took a close look at the decisions of consumers. We found that consumers make their choices by comparing the price of a good with the marginal utility of consuming the good. In other words, consumers compare the marginal benefit of consuming with the marginal cost of consuming.

Firms also compare marginal benefits and marginal costs. The firm's marginal benefits are the additional revenues that it gets from selling more of its product. These marginal benefits are called "marginal revenues." The firm's marginal costs are the additional costs of producing more of its product. These marginal costs are just called "marginal costs." We will get to the revenue side of the picture in Chapter 9. In this chapter, we focus on costs.

If a business firm wants to have something to sell, it must produce some good or service. The goods and services that the firm produces are called *outputs*. In order to produce these outputs, the firm must use *inputs*. For example, in the case of a barber shop, the outputs are haircuts. The inputs are the barbers, the shop, the scissors and combs, and so on.

Variable Inputs and Fixed Inputs

We separate inputs into two broad categories—variable inputs and fixed inputs. *Variable inputs* are inputs whose quantity can be varied during the time period under consideration. *Fixed inputs* are those for which quantity *cannot* be changed during the time period under consideration. An example will help us to understand these definitions.

Let's consider a small Midwestern firm that makes apple cider. The firm is called Cider Space. If the firm wants to hire more workers, it will usually take a few days or a few weeks to find new workers who are willing to work in the cider mill. If we are thinking about the firm's production choices over the next year, then labor will be considered a *variable* input, because one year is the time period under consideration, and the amount of labor can be changed in less than one year. If we're thinking about the firm's production choices over the next year, *any* input that can be altered in less than one year is a variable input.

Labor is certainly an important input into the production of cider at Cider Space. Another important input is the mill itself, which consists of a building with an office, machinery for shredding and squeezing apples, and other equipment. Cider Space has a two-year lease on the mill. Therefore, if we are considering the firm's production choices over the next year, the cider mill itself would be considered a *fixed* input. If we're thinking about the firm's production choices over the next year, *any* input that can't be altered in less than one year is a fixed input.

The distinction between variable inputs and fixed inputs will depend on the length of time that we are thinking about. If we consider the production choices for a firm like Cider Space over the next 10 years, then every input would be considered a variable input.

In the example that we have just given, labor was considered a variable input. In many cases, workers and materials are variable inputs. The number of workers and the amount of materials can usually be changed in a fairly short period of time. However, workers and materials aren't variable inputs in every case. For example, some workers (such as professional athletes) are hired according to long-term contracts. If we are considering a time horizon of one year, and if a professional baseball player has three more years remaining on his contract, then he would *not* be considered a variable input.

Buildings and capital equipment are often fixed inputs. This is because, in many cases, buildings and capital equipment cannot easily be varied in a short period of time. However, buildings and capital equipment aren't fixed inputs in every case. For example, it's sometimes possible to rent a bulldozer, or some other piece of heavy machinery, for as little as half a day. In this case, the bulldozer would be considered a variable input, as long as we are thinking of the firm's production choices over a period of more than half a day.

The Short Run and The Long Run

In the discussion of variable inputs and fixed inputs, the "time period under consideration" played an important role. The distinction between the short run and the long run is related to the time period under consideration. The *short run* is defined as a period of time over which at least one input is fixed. In the *long run*, all inputs are variable.

The length of time that is necessary to take us to the long run will vary from one production process to the next. In heavy industries, such as chemicals, steel, and automobiles, it may take years to design and construct a new factory. In these industries, the long run might be two years, five years, or even ten years. For the child operating a lemonade stand, the long run may be only a few minutes. For many businesses, the long run will be between these extremes, at a few months or a year.

For most of this chapter, we will study production and cost in the short run. Toward the end of the chapter, we'll consider the long run, in which *all* inputs are variable.

Production in the Short Run

Let's continue with the example of Cider Space, the small apple-cider mill. In the discussion that follows, we will assume that Cider Space has one variable input (labor), one fixed input (the mill, with its building and equipment), and one output (apple cider). Of course, in reality, labor isn't the only variable input. The firm also uses electricity, and apples, and other inputs. However, our goal is to keep the example as simple as possible, so we will assume that labor is the only variable input. The ideas developed here can be carried over to the case in which there is more than one variable input.

The mill's output can be measured by the number of gallons of apple cider that are produced in a day. The total number of gallons produced is called *total product*. For any good, the total amount that is produced by a firm can be called the firm's *total product* of that good. Total product is also sometimes called "total physical product." This indicates that we are thinking about an amount of output, rather than a dollar amount.

Another name for total product is *quantity of output*. In this chapter and the following chapters, we will use "Q" as our abbreviation for quantity of output or total product.

When the firm hires more workers, how many additional gallons of apple cider can it produce? *We assume that, as we allow the number of workers to change, the size of the mill is held constant.* This assumption is crucial. In order to focus on the productivity of additional labor, we have to hold constant the firm's other inputs. Therefore, when we allow the number of workers to change, we will assume that the size of the cider mill stays the same, and that the number of apple presses stays the same, and so on.

Table 8.2 shows the relationship between the number of workers and the number of gallons of cider that can be produced in a day. Total product (the total number of gallons produced) is in the second column of the table. The third column has the *marginal product* of labor. (The marginal product is sometimes also called the "marginal physical product.") In this example, the marginal product of labor is the additional number of gallons of apple cider that can be produced, when the firm hires one additional worker, and all other inputs are held constant. The *marginal product* of any variable input is defined as the additional output that is produced when one additional unit of the input is used. In the case of labor, we have

Marginal Product of Labor =

$$\frac{\text{Change in Total Product}}{\text{Change in Labor Input}} = \frac{\Delta Q}{\Delta L}$$

Since "quantity of output" is the same thing as "total product", we could also say

Marginal Product of Labor =

$$\frac{\text{Change in Quantity of Output}}{\text{Change in Labor Input}} = \frac{\Delta Q}{\Delta L}$$

If we were to calculate the marginal product of some other input, we would use a very similar formula. For example, in an aluminum-processing plant, the marginal product of electricity is the change in aluminum output, divided by the change in the amount of electricity that is used. In general, the marginal product of any variable input is the change in the quantity of output, divided by the change in the amount of that variable input, assuming that all other inputs are held constant.

The fourth column of Table 8.2 shows the *average product* of labor. This is sometimes also called "average physical product" or "output per worker". The *average product* of labor is defined by

Average Product of Labor =

$$\frac{\text{Total Product}}{\text{Labor Input}} = \frac{Q}{L}$$

(1) Number of Workers	(2) Quantity of Output = Q = Total Product = Number of Gallons Produced Per Day	(3) Marginal Product = (Change in Total Product)/ (Change in Labor Input)	(4) Average Product= (Total Product) / (Labor Input)	Comment
0	0	—	—	
1	100	100	100	
2	250	150	125	Marg.>Avg. => Avg. ↑
3	375	125	125	Marg.=Avg. => Avg. unchanged
4	450	75	112.5	Marg.<Avg. => Avg. ↓
5	500	50	100	Marg.<Avg. => Avg. ↓
6	525	25	87.5	Marg.<Avg. => Avg. ↓
7	525	0	75	Marg.<Avg. => Avg. ↓
8	500	−25	62.5	Marg.<Avg. => Avg. ↓

Table 8.2 Labor Input and Output for Cider Space

Since "quantity of output" is the same thing as "total product", we could also say

Average Product of Labor =

$$\frac{\text{Quantity of Output}}{\text{Labor Input}} = \frac{Q}{L}$$

If we were to calculate the average product of some other input, we would use a very similar formula. For example, in an aluminum-processing plant, the average product of electricity is the total aluminum output, divided by the amount of electricity that is used. In general, the *average product* of any variable input is equal to the total product, divided by the amount of that variable input.

It's important to understand Table 8.2 in two ways. First, we need to understand it in terms of the numerical relationships among marginal product, average product, and total product. Second, and even more important, we need to understand its economic meaning. In the next few paragraphs, we will discuss the numbers and their economic meaning.

Marginal Product and Total Product. Look at the top row of Table 8.2. If Cider Space doesn't hire any workers, then the firm's total output will be zero. If the firm hires one worker, that worker can produce a total of 100 gallons of apple cider per day. The marginal product of the first worker is 100 gallons. When we consider only the first worker, the average product is also 100 gallons.

If the firm hires a second worker, the total product increases to 250 gallons. This means that the marginal product of the second worker is (250–100) = 150 additional gallons of cider. Marginal product actually increases as we move from the first worker to the second!

Why would the marginal product increase? With only one worker, the same person must perform all tasks. This one person must pick and sort the apples, operate the presses, collect the cider in gallon-size containers, clean

the presses, keep records, answer the phone, and so on, and so on. It would be hard for anyone to juggle so many tasks. When the firm hires a second worker, the two workers can coordinate their activities. One worker could be in charge of picking the apples, keeping records, and putting the cider in containers. The other worker could do the work of running the cider press. In the example of Table 8.2, this specialization means that the marginal product of labor increases when we consider the second worker.

As you read down through Table 8.2, you will see that the marginal product of labor begins to decrease when we add a third worker. As we add more and more workers, the marginal product of labor decreases even farther.

For most of Table 8.2, the marginal product of labor is greater than zero. As long as marginal product is positive, total product will continue to increase. However, when a seventh worker is added, the marginal product of labor is zero. In other words, when the seventh worker is added to the firm's work force, the quantity of output doesn't change. If Cider Space were to bring on an eighth worker, his or her marginal product would actually be negative!

It may seem strange that the marginal product of an additional worker could be zero or even negative. However, it's important to remember that we are holding the size of the cider mill constant as we calculate the marginal product of additional workers. For example, Cider Space only has one apple press. Most of the time, operating the press requires only one or two workers. In addition, when we add more and more workers to a fixed cider mill, it gets harder and harder to coordinate their activities. Workers bump into each other. Tempers flare. Fistfights erupt. Eventually, these problems could mean that the marginal product of labor is zero or negative. In Table 8.2, the seventh worker interferes with the other workers so much that output remains the same as it had been when there were only six workers. The eighth worker interferes with the other workers so much that output decreases.

The Law of Diminishing Returns. It's important to realize that this apple-cider example is not unusual. In fact, lots of production processes have the character that we have just seen. For example, consider the productivity of fertilizer in a cotton field. Hold constant the size of the field, the quality of the soil, the number and quality of seeds, the climate, and so on. As we add a small amount of fertilizer, the marginal product of fertilizer is positive. In other words, more cotton can be grown with a small amount of fertilizer than with no fertilizer. However, as we add more and more fertilizer to the same plot of ground, the additional output that we can squeeze out of the field will get smaller and smaller. Finally, by the time we're dumping several pounds of fer-

tilizer on each square foot of ground, the marginal product will have gone negative. We will have burned the soil so badly that we get *less* output by adding more fertilizer.

In *Real Economics for Real People 8.1*, we consider another case in which marginal product is positive at first, but eventually negative.

We have now considered the marginal product of labor in an apple-cider mill, the marginal product of fertilizer in a cotton field, and the marginal product of study time in an economics course. All three of these production processes are similar in character. In each case, we consider increasing one variable input, while holding *all* other inputs constant. The marginal product of the variable input may actually increase over some range of inputs. In fact, this occurred in the Cider Space example in Table 8.2. The marginal product of the first worker was 100 gallons of apple cider, and the marginal product of the second worker

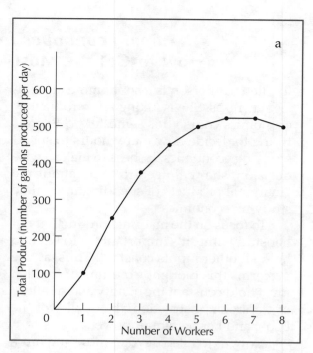

Figure 8.2 Panel (a)
The Total Product of Labor at Cider Space

This graph shows what happens to the output of apple cider, as more workers are added to the production process, while other inputs are held constant. As the number of workers increases from zero to six, the quantity of output increases. However, as more and more workers are added, it becomes more and more difficult to increase output. The total-product curve becomes flatter. Finally, when the seventh worker is added, the quantity of output stays the same. When the eighth worker is added, total product actually decreases.

Figure 8.2 Panel (b)
The Marginal Product of Labor at Cider Space

The marginal product of the second worker is greater than the marginal product of the first worker. However, after the second worker, the marginal product starts to decline. Thus, this production process obeys the Law of Diminishing Returns. Finally, the marginal product of the seventh worker is zero, and the marginal product of the eighth worker is negative.

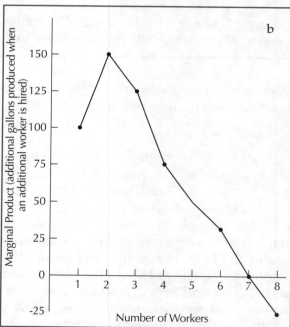

was 150 gallons. However, the marginal product *eventually* decreases. This happens in so many cases that economists refer to the "Law" of Diminishing Returns. The Law of Diminishing Returns is sometimes also called the Law of Diminishing Marginal Returns, or the Law of Diminishing Marginal Product.

The Law of Diminishing Returns states that, when we increase one variable input, *holding constant all other inputs*, the marginal product of that variable input will *eventually* decrease.

A Graph of Marginal Product and Total Product. The relationships between total product and marginal product are graphed in Figure 8.2. In panel (a) of the figure, we see that the total product of Cider Space increases at an *increasing* rate, when we go from the first worker to the second worker. After that, total product continues to increase, but at a *decreasing* rate. Finally, total product stops increasing, and begins to decrease.

In panel (b) of Figure 8.2, we see that the marginal product of labor rises until the second worker, but then falls.

The marginal product of labor is the change in total product, divided by the change in labor input. But this is the same as the definition of the slope of the total-product curve. For example, as we go from the second worker to the third, total product increases by (375–250) = 125 gallons, and labor input increases by 1. Therefore, the slope of the total product curve is (125 / 1) = 125, which is the same as the marginal product of labor. *Marginal product is the slope of the total-product curve.*

Marginal Product and Average Product. Recall the example of a trip from Maine to Texas, from earlier in this chapter. We saw that, when the marginal distance exceeded the average distance from the previous days, the average distance increased. In our example of Cider Space, we see the same sort of thing. The average product of the first worker is only 100 gallons, whereas the marginal product of the second worker is 150 gallons. So, marginal product exceeds average product, and average product rises. The average product of the first two workers is (250 / 2) = 125 gallons of cider per worker, which is greater than the average product of the first worker. *When marginal product is greater than the average product from the previous units, the average product will increase.*

The marginal product of the third worker

is also 125 gallons. If we include a third worker, whose marginal product is the same as the average of the previous two workers, the average product should remain the same. And it does. The average product of the first three workers is (375 / 3) = 125 gallons per worker, which is the same as the average product of the first two workers. This is another general relationship that we will see again and again. *When marginal product equals the average product from the previous units, the average product remains the same.*

Beginning with the fourth worker, the marginal product of labor is below the average product. This pulls the average product down. *When marginal product is less than the average product from the previous units, the average product will decrease.*

These relationships between marginal and average product can be seen in the graph in panel (b) of Figure 8.2. For the first worker, marginal product and average product are the same. For the second worker, marginal product rises, so that it exceeds average product. Thus, the average-product curve slopes upward to the right. For the third worker, marginal and average are once again the same, and the average-product curve is horizontal. *Average product is maximized at a level of input at which that average product equals marginal product.* After the third worker, marginal product is less than average product. Because of this, the average-product curve slopes downward to the right.

Reality Check: Interim Review Questions

IR8-3. Woofer Corporation produces stereo speakers. At the current level of production, the marginal product of labor is less than the average product of labor. Does this mean that the average-product curve will slope upward, or slope downward, or be horizontal, as we move to the right?

IR8-4. Explain the Law of Diminishing Returns.

THE SHORT-RUN COSTS OF PRODUCTION

So far, we've talked about the relationship between inputs and outputs. That's fine, as far as it goes. But a business firm like Cider Space is interested in more than the number of gallons of cider that it can produce. The firm is ultimately interested in the number of *dollars* that it must spend for its inputs. In this section, we show how the firm can begin with information on the productivity of its inputs, and end up with information on the dollar amount of its costs.

Variable Costs and Fixed Costs

In the previous section, we distinguished between variable inputs and fixed inputs. Here, we make a similar distinction between variable costs and fixed costs. **Variable costs are the costs of variable inputs.** If the firm wants to produce more output, it will have to use more variable inputs. For example, one way for the firm to increase output is to use more of the variable input called labor—that is, the firm can increase output by hiring more workers. However, if the firm hires more workers, it will have to pay more wages. Therefore, its variable costs will increase. *Whenever any business firm wants to produce more output, it will have to pay more variable costs.*

Total variable cost is the total of all of the payments to variable inputs. For example, if there were six different variable inputs, total variable cost would include the costs for each of the six. However, in the case of Cider Space, we are assuming that labor is the *only* variable input. Therefore, in this case, total variable cost is the sum of the payments to workers.

Fixed costs are the costs of fixed inputs. Total fixed cost is the total of all of the payments to fixed inputs. Recall that the quantity of a fixed input can't be changed during the time period under consideration. Therefore, *total fixed cost will be the same, regardless of the level of output. Even if output is zero, total fixed cost won't change.* In the case of Cider Space,

the lease on the cider mill itself is the firm's only fixed cost. If the cost of leasing the cider mill is $200 per day, then total fixed cost is $200, *even if output is zero.*

The Relationship Between Total Product and Total Variable Cost

We have just seen that fixed costs and fixed inputs remain the same, even when the level of output changes. Therefore, fixed costs don't have anything to do with changes in the level of output. If we want the quantity of output to increase, we must increase total *variable* cost. We can use our example of the apple-cider mill to illustrate the relationship between total product and total variable cost.

In this example, we assume that labor is the only variable input for Cider Space. Therefore, if the firm wants to produce more apple cider, it must hire more workers. Since Cider Space is very small relative to the labor market in its area, its hiring decisions don't have any effect on overall wage rates in the area. We will assume that the firm takes the wage rate as given: Cider Space can hire as many workers as it wants, at the going market wage.

Notice that this assumption is similar to the assumption that we made regarding consumers, in Chapter 7. We assumed that each individual consumer is small relative to the market. Thus, the consumer can buy as many units as desired, at the going market price. Here, we assume that the firm is small relative to the market, so that it can hire as many workers as desired, at the going market wage rate.

Let's assume that the going market wage rate is $100 per day, for the type of worker that Cider Space might hire. The first worker will cost $100 per day; two workers will cost a total of $200 per day; and so on.

The first three columns of Table 8.3 show the number of workers, the corresponding total product, and the total variable cost.

Notice that Table 8.3 only considers six workers, whereas Table 8.2 had eight workers. The reason for this is that the seventh worker's marginal product is zero, and the eighth worker's marginal product is negative. It would be crazy for a business firm to hire workers who don't create positive marginal product. Therefore, from now on, we won't consider the possibility of a seventh or eighth worker.

Figure 8.3 represents some of the same information that was shown in Table 8.3. Among other things, Figure 8.3 includes a graph of the relationship between total product (that is, the quantity of output) and total variable cost.

Figure 8.3 shows that the graph of total variable cost is *not* a straight line. Here's why: Each additional worker costs an extra $100 per day. Therefore, there is no change in the amount of money that the firm must spend to hire an additional worker, when more workers are hired. However, the marginal product of an additional worker *does* change as the number of workers changes. For example, the first worker's marginal product is 100 gallons, and the second worker's marginal product is 150 gallons.

The total variable cost for the first 100 gallons of cider is $100, which is what Cider Space has to pay to hire one worker. When the

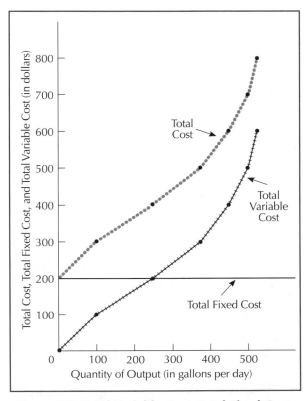

Figure 8.3 Total Variable Cost, Total Fixed Cost, and Total Cost for Cider Space

Fixed inputs do not change as the quantity of output changes. Therefore, the graph of total fixed cost (TFC) is a horizontal line. Total cost (TC) is equal to TFC plus total variable cost (TVC). Since TFC is a constant, the vertical distance between the TVC curve and the TC curve is always the same.

Table 8.3 Total Production Costs for Cider Space

Number of Workers	Quantity of Output = Q = Total Product = Number of Gallons Produced Per Day	Total Variable Cost = $100 (The Daily Wage) x Number of Workers	Total Fixed Cost	Total Cost
0	0	$ 0	$200	$200
1	100	100	200	300
2	250	200	200	400
3	375	200	200	500
4	450	400	200	600
5	500	500	200	700
6	525	600	200	800

firm hires a second worker, its total variable cost doubles, from $100 to $200, but its quantity of output *more* than doubles, from 100 gallons to 250 gallons. In Figure 8.3, this means that the TVC curve gets less steep when we move from an output of 100 gallons to an output of 250 gallons. For similar reasons, the TVC curve gets steeper when we go to higher levels of output. In other words, the TVC curve is relatively flat when the marginal product of the variable inputs is relatively high, and the TVC curve is relatively steep when the marginal product of the variable inputs is relatively low.

Total Fixed Cost, Total Variable Cost, and Total Cost

As we saw in the previous section, total fixed cost is a constant, which doesn't change when the quantity of output changes. Therefore, as shown in Figure 8.3, the graph of total fixed cost is a horizontal line.

Total cost (TC) is equal to total variable cost (TVC) plus total fixed cost (TFC):

TC = TVC + TFC.

Thus, total cost includes total variable cost (which changes when the quantity of output changes), and total fixed cost (which doesn't

change when the quantity of output changes). This means that *any changes in total cost are caused by changes in total variable cost.*

Total cost is also shown in Figure 8.3. Notice that the graph of total cost is parallel to the graph of total variable cost: The vertical distance between the TC curve and the TVC curve is always the same, since the change in total cost is equal to the change in total variable cost.

Average Costs

We have now seen the relationships between total fixed cost, total variable cost, and total cost. These relationships are important, but they aren't the only ones that the business firm cares about. We'll discuss some of the other cost relationships in this section.

Average Variable Cost. *Average variable cost* (AVC) is the amount of variable cost per unit of output. AVC is equal to total variable cost (TVC) divided by total product (Q):

AVC = TVC / Q.

For our example of Cider Space, average variable cost is shown in the third column of Table 8.4. The AVC curve is one of the relationships that are graphed in Figure 8.4.

Table 8.4 Total and Average Costs of Production for Cider Space

Quantity of Output = Total Product (Q) (in Gallons)	Total Variable Cost (TVC) (in Dollars)	Average Variable Cost(AVC) = TVC / Q (in Dollars Per Gallon)	Total Fixed Cost (TFC) (in Dollars)	Average Fixed Cost (AFC) = TFC / Q (in Dollars Per Gallon)	Total Cost (TC) = TVC + TFC (in Dollars)	Average Total Cost (ATC) = TC / Q (in Dollars Per Gallon)
0	$ 0	—	$200	—	$200	—
100	100	1.00	200	2.00	300	3.00
250	200	0.80	200	0.80	400	1.60
375	300	0.80	200	0.53	500	1.33
450	400	0.89	200	0.44	600	1.33
500	500	1.00	200	0.40	700	1.40
525	600	1.14	200	0.38	800	1.52

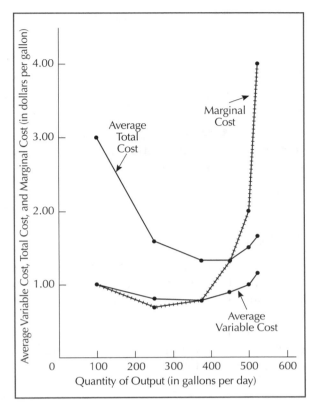

Figure 8.4 Average Variable Cost, Average Total Cost, and Marginal Cost for Cider Space

The marginal *product* of labor increases at first, and then decreases. Since labor is the only variable input, this means that marginal *cost* (MC) decreases at first, and then increases. When MC is below average variable cost (AVC), AVC will decrease. When MC is above AVC, AVC will increase. Therefore, MC crosses AVC at the point where AVC is minimized. Marginal cost also crosses average total cost (ATC) at the point where ATC is minimized. The difference between ATC and AVC is average fixed cost (AFC). AFC decreases as the quantity of output increases. Because of this, the vertical distance between the ATC curve and the AVC curve decreases as the quantity of output increases.

The graph of average variable cost is U-shaped. The downward-sloping portion of the AVC curve is associated with the region of increasing average product, which we saw in Figure 8.2. At the quantity where average product reaches its *highest* point, AVC reaches its *lowest* point. Finally, when average product

starts *downward*, average variable cost heads *upward*.

Thus, in an example like this, where there is only one variable input, average variable cost and average product will always move in opposite directions. Since the firm pays every worker the same wage, AVC will be relatively low when the average worker is very productive. In other words, average variable cost will be low when average product is high. On the other hand, AVC will be high when the average worker is not very productive: Average variable cost will be high when average product is low.

Average Fixed Cost. **Average fixed cost (AFC) is the amount of fixed cost per unit of output.** AFC is given by

AFC = TFC / Q,

where Q is total product. For our example of Cider Space, average fixed cost can be found in the fifth column of Table 8.4.

Remember that total fixed cost is a constant—it doesn't change when there is a change in the level of output. If we take a constant (like TFC) and divide it by a number that keeps increasing (like Q), we get a ratio that keeps decreasing. For example, total fixed cost for Cider Space is $200 per day. If Cider Space were to produce only one gallon of apple cider per day, average fixed cost would be ($200 / 1 gallon) = $200 per gallon. If Cider Space were to produce two gallons of apple cider per day, average fixed cost would be ($200 / 2 gallons) = $100 per gallon. The second row of Table 8.4 shows that, if Cider Space were to produce 250 gallons of cider per day, AFC would be ($200 / 250 gallons) = $0.80 per gallon. Thus, *average fixed cost will always decrease when output increases.* At very high levels of output, AFC will get very close to zero.

Average Total Cost. **Average total cost (ATC) is total cost per unit of output.** This includes both fixed costs and variable costs.

We can find ATC in either of two ways. First, we can divide total cost by the quantity of output:

ATC = TC / Q.

For example, when the total product of Cider Space is 100 gallons, total cost is $300. Therefore, average total cost is ($300 / 100 gallons) = $3.00 per gallon. This can be seen in the first row of Table 8.4.

We can get the same result by adding AFC and AVC together:

ATC = AFC + AVC.

For example, when the total product of Cider Space is 100 gallons of cider, average variable cost is $1.00 per gallon, and average fixed cost is $2.00 per gallon. Therefore, average total cost is ($1.00 + $2.00) = $3.00 per gallon.

Sometimes, economists will use the phrase "average cost" to refer to average total cost. In an attempt to avoid confusion, we will always use "average total cost". However, you should know that you may hear the phrase "average cost", and that this is the same as "average total cost".

Average total cost is shown in the seventh column of Table 8.4. It is graphed in Figure 8.4. As you look at Figure 8.4, you will see that we have included average *variable* cost and average *total* cost, but we haven't included average *fixed* cost. This is because the graph would become cluttered and hard to read, if we were to include average fixed cost. However, Figure 8.4 does reveal information about average fixed cost. Remember that ATC = AFC + AVC. If we subtract AFC from both sides of this expression, we see that AFC = ATC - AVC: Average fixed cost is the difference between average total cost and average variable cost. Therefore, at any quantity of output, the vertical distance between the ATC curve and the AVC curve gives us the value of AFC. As quantity increases in Figure 8.4, there is a decrease in the vertical distance between ATC

and AVC. This is another way of saying that average fixed cost decreases when quantity increases.

Marginal Cost

We now come to the most important cost concept of all. ***Marginal cost* is the additional cost that is necessary to produce one additional unit of output.** It is defined as

Marginal Cost =

$$\frac{\text{Change in Total Cost}}{\text{Change in Total Product}} = \frac{\Delta TC}{\Delta Q}$$

Remember that fixed costs don't change when the level of output changes. Consequently, when output changes, the *variable* costs are the only costs that are changing. This means that the change in total cost is exactly equal to the change in total variable cost. Therefore, another way to define marginal cost is

Marginal Cost =

$$\frac{\text{Change in Total Variable Cost}}{\text{Change in Total Product}} = \frac{\Delta TVC}{\Delta Q}$$

Let's calculate marginal cost in the apple-cider example. When Cider Space hires the first worker, the firm gets additional output of 100 gallons of cider, and it has to pay the worker $100. Thus, dividing $100 by 100 gallons of cider, we get marginal cost of $1.00 per gallon. In other words, in this range of Cider Space's output, if the firm wants to produce one additional gallon of cider, it must pay additional costs of one dollar. The second worker produces additional output of 150 gallons, but the additional cost to hire the second worker is still just $100. Thus, in this case, marginal cost is ($100 / 150 gallons) = $0.667 per gallon. The numbers for marginal cost are shown in the last column of Table 8.5. The marginal cost information is also graphed in Figure 8.4.

Table 8.5 Average and Marginal Costs of Production for Cider Space

Quantity of Output = Total Product (Q) (in Gallons)	Average Variable Cost (AVC) = (TVC / Q) (in Dollars Per Gallon)	Average Fixed Cost (AFC) = (TFC / Q) (in Dollars Per Gallon)	Average Total Cost (ATC) = (TC / Q) = (AVC + AFC) (in Dollars Per Gallon)	Marginal Cost (MC) = (Δ TC / Δ Q) (in Dollars Per Additional Gallon)
100	1.00	2.00	3.00	1.00
250	0.80	0.80	1.60	0.67
375	0.80	0.53	1.33	0.80
450	0.89	0.44	1.33	1.33
500	1.00	0.40	1.40	2.00
525	1.14	0.38	1.52	4.00

We have already seen that average product is maximized when average product equals marginal product. A similar relationship occurs here. From Table 8.5 or Figure 8.4, you can see that *average variable cost is minimized when average variable cost equals marginal cost.* In other words, at the quantity where the AVC curve reaches its lowest point, the MC curve will cross the AVC curve.

It's also true that *average total cost is minimized when average total cost equals marginal cost.* That is, if we find the quantity at which the ATC curve reaches its lowest point, the MC curve will cross the ATC curve at that same quantity.

When a business firm is deciding how much to produce, it will continually ask: "If we produce one more unit, can we increase our profit?" If the answer is "no" then the firm will ask: "If we produce one *less* unit, would that increase our profit?" By thinking in this way, the firm will find the level of output at which profit is maximized. Therefore, the firm will always want to concentrate on *marginal* costs and *marginal* revenues. This is why marginal costs are the most important of all.

In the most recent few pages, we have presented a large number of terms and definitions. These are summarized in Table 8.6.

Reality Check: Interim Review Questions

IR8-5. If total fixed cost is $10 and total product is 5 units, what is average fixed cost?

IR8-6. When total product is 10 units, total variable cost is $100. When total product is 11 units, total variable cost is $105. What is the marginal cost of the 11th unit of output?

IR8-7. When total product is zero, total cost is $10,000. What is total fixed cost?

Table 8.6 Summary of Terms and Definitions on Production and Cost

Term	Abbreviation (if any)	Definition	Equation (if any)
Variable input		An input whose quantity can be varied during the time period under consideration	
Fixed input		An input whose quantity *cannot* be varied during the time period under consideration	
Short Run		Period of time during which at least one input is fixed	
Long Run		Period of time during which all inputs are variable	
Total Product	Q	Total output produced by the firm	
Marginal Product	MP	Change in total product divided by change in amount of some variable input	MP = (Change in Q) / (Change in variable input)
Average Product	AP	Total product divided by the amount of some variable input	AP = (Q) / (variable input)
Total Variable Cost	TVC	Total spending by the firm for variable inputs	
Total Fixed Cost	TFC	Total spending by the firm for fixed inputs. TFC does not change as output changes	
Total Cost	TC	Total spending by the firm for both fixed and variable inputs.	TC = TFC + TVC
Average Variable Cost	AVC	Total variable cost per unit of output (equals total variable cost divided by number of units of output)	AVC = TVC / Q
Average Fixed Cost	AFC	Total fixed cost per unit of output (equals total fixed cost divided by number of units of output)	AFC = TFC / Q
Average Total Cost	ATC	Total cost per unit of output and ATC = AVC + AFC	ATC = TC / Q and ATC = AVC + AFC
Marginal Cost	MC	Change in total cost as a result of producing one additional unit of output	$MC = \dfrac{\text{change in TC}}{\text{change in Q}}$

THE LONG-RUN COSTS OF PRODUCTION

In the short run, at least one input is fixed. In the long run, all inputs are variable. In our example of Cider Space, we have thus far looked only at the short run. In the short run, the firm's labor is its variable input, and the cider mill itself is the fixed input.

Let's say that Cider Space has a two-year lease on its building and equipment. This means that the long run is two years for Cider Space. When that lease is up, the firm must decide whether to continue in the same building, with the same equipment. If not, it must decide how big its next cider mill should be. If Cider Space chooses a larger building, then it will have a different set of short-run

average-total-cost curves and marginal-cost curves.

In fact, the firm will potentially have a very large number of short-run average-total-cost curves and marginal-cost curves. Each of these corresponds to a particular size of building. In Figure 8.5, we see a whole family of short-run average-total-cost curves, labeled SRAC, and a whole family of short-run marginal-cost curves, labeled SRMC. Right now, the firm uses a fairly small building. The cost curves for this size of building were shown in Figure 8.4. In Figure 8.5, these are marked "$SRMC_{now}$" and "$SRAC_{now}$".

From Figure 8.5, you can see that the firm

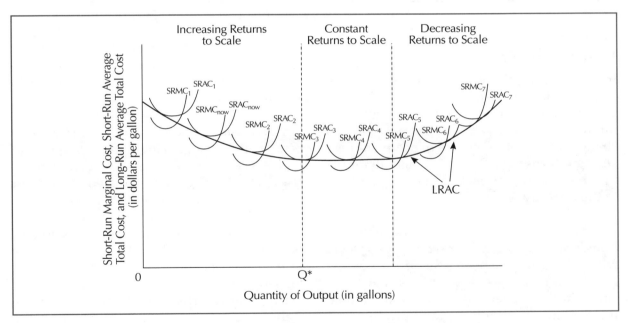

Figure 8.5 Long-Run Average Total Cost for Cider Space

In the long run, *all* inputs are variable. This graph shows several pairs of short-run marginal-cost curves (SRMC) and short-run average-total-cost curves (SRAC), each corresponding to a different size of plant. The long-run average-total-cost curve (LRAC) connects the SRAC curves. At relatively low levels of output, the firm experiences increasing returns to scale, which means that there are decreases in long-run average total cost. Eventually, the firm reaches a level of output at which it is no longer possible to have increasing returns to scale. This level of output is called minimum efficient scale, and it is shown as Q^*. As the level of output increases beyond Q^*, the firm experiences constant returns to scale. In this region, the LRAC curve is a horizontal line. Finally, at even higher levels of output, the firm experiences decreasing returns to scale, which is represented by the portion of the LRAC curve that slopes upward to the right.

would have lower short-run costs if it were to use a somewhat larger mill. Eventually, however, we might get to a mill that is so large that it becomes hard to manage. If so, the short-run costs associated with a very large mill would be higher than the short-run costs associated with a somewhat smaller mill. This is shown in Figure 8.5, where the short-run costs are eventually higher for a larger scale of operations.

Underneath all of the short-run average-total-cost curves in Figure 8.5, we have drawn the long-run average-total-cost curve, which is labeled LRAC. We see that the current size of cider mill does *not* give Cider Space the lowest possible costs. The least-cost cider mill is about twice the size of the current cider mill. This implies that, when its current lease is up, Cider Space should think very seriously about expanding.

Returns to Scale

In constructing the *short-run* cost curves, we hold constant the size of the mill. In constructing the *long-run* cost curves, we allow *all* inputs to change. When we allow *all* inputs to change, we observe **returns to scale**. In measuring returns to scale, we increase all inputs by the same proportion, and see what happens to the quantity of output.

Increasing Returns to Scale. We have **increasing returns to scale** or **economies of scale** when the percentage increase in output is *greater* than the percentage increase in inputs. Under increasing returns to scale, if we double the amounts of all inputs, total product will *more* than double.

When a firm is experiencing increasing returns to scale, what will happen to its costs? To answer this question, let's assume that the firm is small relative to all of the markets in which it buys inputs. If this is the case, then the firm will take input prices as given. If every unit of an input is paid the same as any other unit, then doubling all inputs will dou-

ble the firm's costs. Under increasing returns to scale, when all inputs are increased by the same proportion, output increases by an even greater proportion. Thus, *under increasing returns to scale, when costs double, outputs more than double. This means that long-run average total cost will decrease.* Increasing returns to scale are observed in the left-hand portion of Figure 8.5, where the long-run average-total-cost curve slopes downward to the right.

Constant Returns to Scale. We have **constant returns to scale** when the percentage change in output is *the same* as the percentage change in all inputs. For example, under constant returns to scale, if we double all inputs, the level of output will double. Thus, under constant returns to scale, when costs double, outputs also double. This means that, if the firm is experiencing constant returns to scale, long-run average total cost will stay the same. Constant returns to scale are seen in the area where the LRAC curve is a horizontal line, in Figure 8.5.

Decreasing Returns to Scale. We have **decreasing returns to scale** or **diseconomies of scale** when the percentage increase in output is *less* than the percentage increase in all inputs. In this case, if we double the amounts of all inputs, the output will *not* double. Thus, under decreasing returns to scale, when costs double, outputs will not double. This means that, if the firm is experiencing decreasing returns to scale, long-run average total costs will increase. Decreasing returns to scale are seen in the right-hand portion of Figure 8.5, where the LRAC curve slopes upward to the right.

Firms sometimes encounter decreasing returns to scale when they have difficulty in managing and coordinating the activities of ever-increasing numbers of workers, buildings, machines, and so on. However, for some production processes, decreasing returns don't set in until the firm reaches a very high level of output. For example, studies of the automobile industry have shown that firms can grow to be multi-billion-dollar enterprises before they encounter decreasing returns to scale.

Many production processes have increasing returns to scale, at least up to a certain point. Beyond that point, it is common to have constant returns to scale over a fairly large range of sizes. In a case like this, we say that the firm reaches its *minimum efficient scale* when it no longer has increasing returns to scale. At output levels below the minimum efficient scale, the firm would be able to decrease its long-run average total cost by increasing the scale of its operations. In Figure 8.5, the firm's minimum efficient scale is Q^*.

In *Real Economics for Real People 8.2*, we discuss returns to scale in the supermarket industry.

Reality Check:
Interim Review Questions

IR8-8. The LRAC curve for Corporation X is a horizontal line. What does this imply about the returns to scale for Corporation X?

IR8-9. If Corporation Y were to increase all of its inputs by 20 percent, its output would increase by 30 percent. In this range of output, does Corporation Y have increasing returns to scale, constant returns to scale, or decreasing returns to scale? In this range of output, does Corporation Y's LRAC curve slope upward, or downward, or is it horizontal?

Returns to Scale and International Trade

The idea of scale economies is very important for our understanding of the effects of tariffs and other barriers to international trade. Many economists have attempted to measure the gains from removing trade barriers, using computer simulation models. Most of these models have assumed that production is characterized by constant returns to scale. However, some economists have recently suggested that scale economies play an important role. If there are trade barriers, a firm can survive, even when it is operating at less than the minimum efficient scale. In other words, with trade barriers, firms don't always take advantage of scale economies, and inefficiently small firms can stay in business. On the other hand, if the trade barriers were removed, the firms would be forced to take advantage of scale economies, in order to survive: With no trade protection, the firms would have to minimize their long-run average total cost, or they would go out of business.

Richard Harris, a Canadian economist, has done research using a computer simulation model that has scale economies. He shows that the gains from removing trade barriers for a country like Canada can be very large. A large portion of these gains comes about because, when trade barriers are removed, Canadian firms become more efficient. As the firms take advantage of scale economies, their long-run average total costs go down.

ECONOMIC COSTS VS. ACCOUNTING COSTS

Economists and accountants define costs differently. The difference arises because economists use the idea of opportunity cost, whereas accountants do not.

When an accountant puts together a balance sheet for a firm, he or she will focus on the *explicit* costs of the firm. These are the direct, out-of-pocket costs, such as payments

of wages, purchases of materials, and so on. If the firm has a check stub saying that it paid wages to a worker, the accountant will record the expense. *Accounting cost* is the sum of all of these explicit, out-of-pocket costs.

However, accounting costs don't necessarily include all of the relevant costs. To see this, consider the following example: Lyle

Real Economics for Real People 8.2:
Can Retail Stores Ever Be Too Big?

An average-size discount store covers about 70,000 square feet, or about the size of a major league baseball field. Such a store might have 200 to 300 employees, and might stock as many as 80,000 different items on its shelves.

A large retail establishment like this has some clear cost advantages over a "Mom-&-Pop" operation. With its larger scale of operations, it can afford to take advantage of economies of scale in receiving deliveries and keeping its shelves stocked. It may be possible to have greater specialization among its workers, and this may also make for a more efficient operation. In addition to these cost considerations, a larger retailer may also attract consumers because it can offer the advantages of "one-stop shopping".

So, if an average-size discount store has cost advantages over a small store, does an even larger store have advantages over an average discount store? In other words, do we continue to have increasing returns to scale as the store gets bigger and bigger?

The answer is that we may not. There is some evidence that stores can actually be too big. Although some retailers have been successful with "Super Centers" of 150,000 square feet or more, the experience with even-larger "Hypermarkets" has not always been good. Hypermarkets typically have over 200,000 square feet of floor space, and sometimes even have more than 300,000. They may have as many as 600 workers. At this scale of operations, the problems of management and coordination can get serious. Regardless of cost concerns, hypermarkets can create problems for customers. The prospect of getting lost while wandering among acres and acres of shelves can be daunting to some shoppers.

We don't have enough information to make a blanket statement about whether hypermarkets can succeed. It may be possible for such stores to succeed in some regions of the country, but not in others. Or it may be that improved marketing and management can help to improve the operations of very large stores. However, we do know that some of the nation's largest retailers have been disappointed with the performance of their hypermarkets. Wal-Mart Stores built just four of its Hypermart USA Stores before stopping the program. And Kmart Corporation has sustained losses in its American Fare stores.

Robinson owns an ice-cream store. He doesn't pay himself a salary, as such. Since no explicit payment is made, an accountant would not include Lyle's labor as a cost. From the economist's point of view, though, the time that Lyle spends working at the store is most definitely a cost. It is a cost because of the *opportunity cost* of working at the ice-cream store. If Lyle didn't work at the ice-cream store, he could earn money somewhere else.

Before he opened the ice-cream store, Lyle worked as a loan officer in a bank. If he wants to, he could go back to a job in the financial-services industry, at an annual salary of $40,000. Thus, we would say that the opportunity cost of Lyle's time is $40,000 per year.

Let's say that Lyle's accountant tells him that the ice-cream store's revenues for the year are $200,000, and its out-of-pocket expenses are $150,000. Thus, the accountant would say that Lyle's profit is ($200,000 − $150,000) = $50,000. In other words,

**Accounting Profit =
Total Revenue −
Explicit, Accounting Costs**

However, this calculation gives a misleading impression, because it doesn't include all of the true economic costs. Economists say that *economic costs* are the payments that a firm must make, in order to attract resources away from other activities in which they might be used. Economic costs include the explicit, accounting costs, *and* they also include *implicit* costs, such as the opportunity cost of Lyle's time.

**Economic Costs =
Accounting Cost + Implicit Costs**

Economic profit is equal to total revenue minus all costs, regardless of whether they are explicit or implicit. In other words,

Economic Profit
= Total Revenue − Economic Cost
= Total Revenue − Accounting Costs −
    Implicit Costs
= Accounting Profit − Implicit Costs

Figure 8.6 is a graphical representation of the differences between economic costs and accounting costs.

In our example of Lyle, the owner of an ice-cream store, an economist would say that Lyle has to pay an implicit cost when he runs the ice-cream store. The implicit cost is the opportunity cost of his time, which is $40,000 per year. To find Lyle's true *economic* profit, we subtract the opportunity cost of his time from the accounting profit. This gives us an economic profit of ($50,000 − $40,000) = $10,000.

What if Lyle's accounting profit were only $40,000? In this case, his economic profit from the ice-cream store would be ($40,000 − $40,000) = zero. When you see that Lyle's economic profit is zero, you might think that it's bad

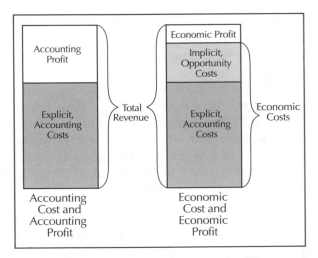

Figure 8.6 Accounting Cost, Accounting Profit, Economic Cost, and Economic Profit

Accounting cost includes only the explicit, out-of-pocket costs that are paid by the firm. Economic cost includes accounting cost, *plus* any implicit opportunity costs. These implicit opportunity costs include a "normal" rate of return on capital investment. Thus, economic cost is greater than accounting cost. Accounting profit is total revenue minus accounting cost, and economic profit is total revenue minus economic cost. Therefore, economic profit is less than accounting profit.

news, but it really is not a problem. When Lyle is making an economic profit of zero in the ice-cream store, it means that he is doing just as well at the ice-cream store as he would have done in his alternative employment in a bank. Thus, there is no reason for Lyle to abandon the ice-cream store.

But what is Lyle's accounting profit were only $20,000? In this case, his economic profit from the ice-cream store would be ($20,000 − $40,000), or −$20,000. We have just seen that an economic profit of zero is OK, but this is a *negative* economic profit, and that is definitely bad news. When Lyle's economic profit from the ice-cream store is −$20,000, he could do a lot better by giving up the ice-cream store and getting a job with a bank.

Economic costs and economic profit provide extremely important information, because they are defined to include opportunity cost. If the business firm is making a positive economic profit, or a zero economic profit, there is no incentive to change its actions. However, if the business firm is making negative economic profits, it should consider the possibility of going out of business. In Chapter 9, we will take a detailed look at the decision to go out of business.

A "Normal" Rate of Return

In the case of Lyle Robinson, the owner of the ice-cream store, the difference between accounting cost and economic cost is the amount that he could earn if he were to work in a bank. In this example, the relevant opportunity cost is the value of the *labor* that is provided by the owner of the firm. In other cases, the value of *capital* can be an important opportunity cost, as well.

Investors expect to earn a positive rate of return on their capital investments. Let's say that the "normal" rate of return on a capital investment is 10 percent per year. If this is the case, then a 10-percent rate of return is the opportunity cost of capital investment. Even though this "normal" rate of return is not an explicit, accounting cost, it certainly is an economic cost. After all, if a firm had not invested in its current line of business, it could have invested in some other line of business. The firm could earn a "normal" return by investing in a portfolio of stocks from many different companies. If the firm is earning less than the "normal" or "average" return, it could do better by going out of business and putting the money where it *does* earn a normal return.

What is a "normal" return on investment? In fact, what is "normal" may change from year to year. However, when you think of a normal return, you might think of a rate of return of 10 percent per year, or 12 percent, or 15 percent.

As a result of this way of thinking, economists say that the firm is making zero *economic* profits, even when it makes a normal return on its capital investment. Let's assume that a normal rate of return is 10 percent per year. Then, if the firm earns an accounting profit of 18 percent per year, it is making an economic profit of (18–10) = 8 percent per year. If the firm earns an accounting profit of 10 percent per year, it is making zero economic profit. Still, if the firm is earning zero economic profit, it should stay in business, because it is doing as well as the market average. Only when the firm is earning a negative economic profit should it think about going out of business. We will return to these issues in Chapter 9.

Sunk Costs

A *sunk cost* is an expenditure that has already been made in the past, and cannot be recovered. As a result, it should not have any influence on our decisions. We make decisions regarding the future, not the past.

Let's think about a firm that buys a new boiler in September, 1973, when the price of oil is low. Because oil is cheap at this time, there isn't much of an incentive to use technologies that will conserve oil. Therefore, the boiler's technology uses a lot of oil. Assume that the boiler is highly specialized, so that this firm can't sell it to some other firm.

One month after the boiler is installed, the Organization of Petroleum Exporting Countries (OPEC) succeeds in raising the price of oil by 300 percent. The firm may *wish* that it hadn't bought the inefficient boiler, but the old boiler is a sunk cost. It has no alternative use, and its opportunity cost is zero. Therefore, it shouldn't have any influence on the firm's decisions. If the firm now wants to buy a more energy-efficient boiler, it should compare the cost of the *new* boiler with the projected savings in fuel costs. The amount that it paid for the *old* boiler is irrelevant. For better or worse, the past has already happened, and we can't change it. Therefore, whenever we make a decision, we are looking toward the future. Yesterday is gone, and we can't get it back.

In *Real Economics for Real People 8.3,* we take a look at another example involving sunk costs.

Reality Check:
Interim Review Questions

IR8-10. Is economic cost greater than, equal to, or less than accounting cost?

IR8-11. Is economic profit greater than, equal to, or less than accounting cost?

IR8-12. Joe's Burger Joint is earning an accounting profit of 6%. The normal rate of return on an investment in the burger industry is 12%. What is Joe's economic profit?

ECONOMICS AND YOU:
IF YOU'VE ALREADY PAID FOR IT,
YOU SHOULDN'T EAT IT UNLESS YOU WANT TO

At the beginning of this chapter, we considered the situation of Allison and Zachary, who paid $8 for an all-you-can-eat spaghetti dinner, only to find that the food was very bad.

Our analysis of sunk costs can help us to understand this situation. Allison and Zachary probably *wish* that they hadn't paid $8. But that money is a sunk cost. Zachary says that he wants to pig out, because he wants to get his "money's worth." But this doesn't make any sense. His money is gone, and no amount of horrible pasta will get the money back.

After Zachary pays at the door, he doesn't have to pay any more money to get more food at Pat's Pasta Palace. In other words, the opportunity cost to Zachary of eating the pasta is zero. If the benefit of eating the spaghetti is greater than zero, he should eat. If not, then he should not eat. If he decides that he doesn't want to eat at Pat's Pasta Palace, he still has other alternatives. If he wants, he can go across the street to Samantha's, and buy food there. If the marginal benefit from eating at Samantha's is greater than the marginal cost, then Zachary will come out ahead.

It was Allison who said "As for getting my money's worth, I kissed my eight dollars goodbye when I paid at the door." Zachary would do well to listen to her. If he tries to get his "money's worth," all he is likely to get is indigestion.

Of course, sunk costs are not the only costs that we have considered in this chapter. Much of our emphasis was on the relationships between production and cost for the business firm. We have made a distinction between fixed inputs and variable inputs, and between fixed costs and variable costs. We have shown how the business firm can calculate its total costs and average costs. Most important of all, we've shown how the business firm can calculate its marginal cost.

For many students, this information on production and costs is not very satisfying. In this chapter, we have said a lot about how to *define* costs, and how to *calculate* them, but we have only said a little about how to *use* this information. It's understandable if this is frustrating. However, you can rest assured that we *will* show how to use this information, especially in Chapters 9, 10, and 11. In those chapters, we will concentrate on how business firms actually behave. Usually, we assume that business firms want to maximize their profits. Profits are equal to the difference between total revenues and total costs. Thus, if we want to know something about profits, we have to know something about costs. Now that you have read this chapter, you have an understanding of costs. In the chapters to come, you will build on that understanding again and again.

Chapter Summary

1. In the short run, at least one input is fixed. The Law of Diminishing Returns describes a production relationship that is often observed in the short run. The Law of Diminishing Returns states that, if we increase one input repeatedly, while holding all other inputs constant, the amount of additional output that we get will eventually decline.

2. Variable costs are the costs that the firm pays for its variable inputs. Fixed costs are the costs that the firm pays for its fixed inputs. The distinction between variable costs and fixed costs is only relevant in the short run. In the long run, all inputs are variable.

3. Marginal cost is the additional cost that the firm has to pay when it produces one additional unit of output. By definition, marginal costs must be variable costs, since fixed costs are paid regardless of the level of production.

4. Short-run average-total-cost curves are often U-shaped. Average total cost decreases when the level of output is small, because average fixed cost goes down when quantity goes up. Eventually, however, average total cost may be pulled up by increasing marginal costs. At the quantity at which average total cost is minimized, average total cost equals marginal cost.

5. In the long run, all inputs are freely variable, so that the firm can adjust its entire scale of operations. We say that the firm has increasing returns to scale if its output more than doubles when all of its inputs double. If the firm has increasing returns to scale, its long-run average-total-cost curve will slope downward to the right. We have constant returns to scale if, when all inputs increase by a given proportion, output increases by that same proportion. If the firm has constant returns to scale, its long-run average-total-curve is a horizontal line. If all inputs increase by the same proportion and output increases by a smaller proportion, we have decreasing returns to scale. In this case, the long-run average-total-cost curve will slope upward to the right.

6. Economists use the idea of opportunity cost. Thus, economic cost is defined to include the "normal" return on a capital investment. Economic profit is defined to be net of this normal return. Economic cost is larger than accounting cost, so that economic profit is less than accounting profit.

Key Terms

Outputs

Inputs

Variable Inputs

Fixed Inputs

Short Run

Long Run

Total Product

Quantity of Output

Marginal Product

Average Product

Law of Diminishing Returns

Variable Costs

Total Variable Cost

Fixed Costs

Total Fixed Cost

Total Cost

Average Variable Cost

Average Fixed Cost

Average Total Cost

Marginal Cost

Returns to Scale

Increasing Returns to Scale

Economies of Scale

Constant Returns to Scale

Decreasing Returns to Scale

Diseconomies of Scale

Minimum Efficient Scale

Accounting Cost

Economic Cost

Economic Profit

Sunk Cost

Key Figure
The key figure for this chapter is Figure 8.4.

Questions and Problems

QP8-1. Use the table below to answer the following questions:

a. What is the average product of labor when two units of labor are employed?
b. What is the marginal product of the third unit of labor?
c. Does the Law of Diminishing Returns apply to the data shown here?

QP8-2. Which of the following is a short-run decision? Which deals with the long run?

a. A mail-order catalog company hires six extra customer-service representatives.
b. A hardware store chain opens up a new store.
c. A corn farmer applies additional fertilizer to a cornfield.
d. A corn farmer cuts down some trees, in order to increase the size of the cornfield.

QP8-3. Fill in the blanks in the first table on the next page.

QP8-4. Explain the distinction between the following pairs of concepts:

a. Economic costs and accounting costs.
b. Economic profits and accounting profits.
c. Short run and long run.
d. Fixed costs and variable costs.

QP8-5. If marginal cost is above average total cost, is average total cost increasing, or decreasing, or constant? How would your answer change if marginal cost is equal to average total cost? What if marginal cost is less than average total cost?

QP8-6. During television broadcasts of professional football games, it is common to announce the attendance and the number of "no-shows" (people who purchased tickets but who did not come to the stadium). Explain why it might be rational for a season-ticket holder to be a no-show.

QP8-7. In the diagram below, identify the regions of increasing returns to scale, constant returns to scale, and decreasing returns to scale.

QP8-8. Fill in the blanks in the second table on the next page.
    Now, assume that the wage rate for each of the workers in the table above is $8, and the rental rate for each of the machines is $6.

Units of Labor	Units of Output
0	0
1	10
2	24
3	35
4	43

Quantity Of Output	TVC	ATC	TC	MC
0	0	—	20	—
1	10	_____	30	_____
2	_____	19	38	_____
3	28	_____	_____	10
4	_____	_____	60	12
5	56	12.67	76	_____
6	_____	16	_____	20

Number of Workers	Number of Machines	Units of Output	Marginal Product of Labor	Average Product of Labor
1	4	3	—	_____
2	4	_____	4	3.5
3	4	12	_____	_____
4	4	18	_____	4.5
5	4	_____	_____	5.0
6	4	_____	8	5.5

a. What is average variable cost when the number of workers is 3?

b. What is average fixed cost when the number of workers is 3?

c. What is average total cost when output is 12?

QP8-9. If the marginal product of labor is the same for every worker, what can be said about the average product of labor?

Chapter 9

Perfect Competition

ECONOMICS AND YOU:
CAN YOU MAKE A BUNDLE IN THE STOCK MARKET?

Frank Owens and Jenny Krueger work for a software-consulting firm. In their spare time, they like to "play the stock market". They read *Barron's*, the Wall Street *Journal,* and other financial publications, looking for hot ideas. Then, they buy the stocks of companies that they think will do unusually well.

Over lunch one day, Frank says "I'm a smart guy. I think I can pick stocks that will do better than the market average for the next year." But Jenny isn't so sure. OK, she says, it's true that your stock picks have made good money in the last few years. But in the 1990s, nearly everyone has done well in the stock market. The Dow Jones Industrial Average (DJIA), which is the most widely quoted measure of stock-market performance, *quadrupled* between January, 1990, and January, 2000! But Frank didn't just predict that his stocks would do *well*. He predicted that his stocks would do *better than average*. We'll see that it might not be very easy to do this, even for a smart guy like Frank.

The DJIA measures the performance of the stocks of 30 large companies that are listed on the New York Stock Exchange (NYSE). Stock markets, such as the NYSE, are examples of what we call "competitive" markets. It's relatively easy to get involved in the stock market, and millions of investors do so. Because so many investors are competing against each other, it may be difficult to do much better than average.

Most of this chapter is devoted to a discussion of "perfectly competitive" markets. We'll develop the theory of the perfectly competitive firm, by working through an example of a company that produces apple cider. (This example was first introduced in Chapter 8.) At the end of the chapter, we will return to the case of the stock market.

At the beginning of Chapter 8, we said that many students find that chapter to be relatively difficult. The same is true for this chapter on perfect competition. Therefore, once again, it's important to go one step at a time: This chapter contains many details, but you should be able to learn the details if you work on them in a systematic way. You may need to go slowly, but don't worry. If you keep at it, you will master the material.

MARKET STRUCTURES

Not all markets are perfectly competitive. In fact, perfect competition is only one of four *market structures*. The term *"market structure"* refers to the way in which the firms in a market relate to each other, and to their buyers. The four market structures are:

- perfect competition or pure competition,
- monopoly,
- monopolistic competition, and
- oligopoly.

In this section, we'll briefly describe the characteristics of the four market structures. Then, in the rest of the chapter, we will take a closer look at perfectly competitive firms and markets.

Perfect Competition

In *perfect competition* or *pure competition*, the market has many firms, and each firm is small relative to the market. Some of the best examples of perfect competition are in agriculture. For instance, more than a million American farms grow grain. Perfect competition can also be found in some other parts of the economy. For example, the cotton-weaving industry has more than 200 firms, and the men's work-clothing industry has nearly 300. There are about 10,000 sawmills in the lumber industry. Stock exchanges, commodity markets, and foreign-exchange markets are also highly competitive, with thousands of sellers.

Another characteristic of perfectly competitive firms is that they produce a *standardized product*, or *homogeneous product*. For example, in the market for winter wheat, Farmer Olson's wheat is virtually identical to Farmer Johnson's wheat.

Since perfectly competitive firms are all small relative to the market, and since they produce homogeneous products, the individual firms are unable to control the prices of the goods that they sell. If Farmer Olson were to raise his price above Farmer Johnson's price, Olson would lose all of his customers.

Changes in *market* supply or *market* demand will lead to changes in *market* price. However, the individual *firm* can't do anything to change the price.

In a perfectly competitive industry, it's relatively easy for new firms to start up. We say that perfectly competitive markets are characterized by *free entry* into the industry: If profits are high, new firms will enter the industry. This will increase the market supply of the product, and will drive the price down, until firms are no longer making economic profits.

Perfectly competitive markets are also characterized by *free exit* from the industry: If firms are losing money, some of them will go out of business. This will decrease market supply and drive up the price, until firms are no longer suffering economic losses.

Monopoly

Perfect competition is at one end of the spectrum of market structures. The opposite end of the spectrum is occupied by *monopoly*, in which there is only one firm in an industry. Some of the best examples of monopolies are in the utilities that provide electric power, or water and sewerage services, or natural gas. In many communities, these services are only provided by one company. Also, most cities have only one cable-TV franchise. Monopolies can also be found at football and baseball stadiums, and in college dormitories: At many of these places, food and beverages are only provided by one company.

If a monopoly is to be maintained over time, there must be some very significant *barriers to entry*, which keep new firms from entering the industry. (If there were no barriers to entry, new firms would enter the market, and the monopoly wouldn't be a monopoly any more.) Sometimes, the barriers to entry have to do with the high cost of setting up a new company. Sometimes, the barriers are the result of legal restrictions, such as patents and exclusive franchise arrangements.

The monopolist's output must not have very close substitutes: If the output has close substitutes, then the firm isn't really a monopoly. For example, the Coca-Cola company is the only producer of the drink known as "Coke", but this doesn't mean that this company is a monopolist. Many consumers view other soft drinks, such as Pepsi Cola and RC Cola, as close substitutes for Coca-Cola. Therefore, instead of saying that the Coca-Cola company is a monopolist in the market for "Coke", we would say that the Coca-Cola company is only one of several firms in the soft-drink market.

We will discuss monopoly in more detail in Chapter 10.

Monopolistic Competition

Perfect competition is at one extreme, and monopoly is at the other extreme. However, most industries fall *in between* the definitions of perfect competition and monopoly. There are two categories of "in-between" market structures. These are called *monopolistic competition* and *oligopoly*.

First, let's talk about monopolistic competition. Ice-cream stores and gasoline stations have some of the characteristics of perfect competition, but they are also different in one important way. The difference is that ice-cream stores and gasoline stations sell *differentiated products,* whereas perfectly competitive firms sell homogeneous, standardized products. When the firms in a market produce goods that have noticeable differences in quality, or location, or service, we say that the market is characterized by **differentiated product**.

For example, one gasoline station may be located right next to the freeway exit ramp, while it might be harder to get to another gasoline station. As a result, the conveniently located station may be able to charge higher prices, without losing all of its customers. Also, one ice-cream store may have more flavors than another store, or it may have a nicer atmosphere. Because of these characteristics, it may be possible for one ice-cream store to charge higher prices, without losing all of its customers. In other words, some gasoline stations and ice-cream stores may be able to control their selling prices, at least to a small degree. (Remember that perfectly competitive firms have no control over price.)

Ice-cream stores and gasoline stations are engaged in *monopolistic competition.* **Monopolistic competition** is similar to perfect competition, in that there are many firms in an industry, and each firm is relatively small, and it's easy to enter the industry or exit from it. The big difference is that monopolistically competitive firms have differentiated products.

Many of the best examples of monopolistic competition are in retailing, because differences in location and the quality of service can be extremely important to retail firms. Monopolistic competition applies to clothing stores and grocery stores, as well as to ice-cream stores and gasoline stations. We will discuss monopolistic competition in detail in Chapter 11.

Oligopoly

Perfect competition and monopolistic competition are both characterized by free entry and exit, and both have a relatively large number of firms. In many important industries, however, there are only a few firms. For example, the automobile industry is dominated by Daimler Chrysler, Ford, General Motors, Honda, Nissan, Toyota, Volkswagen, and a few other large firms. The commercial-aircraft-manufacturing industry includes only two firms: Boeing (of Seattle, Washington), and a European consortium called Airbus.

The automobile industry and the commercial-aircraft-manufacturing industry are examples of *oligopoly*. When a market has only a few firms, we say that it is an *oligopoly*. Many of the best examples of oligopoly are in manufacturing. The photographic-film industry is also an oligopoly, led by Kodak and Fuji. The breakfast-cereal industry is an oligopoly, dominated by General Foods, General Mills, Kellogg, Nabisco, Post, Quaker, and Ralston-Purina.

Whereas competitive industries are characterized by free entry, oligopolies usually have significant barriers to entry. In many cases, the entry barriers have to do with the high costs of setting up a new firm: In steel, automobiles, oil, and other oligopolistic industries, it is often necessary to invest billions of dollars to compete effectively. This means that it's difficult (but not necessarily impossible) for new firms to enter the industry.

The products of oligopolistic firms may be standardized (as in the case of the oil industry), or they may be differentiated (as in the case of the automobile industry and the breakfast-cereal industry).

Because oligopolistic industries have relatively few firms, the firms are very much aware of each other. For example, when General Motors brings out a new model of car, Ford's engineers take it apart, piece by piece. They analyze the car in the smallest detail, looking for technological improvements and ways to cut costs. The automobile firms are also very much aware of each other's TV commercials and other marketing strategies. In oligopolistic industries, firms are *interdependent,* so that strategy becomes important. We will discuss oligopolies and their strategies in Chapter 11.

Sometimes, the firms in an oligopolistic industry try to cooperate with each other. When oligopolistic firms cooperate with each other, we say that they are engaged in *collusion*. If the firms can collude with each other, they may be able to maintain higher prices and higher profits. However, collusion is illegal in the United States. The laws don't eliminate collusion, but they probably mean that we have less collusion than we would otherwise have. We will discuss the laws against collusion in Chapter 12.

The characteristics of the four market structures are summarized in Table 9.1.

Reality Check:
Interim Review Questions

IR9-1. Name the four types of market structure, and give an example of an industry of each type.

IR9-2. In a perfectly competitive market, do the firms have differentiated products? What about the firms in a monopolistically competitive market?

THE IDEAL OF PERFECT COMPETITION

Here again are the key characteristics of a perfectly competitive market:

- many firms, each of which is small relative to the market,

- output that is standardized, or homogeneous, and

- free entry and exit.

We now discuss these characteristics (and some others) in greater detail.

A Large Number of Firms, Each of Which Is Small Relative to the Market

Our first assumption is that perfectly competitive industries have a large number of firms, *each* of which is small relative to the market. If there were one huge firm and hundreds of tiny ones, we wouldn't have a perfectly competitive industry, because the one huge firm would be able to manipulate the price.

Table 9.1 Characteristics of the Different Market Structures

Market Structure	Number Of Firms	Product Differentiation	Ability Of Firms To Control Price	Barriers To Entry	Examples
Pure Competition or Perfect Competition	Many	None: Products Are Standardized	None	None	Agriculture, Sawmills, Some Financial Markets, Some Textiles
Monopolistic Competition	Many	Products Are Differentiated	Depends on Product Differentiation	None	Retailing, Some Manufacturing, Some Publishing
Oligopoly	Few	Can Be Either Standardized or Differentiated	Depends on Interaction Between Firms: Can Be Substantial If Firms Can Collude	Major Barriers	Steel, Automobiles, Breakfast Cereals, Oil, Aircraft Manufacture, Some Chemicals
Monopoly	One	Product Must Not Have Close Substitutes	Very Substantial	Barriers Must Be Very Strong	Electric Utilities, Some Pharmaceuticals

Standardized Product

Another important assumption is that perfectly competitive firms produce an output that is standardized, or homogeneous. What would happen if outputs *weren't* homogeneous? If different firms were to make significantly different products, we would observe two effects. First, if one firm's products are viewed as having higher quality, that firm might be able to raise its price, without losing all of its customers. Second, the firms might engage in non-price competition, such as advertising. When we observe a lot of advertising, as in the automobile industry and the beer industry, we know that we aren't dealing with perfectly competitive firms. If an industry were perfectly competitive, we would observe very little non-price competition, and every firm would charge the same price.

Price-Taking Firms

If a firm is small relative to the market, and if its product is the same as the product of the other firms, then the firm won't have any power to influence the price. It will just take the market price as given. A *price-taking firm* is one that accepts the market price. By assuming that firms are small and that they produce homogeneous products, we are assuming that perfectly competitive firms are price takers.

If a firm is able to control its price, we say that the firm has *market power*. However, a perfectly competitive, price-taking firm does not have any market power.

Freedom of Entry and Exit

We assume that there are no significant barriers to entry into a perfectly competitive industry.

If there are high profits in a perfectly competitive industry (as in the case of the markets for some computer components), new firms will enter the industry. When new firms enter, there is an increase in market supply. This will drive prices down, and the lower prices will lead to reduced profits.

Conversely, if an industry is experiencing economic losses (as in some parts of agriculture), some firms will exit from the industry. When firms exit from the industry, there is a decrease in market supply. This will increase prices, which means that the losses will be reduced.

Perfect Information

If a perfectly competitive market is to work properly, consumers must have accurate information about the market price. After all, if a consumer doesn't *know* the prices that are being charged by different firms, he or she might end up paying a price that is too high. We assume that consumers have all the information that they need, in order to make intelligent decisions.

In fact, as time passes, more and more markets are characterized by perfect information. As consumers make more use of toll-free telephone numbers, Internet shopping, and other services, they have more and more access to accurate information.

Reality Check: Interim Review Question

IR9-3. A perfectly competitive firm has several characteristics. Which of these characteristics are important in making the firm a price-taking firm?

DEMAND AND REVENUE FOR PERFECTLY COMPETITIVE FIRMS

In Chapter 8, we studied the production and cost relationships of Cider Space, a small manufacturer of apple cider. The market for apple cider is perfectly competitive: It's relatively easy to enter the industry, which has many firms. In this section, we will study the demand and revenue relationships for Cider Space. Later in this chapter, we'll put the cost information together with the revenue information. When we know about both costs and revenues, we can determine whether the firm will make a profit.

Perfectly Elastic Demand for the Output of the Price-Taking Firm

In a typical year, Cider Space produces about one-tenth of one percent of the apple cider that is sold in the Midwest. What will happen if Cider Space were to try to drive up the market price of cider, by reducing the quantity of its output? Since Cider Space only produces one-tenth of one percent of the market output, even a ten-percent reduction in the *firm's* quantity will mean that the *market* quantity will go down by only one-hundredth of 1%.

This means that Cider Space will have great difficulty in raising the market price. For all practical purposes, the firm must take the market price as given. Therefore, *the demand for the individual firm's output is perfectly elastic: The firm can sell as many units as it wants to sell, at the going market price.*

It's very important to keep this straight: *Even though the* market *demand may be relatively inelastic, the demand for the output of a perfectly competitive* firm *is perfectly elastic.* The individual firm is a price taker, with no control over the market price. We will assume that *all* perfectly competitive firms are price takers, regardless of whether they are apple-cider mills, barley farms, textile companies, clothing companies, or other firms.

The Revenue Curves for the Perfectly Competitive Firm

The market price is the *only* information that we need to know about the revenues of a perfectly competitive firm. Currently, the market price of apple cider is $2 per gallon. On the basis of this information, we can construct the various revenue schedules for Cider Space. These revenue schedules are shown in Table 9.2, and the corresponding revenue curves are graphed in Figure 9.1.

Cider Space can sell as many gallons of cider as it wants to sell, at the market price of $2 per gallon. If the firm sells one gallon per day, the price is $2 per gallon. If the firm sells 100 gallons per day, the price is still $2 per gallon. Thus, the firm's demand curve in panel (a) of Figure 9.1 is just a horizontal line at the price of $2.

In a perfectly competitive industry, the market demand curve is downward sloping as we move to the right, but the demand curve facing an individual firm is perfectly horizontal.

Marginal Revenue. **Marginal revenue (MR) is the extra amount of money that the firm receives, when it sells one more unit of output.** For managers of any company, marginal revenue is an extremely important piece of information. When Cider Space sells its first gallon of cider, it receives $2. When it sells its second one, it gets another $2. When it sells its hundredth gallon of cider, the extra revenue is still $2. Thus, Cider Space's marginal revenue is $2 for each additional gallon of cider, regardless of how many gallons are produced by the firm. *For any perfectly competitive firm, marginal revenue is given by the market price.*

If we graph the marginal-revenue curve (as in panel (a) of Figure 9.1), we get a horizontal line at $2. For the perfectly competitive firm, the demand curve and the marginal-revenue curve are identical.

Total Revenue. **Total revenue is the total number of dollars that the firm receives from all sales of its product.** If Cider Space were to sell only one gallon of cider, then its total

Table 9.2 Revenue Information for Cider Space

Quantity of Apple Cider Produced (Gallons Per Day)	Price Of Apple Cider, In Dollars Per Gallon	Marginal Revenue, In Dollars Per Additional Gallon	Average Revenue, In Dollars Per Gallon	Total Revenue, In Dollars
0	$2	—	—	$0
1	$2	$2	$2	$2
2	$2	$2	$2	$4
3	$2	$2	$2	$6
.	.	.	.	.
.	.	.	.	.
.	.	.	.	.
100	$2	$2	$2	$200
250	$2	$2	$2	$500
375	$2	$2	$2	$750
450	$2	$2	$2	$900
500	$2	$2	$2	$1000
525	$2	$2	$2	$1050

Figure 9.1 Panel (a)
Marginal Revenue and Average Revenue
for Cider Space

A perfectly competitive firm, such as Cider Space, can sell as many units as it wants to sell, at the market price. Because of this, the additional revenue that the firm gets from selling one more unit is always equal to the market price. This means that the firm's marginal-revenue curve and average-revenue curve are both horizontal lines.

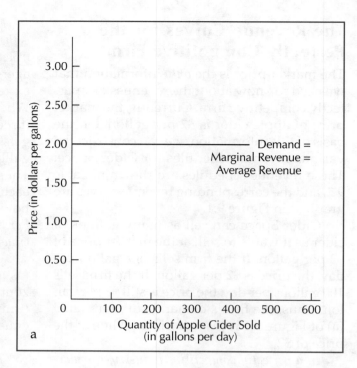

a

Figure 9.1 Panel (b)
Total Revenue for Cider Space

Total revenue is the total amount of money that a firm receives from selling a product. Total revenue equals price multiplied by quantity. A perfectly competitive firm can sell as many units as it wants to sell, at the market price. Therefore, the total-revenue curve is a straight line, whose slope is the market price.

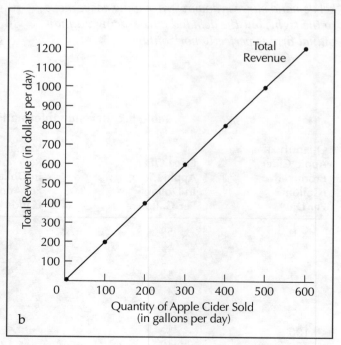

b

revenue would be (1 gallon)x($2 per gallon) = $2. If two gallons were sold, total revenue would be (2)x($2) = $4. If the firm were to sell 100 gallons of cider, its total revenue would be (100)x($2) = $200. *We calculate total revenue by multiplying the price by the quantity*:

TR = (P)(Q).

In panel (b) of Figure 9.1, the total-revenue curve is an upward-sloping straight line. The slope of the total-revenue curve is the marginal revenue, which is the same as the market price.

Here is another way to express the relationship between total revenue and marginal revenue. Marginal revenue is the change in total revenue divided by the change in output:

MR = (ΔTR) / (ΔQ).

Average Revenue. Finally, *average revenue is the average number of dollars per unit that the firm receives.* Average revenue is total revenue divided by the quantity sold:

AR = TR/Q.

Remember that total revenue is price multiplied by quantity. Therefore,

AR = (TR/Q) = ((PQ)/Q) = P.

In other words, *average revenue is equal to the price.*

We also graph average revenue in panel (a) of Figure 9.1. Average revenue is identical to marginal revenue, and they are both identical to the demand curve for the perfectly competitive firm. For *any* perfectly competitive firm, average revenue and marginal revenue are given by the price.

Reality Check: Interim Review Questions

IR9-4. A manufacturer of corn flakes knows that if it produces 1,000,000 boxes, it can sell them for a price of $2.50 each. However, if the firm wants to produce 100,000 additional boxes of corn flakes, the firm will have to cut its price to $2.40 per box. Is this a perfectly competitive firm?

IR9-5. For a perfectly competitive firm, what is the relationship between price, marginal revenue, and average revenue?

HOW THE PERFECTLY COMPETITIVE FIRM BEHAVES IN THE SHORT RUN

In Chapter 8, we described the cost curves of business firms. Here in Chapter 9, we have described the perfectly competitive firm's revenues. Next, we put the revenues and costs together. When we look at revenues and costs at the same time, we can understand the perfectly competitive firm's decision about how much to produce.

In the rest of this chapter, and in the next few chapters, we'll use the cost concepts from Chapter 8 very often. Again and again, we'll use marginal cost, average variable cost, and average total cost. If you're not sure that you understand the cost curves, this would be the best time to go back for a brief review of Chapter 8.

The Goal of Profit Maximization

To understand the behavior of the firm, we need to have some idea of what it is trying to accomplish. *We assume that firms maximize their economic profits.* Economic profits are equal to the difference between total revenue and total cost:

Profit = TR - TC.

The assumption of profit maximization is not completely correct all of the time. Some firms may be sloppy and wasteful. In addition, some firms may desire to increase their share of the market, and this may mean that they don't maximize their profits immediately. And yet, the assumption of profit maximization is probably pretty close to the truth. After all, firms that do maximize profits will be more likely to stay in business. Firms that consistently don't maximize profits will be more likely to go bankrupt.

Finding the Maximum Profit by Comparing Total Revenue and Total Cost

We have already seen the revenues of Cider Space, in Table 9.2 and Figure 9.1. Table 9.3 repeats some of the numbers from Table 9.2, and adds some additional information. You can tell that Cider Space is a perfectly competitive firm, because the price of apple cider is the same ($2 per gallon) for every possible level of output for the firm. When we multiply the price by the quantity, we get the firm's total revenue, which is shown in column (3) of Table 9.3.

The cost information for Cider Space was given in Tables 8.3, 8.4, and 8.5. Some of those numbers are repeated here, in columns (4)–(7) of Table 9.3.

You may recall that, when we developed these cost relationships in Chapter 8, we started

by looking at the output of each additional worker. The marginal product of an extra worker is *not* a constant. This is why the quantity of output, shown in column (1) of Table 9.3, doesn't increase by the same amount as we go from one row of the table to the next. However, each worker receives the same wage rate. Therefore, total variable cost, shown in column (5) of Table 9.3, *does* increase by the same amount as we go from one row to the next.

The firm's total costs are shown in column (7) of Table 9.3. These are equal to its total fixed costs (shown in column (6)), plus its total variable costs (shown in column (5)): TC = TFC + TVC.

We calculate the profits for Cider Space, by subtracting total cost from total revenue: Profit = TR - TC. Profits are shown in column (8) of Table 9.3. When the firm produces only a small quantity of output, total cost is greater than total revenue. This means that the firm's profits are negative: Cider Space will suffer a loss if it produces only a small amount of apple cider.

However, if the firm were to increase its output, it would eventually earn a profit. As shown in column (8) of Table 9.3, profits continue to increase until the firm is producing 450 gallons of cider per day. At this quantity,

Table 9.3 Revenues, Costs, and Profits for Cider Space, When the Price Is $2 Per Gallon

(1) Q	(2) P	(3) TR	(4) MC	(5) TVC	(6) TFC	(7) TC	(8) Profit
Quantity of Apple Cider, In Gallons Per Day	Price, In Dollars Per Gallon = Marginal Revenue = Average Revenue	Total Revenue, In Dollars (= PxQ)	Marginal Cost, In Dollars Per Additional Gallon	Total Variable Cost, In Dollars	Total Fixed Cost, In Dollars	Total Cost, In Dollars (=TFC+TVC)	Profit, In Dollars (=TR-TC)
0	$2.00	$ 0	—	$ 0	$200	$200	−$200
100	$2.00	$ 200	$1.00	$100	$200	$300	−$100
250	$2.00	$ 500	$0.67	$200	$200	$ 40	$100
375	$2.00	$ 750	$0.80	$300	$200	$500	$250
450	$2.00	$ 900	$1.33	$400	$200	$600	$300
500	$2.00	$1000	$2.00	$500	$200	$700	$300
525	$2.00	$1050	$4.00	$600	$200	$800	$250

profit is $300 per day. Profit remains at $300 when the firm increases output from 450 gallons per day to 500 gallons per day. If the firm were to increase its output beyond 500 gallons per day, profits would fall.

You may be bothered by the fact that there is not a *unique* profit-maximizing quantity. The maximum profit of $300 is earned when the firm produces 500 gallons per day, but the same level of profit is also earned when the firm produces 450 gallons per day. Will the firm produce 450 gallons, or 500? We assume that Cider Space will go ahead and produce 500 gallons per day. We will discuss this in more detail below.

Graphical Analysis of Profit Maximization

Figure 9.2 contains some of the information from Table 9.3. The total-revenue curve is a straight line, as it should be for any price-taking firm. In Figure 9.2, *profits are the vertical distance between the total-revenue curve and the total-cost curve.* Profits are largest at the quantity where this vertical distance is greatest. Figure 9.2 shows that the vertical distance between the two curves is greatest when the quantity of output is 500 gallons of cider per day. This means that the profit-maximizing quantity is 500 gallons per day, which is the same answer that we got from looking at Table 9.3.

In Figure 9.2, the maximum profit occurs at the quantity where the slope of the total-revenue curve is equal to the slope of the total-cost curve. In other words, *at the profit-maximizing quantity, the total-revenue curve (TR) is parallel to the total-cost curve (TC).*

Let's think about this, by considering cases in which the TR curve and the TC curve are *not* parallel. For example, as quantity increases from 250 gallons to 375 gallons, the TR curve is steeper than the TC curve. That is, the vertical distance between the two curves is getting larger. Therefore, as output increases from 250 gallons per day to 375 gallons per day, profit is increasing. *If profit is increasing, the firm can't be at the maximum profit.*

On the other hand, as quantity increases from 500 gallons per day to 525 gallons per day,

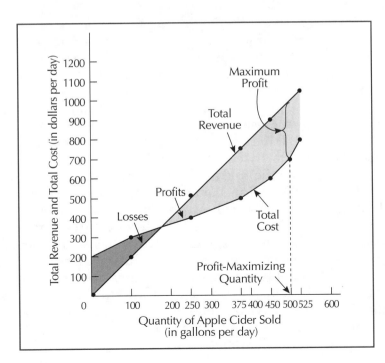

Figure 9.2 Total Revenue, Total Cost, and Profit for Cider Space

The firm's profit-maximizing quantity is found where the vertical distance between the total-revenue curve and the total-cost curve is greatest. This occurs at the quantity where the TR curve is parallel to the TC curve. In the case of Cider Space, the firm maximizes profit by producing 500 gallons of apple cider per day.

the TR curve is flatter than the TC curve: The slope of the TR curve is *less* than the slope of the TC curve, so that the vertical distance between the two curves is shrinking. Therefore, as output increases from 500 gallons per day to 525 gallons per day, profit is falling. *If profit is falling, the firm can't be at the maximum profit.*

So, profit can't be maximized if the TR curve is steeper than the TC curve, and profit also can't be maximized if the TR curve is less steep than the TC curve. This leaves us with only one possibility: *If profits are to be maximized, the slope of the TR curve must be the same as the slope of the TC curve.* In Figure 9.2, the two curves have the same slope between the quantities of 450 gallons per day and 500 gallons per day, and this is the region in which profits are maximized.

Finding the Maximum Profit By Comparing Marginal Revenue and Marginal Cost

In the preceding section, we calculated profit by subtracting *total* cost from *total* revenue. We then studied the profit numbers, to find the profit-maximizing level of output. This method is OK, but a different method is even better. Our second method uses *marginal* revenue and *marginal* cost.

Since Cider Space is a perfectly competitive firm, its marginal revenue is equal to the market price. Marginal revenue (MR) is $2 for each additional gallon of apple cider. But marginal cost (MC) is only $1 for each of the first 100 gallons produced. Therefore, MR is greater than MC for the first 100 gallons, so it makes sense for the firm to produce and sell those units. Whenever a firm can spend only $1, to get $2 of extra revenue, it should do so.

As Cider Space increases its output from 100 gallons per day to 250 gallons per day, and to 375 gallons, and to 450 gallons, MR continues to be greater than MC, so the firm should also produce and sell those units. *When MR is greater than MC, firms should expand their output.*

As the firm increases its output from 450 gallons per day to 500 gallons per day, MR is exactly equal to MC. Even though profit doesn't change as Cider Space increases its output from 450 gallons to 500 gallons, we assume that the firm will go ahead and produce 500 gallons per day.

However, if Cider Space were to increase its output from 500 gallons per day to 525 gallons per day, MR would be $2 and MC would be $4. It doesn't make sense for the firm to produce apple cider for an additional cost of $4 per gallon, when the stuff can only be sold for $2 per gallon. Therefore, Cider Space won't produce any more than 500 gallons per day. *When MC is greater than MR, firms should not produce more.*

The Rule for Profit Maximization: Marginal Revenue Equals Marginal Cost

We can now state the rule by which the profit-maximizing, perfectly competitive firm chooses its quantity. We call it the **MR = MC Rule**:

If a perfectly competitive firm is to maximize its profits, it should produce the quantity at which marginal revenue equals marginal cost. In symbols, **MR = MC**. *Since the perfectly competitive firm's marginal revenue is its price (MR = P), it follows that MR = MC = P. Thus, we can also say that the firm should produce the quantity at which price equals marginal cost. In symbols, P = MC.*

If there is no level of output at which price is exactly equal to marginal cost, we would state the rule as follows: The perfectly competitive firm should maximize profits by producing the highest quantity at which MR>MC.

This isn't the first time that we've seen a rule like this. Back in Chapter 7, which dealt with consumer behavior, we saw that the consumer should set marginal utility equal to price. This is really very similar to the MR=MC rule for the perfectly competitive firm. In each case, economic activity is expanded until *marginal benefit equals marginal cost.* For the consumer, the marginal benefit from consuming more of a good is called marginal utility, and the marginal cost is the price that must be paid to buy the good. For the perfectly competitive firm, the marginal benefit from producing and selling more of a good is called marginal revenue, and the marginal cost is just called marginal cost.

The MR = MC rule can also be shown graphically. Figure 9.3 shows the MR curve and MC curve for Cider Space. The MC curve looks like a bunch of stair steps, rather than a smooth line. The MC curve is the same as the MR curve between 450 gallons per day and 500 gallons per day, which is where profits are maximized.

We now have two ways of finding the profit-maximizing quantity for a perfectly competitive firm. (1) Profits are maximized where the vertical distance between the TR curve and the TC curve is greatest. (2) Profits are maximized where the MC curve crosses the MR curve.

These two statements are very closely related. Remember that marginal revenue is the slope of the total-revenue curve, and marginal cost is the slope of the total-cost curve.

When we say that MR equals MC, this is *the same* as saying that the slopes of the TR and TC curves are equal. When the slopes of the two curves are equal, the vertical distance between them is greatest. In other words, the two ways of finding the profit-maximizing quantity will always get the same answer! If we find the quantity at which MR = MC, we will also have found the quantity at which (TR – TC) is greatest.

Even though the two ways of finding the profit-maximizing quantity will give us the same result, one method will usually be more useful. It's often much easier to think in terms of *marginal* revenues and costs. If MR > MC, the firm ought to expand output; if MR < MC, the firm ought to cut back. If MR = MC, the firm is maximizing profits.

Another Example

Let's face it—This chapter presents a lot of material for you to digest. To help you to solidify your understanding, we'll now present another numerical example.

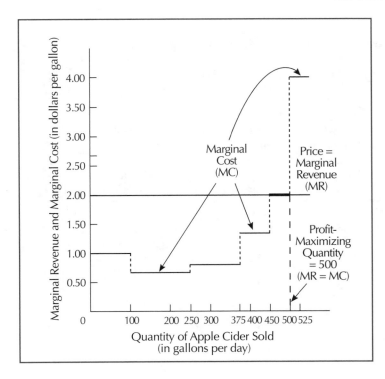

Figure 9.3 Marginal Revenue, Marginal Cost, and the Profit-Maximizing Quantity of Output for Cider Space

Any firm that wants to maximize profits will produce the quantity at which MR = MC. For a perfectly competitive firm like Cider Space, marginal revenue is the market price. Therefore, the perfectly competitive firm will maximize profits by producing the quantity at which P = MC.

American Gizmos, Inc., is a perfectly competitive producer of gizmos. The firm's costs and revenues are shown in Table 9.4. The market price of a gizmo is $5, so that the firm's marginal revenue is $5, and its average revenue is also $5. The firm's marginal cost is $1 for the first gizmo, $2 for the second gizmo, $3 for the third gizmo, and so on. Total variable cost is the sum of all of the marginal costs. Therefore, when three gizmos are produced, total variable cost is ($1+$2+$3) = $6. American Gizmos has no fixed costs, so that its total cost is equal to its total variable cost.

American Gizmos should produce at least one gizmo, since the MR of the first gizmo is $5, while the MC is only $1. By similar reasoning, American Gizmos should also produce a second, third, and fourth gizmo. The MR of the fifth gizmo is $5, and the MC is also $5. Profits don't increase by adding the fifth gizmo, but profits don't decrease, either. We assume that the firm will go ahead and produce the fifth gizmo. However, the MC of the sixth gizmo is $6, which is greater than the MR. Therefore, the firm should *not* produce the sixth gizmo. American Gizmos will maximize its profits by producing and selling five gizmos. As shown in column (8) of Table 9.4, the firm will earn profits of $10.

By comparing MR and MC, we have seen that American Gizmos maximizes profit by producing five gizmos. This is shown in panel (a) of Figure 9.4. We can also get the same answer by comparing *total* revenue with *total* cost, as shown in panel (b) of Figure 9.4. The vertical distance between the TR curve and the TC curve is greatest at a quantity of five gizmos, so that five gizmos is the profit-maximizing quantity.

The Firm's Profits: Further Graphical Analysis

When we compared total revenue and total cost in Figure 9.4(b), we could actually show the *amount* of profit, because profit is the vertical distance between the TR curve and the TC curve. Profits are measured in dollars, and

Table 9.4 Revenues, Costs, and Profits for American Gizmos, Inc.

(1) Q Quantity of Gizmos Per Day	(2) P Price, In Dollars Per Gizmo = Marginal Revenue = Average Revenue	(3) TR Total Revenue, In Dollars (= PxQ)	(4) MC Marginal Cost, In Dollars Per Additional Gizmo	(5) TVC Total Variable Cost, In Dollars	(6) TFC Total Fixed Cost, In Dollars	(7) TC Total Cost, In Dollars (=TFC+TVC)	(8) Profit Profit, In Dollars (=TR-TC)
0	$5	$ 0	—	$ 0	$0	$ 0	$ 0
1	$5	$ 5	$1	$ 1	$0	$ 1	$ 4
2	$5	$10	$2	$ 3	$0	$ 3	$ 7
3	$5	$15	$3	$ 6	$0	$ 6	$ 9
4	$5	$20	$4	$10	$0	$10	$10
5	$5	$25	$5	$15	$0	$15	$10
6	$5	$30	$6	$21	$0	$21	$ 9
7	$5	$35	$7	$28	$0	$28	$ 7
8	$5	$40	$8	$36	$0	$36	$ 4
9	$5	$45	$9	$45	$0	$45	$ 0

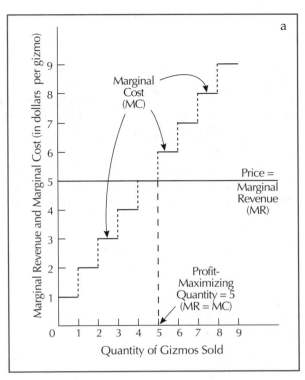

**Figure 9.4 Panel (a)
Marginal Revenue, Marginal Cost, and the Profit-Maximizing Quantity of Output for American Gizmos**

Any firm will maximize profits by choosing the quantity at which MR = MC. In the special case of a perfectly competitive firm, such as American Gizmos, marginal revenue is the price. Therefore, American Gizmos maximizes profits by producing five gizmos: At this quantity, P = MR = MC.

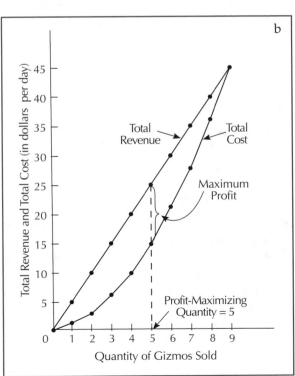

**Figure 9.4 Panel (b)
Total Revenue, Total Cost, and Profit
for American Gizmos**

The firm's profit-maximizing quantity is found where the vertical distance between the total-revenue curve and the total-cost curve is greatest. In the case of American Gizmos, the firm maximizes profit by producing five gizmos per period.

Figure 9.4(b) has *dollars* on the vertical axis. However, in Figure 9.4(a), the vertical axis shows *dollars per unit*. So far, in Figure 9.4(a), we've only shown the profit-maximizing *quantity*; we haven't yet shown how large the profits are. Fortunately, it only takes one more step for us to draw the amount of profits in a graph like Figure 9.4(a).

Revenue per unit, which is also called average revenue, is total revenue divided by quantity. The average revenue for a competitive firm is the price of its output. *Cost per unit*, which is also called average total cost, is total cost divided by quantity. *Profit per unit*, which is also called average profit, is equal to (revenue per unit) minus (cost per unit). In other words,

**Average Profit =
Average Revenue − Average Total Cost.**

Next, if we use the fact that average revenue is equal to price for the perfectly competitive firm, we can say that

Average Profit = P − ATC.

Now, if we multiply average profit by quantity, we get back to total profit:

**Profit = (Average Profit)x(Q) =
(P − ATC)x(Q).**

As an example, let's return to the case of Cider Space. We have already seen that the firm's profit-maximizing quantity is 500 gallons of apple cider per day. Table 9.3 shows that the firm's total cost is $700 when the quantity is 500 gallons per day. Therefore, average total cost is ($700/500 gallons), which is $1.40 per gallon. If we take the price of $2 per gallon, and subtract the average total cost of $1.40 per gallon, we get an average profit of $0.60 per gallon. Multiplying the average profit by the quantity gives us a total profit of

($0.60 per gallon)x(500 gallons per day) = $300 per day.

For much of the rest of this chapter, we will draw smooth marginal-cost curves. When the curves are smooth, there will be a *unique* profit-maximizing quantity. *Graphically, profits are maximized at the quantity where the MR curve crosses the MC curve.* Panel (a) of Figure 9.5 shows the profits for a firm that is making positive economic profits. (This type of diagram would apply to Cider Space, or to any other firm that is earning positive economic profits.) *In a diagram like this, profit is the area of a rectangle. The base of the rectangle is the quantity sold by the firm, and the rectangle's height is the difference between price and average total cost.*

In Figure 9.5(a), we can tell that the firm is making positive profits, because P > ATC at the profit-maximizing quantity, Q*. If P = ATC at the profit-maximizing quantity, then the firm is making zero economic profits, as in Figure 9.5(b). In this case, there isn't any rectangle to represent profits, because profits are zero. The firm will suffer economic losses when P < ATC at the profit-maximizing quantity, as in panels (c) and (d) of Figure 9.5.

Reality Check:
Interim Review Questions

IR9-6. At its current level of output, a farm's marginal cost of producing hogs is less than the price of hogs. Should the firm expand output, or reduce output, or keep output the same?

IR9-7. Profits are maximized at the quantity where MR equals MC. Also, profits are maximized at the quantity where the TR curve is parallel to the TC curve. Explain why these two methods of finding the profit-maximizing quantity will lead us to the same answer.

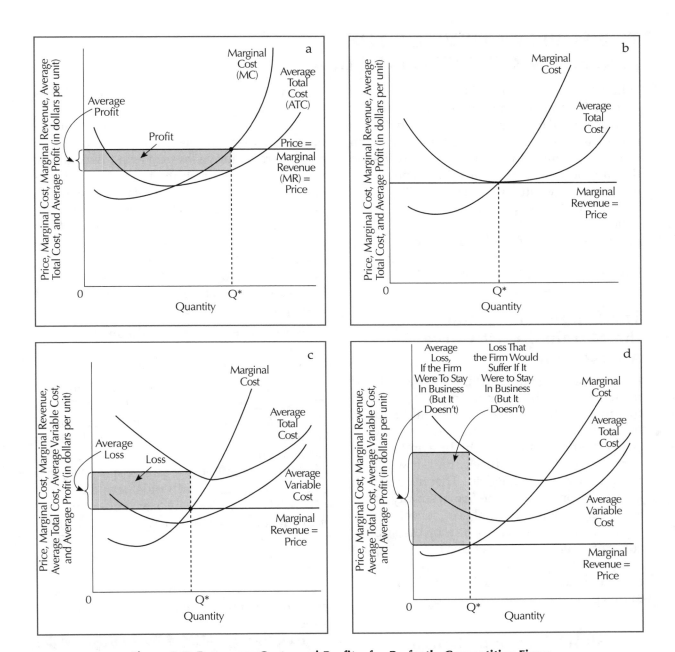

Figure 9.5 Revenues, Costs, and Profits, for Perfectly Competitive Firms

The profit-maximizing quantity is always found where MR = MC. If P > ATC at the profit-maximizing quantity (as in panel (a)), the firm is making positive economic profits. If P = ATC at the profit-maximizing quantity (as in panel (b)), the firm is making zero profit. If P < ATC at the profit-maximizing quantity (as in panels (c) and (d)), the firm is suffering losses. If the firm is suffering losses, it will stay in business if P > AVC (as in panel (c)). If P < AVC at the profit-maximizing quantity (as in panel (d)), the firm should shut down.

THE SUPPLY CURVE OF THE PERFECTLY COMPETITIVE FIRM

When the market price is $2 per gallon of cider, Cider Space maximizes its profits by producing 500 gallons per day. But what if the price were to rise to $4 per gallon? The firm would still want to maximize its profits, so that it would still set P=MR=MC. The profit-maximizing quantity would rise to 525 gallons per day. If the price were to fall to $1.33 per gallon, quantity would decrease to 450 gallons per day. For each of these market prices, Cider Space will maximize its profits by producing the quantity at which P = MR = MC.

The Supply Curve and the Marginal-Cost Curve: A First Look

In the preceding paragraph, we have outlined the relationship between the market price and the quantity that Cider Space would supply. In other words, we've described how to construct the firm's supply schedule and supply curve! If the firm produces at all, it will find the quantity at which P=MC. Therefore, at first glance, it appears that the firm's supply curve is the same as its marginal-cost curve.

However, this description of the supply curve of a perfectly competitive firm isn't quite complete. The problem is that the firm may go out of business if the price is very low. We turn to this problem in the next section.

The Short-Run Shut-Down Decision of the Perfectly Competitive Firm

Earlier in this chapter, we considered the case in which the price of apple cider is $2 per gallon. When the price is this high, Cider Space is able to earn a profit. However, if the price were to fall far enough, the firm would suffer losses.

Let's assume that the price is low, and that Cider Space is losing money.

You might think that the firm would go out of business immediately if its economic profits are negative, but this isn't necessarily the case. If the firm shuts down, its total revenue will go to zero, but its total costs will still be greater than zero. This is because *the firm has to pay its total fixed costs, even if it produces nothing*. If the firm shuts down, it will have losses equal to its total fixed costs. On the other hand, if the firm stays in business, its losses are equal to the difference between total cost and total revenue:

Losses if Firm Stays in Business = TC – TR

Losses if Firm Shuts Down = TFC

So, the firm's choice depends on whether TFC is larger than (TC – TR). *If TFC < (TC – R), the firm should quit producing*, because its losses from shutting down are smaller than its losses from staying in business.

Now, remember that total cost (TC) equals total variable cost (TVC) plus total fixed cost (TFC): TC = TVC + TFC. If we substitute this into our earlier expression, we see that the firm should *shut down if TFC < (TFC + TV – TR)*. Now, we subtract TFC from each side of the inequality. The firm should *quit producing if 0 < (TVC – TR)*. Finally, if we add TR to both sides of this inequality, we see that the firm should *shut down if TR < TVC*.

Now, we can describe the ***short-run shut-down decision*** for the perfectly competitive firm: *The firm should go out of business if total revenue is less than total variable cost. This is equivalent to saying that the firm should go out of business if average revenue (which is equal to price) is less than average variable cost.* If the price isn't even high enough for the firm to cover its *variable* costs, it's time to go out of business.

Earlier in this chapter, Table 9.3 showed that Cider Space would earn positive economic profits if the price of apple cider were $2 per gallon. In Table 9.5, we provide much the same information as in Table 9.3, except we assume that the price of apple cider is only $0.80 per gallon (that is, 80 cents per gallon). Column (9) of Table 9.5 shows that Cider Space would suffer losses at *any* level of output. (In other words, profits are always less than zero, regardless of how many gallons the firm produces.) Therefore, the firm will need to consider whether to shut down.

If Cider Space is to stay in business at all, it should produce the quantity of apple cider at which P = MR = MC. Price, which equals marginal revenue, is $0.80 per gallon, and marginal cost is also equal to $0.80 per gallon at a quantity of 375 gallons per day. The firm should shut down if price is less than average variable cost, at this quantity. However, column (6) of Table 9.5 shows us that the firm's average variable cost is also $0.80 per gallon, when the quantity is 375 gallons per day. Thus, when the price is $0.80 per gallon, Cider Space is just barely able to cover its variable costs.

For the time being, if the price is at or above $0.80 per gallon, the firm should stay in business. If price is below $0.80 per gallon, the firm should go out of business right now.

Why would a firm like Cider Space stay in business, even if it is suffering losses? The reason is that its losses would be even worse if it were to shut down. The fixed costs of Cider Space consist of leases on buildings and equipment. What if Cider Space's leases end at the end of the year? The firm has the option of not renewing its leases, so that it could go out of business at the end of the year, if it wants to. The firm's decision will depend on whether it believes that it can turn its losses into profits by next year. If demand is projected to increase, or if Cider Space thinks it can find a way to cut its costs, it should try again next year. If not, it would be best to go out of business when the leases are up.

Panels (c) and (d) of Figure 9.5, on p. 205, show two possibilities for firms that are suffering losses. Unlike panels (a) and (b), panels (c) and (d) include the average-variable-cost curve, because the shut-down decision depends on whether price is below average

Table 9.5 Revenues, Costs, and Profits for Cider Space, When the Price Is $0.80 Per Gallon

(1) Q	(2) P	(3) TR	(4) MC	(5) TVC	(6) AVC	(7) TFC	(8) TC	(9) Profit
Quantity of Apple Cider, In Gallons Per Day	Price, In Dollars Per Gallon = Marginal Revenue = Average Revenue	Total Revenue, In Dollars (= PxQ)	Marginal Cost, In Dollars Per Additional Gallon	Total Variable Cost, In Dollars	Average Variable Cost, In Dollars Per Additional Gallon	Total Fixed Cost, In Dollars	Total Cost, In Dollars =TFC+ (TVC)	Profit, In Dollars (=TR-TC)
0	$0.80	$ 0	—	$ 0	—	$200	$200	–$200
100	$0.80	$ 80	$1.00	$100	$1.00	$200	$300	–$220
250	$0.80	$200	$0.67	$200	$0.80	$200	$400	–$200
375	$0.80	$300	$0.80	$300	$0.80	$200	$500	–$200
450	$0.80	$360	$1.33	$400	$0.89	$200	$600	–$240
500	$0.80	$400	$2.00	$500	$1.00	$200	$700	–$300
525	$0.80	$420	$4.00	$600	$1.14	$200	$800	–$380

variable cost. In panel (c), price is greater than average variable cost, so that the firm should stay in business. In panel (d), however, price is less than average variable cost. Thus, if the firm's cost and revenue curves are like the ones shown in panel (d), the firm should shut down.

In the long run, the firm is free to choose any scale of operations, including an output of zero. So, just because a money-losing firm stays in business for the time being, it does not follow that it will stay in business indefinitely.

In *Real Economics for Real People 9.1*, we discuss some of the changes that have occurred in American agriculture, as farms have decided to go out of business.

The Short-Run Supply Curve of the Perfectly Competitive Firm

We now can give a complete description of the perfectly competitive firm's *short-run supply curve*: *When price is greater than or equal to average variable cost, the supply curve is the marginal-cost curve. When price is less than average variable cost, the firm will shut down, and its quantity supplied will be zero.*

The perfectly competitive firm's short-run supply curve is shown in Figure 9.6. When the price is greater than or equal to average variable cost, the firm will produce a positive

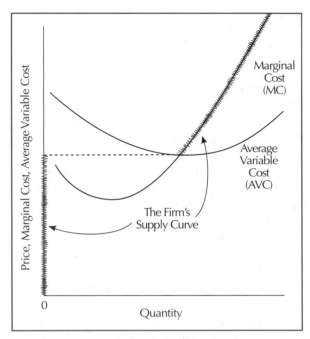

**Figure 9.6 The Short-Run Supply Curve
for a Perfectly Competitive Firm**

If price is greater than or equal to average variable cost (AVC), then the firm will produce a positive quantity of output. If a positive quantity is produced, the quantity will be given by the marginal-cost curve (MC). This is why a portion of the perfectly competitive firm's supply curve is the same as a part of the MC curve. However, if price falls below AVC, the firm's best decision is to shut down. This means that the firm's output will be zero, so that a portion of the firm's supply curve is on the vertical axis.

quantity. The firm will choose the quantity at which price equals marginal cost, which means that this portion of the supply curve is the same as the MC curve. However, when the price is less than average variable cost, the firm will stop producing. This is why a part of the firm's supply curve is on the vertical axis, because all points on the vertical axis have a quantity of zero.

Reality Check:
Interim Review Questions

IR9-8. Jones and Company is a perfectly competitive firm, which makes men's dress shirts. The market price is $20 per shirt. Average total cost is $24 per shirt, and average variable cost is $16 per shirt. Is the firm making profits or losses? If it is suffering losses, should it go out of business in the short run?

IR9-9. How would your answer to question 8 change if you were told that average variable cost is $22 per shirt, while price is still $20 per shirt, and average total cost is still $24 per shirt?

THE SHORT-RUN MARKET SUPPLY CURVE

We construct the short-run *market supply curve* in a perfectly competitive industry by adding together the supply curves for all of the individual firms. The market supply curve for winter wheat is the sum of the supply curves for all wheat farmers, and the market supply curve for men's loafers is the sum of the supply curves for all shoe manufacturers. If a perfectly competitive industry has 100 firms, and if each firm is willing to produce five units when the price is $10 per unit, then

the quantity supplied in the market is (100 firms)x(5 units per firm) = 500 units when the price is $10. Graphically, we add the supply curves of the individual firms horizontally to get the market supply curve.

This is basically the same procedure that we used in Chapter 7, where we formed the market *demand* curve, by adding together the individual demand curves for all of the consumers in the market.

CHANGES IN THE NUMBER OF FIRMS IN A PERFECTLY COMPETITIVE INDUSTRY

Modern industries are dynamic, with lots of changes over time. Sometimes new firms start up, and sometimes the existing firms shut down. We need to take a closer look at why the number of firms might change, and we need to study what happens as a result.

Profits and Entry into the Industry

In one of our examples from earlier in this chapter, Cider Space was earning positive economic profits. But those profits can't be sustained for long, because it's easy for new firms to enter a perfectly competitive industry. If the existing firms are earning positive economic profits, new firms will want to get in on the action.

What will happen when new firms come into the industry? Since the market supply curve is the sum of the supply curves of the individual firms, *an increase in the number of firms will shift the industry supply curve to the right.* Like any rightward shift in the market supply curve, this will cause an increase in the equilibrium quantity, and a decrease in the equilibrium price.

This process is illustrated in Figure 9.7, for the market for 3.5-inch computer diskettes. Panel (a) of Figure 9.7 shows the situation faced by an individual firm, called Disk-o-Tech, while panel (b) shows the entire market. Let's say that the original market price for a particular type of diskette is $0.80 per diskette, and that this is high enough that the firms can earn positive economic profits. These profits

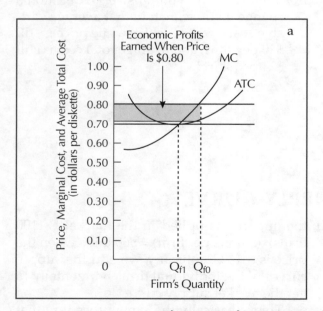
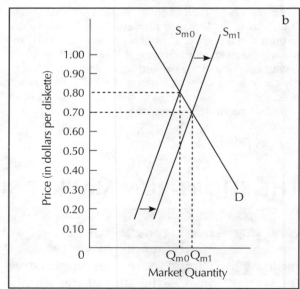

Figure 9.7 The Response of the Firm and the Market, When Positive Economic Profits Are Being Made

When the price of a diskette is $0.80, positive economic profits are earned. For the individual firm, profits are the shaded region in Panel (a). As a result of the profits, new firms enter the industry, which pushes the market supply curve to the right, from S_{m0} to S_{m1} in Panel (b). This lowers the market price to $0.70. When the price is $0.70 per diskette, Panel (a) shows that the firm's profit-maximizing quantity is Q_{f1}. At this quantity, P = ATC, so that the firm is earning zero economic profits. Entry into the industry has eliminiated the economic profits.

are indicated by the shaded rectangle in panel (a) of the figure. Disk-o-Tech produces Q_{f0}, and the market quantity is Q_{m0}. (Note that, in the two panels of Figure 9.7, the horizontal axes aren't drawn to the same scale.)

In response to the positive economic profits, new firms will enter the industry. This will shift the market supply curve for diskettes to the right, from S_{m0} to S_{m1}, as shown in panel (b) of Figure 9.7. The price will continue to drop until the economic profits have been eliminated. In the case shown, economic profits will fall to zero when the price drops to $0.70 per diskette. The individual firm's quantity drops from Q_{f0} to Q_{f1}, and the market quantity increases from Q_{m0} to Q_{m1}. Disk-o-Tech and the other individual firms will actually produce slightly fewer diskettes in the long-run equilibrium than they did before the new firms entered. However, even though each individual *firm* produces less, there are enough new firms that the total *market* quantity will rise.

Losses and Exit from the Industry

We have just seen that economic *profits* will bring new firms into the industry, and that this will drive prices down. If the firms in an industry are having economic *losses*, the process runs in reverse.

Consider the Renkowski family farm, which is earning an *accounting* profit of $1000 per year from its soybean operation. Even though the farm is making an accounting profit, which means that its revenues are greater than its explicit, out-of-pocket costs, it is still doing very poorly. The Renkowski farm is making enough to cover its out-of-pocket costs, but it isn't making enough to cover its opportunity costs. Therefore, the firm is earning a negative *economic* profit. Its return on investment is very low, relative to what other investments are earning. In addition, the family members are putting in long hours, but they aren't earning the kind of money that they might earn in other occupations.

Panel (a) of Figure 9.8 shows the situation faced by the Renkowski family farm, while panel (b) shows the entire market. (As in Figure 9.7, the horizontal axes aren't drawn to the same scale.) Let's say that the original market price for soybeans is $6 per bushel. The individual farm produces a quantity of Q_{f0}, and the market quantity is Q_{m0}. At the price of $6 per bushel, farms are suffering economic losses. These losses are indicated by the shaded rectangle in panel (a) of Figure 9.8.

After considering the prospects for the future, some of the farms will decide to go out of business. However, we assume that the Renkowskis decide to stay in business. This might happen, for example, if the Renkowskis are more optimistic about the future than are some other farming families. Another possibility is that different farms have slightly different cost curves, so that the price is below average variable cost for some farms, but not for the Renkowski farm.

When some farms go out of business, the market supply curve shifts to the left, as shown in panel (b) of Figure 9.8. The price will rise until the economic losses are gone. In the case shown, economic profits will rise to zero when the price increases to $7 per bushel. The firm's quantity goes up from Q_{f0} to Q_{f1}, and the market quantity decreases from Q_{m0} to Q_{m1}.

Because of free entry and exit, perfectly competitive industries will always be moving in the direction of zero economic profits. If firms are making positive economic profits, new firms will enter, and this will compete the profits away. If firms are experiencing losses, some will leave the industry. This will raise the price until the remaining firms can earn zero economic profits.

In *Real Economics for Real People 9.2*, on p. 213, we discuss a policy debate that has to do with the problems that workers face when industries are shrinking.

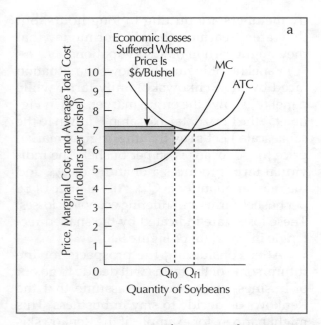
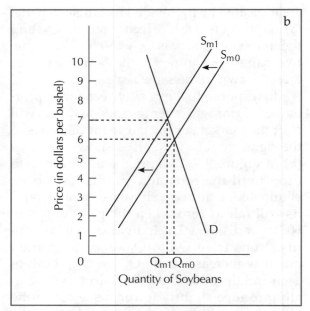

Figure 9.8 The Response of the Firm and the Market,
When Economic Losses Are Being Made

When the price of a bushel of soybeans is $6, firms are suffering economic losses. For the individual firm, losses are the shaded region in Panel (a). As a result of the losses, some firms go out of business. This pushes the market supply curve to the left, from S_{m0} to S_{m1} in Panel (b). This raises the market price to $7 per bushel. When the price is $7 per bushel, Panel (a) shows that the firm's profit-maximizing quantity is Q_{f1}. At this quantity, P = ATC, so that the firm is earning zero economic profits. Exit from the industry has eliminiated the economic losses.

Reality Check:
Interim Review Question

IR9-10. Currently, all of the firms in a perfectly competitive industry are earning economic profits. In response to these profits, what will happen in the future to (a) the number of firms in the industry, (b) the market price, and (c) the level of profits in the industry?

LONG-RUN INDUSTRY SUPPLY CURVES

In the *long run*, we assume that entry and exit will always lead us to the zero-profit situation. When we draw the *long-run supply curve* for an industry, we concentrate on the relationship between the size of the industry (assuming zero economic profits) and the costs of the individual firms. We can identify three special cases. These are:

* constant-cost industries,
* increasing-cost industries, and
* decreasing-cost industries.

Constant-Cost Industries

Even if the bicycle industry were to double in size, it probably wouldn't have any effect on the prices of the labor, steel, rubber, and plastic that are used in making bicycles. The cost of building a bicycle would not change as the size of the industry changes. In a case like this, the *industry's long-run supply curve is a horizontal line*. In other words, long-run industry supply is perfectly elastic.

When we assume that the long-run industry

Real Economics for Real People 9.2:
Should Businesses Be Required to Give Advance Notice of Layoffs?

Free entry is crucial to the operation of competitive industries, because it guarantees that positive economic profits will be competed away. Free exit is just as important, because free exit is the way in which losses are eliminated. If firms cannot leave an industry easily, then they will know that they may be stuck in an unprofitable position for a long time. Therefore, the firms may be less willing to get into the industry in the first place.

Freedom of exit is at the heart of an important debate in the past few decades. On one side of the debate are those who believe that business firms have a responsibility to notify their workers in advance, when they are planning layoffs or plant closings. On the other side are those who believe that firms should be able to leave an unprofitable industry quickly, so that economic activity can be carried on more efficiently.

In 1988, Congress passed the Worker Adjustment and Retraining Notification Act (WARN), despite the objections of President Reagan. This law requires employers with more than 100 employees to give at least 60 days' advance notice of plant closings or mass layoffs. (Some States and cities have stricter requirements, often including a 90-day notification period.) In addition to the exemption for firms with fewer than 100 employees, there are also exemptions for firms in special circumstances. Seasonal layoffs, which are common in agriculture and construction, are excluded from the law, as are layoffs caused by natural disasters. Also excluded are companies that are trying to find new financing in order to avoid bankruptcy. This is because an announcement of a plant closing or layoff might make it hard to obtain the financing.

Critics of the law say that it puts an unfair burden on the very businesses that are most in need of help. With the notification requirements, firms have the unpleasant choice of continuing to suffer losses for two more months, or paying workers up to two months' additional wages. Thus, the notification requirement for a single plant could push an entire firm into bankruptcy.

However, it appears that WARN hasn't caused too much dislocation so far. The many exclusions were designed to reduce the disruption that the law would cause for businesses. In fact, some firms have complied with the law, even though they were eligible to be excluded from its provisions. Nevertheless, mandatory notification laws will probably continue to be debated. Some proposals in Congress would extend the law to a six-month notification period, with four weeks of severance pay for each year of employment, health-care benefits for 18 months, and up to $10,000 in job-training benefits.

However, even these requirements look small when compared with some of the ones in Europe. In Italy, for a 45-year-old worker with 20 years of service who is currently earning $50,000 per year, a company must pay termination benefits of $130,000. In future debates, critics of these policies will surely point to the strict laws in Europe, where the number of jobs has increased much more slowly than in the United States.

supply curve is perfectly elastic, we are assuming that the industry in question is a *constant-cost industry*. This is a reasonable assumption when an industry's demand for factors of production is small relative to the total demand for those factors. In fact, until now, we have always assumed that expansion of an industry will not affect production costs. In other words, we have assumed that neither entry nor exit will have any effect on the long-run average-cost curves of the firms in the industry. Basically, we have assumed that all industries are constant-cost industries. However, there are other possibilities, and we discuss them below.

Increasing-Cost Industries

If the fishing industry were to expand, it might reduce the size of schools of fish, so that the costs of catching more fish would go up. In a case like this, the *long-run industry supply curve will slope upward*. When the long-run supply curve slopes upward, we say that the industry is an *increasing-cost industry*. In an increasing-cost industry, long-run average cost will increase as output increases. If the automobile industry were to expand greatly, it might push up the prices of steel, rubber, and other inputs into the production of automobiles. If this were to happen, we would say that the automobile industry is also an increasing-cost industry.

Decreasing-Cost Industries

Some industries have average costs that *decrease* when output increases. These are called *decreasing-cost industries*. The growth of the computer industry has led to improvements in operating-system software, and this has helped to reduce the overall cost of producing computers. During frontier times, the growth of agriculture in a newly-developed region of the country would eventually lead to the development of improved transportation networks, which would then reduce the costs of production for the farmers. For a decreasing-cost industry, *the long-run industry supply curve will slope downward*.

THE EFFICIENCY OF PERFECT COMPETITION

Since only a few industries are perfectly competitive, it may seem strange that we study perfect competition before we study any other market structure. One reason for this is that perfectly competitive markets lead to some very good results. In the language of economists, perfect competition tends to lead to "efficient" outcomes.

Average Total Cost Is Minimized

We can demonstrate the efficiency of perfect competition in several ways. One aspect of efficiency is that *perfectly competitive firms will produce for the minimum cost per unit*. In other words, average total cost will be minimized under perfect competition.

In order to understand this, recall two things about perfectly competitive firms. First, they maximize their profits, which means that they produce the quantity at which *price equals marginal cost*. Second, firms earn zero profits in the long run. When profits are zero, *price equals average total cost*. Since P = MC *and* P = ATC, it follows that MC = ATC. But ATC reaches its minimum point at the quantity where MC = ATC. Therefore, if MC = ATC, it must be true that ATC is minimized!

You can see this graphically by taking another look at Figure 9.5(b), or Figure 9.7(a), or Figure 9.8(a). Since Figure 9.8(a) is the most recent of the three, we'll concentrate on it. When the price is $7, the Renkowski family farm produces Q_{f1}, and earns zero profit. Figure 9.8(a) shows that Q_{f1} is the quantity at which price, marginal cost, and average total cost are all equal. *The average-total-cost curve is at its minimum point!*

Cost minimization is a very desirable property of perfectly competitive markets. After all, if we don't minimize costs, we are being wasteful. This cost minimization comes about automatically, through the normal workings of the market.

Deadweight Loss Is Avoided

Figure 9.9 shows the supply and demand curves, in the perfectly competitive market for cotton sheets. As usual, the market equilibrium is given by the intersection of the supply curve and the demand curve, so that the perfectly competitive market quantity is Q^*.

The marginal benefit from consumption of sheets is represented by the demand curve, and the marginal cost of production is represented by the supply curve. Since supply equals demand at the competitive equilibrium, a perfectly competitive market will produce the quantity that sets marginal benefit equal to marginal cost.

What would happen if society were to produce and consume some quantity other than Q^*? For example, what if the government were to institute a quota system, making it illegal for consumers to buy more than Q_1? In Figure 9.9, when the quantity falls to Q_1, we give up consumption of all cotton sheets between Q_1 and Q^*. For each of these sheets, marginal benefit (given by the demand curve) is greater than marginal cost (given by the supply curve).

Compared with the perfectly competitive equilibrium, Q_1 is associated with a *deadweight loss*. Society is worse off consuming Q_1 than consuming Q^*. The ***deadweight loss*** is the difference between how well off we are under perfect competition and how well off we are at some other quantity. Graphically, the deadweight loss is represented by the shaded triangle in Figure 9.9. We get a deadweight loss

because we don't consume the cotton sheets between Q_1 and Q^*, even though each of those sheets would give us more benefits than costs. The triangle of deadweight loss in Figure 9.9 is the sum of all of the losses that result from consuming Q_1, instead of Q^*.

For many people, it makes sense that we will suffer a deadweight loss if we reduce quantity *below* the perfectly competitive level. It may be a little more surprising that we also suffer a deadweight loss by increasing quantity *above* the perfectly competitive level. If we were to produce and consume more than Q_1 in Figure 9.9, the marginal benefit of any

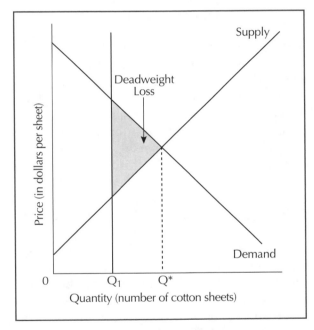

Figure 9.9 The Deadweight Loss When Quantity Is Reduced Below Its Perfectly Competitive Level

In a perfectly competitive market for cotton sheets, the equilibrium quantity is Q^*. The demand curve represents the marginal benefit to society's consumers, and the supply curve represents the marginal cost to society's producers. For quantities of sheets between Q_1 and Q^*, the marginal benefit is greater than the marginal cost. Therefore, if we only produce and consume Q_1, we will suffer a deadweight loss. The deadweight loss is the difference between marginal benefit and marginal cost, added over all of the units from Q_1 to Q^*.

additional sheets would be less than the marginal cost. In fact, *any* deviation from the perfectly competitive quantity will lead to a deadweight loss.

Again and again, we have seen that the way to maximize something is to set marginal benefit equal to marginal cost. Here, the best choice for society is to produce and consume the quantity at which marginal benefit equals marginal cost. Therefore, the best choice for society is the perfectly competitive equilibrium quantity, Q*!

Reality Check:
Interim Review Question

IR9-11. Why does a deadweight loss occur when the market quantity is increased beyond the competitive equilibrium level?

ECONOMICS AND YOU: BEATING THE STOCK MARKET MAY BE HARDER THAN YOU THINK

At the beginning of this chapter, we told about Frank and Jenny, who were discussing whether it would be possible to beat the stock market. Certainly, *some* investors are able to pick stocks that do better than the market as a whole. If no one ever did better than average, the stock market would be pretty dull.

However, if Frank, or Jenny, or anyone else, is to beat the market *systematically*, it's necessary to have special information or special ability. Getting special information is harder than you might think. If you see a stock-market analysis in the pages of the Wall Street *Journal*, you should remember that a few million other investors will see the same story on the same day. By the time a piece of information gets into the papers, it's probably too late to help you very much. Everybody else will be reacting to the same information. You may be able to earn a *good* rate of return on your investments, but it will be hard to do much *better* than the others.

If it's hard to obtain special information, it's even harder to bring special abilities to bear in the marketplace. Many billions of dollars change hands every day at the New York Stock Exchange. When that kind of money is involved, lots of very smart people will buy and sell in the market. You would have to be an extraordinary market analyst, in order to be smarter than all of these other folks.

In fact, Wall Street occasionally produces some spectacular successes. One of the best-known is the Fidelity Magellan mutual fund. Investors who bought shares in Fidelity Magellan were hoping that the fund's managers would buy stocks that would outperform the market. And, for a while, that's exactly what Magellan's managers did! One popular way of charting a fund's performance is to compare its total return with the total return on the Standard and Poor's 500-stock index (S&P 500), which measures the performance of the stocks of 500 important companies. From 1977 to 1990, under the management of Peter Lynch, Fidelity Magellan had an average rate of return of 29.2 percent per year, compared with only 15.8 percent per year for the S&P 500! Morris Smith served as fund manager from 1990 to 1992, and he beat the market, too. Jeffrey Vinik took over in 1992, and he beat the S&P 500 by nearly nine percentage points in his first year.

By 1993, however, even Magellan was falling behind. Vinik resigned as fund manager in 1996, after three years of returns that were below those of the S&P 500. In 1997, Magellan closed its doors to new investors. More and more, it looks as if Magellan's early success would be hard to duplicate.

Magellan isn't the only fund that has trouble beating the market. In fact, *most* mutual funds aren't able to outperform the S&P 500.

The Wall Street *Journal* holds a contest

every month, in which stock-market professionals pick certain stocks. The performance of those stocks over the next six months is compared with the performance of a group of stocks that are chosen by throwing darts at a dartboard. The professionals often beat the dart throwers, but they don't always do so. For example, in the 12 contests that ended from May, 1992, to April, 1993, the darts averaged a 4.2% *increase*, while the professionals averaged a 2.7% *loss.* The darts won seven of the 12 contests during that period.

This is the way it is with competitive markets, where information is freely available, and the individual players are all small relative to the market. Just as it's hard for one player in the stock market to do better than average systematically, it's also hard for one wheat farmer to do better than the average wheat farmer systematically. It's also hard for one small textile firm to do better than the average small textile firm systematically. In a perfectly competitive market, you may do well, but it will be hard to do better than everybody else.

Chapter Summary

1. Economists distinguish among four types of market structure. These are perfect competition, monopoly, monopolistic competition, and oligopoly.

2. There are many firms in a perfectly competitive market, and each firm is small relative to the market. The firms produce standardized, or homogeneous, output. As a result of these two characteristics, the firms are price takers: They take the market price as given. Perfectly competitive markets are also characterized by free entry and exit, and by perfect information.

3. Since the perfectly competitive firm is a price taker, the demand for the firm's product is perfectly elastic. Even though the *market* demand curve slopes downward, the demand curve facing the *individual firm* is a horizontal line. The height of the firm's demand curve is given by the market price.

4. Marginal revenue for the perfectly competitive firm is given by the market price, and average revenue is also given by the market price. Thus, the individual firm's marginal-revenue curve and its average-revenue curve are both the same as the firm's demand curve.

5. If any firm is to maximize profits, it will produce the quantity at which marginal revenue equals marginal cost. For a perfectly competitive firm, marginal revenue equals the price. Thus, the perfectly competitive firm will maximize profits by producing the quantity at which price equals marginal cost.

6. The short-run supply curve for the perfectly competitive firm is the same as the firm's marginal-cost curve, so long as the marginal-cost curve is above the average-variable-cost curve. When price is less than average variable cost, the firm will shut down, and its quantity supplied will be zero.

7. The industry supply curve is formed by horizontally adding the supply curves of the individual firms.

8. If positive economic profits are being earned in a perfectly competitive industry, new firms will enter. This will increase industry supply, and will drive down the market price until the profits have been eliminated. If firms are suffering economic losses, some firms will leave the industry. This will increase the market price until firms are once again able to earn zero economic profits. The long-run tendency of a perfectly competitive industry is toward zero economic profits.

9. For a constant-cost industry, the long-run industry supply curve is a horizontal line. For an increasing-cost industry, the long-run industry supply curve slopes upward. For a decreasing-cost industry, the long-run industry supply curve slopes downward.

10. Perfect competition leads to some very attractive outcomes. First, in the long run, average total costs will be maximized. Second, at the perfectly competitive output marginal benefit equals marginal cost. At any other level of output, there will be a deadweight loss.

Key Terms

Market Structure

Perfect Competition

Standardized or Homogeneous Product

Free Entry

Free Exit

Monopoly

Barriers to Entry

Monopolistic Competition

Oligopoly

Differentiated Products

Collusion

Price-Taking Firm

Market Power

Marginal Revenue

Total Revenue

Average Revenue

Profit Maximization

MR = MC Rule

Short-Run Shut-Down Decision

Short-Run Supply Curve

Market Supply Curve

Long Run

Long-Run Supply Curve

Constant-Cost Industry

Increasing-Cost Industry

Decreasing-Cost Industry

Deadweight Loss

Key Figures

The key figures for this chapter are Figures 9.5(a), 9.5(b), 9.5(c), and 9.5(d).

Questions and Problems

QP9-1. XYZ Corporation is currently producing 1000 units of output. The marginal cost of one additional unit is $10, and the mar-ginal revenue is $12. Is the firm maximizing profits? If not, should it produce more or less?

QP9-2. The following table gives information on the costs of a perfectly competitive firm.

Quantity	Total Cost	Marginal Cost
0	20	—
1		5
2		3
3		5

a. When two units are produced, what is average variable cost?
b. When three units are produced, what is average total cost?
c. When two units are produced, what is average fixed cost?

QP9-3. List the characteristics of a perfectly competitive firm. What sets the perfectly competitive firm apart from the monopolistically competitive firm?

QP9-4. What type of market structure would apply most closely to each of the following firms?

a. Boeing Corporation, a producer of commercial aircraft.
b. A corn farm in Illinois.
c. A gasoline station on Interstate 80, in Auburn, California.
d. An electric power utility.

QP9-5. Fill in the blanks in the table at the top of the next page.

QP9-6. Explain why the perfectly competitive firm's supply curve coincides with its marginal cost curve. Why does the firm supply a quantity of zero when the price is less than average variable cost?

Quantity	Price	Marginal Revenue	Average Revenue	Total Revenue
1	$5	_____	_____	_____
2	5	_____	_____	_____
3	5	_____	_____	_____

QP9-7. The perfectly competitive firm whose supply schedule is shown in the following table is one of 1000 identical firms in its industry. Using this information, write down the market supply schedule for the entire industry.

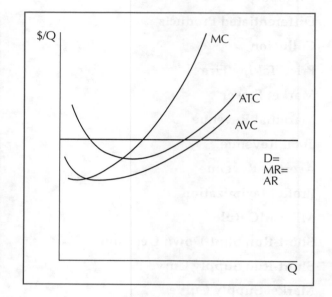

Price	Firm Supply	Industry Supply
$0	0	_____
1	5	_____
2	10	_____
3	15	_____

QP9-8. A perfectly competitive market has 100 identical firms. The curves for one such firm are shown above right. In the future, what would you expect to happen to the industry? Assuming that it stays in business, what would happen to the individual firm?

QP9-9. In the righthand column are the cost curves for another perfectly competitive firm, from another industry with many identical firms. What would we expect to happen to the industry? Assuming that it stays in business, what would happen to the individual firm?

QP9-10. Complete the following table. Assume that the firm is a perfect competitor. What is the profit-maximizing level of output for the firm? How much profit does it earn?

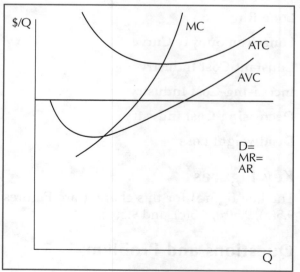

Quantity	Total Cost	Marginal Cost	Price	Marginal Revenue	Average Revenue	Total Revenue	Profit
0	$10	—	$10				
1		$6					
2		4					
3		5					
4		7					
5		10					
6		14					
7		19					
8		25					
9		32					

Chapter 10

Monopoly

ECONOMICS AND YOU:
DIALING FOR DOLLARS IN THE TELEPHONE MARKETS

Tamika Chandler makes lots of long-distance telephone calls. From her home in Atlanta, she calls her parents in Chicago, one set of grandparents in Mississippi, and another set of grandparents in Tennessee. Now that she has graduated from college, Tamika also keeps in touch with her college roommates, who have moved to Los Angeles, Detroit, and Baltimore.

Because she is on the phone so much, Tamika keeps careful track of her long-distance telephone bills. She used to subscribe with AT&T, which is the largest provider of long-distance service. But then she learned of a discount plan that allowed her to save money by subscribing with MCI. As the long-distance phone companies have continued to compete with each other, Tamika has continued to find new ways to save. In the last couple of years, she has switched from MCI to Sprint, and then back to MCI.

The long-distance market offers choices for consumers. It isn't a *perfectly* competitive market, like the ones that we discussed in Chapter 9, because the long-distance carriers are large. Nevertheless, consumers do have choices. None of the long-distance companies can charge prices that are too far out of line,

because customers are free to switch to other carriers.

The situation is starkly different in the market for local telephone service. BellSouth is the only provider of local phone service for Tamika, as well as for virtually everyone in a nine-State area, stretching from Louisiana to Florida to Kentucky. All across the country, most people can only get local phone service from one company. Most Pennsylvanians have no choice but to buy from Bell Atlantic, and most Texans have no choice but to buy from SBC.

When there's only one seller in a market, we say that the firm is a *monopoly*. In this chapter, we'll see that monopolies usually don't behave nearly as well as perfectly competitive industries. If there aren't any other firms in the industry, then the monopoly knows that it can raise its prices and not lose its customers to other firms. As a result, monopolies tend to charge higher prices than competitive firms would charge.

The local telephone companies are not the only examples of monopoly. The United States Postal Service has a monopoly on the delivery of first-class mail. Most communities have only one cable-TV firm, and many parts of the country also have local monopolies in the markets for electric power, natural gas, and water. Many professional sports franchises are regional monopolies: If you're in the Denver area and you want to see a major-league baseball game in person, your only choice is to see one of the home games of the Colorado Rockies. If you go to Yosemite National Park in California, you will find that virtually *all* services are provided by a monopoly called Yosemite Concession Services Corporation. This firm provides hotel rooms, cabins, restaurants, snack stands, gasoline stations, bus services, grocery stores, gift shops, sports shops, vending machines, guided tours, horse stables, and other services.

In this chapter, we'll discuss monopoly. We begin by describing the characteristics of monopoly, and then we describe the way in which monopolies maximize their profits. Finally, we provide some comparisons between the behavior of monopolies and the behavior of competitive firms.

CHARACTERISTICS OF MONOPOLY

If an industry is to be a monopoly, it has to have several characteristics:

- The industry must have only *one firm*.

- The firm must have *barriers to entry*, so potential competitors are unable to enter the industry.

- There must be *no close substitutes* for the firm's product.

Let's discuss these characteristics of monopoly in greater detail.

Only One Firm

Perfectly competitive firms are price takers, but monopolists are *price makers*: Because there is only one firm in the industry, the monopolist may be able to increase its profits by raising prices. Another way to say this is that the monopolist has *market power*, whereas the perfectly competitive firm has no market power.

Monopolies have the greatest amount of market power that we can imagine, but they aren't the only firms with market power. In later chapters, we will talk about monopolistically competitive firms and oligopolistic firms. These firms also have some market power, although they don't have as much market power as monopolies have.

Some industries have one firm that controls the overwhelming majority of the market, even though it isn't literally the *only* firm. For example, Microsoft Corporation produces more than 90 percent of the operating systems for personal computers. Therefore, according to our definition, Microsoft isn't a true monopoly. However, Microsoft's position is so dominant that it can behave in about the same way that a true monopoly would behave. Firms like Microsoft could be called "near monopolies". In this chapter, we'll look at "near monopolies", as well as true monopolies.

Barriers to Entry

A monopoly can only succeed if it has some way to keep out competitors. In the next few paragraphs, we'll discuss some of the many ways in which monopolists may be able to keep competitors from entering the market.

Legal Barriers. One way to keep out potential competitors is to have legal barriers to entry, such as patents and exclusive licenses. A *patent* gives an inventor a monopoly on his or her invention. Patents are extremely important for companies like Dupont, General Electric, and Xerox. These firms take great care to make sure that other firms don't threaten the patent monopoly by cheating on their patents.

Real Economics for Real People 10.1:
Monopoly in the Market for an AIDS Drug

Article I, Section 8 of the United States Constitution allows Congress "to promote the progress of science and useful arts, by securing for limited times to authors and inventors the exclusive right to their respective writings and discoveries". By law, the company that owns a patent gets a monopoly for a period of 17 years. Other firms can't infringe on the patents without breaking the law. When a company acquires a patent, it gets monopoly power.

Glaxo Wellcome Company owns the patent on the drug AZT, which is used in the treatment of AIDS. Like any successful monopolist, Glaxo Wellcome has used its position to earn hefty profits. A year's dose of AZT for one patient costs as much as $2500, which is far more than the cost of production.

Two other companies have said that they would sell AZT for a much lower price, if they were allowed to do so. These companies (Barr Laboratories, of Pomona, New York, and Novopharm, of Schaumburg, Illinois) challenged Glaxo Wellcome's patent in a lawsuit. They pointed out that AZT was the result of a very complex development process. Much of the research work was carried out by government researchers who were *not* employees of Glaxo Wellcome. However, courts have upheld Glaxo Wellcome's patent. AIDS patients will have to pay monopoly prices for AZT until the year 2005, when the patent expires. However, between now and the time that the AZT patent expires, AIDS patients will be able to get some relief from another source. In recent years, many other drugs have been developed. Consequently, some patients do not have to rely exclusively on AZT. Even after a patent expires, however, it's still possible for the inventor to produce successfully. For example, the Bayer Company had the patent on aspirin. The patent expired in 1917, and many other companies rushed in to produce aspirin. But Bayer still produces aspirin to this day. Therefore, Glaxo Wellcome will probably continue to produce AZT, even after the patent runs out.

The AZT case raises some tough problems of economic policy. New products (such as AZT) can be very valuable to society. Therefore, it may make sense to give incentives for research and development. Patent monopoly is one way to give such incentives. If the incentive of monopoly had not been there, it's possible that AZT wouldn't have been developed in the first place.

How much incentive is enough? If the period of patent monopoly were shortened, would we still get valuable research, without having to pay so much for so long? It's hard to say for sure. In any event, however, there doesn't seem to be much public pressure for major changes in the patent laws at this time.

In *Real Economics for Real People 10.1,* we discuss the controversy surrounding the patent monopoly on AZT, a drug that is used in the treatment of acquired immune deficiency syndrome (AIDS).

Another type of legal barrier to entry is the *exclusive franchise*. An exclusive franchise is a business arrangement under which only one firm is allowed to produce in a particular territory. For example, professional sports teams have monopoly power in their regional markets because they have exclusive franchises.

Also, the law sometimes gives monopoly power to government agencies. We've already mentioned the Postal Service monopoly. In many States, the State government gives itself a monopoly in liquor sales. Many States also give themselves monopolies in the market for lottery games. In Japan, a government agency runs monopolies on salt and tobacco. In the socialist economies of Cuba and North Korea, *most* industries are organized as government-run monopolies.

Natural Monopoly: Cost Advantages As Barriers to Entry

So far, we have spoken of *legal* barriers to entry. In virtually every case of legal barriers, competitors could enter the market successfully, *if* it were legal to do so. For example, when a patent expires, new firms usually enter the market quickly. Another example is that if the State of Pennsylvania were to stop giving itself a monopoly in the retail liquor business, many private liquor stores would probably open their doors in a very short time.

However, in some cases, the barrier to entry has to do with a cost advantage for the monopolist. If a single firm can produce at a lower average total cost than any combination of two or three or more firms, then we say that the firm is a *natural monopoly*.

Economists are often quite critical of legal barriers to entry. We expect that these barriers will lead to higher prices and less consumer satisfaction, relative to what would occur if the industry were competitive. But things aren't so clear-cut in the case of natural monopoly. If a natural monopoly were replaced by a group of competing firms, those firms would have higher costs. As a result, there's no guarantee that breaking up a natural monopoly will help consumers. We'll discuss natural monopoly in more detail, later in this chapter. In fact, however, natural monopoly is rare. Most monopolies rely on legal barriers, rather than on cost advantages.

No Close Substitutes for the Monopolist's Product

The first characteristic of a monopoly is that the market has only one firm. The second is that there are barriers to entry. The third characteristic is that, *if a firm is to have monopoly power, there must not be any close substitutes for its product.* For example, Daimler Chrysler Corporation is the world's only manufacturer of the Dodge Caravan, but it isn't very useful to think of Daimler Chrysler as a monopolist. Instead, we think of Daimler Chrysler as competing in the minivan market with Toyota (which produces the Previa), Ford (which produces the Ford Aerostar and Mercury Villager), and other companies. The Previa and the Villager aren't identical to the Caravan, but they are reasonably close substitutes.

The "company store" is an example of a monopoly that can be maintained because it is difficult for consumers to buy substitute products. In some isolated rural areas, there is only a single grocery store. Such a store can sometimes charge monopoly prices, because it's very costly for consumers to get to other stores. In John Steinbeck's novel, *The Grapes of Wrath* (set in the 1930s), the Joad family find themselves trying to buy hamburger from such a store. The Joads complain that the prices are one-third higher than at other locations. The store clerk admits that the prices are high. But he explains that the Joads would have to use a gallon of gasoline to reach another store, and they don't have enough money to buy a gallon of gasoline. Basically, the clerk is saying that the store can afford to charge monopoly prices, because it would cost a lot to go to another store. Therefore, from the Joads' point of view, the other stores aren't close substitutes for the company store.

In the 60 years since the time of *The Grapes of Wrath,* the American population has become more urbanized, more affluent, and more mobile. These days, for most Americans, it's inexpensive to choose among several different stores. Since most people can shop at a variety of stores that are close substitutes for each other, it won't be possible for any one store to exercise monopoly power. As a result, the situation faced by the Joads has (fortunately) become increasingly rare.

Occasionally, a large firm or a wealthy individual will attempt to buy so much of a resource that monopoly control is achieved. This is called "cornering the market". For example, in 1991, the Wall-Street firm of Salomon Brothers cornered the market in an auction of $12 billion of United States Treasury notes. In fact, the Treasury Department has rules that prohibit any individual firm from buying more than 35 percent of the notes at any particular auction. Nevertheless, Salomon Brothers violated the rules and acquired more than 85 percent of the notes sold on May 22, 1991. Other firms had accepted orders from customers, under the assumption that Salomon Brothers would *not* corner the market (that is, the other firms assumed that Salomon Brothers would not violate the rules). Since these other firms had promised to provide their customers with Treasury notes from that particular auction, there wasn't any available substitute. In order to meet their obligations to their customers, these other firms had to pay inflated prices to Salomon Brothers. The other firms suffered losses of more than $100 million. When news of the "squeeze" got out, a scandal erupted, and several Salomon Brothers executives were forced to resign.

The market for rough diamonds is another example of a monopoly that arises from control of resources for which there are few substitutes. In the eyes of many buyers, there are simply no close substitutes for diamonds: You don't give your fiancee a sapphire engagement ring; you give her the real thing. Because of the lack of substitutes, any firm that controls most of the world's diamonds will have a monopoly position. In fact, most of the world's diamonds are controlled by the South African firm of DeBeers Consolidated Mines. However, in *Real Economics for Real People 10.2, on p. 228*, we see that DeBeers's monopoly position is threatened by competitors.

Reality Check: Interim Review Question

IR10-1. Anheuser-Busch, Inc., is the only producer of Budweiser beer. Would you say that Anheuser-Busch is a monopolist?

THE DEMAND FOR THE OUTPUT OF A SINGLE-PRICE MONOPOLY

Slam Dunk State College is famous for its basketball teams, which play their home games in the Slam Dunk Coliseum. Like many other sports arenas, the Coliseum runs its food and beverage service as a monopoly. Fans aren't allowed to bring their own food or drinks into the Coliseum. If the fans get hungry and thirsty, they can only buy from Coliseum Enterprises, Inc. To understand the behavior of a monopolist, let's study the market for hot dogs at the Slam Dunk Coliseum.

Coliseum Enterprises is what we call a *single-price monopoly*, which means that the firm sells all of its hot dogs at the same price. This is because it's very hard for the firm to distinguish the customers who are willing to pay a lot of money for a hot dog from those who aren't willing to pay very much. Near the end of this chapter, we'll discuss *price discrimination*, under which a firm will sell the same product to different customers at different prices. *If* a firm is able to distinguish among its customers on the basis of how much they are willing to pay, the firm can increase its profits by engaging in price discrimination.

Real Economics for Real People 10.2:
Letters And Diamonds: How Monopoly Can Slip Away

A monopolist's product must not have close substitutes, and there must not be other sources of supply. If a substitute product appears, or if alternate sources of supply become available, the monopolist is in trouble.

One case in point is the United States Postal Service. The Constitution gives Congress the power to "establish post offices and post roads". This has usually been interpreted as meaning that the Postal Service should have a monopoly in the delivery of first-class mail.

The Postal Service has used its monopoly in an unusual way. Most monopolies would try to maximize their profits. However, for many years, the Postal Service had *losses*, which were covered with tax dollars. After the government subsidies were removed, the Postal Service was forced to become more efficient, but its profits were still fairly modest in most years. Instead of making high profits, the Postal Service has used its monopoly power to grant high wage rates for its workers. One study suggested that Postal-Service workers are paid 84 percent more than comparable workers in other mailrooms.

For years, the Service has faced competitors in practically every area except first-class mail. (For example, United Parcel Service and other firms have taken over most of the market for small package delivery.) And now, the first-class mail monopoly is threatened, too. The threats come from overnight delivery services, electronic mail, and fax machines. From the point of view of many customers, these are close substitutes for first-class letters. As faxes, e-mail messages, and overnight delivery become cheaper and more widely available, it will become harder and harder for the Postal Service to keep its customers. The challenge for the Postal Service is to continue to become more efficient, so that it can continue to guarantee service to every home in America, without suffering large losses.

Another case of a threatened monopoly is in the diamond market. Strictly speaking, DeBeers Consolidated Mines is only a near monopoly, since it only controls about 80 percent of the world market in rough diamonds. However, this 80-percent share is large enough that DeBeers has been able to behave like a monopolist.

DeBeers can only keep its monopoly position if it maintains control over the vast majority of supplies. However, in the early 1990s, the diamond market began to be flooded by new supplies that weren't under the control of DeBeers. Most of the new supplies came from Angola and from the new nations of the former Soviet Union. These new supplies would tend to depress prices. In order to keep prices high, DeBeers bought more than $200 million of new diamonds in 1991 and 1992. Also, the firm has negotiated agreements with Russian diamond producers, in an effort to keep control over as much of the market as possible.

Only time will tell whether DeBeers will be able to maintain its monopoly position. If it can't, the resulting price cuts will be bad for DeBeers, but good for people who want to buy wedding rings and other diamond jewelry.

The Postal Service and DeBeers are both protected by barriers to entry, but these barriers are incomplete. A monopoly firm is only secure if it is shielded by *strong* barriers to entry. If the barriers are leaky, competitive forces will challenge the monopolist again and again.

The Monopoly Firm's Demand Curve

Since Coliseum Enterprises is a monopolist, *it faces the* entire *market demand for hot dogs at the Coliseum. The demand curve for the firm's output is the same as the market demand curve.*

Table 10.1 shows the demand schedule for the hot-dog monopoly at Slam Dunk Coliseum. In order to keep the numbers manageable, we show the demand schedule for hot dogs *per minute.*

If hot dogs were priced above $5.00 each, no one would be willing to buy. If the price were $5.00, the basketball fans would be willing to buy one hot dog per minute. When the price falls to $4.50, the quantity demanded would increase to two hot dogs per minute. In fact, every time the price falls by 50 cents, the quantity demanded increases by one hot dog per minute.

The demand facing a monopolist is fundamentally different from the demand facing a perfectly competitive firm. As we saw in Chapter 9, the perfectly competitive firm can sell as many units as it wants to sell at the mar-

ket price. On the other hand, *if a single-price monopolist wants to sell more output, it has to decrease the price on* all *units that it sells.*

Marginal Revenue, Total Revenue, and Average Revenue for the Single-Price Monopolist

In Chapter 9, we learned about marginal revenue, which is a very important concept for the business firm. Marginal revenue is the additional amount of money that the firm receives, if it sells one more unit of output. Marginal revenue is constant for the perfectly competitive firm, because the firm can sell as many units as it wants to sell at the market price. *For the monopolist, however, marginal revenue will decrease as quantity increases.* We can see this by working through the example of hot dogs at Slam Dunk Coliseum.

Marginal Revenue and Total Revenue. Table 10.1 shows the demand schedule for hot dogs at Slam Dunk Coliseum, and it also shows total revenue and marginal revenue. We get total revenue by multiplying the price by

Table 10.1 Demand, Total Revenue, and Marginal Revenue for Hot Dogs At Slam Dunk Coliseum

P Price (In Dollars Per Hot Dog)	Q Quantity Demanded (Hot Dogs Per Minute)	TR Total Revenue (= P x Q)	MR Marginal Revenue (= Change in TR/ Change in Q)
$5.50	0	$0	—
5.00	1	5	$5
4.50	2	9	4
4.00	3	12	3
3.50	4	14	2
3.00	5	15	1
2.50	6	15	0
2.00	7	14	−1
1.50	8	12	−2
1.00	9	9	−3
0.50	10	5	−4
0.00	11	0	−4

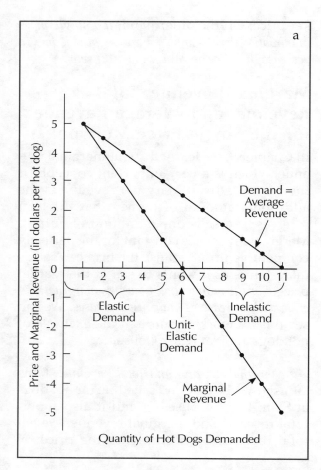
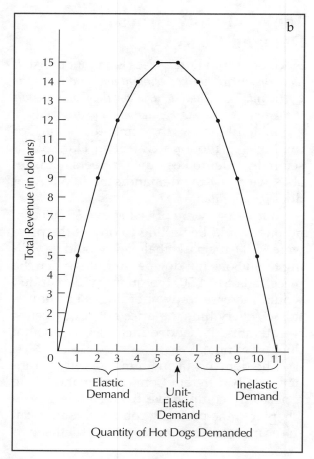

Figure 10.1 The Demand Curve, Marginal-Revenue Curve, and Total-Revenue Curve for Coliseum Enterprises, Inc.

Since Coliseum Enterprises is a monopolist, it faces the entire downward-sloping market demand curve for hot dogs. The demand curve is shown in panel (a). The demand curve could also be called the average-revenue curve.

The total-revenue curve shows the total sales revenue that the firm receives from all of its sales of hot dogs. The total-revenue curve is shown in panel (b). For a downward-sloping demand curve, the total-revenue curve will rise at first, and then fall.

The marginal-revenue curve shows the additional sales revenue that the firm receives, when it sells one additional hot dog. The marginal-revenue curve is shown in panel (a). For a downward-sloping demand curve, the marginal-revenue curve will always be below the demand curve. When the demand curve is a straight line, the marginal-revenue curve will be exactly twice as steep as the demand curve.

Marginal revenue is the change in total revenue when one additional hot dog is sold. Thus, marginal revenue represents the slope of the total-revenue curve. When total revenue slopes upward, marginal revenue is positive. This occurs when demand is elastic. When the total-revenue curve reaches its peak, marginal revenue is zero. This occurs when demand is unit elastic. When total revenue slopes downward, marginal revenue is less than zero. This occurs when demand is inelastic.

the quantity. In symbols, TR = (P)x(Q). *Marginal revenue is the change in total revenue, when quantity increases by one unit. Equivalently, marginal revenue is the change in total revenue divided by the change in quantity.* In symbols, MR = ΔTR / ΔQ.

For the first hot dog sold at Slam Dunk Coliseum, the maximum price that consumers would be willing to pay is $5. Therefore, if one hot dog per minute were sold, total revenue per minute would be $5: TR = (P)x(Q) = ($5 per hot dog)x(1 hot dog) = $5. The marginal revenue for the first hot dog sold is also $5: When the number of hot dogs increases from zero to one, total revenue increases from $0 to $5, so that the marginal revenue for the first hot dog is ($5 – $0) = $5.

If Coliseum Enterprises were to sell two hot dogs per minute, the firm would have to drop the price to $4.50. Total revenue would now be ($4.50 per hot dog)x(2 hot dogs) = $9.00 per minute. Total revenue increases from $5 to $9 when the firm sells a second hot dog, so that the marginal revenue for the second hot dog is ($9 – $5) = $4. If Coliseum Enterprises were to sell a third hot dog, the price would have to fall to $4. Total revenue would be ($4)x(3) = $12, and marginal revenue would be ($12 – $9) = $3.

The information in Table 10.1 is graphed in Figure 10.1. Panel (a) of the figure shows the demand curve and marginal-revenue curve for the hot-dog monopoly. *When the demand curve is a straight line, as in this case, the marginal-revenue curve is exactly twice as steep as the demand curve.*

Panel (b) of Figure 10.1 shows the total-revenue curve for the hot-dog monopoly. *Since marginal revenue is the change in total revenue when one additional unit is sold, the marginal-revenue curve is the slope of the total-revenue curve.* This relationship is similar to some other relationships that we have seen in earlier chapters. For example, in Chapter 8, we saw that marginal cost is the slope of the total-cost curve. In Chapter 7, we saw that marginal utility is the slope of the total-utility curve.

The slope of the total-revenue curve is positive when total revenue is increasing. This means that marginal revenue must be positive when the total-revenue curve slopes upward to the right.

In this example, total revenue increases until the quantity reaches 5 hot dogs per minute. If Coliseum Enterprises were to sell five hot dogs per minute, it would charge $3 per hot dog, and total revenue would be (5)x(3) = $15. If the firm were to sell a sixth hot dog per minute, it would have to reduce the price from $3.00 to $2.50. Now, total revenue would be (6)x($2.50) = $15. The increase in quantity is exactly offset by the reduction in price, so that total revenue remains unchanged. Therefore, the marginal revenue of the sixth hot dog per minute is zero. When quantity increases from five to six, total revenue is maximized, and the slope of the total-revenue curve is zero.

If the quantity goes above six, total revenue actually decreases. When the total-revenue curve slopes downward to the right, marginal revenue is negative.

Average Revenue. In Chapter 9, on perfect competition, we defined average revenue. Recall that the definition of average revenue is similar to the definitions of other averages that we have seen: ***Average revenue*** is total revenue divided by the number of units sold. In symbols, AR = TR/Q.

A few paragraphs ago, we saw that total revenue is the price multiplied by the number of units sold: TR = (P)x(Q). If we put the expression for AR together with the expression for TR, we have AR = TR/Q = (P)x(Q) / Q = P. For the single-price monopolist, *average revenue equals price.* (Average revenue is also equal to price for a perfectly competitive firm, because a perfectly competitive firm will also sell all units at the same price.)

Now, recall that a demand curve is a graph of the relationship between price and quantity demanded. Since average revenue is the price, *the average-revenue curve is identical to the demand curve for the firm's output.* In Figure 10.1(a), we see that the average-revenue curve (that is, the demand curve) slopes downward, and the marginal-revenue curve slopes downward more steeply. This is yet another example of the relationships between marginal quantities and average quantities—When marginal revenue is less than average revenue, average revenue will be decreasing.

Total Revenue, Marginal Revenue, and the Elasticity of Demand

If you aren't clear about how to calculate and use elasticities, this would be a good time to take another look at Chapter 6.

Here is a brief review of the relationship between price, quantity, total revenue, and the own-price elasticity of demand: Whenever we move downward and to the right along a demand curve, the quantity demanded increases and the price decreases. Since total revenue is price multiplied by quantity, we have two opposite influences on total revenue. By itself, the decrease in price will tend to *decrease* total revenue. However, the increase in quantity will tend to *increase* total revenue. The net effect on total revenue will depend on whether the price decrease is stronger or weaker than the increase in quantity.

If the percentage increase in quantity demanded is larger than the percentage decrease in price, we say that demand is *elastic.* When demand is elastic, total revenue will increase when quantity increases. If the percentage increase in quantity demanded is equal to the percentage decrease in price, we say that demand is *unit elastic.* When demand is unit elastic, total revenue will not change. Finally, if the percentage increase in quantity demanded is smaller than the percentage decrease in price, we say that demand is *inelastic.* When demand is inelastic, total revenue will decrease when quantity increases.

Now that we have reviewed the elasticity concepts, we can divide the total-revenue and marginal-revenue curves in Figure 10.1 into three regions, which are closely related to the own-price elasticity of demand.

- *Total revenue increases* as we move from a quantity of zero to a quantity of five, and this means that *marginal revenue is positive.* Since the increase in quantity is associated with an increase in total revenue, we know that *demand is elastic.* This corresponds to the region on the left of Figure 10.1.

- *Total revenue is constant* as we move from Q=5 to Q=6, and this means that *marginal revenue is zero.* Since total revenue is unchanged, *demand is unit elastic.*

- When quantity increases above six, *total revenue is declining,* and this means that *marginal revenue is negative.* Since the increase in quantity is associated with a decrease in total revenue, *demand is inelastic.* This corresponds to the region on the right of Figure 10.1.

We've now looked at the monopolist's revenues. The next step is to combine this information on revenues with information on costs, so that we can study profits.

Reality Check: Interim Review Questions

IR10-2. Marginal revenue is a constant for a perfectly competitive firm. However, for a monopolist, marginal revenue decreases when sales increase. Explain why this is so.

IR10-3. Colossal Corporation is a monopolist. If the firm were to sell one more unit of output, its total revenue would increase. Is Colossal Corporation's marginal revenue greater than zero or less than zero? Is the firm facing elastic demand or inelastic demand?

THE PRICE AND QUANTITY DECISIONS OF THE SINGLE-PRICE MONOPOLIST

In Chapter 9, on perfect competition, we saw that there are two ways to think about how the firm chooses its profit-maximizing quantity: We can compare *total* revenue and *total* cost, or we can compare *marginal* revenue and *marginal* cost. We'll do the same here for monopolies. We begin by comparing total revenue and total cost. Later, we will compare marginal revenue and marginal cost.

The Monopolist's Profit-Maximizing Decisions: Comparing Total Revenue and Total Cost

In Table 10.2, we repeat the revenue information from Table 10.1, and we also add some information on costs. We want to concentrate on the most important things, so we will assume that Coliseum Enterprises has a simple cost structure. If one hot dog per minute is produced, total cost is $1. If two are produced, total cost is $2. If 47 hot dogs are produced, total cost is $47, and so on. In other words, the firm has no fixed costs, and its marginal costs are constant. For *each* additional hot dog, the marginal cost is $1.

Total variable cost is the sum of the marginal costs. Since there are no fixed costs, total cost is equal to total variable cost. Therefore, in this special example, total cost is also the sum of the marginal costs.

Profit is total revenue minus total cost. When Coliseum Enterprises sells one hot dog per minute, total revenue is $5, total cost is $1, and profit is ($5 − $1) = $4. Since the first hot dog gives positive profit, the firm will sell at least one hot dog. If the firm were to sell a second hot dog, total revenue would increase to $9, total cost would go to $2, and profit would rise to ($9 − $2) = $7. Since the profit is higher with two hot dogs than with one, it makes sense for the firm to sell at least two hot dogs.

We can continue to think in this way until we find the quantity with the maximum profit. The maximum profit in this example is $10, at a quantity of 4 or 5 hot dogs per minute. As in Chapter 9 on perfect competition, we assume

Table 10.2 Revenues, Costs, and Profits for Hot Dogs At Slam Dunk Coliseum

P Price	Q Quantity Demanded	TR Total Revenue	MR Marginal Revenue	TC Total Cost	MC Marginal Cost	Profit (= Total Revenue Minus Total Cost)
$5.50	0	$0	—	$0	—	$0
5.00	1	5	$5	1	$1	4
4.50	2	9	4	2	1	7
4.00	3	12	3	3	1	9
3.50	4	14	2	4	1	10
3.00	5	15	1	5	1	10
2.50	6	15	0	6	1	9
2.00	7	14	−1	7	1	7
1.50	8	12	−2	8	1	4
1.00	9	9	−3	9	1	0
0.50	10	5	−4	10	1	−5
0.00	11	0	−5	11	1	−11

(handwritten annotation in TC header: "TC = TVC (no TFC)")

that the firm will produce the larger amount: Coliseum Enterprises will produce and sell five hot dogs per minute.

The information on total revenue and total cost, from Table 10.2, is graphed in panel (a) of Figure 10.2. The vertical distance between the total-revenue curve and the total-cost curve is the firm's profit. Thus, the firm will maximize its profits by producing the quantity at which the vertical distance between the TR curve and the TC curve is greatest. As we showed in Chapter 9, the vertical distance between two curves is maximized where the two curves are parallel. In other words, the distance between the curves is greatest when the slope of the total-revenue curve is the same as the slope of the total-cost curve. This occurs at a quantity of five hot dogs per minute, so that the profit-maximizing quantity is five hot dogs per minute.

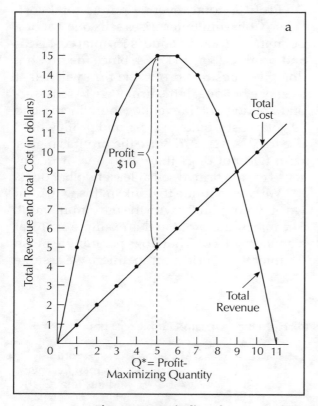
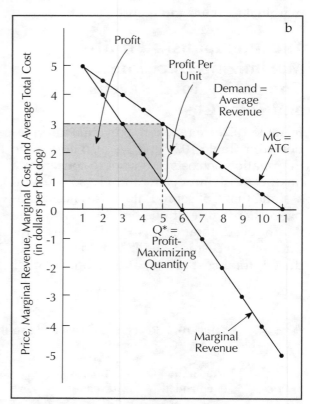

Figure 10.2 Finding the Level of Output and Profit for Coliseum Enterprises

In panel (a), profit is the vertical distance between the total-revenue curve and the total-cost curve. The profit-maximizing quantity of output is the quantity at which this vertical distance is the greatest. In this case, the profit-maximizing quantity of output is five. In other words, Coliseum Enterprises maximizes its profits by selling five hot dogs per minute.

Panel (b) shows the marginal-revenue and marginal-cost curves. The profit-maximizing quantity is at the intersection of these curves. (Once again, the profit-maximizing quantity is five hot dogs per minute.) The firm's profit per unit is the difference between price and average total cost, at the profit-maximizing quantity. If we multiply profit per unit by the quantity, we get the firm's profit, which is the shaded area in panel (b).

The Monopolist's Profit-Maximizing Decisions: Comparing Marginal Revenue and Marginal Cost

In the preceding section, we studied the information on *total* revenue and *total* cost, from Table 10.2. That table also contains information on *marginal* revenue and *marginal* cost. In Chapter 9, we learned that *any firm will maximize profits by producing the quantity at which marginal revenue equals marginal cost*. From Table 10.2, we can see that MR = MC when Q = 5. At this quantity, both MR and MC are $1 per additional hot dog. The graph is found in panel (b) of Figure 10.2.

We find the same profit-maximizing quantity, regardless of whether we look at *total* revenue and cost, or *marginal* revenue and cost. This makes a lot of sense, if we consider the close relationship between total quantities and marginal quantities. Marginal revenue is the slope of the total-revenue curve, and marginal cost is the slope of the total-cost curve. As a result, *when marginal cost equals marginal revenue, total cost will have the same slope as total revenue, and profit will be maximized.*

Using Graphs to Calculate Profit

How much profit does Coliseum Enterprises make? In Chapter 9, on perfect competition, we learned that *profit per unit is price minus average total cost*. It would be valuable to use panel (b) of Figure 10.2 to show the firm's profit. If we are to do this, we need to identify the firm's price and its average total cost.

First, let's find the price. The profit-maximizing quantity is five hot dogs. At this quantity, how much are consumers willing to pay? The answer comes from the demand schedule, which is found on the left side of Table 10.2. When Q = 5, consumers are willing to pay $3 per hot dog, and this is the price that the monopolist will charge. Even though the

marginal cost of producing the fifth hot dog is only $1, the price will be $3.

Next, let's find the average total cost for Coliseum Enterprises, Inc. The firm has no fixed costs, which means that average total cost and average variable cost will be the same in this example. Average variable cost is the average of all of the marginal costs. If the marginal cost for the first hot dog is $1, and the second hot dog also has marginal cost of $1, then the average variable cost for the two will be $1. Since marginal cost stays constant at $1 for each additional hot dog, average *variable* cost will also stay constant at $1 per hot dog. With no fixed costs, average *total* cost in this example will also be $1 per hot dog.

We now know that Coliseum Enterprises will sell five hot dogs per minute at a price of $3 each, and that its average total cost is $1 per hot dog. Profit per hot dog is (P – ATC), or ($3 – $1), or $2. When we multiply the profit per hot dog by the number of hot dogs, we get the firm's profit. This is ($2 per hot dog)(5 hot dogs per minute) = $10 per minute.

The firm's profit is drawn in panel (b) of Figure 10.2. Profit per hot dog is the vertical distance between the price of $3 and the average total cost of $1. The number of hot dogs per minute is 5, which is shown on the horizontal axis. If we multiply profit per hot dog (on the vertical axis) by the number of hot dogs per minute (on the horizontal axis), we get a rectangle for the firm's profit per minute. This profit rectangle is the shaded area in panel (b) of Figure 10.2.

More Examples of Revenues, Costs, and Profits for Monopolies

Coliseum Enterprises has a simple cost structure. The firm has no fixed costs, and it has constant marginal costs. Figure 10.3 shows a somewhat more involved set of cost and revenue curves. The information in Figure 10.3 is for Monolithic Pharmaceutical Company, which has a patent on a drug called soma. The patent gives Monolithic a monopoly in the soma market. Monolithic has fixed costs, and it also has increasing marginal costs. We can tell that the firm has fixed costs by looking at panel (a) of Figure 3: Total cost is positive, even when output is zero. This graph also reveals that the firm has increasing marginal costs, because the slope of the total-cost curve becomes larger and larger as we move to the right in the diagram.

Even though the details of Figure 10.3(a) are different from the details of Figure 10.2(a), the basic idea is still the same. Profit is the vertical distance between the total-revenue curve and the total-cost curve. Profit is maximized when the firm produces the quantity at which the total-revenue curve is parallel to the total-cost curve. In the figure, the profit-maximizing quantity is Q*.

Panel (b) of Figure 10.3 has the *marginal* cost and revenue curves for Monolithic Pharmaceutical Company. Monolithic has a U-shaped average-total-cost curve (ATC), in contrast to the horizontal cost curves of our example of Coliseum Enterprises. As always,

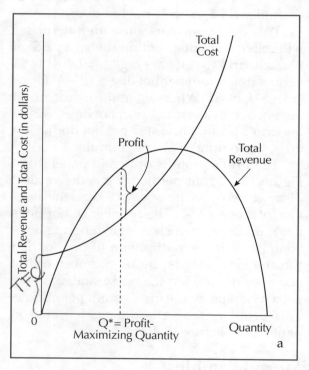 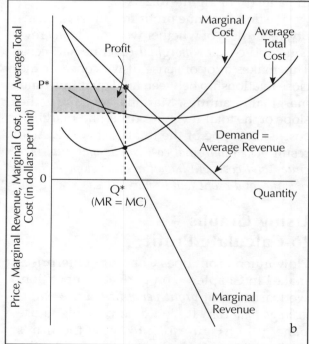

Figure 10.3 Finding the Level of Output and Profit for Monolithic Pharmaceutical Company

In panel (a), profit is the vertical distance between the total-revenue curve and the total-cost curve. The profit-maximizing quantity of output is the quantity at which this vertical distance is the greatest. In this case, the profit-maximizing quantity of output is Q*. In other words, Monolithic Pharmaceutical Company maximizes its profits by producing Q* units of soma.

Panel (b) shows the firm's marginal-revenue and marginal-cost curves. The profit-maximizing quantity, Q*, is at the intersection of these curves. The corresponding price is P*. The firm's profit per unit is the difference between price and average total cost, at the profit-maximizing quantity. If we multiply profit per unit by the quantity, Q*, we get the firm's profit, which is the shaded area in panel (b).

the ATC curve reaches its minimum when ATC = MC.

Figures 10.2(a) and 10.3(a) are basically similar, and this is also true for Figures 10.2(b) and 10.3(b). Here are some of the similarities between Figure 10.2(b) and Figure 10.3(b):

- The firm still finds its profit-maximizing quantity by looking for the quantity at which the MR curve intersects the MC curve.

- Once the profit-maximizing quantity is found, we still go up to the demand curve to find the price.

- Then, we determine profit per unit by subtracting average total cost from price.

- Once again, the profit is shown as a shaded rectangle. The base of the rectangle is the profit-maximizing quantity, while the height of the rectangle is the vertical distance between price and average total

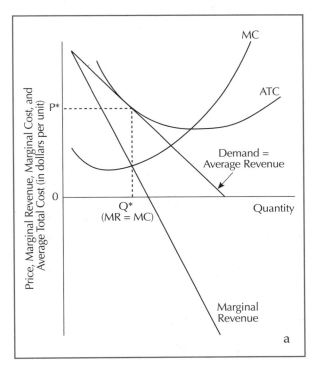

Figure 10.4 Panel (a)
Output and Profit For Enormous Corporation,
Which Earns Zero Economic Profit

Like any firm, Enormous Corporation will maximize profits by producing the quantity at which marginal revenue equals marginal cost. In this case, the quantity is Q*, and the corresponding price is P*. Profit per unit is the difference between price and average total cost. In this case, at Q*, price is exactly equal to average total cost. Therefore, Enormous Corporation is making zero economic profit.

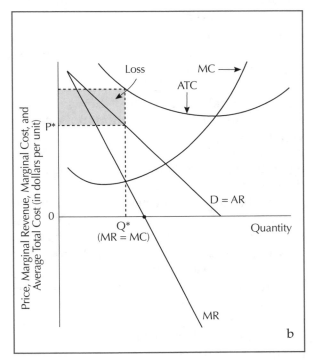

Figure 10.4 Panel (b)
Output and Profit For Gigantic Corporation,
Which Earns Negative Economic Profit

Like any firm, Gigantic Corporation will maximize profits by producing the quantity at which marginal revenue equals marginal cost. In this case, the quantity is Q*, and the corresponding price is P*. Profit per unit is the difference between price and average total cost. In this case, at Q*, price is less than average total cost. Therefore, Gigantic Corporation is making negative economic profit. In other words, the firm is suffering losses. The losses are represented by the shaded area in the figure.

cost, evaluated at the profit-maximizing quantity. Monolithic Pharmaceutical Company makes a positive profit, just as Coliseum Enterprises did.

So far, we've only studied monopolies that are making positive economic profits. Monopolies do indeed often make very large profits, but there's no guarantee that a monopoly will always earn profits. If costs are relatively high, and/or if demand is relatively low, the monopoly firm may not be able to make economic profits. Figure 10.4(a), on p. 237, shows the cost and revenue curves for a monopolist called Enormous Corporation. In this case, the monopoly is just breaking even, earning zero economic profit. Price and average total cost are equal at the profit-maximizing quantity, and this means that the firm has zero profit per unit. Finally, Figure 4(b) shows the cost and revenue curves for a monopoly called Gigantic Corporation, which is actually suffering economic losses: Price is *less* than average total cost. The shaded area represents the firm's economic losses.

In Chapter 9, on perfect competition, we showed that the perfectly competitive firm will produce at minimum average total cost. However, Figures 10.3(b) and 10.4 show that this is not the case for the monopolist. It's *possible* that a monopoly might produce at minimum average total cost, but it would only be a coincidence. In general, we don't expect that monopolies will locate at the minimum point on their ATC curves.

The Monopolist Raises Price Until Demand Is Elastic

Figure 10.1 showed that the monopolist's demand curve can be divided into three regions: At relatively low quantities, demand is elastic, which means that marginal revenue is positive. At high quantities, demand is inelastic, so that marginal revenue is negative. In between, there will be a quantity at which

demand is unit elastic, and marginal revenue is zero.

We've also seen that any monopolist will produce the quantity at which MR = MC. Since marginal cost is always positive, and since marginal revenue equals marginal cost at the profit-maximizing quantity, it follows that *marginal revenue must be positive at the monopolist's profit-maximizing quantity*. Now, marginal revenue can only be positive if demand is elastic. This means that *demand must be elastic at the monopolist's profit-maximizing quantity. The monopolist will raise prices until demand becomes elastic.*

Here's another way to understand the ideas of the last paragraph: Business firms are always asking themselves whether they can make more profit by producing and selling one more unit. Producing one extra unit is always costly—marginal cost has to be positive. Therefore, the firm can't possibly be maximizing its profits unless marginal revenue is also positive. If marginal revenue were negative, then the firm could always do better by reducing its output. Reducing output would save costs *and* increase revenue. This is why the monopolist will never choose a quantity at which demand is inelastic. Instead, the monopolist will always choose to move into the elastic region of its demand curve.

The Monopolist Has No Supply Curve

A supply curve is a graph of the relationship between price and quantity supplied. For any price, a supply curve will identify the *unique* quantity that a firm will bring to market. But monopolists don't have any such unique relationship between price and quantity supplied, because the monopolist's behavior depends on the shape of the demand curve. Give a monopolist a different demand curve, and the firm will change to a different quantity supplied. Because of this, it doesn't make sense to talk of the monopolist's supply curve.

IR10-4. A monopolist will produce the quantity at which marginal cost equals _____.

IR10-5. Does a monopoly firm have a supply curve? Why, or why not?

IR10-6. Explain why the monopolist will produce a quantity at which demand is elastic.

ECONOMIC EVALUATION OF MONOPOLY

In Chapter 9, we studied the behavior of perfectly competitive firms. We've now studied the behavior of monopolies. It's time to combine our understanding of these two market structures, so that we can learn how to measure the damage done by monopoly.

Let's return to the Slam Dunk Coliseum, where Coliseum Enterprises has a monopoly on the sale of hot dogs. Earlier in this chapter, we saw that this firm would maximize its profits by charging $3 per hot dog, and selling five hot dogs per minute. With average total costs of $1 per hot dog, the firm would make a profit of $2 on every hot dog sold. This information was shown in Figure 10.2(b), part of which is reproduced here as part of Figure 10.5. In this figure, $P_m = \$3$ is the monopolist's price, and $Q_m = 5$ is the monopolist's quantity. The firm's profit per minute is ($2 per hot dog)x(5 hot dogs per minute), for a total profit of $10 per minute. The monopoly profit is represented by the rectangle DEFC, in Figure 10.5.

What would happen if Coliseum Enterprises were to lose its exclusive franchise? What if anyone could come in and start selling hot dogs competitively? When we discussed perfect competition in the previous chapter, we learned that the perfectly competitive firm's supply curve is its marginal-cost curve. In this example, the marginal-cost curve is a horizontal line at $1 per hot dog. Therefore, if hot dogs were sold competitively, each competitive firm's supply curve would be a horizontal line at $1, and the market supply curve would also be a horizontal line at $1. This sup-

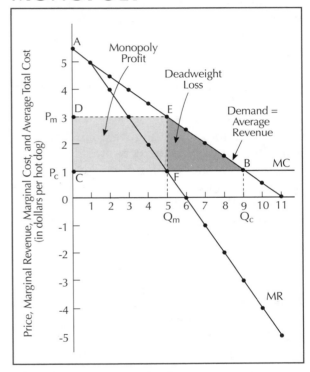

Figure 10.5 The Deadweight Loss of Monopoly

If the hot-dog market is run as a monopoly, the profit-maximizing quantity is Q_m, and the corresponding price is P_m. If the market is organized according to perfect competition, the market equilibrium quantity is Q_c, and the corresponding price is P_c. With perfect competition, the firms earn zero economic profits. With monopoly, the firm earns a positive economic profit of DEFC. For the units between Q_m and Q_c, the marginal benefit of consumption is greater than the marginal cost of production. Therefore, society is worse off when we consume Q_m units, instead of Q_c units. The loss from consuming only Q_m units is called the deadweight loss of monopoly. The deadweight loss is represented by the triangle, EBF.

ply curve intersects the demand curve at a quantity of 9 hot dogs per minute. In Figure 10.5, $P_c = \$1$ is the competitive price, and $Q_c = 9$ is the competitive quantity. If competition were allowed, economic profits would be zero. With competition, the price would be $1, and average total cost would be $1, and all of the firms would just break even.

It's clear that *producers are better off under monopoly*: The monopolist gets economic profits, whereas there aren't any economic profits with perfect competition. On the other hand, *consumers are worse off under monopoly*. They pay higher prices, and they buy a lower quantity.

In fact, *the consumer's losses are greater than the monopolist's gains.* In other words, *society as a whole is made worse off by monopoly.* We can see this by looking at Figure 10.5. The marginal benefit of hot-dog consumption is represented by the demand curve, and the marginal cost of hot-dog production is represented by the marginal-cost curve. For every unit between Q_m, the monopoly quantity, and Q_c, the competitive quantity, marginal benefit is greater than marginal cost. Therefore, society should produce and consume Q_c. If we produce and consume Q_m, instead of Q_c, we suffer a loss. The loss is the sum of the differences between marginal benefit and marginal cost, for all units from Q_m to Q_c. The loss, which is represented by the triangle EBF in Figure 10.5, is called the *deadweight loss* of monopoly. The ***deadweight loss*** of monopoly is the amount by which society is worse off, as a result of having monopoly instead of competition. The base of the deadweight-loss triangle is $(9-5) = 4$. The height of the triangle is $(\$3-\$1) = \$2$. Thus, the area of the triangle is $(0.5)(4)(\$2) = \$4$. The deadweight loss is $4 per minute. This is fairly large, when we consider that the total cost of production is only ($1 per hot dog)(5 hot dogs per minute) = $5 per minute.

The losses caused by monopoly can be large. Some economists have estimated that the transfer to monopolists, in terms of higher profits, might be between 2 percent and 3 percent of gross domestic product. The deadweight loss of monopoly might be of similar size. In other words, the deadweight loss of monopoly in the United States might be as large as $100 billion per year, or even $200 billion per year.

Using this example, we've identified four effects of monopoly:

- The monopolist charges higher prices than perfect competitors would charge.

- Because of the higher prices under monopoly, a lower quantity is bought and sold under monopoly than under competition.

- The monopolist earns profits in the long run, whereas perfectly competitive firms will only earn a normal return. That is, competitive firms will earn zero economic profits in the long run.

- Monopoly causes a deadweight loss.

In the next few sections, we'll look at some other possible effects of monopolies.

Do Monopolies Keep Their Costs under Control?

In the previous section, we analyzed the differences between competition and monopoly, *assuming that the cost curves were the same in the two cases.* But monopolies might also be wasteful, in the sense that they don't produce the most possible output with their resources. It takes hard work to control costs, and to use the latest technologies. If your firm is a secure monopoly, you'll be tempted to take leisurely coffee breaks and long lunches.

The workers of the monopoly firm probably don't have as much incentive to work hard as they would if they worked for a competitive firm, and the managers don't have as much incentive to adopt the latest and most efficient techniques. This lack of incentives can lead to wasted resources.

Real Economics for Real People 10.3:
Can We Get Better Education
by Reforming the Public School Monopolies?

In 1960, American public schools spent an average of $472 per student. By 1995, this figure had grown to $5907. Even after correcting for inflation, per-pupil expenditures increased by a whopping 143 percent over this period.

What did we get in return for all of this extra spending? For one thing, we got less-crowded classrooms. The average pupil/teacher ratio dropped from 25.8 in 1960 to 17.4 in 1995. Also, teacher salaries rose substantially. Teacher salaries are now about two-thirds higher than the pay of the average worker.

In spite of the additional spending, however, the public schools don't seem to have achieved much improvement in the education received by children. Test scores have shown very little improvement in recent decades. Research doesn't find any clear relationship between student achievement and class size, or teacher salaries, or teacher experience.

Public schools in America have a significant degree of monopoly power, and this may be a part of the problem. In almost all communities, taxpayers are required to pay taxes that are used to subsidize public schools, and most families use this subsidy to send their children to public schools, free of charge. Private schools do exist in some communities, but individual parents have to pay private-school tuition out of their own pockets. The cost difference between non-subsidized private schools and subsidized public schools is often very great, so that low- and middle-income families really have very little choice. As a result, the public schools have an effective monopoly in providing schooling for the children of many families.

Many economists have suggested that monopoly power allows the public schools to waste resources. In other words, the public-school monopolies are accused of X-inefficiency. Protected by their monopoly status, the public schools have little incentive to adopt innovative teaching techniques, or to weed out poor teachers, or to control costs. For example, public schools tend to have larger bureaucracies than comparable private schools. The New York City public schools have about 10 times as many students as the Catholic schools in New York, but the public schools have about 200 times as many administrators.

Because public schools have used more resources and produced disappointing results, reformers are increasingly challenging the monopoly status of the public schools. In recent years, many proposals for *voucher systems* have been introduced. The idea is that tax dollars would be used to give every child a voucher, which could be used at *any* school, including schools that are not operated by governments. The vouchers would give parents the ability to send their children to different schools, without having to move to a new school district. This would inject an element of competition and choice into the school system. If a school had a reputation for poor-quality instruction, it would have difficulty in attracting students.

School choice isn't a magical solution to the problems facing the educational system. Students will still have to do their homework in order to do well, regardless of whether they attend monopoly schools or competitive schools. Still, as long as many parents believe that the public schools aren't doing a good job, it seems very likely that the idea of school choice will continue to attract a lot of attention.

ful, because it has a reduced incentive to use resources wisely, the waste is sometimes called *X-inefficiency*.

Many studies have shown that X-inefficiency can be important. For example, some electric power utilities are monopolies, while others are not. One study showed that the power companies that faced competition had unit costs that were about 11 percent lower than the monopolies' costs. Another example is the British glass-bottle industry, which had a price-fixing agreement that allowed the firms to share in monopoly profits. When this agreement broke down, the firms had to learn how to compete. They introduced modern equipment, and output per worker went up by nearly 100 percent!

We have now seen that *monopolies cause three distinct types of inefficiency.* The deadweight loss occurs because the monopolist charges prices above marginal cost. The second type of inefficiency comes from the fact that the monopoly doesn't usually produce at the minimum point of its average total cost curve. Finally, the monopoly may be guilty of X-inefficiency.

In *Real Economics for Real People 10.3,* on p. 241, we consider the effects of monopoly on efficiency in public education.

Reality Check: Interim Review Question

IR10-7. When compared with the situation under perfect competition, will consumers be better off or worse off under monopoly?

CAN WE SAY ANYTHING GOOD ABOUT MONOPOLY?

So far, we've seen that monopolies tend to raise prices and reduce quantities. Monopolies generate deadweight losses, and they tend to be less efficient than competitive firms. It's not a pretty picture. In this section, we'll consider whether there are any situations in which monopolies may not be so bad.

Natural monopoly

In our example of the hot-dog market at the Slam Dunk Coliseum, we assumed that average total cost was constant. In other words, the average-total-cost curve was drawn as a horizontal line. In a situation like this, monopolies wouldn't have any cost advantage over competitive firms. But what if average total cost were decreasing over the entire range of output? Figure 10.6 shows the cost curves for a firm of this type. From earlier chapters, we know that marginal cost will be less than average total cost, if average total cost is decreasing. In Figure 10.6, ATC slopes downward to the right, and MC is always below ATC.

An industry is a *natural monopoly* if a single firm could produce at lower average total cost than could any combination of two or more smaller firms. Because of this cost advantage for the natural-monopoly firm, it might be able to sell at a *lower* price than any combination of competitive firms would.

Still, if the natural monopoly is left to its own devices, it will charge prices that are greater than its marginal costs. There is no guarantee that a natural monopoly will charge lower prices than competitive firms would have charged. This presents a tough problem for public policy. On the one hand, if it avoids X-inefficiency, the natural monopoly can produce at lower cost. On the other hand, it won't necessarily pass those lower costs on to consumers in the form of lower prices. Because of this problem, many governments have chosen to regulate the industries that were believed to be natural monopolies. In Chapter 12, we will discuss the regulation of natural monopolies in greater detail.

However, some industries that have tra-

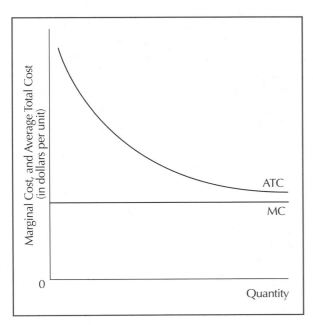

**Figure 10.6 The Cost Curves
for a Natural Monopoly**

In a natural monopoly, the average-total-cost curve is decreasing, throughout the entire range of output. This means that the natural monopoly can produce at a lower average cost than any combination of two or more smaller firms. Since ATC is always decreasing, the marginal-cost curve must always be below the ATC curve.

ditionally been treated as natural monopolies may not really be natural monopolies. The most important such case is the industry that generates and transmits electric power. For most of this century, governments have given regional monopolies to the electric-power utilities. In the 1980s, though, many small, independent power plants began to generate electricity at costs that were *lower* than those of the monopoly utilities. If small firms can produce at lower cost than large firms, then the industry cannot be a natural monopoly. It now appears that the electric-power industry may not have been a natural monopoly at all. The industry was monopolized, but the source of the monopoly was government restrictions, rather than cost advantages.

Partly as a result of this evidence, the Energy Policy Act of 1992 brought greater competition to electric-power transmission, by forcing utilities to transmit the electricity of other companies on their transmission lines. All across the country, state governments are now moving in the direction of allowing more competition in the electric-power industry. The changes have been most dramatic in California and the New England states, where governments have encouraged competition by requiring the old monopolies to sell off some of their plants. It is possible that most consumers in the United States will be able to choose their electric-power provider in a few years.

In theory, natural monopolies have the potential to perform better than the industry could do if it were organized competitively. However, as a practical matter, it appears that very few industries actually fit the definition of a natural monopoly.

Innovation

We've already seen that patents give temporary monopoly power. This means that firms that invent new products will be rewarded with monopoly profits, at least for a while. We don't know for sure what would have happened if the promise of monopoly profits had not been there. But it's possible that the firms work harder on their research efforts, because they believe that they will earn monopoly profits as a result. If this is the case, then patent monopoly may be socially useful.

Quite apart from patent monopoly, some economists emphasize that large-scale firms have advantages in research and development. More than a century ago, Thomas Edison worked by himself in creating some of his inventions. Gradually, however, Edison's operation became larger and larger. Today, research is often carried out in big laboratories, with large teams of scientists. Small firms will be at a big disadvantage in carrying out this kind of research.

The economist Joseph Schumpeter is best-known for advocating the idea that economic progress requires large-scale organizations. In his book, *Capitalism, Socialism, and Democracy*, Schumpeter says that large-scale establishments have "come to be the most powerful engine of (economic progress) . . . In this respect, perfect competition is not only impossible but inferior, and has no title to being set up as a model of ideal efficiency."

Schumpeter's ideas do have some merit. Many innovations are developed by large-scale organizations, some of which are monopolies or near-monopolies. For example, a century ago, John D. Rockefeller's Standard Oil Company had a near-monopoly in refining and distributing petroleum products. Standard Oil improved the pipeline system, and the price of kerosene actually decreased.

However, it's important not to carry Schumpeter's ideas too far. Many innovations are still developed by small teams of inventors. Also, in many cases, monopolies have not been very good innovators. For example, for most of the 20th century, the American Telephone and Telegraph Company (AT&T) had a monopoly in producing telephone equipment. AT&T took a long time to implement several important technological improvements. The firm was slow to replace live operators with dial telephones in the 1940s, and slow to introduce electronic switching in the 1960s. The designs for telephone receivers were improved greatly in the 1970s, with automatic redialing, memory dialing, and so on. But this only occurred *after* the Federal Communications Commission ordered AT&T to let its customers use non-AT&T equipment.

Why are some monopolies good at introducing new techniques, while others aren't so good? The answer may lie in the fact that some monopolies feel safer than others. AT&T was protected from competition by laws and regulations, and this may have contributed to a feeling of complacency. On the other hand, Microsoft Corporation has not depended on legal barriers to entry. Instead, Microsoft has achieved its strong position by other means. Some of Microsoft's success has been due to very aggressive business tactics, some of which may be illegal. On the other hand, it is also true that Microsoft has developed many useful products. Microsoft's executives probably realize that their near-monopoly could be eroded quickly if they don't continue to innovate.

If a monopoly is protected by airtight barriers to entry, it will be tempted to slack off and take it easy. Larger firms do have some advantages in research and development, but it's important that the firm not feel too safe and comfortable.

Summary

On balance, we aren't left with a very good impression of monopolies. Some monopolies may be able to achieve technological breakthroughs, but not all have done so. Natural monopolies may have a cost advantage, but it appears that natural monopolies are rare in reality. In most cases, monopolies lead to high prices, reduced output, and inefficiency.

Reality Check: Interim Review Questions

IR10-8. Describe the shape of the average-total-cost curve for a natural monopoly.

PRICE DISCRIMINATION

Until now, this chapter has dealt with "single-price monopolies", which sell to all of their customers at the same price. But there are actually lots of firms that charge different prices to different customers, for the same service. Many movie theaters allow children to pay less than adults. Many restaurants give discounts to Senior Citizens. When different customers are charged different prices for the same good or service (even though the costs of production are the same), we say that the firm is practicing *price discrimination*.

Store coupons are another example of price discrimination. If you go to your local grocery store without a coupon, you might pay $3.39 for a box of Raisin Nut Bran. But it you have a "75 cents off" coupon, you only have to pay ($3.39 – $0.75) = $2.64 for the identical item. Some customers cut coupons out of the Sunday newspaper, and they get to buy the cereal for a lower price. Other customers, who don't have a coupon when they go to the store, end up paying a higher price for an identical product.

Most colleges and universities practice price discrimination by offering financial aid to some (but not all) students. Doctors, lawyers, social workers, and other professionals often practice price discrimination by using a "sliding fee scale", which means that they charge higher prices to higher-income clients.

The passenger-airlines industry is well known for practicing price discrimination. Most airlines offer lower fares to passengers who stay at their destination over a Saturday night. Sometimes, lower fares are only available to those who book their tickets well in advance. Sometimes, the passenger has to stay for at least a week or two in order to qualify for the lower fare.

Since we believe that firms desire to maximize profits, it must be that firms engage in price discrimination because they believe that

doing so will increase their profits. The basic idea is that *the firm may be able to increase its profits if it can somehow charge a higher price to those who are willing to pay more, and a lower price to those who aren't willing to pay as much.*

Shortly, we'll say more about exactly how the price-discriminating firm can increase its profits. For now, however, let's list the conditions that have to exist, if a firm is to engage in successful price discrimination.

Conditions Necessary for Price Discrimination

In principle, *all* firms would like to price discriminate, because doing so would increase their profits. But many firms find it impossible to practice price discrimination successfully. If a firm is to increase its profits through price discrimination, several conditions must be met.

- The firm must have some market power.
- The firm must be able to estimate which customers are willing to pay more.
- It must be difficult or impossible for customers to re-sell to other customers.

Let's think about these three conditions in more detail.

Market Power. Remember the characteristics of perfectly competitive firms: They're small relative to the market, and their outputs are homogeneous, or standardized. Because of these characteristics, perfectly competitive firms are *price takers*. If one competitor tries to sell her corn crop at a higher price than the market price, she will lose all of her customers. Since perfect competitors are price takers, *perfectly competitive firms cannot practice price discrimination.*

Some price-discriminating firms are monopolies. For example, many electric-power monopolies charge different prices to different customers. However, some price-discriminating firms aren't monopolies. Thus, even though monopolies are the main focus of this chapter, our discussion of price discrimination doesn't apply only to monopolies. Price discrimination can also be practiced by oligopolistic and monopolistically competitive firms, which are discussed in the next chapter. The key thing is that *price discrimination can only succeed if the firm has some market power.* Either the firm must have a differentiated product, or it must be large relative to the market, or both.

In each of the examples of price discrimination given above, the firms do indeed have market power. Store coupons are issued by the breakfast-cereal manufacturers, such as General Mills and Kellogg. These firms are large relative to the market, and they also have some market power because their products are differentiated. Passenger airlines also have market power.

The Firm Must Be Able to Estimate Which Customers Are Willing to Pay More. The idea of price discrimination is to charge higher prices to those customers who are willing to pay more. Therefore, the sellers need to have some way of determining who's willing to pay more, and who isn't. In the case of store coupons for breakfast cereal, the customer has to go to the trouble of cutting out the coupon and carrying it to the store. If you cut out coupons, you have revealed that lower prices are important to you. In other words, coupon cutters reveal that they are relatively sensitive to price differences. If you don't go to the trouble of clipping the coupon, you have revealed that you don't care as much about getting a lower price, which means that you are relatively insensitive to price changes.

Passenger airlines distinguish their customers on the basis of the length of the stay at the destination city. Generally speaking, the airlines have found that business travelers are willing to pay more than vacationers. This is why lower prices are often charged to customers who are willing to stay over a Saturday night. Since business travelers are especially eager to get home for the weekend, they don't like to stay over Saturday night, even if they could save money by doing so. Similarly, some airlines charge less for a longer stay. If you stay at the same destination for two weeks, you're probably a vacationer. Also, in some cases, cheap fares are only available to those who book their reservations a week or more in advance. Travelers who make their reservations at the last minute have to pay higher prices. Most often, these travelers either have an emergency, or they are too disorganized to make their reservations in advance. In either case, those who book at the last minute are likely to be willing to pay more.

Ideally, breakfast-cereal manufacturers and passenger airlines would like to distinguish among their customers *perfectly*. The makers of Cheerios would like to identify those consumers who are willing to pay *exactly* $4.73, for example, and charge them exactly that much. If a firm were able to charge the exact maximum that each customer is willing to pay, we would say that the firm is engaged in *perfect price discrimination*. Cereal coupon schemes don't go this far—they are a very imperfect way of distinguishing among customers. Nevertheless, coupon schemes do help the cereal firms to identify their high-paying and low-paying customers.

In many cases, it's very hard for firms to tell which of their customers are willing to pay more. For example, hardware stores can't easily judge high-paying from low-paying customers. Consequently, most hardware stores charge *all* of their customers the same price for the same item. In other words, there is no price discrimination at most hardware stores: You pay more for a circular saw than for a screwdriver, but everyone who buys a particular kind of circular saw pays the *same* price.

It Must Be Difficult or Impossible for Customers to Re-sell the Product. If it were possible for customers to buy large quantities of discounted merchandise, and then re-sell them, the whole purpose of the price-discrimination scheme would be defeated. One example of an attempt to avoid re-selling is that movie theaters only sell one ticket per customer. Consequently, even if a child gets a discount price, he or she won't be able to re-sell movie tickets in large quantities.

Sometimes, however, buyers are able to do a substantial amount of re-selling. A supermarket in Udine, Italy, started to offer a 20-percent discount to Senior Citizens in 1995. At first, the store's managers thought the plan was a success. However, they discovered that teams of grandmothers were loading up carts of groceries, carrying them out of the store, and re-selling to younger folks. The younger shoppers saved money, the older shoppers made a small fortune, and the store discovered that it wasn't increasing its profits as much as it had hoped. Soon, the Italian supermarket quit offering the Senior Citizen discount. In most cases, if a price-discriminating firm learns that customers are doing lots of re-selling, the firm is likely to stop its attempt at price discrimination.

The Role of Demand Elasticities in Price Discrimination

If a firm could engage in perfect price discrimination, it would have the potential to make enormous profits. Of course, in most cases, firms can't distinguish among their customers perfectly. But there is still plenty of room for increasing profits, even when a firm can't tell its customers apart perfectly.

For example, let's consider the airlines. They certainly can't read the minds of all of their customers. Still, they manage to discriminate on the basis of certain characteristics that are rough indicators of willingness to pay. If you arrange your flight months in advance, and if you plan a two-week stay, then the airlines can guess that you are probably a vacation traveler. As such, you are probably sensitive to price. In other words, your demand is probably relatively *elastic*.

On the other hand, what if you were to call an airline on a Monday, and say that you need to fly on Tuesday and be back by Wednesday? In this case, the airline will guess that you are a business traveler, so that you are insensitive to price. In other words, your demand is probably relatively *inelastic*.

The trick is to *charge higher prices to customers who have relatively* inelastic *demands, and charge lower prices to those who have relatively* elastic *demands.* When price is increased for those with inelastic demand, total revenue goes up. Similarly, when price is decreased for those with elastic demand, total revenue goes up. All of the price-discrimination schemes that we listed earlier in this section have the same character: They find ways to charge higher prices to those with less elastic demand.

When firms give a discount to Senior Citizens, they would like their customers to believe that they do it out of the goodness of their hearts. However, we now see that price discrimination is more accurately viewed as a method of trying to increase profits. Firms may indeed have respect for their elders, but all we know for sure is that they believe that Senior Citizens have relatively elastic demand. If the firms were really motivated by charity, rather than by profit, they would give the same low prices to *all* of their customers, and not just to Senior Citizens.

Reality Check:
Interim Review Questions

IR10-9. Do perfectly competitive firms engage in price discrimination? Why, or why not?

IR10-10. Explain why price-discriminating firms charge higher prices to customers with relatively inelastic demand.

ECONOMICS AND YOU: COMPETITION, MONOPOLY, AND THE FUTURE OF TELECOMMUNICATIONS

We began this chapter with a discussion of Tamika Chandler, who can choose among several different suppliers of long-distance telephone services. However, she faces a monopoly in local phone service. We end this chapter by returning to our discussion of the telecommunications industry. This industry has a long history of monopoly, but competition has increased during the last few decades. The increases in competition have resulted from new technologies, as well as from changes in government policy.

Alexander Graham Bell invented the telephone in 1876. When he received a patent, it gave the Bell Telephone Company a monopoly in the telephone business. Even after the telephone patent expired in 1894, the Bell System maintained a monopoly in virtually all phases of telephone service for most of the next century. Bell monopolized equipment manufacturing and long-distance phone service, and it also monopolized many local telephone markets through its local operating companies.

Bell's monopoly position began to erode in the late 1960s and early 1970s. The Federal Communications Commission (FCC) allowed a new company, MCI, to begin to compete in long-distance service. The FCC also allowed telephone subscribers to use non-Bell equipment. This allowed new firms to introduce new technologies, such as microwave transmission, fiber-optic transmission, and cellular telephones. Many of the new inventions weakened the Bell monopoly.

In 1974, the U.S. government sued under the antitrust laws. (The antitrust laws are designed to combat monopoly. We'll discuss these laws in detail in Chapter 12.) This monumental court case was settled in 1982, in a way that led to the break-up of the Bell System. The local operating companies were re-organized into seven regional holding companies, which were nicknamed the "Baby Bells". These companies were separated from the long-distance company, American Telephone and Telegraph (AT&T).

After the mid–1980s, long-distance telephone service became increasingly competitive. MCI, Sprint, and a host of smaller firms offered discount prices. This forced AT&T, the former long-distance monopoly, to lower its prices as well.

However, local phone service presented a dramatically different picture. Each of the Baby Bells maintained a near-monopoly in its own region. The United States now had seven regional monopolies in local telephone service, instead of one nationwide monopoly. Customers were still forced to pay monopoly prices.

This situation led Congress to pass the Telecommunications Act of 1996. The idea was for the Baby Bells to get involved in long-distance service, and for the long-distance companies to get involved in local service. This would lead to a competitive free-for-all, resulting in lower prices and better services for telephone users.

Unfortunately, it hasn't yet worked out that way. The 1996 law requires the Baby Bells to demonstrate that their local markets are open to competition, *before* they are allowed to compete in the long-distance market. So far, not a single Baby Bell has met the requirements. In fact, the Baby Bells have actively fought against competition, by making it difficult for long-distance companies to hook up customers for local service. The Baby Bells appear to be more interested in preserving their local monopolies than in competing in the long-distance market.

In fact, much of the energy of these telephone giants has gone into merging with each other, rather than competing. Bell Atlantic paid $26 billion to take over Nynex in 1997, creating a combined Baby Bell that monopolizes local service from Virginia to Maine. In the same year, SBC Communications bought Pacific Telesis for $17 billion, creating a local-service monopoly that serves California, Texas, and five other States. SBC has also been involved in merger talks with Ameritech (the Baby Bell for the Great Lakes region), and even with AT&T itself.

If the present trend continues, it's possible that we will end up with a giant monopoly, much like the AT&T that dominated telephone service until the 1970s and 1980s. If so, the results for customers aren't likely to be very good. A new monopoly would probably be very reluctant to cut prices. To avoid that possibility, Congress may need to take further action. For example, Congress may have to strengthen the requirements for the Baby Bells to connect customers to competing firms.

A truly competitive market for local telephone service *can* be achieved, and many analysts believe that we will reach it some day. The question is when.

Chapter Summary

1. There is only one firm in a monopolized market. If the firm is to remain a monopoly, it must be protected by barriers to entry. In addition, there must not be any close substitutes for the product of the monopolist.

2. Monopolists are sometimes protected from competition by legal barriers to entry, such as patents or exclusive franchise arrangements. In the case of a natural monopoly, the barrier to entry is the firm's cost advantage.

3. Whereas the perfectly competitive firm has a horizontal demand curve for its product, the monopoly firm faces the entire market demand curve, which slopes downward to the right.

4. The marginal revenue of the monopolist is the amount of extra sales revenue that it receives, when it sells one extra unit of output. The monopolist's marginal-revenue curve slopes downward to the right. In the case of a straight-line demand curve, the marginal-revenue curve is twice as steep as the demand curve. When marginal revenue is positive, demand is elastic. When marginal revenue is zero, demand is unit elastic. When marginal revenue is negative, demand is inelastic.

5. The monopolist maximizes profit by producing the quantity at which marginal revenue equals marginal cost. The firm then sells at the price given by the demand curve.

6. The price chosen by the monopolist will depend on the shapes of the demand and marginal-revenue curves. There is no unique relationship between quantity and price. Therefore, the monopoly firm does not have a supply curve.

7. Compared with a perfectly competitive industry, a monopolized industry will charge a higher price, sell a lower quantity, and make larger economic profits. Because of the higher price and lower quantity, consumers will be worse off when the industry is monopolized than when it is perfectly competitive. The consumer's loss is larger than the monopolist's profit. As a result, society as a whole is worse off. The loss due to monopoly is called the deadweight loss of monopoly.

8. Monopolists may be able to survive, even if they do not control their costs. If they are wasteful, they create "X-inefficiency".

9. A price-discriminating firm is one that sells the same product at different prices to different customers, even though there are no differences in costs. To engage in successful price discrimination, a firm must have some ability to control the price, it must have some way of distinguishing customers on the basis of willingness to pay, and it must be able to prevent its product from being re-sold. If these conditions are met, the firm will increase its profits by selling at higher prices to those with relatively inelastic demands, and selling at lower prices to those with relatively elastic demands.

Key Terms

Monopoly

Price Makers

Market Power

Patent

Exclusive Franchise

Natural Monopoly

Single-Price Monopoly

Price Discrimination

Average Revenue

Deadweight Loss

Key Figure

The key figures for this chapter are Figures 10.3(a) and 10.3(b).

Questions and Problems

QP10-1. Different monopolies are protected by different barriers to entry. Name as many barriers to entry as you can. Which of these barriers to entry (if any) makes society better off?

QP10-2. What is the difference between the demand curve facing a perfectly competitive firm and the demand curve facing a monopoly firm? What is the difference between the marginal-revenue curve facing a perfectly competitive firm and the marginal-revenue curve facing a monopoly firm? Why are the curves different?

QP10-3. AAAA Corporation has a monopoly in the production of gizmos. Financial analysts calculate that the elasticity of demand for AAAA's gizmos is 0.4, which means that the demand is inelastic. What does this imply about the marginal revenue of selling one additional gizmo? How would your answer change if the demand for gizmos were unit elastic? What if the demand for gizmos were elastic?

QP10-4. In the previous question, it was stated that AAAA Corporation (a monopoly firm) faces a demand curve with an elasticity of 0.4. Is the firm maximizing its profits? If the firm is not maximizing profits, and if it desires to maximize profits, how would it change its level of output?

QP10-5. Below is a demand schedule in the market for zolotkas:

a. Assume that the firm does *not* practice price discrimination. Fill in the columns for total revenue and marginal revenue.

b. Assume that marginal cost is a constant: At any quantity, MC = $3 per additional

$$TR = P \cdot Q \qquad MR = \frac{\Delta TR}{\Delta Q}$$

$$TC = TVC$$
$$TC = \Sigma MC$$

Price	Quantity Demanded	Total Revenue	Marginal Revenue	Marginal Cost	TFC	Total Cost	Profit TR-TC
$10	0	0	—	—	15	—(15)	—(-15)
9	1	9	9	3	15	3(18) 6	(-9)
8	2	16	9	3	15	6(21) 10	(-5)
7	3	21	5	3	15	9(24) 12	(-3)
6	4	24	3	3	15	12(27) 12	(-3)
5	5	25	1	3	15	15(30) 10	(-5)
4	6	24	-1	3	15	18(33) 6	(-9)
3	7	21	-3	3	15	21(36) 0	(-15)
2	8	16	-5	3	15	24(39) -8	(-23)
1	9	9	-7	3	15	27(42) -18	(-33)
0	10	0	-9	3	15	30(45) -30	(-45)

unit. Also, assume that there are no fixed costs. Fill in the columns for marginal cost and total cost.

c. What is the firm's profit-maximizing quantity of output? What price does the firm charge? How much profit does the firm make? MR=MC $6-$12

d. Verify that we get the same profit-maximizing quantity, regardless of whether we compare *total* revenue and cost, or *marginal* revenue and cost.

e. Now, assume that the firm has fixed costs of $15, but that all of the other information on costs and revenues stays the same. How does this affect your answers about the firm's profit-maximizing quantity of output, price, and profit?

QP10-6. Return to the demand schedule of the previous question. Now, however, assume that the firm is able to practice perfect price discrimination. In other words, it can charge $9 to the first customer, $8 to the second customer, $7 to the third customer, and so on.

a. Now, re-calculate total revenue and marginal revenue.

b. Assuming that the firm has no fixed costs, what is its profit-maximizing quantity of output? What is its price? How much profit does it earn?

c. Assume that the firm has fixed costs of $15. How does this affect your answers about the firm's profit-maximizing quantity of output, price, and profit?

d. What are the differences between the single-price monopoly of the previous question, and the price-discriminating monopoly of this question? Who is better off with price discrimination, and who is better off with the single-price monopoly?

QP10-7. Once again, return to the demand schedule from question (5). This time, however, assume that the industry is perfectly competitive.

a. If the marginal cost of production is $3 for any firm, and if every firm has zero fixed costs, what are the market equilibrium price and quantity?

b. Compare this price and quantity with the price and quantity that would occur with a single-price monopolist (as in question (5)).

c. Next, compare this equilibrium price and quantity with the various prices and the quantity that would occur with a perfectly price-discriminating monopolist (as in question (6)).

QP10-8. Draw graphs showing the relevant information on demand, marginal revenue, marginal cost, quantity, price, and profit, for each of the three cases described in the previous three questions. The graphs should have quantity on the horizontal axis, and dollars per unit of quantity on the vertical axis.

QP10-9. It is observed that a firm is making very large positive economic profits. Does this imply that the firm must be a monopoly?

QP10-10. John Q. Monopolist inherits a monopoly firm from his parents. He knows that a monopolist has market power. On this basis, he decides that it is best for the firm to charge the highest possible price that can be charged, without driving the quantity demanded all the way down to zero. Comment on this strategy.

QP10-11. A movie theater charges $3 for all seats for its shows at 4 p.m. The theater charges $6 for all seats for its shows at 8 p.m. Is this price discrimination? Why or why not?

QP10-12. A hardware store is having a "buy one, get the second one for half price" sale on screwdrivers. This means that all customers must pay $10 for the first screwdriver, but, if they want a second screwdriver, the price will only be $5 more. Is this price discrimination? Why or why not?

Chapter 11

Monopolistic Competition and Oligopoly

ECONOMICS AND YOU: FROSTED FLAKES AND COUNT CHOCULA; CHIPS AHOY AND OREOS

When you walk past the breakfast cereals in your grocery store, what do you see? There are Frosted Flakes and Cinnamon Toast Crunch, Grape Nuts and Mueslix, Shredded Wheat, Frosted Mini-Wheats, and Frosted Wheat Bites. This certainly *isn't* a perfectly competitive world, where one farmer's wheat is identical to another farmer's wheat. This is a world of *product differentiation*, in which the different firms in an industry make products that are noticeably different.

If you look closely, you'll also see that there are only a few firms in the breakfast-cereal market. The market certainly isn't a monopoly, but it is dominated by a few giants: Kellogg, General Foods, General Mills, Post, Ralston, Quaker, and Nabisco have the lion's share of the market. Once again, this is not the perfectly competitive world, because perfect competition involves hundreds or thousands of small firms. Instead, this is a world of competition among the few.

In short, the breakfast-cereal industry is different from the perfectly competitive ideal in two important ways: (1) the products are differentiated, and (2) there are only a few firms.

In fact, *most* American industries have at least one of these two characteristics. The automobile industry has differentiated products, and most of the world's production is generated by General Motors, Ford, Daimler Chrysler, Toyota, Nissan, Honda, Volkswagen, and a few other firms. The steel industry does *not* have a great deal of product differentiation, since steel from one part of the world is very similar to steel from another part. However, the steel industry *is* dominated by a relatively small number of firms.

Each industry is unique, and no simple model can hope to tell us everything that we want to know about every industry. And yet, certain basic patterns do emerge. Economists have found it convenient to classify industries into four broad categories, based on the way in which the firms interact with each other in a given industry. These four categories are called *market structures*.

We've already studied two market structures—perfect competition and monopoly. The third market structure is *monopolistic competition*. When we study monopolistic competition, we are concerned with the effects of product differentiation. The final market structure is *oligopoly*. When we study oligopoly, there's more emphasis on the interactions among a small number of firms.

If we consider monopolistically competitive industries and oligopolies together, we sometimes speak of industries that are characterized by *imperfect competition*.

Before we begin to study the *theories* of imperfect competition, we need to know more about the *facts*. In the next section, we will take a look at the sizes of business firms, both in the United States and in the rest of the world. Then, we'll think about how to measure the extent to which industries are dominated by a small number of firms. After that, we develop some ways of thinking about monopolistic competition, and we begin the study of oligopoly.

GIANTS OF THE ECONOMY

Table 11.1 shows some information on the largest corporations in the United States, for 1999. The largest is General Motors, which had sales of more than $189 *billion*. To put this into perspective, General Motors' sales are more than the entire value of *all* of the output produced in Indonesia, a country with more than 200 million people. In fact, General Motors is bigger than *most* of the world's countries. Only about two dozen countries have a total output that is worth more than the output of General Motors.

Table 11.1 gives an indication of the diversity of the largest enterprises in the United States economy. In a country that travels by automobile, it is probably not surprising that two of the top 20 companies (General Motors and Ford) are auto manufacturers, and two (Exxon Mobil and Enron) are energy companies. The top 20 also includes two retailers (Wal-Mart and Sears), five financial-services companies (Citigroup, Bank of America, State Farm, American International, and TIAA-CREF), three computer companies (IBM, Hewlett-Packard, and Compaq), and two telecommunications firms (AT&T and SBC Communications). Rounding out the top 20 are a producer of everything from aircraft engines to light bulbs (General Electric), an aircraft manufacturer (Boeing), a producer of food and tobacco products (Philip Morris), and a grocery company (Kroger).

In recent years, there has been a wave of mergers and acquisitions among large corporations, and this is reflected in the figures for the companies represented in Table 11.1. For example, Exxon and Mobil merged to create one giant energy company, Exxon Mobil. Citicorp and Travelers merged to create a bigger financial-services firm, called Citigroup, and SBC Communications acquired some other firms, to create a bigger telecommunications company.

It's also interesting to note some of the companies that are *not* in the Top 20. For example, some people might be surprised that Chrysler Corporation isn't on the list. The reason is that Chrysler can't be on this list of the top corporations *in the United States,* because of its merger with Daimler, a German company. Some might also be surprised that Microsoft Corporation is not on the list. In fact, however, Microsoft's sales were only about $20 billion in 1999, which put it in 84th place. On the other hand, Microsoft had an unusually high profit margin. Microsoft managed to squeeze nearly $8 billion of profits from its $20 billion of sales. This compares with General Motors, which had profits of only about $6 billion from sales of $189 billion.

Measurement of Market Concentration

Table 11.1 gives us some idea of the enormous scale of operations of today's global enter-

Table 11.1 The 20 Largest Industrial Corporations in the United States, 1999

Company	City of Headquarters	1999 Revenues (in billions of dollars)
1. General Motors	Detroit, Michigan	$189.1
2. Wal-Mart Stores	Bentonville, Arkansas	166.8
3. Exxon Mobil	Irving, Texas	163.9
4. Ford Motor	Dearborn, Michigan	162.6
5. General Electric	Fairfield, Connecticut	111.6
6. Int'l. Business Machines	Armonk, New York	87.5
7. Citigroup	New York, New York	82.0
8. AT&T	New York, New York	62.4
9. Philip Morris	New York, New York	61.8
10. Boeing	Seattle, Washington	58.0
11. Bank of America Corp.	Charlotte, North Carolina	51.4
12. SBC Communications	San Antonio, Texas	49.5
13. Hewlett-Packard	Palo Alto, California	48.3
14. Kroger	Cincinnati, Ohio	45.4
15. State Farm Insurance	Bloomington, Illinois	44.6
16. Sears Roebuck	Hoffman Estates, Illinois	41.1
17. American International	New York, New York	40.7
18. Enron	Houston, Texas	40.1
19. TIAA-CREF	New York, New York	39.4
20. Compaq Computer	Houston, Texas	38.5

Source: *Fortune*, April 17, 2000

prises. But if we really want to understand what's going on with these big firms, we need to learn more about how they *interact* with each other. That means that we will need to focus on firms *within a particular industry.* (After all, General Motors and IBM are both gigantic corporations, but they don't really interact very much, because most of GM's products are very different from most of IBM's products.)

The nature of the interaction among firms will depend on the number and size of firms in the industry. If an industry is dominated by a small number of firms, we say that it is a *concentrated* industry.

Concentration Ratios. The most popular method of measuring an industry's degree of competitiveness is the *four-firm concentration ratio*. To calculate this ratio, we divide the total sales of the four largest firms by the total sales for the entire industry. Finally, we multiply by 100, in order to convert to a percentage:

Four-firm concentration ratio = ((Sales of 4 largest firms) ÷ (Sales of all firms)) x 100.

The *eight-firm concentration ratio* is calculated in the same way, except that it involves the *eight* largest firms.

The Census Bureau publishes the concentration ratios that are used most widely. Unfortunately, these concentration ratios have some problems. First of all, they only look at firms *in the United States*. But we know that the competitive environment in an industry is affected by competition from other countries. Thus, these concentration ratios make it appear that some industries are highly concentrated, whereas they are really quite competitive.

A second problem can be illustrated by an example: Consider industry A, in which the biggest firm has 65% of the market, and seven smaller firms each have 5% of the market. The four-firm concentration ratio for industry A is 80%. Now, consider industry B, in which there are five firms, each with 20% of the market. The four-firm concentration ratio for industry B is also 80%. However, even though the two industries have identical concentration ratios, they may behave in very different ways. Industry A has one giant firm, which may be able to act nearly like a monopolist. On the other hand, it's possible that the firms of industry B may act in a fairly competitive way. The basic problem is that the concentration ratio doesn't use all of the available information.

The Herfindahl Index. An alternative way to measure concentration is the ***Herfindahl index***, named for O.C. Herfindahl. To calculate the Herfindahl index, we take the sum of the squares of the market shares for the firms in the industry, where the market shares are expressed as percentages. For example, a monopoly firm has a market share of 100%, so that a monopolized industry has a Herfindahl index of $(100^2) = 10,000$. This is as high as the index can go. For industry A, from the preceding paragraph, the index is $(65^2) + (5^2) + (5^2) + (5^2) + (5^2) + (5^2) + (5^2) + (5^2) = 4400$. For industry B, the index is $(20^2) + (20^2) + (20^2) + (20^2) + (20^2) = 2000$. While the four-firm concentration ratio makes these two industries look the same, the Herfindahl index indicates that industry A is more concentrated.

In recent years, the Justice Department has indicated that it will probably not challenge mergers that would leave the Herfindahl index at a value of less than 1000. This indicates that the Justice Department believes that this index is a good measure of industrial concentration.

Comparing Concentration Ratios and the Herfindahl Index. In Table 11.2, we show the four-firm concentration ratio, the eight-firm concentration ratio, and the Herfindahl index, for some important industries in the United States. These figures are from the 1987 Census of Manufactures.

Table 11.2 shows that American industry is tremendously varied. The industry that produces washing machines and other household laundry equipment is *highly* concentrated. The four-firm concentration ratio is 93, which means that 93% of the market is controlled by only four firms! The Herfindahl index is 2855, which is very high. On the other hand, the industry that produces women's, misses', and juniors' dresses is much less concentrated. The four-firm ratio is only 6, and the Herfindahl index is only 24.

When we compare two industries, the one with the higher concentration ratio is usually also the one with the higher Herfindahl index. However, there are some exceptions. The photographic-equipment-and-supplies industry has *lower* concentration ratios than the breakfast-cereal industry, but it has a *higher* Herfindahl index. This is because one giant firm (Eastman Kodak) has such a big influence on the Herfindahl index in photographic equipment and supplies.

Table 11.2 gives the impression that the newspaper industry is not very concentrated. However, most newspapers are only sold in a single region of the country. Within their local regions, many newspapers have a monopoly or near-monopoly. This reminds us that the concentration ratios and the Herfindahl index are measures of concentration at the *national* level. This may be misleading for industries that are primarily *local* in nature.

In the next few pages, we will discuss the economics of monopolistically competitive industries. Although these industries are not perfectly competitive, they usually aren't very concentrated. Later in this chapter, we'll begin to study oligopolistic industries, which can be *highly* concentrated.

**Table 11.2 Measures of Industrial Concentration in Selected Industries, for 1987
(Ranked by Herfindahl Index)**

Industry	Four-Firm Concentration Ratio	Eight-Firm Concentration Ratio	Herfindahl Index (For 50 Largest Firms)
Household laundry equipment	93	99+	2855
Photographic equipment and supplies	77	84	2241
Cereal breakfast foods	87	99	2207
Primary aluminum	74	95	1934
Aircraft	72	92	1686
Motorcycles, bicycles, and parts	66	74	1453
Synthetic rubber	50	76	920
Lawn and garden equipment	52	71	883
Paper mills	33	50	432
Newspapers	25	39	250
Wood office furniture	26	37	248
Men's and boys' shirts	22	32	194
Sheet metal work	10	14	43
Women's, misses', and juniors' dresses	6	10	24

Reality Check: Interim Review Question

IR11-1. The grizbot industry has 10 firms, each of which controls 10 percent of the market.

Calculate the four-firm concentration ratio, the eight-firm concentration ratio, and the Herfindahl index for this industry.

CHARACTERISTICS OF MONOPOLISTIC COMPETITION

The theory of monopolistic competition was developed in the 1930s, by Edward Chamberlin (an American) and Joan Robinson (an Englishwoman). We can identify several characteristics that monopolistically competitive industries have in common. These include

- a large number of producers,

- easy entry and exit,

- product differentiation, and

- frequent use of non-price competition.

Let's look at each of these features in turn.

Many Firms

In an earlier chapter, we saw that a perfectly competitive industry has many firms. The same is true for an industry with monopolistic competition. Some of the best examples of monopolistic competition are in retailing. Most Americans can easily go to dozens of different gasoline stations, or fast-food restaurants, or clothing outlets.

Easy Entry and Exit

Another of our assumptions regarding perfect competition was that it is easy for firms to enter the industry when positive economic profits are being earned, and easy for firms to exit when losses are being suffered. In this way, a perfectly competitive industry will be driven toward zero economic profits.

Free entry and exit also apply to monopolistically competitive industries. This means that these industries will also tend toward zero economic profits in the long run. Once again, some of the best examples are in retailing. It's often possible to set up a new burger franchise for an investment of thousands of dollars, instead of millions. Think about opening an ice-cream store, compared with starting up a manufacturer of commercial aircraft. Entry is relatively easy in the retail ice-cream business (which we think of as monopolistically competitive). But entry is extremely costly in the aircraft industry (which we think of as oligopolistic).

Product Differentiation

So far, we've seen that monopolistic competition shares some of the characteristics of perfect competition. But perfectly competitive firms produce homogeneous, standardized products, whereas monopolistically competitive firms produce differentiated products.

Product differentiation can come in many forms. Firms often differentiate themselves on the basis of location, or product quality, or service.

Location. If one gasoline station is located right next to the freeway exit ramp, it will be easy to drive in and fill up quickly. Even if another gas station is located only a few blocks away, it may not be so convenient. Consumers take location into consideration, and so they will have greater demand for gasoline from the conveniently located station. This is why we sometimes see one station charging, say, $1.32 for a gallon of regular unleaded gas, while a station a block away only charges $1.30. Some people are willing to pay a little

extra, in order to save time and trouble. The amount of the price difference will depend on the degree of difference in convenience.

The same is true in many other monopolistically competitive industries. Some people find it more convenient to buy eyeglasses and frames from a store in a shopping mall, rather than from some other store. Therefore, the mall stores may be able to charge higher prices than other stores.

Product Quality and Service. Most shopping malls have literally dozens of stores that sell clothing. Some have lots of selection; others have less. Some have friendly, courteous salespeople; others don't. Some have jackets that are made of finest linen and fully lined; others have unlined polyester. For all of these reasons, shoppers perceive that the different clothing stores are *not* perfect substitutes for each other. If you want the highest quality, you'll have to pay more. If you don't need such high quality, you may be able to save a lot of dollars.

Many other industries have differences in quality. Some restaurants have starched white tablecloths; others offer an ordinary atmosphere. Some photo developers offer one-hour service; others don't. In all of these cases, consumers will have different demand for the products of the different firms, depending on the perceived differences in quality.

Advertising. In a perfectly competitive industry, it's understood that firms produce homogeneous, standardized outputs. As a result, Farmer Jones doesn't have much reason to put up a billboard advertising his wheat. But under monopolistic competition, buyers recognize that the products are not the same. As a result, firms may decide to engage in *advertising.* When a firm advertises its products, it tries to push its demand curve outward. If it is successful, the firm will be able to sell a larger quantity, at a higher price.

Advertising is one form of *non-price com-*

petition. Firms still do use price as a competitive weapon, but the buyers' perceptions of product differences will also have an important effect. Many monopolistically competitive firms try to shape those consumer perceptions through advertising.

Real Economics for Real People 11.1 shows that some product differentiation is more imaginary than real, and *Real Economics for Real People 11.2* discusses the advantages and disadvantages of advertising.

Real Economics for Real People 11.1:
Let the Buyer Beware of Product Differentiation

Product differentiation is often a good thing. For example, the automobile market offers station wagons, minivans, and pickups for those who want to haul around a lot of people or a lot of goods. But the market also offers subcompacts for those who don't need as much space. Some people prefer muscled sports cars, while others prefer conservative sedans, and the market caters to both tastes.

The market for cough-and-cold medicines is highly differentiated. There are syrups, tablets, gels, and nasal sprays. Some medicines treat flu symptoms; others don't. Some give 12-hour relief; some work for only four or six hours. Once again, it's probably beneficial to have different products for different needs.

However, some of the differentiation in the cough-and-cold market may not be worth very much to the consumer. On a recent trip to the local pharmacy, we found three liquid cough-and-cold medicines with *identical* active ingredients. The adult dose for each medicine includes exactly 30 milligrams of the *same* cough suppressant, and exactly 60 milligrams of the *same* decongestant. Thus, the only product differentiation involves brand name, the taste of the syrup, the color of the package, etc.

All of these medicines were sold in four-ounce bottles. One sold for $5.69 per bottle, one for $4.99, and the other for $4.49. Thus, if we compare the $5.69 bottle with the $4.49

bottle, there is a price gap of nearly 27 percent. But the price differences don't end there. The ingredients of the $4.99 bottle were more heavily diluted by the syrup. Even though all of the bottles have the same number of ounces, they don't all have the same amount of active ingredients. Consequently, if we were to adjust the price of the $4.99 bottle, in order to make it comparable with the other two, the "true" price of the $4.99 bottle would jump to $6.65. If we compare this with the $4.49 bottle, there is a price gap of more than 48 percent. The brand that sold for $4.49 in a four-ounce bottle also offered an eight-ounce bottle, for $7.49. If we compare the price per unit of medicine, between this "giant economy size" and the most expensive brand, there is a price difference of more than 77 percent!

It may be that some customers really make a wise decision when they buy the more expensive brands. (Maybe they have doubts about whether the less-expensive brands are really of equal quality.) But it's also possible that some customers would have come to a different decision, if they had read the labels carefully.

In a world of homogeneous products, there isn't much reason to shop around. However, many of our expenditures are devoted to differentiated products. In this type of environment, it pays to shop wisely.

PRICES AND OUTPUTS WITH MONOPOLISTIC COMPETITION

Now that we have discussed the *characteristics* of monopolistically competitive firms, it's time to analyze their *behavior,* as they interact with each other in the marketplace.

The Firm's Demand Curve

When we discussed *perfect* competition, we learned that the individual firm's demand curve was given by the market price. Since all perfectly competitive firms face the same market price, it has to be true that all perfectly competitive firms face the same demand curve. The reason for this is that perfectly competitive firms all produce the same homogeneous output.

However, because of product differentiation, *each monopolistically competitive firm faces its own, unique demand curve.*

Jean's Jeans is a monopolistically competitive firm, selling blue jeans and other clothing items. Jean's has a convenient location, free parking, and a reputation for friendly service. Even though there are plenty of other clothing stores in the area, Jean's good reputation means that the store can raise its price somewhat, without losing all of its customers.

In other words, *the demand curve for a monopolistically competitive firm is downward sloping.* This is shown in Figure 11.1, where the demand curve for Jean's Jeans slopes downward. Our analysis of monopolistic competition will be very similar to our analysis of monopoly, since monopolists also face a downward-sloping demand curve. As we saw in the chapter on monopoly, a downward-sloping demand curve means that the marginal-revenue curve (MR) is also downward sloping. As shown in Figure 11.1, the downward-sloping MR curve for Jean's Jeans is always below the demand curve.

However, even though monopolistic competitors and monopolists both face downward-sloping demand curves, they aren't identical. The reason for this is that the monopolist doesn't have any rivals. On the other hand, the monopolistic competitor has lots of rivals, so that a monopolistic competitor like Jean's Jeans will only have a limited ability to raise its price. If it raises its price very much, the monopolistically competitive firm will lose lots of customers. Therefore, even though the demand curve for Jean's Jeans slopes downward, it is fairly flat.

Profit Maximization in the Short Run

We always assume that firms want to maximize their profits. Like *any* profit-maximizing firm, Jean's Jeans will *choose the quantity at which marginal revenue equals marginal cost.* This quantity is given by Q_0 in Figure 11.1. When we go from Q_0 up to the demand curve, we find that Jean's will sell at a price of P_0.

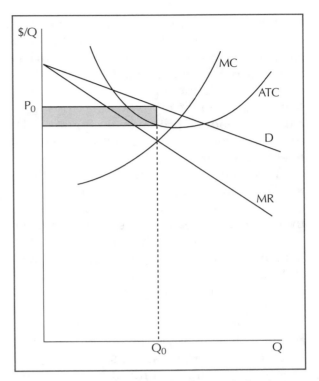

Figure 11.1 Short-Run Profit Maximization for Jean's Jeans

The monopolistically competitive firm maximizes profit by choosing the quantity at which marginal revenue (MR) equals marginal cost (MC). This gives a quantity of Q_0, and a price of P_0. Profit per unit is P_0 minus average total cost (ATC). Total profit for the firm is given by the shaded area.

In earlier chapters, we learned that economic profit per unit is equal to price minus average total cost (ATC). In Figure 11.1, when the quantity is Q_0, price is greater than ATC. This means that Jean's Jeans is earning positive economic profits. (If price had been less than ATC, Jean's would have had economic losses.) The amount of profit is represented by the area of the shaded rectangle in Figure 11.1.

The Long Run: Zero Economic Profits

Figure 11.1 represents a *monopolistically competitive firm* in the short run, but it is basically the same as the short-run profit picture for a *monopolist*. However, that's the end of the story for a monopolist, since the monopoly firm has no rivals. But remember that there are no barriers to entry in monopolistic competition. If Jean's Jeans and the other existing firms were earning economic profits (as in Figure 11.1), then there would be an incentive for new firms to enter the market.

When new firms enter the retail clothing market, there will be an effect on the demand curve facing Jean's Jeans. At any given price, the quantity that Jean's can sell will be smaller than it was before. This means that the demand curve and MR curve for Jean's will shift to the left, as shown in Figure 11.2. The new equilibrium price and quantity are P_1 and Q_1.

Entry into the industry will continue for as long as there is any incentive for new firms to enter the market. In other words, this process will continue until the firms in the market are making zero economic profits. *The long-run tendency of a monopolistically competitive industry is toward zero economic profits.*

Profit per unit is equal to price minus ATC. If the firm has zero economic profit, then price must equal ATC. In Figure 11.2, Jean's is earning zero economic profits, since the ATC curve is just touching the demand curve at a quantity of Q_1 and a price of P_1.

"Excess Capacity" and the Value of Differentiated Products

If the ATC curve for Jean's Jeans is tangent to the demand curve, it has to be true that the ATC curve is downward-sloping (since the firm's demand curve slopes downward). This means that *the monopolistically competitive firm does not minimize its average total costs.* If the firm were to minimize its costs per unit, it would have to increase its output to a larger quantity than Q_1.

Over the years, monopolistically competitive firms have been criticized because they

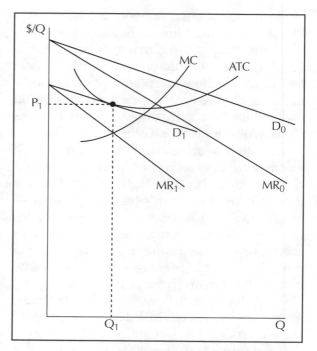

Figure 11.2 Long-Run Profit Maximization for Jean's Jeans

If the existing monopolistically competitive firms are making positive economic profits, new firms will enter the industry. This will shift the demand curve and marginal-revenue curve for an existing firm from D_0 and MR_0 to D_1 and MR_1. The new profit-maximizing price and quantity will be P_1 and Q_1. Price equals average total cost, which means that total profits are now zero because of the increased competition from new firms.

don't minimize costs. It has been said that these firms have *excess capacity*, since they could reduce their average total costs by expanding. Another way to state the criticism is this: Monopolistically competitive industries have too many firms, each of which is too small.

However, many economists have concluded that "excess capacity" is not really a very strong criticism of monopolistic competition. First of all, excess capacity may just not be a very big deal. Even though average total costs aren't minimized, they may be *close* to their minimum values. Remember that the demand curve facing the firm will usually be fairly flat. (Product differentiation may give the firm a little bit of market power, but it doesn't usually give a tremendous amount of market power.) If the firm's demand curve is fairly flat, then the ATC curve will probably be close to its minimum point, as in Figure 11.2. In other words, the difference between the firm's *actual* ATC and its *minimum* ATC may be very small.

Second, even though the firms may not minimize their costs, they *do* produce a wide variety of products. If you can even imagine a world of no product differentiation, it would be a very boring place. Every ice-cream store would sell only vanilla. There would be exactly one style of shirt, one style of pants, one style of shoes. Every radio station would have the same format. If "excess capacity" is the price that we pay for product differentiation, it may well be worthwhile.

CHARACTERISTICS OF OLIGOPOLY

We have now completed our discussion of monopolistic competition. Our next goal is to learn about oligopoly, which is the other "in-between" market structure. Earlier in this chapter, we saw that monopolistically competitive firms have free entry and exit, a large number of sellers, product differentiation, and non-price competition. The features of oligopoly are rather different. In particular, oligopolistic industries are characterized by

- a small number of firms,
- barriers to entry, and
- strategic interdependence among firms.

Let's take a look at these features in turn.

Few Firms

Oligopoly refers to an industry in which there are only a few sellers. (One special case of oligopoly is *duopoly*, in which there are exactly two sellers.) Earlier in this chapter, Table 11.2 presented concentration ratios and Herfindahl indices for several important industries, some of which are dominated by a relatively small number of firms.

Among the industries listed in that table, several would certainly be classified as oligopolistic. For example, household laundry equipment is dominated by Maytag, Whirlpool, and a few other brands. Other oligopolistic industries include automobile tires, cigarettes, greeting cards, malt beverages, and telephone and telegraph apparatus.

Barriers to Entry

Perfect competition and monopolistic competition are similar, in that they both have free entry and exit. But oligopoly is more like monopoly, in that there are usually significant barriers to entry into the industry.

Size as a Barrier to Entry. Oligopolistic firms are often very large. Sometimes the large scale of operations can be a barrier to entry. The investment needed to start a new firm in most oligopolistic industries runs to many millions of dollars, and it can even run into the billions. If you want to set up a new firm to make automobiles, you would have to hire thousands of engineers and technicians. It would take years before you could roll out a car that could compete in tomorrow's market.

Reputation and Experience. Most oligopolistic firms have had years of experience with their customers. Their salespeople have detailed knowledge of the customers' needs, and this knowledge can be extremely effective in competing with rival firms. Even if a new firm could make automobiles that are better than those currently produced by General Motors, Ford, and the other firms in the industry, the new firm would have to convince a skeptical group of buyers. The relationships between the existing firms and their customers can be an important barrier to entry.

Interdependence

In perfect competition, the firms are very passive. Each firm is so small that it can't do anything to affect the market price. The firms are more active under monopolistic competition. Since the firms have differentiated products, they have some market power. They will try to exploit that market power, in an effort to increase their profits.

With oligopoly, the firms have even more market power. Oligopolistic industries have only a few firms, and this means that the firms are very much aware of each other. If one firm changes its price, the other firms have to decide whether they will change their prices in a similar way. If one firm starts a campaign of research and development, or brings out a new product, the other firms must decide how to respond. Thus, oligopolies have an element of strategic interdependence that is mostly missing from perfectly competitive or monopolistically competitive industries.

Since oligopolistic industries have barriers to entry, they may be able to earn economic profits for a very long time. However, the amount of profit will depend on whether the firms engage in *collusion*. When we say that firms collude, we mean that they cooperate with each other. If the firms cooperate by promising not to cut prices, they may be able to make the kind of profits that a monopoly firm would make. On the other hand, if each firm cuts prices in an attempt to gain a larger market share, prices may fall to the levels that we would expect for perfectly competitive firms.

Advertising by Oligopolists. Earlier in this chapter, we said that advertising and other forms of non-price competition are essential features of monopolistic competition. Some important oligopolistic industries do *not* engage in much advertising or other non-price competition. (The crude-oil industry is a good example.) However, many of the most important oligopolies have a lot of product differentiation, and therefore they tend to do a lot of advertising.

The heaviest advertiser in the nation is Procter & Gamble Co., the Cincinnati-based firm that makes laundry detergent, toothpaste, and many other consumer products. In 1996, Procter & Gamble spent over $2 *billion* on advertising. Philip Morris, the food-and-tobacco company, also spent more than $2 billion on advertising. Thus, the amount spent on *advertising* by each of these two firms is greater than the *entire* output of Burundi, or Tajikistan, or Niger, or any of several other countries.

In Table 11.3, we list some more of the American firms that did the most advertising in 1996. The list is a who's-who of oligopolistic firms. Table 11.3 lists the big advertisers in four industries (retailing, automobiles, food products, and pharmaceuticals), since these include many of the largest advertisers.

We summarize the features of imperfectly competitive firms in Table 11.4.

Table 11.3 Some Leading Advertisers in the United States in 1996

Industry	Firm	Spending on Advertising in 1996
Retailing	Sears, Roebuck & Co.	$1,317 million (= $1.317 billion)
	J.C. Penney Co.	808 million
	Federated Department Stores	571 million
	Dayton Hudson Corp.	544 million
	May Department Stores Co.	400 million
	Kmart Corp.	380 million
	Wal-Mart Stores	343 million
Automobiles	General Motors Corp.	$2,373 million (= $2.373 billion)
	Chrysler Corp.	1,420 million (= $1.42 billion)
	Ford Motor Co.	1,179 million (= $1.179 billion)
	Toyota Motor Corp.	800 million
	Nissan Motor Co.	557 million
	Honda Motor Co.	516 million
Food Products	PepsiCo	$1,269 million (= $1.269 billion)
	McDonald's Corp.	1,075 million (= $1.075 billion)
	Coca-Cola Co.	612 million
	Kellogg Co.	595 million
	Anheuser-Busch Cos.	577 million
	Mars Inc.	558 million
	General Mills	483 million
	Nestle SA	403 million
	Sara Lee Corp.	322 million
	Quaker Oats Co.	321 million
	H.J. Heinz Co.	306 million
	Ralston Purina Co.	302 million
	Hershey Foods Corp.	282 million
Pharmaceuticals & Medical	Warner-Lambert Co.	$1,086 million (= $1.086 billion)
	Johnson & Johnson	1,053 million (= $1.053 billion)
	Unilever NV	949 million
	Bristol-Myers Squibb Co.	604 million
	SmithKline Beecham	420 million

Source: *Advertising Age,* September 29, 1997.

Table 11.4 Characteristics of Monopolistic Competition and Oligopoly

Monopolistic Competition	Oligopoly
1. Many Firms	1. Few Firms
2. Free Entry and Exit	2. Barriers to Entry
3. Product Differentiation	3. Products May Be Differentiated or Homogeneous
4. Advertising and Other Non-Price Competition	4. May or May Not Have Non-Price Competition
	5. Strategic Interdependence

IR11-5. An industry has 75 firms. Is this industry an oligopoly? Why or why not?

STRATEGIC INTERDEPENDENCE

Now that we have outlined the *characteristics* of oligopoly, it's time to begin to learn more about the *behavior* of oligopolistic firms. We start our study by looking at a couple of important aspects of oligopolistic interdependence. Then, we use the tools of "game theory" to think about collusion. Third, we'll talk about whether an industry that appears to be oligopolistic might actually be fairly competitive, because of the *threat* of entry by new firms.

Adam Smith, the great Scottish economist, once wrote, "people of the same trade seldom meet together, even for merriment and diversion, but the conversation ends in a conspiracy against the public, or in some contrivance to raise prices." In other words, firms are often tempted to collude with each other.

The firms in an oligopolistic industry may be able to form a *cartel*, which is an agreement that sets the industry price. The ultimate goal of every cartel is to act as a *shared monopoly*, which means that the cartel firms would charge the same price that a monopolist would charge. This will maximize the profits of the industry as a whole.

If the cartel members desire to charge the monopoly *price,* then they will have to restrict output to the monopoly *quantity.* Consequently, cartel agreements usually try to restrict quantity, by specifying the amount that can be produced by each firm.

However, if a cartel is successful in charging the monopoly price, some of the firms may be tempted to cheat on the cartel. If one firm can secretly lower its price slightly, it can increase its own profits at the expense of the other cartel members. If enough firms do

enough cheating, the price will fall and fall. If the cartel breaks down completely, the price will eventually fall all the way to the competitive price.

Thus, every cartel faces a difficult dilemma: *Once a firm is a member of a cartel, it has an incentive to cheat, but cheating can destroy the cartel.* This is good news for consumers, but bad news for the cartel members.

Game Theory

In the last few decades, economists and other social scientists have developed a framework, called *game theory,* for thinking about a wide variety of situations. *Game theory* is the study of how people and organizations interact with each other in strategic situations. A game-theoretic analysis involves identifying the "players" in the game, and the rules of the game. Then, the analysis will specify the *payoffs* that accompany various outcomes. On the basis of the rules and the payoffs, each player will develop a set of *strategies* that will determine how they will play the game.

These game-theoretic ideas can be illustrated by thinking about a game of poker. Each player in a poker game knows the rules of the game: In poker, two pair beats one pair, three of a kind beats two pair, and so on. At the end of each hand, the player with the best hand wins all the money that has been bet. After the cards are dealt, each player assesses the strength of his or her own hand. Each player will make some guesses about whether his or her cards are likely to beat the cards held by the other players. On that basis, each player must develop a strategy. The player can fold (that is, quit the game), or continue to bet. As the play develops, other players will discard old cards, draw new cards, and bet. Based on these actions, each player may revise his or her strategy.

Poker is a *zero-sum game*. On each hand, the amount that is lost by some players is exactly equal to the amount that is won by other players. However, some games are *non-zero-sum games*, because the sum of the gains and losses can be positive or negative.

The Prisoner's Dilemma. One famous non-zero-sum game is called the *Prisoner's Dilemma*. The standard story of the Prisoner's Dilemma goes something like this: Sneaky Sam and Harry the Heist are arrested during the commission of a burglary. The evidence against them is overwhelming. There are eye-witnesses, and Harry and Sam are caught with burglary tools. The police and prosecutors have no doubt that they will be able to get a conviction on the charge of breaking and entering.

However, the police and the prosecutors suspect that these two men may also be the culprits in a whole series of other crimes. But the evidence in the other crimes is not so clear-cut, and it won't be possible to get a conviction for the other crimes, unless one or both of the men confesses.

The police and prosecutors keep the two men in separate jail cells, so that they won't be able to communicate with each other. In separate discussions with Sam and Harry, the authorities emphasize that they want the men to cooperate, by confessing. To each of the prisoners, they say "If you confess to all of these crimes, and the other guy doesn't confess, we'll let you go free, and he will be sent to prison for 20 years. If both of you confess, you will each get a sentence of five years in prison. If you don't confess, but the other guy does confess, he will go free and you will be sent to prison for 20 years. If neither of you confesses, we still have enough evidence to

convict you of this one burglary, and both of you will be sent to prison for 2 years."

In other words, the authorities describe a "payoff matrix" to each of the men. The payoff matrix tells what will happen, depending on whether the men confess. The payoff matrix is shown in Figure 11.3.

Let's consider Sneaky Sam's decision about whether to confess. It's possible for him to subdivide this decision into two parts. The first part has to do with the situation in which Harry (the other prisoner) confesses. The second part has to do with the situation in which Harry *does not* confess.

If Harry confesses, Sam can confess and get a sentence of five years, or he can not confess and get a sentence of 20 years. Not surprisingly, Sam wants to get the lightest possible sentence. Therefore, if Harry confesses, Sam's choice will be to confess.

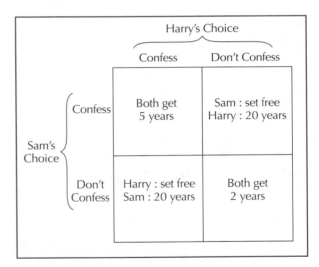

**Figure 11.3 The Payoff Matrix
in the Classic Prisoner's Dilemma**

If each prisoner confesses, they will each get a five-year prison sentence. If neither confesses, they will each receive a two-year prison sentence. If one confesses and the other does not, the one who confesses will be set free, while the one who does not confess will receive a 20-year sentence. This structure of payoffs will give each man an incentive to confess, regardless of what the other man does.

If Harry does not confess, Sam can confess and go free, or he can not confess and get a sentence of two years. Therefore, if Harry doesn't confess, Sam's choice will be to confess.

This is the remarkable result of the Prisoner's Dilemma: Regardless of whether Harry confesses, Sam's best choice will be to confess. In another prison cell, Harry faces the identical problem. If Sam confesses, Harry's best choice is to confess. If Sam doesn't confess, it is still in Harry's interest to confess.

Because of the payoff matrix presented by the police and the prosecutors, each of the prisoners will decide to confess. It doesn't matter whether they are actually guilty of the other crimes. Their own selfish interest will lead each of them to confess. As a result, each of them will confess, and they will both get five years in prison. This is *not* the optimal choice for the two men as a group. As a group, they would be better off if they could agree not to confess. In this case, they would each be sentenced to two years in prison, instead of five years. This is why the Prisoner's Dilemma is a non-zero-sum game: Harry and Sam *both* lose as a result of their inability to cooperate.

This is an unusual result, and a very interesting one. If the two men could cooperate, and agree not to confess, they would each have to spend only two years in prison. However, it is in the selfish interest of each man to confess, which means that they will each have to spend five years in prison. Their inability to cooperate has made them worse off. (Clearly, the Prisoner's Dilemma is very different from the "Invisible Hand". The idea of the Invisible Hand, introduced much earlier in this book, is that there will be good outcomes for society as a whole, even though everyone is pursuing his or her own interest.)

Application of the Prisoner's Dilemma to Oligopoly. At this point, you may be wondering what this Prisoner's Dilemma stuff is doing in a chapter on monopolistic competition and oli-

gopoly. The answer is that the idea of the Prisoner's Dilemma can be applied to a wide variety of problems, including the problem facing a group of oligopolists who are trying to act as a cartel. We will consider the simplest version of this problem, in which there is a duopoly (an oligopoly with only two firms). The two firms are Colossal Corporation and Immense Industries. The payoff matrix for the two firms is shown in Figure 11.4.

If both of the firms cooperate with the cartel agreement, they will act as a shared monopoly. They will cut back on output and raise prices, and each firm will earn $30 million in (economic) profits. If both of the firms cheat on the cartel agreement by secretly increasing sales, they will produce the same output that would be produced if the industry were perfectly competitive, and each of the firms will earn zero profits. On the other hand,

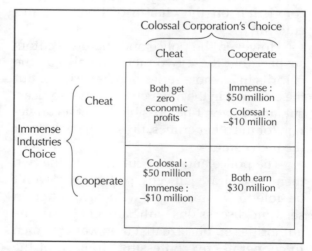

Figure 11.4 The Payoff Matrix for Duopoly Firms

If both firms cheat on the cartel agreement, they will each earn zero (economic) profits. If neither firm cheats, each will earn profits of $30 million. If one cheats and the other does not cheat, the firm that cheats will earn profits of $50 million, while the firm that cooperates with the agreement will suffer losses of $10 million. This structure of payoffs will give each firm an incentive to cheat on the cartel agreement, regardless of what the other firm does.

if one firm cooperates with the agreement, and the other cheats, the cheating firm will increase its share of the market, at the expense of the other firm. The cheating firm will earn $50 million in profits, and the cooperating firm will suffer losses of $10 million.

Let's analyze the decision facing Immense Industries. First, let's look at the payoffs that will occur for Immense Industries, if Colossal Corporation cheats on the agreement. If Colossal cheats, then Immense can also cheat, in which case Immense will earn zero profits. The other possibility is that Immense can cooperate with the agreement, and lose $10 million. Of course, earning zero profits is better than suffering losses of $10 million. Therefore, if Colossal Corporation cheats on the agreement, Immense Industries will be better off if it also cheats.

Now, let's look at the payoffs for Immense Industries, if Colossal Corporation cooperates with the cartel agreement. If Colossal cooperates and Immense cheats, then Immense will earn profits of $50 million. If Colossal cooperates and Immense also cooperates, then Immense will earn profits of $30 million. Here, too, it is in the selfish interest of Immense Industries to cheat on the cartel agreement.

In summary, if Colossal Corporation cheats, it is in the selfish interest of Immense Industries to cheat. If Colossal Corporation cooperates with the cartel agreement, it is still in the selfish interest of Immense Industries to cheat. Regardless of what Colossal Corporation does, it is in the interest of Immense Industries to cheat. Therefore, Immense Industries will cheat. Since Colossal Corporation faces the same payoff matrix, it will also cheat on the agreement. The result is that both firms will cheat, and each will earn zero profits.

Earlier, in the example of Sam and Harry, we saw that each man would confess, even though the two of them would be better off if they could somehow agree not to confess. Our application of the Prisoner's Dilemma to oligopoly is similar. Each firm will cheat on the cartel agreement, even though the two firms would be better off if they could somehow agree not to cheat.

Mechanisms for Tacit Collusion. If oligopoly firms could cooperate with each other, they might be able to increase their profits greatly. With so much money on the line, it's no surprise that oligopolists are always looking for ways to cooperate. In the next few paragraphs, we will discuss some of the methods of cooperation.

In the United States, collusion is illegal. The laws against collusion are known as the "antitrust laws", and we will discuss them in detail in the next chapter. If American firms are to avoid getting caught by the government, they must engage in *secret* or *tacit* collusion. Over the years, firms have used a number of imaginative schemes in their efforts to collude. Here are a few examples. (We'll study collusion some more in the next chapter.)

Basing-Point Pricing. In the 1920s, American steel manufacturers developed a price-fixing scheme called "Pittsburgh Plus". All producers agreed that the price of steel in, say, Nashville, Tennessee, would be equal to the price at a steel mill in Pittsburgh, plus the charge for shipping the steel from Pittsburgh to Nashville. *All* producers used this formula, regardless of whether their mills were in Pittsburgh, or Birmingham, Alabama, or Gary, Indiana.

The Pittsburgh-Plus pricing scheme is an example of *basing-point pricing*. Basing-point pricing is an attempt to allow the cartel members to collude on prices, by reducing the number of prices that must be agreed upon. The Pittsburgh-Plus system was finally stopped because of an antitrust order in 1924. In the meantime, however, this scheme made it easier for the steel companies to collude, since they only needed to agree on the price at Pittsburgh. If they hadn't used such a scheme, then each manufacturer would have been able to quote a different price to customers in different locations. This would have made it necessary for the firms to agree on thousands of prices, instead of just one. Without Pittsburgh Plus, it would have been much more difficult to collude.

The Great Electrical Equipment Conspiracy. One of the most elaborate price-fixing schemes in history involved the manufacturers of turbine generators, transformers, and other electrical equipment, during the 1950s. General Electric, Westinghouse, and Allis-Chalmers were the biggest players in the industry, but at least 29 companies were involved.

These firms used different price-fixing schemes for different products. The most imaginative scheme had to do with the prices of high-voltage switchgear. This was known as the "phases of the moon" scheme. The firms first decided on their market shares. Then, in order to achieve those market shares, they arranged for each firm to be the low bidder on a specified number of contracts. The firms would rotate into the low-bidding position for two-week periods, according to the phases of the moon. This gave the *appearance* of competition, even though it was the result of collusion.

Ultimately, however, the collusion couldn't be sustained. In some cases, firms cheated on the agreements, causing the agreement to break down into a price-cutting war. In addition, the government found out about the conspiracy. (After all, if no one had ever found out about it, we wouldn't be writing about it here!) Seven executives went to jail, and the companies eventually had to pay fines and damages of about $400 million.

Collusion in the Airline Industry. Some airlines share the same computerized reservation systems. This may allow them to signal information to each other about their pricing intentions. By sending information in this way, the airlines may be able to collude to raise prices.

A great many industries have stories of price-fixing agreements. Although most cartels eventually break down, it may be possible for oligopoly firms to earn hefty profits for a long time. Price fixing is more difficult in the United States than in many other countries, because of the antitrust laws. Still, we will probably continue to see occasional attempts to fix prices, for as long as the human imagination can dream up collusive schemes.

Real Economics for Real People 11.3 discusses the most famous cartel of all.

Real Economics for Real People 11.3:
The Rise, Fall, and Rise of OPEC, the World's Most Famous Cartel

Few industries have had a more profound effect on the modern economy than the petroleum industry. Industries, automobiles, and homes all require energy, which often comes from petroleum products. In recent years, the U.S. economy has consumed about 18 million barrels of oil *per day*. (About half of this oil is produced domestically, and the rest is imported.)

Unfortunately, the oil industry has a long history of collusive behavior. Right after the Second World War, the world market was dominated by the "Seven Sisters": Exxon, Texaco, Gulf, Chevron, Mobil, British Petroleum, and Royal Dutch/Shell. Through a series of joint ventures, they developed the huge oil fields in Kuwait, Saudi Arabia, and Iran. Because of these joint ventures, the companies were reluctant to compete aggressively with each other.

Thus, the oil industry of the 1940s and 1950s was a cozy, profitable oligopoly. But high profits will always be an incentive for other producers to enter the market. In 1954, several smaller, independent oil companies got a foothold in Iran. By 1960, the Seven Sisters were losing their grip on the world market, and prices began to fall.

However, falling prices meant falling tax revenues for the host countries. In an effort to halt the price cuts, the Organization of Petroleum Exporting Countries (OPEC) was formed in 1960.

OPEC didn't have much influence at first. By the early 1970s, however, the oil-producing countries became more aggressive. Algeria, Libya, and Iraq all nationalized their oil fields. The Seven Sisters' oligopoly had been effectively replaced by an oligopoly of Middle-Eastern governments. Finally, in 1973, OPEC made big cuts in the supply of crude oil. Prices soared from about $3 per barrel to about $10 per barrel. In 1979, further reductions in supply sent prices soaring to more than $30 per barrel.

But OPEC, like most cartels, couldn't ride high forever. The high prices encouraged conservation: more fuel-efficient cars, homes, and industrial processes. The high prices also made it profitable for non-OPEC producers to increase their exploration and drilling for oil. These activities take a long time, but large quantities of oil eventually began to flow in from Alaska, Mexico, Norway, and other oil fields. OPEC controlled about 55% of the world's crude-oil production in 1973, but only about 30% by 1985.

In addition, many OPEC members were cheating on the cartel, by exceeding their production quotas. This led to disagreements within the cartel. In an effort to keep prices up in the early 1980s, Saudi Arabia decreased its production by several million barrels per day. Finally, Saudi Arabia got tired of trying to carry the entire cartel, and it increased its production in late 1985. This was probably an attempt to punish the countries that had been cheating. Prices soon tumbled, briefly falling as low as $6 per barrel. For most of the 1980s and 1990s, after adjusting for inflation, prices were lower than they were in 1974.

It has happened again and again, in oil and many other industries: Cartels are often able to raise prices for a time, but they eventually lose control over the market, and prices come back down. However, it would probably be a bad idea for oil-importing countries (such as the United States) to get too complacent. The relatively low prices discouraged energy conservation, and the low prices also led to a reduction in exploration by the non-OPEC countries. When Mexico and Norway began to cooperate with OPEC in 1998, the oil-producing countries succeeded in reducing production for the first time in more than a decade. World output went down by about 5 million barrels per day, and the price of oil surged from $10 per barrel to more than $30 per barrel.

Will the prices stay that high? Probably not. In fact, after a few weeks, the price fell back to about $26 per barrel. In all likelihood, the same forces that led to the collapse of oil prices in the mid–1980s will eventually send prices lower again.

Contestable Markets

We began this chapter by discussing measures of concentration, and we've consistently implied that more concentration is a bad thing. It is true that higher concentration is *often* associated with higher prices and lower quantities, but this may not *always* be true. Here are a couple of exceptions:

1. An increase in concentration may not be much of a problem, if the industry is still relatively unconcentrated (even after the increase). Earlier in this chapter, we saw that the women's, misses', and juniors' dress industry is very unconcentrated, with a four-firm concentration ratio of 6. If two dressmaking companies were to merge, the concentration ratio might go up to 7 or 8. This is probably not a big deal. The industry would almost certainly still be highly competitive.

2. Even when an industry appears to be fairly concentrated, it still may operate in a competitive manner if it would be easy for new firms to enter the market. During the last two decades, economists have developed a theory of *contestable markets*, to describe oligopolies in which it is easy to enter. If entry is relatively easy, then a market may be "contestable", even if it has only a small number of firms.

The theory of contestable markets has been applied to the commercial airlines industry. (Don't confuse the commercial *airlines* industry with the commercial *aircraft* industry. Commercial *aircraft* are manufactured by a very small number of firms. By the late 1990s, Boeing and Airbus were the only firms left in the industry. These firms are protected by substantial barriers to entry. Commercial *airlines* include companies that carry air passengers, such as United, American, Delta, Northwest, and many others.)

Over some routes, the airlines industry is highly concentrated. Nevertheless, since it's fairly easy to begin service on a route, the existing airlines may not be able to raise prices as far as they otherwise would. According to the theory of contestable markets, even an industry with only one existing firm might sometimes behave fairly well, if the existing firm believes that other firms could enter easily. The existing firm would not charge the monopoly price, since this would quickly bring a rival firm into the market.

Reality Check: Interim Review Questions

IR11-6. In earlier chapters, we emphasized the fact that trade can make everyone better off. In the language of game theory, is trade a zero-sum game, or a non-zero-sum game?

IR11-7. Can game theory be used to understand a perfectly competitive industry? Why or why not?

IR11-8. What is a shared monopoly?

IR11-9. Company A and Company B form a duopoly. When you go to the store, you notice that Company A's products are on sale for one week. Then, the sale on Company A's products ends, and Company B's products go on sale for one week. The pattern continues, with the firms having sales on alternate weeks. Could this be a scheme for tacit collusion? If so, is it likely to be effective?

ECONOMICS AND YOU:
THE JOYS OF DISCOUNT SHOPPING

Regardless of what else you might say about them, the 1990s have been a great time to shop. In one market after another, vigorous competition has kept consumers happy with low prices. These good times for the consumer have come from two main sources: discount *brands* and discount *stores*.

In many cases, the average consumer can't even name the discount brands that he or she buys. These discount brands (sometimes called "store brands" or "private label products") do not receive the kind of heavy advertising that goes to the better-known "national brands". The discounters' strategy is simple: Generate sales by slashing prices. Quite often, it's a strategy that works. In the market for frozen orange juice, the various private labels get more sales revenue than Minute Maid or Tropicana. In the market for cough-and-cold remedies, private label products lead the pack, ahead of Robitussin, NyQuil, Alka-Seltzer Plus, or any of the other name brands.

When the discount brands are successful, they inevitably put pressure on the better-known brands. The better-known brands often have little choice but to cut their own prices. For example, discount cigarette brands were non-existent in 1981, but they grew to 30% of the American market by 1992. In response, prices were cut by the makers of Marlboro.

Discount brands are often found on the same shelf as higher-priced brands. In a discount store, however, practically everything is marked down. One of the most successful discount-store chains is Wal-Mart, which grew from a single store in Arkansas until it became the largest retailer in the world. Affiliated with Wal-Mart are the Sam's Club stores, which are one of a number of deep-discounting warehouse stores. For a modest annual fee, the members of Sam's Club, Price Club, and other clubs get to roam down aisle after aisle of heavily discounted merchandise. At the same time, deep-discounting drug-store chains, such as Phar-Mor, have added extra pressure to the market. This pressure has been felt by the traditional supermarket chains, which have been forced to lower their own prices.

Even with all of this discounting, it still is true that most of the markets in the United States economy are *not* perfectly competitive. There still is product differentiation, there still are markets with relatively few firms, and there still are barriers to entry. Nevertheless, the trend is definitely toward markets that are closer to the perfectly competitive ideal. For price-conscious consumers, this is great news.

Chapter Summary

1. Industrial concentration is often measured by the four-firm concentration ratio or the eight-firm concentration ratio. These measures do not account for the relative sizes of firms *within* the four largest firms or the eight largest firms. The Herfindahl index attempts to deal with this problem.

2. A monopolistically competitive industry has a large number of firms, which have free entry into and exit from the industry. These firms sell products that are differentiated on the basis of location and/or product quality and service. This product differentiation leads to the frequent use of advertising and other forms of non-price competition.

3. Because of product differentiation, the monopolistically competitive firm faces a downward-sloping demand curve (unlike the flat demand curve of the perfectly competitive firm). The firm maximizes its profits by choosing the quantity at which marginal revenue equals marginal cost.

4. If firms in a monopolistically competitive industry are earning positive economic profits, then new firms will enter. If the existing firms have economic losses, some of them will exit the industry. Thus, the long-run tendency in a monopolistically competitive industry is toward zero economic profit.

5. In the long run, monopolistically competitive firms will not minimize their average total costs: If the individual firms were to produce more, their average costs would decline. This is called "excess capacity". However, on the positive side, it must be remembered that monopolistic competition does provide the benefits of product differentiation.

6. Oligopolistic industries have relatively few firms, and they have barriers to entry. When we study oligopoly, the emphasis is on the strategic interdependence among the firms.

7. Oligopolies often attempt to establish cartels, for the purpose of raising prices and profits. If a cartel is successful, the total profits of the cartel members will be maximized (that is, the firms will make monopoly profits). However, the individual members of the cartel will often have an incentive to cheat, by secretly reducing prices. As a result, cartels tend to break down.

8. The incentive for oligopoly firms to cheat on a cartel agreement can be studied using the Prisoner's Dilemma, which is a type of non-zero-sum game.

9. The theory of contestable markets suggests that concentrated industries may still behave in a fairly competitive fashion, if the existing firms believe that it would be easy for new firms to enter the market.

Key Terms

Product Differentiation

Market Structure

Monopolistic Competition

Oligopoly

Imperfect Competition

Concentration

Four-Firm Concentration Ratio

Eight-Firm Concentration Ratio

Herfindahl Index

Advertising

Non-Price Competition

Excess Capacity

Duopoly

Strategic Interdependence

Collusion

Cartel

Payoff

Strategy

Zero-Sum Game

Non-Zero-Sum Game

Prisoner's Dilemma

Basing-Point Pricing

Contestable Markets

Questions and Problems

QP11-1. In alphabetical order, the four market structures are monopolistic competition, monopoly, oligopoly, and perfect competition. Rank them from most competitive to least competitive.

QP11-2. Compare the elasticity of demand for a monopolistically competitive firm's product with the elasticity of demand for a perfect competitor. Compare both of these with the elasticity of demand for a monopolist.

QP11-3. If we look at the concentration ratios for the nation as a whole, the airlines industry is not extremely concentrated. However, if we concentrate on specific cities, we see that Northwest dominates the flights into and out of Detroit and Minneapolis, USAir dominates Pittsburgh, and TWA dominates St. Louis. In your opinion, should we focus our attention on con-

centration at the national level, or should we focus on local markets?

QP11-4. Assume that an industry has five firms. In percentage terms, the market shares are as follows: 30%, 25%, 20%, 15%, 10%. Calculate the Herfindahl index. Discuss the advantages and disadvantages of the four-firm concentration ratio, the eight-firm concentration ratio, and the Herfindahl index.

QP11-5. Assume that a perfectly competitive firm has a U-shaped average-total-cost curve. Graph the long-run price and quantity for this firm (after entry or exit have led to zero economic profits). Now, assume that a monopolistically competitive firm has exactly the same average-total-cost curve. Graph this firm's long-run price and quantity. Compare the long-run prices and quantities for the two market structures.

QP11-6. The cola industry is dominated by Coca-Cola and Pepsi. Together, these firms control about 90% of the production of cola drinks in the United States. One could imagine an alternative scenario, under which Coke and Pepsi lost market share to low-priced store brands. Discuss the advantages and disadvantages of these two situations.

QP11-7. The steel industry was once characterized by "price leadership". U.S. Steel (now USX Corp.) would announce a change in prices. Within a matter of days, virtually all of the other firms would follow. Could this pattern of price leadership be explained as a mechanism of tacit collusion?

Chapter 12

Market Power, Regulation, and Antitrust

ECONOMICS AND YOU:
A DAY IN THE REGULATED LIFE

Alan Altobelli is a travelling salesman. He wakes up in a hotel room in Altoona, Pennsylvania, and makes a few phone calls over a telephone system that is regulated by the Federal Communications Commission (FCC). He also watches television programs that are regulated by the FCC. The TV runs on electricity, which is regulated by Pennsylvania authorities and by the Federal Energy Regulatory Commission (FERC).

Alan's allergy medicine is approved by the Food and Drug Administration (FDA). Many of the items on his breakfast plate have been inspected by the U.S. Department of Agriculture (USDA). After breakfast, he drives to a factory to meet his client for the day. The workers at the factory have a contract that conforms to the regulations of the National Labor Relations Board (NLRB). The emissions from the factory smokestack are regulated by the Environmental Protection Agency (EPA). The factory uses safety procedures that are mandated by the Occupational Safety and Health Administration (OSHA).

At day's end, Alan drives to the airport, and buys toys for his daughter and son at the gift shop. The toys are manufactured according to the standards of the Consumer Product Safety Commission (CPSC). Finally, Alan flies home on a flight that is regulated by the Federal Aviation Administration (FAA).

FCC, FERC, FDA, USDA, NLRB, EPA, OSHA, CPSC, FAA: All day long, our economic lives are regulated by government agencies. In this chapter, we will look at some of the government rules, and we'll study their effects on the private economy. We focus on three areas of government involvement in the economy.

First, we study an area that is usually called economic regulation, or industrial regulation. *Economic regulation* includes the regulation and deregulation of prices and quantities, in industries such as utilities, airlines, and trucking. Second, we look at some aspects of social regulation, including rules for health and safety. Finally, we consider the *antitrust laws*, under which it is possible for the government to break a large firm into smaller pieces, in order to overcome the problems of monopoly.

Our discussion of government involvement in the economy will not end with this chapter. In Chapter 13, we discuss minimum-wage laws and other aspects of government involvement in the labor market. In Chapter 16, we discuss the effects of the taxes that are used to finance government operations. In Chapter 17, we discuss government efforts to regulate air pollution, water pollution, garbage disposal, and similar problems.

REGULATION OF PRICES AND QUANTITIES

In this section, we will talk about several types of regulation, including:

- Price regulations

- Requirements that firms provide certain services

- Restrictions on entry into an industry

Price regulation is one of the most widespread types of regulation of business. We've already studied some price controls (such as rent controls, agricultural price supports, and so on.) in an earlier chapter. In this chapter, we'll study price regulation of the utility firms that provide electricity, natural gas, or water, as well as price regulations of airlines, trucking companies, and other industries.

In many cases, governments require the regulated firms to provide certain types of service. For example, airlines were once required to serve many smaller communities, even if the service was unprofitable. This amounts to a restriction on *exit* from the industry. Governments also regulate industries by putting restrictions on *entry*. For instance, many cities put severe limits on entry into the taxicab industry.

Are these regulations good or bad? The answer will depend on the nature of the industry. If the industry has the potential to be competitive, then it may not make much sense to regulate. After all, competition tends to deliver good outcomes, *without* any government interference. However, if the industry is a natural monopoly, government regulation may be better for society. We begin by looking at the regulation of natural monopolies.

Regulation of Natural Monopolies

In Chapter 10, we learned that an industry is a natural monopoly if a single firm can always produce at lower average total cost than can any combination of two or more smaller firms.

Economists have long thought that electric-power utilities are among the best examples of natural monopoly. In the discussion that follows, we will *assume* that Gigantic Power Company is a natural monopoly. (However, some new evidence suggests that electric power utilities might have the potential to be competitive. We'll discuss this evidence at the end of this section.)

The cost curves for Gigantic Power Company are shown in Figure 12.1. Since the average-total-cost curve is always decreasing as we move from left to right in the diagram, we have a natural monopoly. If average total cost (ATC) is always decreasing as we move to higher outputs, then marginal cost (MC) must always be below average total cost. Therefore, in Figure 12.1, MC < ATC. Since Gigantic Power is a monopoly, it faces the downward-sloping market demand curve. The marginal-revenue curve (MR) slopes downward even more steeply than the demand curve (D). These curves are also drawn in Figure 12.1.

There are many possible combinations of price and quantity. We will discuss three of these possibilities:

- Monopoly profit maximization

- Marginal-cost pricing

- Average-cost pricing

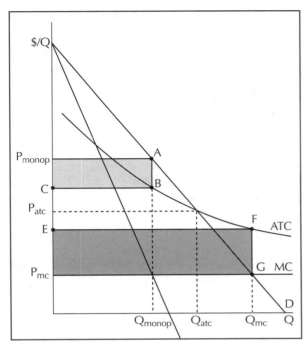

Figure 12.1 Prices, Quantities, and Profits of a Natural Monopoly, Under Different Regulations

If the natural monopolist is allowed to maximize profits without any regulation, the price will be P_{monop}, the quantity will be Q_{monop}, and economic profits will be the rectangle $P_{monop}ABC$. If a regulatory agency forces the firm to price according to marginal cost, the price will be P_{mc}, and the quantity will be Q_{mc}. The firm will have economic losses, which will be the rectangle $P_{mc}EFG$. If the regulator gets the firm to price according to average total cost, the price will be P_{atc}, the quantity will be Q_{atc}, and economic profits will be zero.

Monopoly Profit Maximization. What will happen if we just let Gigantic Power maximize its profits, without any interference from government? The intersection of the MR curve and the MC curve determines the monopolist's profit-maximizing level of output. This gives a quantity of Q_{monop}. At this quantity, the demand curve tells the firm that it can charge a price of P_{monop}. Gigantic Power's economic profits are shown by the rectangle, $P_{monop}ABC$.

If the government doesn't intervene, that is the end of the story. But governments don't appear to believe that profit-maximizing monopolization is a good policy. Consumers pay high prices and consume low quantities, while the monopolist gets profits. This is both economically inefficient and politically unpopular.

Marginal-Cost Pricing for the Natural Monopoly. If the government does decide to intervene, what should it do? The economist's instinct is to say that price (P) should be set equal to marginal cost. If the government forces Gigantic Power to use marginal-cost pricing, we will get a price of P_{mc}, and a quantity of Q_{mc}. From the point of view of the consumer, this is a lot better than allowing the monopoly to maximize its profits. The consumer can buy more units, because the price is much lower. Consumer surplus will be much larger.

Unfortunately, there's a problem with requiring a natural monopoly to set P=MC. Marginal cost is below average total cost for the natural monopolist. If price equals marginal cost, and if marginal cost is less than average total cost, then price must be less than average total cost. Since profit per unit is the difference between price and average total cost, the firm will suffer economic losses. The losses are shown by the rectangle, $P_{mc}EFG$.

If Gigantic Power is required to have losses year after year, it will go out of business. The firm won't keep producing unless the government covers the losses. This will probably involve raising taxes on some other part of the economy. As we shall see in Chapter 16, taxes lead to inefficiencies of their own. (And taxes aren't very popular politically, either.)

Average-Cost Pricing for the Natural Monopoly. So far, we've shown that monopoly profit maximization has its problems, and that marginal-cost pricing has *its* problems, too. There is one other alternative, although it has difficulties of its own. If the government requires Gigantic Power to set P=ATC, then we get a price of P_{atc}, and a quantity of Q_{atc}. Since profit per unit is the difference between price and average total cost, the firm will earn zero economic profit.

In theory, average-cost pricing is very attractive. It gives consumers a better deal than they would get from monopoly profit maximization. It also avoids the problem of economic losses that would occur under marginal-cost pricing. In practice, however, average-cost pricing creates difficulties. The trouble is that other firms aren't there to *force* the firm to earn zero economic profits. Instead, the government tries to *guarantee* a price that will lead to zero economic profits. In other words, the government tries to guarantee a normal rate of return for the firm. (Average-cost pricing is sometimes called guaranteed-rate-of-return regulation.)

Practical Problems in Regulation. As a practical matter, setting a price that will guarantee a normal rate of return is very tricky. In order to know what price to set, *the regulatory agency needs very detailed information on the utility firm's costs.* But the firm itself provides most of those cost data. The firm has an incentive to use clever accounting techniques, in order to make its costs appear to be higher than they really are. The firm will also have very little incentive to keep its costs tightly under control.

A second problem is that *the regulators may come to identify more with the firm than with the consumers.* It's easy to see how this might happen. The people at the regulatory agency work very closely with the people at the utility firm. It's only natural for friendships to form. As a result, the commission may be "co-opted" or "captured" by the firm that it is supposed to regulate. The regulators may be tempted to allow prices that are higher

than those that would lead to zero economic profits.

A third problem is that *the rate-setting process is very slow.* If economic conditions change, the prices that the utility are allowed to charge may not keep pace. This problem is called *regulatory lag.* If the firm installs new, cost-reducing technologies, it can make higher profits until the regulatory commission forces it to lower its rates. But if inflation is unexpectedly rapid, the firm's profits may be depressed until the commission allows higher rates to be charged.

We've now seen that natural monopolies create problems, no matter how we try to regulate them. Before we turn to a different subject, however, we should ask whether electric power utilities are really natural monopolies at all. If they aren't really natural monopolies, then we would do best to let them compete.

Is There a Competitive Future for the Electric-Power Industry?

In the late 1970s and early 1980s, some large factories began to build their own power plants. In many cases, these small power plants had lower costs than the bigger plants of the utilities. This suggests that the utilities may *not* truly be natural monopolies. However, these independent power plants couldn't sell to far-away customers, because the big utilities owned almost all of the high-voltage transmission lines. In other words, monopoly in the *transmission* of electric power helped to prop up monopoly in the *generation* of power.

But everything changed as a result of a new federal law passed in 1992. The Energy Policy Act required utilities to transmit other companies' electricity on their power lines. This allows low-cost producers to compete for customers. As a result, big industrial customers and some city governments are insisting on rate cuts from their electricity suppliers. Now that local utilities are no longer protected from competition, the industry is beset by mergers.

In 1994, the California Public Utility Commission proposed to allow homeowners to choose their own power company, beginning in 2002. In a few years, families may choose among power companies, in the same way that they now choose among long-distance telephone companies. We may one day decide that the solution to the problems of utilities is a healthy dose of competition.

In *Real Economics for Real People 12.1*, we discuss some other problems that can arise in regulated industries.

Reality Check: Interim Review Questions

IR12-1. A natural monopolist is required to use marginal-cost pricing. Will its economic profit be positive, negative, or zero?

IR12-2. For a natural monopoly, rank (1) monopoly profit maximization, (2) average-cost pricing, and (3) marginal-cost pricing, according to the prices that will be charged.

IR12-3. For a natural monopoly, rank (1) monopoly profit maximization, (2) average-cost pricing, and (3) marginal-cost pricing, according to the quantities that will be produced.

Real Economics for Real People 12.1: How Cable TV Rates Went Up, When Regulators Tried to Make Them Go Down

After several years of unregulated price increases in the cable-television industry, Congress passed the Cable Act of 1992. The law, which was passed over President Bush's veto, set prices for "basic cable" packages that were lower for most customers. However, the law left all sorts of loopholes:

- The law set *minimum* rates. Although these rates represented price reductions for many cable customers, they meant price *increases* for some others. In Connecticut, Continental Cablevision raised rates to the new minimum.

- Time Warner's cable operation in Milwaukee didn't change its price for "basic" cable, but it did remove four channels from the "basic" package. Customers who wanted to receive these four channels (including the Discovery Channel) would have to pay an additional

$2.20 per month. Since most of the law relates only to basic cable packages, the cable companies have an incentive to remove channels from basic cable, and add them to other, unregulated categories of service.

- In Los Angeles, before the law was passed, Century Communications Corp.'s cheapest rate was $16.30, for which buyers received a package of *23* channels. After the law, the cheapest rate rose to $24.67, for *31* channels. According to the rules of the 1992 Cable Act, the cable companies have an incentive to change the number of channels, so that higher rates can be charged.

In short, regulation is almost never an easy task. If the regulated industry sells a wide variety of products, the regulator's job gets even tougher.

REGULATION AND DEREGULATION
IN POTENTIALLY COMPETITIVE INDUSTRIES

There may be practical problems in regulating monopolies, but at least there's a good reason to try to regulate them: If a monopoly is left to its own devices, it will usually reduce its output and charge high prices. However, American government agencies have often regulated the prices of industries that aren't monopolies by any stretch of the imagination. Our next step is to study the regulation of competitive industries.

Federal Regulation of Railroads and Trucking

When the Interstate Commerce Commission (ICC) was organized in 1877, the railroad industry was the first to be regulated. The railroad industry wasn't the most competitive, but it also wasn't a monopoly. Under ICC regulation, the existing railroads were protected from competition. If a railroad wanted to enter a new market and charge a lower price, it now had to get the ICC's permission.

As a result of the ICC, railroad competition was stifled, and high prices tended to provide comfortable profits. By the 1930s, however, the railroads were facing competition from unregulated truckers. But instead of allowing trucks and railroads to compete, the ICC extended its regulations to the trucking industry. As a result, it became much harder for trucking firms to cut prices.

By the 1970s, the ICC's policy of high prices was under attack. Economists led the charge, saying that competition would deliver better results for consumers. The Federal government engaged in *deregulation* of trucking and railroads in the late 1970s and early 1980s, by removing some of the rules that had restricted competition.

Deregulation allowed trucking and railroad firms to compete by charging lower prices. The gains to consumers from trucking deregulation have been estimated at $30 billion *per year*, and the gains from railroad deregulation have been estimated at $15 billion *per year*.

State Regulation of Trucking and Railroads

One problem with the first wave of transportation deregulation is that it only applied to *interstate* trips. But most States continued to regulate the trips that occurred completely within their borders. This meant that prices for *intrastate* trips were often much higher than prices for trips that did not cross State lines.

For example, a company in Beaumont, Texas, paid $297 to ship fire hydrants to Texarkana, Arkansas. Since the trip crossed a State line, it was not regulated by Texas authorities. However, if the company wanted to ship a fire hydrant to Texarkana, *Texas* (which is right next to Texarkana, Arkansas), it would have to pay a regulated price of $603.

As a result of regulation by the States, many shipping firms go far out of their way in order to cross State lines. Instead of going straight from Grand Rapids, Michigan, to Detroit, Michigan, one company would send shipments through South Bend, Indiana. In this way, it created two unregulated interstate trips, instead of one regulated intrastate trip. Similarly, a Virginia company would ship through Landover, Maryland, in order to avoid Virginia's regulators.

Finally, in 1994, Congress overrode the regulations of the States, in order to allow competition in trucking *within* States.

Regulation and Deregulation in the Airline Industry

The 1930s brought an explosion of price and quantity regulation by the Federal government, as shown in Table 12.1.

Table 12.1 Some Federal Agencies Involved in Economic Regulation

Agency	Area of Interest
Interstate Commerce Commission (1887)	Railroads, trucks, and water carriers. Also had responsibility for telephone service from 1910–1934, and for oil pipelines from 1906–1977.
Federal Communications Commission (1934)	Telephones, television broadcasting, radio broadcasting, and cable television.
Securities and Exchange Commission (1934)	Stocks, bonds, and other securities.
Federal Power Commission (1935, renamed Federal Energy Regulatory Commission in 1977)	Electricity and natural gas. After 1977, inherited responsibility for oil pipelines.
Civil Aeronautics Board (1938, disbanded in 1983)	Airlines.

One of the agencies that opened its doors in the 1930s was the Civil Aeronautics Board (CAB). The CAB set maximum and minimum airline fares, and it controlled entry and exit in airline markets. Between 1938 and 1978, the CAB received dozens of applications from new firms that wanted to enter the industry. The CAB turned down every single application. The effect of the CAB's airline regulation was similar to the effect of railroad and trucking regulation by the ICC. Where airline fares were regulated by the CAB, they tended to be higher than they would have been with competition.

Recall that most States continued to regulate trucking, even after the Federal government had deregulated. As a result, in the 1980s, trucking prices were often much higher for *intrastate* trips than for *interstate* trips. For many years, the airline industry had exactly the opposite arrangement, because CAB regulation only applied to interstate flights. The prices of *intrastate* airline trips were generally not regulated, so that intrastate flights were much cheaper than *interstate* flights of similar distance. One study of airfares in 1972 showed that, for flights of about 350 miles, interstate fares averaged about 93 percent higher than intrastate fares within the state of California.

As a result of CAB regulation of interstate flights, the airlines weren't able to compete on the basis of price. So they competed on the basis of service, by offering more flights, fancier meals, more flight attendants, and so forth. But these arrangements were very costly.

By the mid–1970s, there was growing political pressure for deregulation of the airlines. Congress passed a deregulation law in 1978. New firms entered the industry, and the existing firms re-organized their fare and route structures.

One major *unanticipated* consequence of deregulation was that the airlines developed *hub-and-spoke route systems*. Under this system, the airlines sent more traffic through their "hubs". Delta established a hub in Atlanta, Northwest in Minneapolis, USAir in Pittsburgh, United in Chicago, Continental in Houston. By concentrating traffic at the hubs, the airlines were able to use larger, more efficient aircraft. In this way, the airlines were able to offer more frequent flights over many routes, at the same time that they lowered their prices!

The move to hub-and-spoke systems was not predicted beforehand. This reveals an important point: We can't always predict what will happen as a result of deregulation. By unleashing the forces of competition, deregulation gives incentives for creativity and innovation.

Not all airline customers are better off than they were before deregulation, however. Before deregulation, the CAB established fares that were *above* cost for flights of over 400 miles, but *below* cost for shorter flights. In this way, passengers on longer flights were forced to subsidize passengers on shorter flights. When deregulation came, this type of ***cross-subsidization*** was no longer required. Thus, prices increased for some passengers.

However, it appears that airline passengers as a group were made much better off as a result of deregulation. One study for 1977 suggests that airline regulation cost consumers nearly $10 billion per year.

In *Real Economics for Real People 12.2*, we discuss some problems that have occurred in other regulated industries.

The Politics and Economics of Regulation

We've talked about economic regulation of utilities, railroads, trucking firms, airlines, taxicabs, and cosmetologists. Although economic regulations may have good effects, they often seem to be helpful only to a relatively small group. For society as a whole, some of these regulations lead to losses of many billions of dollars per year.

How can we explain regulations that, on balance, make society worse off? We can get a few answers by learning about the "economic theory of regulation", which was developed by George Stigler and other economists. The economic theory of regulation starts by recognizing that the power to coerce is the most fundamental resource of government. An interest group (such as the taxicab owners) can make itself better off, if it can get the government to use its coercive powers in a particular way (such as by restricting entry into the taxicab industry).

How does an interest group get the government to do its bidding? The economic theory of regulation stresses that legislators want to maximize their political support. Entry restrictions in the taxicab industry do make consumers worse off, but the loss to any individual consumer is probably small, and it's probably difficult to organize the consumers into a powerful lobbying group. On the other hand, each existing taxicab firm has a very large stake in the outcome. Because the number of firms is relatively small, it won't be very hard for the firms to organize, so that they can pressure the government effectively.

When we view regulations in this way, we see that they are likely to be most helpful to small, easily organized interest groups, especially if those groups feel very strongly. Regulations are likely to hurt large, diffuse groups whose desires aren't very strong. According to the economic theory, regulations *may* be socially beneficial, but there is no reason to believe that they will always be good for the nation as a whole. A regulation may be approved, even if it hurts a lot of people, and only helps a few.

Reality Check: Interim Review Questions

IR12-4. What is cross-subsidization?

IR12-5. It is commonly believed that businesses dislike regulation. However, in some cases, businesses may actually prefer regulation. Under what circumstances would you expect a business to desire to be regulated?

Real Economics for Real People 12.2:
Cabs and Cornrows: The Effects of Licensing Regulation

If you want to operate a taxicab legally in New York City, you have to have a medallion. The city government issues fewer than 12,000 medallions. There are fewer medallions now than there were in 1937, even though the city's economy has grown a lot since then. By controlling the number of medallions, the city effectively controls entry into the industry. The city also regulates the fares that the taxis can charge.

If you want to enter the industry, you have to pay the market price for a medallion, which is around $140,000. This indicates that the regulated fares are high enough to generate substantial economic profits. (Otherwise, no one would be willing to pay that kind of money to get into the industry.)

The story is similar in many other cities. Baltimore, Boston, Chicago, and San Francisco all restrict entry into the taxicab industry, using systems similar to the one in New York. San Francisco has about the same population as Washington, D.C., but San Francisco restricts entry into the industry, while the nation's capital does not. The difference is dramatic: In 1983, there were only 711 cabs in San Francisco, compared with 8600 in Washington, D.C.

The main winners from taxicab regulation are the existing firms, which get economic profits. The chief losers are the consumers. Restricting the number of taxicabs causes special problems for people who are elderly, or handicapped, or who don't own cars. A Transportation Department study estimated that taxicab restrictions cost consumers nearly $800 million per year.

Another group hurt by taxicab regulations are those who would like to earn a living by driving a cab, but are prevented from doing so. It's estimated that removing the restrictions would create 38,000 jobs in the taxi industry.

Driving a cab isn't the only profession with restrictions on entry. Dozens of professions require some sort of licensing or certification. In many States, you need a license to practice as a barber, beautician, or cosmetologist. For instance, Washington, D.C., has a Board of Cosmetology, which regulates hair salons. The members of the Board are all owners of existing salons. In order to get a license, it's necessary to pay $5000 and take a nine-month course of study. The beautician exam involves hairstyles that were popular in the 1930s, but nothing on braiding, which is more popular today.

Usually, regulators say that licensing regulations protect the public, by ensuring that professionals are adequately trained. This makes the most sense for doctors and other professionals who are doing complicated work that affects the public safety. However, entry restrictions also serve to increase the profits of the existing firms, by eliminating potential competitors. It seems likely that the Cosmetology Board does more to support the profits of the existing firms than to protect the public. The owner of a new company challenged the regulations, saying "We're not talking about gene splicing or test-tube babies or something complicated here. We're talking about hair-braiding."

SOCIAL REGULATION

Before 1970, the Food and Drug Administration (FDA) was the only agency involved in "social regulation" of health and safety. But several new regulatory agencies were founded in the early 1970s. These include the Occupational Safety and Health Administration (OSHA), which deals with health and safety in the workplace, and the Consumer Product Safety Commission (CPSC), which regulates products like household appliances and children's toys.

Another agency of social regulation is the Environmental Protection Agency (EPA), which is mainly concerned with industrial pollution. We will deal with pollution and the EPA in Chapter 17. Table 12.2 summarizes information about some of the Federal social-regulation agencies.

OSHA and Regulation of Health and Safety on the Job

In the United States in 1930, there were 15.4 work-related accidental deaths for every 100,000 people. By 1940, the number of accidental deaths on the job had dropped to 12.9 per 100,000 population. The work-related accidental death rate continued to fall, to 10.2 in 1950, 7.7 in 1960, 6.8 in 1970, 5.8 in 1980, and 4.0 in 1990.

Most of this decrease in job-related accidental deaths occurred *before* OSHA was established in 1970. Most statistical studies indicate that OSHA has only had a small effect on death rates. This leaves us with two questions: First, why did on-the-job safety improve even without government regulation? Second, why didn't OSHA have a bigger effect?

The Market for Job Safety. Let's assume that you understand that there is a greater chance of getting injured on one job than on other jobs, and let's also say that you're able to choose among a variety of different jobs. Then, the only way that an employer can get you to take the riskier job is by offering a higher wage rate. This gives employers an incentive to improve safety on the job, even without government regulation.

The market incentives for a safer workplace have grown stronger over the years. During the 20th century, labor markets have become more competitive than they were before, so workers have more opportunities to avoid dangerous jobs. Also, the American population has become much more affluent over the last couple of generations. When incomes go up, it appears that the "demand for safety" goes up as well. So it really isn't very surprising that the accidental death rate

Table 12.2 Some Federal Agencies Involved in Social Regulation	
Agency	**Area of Interest**
Food and Drug Administration (1906)	Food, drugs, medical devices, and cosmetics.
Occupational Safety and Health Administration (1971)	Health and safety in the workplace.
Environmental Protection Agency (1971)	Air and water pollution, toxic waste.
Consumer Product Safety Commission (1972)	Safety of toys, appliances, and other products used in the home.

on the job was reduced by more than half from 1930 to 1970.

The Successes and Failures of OSHA. The preceding paragraphs suggest that the market will often provide on-the-job safety, even if there is no regulation. However, the market will only work well if workers are well informed about the risks. This means that one of the most important functions for an agency like OSHA is to provide information.

In fact, providing information has been the key to some of OSHA's greatest successes. Chemical companies must now put labels on containers of some kinds of chemicals, and workers are trained in handling certain chemicals.

Unfortunately, OSHA has also been beset by problems. The problems include:

- frivolous, nitpicking regulations,

- regulations that don't give firms much flexibility,

- regulations that are extremely costly to comply with, and

- an enforcement effort that is too small to have much effect.

In the early days of OSHA, the agency issued over 4000 industry standards. Many of these, such as the standards for portable toilets for cowboys, were viewed as being silly. In one case, an employer was cited by OSHA for not giving life jackets to the workers who were building a bridge, even though the riverbed below the bridge was dry. In order to improve OSHA's credibility, the Carter Administration eliminated or modified nearly 1000 of the regulations in 1978.

Another problem is that OSHA regulations are often written in a very rigid way. For example, the OSHA regulation for handrails has specific requirements for height, spacing of posts, thickness, and clearance from the wall. An alternative approach would be for OSHA to specify performance standards, and let firms achieve the standards in the way that they see fit. OSHA has moved very gradually to allow greater flexibility. In 1984, the agency issued standards for controlling the build-up of dust within grain elevators, and it gave employers considerable flexibility in how to reach the standards. But OSHA still has a long way to go: Many of the regulations are still written in a very inflexible manner.

On many occasions in this book, we have stressed the importance of thinking in terms of the *marginal* benefits and *marginal* costs of an economic action. If we were to design OSHA's regulations in the best possible way, we would want to achieve a balance between the marginal benefits and marginal costs of each regulation. But the legislation that created OSHA doesn't say anything about taking costs into account.

The basic approach has been that firms are supposed to comply with the regulations if it's at all possible, regardless of cost. As a result, some OSHA regulations would certainly not survive, if they were subjected to a serious analysis of costs and benefits. For instance, it has been estimated that the OSHA arsenic standard costs as much as $70 million per life saved.

It appears that OSHA is more aware of cost considerations than it once was. Nevertheless, we are unlikely to get a fully sensible set of regulations unless Congress changes the law, so that cost concerns can be taken into account directly.

Finally, one reason that OSHA has only had a very modest effect is that its enforcement effort is so small. In any given year, inspectors only visit the workplaces of about 3 million workers, out of a workforce of more than 100 million. The average inspection leads to fines of only about $100. This just isn't big enough to give employers a strong financial incentive to improve safety.

What does the future hold? If OSHA were to strengthen its enforcement efforts, while at the same time taking the costs of compliance into account, we could hope for further improvements in workplace safety. Of course, experience suggests that some improvements would be likely, regardless of what is happening at OSHA.

Product Safety Regulation

Since early in the 20th century, the Food and Drug Administration has regulated food products, drugs, medical devices, and cosmetics. More recently, the Consumer Product Safety Commission has regulated toys and other products.

Seat Belts, Safety Caps, and the Role of Human Behavior. In trying to understand the effects of any product-safety regulation, it's important to remember that human behavior plays an important role. If a toy has sharp edges, parents may take special precautions in order to reduce the chance of an accident. If the toy is made safer, parents may be less careful. The ultimate effect on the number of accidents will depend on *both* the inherent safety of the toy and on the extent to which people take care.

Automobile safety regulations are one important example of this. If the roads are wet and slippery, most people will slow down. This tells us that people adjust their behavior to the safety conditions that they perceive. Studies have shown that, when seat belts were made mandatory, the average driving speed increased. As a result, the actual improvement in safety was not as great as it would have been, if people had continued to drive at the same speeds.

On balance, automobile safety regulations have helped to reduce injuries and deaths. It's possible that the increased safety has been so great that it would justify the additional cost, which can run to a few thousand dollars per car. However, it isn't always the case that safety regulations improve safety. "Child-resistant" caps on medicine containers are difficult to open, even for many adults. Some

families respond to this by leaving the caps off. There is some evidence that the number of poisonings may have actually *increased* since the introduction of the child-resistant cap.

The examples of seat belts and safety caps tell us that safety is not just a matter of technology. It's also a matter of behavior. If future safety efforts are to be more successful, they will need to involve teaching people to act in a safe way, in addition to merely concentrating on safety technology.

Uncertainty and the Regulation of Medical Treatments. Finally, it's important to keep in mind that the scientific evidence about safety is often uncertain. This uncertainty causes big problems for the Food and Drug Administration (FDA), which is heavily involved in regulating drugs and medical devices.

One example of the problem is the recent controversy over silicone breast implants, which are widely used by women who have had a mastectomy. In the 1980s and early 1990s, there were several highly publicized cases of women who had had implants, who then developed medical problems. One of the most serious of these problems was a skin-hardening disease called scleroderma. The question is whether the breast implants caused the diseases, or whether the diseases would have happened anyway. This is a difficult question to answer, since any large population will have at least a few people who develop diseases.

In the early 1990s, the FDA came down on the side of those who said that the silicone implants were responsible for the diseases. As a result, the implant manufacturers put together a fund of $4.3 billion to settle lawsuits. (About $1 billion of this total would go to trial attorneys.) The manufacturers also dropped out of the business.

However, in June, 1994, a study published in the *New England Journal of Medicine* found "no association between breast implants and the connective-tissue diseases and other disorders. . . ". In other words, these medical researchers suggested that the FDA had made the wrong decision, because the silicone implants didn't really cause the problems that they were accused of causing. The relationship between breast implants and diseases is still controversial, and further study will be needed before we can be really certain.

An agency like the FDA can make two very different kinds of mistake. First, it can disapprove products that are really beneficial. (The previous paragraph suggests that this may have happened in the case of breast implants.) Second, the agency can approve products that are harmful. Mothers who took the drug thalidomide during pregnancy gave birth to terribly deformed children. These "thalidomide babies" are a strong reminder of the dangers of this second type of mistake.

Ultimately, the FDA would like to avoid both types of mistake. This is a very hard task, however, since the scientific evidence is often uncertain. The consensus seems to be that the FDA is more afraid of approving a harmful drug than of failing to approve a helpful one.

Thus, the FDA usually takes a very conservative approach. New drugs and devices are subjected to a very long and exacting approval process.

This cautious approach is understandable, given the politics of the situation. The FDA probably has more to lose by approving a bad drug or device, than by failing to approve a good one. Those who are hurt by a bad drug or device are likely to be highly vocal and organized. Those who are hurt by the absence of a device that has never been approved are less likely to pressure the FDA. (One exception to this is the well-organized campaign for the FDA to move faster in approving drugs that might help AIDS patients.)

Reality Check: Interim Review Question

IR12-6. Let's say that an occupational safety regulation is expected to save one life per year. If the annual cost of this regulation were $1 million, do you think it would be beneficial to adopt the regulation? What if the cost were $10 million, or $100 million, or $1 billion, or $1 trillion?

ANTITRUST IN ACTION

Government regulation of business is a worldwide phenomenon. Nearly every nation regulates businesses, and the regulations found in many other countries are similar to those found in the United States. Now, we move to consider the antitrust laws, which are an American invention that has been pursued further in the United States than anywhere else.

In the 1870s and 1880s, giant monopolistic organizations called "trusts" came to dominate many American industries, including petroleum, tobacco, sugar, meatpacking, and coal. The business practices of trusts caused a great deal of resentment. The public outcry led to the passage of the first antitrust law, the Sherman Antitrust Act of 1890.

The Sherman Act of 1890

The original antitrust law was named for Senator John Sherman of Ohio. Section 1 of the *Sherman Act* prohibits "(e)very contract, combination . . . or conspiracy, in restraint of trade. . . ". This makes it illegal for competing companies to collude to fix prices. Section 2 of the Sherman Act prohibits monopoly or attempting to monopolize. Under the Sherman Act, either private parties or the Justice Department could bring lawsuits aimed at eliminating price fixing or monopoly.

The enforcement of the Sherman Act got off to a very slow start. In fact, the period from 1890 to 1904 is sometimes called the "merger-to-monopoly wave", because dozens of fairly competitive industries were transformed into monopolies or near-monopolies. During this period, giants such as United States Steel, General Electric, DuPont, Eastman Kodak, American Tobacco, and International Paper came to dominate important markets.

Even when the Sherman Act was used, the effect was often small. For example, a cartel was formed by six manufacturers of cast-iron pipe in 1895, and this arrangement was declared illegal by an Appeals Court. In order to avoid the court ruling, the firms simply merged to form a new company, which controlled three-quarters of the national market. Despite the Sherman Act, the merged firm was allowed to exist.

Finally, in the *Northern Securities Case* of 1904, the Supreme Court used the Sherman Act to rule that two railroads (Northern Pacific and Great Northern) could not merge. In the *Standard Oil Case* of 1911, the Supreme Court broke John D. Rockefeller's Standard Oil Trust into 33 separate companies. (These included the forerunners of such firms as Exxon, Mobil, Socal, and Sohio. Ironically, the two largest pieces, Exxon and Mobil, have recently merged with each other.) A few weeks after the *Standard Oil* decision, the Supreme Court decided the *American Tobacco Case*, by breaking James B. Duke's Tobacco Trust into 16 smaller companies.

The Clayton Antitrust Act of 1914

Even though the Sherman Act had been used successfully on a few occasions, there was still a feeling that the antitrust laws needed to be strengthened. As a result, Congress passed the Clayton Act in 1914. The Clayton Act prohibits some specific practices that we have discussed in earlier chapters, including:

- Price discrimination, when it is not justified on the basis of cost differences.

- Mergers achieved through the acquisition of stock, when the merger reduces competition substantially. (It is important to recognize that many mergers may be perfectly legal.)

A *conglomerate merger* is a merger between two firms in unrelated industries. For example, if a manufacturer of computer equipment merges with a maker of sports equipment, it would be a conglomerate merger. Conglomerate mergers are not much of a concern, because they are unlikely to reduce competition in any important way. It is unlikely that conglomerate mergers would be challenged under the antitrust laws. A *vertical merger* is a merger between a firm and one of its suppliers. For example, a vertical merger would occur if an automobile company were to merge with a maker of tires. Vertical mergers have some potential to reduce competition, but they are still not the most dangerous type of merger. A *horizontal merger* is a merger between two firms that are competing with each other directly in the same industry. It is much more likely that the Clayton Act would be used to challenge a horizontal merger than a vertical merger or a conglomerate merger. Even a horizontal merger is not necessarily a cause for alarm. The damage to competition that occurs as a result of a horizontal merger will depend on the size of the two firms. If both of the firms are small relative to the market, then the degree of concentration of the industry would not be greatly affected. However, if the combined firm would be large relative to the market, then competition might be reduced significantly by the merger.

The Clayton Act also prohibits these other practices:

- *Tying clauses*, under which a seller would only sell one product if the buyer agrees to buy some other product from that same seller. For example, it used to be that if you bought Kodak film, you were also required to buy Kodak developing services.

- *Exclusive dealing arrangements*, under which a dealer agrees to buy all of its supplies from one supplier. For example, Standard Oil Company of California had an exclusive dealing arrangement with several thousand retail gas stations, until this was declared illegal by the Supreme Court.

- *Interlocking directorates*, under which the same person would sit on the Board of Directors of several competing companies.

One other important piece of antitrust law was passed in the same year as the Clayton Act. The *Federal Trade Commission Act* of 1914 created a new agency for dealing with antitrust issues. (Previously, the Department of Justice had been the only agency involved with antitrust.)

Two sections of the Clayton Act were later amended in a major way. The price-discrimination section was changed drastically by the *Robinson-Patman Act* of 1936. This law was designed to protect small businesses from competition from large discount chains. The Robinson-Patman Act made it illegal for large food chains to pay less than small stores for produce, even when the chains could reduce costs by acting as their own wholesalers. Although many of the antitrust laws are generally believed to be beneficial, the Robinson-Patman Act is not. Most of the antitrust laws encourage competition, but Robinson-Patman discourages it. Fortunately for consumers, the Robinson-Patman Act hasn't been enforced very strictly in recent years.

The anti-merger provisions of the Clayton Act had one big loophole. Although the Act made it illegal to acquire *stock*, it still allowed firms to merge by acquiring *physical assets*. This loophole was plugged by the *Celler-Kefauver Act* of 1950.

Table 12.3 has a summary of the major antitrust laws.

Table 12.3 Antitrust Laws in the United States

Law	Important Provisions of the Law
Sherman Act (1890)	Prohibits combinations or conspiracies in restraint of trade. This has been used to outlaw price-fixing conspiracies. Prohibits monopoly, or the attempt to monopolize.
Clayton Act (1914)	Prohibits price discrimination, if the discrimination is not based on cost differences. Prohibits mergers achieved through acquisition of stock. Prohibits "tying clauses", which force a buyer to buy a second product from the same seller. Prohibits "exclusive-dealing arrangements", which force a dealer to buy all of its supplies from one seller. Prohibits "interlocking directorates", under which the same person sits on the Board of Directors of two or more competing companies.
Federal Trade Commission Act (1914)	Forms a new agency to enforce the antitrust laws. The FTC has been especially interested in deceptive business practices.
Robinson-Patman Act (1936)	Changes price-discrimination provisions of the Clayton Act, by prohibiting large retailers from selling at lower prices, even when the different prices arise from lower costs.
Celler-Kefauver Act (1950)	Strengthens anti-merger provisions of Clayton Act by prohibiting mergers through acquisition of physical assets.

Exemptions from the Antitrust Laws

Some activities have been specifically exempted from the antitrust laws. By far the most important exemption applies to labor unions. Without an exemption, much union organizing activity would violate the antitrust laws. Agricultural cooperatives are also exempt from the antitrust laws.

Since 1922, major-league baseball has been given an exemption from the antitrust laws. As a result, major-league baseball is a cartel, and it is perfectly legal. Entry into the cartel is strictly controlled by the existing firms. New firms (called expansion franchises) are sometimes allowed to enter the industry, but only if they receive the approval of the existing firms. Consequently, when entry does occur, it happens in such a way as to maintain the regional monopolies of the existing firms.

Changing Interpretations of the Antitrust Laws

The passage of a law by Congress is only the beginning. The ultimate effect of any law will depend on how it is enforced, and how it is interpreted by the courts. We have already seen that the Sherman Act did not have much effect for more than a decade after its passage. Beginning in 1904, however, there was a period of more aggressive enforcement. This roller coaster has continued for much of the 20th century: Periods of strict interpretation of the antitrust laws have alternated with periods of looser enforcement.

U.S. Steel and the Rule of Reason. In 1920, the Supreme Court issued a landmark ruling in the **U.S. Steel Case**. The Court refused to rule against U.S. Steel, because they said that the firm had not acted badly. The Court thus stated the **Rule of Reason**—a firm would not be found guilty unless it had behaved in an *unreasonable* way. In other words, it wasn't ille-gal for U.S. Steel merely to be a big company. In fact, U.S. Steel (which is now called USX Corporation) had already been losing market share. Its share of the American market had dropped to 52 percent by 1915.

The End of the Rule of Reason. In the **ALCOA Case** of 1945, the Rule of Reason was dramatically reversed. ALCOA (the Aluminum Company of America) had actually performed very well. Aluminum prices had *fallen* on several occasions. Nevertheless, it was ruled that ALCOA had violated the antitrust laws, merely by having a dominant position in the aluminum market. As a result, government-owned aluminum plants were sold to create two new competing firms, Reynolds Aluminum and Kaiser Aluminum.

The *ALCOA* case ushered in a quarter century of aggressive antitrust decisions. Some of these decisions would probably not be made by today's Supreme Court. Two examples are the **Brown Shoe Case** of 1962 and the **Von's Grocery Case** of 1966.

The *Brown Shoe* case involved a merger between Brown and Kinney, two firms in the shoe industry. The *combined* market share of Brown and Kinney was less than five percent of the shoe-manufacturing market in the United States, and less than four percent of the shoe-retailing market. These small market shares don't seem likely to lead to major price increases. Nevertheless, the Supreme Court indicated a desire to stop even a small increase in market concentration.

The *Von's Grocery* case involved two chains of grocery stores in the Los Angeles area. If Von's Grocery and Shopping Bag Food Stores had been allowed to merge, their combined market share would have been only about 7.5 percent. Once again, however, the Court ruled against the merger.

Antitrust Law Since 1970. The *Brown Shoe* and *Von's Grocery* decisions are widely viewed as extreme. By the early 1970s, the Supreme

Court was becoming more moderate, by showing an increased willingness to approve mergers. In 1984, the Justice Department issued new, more lenient guidelines for its antitrust actions.

Whereas antitrust enforcement may have been too strict from the 1940s to the 1960s, it may have become too lenient after that. In the more permissive atmosphere, the 1980s saw many huge mergers and acquisitions: Getty Oil and Texaco, USAir and Piedmont Airlines, DuPont Chemical and Conoco Oil, Philip Morris and Kraft, and Northwest Airlines and Republic Airlines.

Even when the government tried to use the antitrust laws, it was sometimes unsuccessful. In the *IBM Case*, the government charged International Business Machines Corp. with a number of anti-competitive practices. Over a 13-year period, the case generated $200 million in legal costs and a trial transcript of more than 100,000 pages. However, the Justice Department dropped the case in 1982. In the same year, the Federal Trade Commission lost a breakfast-cereal case against Kellogg, General Mills, and General Foods.

In spite of the more permissive antitrust atmosphere of the last few decades, a few important cases were decided by *consent decrees*, which are negotiated settlements between the government and a company. The *Xerox Case* ended in 1975 with a consent decree, under which Xerox Corp. agreed to license its photocopying patents to its competitors.

One of the most famous antitrust cases of recent years is the *AT&T Case*, which was decided by a consent decree in 1982. The decree, which went into effect in 1984, required American Telephone & Telegraph Co. to divest itself of its local telephone operating companies. AT&T still had a very prominent position in *long-distance* service, but *local* service fell to the "Baby Bells": Ameritech, Bell Atlantic, Bell South, Nynex, Pacific Telesis, Southwestern Bell, and USWest.

In 1998, the agribusiness giant Archer Daniels Midland (ADM) was found guilty of price-fixing in the market for lysine. Fines of $100 million were imposed.

One case that has the potential to affect a very important market is the *Microsoft* **Case**. In 1999, Federal District Court Judge Thomas Penfield Jackson issued a "finding of fact", in which he found that Microsoft Corporation had violated the antitrust laws. Specifically, it was found that Microsoft had aggressively used its near-monopoly in the market for personal-computer operating systems, as a means of creating market power in other markets, such as the market for internet-browsing software. In April, 2000, the Justice Department recommended that Microsoft be divided into two pieces, one for its operating-system software, and one for its other software. As of this writing, the case had not been resolved.

A summary of some of the most important antitrust cases is shown in Table 12.4, on p. 294.

Evaluation of Antitrust

In this section, we have seen some of the ups and downs in the history of antitrust. Certainly, this history is imperfect. Not every feature of the law makes sense, and the law has been enforced unevenly over time. Still, we can ask whether the United States economy is better off, as a whole, than it would have been if there were no antitrust laws. Most economists would probably say "Yes".

Without the antitrust laws, we would almost certainly have much less competition in petroleum, tobacco, telecommunications, and many other industries. The antitrust laws have been used to stop price fixing in industries such as those producing steel, electrical equipment, pharmaceuticals, and folding boxes. The antitrust laws have also been used to strike down "tying" practices in a variety of industries, including the movie-distribution industry. On the whole, antitrust law means more choices and lower prices for consumers.

Table 12.4 Some Important Antitrust Cases

Case	Result
Northern Securities (1904)	First major Supreme Court decision involving Sherman Act; Northern Pacific and Great Northern railroads not allowed to merge.
Standard Oil Co. (1911)	Oil trust violates Sherman Act, and is broken into 33 pieces.
American Tobacco Co. (1911)	Tobacco trust violates Sherman Act, and is broken into 16 pieces.
U.S. Steel Co. (1920)	Dominant firm in the industry is *not* guilty. Mere size is not sufficient for a guilty verdict. Decision is a strong statement of the "Rule of Reason".
ALCOA (1945)	Dominant firm *is* guilty, merely because of its size. Decision marks the end of the "Rule of Reason".
Brown Shoe (1962)	Brown Shoe was ordered to sell Kinney Shoe, despite fact that combined firm had less than 5% of U.S. market.
Von's Grocery (1966)	Von's Grocery and Shopping Bag Food Stores are not allowed to merge, despite fact that combined firm had only 7.5% of market in Los Angeles area.
Xerox (1975)	Xerox Corp. ordered to license its patents to its competitors, and change its pricing policies.
IBM (1982)	Case dropped by Justice Department, after 13 years of prosecution.
AT&T (1982)	American Telephone & Telegraph agrees to divest itself of its local operating companies.

The Future of Antitrust

After the merger wave of the 1980s, things calmed down for a few years in the early 1990s. However, mergers and acquisitions were back at record levels in 1994. Lockheed acquired Martin Marietta in a $23-billion deal in the aerospace-defense industry. In entertainment, Paramount was acquired by Viacom, Inc., for $10 billion. As the 1990s roared to a close, mergers and acquisitions continued at a feverish pace. In the automobile industry, Daimler-Benz combined with Chrysler, in a deal valued at more than $40 billion. A $48-billion deal brought British Petroleum together with Amoco. Two of the "Baby Bell" telecommunications companies combined, as SBC Communications acquired Ameritech in a $63-billion deal. The insurance giant, Travelers Group, acquired Citicorp (a banking and financial-services firm, and the nation's leading issuer of credit cards) for $73 billion. And Exxon combined with Mobil in a $79-billion stock swap.

The latest merger wave has been stimulated by many factors, including relatively low interest rates, intense competition from abroad, and a lenient attitude in the Justice Department and the Supreme Court. It's hard to say definitively whether the Justice Department should have been more vigilant, but one can certainly make a powerful argument that lax antitrust enforcement has created the possibility of anti-competitive actions on the part of many giant firms. Still, it's hard to say where the future will take us. Over the last century, merger activity has come in waves. This new wave could end as quickly as it started, if economic and political conditions change.

Several important antitrust cases are now on the horizon. One involves General Electric, the world's largest manufacturer of industrial diamonds, and DeBeers Consolidated Mines, the largest supplier of gem diamonds. In addition, the antitrust exemption of major-league baseball is once again under scrutiny. In *Real Economics for Real People 12.3*, we consider college financial aid, which has been the subject of recent debates in the antitrust field.

Reality Check: Interim Review Questions

IR12-7. What is the common feature of the *Standard Oil*, *American Tobacco*, and *ALCOA* cases? How are these different from the *Brown Shoe* and *Von's Grocery* cases?

IR12-8. How is the Robinson-Patman Act different from the other antitrust laws?

Real Economics for Real People 12.3: Financial Aid and the Antitrust Laws

The *official* price for a year's stay at an elite private college can be $30,000 or more. But many students don't have to pay the full price, because they receive financial-aid packages. By offering price discounts in the form of financial aid, the colleges are engaged in price discrimination.

In order to limit the cost of financial aid, a group of 22 private colleges and universities in the northeast entered into a cartel agreement. Beginning in the 1950s, these colleges would meet every year to compare notes on the financial-aid packages that they offered to students. The goal was for each student's "family contribution" (or net price) to be the same at every school. In this way, the colleges could avoid getting into a "bidding war" for the most promising students.

In 1991, the Justice Department brought an antitrust suit against Massachusetts Institute of Technology (MIT) and the eight Ivy-League colleges (Brown, Columbia, Cornell, Dartmouth, Harvard, Pennsylvania, Princeton, and Yale). The Ivy-League colleges agreed to stop their price-fixing meetings, but MIT defended itself. MIT argued that the cartel led to better opportunities for needy students. In 1993, an Appeals Court issued a ruling favorable to MIT, saying that the arrangement "promoted equality of access to higher education and economic and cultural diversity." The Justice Department soon dropped the case.

The return to price fixing will have many effects. First, the price-fixing system is lucrative for the richest colleges, such as Harvard, Princeton, and Yale, which devote a smaller fraction of their budgets to financial aid than do the less-rich colleges. Second, some students will end up paying lower prices (that is, they will receive more financial aid). Since the existing financial-aid systems are based on financial need, lower-income students will tend to do better (on average) when the present system is preserved. However, some students will end up paying higher prices (that is, they'll get less financial aid). On average, the most exceptional students will end up paying more than they would have paid if price-fixing had ended. For any particular student, the effects of price-fixing will depend on the details of his or her own situation.

ECONOMICS AND YOU: REGULATION, ANTITRUST, AND LONG-DISTANCE TELEPHONE SERVICE

What do the recent changes in telecommunications mean for the consumer? Overall, deregulation has led to big price reductions, especially in long-distance service. The biggest savings will go to those who make a lot of long-distance calls. But deregulation also means that consumers must make choices that they did not have to make when AT&T held a monopoly. The savvy consumer will do much better than the one who doesn't shop for the best deal.

If your *business* makes a large volume of calls, it may make sense to shop around a lot, remembering that the market doesn't only include AT&T, MCI, and Sprint (the "Big Three"). In fact, there are several hundred smaller long-distance companies. Most of these deal with niches in the business market.

If you're just trying to save on your *home* phone bill, you can probably concentrate your attention on the Big Three, and possibly a few other companies. Still, it makes sense to be a smart shopper. The most important thing to do is to get on some kind of discount plan, such as MCI's "5 Cents Everyday". If you're paying the basic rate with no discounts, you could be losing big money.

You can start by calling the customer-service line at your current long-distance carrier. The representative can use a computer to bring up your bills for the last few months. He or she can quickly calculate which plan would be cheapest for you. (This can be seen as a form of price discrimination. If you don't go to the trouble of calling the customer-service line, you reveal that your demand is inelastic, and you get stuck with the basic rate. If you do make the call, you can often get a lower rate.)

If you become dissatisfied with your long-distance carrier, you can always change to another. If you *are* satisfied with your current carrier, and another company sends you a check in an effort to get you to switch, you can call your own company and ask them to match it. They may be willing to bargain with you, in order to keep your business.

Chapter Summary

1. If a natural monopoly is allowed to maximize profits without government regulation, it will charge a high price and sell a low quantity. Prices would be substantially lower if the government were to require the natural monopoly to charge according to marginal cost. However, marginal-cost pricing would cause the firm to have economic losses.

2. Most States have chosen an intermediate strategy of allowing natural monopolists to charge prices according to average total cost. This is sometimes called "guaranteed-rate-of-return regulation". If this is done correctly, the firm will have zero economic profits. However, average-cost pricing may reduce the firm's incentives to innovate or to cut costs aggressively.

3. The electric-power utility industry has been regulated heavily on the grounds that it is a natural monopoly. But recent evidence suggests that the industry may actually have the potential to be competitive.

4. Governments have also regulated many industries that have the potential to be very competitive. These include railroads, trucking, and airlines. During the 1970s and 1980s, these industries were substantially deregulated. Another example of anti-competitive regulation is licensing regulations, which make it excessively difficult to enter many professions.

5. The economic theory of regulation studies the way in which interest groups attempt to make themselves better off, by getting the government to use its coercive powers to their advantage. According to this theory, regulations are likely to help small, easily organized groups that have strong interests. Regulations are likely to hurt poorly organized groups whose interests are not strong.

6. "Social regulations" dealing with health and safety issues increased substantially in the 1970s, with the formation of the Occupational Safety and Health Administration and the Consumer Product Safety Commission. Even without government regulation, firms have an incentive to provide safe workplaces, because they would have to pay higher wages in order to get workers to work in unsafe conditions. Also, when new safety technologies are introduced, people may respond by reducing the amount of effort that they devote to safety. For example, people tend to drive faster when wearing seat belts. This may reduce the ultimate effectiveness of the safety regulations. One of the most difficult problems facing the social-regulatory agencies is that the scientific evidence on health and safety questions is often inconclusive.

7. The American experience with antitrust laws began in 1890 with the Sherman Act. This law prohibited conspiracies in restraint of trade, as well as monopolization and the attempt to monopolize. After an initial period of lax enforcement, the Sherman Act was used to break up the Standard Oil Trust and the American Tobacco Trust in 1911.

8. The antitrust laws were strengthened in 1914 with the creation of the Federal Trade Commission, and with the Clayton Act. The Clayton Act prohibits tying clauses, exclusive dealing arrangements, interlocking directorates, certain types of price discrimination, and certain mergers. The price-discrimination provisions of the Clayton Act were greatly weakened by the Robinson-Patman Act of 1936. The anti-merger provisions of the Clayton Act were strengthened by the Celler-Kefauver Act of 1950.

9. Some activities are exempt from the antitrust laws. These include labor unions,

agricultural cooperatives, and major-league baseball.

10. In 1920, the Supreme Court stated the "Rule of Reason", under which only "unreasonable" activities were illegal. However, the Rule of Reason came to an end in 1945 with the *ALCOA* case. ALCOA was found guilty of violating the antitrust laws, merely because of its size. This trend toward very strict antitrust enforcement continued with the *Brown Shoe* case and the *Von's Grocery* case, in which mergers were prohibited, even though the companies involved were fairly small relative to the market.

11. In the last few decades, antitrust policy has not been as strict as it was in the days of *ALCOA, Brown Shoe,* and *Von's Grocery.* The government finally dropped its antitrust suit against IBM, it lost its suit against the breakfast-cereal manufacturers, and it never tried to stop many of the big mergers of the 1980s and 1990s. However, Xerox Corp. was forced to license its patents to its competitors, and AT&T was forced to divest itself of its local telephone operating companies. In 1999, a Federal judge found that Microsoft Corporation had violated the antitrust laws. The *Microsoft* case has the potential to lead to profound changes in the computer industry.

Key Terms

Economic Regulation

Antitrust Laws

Marginal-Cost Pricing

Average-Cost Pricing

Guaranteed-Rate-of-Return Regulation

Regulatory Lag

Deregulation

Hub-and-Spoke Route Systems

Cross-Subsidization

Sherman Act

Northern Securities Case

Standard Oil Case

American Tobacco Case

Clayton Act

Conglomerate Merger

Vertical Merger

Horizontal Merger

Tying Clauses

Exclusive Dealing Arrangements

Interlocking Directorates

Robinson-Patman Act

Celler-Kefauver Act

Federal Trade Commission Act

U.S. Steel Case

Rule of Reason

ALCOA Case

Brown Shoe Case

Von's Grocery Case

IBM Case

Consent Decrees

Xerox Case

AT&T Case

Microsoft Case

Questions and Problems

QP12-1. Describe the economic theory of regulation. Can you use the theory to understand why trucking was regulated during the 1930s, and then deregulated during the 1970s and 1980s?

QP12-2. What is the "Rule of Reason"? Discuss some of the landmark antitrust cases that marked the beginning and end of the Rule of Reason. Do you think that the Rule of Reason is a good interpretation of the antitrust laws, or would you prefer a more rigid interpretation? Why?

QP12-3. Describe the most important features of the Sherman Act and the Clayton Act.

QP12-4. Suppose that you are the head of the Antitrust Division of the Justice Department. Which of the following cases would you prosecute very aggressively? Which would you consider prosecuting, but only if the Department's resources permit? Which would you definitely not prosecute?

a. A merger between two adjacent soybean farms, each of which has 160 acres planted.
b. A merger between United Airlines and American Airlines.
c. A merger between a manufacturer of potato chips and a chain of auto parts stores.
d. A takeover of 10,000 gasoline stations by Exxon Mobil.

Would you change any of your answers if the firms in question said that they would reap large economies of scale by merging?

QP12-5. Here is a further list of cases. To which of these would you assign the highest priority, which would get lower priority, and which would you not prosecute at all?

a. The simultaneous election of the same person to the Boards of Directors of Daimler Chrysler, Ford, and General Motors.
b. A contract requiring that anyone who buys an automobile from a dealer must also get all of their repair and maintenance work done at the dealership.
c. Meetings between the financial aid committees at several colleges, designed to coordinate their financial-aid offers to students.
d. A charge by small retailers that Wal-Mart is competing unfairly by offering lower prices.

QP12-6. Discuss the similarities and differences between the *Standard Oil* case, the *Xerox* case, and the *AT&T* case.

QP12-7. For which of the following professions would you require very strict licensing regulations? For which would you require minimal licensing? In which cases would you allow completely unregulated entry into the profession?

a. Heart surgeon.
b. Dental hygienist.
c. Barber.
d. Newspaper delivery person.
e. Social worker.
f. Automobile assembly-line worker.

QP12-8. The railroad industry was largely in favor of regulation in the 1880s. However, by the 1950s, they were at least partly in favor of deregulation. What changes might have brought this about?

QP12-9. "If a firm is extremely successful, it will drive its competitors out of business. As a result, the firm will become a monopoly. Thus, the ultimate measure of success for any firm is its ability to become a monopoly. However, the antitrust laws penalize this behavior. Therefore, the antitrust laws are fundamentally inefficient." Comment on this statement.

QP12-10. Sometimes, a member of a regulatory commission will resign, and accept a job with a company in the industry that he or she had formerly regulated. What effect, if any, will this have on the regulatory relationship? Should this practice be allowed?

QP12-11. People who suffer from epileptic seizures are usually given prescription medicines, in an effort to control the seizures. A number of medications have been on the market for many years, but every medication has some side effects. In 1993, the FDA approved a new anti-seizure drug, called felbamate, for use in the United States. Before felbamate was put on the market, it was tested on 1000 subjects, and no severe side effects were found. Within a few months, felbamate was being used by 100,000 people. In the summer of 1994, however, it was discovered that 10 people taking felbamate had developed a rare form of anemia, and two of these had died. The FDA did not pull the drug off the market, but it did issue a strong warning. The FDA suggested that felbamate users should consult with their doctors, and consider switching to another medication.

a. Given that several other medications were already on the market, should the FDA have considered approval for felbamate under any circumstances?
b. Should the FDA have insisted on a larger pre-market test? Remember that testing is costly, so that more testing will ultimately be reflected in higher prices. What will determine the optimal size of a test?
c. After it was discovered that felbamate has a severe side effect in about one case out of 10,000, what course of action do you think the FDA should have pursued? Under what circumstances should the FDA issue an outright ban, instead of a warning?

Chapter 13

Labor Markets

ECONOMICS AND YOU: WHO MAKES BIG BUCKS?

Today, most Americans spend years working for pay. By 1999, about 72 million men had jobs, and so did about 62 million women. For most of these people, the lion's share of their income is from wages and salaries.

Wages and salaries are much higher for some people than for others. An assembly-line worker in an automobile plant is likely to make four times as much as a worker at a fast-food restaurant. A coal miner or a computer programmer would be likely to make three times as much as a worker at a factory that makes blouses. In 1999, the average worker in private industry was earning about $13.25 per hour, plus some benefits, but some workers were working for the minimum wage of $5.15 per hour. At the other end of the spectrum, the actor Mel Gibson charges $25 million for every movie in which he appears. Julia Roberts and Will Smith are close behind, at $20 million. Baseball star Ken Griffey, Jr., makes more than $12 million per year.

In this chapter, we'll learn where these wage differences come from. The answers usually have to do with the workings of supply and demand in the marketplace. We will see how wage differences are caused by the interaction of the supply of labor and the demand for labor.

THE DEMAND FOR FACTORS OF PRODUCTION

Until now, most of the examples in this book have been taken from *goods markets,* which are also called *product markets.* We've talked about the markets for computers and corn and chemicals, for automobiles and steel. These are all *outputs.*

But what about *inputs*? What about the *resources* that are used to produce the computers and corn and chemicals? In order to get an ear of corn to your picnic table, it takes work by a farmer, and it takes farm machinery, farmland, fertilizer, and pesticides. It takes other inputs as well, such as gasoline or electricity to run the machinery. It's necessary to use a wide variety of inputs in the production of virtually any good. Let's look at these inputs more closely.

Labor

The most important input is the work that people do. Without people, there would be no economy at all. Economists use the word *labor* to refer to the work that is done by workers. In this chapter, we will study labor markets in detail.

Capital

No matter how many workers are available, or how hard they work, they won't be very productive if they have to work with their bare hands. The machinery, equipment, structures, and vehicles that people work with are called *capital*. The carpenter's hammer is a piece of capital, and so is the railroad car that brings cattle to market, and so is the warehouse used by a mail-order clothing company. In recent years, business computers have been among the fastest-growing types of capital. We'll discuss capital markets in the next chapter.

Other Inputs

Land is another important input into many production processes, especially in agriculture and real estate. Most production processes use *energy* from oil, natural gas, electricity, and other sources. Finally, most production processes involve *materials*, such as bricks, plastics, and steel.

Labor, capital, land, energy, and materials: We use the term *factors of production* to refer to these inputs. The purpose of this chapter is to begin thinking about the markets in which factors of production are bought and sold. These markets are called *factor markets* or *input markets*. We start by looking at factor demand, for any kind of factor of production. Then, for the rest of this chapter, we focus on labor markets. We look at labor supply, and then we put demand and supply together, so that we can learn about equilibrium in labor markets.

THE DEMAND FOR A FACTOR OF PRODUCTION

In Chapter 7, we learned that the demand for *goods* arises from the fact that the consumer gets utility from consuming those goods. In goods markets, the good is an end in itself.

The demand for factors of production is somewhat different. Consider a construction firm that hires a worker, or rents a bulldozer, or buys a truckload of dirt. The firm does *not* buy these things because it wants to consume them. Instead, the construction firm hires a worker because that worker can help to produce outputs (such as apartment houses or office buildings), which the firm can then sell.

Thus, the factor of production is *not* an end in itself. Rather, it is a means to the end of making money for the firm. This is why we say that the demand for factors of production is a *derived demand*. The demand for factors is *derived* from the demand for goods.

The Firm's Revenue from Using Factor Inputs

What would be the benefit to the firm, if it were to hire one additional worker? First of all, the worker would produce additional output. A worker in a bicycle factory will help to produce more bicycles, and a worker in an oil field will help to produce more oil. However, firms aren't in business to make bicycles or oil; they're in business to make *money*. The ultimate benefit to the firm from hiring one additional worker is that the firm can increase its revenue, by selling the extra output that is made by the extra worker.

We define the *marginal revenue product* of labor as the additional revenue that the firm gets, when it hires one additional worker, and then sells the extra output that is made by that extra worker. The marginal revenue product of capital is defined in a similar way: The marginal revenue product of capital is the extra revenue that the firm makes when it employs one more machine, and then sells the additional output. The marginal revenue products of land, or energy, or materials are all defined similarly.

In the next few paragraphs, we will analyze marginal revenue product in more detail.

Marginal (Physical) Product. This definition of marginal revenue product has two distinct parts: (1) the extra output that is produced, and (2) the additional revenue that comes from selling that output. The extra output that is produced by an extra unit of input is called the ***marginal product***, or ***marginal physical product***, of the factor of production. In the case of a worker in a bicycle factory, her marginal physical product is the number of extra bicycles that are produced, as a result of hiring her. In the case of a worker in an oil field, marginal physical product is the number of extra barrels of oil.

The first few columns of Table 13.1 give some information on the physical productivity of the workers in an Oklahoma oil field. The field is operated by a small firm called Wildcat Drillers. As we add more workers, we get more barrels of oil, as can be seen by looking down the "Total Physical Product" column.

However, as Wildcat Drillers adds more and more workers, there is a decrease in the amount of extra oil that can be produced by adding one extra worker. This can be seen by looking at the "Total Physical Product" (TPP) column. For example, as we go from one worker to two workers, TPP increases from 25 barrels to 40 barrels, for an increase of (40 – 25) = 15 barrels. However, when we go from two workers to three workers, TPP goes from 40 barrels to 52 barrels, for an increase of only (52 – 40) = 12 barrels.

The same information is also conveyed by the "Marginal Physical Product" column. This is because marginal physical product is the change in total physical product, divided by the change in the number of workers.

Number Of Workers	TPP: Total Physical Product Of Labor (In Barrels Per Day)	MPP: Marginal Physical Product of Labor (In Extra Barrels (Per Extra Worker)	MRP: Marginal Revenue Product (In Extra Dollars Per Extra Worker) = MPP x (Price Of Oil)
0	0	—	—
1	25	25	$500
2	40	15	300
3	52	12	240
4	62	10	200
5	70	8	160
6	75	6	120
7	78	3	60
8	80	2	40
9	81	1	20

Table 13.1 Physical Product of Labor and Marginal Revenue Product of Labor For Wildcat Drillers (We Assume That the Firm Is a Perfect Competitor in Its Output Market, and That the Price of Oil Is $20/Barrel)

In Table 13.1, the marginal physical product of oil-field workers decreases when we add more workers. Therefore, the example of Table 13.1 obeys the "law of diminishing marginal product", which we introduced in Chapter 8. Figure 13.1 is a graph of the information on marginal physical product and total physical product, from Table 13.1. The marginal physical product curve in Figure 13.1 slopes downward as we move to the right.

Marginal Revenue. The second part of the definition of marginal revenue product is the additional revenue that the firm gets, when it sells the additional output. This extra revenue is the firm's **marginal revenue**.

As we saw in earlier chapters, the firm's marginal revenue depends on the market structure of its *output* market. For example, let's assume that Wildcat Drillers is very small, compared to the world oil market. Therefore, the firm behaves like a perfect competitor, and it takes the price as given. *For a firm that is perfectly competitive in its output market, marginal revenue is the market price.*

If we assume that the price of oil is $20 per barrel, then the marginal revenue for Wildcat Drillers is $20 for the first barrel, $20 for the second barrel, and $20 for each subsequent barrel. This means that a graph of marginal revenue for this perfect competitor is a horizontal line, as shown in panel (a) of Figure 13.2.

However, some oil producers are large enough that they have some market power. *For a firm that is* not *a perfect competitor in its output market, the marginal revenue curve slopes downward,* as in panel (b) of Figure 13.2.

Marginal Revenue Product. As we said above, marginal revenue product is the additional revenue that the firm gets, when it hires one additional unit of a factor of production and then sells the extra output that is made by that factor. In other words, marginal revenue product (MRP) is equal to marginal physical

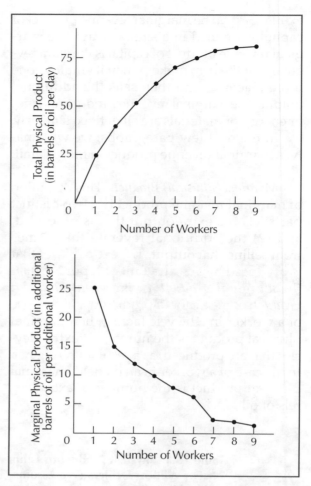

Figure 13.1 Total Physical Product of Labor and Marginal Physical Product of Labor for Wildcat Drillers

As this oil-drilling firm adds more workers, it increases its output. However, the output increases at a decreasing rate. This can be seen in two ways. First, the slope of the total-physical-product curve becomes smaller as we move to the right (that is, the slope becomes smaller when we add more workers). Second, the marginal-physical-product curve decreases as we move to the right.

product (MPP), multiplied by marginal revenue (MR):

MRP = (MPP)x(MR), *for any firm.*

In the special case of a firm that is perfectly competitive in its output market, MR is the same as price. Therefore,

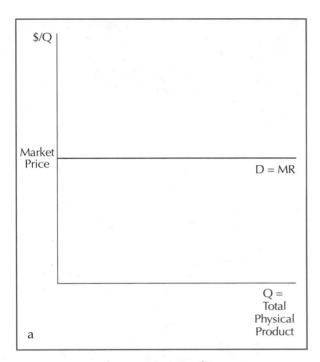

**Figure 13.2 Panel (a)
Marginal Revenue for a Firm That Is
a Perfect Competitor in Its Output Market**

We assume that the perfectly competitive firm is small relative to the market, so that it cannot have any effect on the price. Therefore, the firm takes the market price as given. The firm's demand curve is a horizontal line, and the firm's marginal-revenue curve coincides with the demand curve.

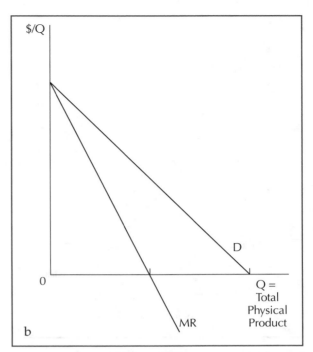

**Figure 13.2 Panel (b)
Marginal Revenue for a Firm That Has
Market Power in Its Output Market**

For a firm with market power in its output market, the demand curve slopes downward to the right. Since the firm must cut its price in order to sell one more unit of output, its marginal revenue is declining. For a straight-line demand curve, the marginal-revenue curve will be twice as steep as the demand curve.

$MRP = (MPP) \times (P)$, *for a firm that is perfectly competitive in its output market.*

In order to calculate the MRP for Wildcat Drillers, we multiply MPP (which decreases) by MR (which is constant and equal to price for this firm, since it is a perfect competitor in its output market). The result is shown in the final column of Table 13.1, and is graphed in Figure 13.3 on p. 306. The MRP curve slopes downward as we move to the right.

We have assumed that Wildcat Drillers is a perfect competitor in its output market, and we've seen that it has a downward-sloping MRP curve. What about the MRP curve for a

firm that has some market power in its output market, so that it *isn't* a perfect competitor? We still use the same formula: MRP = (MPP)x(MR). The MPP curve still slopes downward and to the right, because of the law of diminishing marginal product. And, for a firm with market power, the MR curve *also* slopes downward and to the right. If we combine a downward-sloping MPP curve with a downward-sloping MR curve, we get a downward-sloping MRP curve.

Thus, *the marginal-revenue-product curve can be expected to slope downward as we move to the right, regardless of the market structure in the firm's output market.*

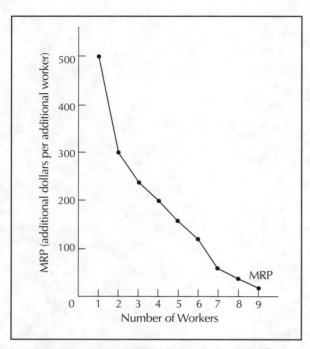

Figure 13.3 The Downward-Sloping Marginal-Revenue-Product Curve for Wildcat Drillers

The marginal-revenue-product curve for Wildcat Drillers is found by multiplying marginal physical product by marginal revenue. The result is a curve that slopes downward as we move to the right.

The Firm's Demand Curve for Factors of Production

In an earlier chapter, we saw that the consumer makes purchase decisions by comparing marginal utility and price. In another earlier chapter, we saw that the business firm makes output decisions by comparing marginal revenue and marginal cost. In each of these cases, the decision was based on a comparison of some type of *marginal benefit* with some type of *marginal cost*. The same basic principle also applies for the firm's input decisions.

Marginal Factor Expense. If Wildcat Drillers were to hire one additional worker, the *marginal benefit* to the firm is the marginal revenue

product of that worker. The *marginal cost* of hiring one more worker is the extra money that the firm has to spend, in order to get one more worker to work for the firm. This extra money is called the *marginal factor expense* of labor. (The marginal factor expense of capital, or of any other input, is defined in a similar way.)

Let's assume that Wildcat Drillers is small, relative to the overall market for oil-field workers. This means that the firm won't be able to affect the market wage rate. In other words, Wildcat Drillers is a perfect competitor in this labor market, and it takes the market wage rate as given.

The market wage rate is $160 per day, so that the additional cost of the first worker hired by Wildcat Drillers is $160 per day. The extra cost of the second worker is also $160 per day, as is the extra cost of the third, or the fourth, or the hundredth worker. *For a firm that is a perfect competitor in the market for a factor of production, marginal factor expense is equal to the price of the input.*

Thus, for a perfect competitor, the marginal factor expense of labor is the wage rate, the marginal factor expense of a bulldozer is the rental price of the bulldozer, the marginal factor expense of land is the rental price of land, and so on.

The Optimal Hiring Decision. Later in this chapter, we'll talk about the case of a firm that is *not* a competitor in an input market. For now, however, let's focus on the competitive firm and its input hiring decision. Table 13.2 shows the marginal revenue product of labor (MRP) for Wildcat Drillers, and it also shows the firm's marginal factor expense of labor (MFE). For the first worker, MRP is $500 per day, and MFE is $160. Since the marginal benefit is far greater than the marginal cost, it follows that the firm should definitely hire at least one worker.

What about a second worker? Here, the MRP is $300 per day, and the MFE is still $160,

Table 13.2 The Optimal Decision of How Many Workers to Hire for Wildcat Drillers

Number of Workers	Marginal Revenue Product (MRP)	Marginal Factor Expense (MFE)	Result	
0	—	—	—	
1	$500	$160	MRP > MFE	(Hire)
2	300	160	MRP > MFE	(Hire)
3	240	160	MRP > MFE	(Hire)
4	200	160	MRP > MFE	(Hire)
5	160	160	MRP = MFE	(Hire)
6	120	160	MRP < MFE	(Don't Hire)
7	60	160	MRP < MFE	(Don't Hire)
8	40	160	MRP < MFE	(Don't Hire)
9	20	160	MRP< MFE	(Don't Hire)

so the second worker should be hired, too. We repeat this reasoning for as long as MRP is equal to or greater than MFE. For Wildcat Drillers, the best decision is to hire five oil-field workers.

The information in Table 13.2 is graphed in Figure 13.4. For a firm that is a perfect competitor in an input market, the marginal-factor-expense curve is a horizontal line. *The optimal input hiring decision is shown by the intersection of the MRP curve and the MFE curve. In the case of a firm that is a perfect competitor in its input market, the optimal hiring decison comes at the intersection of the MRP curve and the horizontal line that represents the input price.*

The Individual Firm's Demand Curve. When the wage rate is $160 per day, Wildcat Drillers should hire five workers, because the fifth worker is the one whose MRP is $160 per day. What would happen if the market wage rate were to rise to $200 per day? The optimal decision still involves setting MRP equal to the wage rate. But now, this comes at a quantity of four workers. On the other hand, if the market wage rate were to fall to $120 per day, Wildcat Drillers should hire six workers.

In every case, the firm's decision is described by a point on its MRP curve. This tells us that, *for the firm that is a competitor in a market for a factor input, the firm's factor-demand curve is given by the marginal-revenue-product curve.* The MRP curve slopes downward, which means that the firm's factor-demand curve is downward sloping as we move to the right.

Market Demand for Factors of Production

In Chapter 3, we saw that, to get the market demand curve for some good or service, we add up the demand curves of individual consumers. We do the same kind of thing to get the market demand curve for a factor of production. To get the market demand curve, we add up the demand curves of the individual firms *horizontally.*

Elasticity of Demand for Factors of Production

We know that the demand curves for inputs such as labor, capital, and land will slope

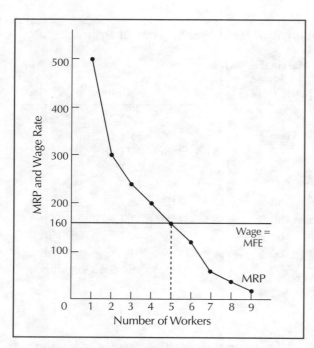

**Figure 13.4 The Optimal Hiring Decision
for Wildcat Drillers**

The marginal benefit from hiring one additional worker
is given by the marginal-revenue-product curve (MRP).
The marginal cost from hiring one additional worker is
given by the marginal-factor-expense curve. Wildcat
Drillers is a perfect competitor in the labor market, so
that its marginal-factor-expense curve (MFE) is a horizontal line, equal to the market wage rate. The firm's
best choice involves hiring the number of workers at
which marginal revenue product is equal to marginal
factor expense. In this graph, the firm chooses the quantity of labor at which the marginal-revenue-product
curve intersects the marginal-factor-expense curve.

downward as we move to the right. But will
they be elastic or relatively inelastic? It makes
a difference. For example, what if the labor-
supply curve shifts? This will lead to one effect
on the equilibrium wage rate if the labor-
demand curve is inelastic, and a very different effect if the labor-demand curve is elastic.

What will the firm do when there is an
increase in the wage rates of factory workers?
In response to the wage increase, employers

may be able to produce the same amount of
output with fewer workers, by using more
robots and more computers. This is called the
substitution effect in factor demand. Generally speaking, if the price of one input
increases, the firm may be able to substitute
away from that input, by using other inputs. If
it's relatively easy to substitute for a particular input, then the demand for that input will
be relatively more elastic.

A second effect on the elasticity of demand
has to do with the demand for the output that
is being produced. If the price of an input goes
up, this will lead to an increase in the firm's
costs, which will lead to an increase in the
equilibrium price of the output. If the *output*
demand is very elastic, then an increase in the
price of the output will lead to a big reduction
in the amount of output that is produced. If
this happens, there will be reduced demand
for *all* factors of production. This is called the
output effect.

So, we see that the elasticity of demand for
factors of production will be larger when (1)
it's easy to substitute one input for another,
and/or (2) the increase in the factor price leads
to a big reduction in output.

In *Real Economics for Real People 13.1*, we
discuss the effects of technological changes on
employment.

Reality Check:
Interim Review Questions

IR13-1. Does the marginal-revenue-product
curve slope upward or downward as we
go to the right?

IR13-2. In a competitive labor market, what is
the relationship between the marginal-revenue-product curve for labor and the
firm's demand curve for labor?

IR13-3. Name the five main categories of factors of production.

We have seen that the demand for a factor of production is affected by the ability of firms to *substitute* toward other factors of production. One of the oldest concerns of workers is that they will lose their jobs, as a result of the introduction of machinery. Indeed, many workers *have* lost their jobs as a result of technological changes. People who wove cloth by hand were replaced by power looms. People who picked cotton and threshed wheat by hand were replaced by farm machinery.

Today, there is much concern that workers will be replaced by computers. This is a legitimate concern, but we need to keep it in perspective. The last few decades have seen tremendous technological changes in the computer field. If these changes were disastrous for the employment of workers, we would expect that the unemployment rate would have risen over time. But the unemployment rate was lower in 2000 than it has been since 1970. Some workers *have* lost their jobs to computers, but others have found jobs in the computer industry, as programmers, software developers, maintenance technicians, and so on.

Moreover, people tend to have *better* jobs, as a result of technological improvements. Imagine a world in which we had decided to "protect jobs", by outlawing technological changes. Since we would not have had any improvements in agricultural techniques, most people would be employed in backbreaking agricultural jobs, in order for society to feed itself.

For society as a whole, technological improvements are the key to a rising standard of living, especially in the long run. However, in the short run, many workers face difficult problems of transition. These problems are greatest for those who have few skills. Several economic studies suggest that capital tends to be a *complement* for highly skilled labor, but a *substitute* for less-skilled labor. This means that new technologies will tend to help skilled workers, while they may not help the unskilled.

Although the situation has improved somewhat in the late 1990s, the real wage rates of less-skilled American workers have been fairly stagnant since the 1970s. The problem is especially severe for those who don't have a high-school diploma. One of the greatest challenges for economic policy is to find ways to reap the benefits of technological improvements, while still protecting those workers who have the fewest skills. We will return to this issue in this chapter, and in Chapters 15 and 16.

LABOR SUPPLY

Labor is certainly the most important of the factor inputs. In most countries, something like two-thirds or three-quarters of national income is paid to workers, in the form of wages, salaries, and benefits. If we want to understand the workings of a modern economy, we have to understand both labor demand and labor supply. In the previous section, we looked at the *demand curve* for labor. Now, we turn to the *supply curve* for labor. In the next section, we'll put them together, so that we can analyze equilibrium in the labor market.

Utility Maximization

In an earlier chapter, we studied the consumer's demand for goods and services. You have a certain amount of money, and you have to decide how much to spend on housing, how much to spend on food, and so on. We suggested that, when people make these choices, their goal is to maximize utility. To maximize utility, your marginal utility per dollar of expenditure must be the same for bananas, and for blue jeans, and for every other good.

We think about labor supply in a similar way. In this case, however, we aren't considering a choice between bananas and blue jeans. Instead, we think of the labor-supply decision as coming from a choice between *labor* and *leisure*. In our model of labor supply, a fixed amount of *time* is allocated between working in the labor market (which we call labor) and doing other things (which we call leisure).

People like leisure. It's fun to spend a week at Disney World, or to watch your favorite TV program, or to take a walk in the park. Unfortunately, there's only a fixed amount of time. Also, the main way in which most people get more money is by giving up leisure, in order to work in the labor market. If we were to devote all of our time to leisure, most of us would have very little money to spend. Thus, we face a tradeoff: More leisure means less money to spend, and *vice versa*. As usual, we end up with a requirement that the marginal something must be equal to the marginal something else. In this case, you would maximize utility by choosing amounts of labor and leisure, such that *the marginal utility of an extra hour of leisure is equal to the marginal utility of the consumption goods that could be bought if you were to work an extra hour.*

The Income Effect:
Non-Labor Income

We've just described the condition that is necessary for the consumer to maximize utility from leisure and consumption. This is fine, but our ultimate goal is more ambitious: We want to say something about how labor supply will change when wage rates change. This will give us the information that we need to draw labor-supply curves.

We start out by asking what would happen when the consumer has a change in her *non-labor income*, which includes transfer payments (such as Social-Security benefits), as well as interest income, dividend income, lottery winnings, and gifts and inheritances. It's easiest to see the effect of non-labor income by thinking about an extreme case. If a long-lost aunt were to leave you a billion dollars, would you work more or less? The answer would vary from person to person, but most people would probably choose to work less. Many would leave the labor market completely. You could buy all sorts of consumer goods with your billion-dollar inheritance, without having to work in the labor market. Usually, people will reduce their labor supply when they have more non-labor income. This is called the *income effect on labor supply*.

Of course, most people who have non-labor income don't have a billion dollars of it. However, it doesn't take a lot of non-labor income to generate an income effect. There will be at least *some* income effect, even with very modest amounts of non-labor income.

Another way to say this is that *leisure is a normal good*: When people get more non-labor income, they tend to take more leisure, which means that they work less.

The Income Effect
of a Change in the Wage Rate

What would happen if your wage rate were to rise? One effect of an increase in wage rates is that you would suddenly be "richer". With a higher wage rate, you would face some new opportunities that weren't there before. For instance, you could now buy the same consumption goods as before, while working less.

You might say to yourself, "I can take more time off, and still put food on the table. So, I'll work less."

The income effect of an *increase* in the wage rate is that people tend to take more leisure, and therefore to *work less.* The income effect of a *decrease* in the wage rate is that people tend to reduce their leisure, which means that they *work more.*

The Substitution Effect of a Change in the Wage Rate

If the income effect were the only thing going on, the story would end with the previous paragraph. However, a change in the wage rate also leads to another important effect, which we call the *substitution effect on labor supply.* To understand the substitution effect, we need to think some more about the role played by the wage rate. When you take one extra hour of leisure, you give up the extra consumption goods that you could have bought, if you would have worked that hour instead. In other words, *we can think of the wage rate as the price of leisure.* If your wage rate were to rise, leisure would be more expensive. (And, if your wage rate were to fall, leisure would be less expensive.) When your wage rate rises, you might say to yourself, "Think of all the stuff I could buy, if I earn wages like these! I can't pass up that kind of money. So, I'll work more."

Throughout this book, we have seen that people tend to change their behavior when prices change. They tend to substitute away from items that become more expensive, and they tend to substitute toward items that become less expensive. The *substitution effect* of an *increase* in the wage rate is that people tend to substitute away from leisure, which means that they *work more.* The substitution effect of a *decrease* in the wage rate is that people tend to substitute toward leisure, which means that they *work less.*

The Overall Effect of a Change in the Wage Rate

In the last few paragraphs, we've described both the income effect and the substitution effect of a wage-rate change. Here is a summary:

- For a wage *increase*, the substitution effect says that work should increase, while the income effect says that work should decrease.

- For a wage *decrease*, the substitution effect says that work should fall, while the income effect says that work should rise.

The overall effect of a wage-rate change will be a combination of the substitution effect and the income effect. If the substitution effect is stronger, then higher wages will bring about more labor supply. However, if the income effect is stronger, higher wages will lead to *less* labor supply. It could go either way. One possibility is that the substitution effect would be larger than the income effect at relatively low wage rates, but smaller at relatively high wage rates. This possibility is graphed in Figure 13.5, on p. 312.

In the lower part of Figure 13.5, where the substitution effect is larger than the income effect, we have an *upward-sloping labor supply curve*. In the upper portion of the figure, the income effect is larger than the substitution effect, and we have a *backward-bending labor supply curve*.

Economists have done many studies of labor supply, to find out more about the sizes of the income effects and substitution effects. Usually, the goal of these studies is to get an estimate for the *elasticity of labor supply with respect to the wage rate* (or just the "labor supply elasticity", for short.) This elasticity is defined as follows:

Labor Supply Elasticity =
(% Change in Labor Supply)/
(% Change in Wage Rate).

The topic is still controversial, but there seems to be a consensus along the following lines:

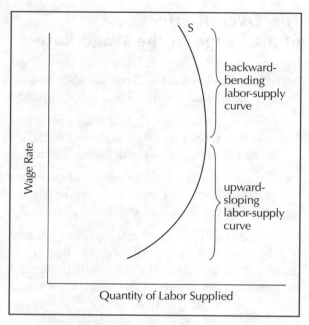

**Figure 13.5 A Labor-Supply Curve
With Changing Slope**

If the substitution effect is greater than the income effect, the labor-supply curve will slope upward as we move to the right. If the income effect is greater than the substitution effect, the labor-supply curve will be backward bending. It is possible for one person's labor-supply curve to have both an upward-sloping portion and a backward-bending portion, as shown here.

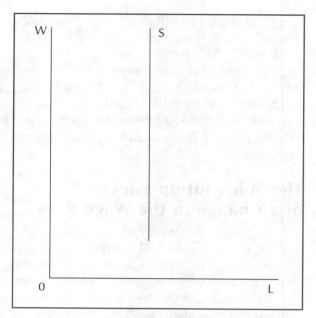

**Figure 13.6 Panel (a)
A Perfectly Inelastic Labor-Supply Curve,
Representative of American Men**

The labor supply of married men is highly inelastic. If the income effect and the substitution effect cancel each other out exactly, the labor-supply curve will be perfectly inelastic, as shown here.

- For married men, aged 25–54, labor supply is *very inelastic.* Most of these men desire to be in the labor force on a full-time basis, usually working between 35 and 45 hours per week. A man in this group might say to himself, "If the wage rate goes up, that's fine. I'll work 40 hours per week. If the wage rate goes down, that's too bad, but I'll still work 40 hours per week." In other words, the income effect and the substitution effect approximately balance each other out.

  For married men, most studies have found a labor-supply elasticity between –0.1 and +0.1. If the labor-supply elasticity is less

than zero, we have a backward-bending labor-supply curve. If the elasticity is greater than zero, we have an upward-sloping curve. Many of the estimated elasticities are right around zero, which would mean that labor supply is perfectly inelastic for this group of workers.

We show a perfectly inelastic labor-supply curve in panel (a) of Figure 13.6.

- For married women, labor supply is probably somewhat more elastic than it is for married men. The labor-supply elasticity for women is probably about +0.2 or +0.3, although this is a controversial subject among economists. For positive elasticities like these, the labor-supply curve is

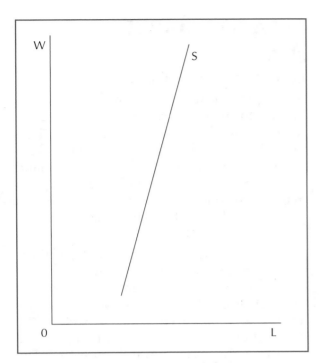

Figure 13.6 Panel (b)
An Upward-Sloping Labor-Supply Curve,
Representative of American Women

For married women, the substitution effect is greater than the income effect, so that the labor-supply curve slopes upward as we move to the right.

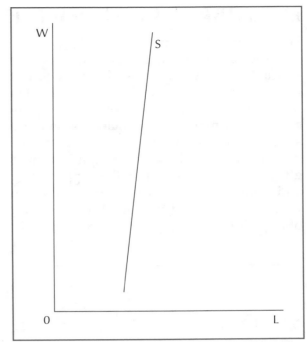

Figure 13.6 Panel (c)
A Slightly Upward-Sloping Labor
Supply Curve, Representative
of the Overall American Labor Market

If we take the weighted average of the labor-supply responses of men and women, we get a labor-supply curve that slopes upward slightly, perhaps with an elasticity of 0.1.

upward sloping, as shown in panel (b) of Figure 13.6.

If we put men and women together, we could find the overall labor supply elasticity for the entire economy. This overall elasticity is probably around +0.1. In other words, *for the labor force as a whole, the substitution effect is slightly more important than the income effect.* If the overall elasticity is +0.1, it means that a 10-percent *decrease* in wage rates would lead to a one-percent *decrease* in the supply of labor. A 20-percent *increase* in wage rates would lead to a two-percent *increase* in labor supply.

Panel (c) of Figure 13.6 shows a labor supply curve with a very modest upward slope, which is probably representative of the American labor force as a whole.

Reality Check:
Interim Review Questions

IR13-4. If the wage rate were to *increase*, would the substitution effect lead toward an increase or decrease in labor supply?

IR13-5. If the wage rate were to *decrease*, would the income effect lead toward an increase or decrease in labor supply?

EQUILIBRIUM IN COMPETITIVE LABOR MARKETS

We began this chapter by looking at the demand for factors of production. Next, we studied labor supply. Now, it's time to put them together. In Figure 13.7, D_0 is a market demand curve, and S_0 is a market supply curve, in the market for oil-field workers. The supply curve is more inelastic than the demand curve. The market equilibrium is given by the intersection of the supply curve and demand curve. Thus, the equilibrium wage rate is W_0 and the equilibrium amount of labor is L_0.

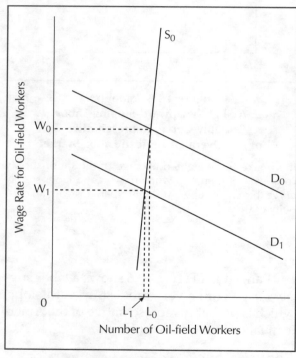

Figure 13.7 The Effect of a Decrease in the Price of Oil on the Market for Oil-Field Workers

At first, the demand curve for oil-field workers is D_0, and the supply curve is S_0. The market equilibrium wage rate is W_0, and the equilibrium amount of labor is L_0. Then, a decrease in the price of oil leads to a leftward shift in the demand curve, from D_0 to D_1. The new equilibrium wage rate is W_1, and the new equilibrium amount of labor is L_1.

Shifts in the Labor-Demand Curve

A competitive firm's demand curve for an input is the marginal-revenue-product curve, which comes from the marginal-physical-product curve and the output price. As a result, it's no surprise that factor-demand curves are shifted when there are changes in marginal physical productivity, or in output prices. Let's look at these in turn.

Changes in Output Prices. In 1986, there was a major drop in the worldwide price of oil. Because of this, the marginal revenue product of oil-field workers was suddenly lower than it had been before. Therefore, the demand curve for oil-field workers shifted from D_0 to D_1, as shown in Figure 13.7. The equilibrium wage fell to W_1.

Whenever an output price falls, we would expect a reduction in the demand for the workers who produce that particular output. This will lead to lower wage rates. On the other hand, if an output price increases, the labor-demand curve will shift to the right, and wages will rise. In fact, this occurred in the oil industry during the 1970s and early 1980s, as rising oil prices increased the demand for oil-field workers.

Changes in Productivity. People get an education for many different reasons. Certainly, one important reason is that educated people have more skills than those who are uneducated. In other words, the educated ones have higher productivity. When you get an education, you are pushing the demand curve for your labor to the right. This is one big reason why wage rates are higher in the United States, Canada, western Europe, and Japan than in the rest of the world: The workers in these countries tend to be more highly educated, and therefore more productive. We will discuss the relationship between education and wages in more detail, later in this chapter.

Immigration and the Supply of Labor

The United States of America is a nation of immigrants. Just about everyone here either came from somewhere else, or is descended from people who came from somewhere else. Until the mid–1800s, most of the immigrants came from Great Britain (voluntarily) or from Africa (in chains). In the middle of the 19th century came waves of immigrants from Germany and Ireland. In the late 19th and early 20th century came still more immigrants, from Italy, Greece, Poland, Russia, and other countries. From 1901 to 1910, a nation of about 80 million people absorbed nearly nine million immigrants. That's an influx of more than 10 percent of the population, in only 10 years!

The immigration laws were made more strict in the 1920s. As a result, immigrants came at a slower rate from the 1920s to the 1960s. However, the immigration laws were loosened again in 1965. Since then, the immigration rate has been higher than it was in the 1950s, but still much less than it was in the early 1900s. In addition, the mix of immigrants has changed: Until 1965, most immigrants came from Europe, but the largest numbers of immigrants in recent years have come from Latin America and from East Asia.

Over the years, there has been a lot of tension between the newcomers and those who were already here. The tensions have often had to do with differences in culture, language, or religion. Just as often, however, the tensions have had to do with economic issues. The most important of these issues is the fear that immigrants will hurt the labor-market performance of the natives.

Has immigration hurt those who were already here? We can begin to think about this question by using supply-demand analysis.

The entrance of new immigrants causes the market supply curve for labor to shift to the right. As shown in Figure 13.8, the rightward shift in the labor-supply curve leads to a decrease in the equilibrium wage rate.

It's important to remember, however, that workers are not all the same. Thus, immigration will have more of an effect in some labor markets than in others, and some native workers will be affected by immigration more than others will. In fact, large numbers of immigrants in the last few decades have been less educated than most of the native population. Consequently, we would expect that recent immigrants would have more of an effect on the livelihoods of less-skilled Americans than on those of greater skill. This appears to be the

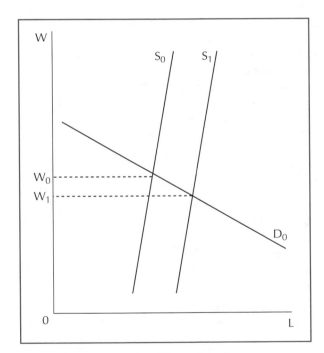

Figure 13.8 The Effect of an Increase in Immigration on the Labor Market

At first, the demand curve for labor in a particular labor market is D_0, and the supply curve is S_0. The market equilibrium wage rate is W_0. Then, immigration leads to a rightward shift in the supply curve, from S_0 to S_1. The new equilibrium wage rate is W_1.

case. There is little evidence that immigration has hurt highly skilled American workers, but one study suggests that the wages of Americans without a high-school education have dropped by as much as 5%, as a result of the influx of relatively poorly educated immigrants.

Still, it's not correct to see the less-skilled immigrants as a heavy weight, dragging down the economy. They provide valuable services (often doing work that native-born Americans are reluctant to do), and they pay taxes. Many of the immigrants own their own homes and businesses. Also, while many of the immigrants are unskilled, some are very highly skilled. During the 1980s, 1.5 million college-educated immigrants arrived in the United States, many with degrees in medicine or engineering. At American universities, nearly half of the new Ph.D.s in the sciences and engineering are foreign-born, and many of these people stay on to contribute strongly to the U.S. economy.

As is so often the case in economics, an overall assessment of immigration would have to consider the pluses and the minuses. The immigrants do contribute to the economy. At the same time, it is true that they are likely to hurt the labor-market chances of native-born Americans who don't have a high-school education. Earlier in this chapter, we mentioned that less-skilled Americans may lose their jobs to computers. Here, we are making a similar statement about the effect of immigration. Most of the economy stands to gain from immigration, just as most of the economy stands to gain from computers. But some will be hurt, especially those with the fewest skills. Unquestionably, these are hard times for American workers with little education, skill, or training. One of the most important economic trends of the past 25 years has been the declining status of less-skilled workers. We will continue to study this trend in Chapter 15, which deals with poverty and income distribution.

Education, Experience, and Wages

Why do people go to college? One big reason is that they believe they will earn more money if they have a college education. The facts are pretty powerful: For men working full time in the United States in 1998, the average earnings for those with a grade-school education were about $23,900 per year. Those with a high-school diploma earned an average of about $32,600 per year, those with a bachelor's degree averaged about $60,600, and those with a professional degree averaged about $117,500 per year. Clearly, *education* has a strong effect on earnings in the labor market.

Experience also has an important effect. As in the previous paragraph, let's focus on those who are full-time workers. For males with a bachelor's degree, aged 25–29, the average earnings in 1992 were about $41,900. The average earnings then rose to about $52,500 for the 30–34 age group, and to about $57,400 for those aged 35–39. At the peak of their careers, male college graduates aged 50–54 were earning about $76,300 per year.

Human Capital. It really isn't very surprising that people make more money when they have more education and experience. After all, the demand for workers will be greater when their marginal revenue products are higher. Since workers with more education and experience tend to be more productive, it follows that the demand for these workers will be relatively greater.

If it didn't cost anything to get an education, then *everyone* would get a lot of education. In fact, however, different people have widely different amounts of education. In 1998, about 134 million Americans earned money in the labor market. Of these, about 16.7 million did not have a high-school diploma, and about 46 million had a high-school diploma but no college education. About 29.9 million had some college, but no degree. About 25.8 million had a Bachelor's degree only, and about 12.1 million had an advanced degree.

We would like to understand why some people get a lot of education, while others don't get very much. In order to do so, we need a theory of investment. The relationships among education, experience, and earnings can be explained by the theory of *human-capital investment*. When we make a human-capital investment, we *invest in ourselves*, in the hope that the human capital will pay off in higher earnings in the future. Human-capital investments can take many forms, but education and on-the-job training are certainly among the most important. Human-capital investments have much in common with other investments, such as investments in factories or delivery vans or warehouses. Whenever we make *any* investment, we reduce our *current* consumption, with the idea of having an increased flow of *future* consumption.

Educational Choices. Sophia is thinking of going to college. To decide whether this is a good human-capital investment, she needs to compare the *benefits* and *costs* of the investment. After graduation, Sophia should be able to earn a higher wage or salary. The higher wages are one of the *benefits* of a college education. (The benefits also include the intellectual satisfaction that goes with an education.)

For Sophia, as for anyone else, there are two basic *costs* of a college education:

- The explicit, out-of-pocket costs, including tuition, fees, and books, and

- The *foregone earnings* associated with going to college. Sophia's foregone earnings are the extra dollars that she would have earned during the years that she was considering going to college, *if* she had decided not to go to college.

For most students, foregone earnings are greater than the explicit costs of college. This is especially true for students at publicly sup-

ported colleges, where tuition payments are lower than they would be without government support.

Figure 13.9 illustrates the decision that Sophia faces, when she decides whether to go to college. A college education will be a wise investment if the value of the benefits (area "B", for benefits, in Figure 13.9) is greater than the value of the costs (area "C", for costs, in the figure).

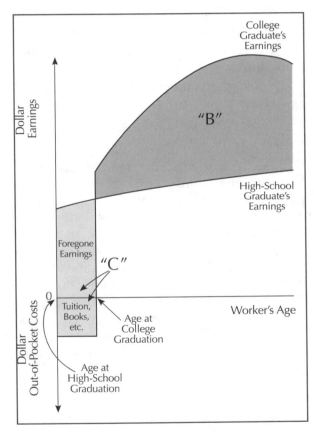

Figure 13.9 The Costs and Benefits of Sophia's College Education

If she goes to college, Sophia will have to pay some out-of-pocket costs for tuition, books, and so on. She will also bear another cost, in the form of foregone earnings. Together, these costs are "C". However, she will gain benefits of "B", in the form of higher earnings after she gets her degree. If the value of B is greater than the value of C, it will make sense for Sophia to go to college.

Figure 13.9 gives us an idea of who will be most likely to go to college:

- Most college students will be young, because young people have a longer period over which to receive the benefits of an education.

- All else equal, college attendance will increase if there is an increase in the difference in earnings between college graduates and high-school graduates.

- All else equal, college attendance will increase if tuition costs go down.

- All else equal, people who place greater value on the future are more likely to go to college. In other words, people who find it hard to plan for the future are less likely to go to college.

Experience and Training. We have seen that those with more education tend to earn more. In addition, earnings grow during the early part of the career, as workers acquire more experience. This can also be explained in terms of human capital. As people work, they learn more about how to cooperate with others in their organization, and they continue to learn more of the technical details of their business. As a result, people acquire human capital when they get work experience, even if their formal schooling has come to an end.

In fact, experience in the labor market causes a sharper increase in earnings for those who have more education. The theory of human capital provides a good explanation for this, as well. People who are faster learners can get more out of a college education. As a result, fast learners are more likely to go to college. But the fast learners are also the ones who can be expected to learn the most on the job!

Compensating Wage Differentials

We have seen that differences in education and experience can lead to wide differences in wage rates. However, some wage differences aren't easily explained by the theory of human capital. For example, people who work the evening shift or the night shift tend to get wages that are about 3 percent higher than those of comparable day-shift workers. Since the skills required for these jobs are the same during the day or night, we can't use the theory of human capital to explain the differences. In this section, we'll develop a way of thinking about wage differences such as these.

Job Characteristics. If all jobs were identical, then every job would pay the same wage rate. But each job has many characteristics, and the characteristics of different jobs tend to be very different. For example:

- Most office jobs are safe, but the job of a police officer or firefighter can be very dangerous.

- Some jobs have a lot of flexibility, whereas an assembly-line job has a very tedious and rigid work schedule.

Let's compare two jobs that are identical in every way, except that one is clean and comfortable, while the other is dirty and unpleasant. The supply curve for the unpleasant job will be further to the left than the supply curve for the pleasant job. Therefore, the two jobs won't have the same equilibrium wage rate. We can only reach an equilibrium if the dirty job has a higher wage rate.

Let's say that the market equilibrium involves a wage rate of $11 per hour for the dirty job, and $10 per hour for the clean job. We say that the $1 difference in wage rates is a *compensating wage differential*. A compensating wage differential is the extra wage that must be paid, in order to attract workers to an unpleasant job.

We began this section with the statement that and night-shift workers earn about 3 percent more than comparable day-shift workers.

In other words, the compensating wage differential associated with and night-shift work is about 3 percent.

The Importance of the "Ceteris Paribus" Assumption. All else equal, a job with unpleasant characteristics will have to pay a higher wage rate, in order to attract workers. It's very important to emphasize the assumption of "all else equal", or "*ceteris paribus*". Our theory of compensating wage differentials *does not* say that everyone with an unpleasant job will get a higher wage than anyone with a nice job. In fact, many of the lowest-paying jobs are boring, dangerous, or dirty. For example, most jobs in poultry-processing plants are fairly

unpleasant, but the wage rates are not much more than the minimum wage, because these jobs don't require much skill.

Still, compensating wage differentials can be seen in the wage rates paid in many jobs, including the wages of different workers at poultry-processing plants. The toughest job of all is that of a "live hanger", who shackles the live chickens as they come into the plant, at a rate of 25 or more per minute. The live hangers are pecked and scratched, and they often develop rashes from contact with the birds. But they earn a few dollars per day more than the other workers in poultry-processing plants.

In *Real Economics for Real People 13.2*, we discuss the compensating wage differentials

---

Real Economics for Real People 13.2: The Effects of Dangerous Working Conditions on Wage Rates

Some jobs are safe; others are dangerous. For example, in logging camps, there is about one death every year for every 1000 workers. If our theory of compensating wage differentials is correct, than a higher likelihood of fatal injury should be associated with a higher wage rate (all else equal).

Economists have done many studies of compensating wage differentials for jobs that have a risk of death. Some of these studies suggest big wage differentials, while others find that the differentials are more modest. But virtually all of the studies find that the wage differentials are in the expected direction: It's necessary to pay higher wages to attract workers to more dangerous jobs.

The estimates of compensating differentials suggest that a firm must pay *each* worker an extra wage of from $35 to $500 more per year, in order to compensate for an extra annual risk of one death per 10,000 workers. This implies that a plant with

10,000 employees could save between $350,000 and $5,000,000 per year in wages, if it were to improve safety by enough to save one life per year.

We conclude that compensating wage differentials serve some very valuable functions for society:

- Compensating differentials give an incentive for workers to take on tasks that are valuable to society, even though they are unpleasant or dangerous.

- Because of compensating differentials, employers have an incentive to improve safety on the job.

Of course, some jobs are inherently dangerous. No matter how much we spend on safety programs, there will still be some deaths on the job. But compensating differentials help to improve the situation, by giving employers a financial incentive to improve working conditions.

that are associated with different degrees of safety on the job.

Reality Check:
Interim Review Questions

IR13-6. Before her award-winning performance in the film "Boys Don't Cry", the actress Hilary Swank earned fairly ordinary wages. Afterward, analysts in the entertainment industry expected that she would get $2 million per movie. In analyzing this change in wage rates, would you say that there was a shift in the demand curve or the supply curve? For the curve that shifted, was there a shift to the right or to the left?

IR13-7. Does immigration shift the demand curve for labor, or the supply curve? In which direction does the curve shift?

IR13-8. Because of compensating wage-rate differentials, do you expect that pleasant jobs will have wage rates that are higher or lower than the wage rates for jobs the are unpleasant but otherwise comparable?

WAGE DIFFERENTIALS BY RACE AND GENDER

So far, we've seen that people tend to earn higher wages if they have more skill, or if they work in unpleasant jobs. But these influences don't necessarily explain all of the variation in wages. Historically, people of different racial, ethnic, and gender backgrounds have had very different levels of earnings.

Differences by Sex

On average, the earnings of women have long been lower than those of men. Back in 1890, the earnings of American women were *less than half* of those of men (for full-time, year-round workers). In the 1960s and early 1970s, this ratio stayed in the range from 56 percent to 60 percent, although the gap closed substantially in the 1980s.

Reasons for the Gender Wage Gap. One reason for the earnings gap between women and men is that many women leave the labor force during their childbearing years. As a result, these women don't get as much labor-market experience as men do. When they return to work, their job skills have often deteriorated.

The theory of human capital says that people are more likely to invest in themselves, if they expect to reap the benefits of those investments over a long period of time. If women expect to be out of the labor force for several years, they may not make the same kind of human-capital investments that men would make. If a woman expects to leave the labor force to raise children, she might not get as much education and on-the-job training as otherwise.

There are other reasons for the gap between men's and women's earnings, as well. First, women don't work as much overtime as men do, and they don't tend to choose occupations that offer high pay but demand long hours. Second, many women are crowded into low-paying occupations that have typically been dominated by females (such as cosmetologists, nurses' aides, and child-care workers). This phenomenon is called *occupational segregation*. Finally, at least some of the wage gap is probably due to outright discrimination, although there is some evidence that the amount of discrimination may be decreasing.

The Recent Increase in the Relative Earnings of Women. In the late 1970s, the gap between women's and men's earnings began to shrink.

From 1976 to 1990, the earnings gap fell by about one percentage point per year. By 1998, for full-time workers, the ratio of women's earnings to men's earnings had risen to about 73 percent. Moreover, *younger* women did best: In 1998, the earnings ratio was more than 82 percent for those in the 25–34 age group.

Several factors explain the surge in women's earnings. For one thing, women are getting more education. In 1977, only 24 percent of young women were college graduates, but this proportion rose to 33 percent by 1989. Also, the rate of return to education has increased dramatically in the last several years. As a result, the 1980s and 1990s have been relatively better times for white-collar workers, and not very good for blue-collar workers. The widening gap between white-collar and blue-collar workers has applied to men as well as to women, but it has helped women relatively, since they aren't in blue-collar jobs as much as men are.

Also, women (especially younger women) are staying in the labor market longer. This means that these women have more reason to get on-the-job training, and their employers also have a greater incentive to invest in them. As a result, the rate of return to experience for women has increased in the last 25 years.

How Much of the Gap Is Due to Discrimination? Even after these increases, women's average earnings are more than 25 percent less than men's. However, much of this difference is due to the fact that men and women still have different levels of education and experience. (In other words, the gap in human capital is smaller than it used to be, but it still isn't zero.) Another substantial part of the difference is due to occupational segregation.

If we control for differences in human capital and occupation, the gender wage gap is probably no more than 10 percent, and may be smaller than that. Some of the remaining gap is probably due to discrimination. But dis-

crimination is very hard to measure. It's difficult to say how much is due to discrimination, and how much is due to other factors that are hard for researchers to observe.

Differences by Race

A century ago, blacks earned less than half of what was earned by whites. However, from the 1930s to the 1970s, there was a tremendous migration of African Americans from the South to the North and West. This was one of the forces that caused the earnings gap between blacks and whites to shrink. But the earnings gap has not changed much since the 1970s. The median earnings for black men who worked full-time, year-round in 1998 was $27,050. For white men, the comparable figure was $36,172. Thus, black men tended to earn about 75 percent as much as white men. This is actually lower than the ratio for 1975, when black men earned 77 percent as much as whites.

We've seen that a big part of the earnings difference between men and women is explained by differences in human capital. The same is true of black-white differentials. Black men still tend to have less education and experience than white men, and this probably explains at least one-third of the gap. Some studies suggest that other factors (such as union membership and region of residence) may explain another quarter of the gap.

This still leaves us with a substantial earnings gap, however: Even after controlling for everything that they can measure, economists still find that black men probably earn no more than about 90 percent as much as comparable white men. It is impossible to say how much of the remaining gap is due to outright discrimination. It may be that the entire gap is due to discrimination. However, some of it may be due to factors that are very hard to measure, such as the quality of schooling. (It's easy to measure the *quantity* of schooling, but much harder to measure *quality*.)

The last few paragraphs have discussed the differences between black and white *men*. There is also a gap between black and white women, although it has been smaller than the men's gap since the 1960s. In 1998, black women earned about 86 percent as much as white women.

On average, Hispanics earn even less than blacks. In 1998, among full-time, year-round workers, Hispanic men earned about 62 percent as much as white men, and Hispanic women earned about 73 percent as much as white women. Not surprisingly, a large part of this gap is explained by differences in language skills. In other words, a Hispanic man who is fluent in English will tend to earn considerably more than a Hispanic man who isn't fluent. Differences in schooling also play a big role.

Reality Check:
Interim Review Question

IR13-9. In the last 25 years, what has happened to the ratio of women's earnings to men's earnings? What has happened to the ratio of earnings for black men to the earnings of white men?

LABOR UNIONS

In many labor markets, individual workers reach individual agreements with their employers. However, in some markets, the workers are organized into *labor unions*, which negotiate with employers about wages, fringe benefits, and working conditions. Many labor unions are also active in political lobbying.

Labor unions are especially powerful in Europe. For example, more than four-fifths of all workers in Sweden are members of unions. But the union movement has never been as strong as that in the United States. The American labor-union movement had some of its greatest successes in the 1930s and 1940s, after the National Labor Relations Act made it easier for unions to organize. At the peak, in the early 1950s, about one-third of workers were union members. However, since the 1950s, there has been a decline in the proportion of workers who are union members. Since the 1950s, the number of unionized workers has stayed about the same, while the labor force has more than doubled in size. In recent years, only about one of every six or seven American workers has been a union member. Still, it would be wrong to say that American unions are unimportant or irrelevant. After all, when we say that one out of every six or seven workers is a union member, we are talking about more than 17 *million* workers. In addition, unions may have powerful effects on *non-union* labor markets. For these reasons, labor unions are an important feature of the economic landscape, and we will study them here.

The decline in union membership is even more pronounced among unions in the private sector. By 1993, only about 11 percent of private-sector workers were members of unions, compared with almost 38 percent of public-sector workers. From 1983 to 1993, private-sector unions *lost* about 2.4 million workers, whereas public-sector unions *gained* about 1.3 million workers.

The Economic Effects of Labor Unions

When asked what unions want, Samuel Gompers of the American Federation of Labor said "More!". However, economists would ask "More of what?". After all, labor unions are complicated organizations, serving social and political functions, as well as economic ones. Even when we concentrate on the economic effects, we can see that it's possible for unions to influence labor markets in many ways.

The economic goals of most unions could include the following:

- Increasing wages;
- Increasing fringe benefits, such as pensions or health insurance;
- Improving working conditions;
- Increasing employment.

Unfortunately for the union, there are tradeoffs among these goals. If the union is successful in raising wages or fringe benefits, it will raise the firm's cost of labor. This will cause the firm to hire fewer workers. In most cases, it appears that unions *do not* maximize employment: They are usually willing to accept some decreases in employment, in return for increased wages.

Figure 13.10 shows some of the effects of a union on wages and employment. At first, the supply and demand curves are S_{0u} and D_{0u} in the union sector, and S_{0n} and D_{0n} in the non-union sector. The wage rate is W_0 in *both* sectors. The level of employment is L_{0u} in the union sector and L_{0n} in the non-union sector.

Now, suppose that the union succeeds in raising the wage rate for union workers from W_0 to W_{1u}. As a result, we move upward and to the left along the labor-demand curve in the union sector. Some workers will lose their jobs in the union sector: The new level of unionized employment is given by L_{1u}.

Eventually, some of the workers who lose their union jobs will start to look for work in the non-union sector. This means that the labor-supply curve in the non-union sector will shift to the right, to S_{1n}. *Because of the increased supply of labor in the non-union sector, the non-union wage rate will fall to W_{1n}.*

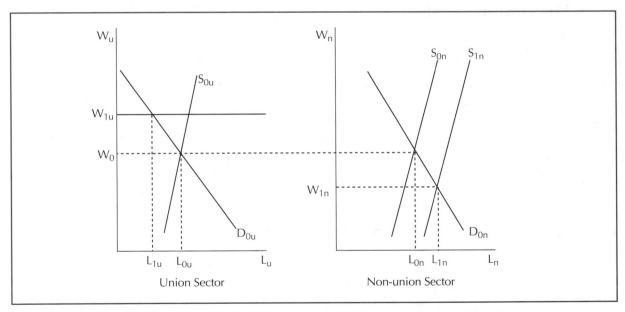

Figure 13.10 The Effects of a Union on Wages and Employment in the Union Sector And in the Non-Union Sector

Without a union, the wage rate is W_0 in each sector. The equilibrium levels of employment are L_{0u} in the union sector and L_{0n} in the non-union sector. When the union raises its wage rate to W_{1u}, the level of unionized employment falls to L_{1u}. Some of the workers who lose their union jobs will seek work in the non-union sector. As a result, the non-union wage rate falls to W_{1n}, and non-union employment increases to L_{1n}.

The Union Wage Gap. We would like to know the size of the wage differential between union and non-union workers (while holding constant any other influences on wages). This wage differential is sometimes called the *union wage gap*.

According to Figure 13.10, the wage gains in the union sector can lead to wage losses in the non-union sector, as displaced workers are forced to seek non-union jobs. This is called the *union spillover effect.* However, there is another effect that works in the opposite direction. Some non-union employers may be willing to pay higher wages, if they believe that this will keep their workers from organizing into a union. This is called the *union threat effect*. The consensus among economists seems to be that, when we put these two effects together, the true wage gap in the United States is between 10 percent and 15 percent.

How Do Unions Deal with Job Losses?

Figure 13.10 shows that some unionized jobs are lost when a labor union raises the wage rate above its equilibrium level. Some workers will get to keep their union jobs, but others will lose theirs. There has to be some system for deciding who gets to keep the union jobs. In other words, there must be a system of *job rationing*.

Many job-rationing schemes have been used over the years. One very popular scheme has been the "seniority system". When layoffs occur, a seniority system preserves the jobs of those who have been on the job for the longest time.

In an effort to limit the job losses, unions also try to affect the labor-demand curves that they face. The union can reduce job losses if it can *make the demand curve for union labor more inelastic.* Job losses can also be limited if the union can *push the demand curve for union labor to the right.*

Here are some of the tactics that unions have used, to increase the demand for their own labor, and/or decrease the demand for competing non-union labor:

- *Unions typically support increases in the minimum wage.* If the government enforces a relatively high minimum wage, it will be hard for employers to substitute low-wage workers for higher-paid union workers.

- *Unions often try to limit imports.* Unions were vocal in their opposition to the North American Free Trade Agreement, as well as to other reductions in trade barriers.

- *Unions sometimes try to encourage people to buy union-made products.* For example, union-sponsored TV commercials urge shoppers to "look for the union label".

MONOPSONY IN LABOR MARKETS

In earlier chapters, we studied market power on the *seller's* side of the market. Monopolists and oligopolists can use their market power to raise their profits. Here, we will look at market power on the *buyer's* side of the market. A *monopsony* exists when there is only one buyer in a market. *Oligopsony* refers to markets with only a few buyers.

Some of the best examples of monopsony and oligopsony occur in labor markets, which is why we study them here. For example, in isolated Appalachian communities, a coal-mining firm may be the only large employer in town. If a firm is to exercise monopsony power, the workers must find it difficult to move in search of better job opportunities. The coal miners might be immobile because they're reluctant to leave their home region, or because they have relatively few skills.

Professional sports provides other examples of labor markets with monopsony or oligopsony power. Before the 1970s, major-league baseball players were effectively tied to only one team. The players weren't allowed to sell their services to the highest bidder. Obviously, this gave the teams tremendous bargaining power in determining player salaries. More recently, players have acquired much greater freedom, as a result of "free-agency" rules. But the player's ability to choose an employer is still limited, in virtually all professional sports.

Next, we will learn about the theory of decision-making for monopsony firms.

Marginal Factor Expense for the Monopsonist

In a perfectly competitive labor market, the individual firm is too small to manipulate the wage rate. Therefore, the firm takes the market wage as given. In a monopsonistic labor market, however, the firm is a "wage maker". The firm faces the entire *market* labor-supply curve, and this has important effects on its hiring behavior.

Let's assume that the market labor-supply curve slopes upward. In other words, the only way to get more workers to supply their labor is to raise the wage rate. *If the monopsony firm wants to hire one additional worker, it has to pay all of its workers a higher wage rate.*

Table 13.3 shows the labor-supply schedule that faces Big Brother, Inc., which is the only employer in its town. If the wage rate is less than $6 per hour, nobody will show up for work. At a wage rate of $6, one worker will come to work for Big Brother. If we multiply the number of workers (one) by the wage rate ($6), we get *total factor expense,* which is $6 in this case.

The *marginal factor expense* is the *extra* amount of money that the firm has to pay, in order to employ one additional unit of a factor of production. In the case of labor, the marginal factor expense is the extra amount of money that the firm has to pay, in order to get one additional worker to come to work. Marginal factor expense is defined as the change in total factor expense, divided by the change in the quantity of labor:

Marginal Factor Expense = (Δ Total Factor Expense) / (Δ Labor).

In the example of Table 13.3, marginal factor expense is $6 for the first worker hired. If Big Brother, Inc., wants to hire a second worker, it has to raise the wage from $6.00 to $6.50. It's important to remember that the increase in the wage rate will apply to *all*

Table 13.3 The Labor-Supply Schedule and Marginal Factor Expense, for Big Brother, Inc.

Number of Workers (L)	Wage Rate (W)	Total Factor Expense (TFE) (= WL)	Marginal Factor Expense (ΔTFE/ΔL)
0	$5.50	$0	—
1	6.00	6	$6
2	6.50	13	7
3	7.00	21	8
4	7.50	30	9
5	8.00	40	10

workers—not only will the second worker get the higher wage, but the first worker will get a wage increase. When we multiply the number of workers (two) by the wage rate ($6.50), we find that total factor expense has risen to $13. To get *marginal* factor expense, we then subtract $6 (which was the total expense when there was only one worker) from $13 (which is the total expense when there are two workers). The result is that the marginal factor expense of the second worker is $(13 − 6) = $7.

In this example, when the firm hires a second worker, the wage rate increases by 50 cents per hour, but marginal factor expense increases by $1. This trend continues in the rest of Table 13.3. Whenever Big Brother wants to hire one additional worker, it is necessary to raise the wage rate by 50 cents, but marginal factor expense increases by $1.00.

The labor-supply schedule of Table 13.3 is graphed as a labor-supply curve (called S) in Figure 13.11, and the marginal-factor-expense curve is shown as MFE. In this case, with a straight-line labor-supply curve, the slope of the marginal-factor-expense curve is exactly twice as great as the slope of the labor-supply curve. (This may remind you of the relationship between demand and marginal revenue for the monopolist. When the monopolist's demand curve is a straight line, the marginal-revenue curve is twice as steep as the demand curve.)

The Monopsonist's Hiring Decision

In the last several chapters, we've studied several of the problems facing economic decision-makers. The utility-maximizing consumer buys the quantity at which marginal utility is equal to the price of the good. The profit-maximizing firm produces the quantity at which marginal revenue equal is to marginal cost. *In each of these problems, the solution involves setting some kind of marginal benefit equal to some kind of marginal cost.*

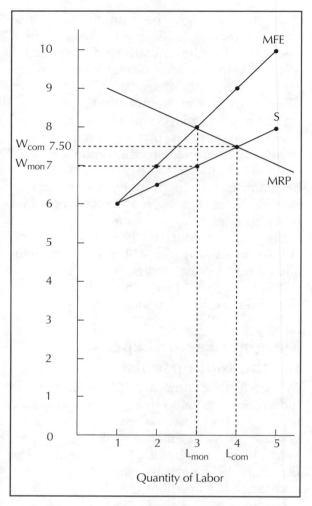

Figure 13.11 The Labor-Supply Curve and Marginal-Factor-Expense Curve for Big Brother, Inc., and the Firm's Hiring Decision

Big Brother, Inc., is a monopsonist. The firm's labor-supply curve is S, its marginal-factor-expense curve is MFE, and its marginal-revenue-product curve is MRP. The firm's best choice is to hire L_{mon} workers, because this is the quantity of labor at which MRP = MFE. The firm then pays a wage rate of W_{mon}, given by the labor-supply curve. Note that the wage is less than the worker's marginal revenue product. If the firm were a perfect competitor in the labor market, it would pay a wage of W_{com}.

The case of the monopsonist is no exception. For the monopsonist, the marginal benefit of hiring one additional worker is the marginal revenue product. The marginal cost of hiring one extra worker is the marginal factor expense. Thus, *the monopsony firm should hire the number of workers at which marginal revenue product (MRP) equals marginal factor expense (MFE)*. In Figure 13.11, the intersection of the MRP curve and the MFE curve tells us that Big Brother, Inc., should hire L_{mon}, which means that three workers will be hired.

The labor-supply curve shows the relationship between the wage rate and the number of workers who will be willing to supply their labor. Therefore, the supply curve tells us that Big Brother will pay a wage rate of W_{mon}. In this case, the wage rate is $7 per hour.

Figure 13.11 also shows the outcomes that would have occurred if this labor market had been competitive. In the competitive case, equilibrium would be given by the intersection of the supply curve and the MRP curve. This would have led to the hiring of four workers, each of whom would have received a wage of $7.50 per hour. Thus, relative to the case of competition, monopsony leads to a lower level of employment *and* a lower wage rate.

Figure 13.11 shows us that *the monopsonist's workers are paid less than their marginal revenue product*. This is sometimes called **monopsonistic exploitation**. The monopsonist's market power allows it to "exploit" the workers, by paying them less than their MRP.

In *Real Economics for Real People* 13.3 on p. 328, we discuss the wages paid to college athletes. These wages are affected by the fact that the employers (colleges and universities) have a lot of market power.

Reality Check:
Interim Review Questions

IR13-10. What effect does the union spillover effect have on the wages paid by non-union firms? What effect does the union threat effect have on the wages paid by non-union firms?

IR13-11. For a monopsonistic firm that faces an upward-sloping labor-supply curve, is the marginal-factor-expense curve above or below the labor-supply curve?

IR13-12. What is monopsonistic exploitation?

ECONOMICS AND YOU:
SOME WORKERS GET BIG BUCKS, AND SOME DON'T

Again and again in this book, we have seen that prices are higher when there is a lot of demand, or when supply is relatively small.

The wage rate is the price at which a worker is hired. If you want a higher wage rate, you need to be working in a labor market where demand is strong, or you have to be working in a labor market where your skills are in relatively short supply.

Of course, one way to do that is to have unique and highly desirable talents. (If you have very unusual talents, then the supply of your skills is small. If those talents are highly desirable, then there will be a lot of demand.) For example, if you are seven feet tall and can move with strength and speed and grace, you may be able to make a lot of money in the National Basketball Association. If you are extremely attractive physically, you may be able to make a lot of money as a fashion model.

But very few people have the body to be a champion athlete, and very few are gorgeous enough to appear on the cover of *Cosmopolitan*. For more ordinary people, the best prescription for high wages is to acquire human capital. People with a lot of human capital are able to earn higher wages, because of labor supply and labor demand. It takes time and effort to acquire a lot of human capital. Since not everyone will go to the trouble to get a lot of education and experience, it follows that those who *do* get education and experience will have skills that are somewhat special, and somewhat limited in supply. In addition, education and experience make us more productive, which means that there will be more demand for our skills. So, here's the secret: Stay in school, and concentrate on your studies. Then, when you get a job, work hard, and make the most of your experience. More than any other things, education and experience are the pathway to earning more money.

Chapter Summary

1. The factors of production include labor, capital, land, energy, and materials. The demand for these factors of production, or inputs, is derived from the demand for the goods that they produce.

2. The marginal revenue product of a factor of production is the extra money that the firm makes when it hires one additional unit of a factor input, and then sells the additional output created by that additional input. In other words, the marginal revenue product equals the marginal physical product, multiplied by the marginal revenue. The marginal-revenue-product curve for a factor of production slopes downward as we move to the right.

3. The marginal factor expense of a factor of production is the extra money that the firm has to pay, in order to hire one additional unit of the factor. If the firm is a competitor in its input market, marginal factor expense will be the price of the input.

4. For the firm that is a competitor in its input market, the demand curve for a factor of production is the marginal-revenue-product curve.

5. The market demand curve for a factor of production is found by adding horizontally the demand curves of the individual firms.

6. The demand for a factor of production is more elastic when it is easier to substitute other inputs for the input whose price is changing. Factor demand is also more elastic when the good being produced by the factor of production is more elastic.

7. A change in the wage rate has two effects on labor supply. The substitution effect leads to an increase in labor supply when the wage rate increases. The income effect goes in the opposite direction: The income effect of an increase in the wage rate will lead to a reduction in labor supply. For men, the income effect and substitution effect approximately cancel each other out, so that the labor-supply elasticity is very close to zero. For women, the substitution effect appears to be stronger, so that the labor-supply elasticity may be something like 0.2 or 0.3.

8. If the price of the output increases, or if productivity increases, then the demand curve for a factor of production will shift to the right. This will tend to increase factor prices. If the demand curve were to shift to the left, factor prices would fall.

9. The theory of human capital says that people will invest in education or on-the-job training, if the value of the benefits is greater than the value of the costs. In fact, labor-market earnings are substantially higher for those with more education and experience.

10. A compensating wage differential is the extra wage rate that must be paid (all else equal), in order to attract a worker to a job that is unpleasant. Dangerous jobs, night jobs, and jobs with other unpleasant characteristics do pay higher wage rates, all else equal.

11. As recently as the mid–1970s, women's earnings were only about 55 percent of men's earnings in the United States. Since then, the gap has narrowed, and the earnings ratio now stands at about 73 percent. This is explained primarily by the fact that women are now getting more education and experience. Most of the remaining gap is due to the fact that there are still differences in education and experience. Part of the gap is probably the result of discrimination.

12. On average, black males earn about 75 percent as much as white males in the

United States. This gap has stayed about the same since the 1970s. The gap is smaller for women: Black females earn about 86 percent as much as white females. Hispanics earn even less than blacks. With both of these groups, differences in human capital explain a large portion of the earnings differences. For Hispanics, much of the difference is also explained by lack of proficiency in English. It's likely that the remaining gaps are partly the result of unmeasured influences, and partly the result of discrimination.

13. The American labor-union movement had some of its greatest successes in the 1930s and 1940s, after the National Labor Relations Act made it easier for unions to organize. At the peak, in the early 1950s, about one-third of workers were union members. However, since the 1950s, there has been a decline in the proportion of workers who are union members. By 2000, only about one-seventh of the work force was in unions. In the last few decades, the only source of union growth has been public-employee unions.

14. Unions typically attempt to increase wage rates, relative to the wages that would have prevailed in the absence of the union. If the union is successful in raising wages, the unionized firms may reduce their employment. If the displaced union workers go to work for non-union firms, the wages at the non-union firms will be reduced. In an attempt to limit the job losses, unions try to reduce the elasticity of demand for their labor, or they try to shift the labor-demand curve to the right.

15. A monopsony occurs when there is only one buyer in a market. If there are only a few buyers, the market is an oligopsony. Monopsony or oligopsony can lead to market power on the buyers' side of the market. A monopsonist in a labor market will choose to hire workers up to the point at which the marginal revenue product equals the marginal factor expense.

16. A monopsonist or oligopsonist will pay workers less than their marginal revenue product. This is called "monopsonistic exploitation".

Key Terms

Labor

Capital

Land

Energy

Materials

Factors of Production

Factor Markets, Input Markets

Marginal Physical Product

Marginal Revenue

Marginal Revenue Product

Marginal Factor Expense

Substitution Effect (in Factor Demand)

Output Effect

Leisure

Non-Labor Income

Income Effect

Substitution Effect (in Labor Supply)

Upward-Sloping Labor-Supply Curve

Backward-Bending Labor-Supply Curve

Elasticity of Labor Supply with Respect to the Wage Rate

Human Capital Investment

Foregone Earnings

Compensating Wage Differentials

Occupational Segregation

Labor Unions

Union Spillover Effect

Union Threat Effect

Union Wage Gap

Monopsony

Oligopsony

Total Factor Expense

Marginal Factor Expense

Monopsonistic Exploitation

Questions and Problems

QP13-1. Explain how the marginal-revenue-product curve for a perfectly competitive firm is different from the marginal-revenue-product curve for a firm that is a monopolist in its output market. In what direction do these marginal-revenue-product curves slope?

QP13-2. Explain the difference between the income effect on labor supply and the substitution effect on labor supply. If the income effect is stronger than the substitution effect, what kind of labor-supply curve will we have? If the income effect and the substitution effect are of equal strength, what will be the shape of the labor-supply curve?

QP13-3. What factors of production are involved in producing an automobile?

QP13-4. Italy's Luciano Pavarotti is one of the most popular opera singers in the world. His splendid voice and vibrant personality combine to make him instantly recognizable all over the world. Joe Dokes flips hamburgers at the Shazam Burger restaurant in Anytown, U.S.A. For which of these workers do you believe that the labor-demand curve would be more elastic? Why?

QP13-5. The "Mariel boatlift" brought more than 100,000 Cubans to the United States in 1980. More of these people ended up in the Miami metropolitan area than in any other part of the country. What do you expect would be the effect on the equilibrium wage rate for less-skilled workers in the Miami area? What would be the effect on the equilibrium quantity of labor in the Miami area? How would your answer change if you were to learn of a recent study, which indicates that the immigration from Cuba was coupled with a substantial reduction in the number of people moving from other parts of the United States to the Miami area? What effects would you expect for other labor markets in the United States?

QP13-6. The marginal physical product of labor for firm A is given by $MPP_L = 10 - L$. Like all of the firms in the market, firm A is a perfect competitor in both its output and input markets. The price of firm A's output is $10 per unit. Draw the firm's marginal-revenue-product curve.

QP13-7. Sam, who studied through four years of college and five years of graduate school, earns $39,000 per year as an Assistant Professor of Classics. Zelda, who has only a high-school diploma, earns $50,000 per year by repairing telephone wires. How can this be? You should be able to come up with at least three or four influences that could help to explain this earnings comparison.

QP13-8. The International Pencil Sharpener Workers Union (IPSWU) succeeds in raising the wage rate for its workers above the rate that would have occurred otherwise. However, this leads to substantial layoffs for IPSWU members. Eventually, many of these workers seek work elsewhere. What will happen in the markets where these displaced workers end up?

QP13-9. In a competitive labor market, the labor-supply curve facing the individual firm is the same as the firm's marginal-factor-expense curve. However, in a monopsonized labor market, the marginal-factor-expense curve is higher than the labor-supply curve. Explain why this is the case.

QP13-10. Should college football players be paid a salary? Why, or why not?

Chapter 14

Capital Markets

ECONOMICS AND YOU: WHO WANTS TO BE A BILLIONAIRE?

In Chapter 13, we discussed the market for labor, which is the most important factor of production. In this chapter, we'll discuss the market for capital, which is also a very important factor of production. Capital includes the machinery and equipment, office buildings, warehouses, factories, delivery vans, railroad cars, and other such stuff that is used in the production process.

The analysis in this chapter will be shaped by one very big difference between labor markets and capital markets. The Thirteenth Amendment to the United States Constitution makes slavery illegal. As a result, it is not possible to own a worker. This means that all labor contracts are in the nature of rental contracts, rather than ownership contracts. However, it is possible to own machines. Our discussion of capital markets has to reflect the fact that capital ownership involves long-lived decisions. Thus, the most important part of this chapter will consider how to compare dollar values that occur at different times.

Much of the nation's capital stock is owned by corporations and other businesses. These businesses, in turn, are owned by people. The people who invest their money in businesses would not do so, unless they expected to earn a return on their investments. The return on a capital investment can come in many forms. If you buy a bond, you will receive *interest payments*. If you buy a share of stock in a corporation, you may receive *dividends*. If the price of the stock goes up, then you will also receive a *capital gain*. If you buy a piece of real estate, you will receive *rents*.

When we talk about stock dividends and capital gains, we are talking about a type of income that is not received by the average household. Relative to labor income, capital ownership tends to be much more highly concentrated in the hands of a few. When we say that Microsoft Corporation's Bill Gates is the richest person in the world, we aren't referring to his salary. We're referring to the value of his holdings of Microsoft stock. The richest people in the world are all owners of very substantial amounts of capital wealth.

So, if you want to be a billionaire, don't expect to get there on the basis of your salary alone. The really rich folks own capital.

THE SUPPLY OF LOANABLE FUNDS

The stock of capital is fixed at any one moment, since it takes time to produce new capital. In other words, the supply of capital cannot change in the very short run. In the short run, the supply of capital is perfectly inelastic with respect to prices.

However, over time, it's possible to build new buildings and install new machines. Thus, when we discuss the supply of capital, we often focus on the supply of *new* capital, which we call **capital investment**.

Where do businesses get the money for new capital investments? There are a variety of sources, but one of the most important is the **market for loanable funds**. Private households save, and entrust their money to financial institutions, such as banks, insurance companies, and so on. The financial institutions then make loans to businesses.

In every market, there is a price that will achieve equilibrium. In the labor market, the key price was the wage rate. In the market for loanable funds, the key price is the interest rate. Thus, if we were to draw a supply curve for loanable funds, we would graph the relationship between the interest rate and the amount of loanable funds that were being saved.

In Chapter 13, we saw that a change in the wage rate leads to an income effect on labor supply, as well as a substitution effect on labor supply. We have a similar story when we consider the effect of a change in the interest rate on the savings decisions of households. Once again, there is an income effect and a substitution effect. When the interest rate rises, today's consumption becomes relatively more expensive, and future consumption becomes relatively cheaper. The substitution effect of an increase in the interest rate will lead people to substitute away from today's consumption, which means that they will save more.

However, an increase in the interest rate also makes us "richer", in that it is possible to consume more in the present and more in the future. The income effect of an increase in the interest rate leads people to save less.

Once again, the income effect and the substitution effect go in opposite directions. The subject is highly controversial among economists, but the consensus seems to be that the income effect and the substitution effect approximately cancel each other out. The elasticity of saving with respect to the interest rate may be positive, but it is probably not much greater than zero.

In Figure 14.1, we show a fairly inelastic supply curve for savings.

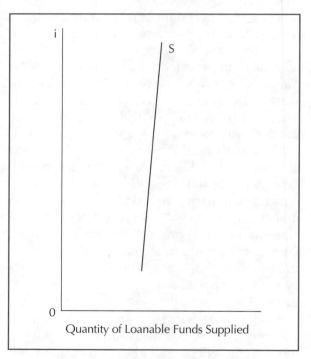

Figure 14.1 The Supply of Loanable Funds

When interest rates change, the substitution effect on savings goes in one direction, while the income effect goes in the opposite direction. Overall, the substitution effect is probably slightly stronger than the income effect. This means that the savings supply curve will slope upward as we move to the right.

IR14-1. If the interest rate increases, will the substitution effect cause saving to increase or decrease?

IR14-2. If the interest rate decreases, will the income effect cause saving to increase or decrease?

PRESENT DISCOUNTED VALUE AND THE DEMAND FOR LOANABLE FUNDS

As we pointed out in the previous section, it is possible to rent certain types of capital. However, it is also possible to own capital. If you are thinking about buying a piece of capital, you have to be thinking about the entire flow of returns that you will receive, over the life of the asset. This makes it necessary to compare dollar values that are received at different times. Economists and financial analysts use a concept called *present discounted value,* to facilitate comparison of dollar amounts in different time periods.

Present Discounted Value

If you receive one dollar today, it is worth exactly one dollar today. However, if you receive one dollar today, it is worth *more* than one dollar a year from now. This is because you can take the dollar and put it in a savings account, or in a money-market fund, or in government bonds, and it will earn interest.

Therefore, if i is the interest rate, then:

$1 today = $(1 + i)$ in one year.

For example, if the interest rate is 6%, or 0.06, then $1 today has the same value as $1.06 in one year.

If we turn this around, we can see that, if you receive one dollar in a year, it is worth *less* than one dollar today. If we divide both sides of the above equation by $(1 + i)$, we have:

$(1/(1+i))$ today = $1 in one year.

For example, if the interest rate is 6%, or 0.06, then $1 received in one year will have the same value as $(1/(1.06))$ today, which is about 94.3 cents. If the interest rate is 10% or 0.10, then $1 received in one year will have the same value as $(1/(1.10))$ today, which is about 90.9 cents.

Economists use the phrase "present discounted value" to refer to calculations such as those in the preceding equation. The **present discounted value** of a future payment is the maximum amount that a person should be willing to pay *today,* in order to receive that payment in the *future.* For example, the present discounted value of $1, received in one year, is $(1/(1+i))$.

Now, what if you put $1 in the bank, and leave it in your account for *two* years? At the end of one year, the $1 has grown to $(1 + i)$. During the second year, you earn interest on the original principal of $1, *and you also earn interest on the accumulated interest.* Thus, at the end of two years, $1, doesn't just grow to $(1 + 2i)$. Instead it grows to $(1+i)^2$, which is $(1+2i+i^2)$. For example, if the interest rate is 6%, or 0.06, $1 today will grow in two years to $(1.06)^2$ or $1.1236. If the interest rate is 10%, or 0.1, $1 today will grow in two years to $(1.1)^2$ or $1.21. If you put $1 in your bank account today, and if you then leave the money in the bank without withdrawing any of the interest or principal for three years, the $1 will grow to $(1+i)^3$. In general, if you put $1 in your account today, and leave it in the account for N years, the \$1 will grow to $\$(1+i)^N$.

The Miracle of Compound Interest and the Rule of 72

Because you earn interest on the accumulated interest, as well as on the principal, the value of an investment can grow with surprising speed. This is the "miracle of compound interest". If you invest \$1 today, and let it accumulate at an interest rate of 6%, you will have \$2 in a little less than 12 years. In other words, at an interest rate of 6%, you would double your money in about 12 years. At an interest rate of 10%, it only takes a little more than 7 years to double your money. (Not surprisingly, the time necessary to double your money is less when the interest rate is greater.) Table 14.1 gives the amount of time that it takes to double your money, for different values of the interest rate.

Notice that, if we multiply the interest rate (in percentage points) by the number of years that it takes to double your money, we always get a number close to 72. For example, for an interest rate of 5 %, it takes a little more than 14 years to double your money. If we multiply 5 by 14, we get 70. At an interest rate of 8%, it takes about 9 years to double your money, and if we multiply 8 by 9, we get 72. At

an interest rate of 12%, it takes a little more than 6 years to double your money, and if we multiply 12 by 6, we get 72. This is *the Rule of 72*: over a fairly wide range of interest rates, the number of years to double your money is approximately equal to 72 divided by the interest rate.

The General Formula for Present Discounted Value

Earlier in this section, we introduced the concept of present discounted value, and applied it in the case of a payment that is to be received one year in the future. Next, we showed how compounding can lead an investment to grow over a period of many years. Now, we put the two parts together. The present discounted value of \$1, received in two years, is $\$(1/(1+i)^2)$. More generally, if we use PDV for present discounted value, the PDV of \$1, received in N years, is $\$(1/(1+i)^N)$.

The most general expression of the formula is this: **The PDV of \$X, received in N years, is $\$(X/(1 + i)^N)$**. Thus, if the interest rate is 8%, or 0.08, the PDV of \$1000, to be received in 5 years, is $\$(1000/(1.08)^5)$, which is about \$680.58.

If the interest rate is relatively high, and/or if the number of years is large, then the PDV of a sum that is to be received in the future can be surprisingly small. For example, if the interest rate is 8%, or 0.08, then the present discounted of one dollar that is to be received in 10 years is $\$(1/(1.08)^{10})$, which is only about 46.3 cents. If the interest rate is 10%, then the PDV of one dollar that is to be received in 10 years is $\$(1/(1.1)^{10})$, which is only about 38.6 cents. If the interest rate is 10%, then the PDV of one dollar that is to be received in 20 years is $\$(1/(1.1)^{20})$, which is about 14.9 cents.

In *Real Economics for Real People 14.1*, we use the concept of present discounted value to think about the value of payments under the lottery.

	Table 14.1	
Interest Rate	**Approximate Amount of Time To Double Your Money**	
4%	17 years,	8 months
5%	14 years,	2 months
6%	11 years,	11 months
7%	10 years,	3 months
8%	9 years,	0 months
9%	8 years,	0 months
10%	7 years,	3 months
11%	6 years,	8 months
12%	6 years,	1 months

Real Economics for Real People 14.1:
How Much Do You Really Win, When You Win the Lottery?

In May, 2000, the largest lottery jackpot in history was awarded in the Big Game drawing. The jackpot was announced at $350 million. But was the jackpot really worth $350 million? The winners were given the option of receiving the money over a period of 26 years, or receiving an immediate payment of substantially less than $350 million. This indicates that the administrators of the lottery have a clear understanding of the concept of present discounted value.

Most states now have lotteries, and these lotteries typically pay out their prizes over a period of many years. The most common pay-out period is 20 years. Let's say that you win the lottery, and that the State government says that your prize is $20 million. This is a bit misleading. In fact, what they mean is that they will pay you $1 million per year in each of 20 years. That is very different from paying the entire $20 million right now. If the entire $20 million were paid right now, its PDV would be exactly $20 million. (Payments that happen right now do not have to be discounted.) However, when the actual payment is $1 million per year for 20 years, the PDV will be much lower.

Let's calculate the PDV of a stream of 20 payments of $1 million dollars each, where the first one happens right now, the second one happens in one year, the third one happens in two years, and so on, and the final payments happens 19 years from now. The PDV of the first payment is exactly $1 million. Since the first payment occurs now, its PDV is always $1 million, regardless of the interest rate.

The PDV of the second payment is ($1 million/ $(1 + i)$). If the interest rate is 8 percent, or 0.08, then the PDV of the second payment is ($1 million/ (1.08)), which is about $925,926. The PDV of the third payment is ($1 million/ $(1 + i)^2$), because it occurs two years into the future. If the interest rate is 8 percent, or 0.08, then the PDV of the third payment is ($1 million/ $(1.08)^2$), which about $857,339. The PDV of the twentieth and final payment is ($1 million / $(1 + i)^{19}$), because it occurs 19 years into the future. If the interest rate is 8 percent, or 0.08, then the PDV of the final payment is ($1 million / $(1.08)^{19}$), which is about $231,712.

To get the present discounted value of the entire stream of 20 payments, we add together each of the pieces. The PDV of the entire stream is

($1 million) + ($1 million / $(1 + i)$) +
($1 million / $(1 + i)^2$) + . . . +
($1 million / $(1 + i)^{19}$).

If the interest rate is 8%, this PDV is about $10,603,599. If the interest rate is 10%, this PDV is about $9,364,920.

If you win the lottery, the authorities will say that you have won $20 million. However, you may only have won about half of that, in present discounted value. If you win a stream of 20 annual payments of $1 million each, and you offer to sell this to a bank in return for a single up-front payment, they will only be willing to pay a fraction of $20 million.

Using Present Discounted Value to Make Investment Decisions

Another important application of the concept of present discounted value applies to firms that are deciding whether to make an investment, such as building a new chemical factory. For most investments, the costs come at the beginning of the life of the project, and the revenues come later. In the case of a new chemical factory, it might take a year or more before the factory is ready to produce chemicals. During this time, the firm incurs costs, but does not receive any revenues. Only after the factory is built will the firm be able to earn any revenues from the factory.

If the costs happen at the very beginning of the project, then they will not have to be discounted. However, if the revenues don't come until several years later, they will indeed have to be discounted.

It is beneficial for a firm to undertake an investment project if the project has net present discounted value that is equal to or greater than zero. We define the net present discounted value as

Net PDV = PDV (Revenues) – PDV (Costs)

We define today's revenues as R_0. Similarly, we define revenues that are to be received in one year as R_1, and we define revenues that are to be received in two years as R_2, and so on. We define today's costs as C_0, and we define costs that are to be incurred in one year as C_1, and so on. Then, the net present discounted value is represented by

Net PDV = $(R_0 - C_0) + (R_1 - C_1)/(1+i)$ + $(R_2 - C_2)/((1+i)^2) + (R_3 - C_3)/((1+i)^3)$ + . . .

Let's consider a project for which all costs come immediately, and all revenues come in exactly one year. For example, what if the project costs $1000, and the revenues (one year later) are $1100? The net PDV of this project is

($1100 / (1 + i))–$1000.

Note that the costs are *not* discounted, because they happen today, while the revenues *are* discounted, because they happen in the future.

If the interest rate is 7%, or 0.07, then the net PDV of the above project will be ($1100 / 1.07)–$1000, which equals about $28.04. In a case like this, in which the net PDV is positive, it is in the firm's interest to undertake the project.

If the interest rate is 10%, or 0.1, then the net PDV of the above project will be ($1100 / 1.1)–$1000, which equals exactly zero. In a case like this, the firm doesn't get a big surplus from the project, but it still breaks even, and it would be acceptable for the firm to undertake the project.

However, if the interest rate takes on any value that is greater than 10%, the net PDV of this project will be negative. In this case, the value of the firm will actually be smaller if it undertakes the project. Firms should not proceed with projects that have negative net PDV.

An Example

Let's say that your company is considering four separate projects. Each one has a cost, which is incurred today, of exactly $1000. Whereas each project has exactly the same cost, they have different revenues. In every case, however, the revenues are to be received one year from now. Table 14.2 shows the net present discounted values for each of the four projects, under different assumptions about the interest rate that should be used to discount the future.

Table 14.2 shows that, if the interest rate is only four percent, each of the four projects has positive net present discounted value. Consequently, at an interest rate of four percent, all four projects will be undertaken. If the interest rate is seven percent, three of the projects still have positive net present discounted value, but one of them now has negative net PDV. Therefore, at an interest rate of seven percent, only three of the projects will be undertaken.

Table 14.2 An Example of the Relationship Between the Interest Rate and the Number of Investment Projects Undertaken

Project Number	Cost Today	Revenue In One Year	Net Present Discounted Value (rounded to the nearest dollar) for interest rate of:			
			4%	7%	10%	13%
1	$1000	$1150	$106	$75	$45	$18
2	$1000	$1120	$77	$47	$18	-$ 9
3	$1000	$1090	$48	$19	-$ 9	-$35
4	$1000	$1060	$19	-$9	-$36	-$62

When the interest rate rises to 10 percent, only two projects will be undertaken. Finally, at an interest rate of 13 percent, only one of the projects will be undertaken.

These results are graphed in Figure 14.2. In this figure, the interest rate is on the vertical axis, and the number of projects undertaken is on the horizontal axis. The figure displays an inverse relationship between the interest rate and the number of projects undertaken. This is a graph of the demand for loanable funds. Like most demand curves, it slopes downward as we go to the right.

Reality Check: Interim Review Questions

IR14-3. What is the present discounted value of $100, to be received one year from now, if the interest rate is 5%? What if the interest rate is 10%? What if it is 20%?

IR14-4. What is the present discounted value of $100, to be received *ten* years from now, if the interest rate is 5%? What if the interest rate is 10%? What if its is 20%?

IR14-5. You are given the opportunity to invest $100 in a capital investment project. You are certain that the revenues, to be received in one year, are $110. If the interest rate is 5%, should the project be undertaken? Would your answer change if the revenues of $110 were to be received in three years?

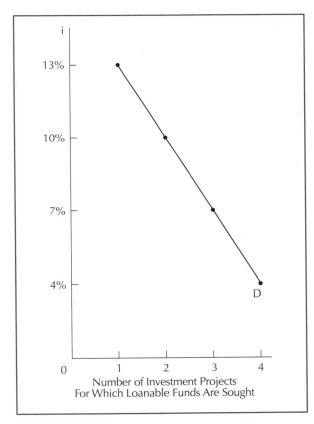

Figure 14.2 The Demand for Loanable Funds

When the interest rate is four percent, four projects will be undertaken by the firm. When the interest rate rises to seven percent, only three projects will be undertaken. At an interest rate of 10 percent, two projects are undertaken. At an interest rate of 13 percent, only one project is approved. The result is a downward-sloping demand curve for loanable funds.

CAPITAL-MARKET EQUILIBRIUM

Figure 14.1 showed us a supply curve for loanable funds. The curve is upward sloping (although fairly steep). And now we have seen Figure 14.2, which has a downward-sloping demand curve for loanable funds.

By now, you can probably guess what we are going to do next. We are going to put the supply curve together with the demand curve, to find equilibrium in the market for loanable funds. This is shown in Figure 14.3. In this figure, the interaction of supply and demand determines the equilibrium interest rate. The equilibrium interest rate is i_0, and the equilibrium quantity of loans is I_0.

Usury Laws

Most State governments have ***usury laws***, which place a ceiling on the interest rates that can be charged. The effects of these laws are similar to the effects of the other price ceilings that we studied in Chapter 4. If the usury ceiling is above the equilibrium interest rate, then the usury law will not have any effect. However, if the usury ceiling is below the equilibrium interest rate, the equilibrium rate will then be illegal. Figure 14.4 shows what will happen if the usury law is enforced. With the interest-rate ceiling below the equilibrium interest rate, the quantity of loanable funds

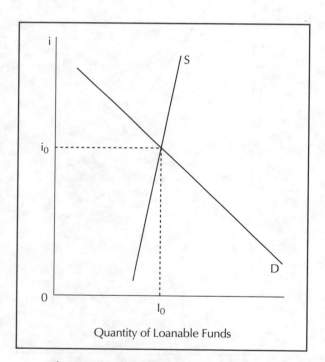

Figure 14.3 Equilibrium in the Market for Loanable Funds

As in any market, the equilibrium price and quantity are determined by the intersection of the supply curve and the demand curve. In the case of the market for loanable funds, the supply curve, S, and the demand curve, D, determine the equilibrium quantity of investment, I, and the equilibrium interest rate, i.

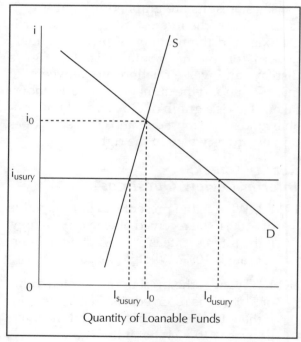

Figure 14.4 The Effects of a Usury Ceiling

The equilibrium interest rate is i_0, and the equilibrium quantity of investment is I_0. An interest-rate ceiling is enforced at i_{usury}. As a result, the quantity of loanable funds demanded increases to Id_{usury}, and the quantity of loanable funds supplied decreases to Is_{usury}. Therefore, there is a shortage of credit.

demanded will increase, and the quantity of loanable funds supplied will decrease. As a result, there will be a shortage of credit.

When there is a shortage of credit, there will not be enough funds to provide loans for all of the people or firms that want to borrow money at the prevailing interest rate. In ordinary times, with no usury ceiling, the market does an excellent job of allocating credit. However, the usury ceiling destroys the market's ability to serve as a rationing device. The usury law will make it necessary for other devices to be used to ration credit. Some financial institutions may simply issue loans on a first-come, first-served basis, until their funds run out. Others may allocate loans on the basis of racial prejudices, or on the basis of personal connections, or according to any of a number of other schemes.

ECONOMIC RENT

Let's suppose that a piece of earth-moving equipment can be hired for $100 per hour. If the market price were to drop to $99.99, would the owners of the equipment still hire it out as they did before? What about a worker who is earning $15 per hour: If his wage were to drop to $14.99, would he stay on, or would he hunt for a new job?

Many factors of production would remain in their present employment, even if they were to receive a lower level of payment. We define *economic rent* as the difference between the amount that a factor is actually paid, and the minimum amount that the factor would have to be paid in order to keep it in its present employment. Let's return to the piece of machinery that is paid $100 per hour. We assume that its owners would continue to allow it to be used where it is currently being used, even if it were to receive as little as $90 per hour. This means that the machinery receives $(100–90) = $10 per hour of economic rent.

This terminology is probably a bit confusing. After all, we are used to hearing the word "rent" used in a very different way. "Rent" is usually taken to mean the *entire* payment that is received each period by the owners of a piece of land or an apartment building. In order to keep the confusion to a minimum, it's important to say *economic* rent, if that's what we mean.

In *Real Economics for Real People 14.2*, we discuss an example of economic rent.

Real Economics for Real People 14.2:
Economic Rent for the Employees of International Organizations

The United States is home to many international organizations, such as the United Nations, the International Monetary Fund (IMF), and the World Bank. Not surprisingly, these organizations have a tradition of hiring workers from all over the world. In addition, they have rules that require them to pay the same wage rates to workers from different countries who do similar jobs. What will happen as a result of these rules?

First, consider an economist from the African nation of Zambia. From the point of view of this person, who hails from a very poor country, the opportunity to work for the IMF in Washington, D.C., looks extremely good. It might be possible to get him to come to Washington for a salary that is modest by American standards.

Next, let's think about an economist from Paris, France. She lives in a city with the Louvre Museum, the Notre Dame Cathedral, some of the finest restaurants in the world, beautiful parks, and so on, and so on. Many French men and women consider Washington, D.C., to be something of a cultural backwater, when compared with Paris.

Consequently, it will take a very high wage rate to coax the Parisian to come to Washington. For an economist with 10 years of experience, the World Bank and the IMF pay salaries of well over $80,000 per year, *tax-free*. These salaries are equivalent to something like $120,000 of taxable income.

So we have three facts: (1) It takes a high salary to get someone to come to Washington from Paris. (2) The IMF requires itself to have an internationally diverse labor force, which means that they have to have people from France, as well as people from poorer countries. (3) The IMF will pay the same wage to all comparable workers, regardless of their country of origin. For the French economist, there might not be much economic rent. However, in many cases, the salaries paid will be far higher than they would have needed to be. The worker from Zambia would have been willing to work for much less than he or she is paid. In other words, for many of the workers at these organizations, a large portion of salary can be considered to be *economic rent*.

Chapter Summary

1. In the short run, the supply of capital is fixed. Over time, the supply of capital can increase, as a result of new capital investment. Many capital investments are financed in the market for loanable funds. The substitution effect of an interest rate change on the supply of savings leads to a higher amount of saving, when the interest rate increases. The income effect of an interest rate change on the supply of savings leads to a lower amount of savings, when the interest rate increases. Overall, the income effect and the substitution effect probably come close to canceling each other out, so that the supply of loanable funds is probably fairly inelastic with respect to the interest rate.

2. The present discounted value of a future payment is the maximum amount that a person should be willing to pay today, for the privilege of receiving that payment in the future.

3. The Rule of 72 states that, over a fairly wide range of interest rates, the number of years to double your money is approximately equal to 72 divided by the interest rate.

4. The net present discounted value of a capital-investment project is equal to the present discounted value of the revenues from the project, less than the present discounted value of the costs of the project. If the net present discounted value of a project is zero or positive, it is in the firm's interest to undertake the project. However, if the net present discounted value of a project is negative, the firm should not undertake the project.

5. A usury law is an interest-rate ceiling. If the usury law is below the equilibrium interest rate, then there will be a shortage of credit.

6. We define economic rent as the difference between the amount that a factor is actually paid, and the minimum amount that the factor would have to be paid in order to keep it in its present employment.

Key Terms

Interest Payments

Dividends

Capital Gains

Rents

Capital Investment

Market for Loanable Funds

Present Discounted Value

The Rule of 72

Usury Law

Economic Rent

Questions and Problems

QP14-1. Ms. Zylks will receive a series of payments from the estate of her great aunt. Each of the three installments is to be $10,000. The first arrives today, the second arrives one year from now, and the third arrives two years from now. The interest rate is 8%. Calculate the present discounted value of this stream of cash flows.

QP14-2. XYZ Corporation is considering whether to undertake a new capital investment project. Analysts at XYZ have determined that the project will cost $300 million, and that it will generate revenues of $330 million, exactly one year after the costs are incurred. What is the present discounted value of the project if a discount rate of 8% is used? What about 10%? 12%? Under what conditions should XYZ undertake the project?

QP14-3. In the early 1980s, Lee Iacocca (whose name is an acronym for "*I Am Chairman Of Chrysler Corporation of America*") accepted a salary of $1 per year. In later years, when Chrysler was doing better, his salary and bonuses came to more than $10 million per year. Does this indicate that all but $1 of his later salary was economic rent?

QP14-4. The supply curve for cement-mixer trucks is given by $Q_s = 0.1P$. The demand curve is given by $Q_d = 100-0.1P$. What are the equilibrium price and quantity of cement-mixer trucks?

QP14-5. The equilibrium interest rate is 6%. A usury ceiling is established at 20%. What effect, if any, will this usury law have on the market? How would your answer change if the usury ceiling were at 5%?

QP14-6. The interest rate is 6%. At this rate, approximately how many years will it take to double one's money? How would your answer change if the interest rate were 10%?

Chapter 15

Income Distribution and Poverty

ECONOMICS AND YOU: WILL THE POOR ALWAYS BE WITH US?

At the very beginning of this book, we saw that any economic system must make three fundamental decisions. The economy must decide *what* gets produced, *how* it gets produced, and *for whom* it gets produced. Since then, we have concentrated on "what" and "how", and we've seen that a private-market economy can deliver goods and services in a very efficient manner.

But what about the "for-whom" decision? Who gets the goods? Unfortunately, there's no guarantee that a private-market economy will lead to an income distribution that people consider fair or desirable. The market economy could generate a highly unequal distribution of income. A relatively small number of people might live in great luxury, while most people subsist in relative poverty. This might be an *efficient* economy, but many people would say that it isn't a *good* one. In fact, most countries use government policies in an effort to reduce poverty and inequality.

In this chapter, we take a look at the distribution of income, and the problem of poverty. Why talk about income distribution now? The reason is that labor and capital are the main sources of income for most people, and we have just finished studying labor markets and capital markets. Thus, it is only now that we have the tools to study income distribution in a serious way.

Regardless of whether we study income distribution at the beginning of the book, or at the end, it is a very important topic. Throughout most of human history, most people have struggled to survive. However, as a result of the tremendous economic growth of the last century, it is now possible to imagine a world without poverty. In this chapter, we will take a look at some of the policies that have been used in the "war on poverty", in an attempt to get a clearer understanding of the way toward a poverty-free world.

SOME FACTS ABOUT THE DISTRIBUTION OF INCOME

Table 15.1 describes the income distribution in the United States. For each year shown, the population is divided into five groups, each of which has 20 percent of the households. About 49 percent of all income was received by the highest-income group in 1998. The lowest-income group also had 20 percent of the households (just like the top group), but these poorer households received less than four percent of all income.

Table 15.1 shows that the distribution of income became *more unequal* from the mid–1970s to the mid–1990s. In 1975, the lowest-income 80 percent of the population received 56.8 percent of all income. By 1998, this group's share had shrunk to 50.8 percent of income. Over the same period, the share of the top 20 percent of the population went up from 43.2 percent of all income to 49.2 percent. In other words, from 1975 to 1998, the American economy changed in such a way that 6 percent of all income got shifted away from the bottom 80 percent of the population to the top 20 percent.

This may not seem like a big change. However, 6 percent of the total income of all households amounts to more than $400 billion every year. If the distribution of income had remained the same after 1975, the top 20 percent would have received over $400 billion *less* in 1998, and the bottom 80 percent would have received over $400 billion *more*. That's a lot of money.

However, it's important to keep in mind that the income distribution doesn't always become more unequal. Even though the income distribution became more unequal from about 1975 to about 1995, the increase in inequality has slowed nearly to a stop in the last half of the 1990s. Moreover, if we go a bit farther back in history, there is at least one period of rapid *equalization*. From the late 1920s to the early 1950s, the income distribution in the United States became more equal, to an extent that is greater than the disequalization that occurred from 1975 to 1995. In large part, the great equalization of the early 20th century was due to a phenomenal increase in education levels. In 1910, only a little more than 10 percent of American teenagers were graduating from high school. By 1940, this number had increased to about 60 percent.

Table 15.1 Shares of Aggregate Income Received by Each 20 Percent of Households in the United States, for Selected Years from 1967 to 1998

	Percent of Aggregate Income Received by:				
Year	Lowest 20 Percent	Second-Lowest 20 Percent	Third 20 Percent	Fourth 20 Percent	Highest 20 Percent
1967	4.0%	10.8%	17.3%	24.2%	43.8%
1970	4.1	10.8	17.4	24.5	43.3
1975	4.4	10.5	17.1	24.8	43.2
1980	4.3	10.3	16.9	24.9	43.7
1985	4.0	9.7	16.3	24.6	45.3
1990	3.9	9.6	15.9	24.0	46.6
1995	3.7	9.1	15.2	24.0	48.7
1998	3.6	9.0	15.0	23.2	49.2

Source: U.S. Bureau of the Census, *Current Population Reports,* P60–206, September, 1999.

This meant that there was a large increase in the supply of relatively more-skilled workers, and a large decrease in the supply of relatively less-skilled workers. As a result, the wages of less-skilled workers increased substantially, relative to the wages of highly skilled workers. The share of income received by the top quintile of the income distribution fell by more than 10 percentage points from the late 1920s to the early 1950s.

The Lorenz Curve and the Gini Ratio

Unfortunately, it isn't easy to use the numbers in the last few paragraphs, because they are so unwieldy. It would be more convenient if we could discuss the income distribution by referring to a single number. In this section, we develop a single number that can describe the degree of inequality in any distribution.

The Lorenz Curve. We begin by graphing the entire income distribution, as shown in Figure 15.1. On the horizontal axis of this figure, the population is lined up in order of income. The lowest-income household is introduced at the far left, while the highest-income household is introduced at the far right.

With the population lined up in this way, the horizontal axis measures the "cumulative proportion of the population". For example, if we start at the left end of the diagram, and go 30 percent of the way toward the right end, we are considering the 30 percent of the population with the lowest incomes. Thus, the horizontal axis can take on a value from zero to one (that is, from zero percent to 100 percent).

The vertical axis of Figure 15.1 shows the "cumulative proportion of income". If we start at the bottom of the diagram, and go 40 percent of the way toward the top, we are considering 40 percent of the economy's income. The vertical axis also takes on values from zero to one.

The *Lorenz curve* shows the proportion of income going to each part of the population.

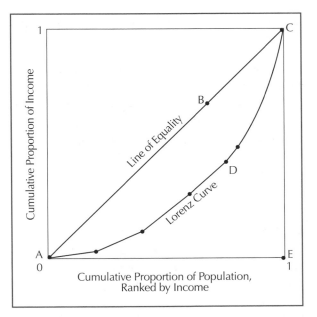

Figure 15.1 The Lorenz Curve

The Lorenz Curve for income is a graph of the relationship between the cumulative proportion of the population and the cumulative proportion of income. The Gini Ratio is calculated by dividing the area between the Line of Equality and the Lorenz Curve by the entire area under the Line of Equality. In other words, the Gini Ratio is equal to ABCD/ACE.

For example, let's say that the lowest-income 20 percent of the population gets 3.6 percent of the income. Then, one of the points on the Lorenz curve would be 20 percent of the way from left to right, and 3.6 percent of the way from bottom to top. In other words, (0.2, 0.036) would be a point on the Lorenz curve. Figure 15.1 shows a Lorenz curve for the United States in 1998.

The Gini Ratio. As a standard for comparison, we could think of an economy in which income is distributed completely equally. Thus, if we were to take *any* 10 percent of the households in this type of economy, they would get exactly 10 percent of the income. In a hypothetical, completely equal economy, the Lorenz curve would be a straight line, slanting upward and to the right at a 45-degree angle. This is the "Line of Equality" in Figure 15.1.

There is a crescent-shaped space between the Lorenz curve and the Line of Equality. In Figure 15.1, the area of this crescent is ABCD. If we divide ABCD by the area of the triangle, ACE, we get the *Gini Ratio*, or *Gini Coefficient*, or *Gini Index*. (Gini is pronounced JEE-nee.) The Gini Ratio is the best-known measure of inequality in an income distribution.

The Gini Ratio in the United States

In a completely equal economy, there would not be any space between the Lorenz curve and the Line of Equality. Thus, the Gini Ratio would be exactly zero. At the other extreme, if one individual had virtually all of the income, the Gini Ratio would be nearly 1.0. When the income distribution is *more unequal,* the Gini Ratio is *higher.* In recent years, the Gini Ratio has been in the neighborhood of 0.4 to 0.5 in the United States.

We've seen that the share of income received by lower-income households has been falling in the United States, whereas the share received by higher-income households has been rising. We expect that this would *increase* the Gini Ratio, since higher Ginis are associated with more unequal distributions of income. In fact, the Gini Ratio increased from 0.397 in 1975 to 0.428 in 1990, and to 0.456 in 1998.

This may seem like a small increase in the Gini Ratio. But even a small change in the Gini is associated with a redistribution of billions and billions of dollars every year.

International Comparisons of Income Inequality

The United States has a distribution of income that is more equal than that of many countries, but less equal than that of many other countries. The European economies tend to have an income distribution that is *more equal* than that of the U.S. In one recent study, the Gini Ratio was lower in Germany, Hungary, Sweden, and the United Kingdom than it was in the United States. Japan is also more equal than the U.S. Many of these countries have Gini Ratios that are closer to 0.3.

On the other hand, the poorer countries of Asia, Africa, and Latin America tend to be *more unequal.* Brazil, Indonesia, Ivory Coast, Mexico, and the Philippines all have Gini Ratios that are substantially higher than that of the United States. Brazil is the most unequal of all, with a Gini of 0.6. In Brazil, the highest-income 10 percent of the population has *more than half* of the income!

Reality Check: Interim Review Questions

IR15-1. From the middle 1970s to the middle 1990s, did the share of income received by the top 20 percent of households increase, or decrease, or stay the same?

IR15-2. The Lorenz Curve for country A is below the Lorenz Curve for country B. (In other words, the Lorenz Curve for country B is closer to the Line of Equality.) Which country has a higher Gini Ratio?

THE CAUSES OF INCOME INEQUALITY

So far, we have looked at some of the *facts* about the income distribution. However, it's important to go beyond the facts: We need some *explanations* for why income is distributed as it is. Of course, some of the variation is just due to luck. (For example, some of today's millionaires got rich by winning lotteries.) But much of the variation in incomes is due to other factors, which we will study now.

Differences Over the Lifetime

In Chapter 13, on labor economics, we saw that workers tend to get higher wages as they get older, because older workers have more experience. Consider Bob, who is 55 years old, and his 25-year-old son, Joe. Bob has worked his way up to a management position, and he earns $60,000 per year. Joe is just starting out as a trainee, and he earns $25,000 per year.

On the surface, it looks as if Bob is a lot better off than his son. However, Bob is at the peak of his career, and is unlikely to get any more big raises. On the other hand, Joe can expect to have rapidly rising earnings over the next several years. Joe may make just as much as his father is making (or even more), when he gets to his father's age. In other words, *some of the inequality in* annual *incomes is just due to the fact that people are of different ages.*

Here is another reason to think that we might get a very different picture if we look at *lifetime* incomes, rather than *annual* incomes: In any given year, some people have an unusually good year. (For example, a construction contractor might land a big project.) On the other hand, some people have an unusually bad year. (For example, a textile worker might be unemployed for a few months). Over the lifetime, the good years and bad years tend to average out.

Because of the ups and downs in income over the lifetime, *the distribution of lifetime income is much more equal than the distribution of annual income.* One study for Canada found that the Gini Ratio for *annual* income was 0.37, while the Gini Ratio for *lifetime* income was only 0.18. Thus, about half of the inequality that we see in annual incomes will go away if we take the lifetime perspective.

Reasons for the Increase in Earnings Inequality

Most of the nation's income is in the form of earnings in the labor market. Therefore, it's understandable that the rise in *income* inequality has had a lot to do with an increase in the inequality of labor earnings. In turn, the changes in the distribution of labor earnings have been caused by changes in labor supply and labor demand.

Changes in Labor Supply. The "Baby Boom" refers to the people who were born during the years of high birth rates in the United States, from 1946 to 1964. When the bulk of the Baby-Boom generation hit the labor market in the 1970s, there was a big increase in the supply of young workers, and especially of workers with a college education. This meant that the wage rates for college-educated workers tended to decline. The gap in wages between college-educated workers and high-school-educated workers fell sharply in the 1970s.

By the early 1980s, most of the Baby Boomers were already in the labor force. There was a big drop in the number of new workers with a college education. This is shown in panel (a) of Figure 15.2, on page 350, as a shift in the supply curve of college-educated workers. The supply curve shifts to the left, from S_0 to S_1. With fewer college-educated workers coming into the market, there was an increase in the wage premium for a college education. The supply shift increased the wages of college-educated workers from w_0 to w_1.

Changes in Labor Demand. At the same time that the *supply* of workers was changing, there were major changes in labor *demand*. Throughout the 1980s, there were decreases in demand for workers with only a high-school education, and for high-school dropouts. The reasons include:

- *Technological change.* For a variety of reasons, including the increasing use of computers in the workplace, there was less demand for less-skilled workers.

- *Competition from abroad.* Imports were very high during the 1980s. The American workers who were most affected were the

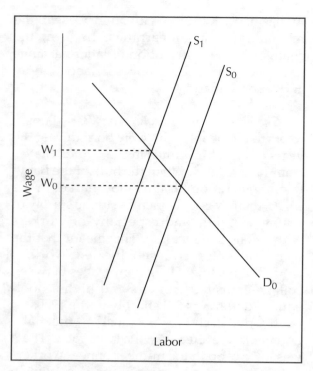

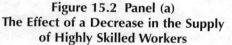

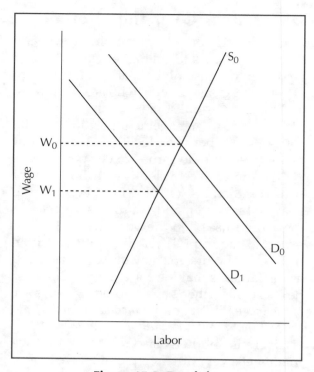

Figure 15.2 Panel (a)
**The Effect of a Decrease in the Supply
of Highly Skilled Workers**

As of 1975, the supply curve for college-educated workers is S_0. The demand curve is D_0. The equilibrium wage rate for college-educated workers is w_0. In the late 1970s and early 1980s, the rate of growth of the college-educated work force slows down greatly. This can be represented as a leftward shift in the supply curve, from S_0 to S_1. As a result, there is an increase in the equilibrium wage rate for college-educated workers, from w_0 to w_1.

Figure 15.2 Panel (b)
**The Effect of a Decrease in the Demand
for Less-Skilled Workers**

As of 1975, the demand curve for high-school-educated workers is D_0. The supply curve is S_0. The equilibrium wage rate for high-school-educated workers is w_0. In the late 1970s and early 1980s, as a result of technological changes and other forces, there is a decrease in the demand for high-school-educated workers. This can be represented as a leftward shift in the demand curve, from D_0 to D_1. As a result, there is a decrease in the equilibrium wage rate for high-school-educated workers, from w_0 to w_1.

production workers in the manufacturing industries, who tended to have only a high-school education.

- *The Shift from Manufacturing to Services.* Many of the highest-paying jobs for workers with a high-school education have been in the manufacturing sector. But the proportion of the economy that is devoted to manufacturing has been dropping for decades, and the service sector has been

increasing. As manufacturing declines, so does the number of highly paid manufacturing jobs.

All of these forces combined to decrease the demand for less-educated workers. This is shown in panel (b) of Figure 15.2 as a shift in the demand curve for high-school-educated workers. The demand curve shifts to the left, from D_0 to D_1. This leads to lower wages for these workers: Their wage drops from w_0 to w_1.

Panel (a) of Figure 15.2 shows an *increase* in the wages of college-educated workers. Panel (b) shows a *decrease* in the wages of high-school-educated workers. Taken together, these changes mean that the wage premium for a college education soared during the 1980s. This was probably the most important cause of the increase in inequality.

The Decline of Unions. As we discussed in Chapter 13, the union movement has been losing strength for many years. Since many union members have only a high-school education, the decline of unions would tend to reduce the wages of workers with a high-school educa-tion, relative to the wages of college-educated workers. The weakening of unions is proba-bly responsible for about 15 percent of the increase in the premium for a college educa-tion. Thus, the decline of unions has also con-tributed to the increase in inequality.

Reality Check: Interim Review Questions

IR15-3. Is lifetime income distributed more or less equally than annual income?

IR15-4. If there is an increase in the demand for more highly skilled workers, will earn-ings inequality increase or decrease?

THE DISTRIBUTION OF WEALTH

So far, we've studied the distribution of *income*. A household's income is the amount that it receives *over a particular period of time.* For example, consider the Olson family's income. Members of the family earned $40,000 in the labor market in 1999, and they also received $2000 of interest on a savings account. If there were no other sources of income in the year, then we would say that the family had $42,000 of income *in this particular year—1999.*

It's clearly important to study the distri-bution of income. But income isn't the only thing that we might be interested in: It's also interesting to learn about the distribution of *wealth.* A household's **wealth** is the total amount of assets that the household owns *at a particular moment in time.*

Now, consider the Olson family's wealth. First of all, the Olsons own a house. As of December 31, 1999, the net value of their stake in the house was $50,000 (after we subtract the amount they still owe on their mortgage). On that particular day, they also had checking and savings accounts, with balances of $20,000. Finally, the family owns two cars, some jew-elry, and other household items, which were then valued at $40,000. If we add together the value of the house, the checking and savings accounts, and the household items, we get $50,000 + $20,000 + $40,000 = $110,000. Assum-ing that the Olsons didn't own anything else of value, we would say that their household wealth was $110,000 *at that particular moment—December 31, 1999.*

The Highly Unequal Division of Wealth

Wealth is distributed much *more unequally than income.* The poorest half of the American pop-ulation owns almost no wealth. (In fact, the people at the very bottom have *negative* wealth, because their debts are greater than their assets.) As we move up to the middle and upper-middle classes, we see many families who have modest amounts of wealth, much of it in homes. In 1989, the poorest 80 percent of households owned only about 15 percent of the nation's wealth.

The people at the top have an extraor-dinary share of the nation's wealth. In 1989, the top five percent of wealthholders had about 61 percent of total wealth. Even more astonishing is the fact that the top one-half of one percent owned more than 31 percent of the wealth!

The Gini Ratio for wealth is usually found to be around 0.8 or 0.85. This is *far* more unequal than the Gini Ratios of about 0.4 that we saw for income.

Changes over Time in the Distribution of Wealth

Earlier, we saw that the distribution of income became more unequal during the 1980s. The same thing happened to the distribution of wealth. One study reports that the Gini Ratio for wealth was about 0.80 in 1983 (which is the same as it had been in 1962). However, the Gini had risen to 0.84 by 1989.

Table 15.2 gives some information on the changes over time in the distribution of wealth. The bottom 80 percent of wealthholders lost

more than three percentage points of the total from 1983 to 1989, while the top one-half of one percent gained more than five percentage points.

Why did the distribution of wealth become so much more unequal during the 1980s? One big reason is that stock prices grew more rapidly than home prices. This helped the rich (who have much of their wealth in stocks) relative to the middle classes (who have much of their wealth in homes).

Real Economics for Real People 15.1 takes a closer look at the top end of the wealth distribution.

Reality Check: Interim Review Question

IR15-5. Is wealth distributed more equally than income, or less equally?

POVERTY

So far, we've talked about the *entire* distribution of income and wealth. But the people at the *bottom* of the income distribution have special problems, and they deserve special attention. When we focus on the people at the bottom of the income distribution, where people may not have enough income to meet certain basic needs, we talk about *poverty*.

In the United States, poverty has an official definition, which was developed by Mol-

lie Orshansky of the Social Security Administration during the 1960s. The official "poverty threshold", or "poverty-line income" depends on family size, and it is updated every year to account for inflation. In 1998, the poverty line stood at $8316 for a one-member family, $16,660 for a four-member family, and $28,166 for an eight-member family. If your family's money income is less than the poverty line (even by one dollar), then everyone in the

	Percent of Wealth Owned by:				
Year	Lowest 20 Percent	Second-Lowest 20 Percent	Third 20 Percent	Fourth 20 Percent	Highest 20 Percent
1962	−0.7%	1.0%	5.4%	13.4%	81.0%
1983	−0.3	1.2	5.2	12.6	81.3
1989	−1.4	0.8	4.6	11.5	84.6

Table 15.2 Shares of Wealth Owned by Households in the United States, for Selected Years From 1962 to 1989

Real Economics for Real People 15.1:
The Rich, the Very Rich, and the Super-Rich

Overall, the United States is a very wealthy nation, but the distribution of that wealth is highly unequal. When we combine these two facts, it's clear that some Americans must be *very* rich. In 1998, the richest person in America was Bill Gates of Microsoft Corporation, the computer software maker. Gates's net worth was estimated to be $58 *billion*. In Table 15.3, we list the 20 Americans with the most wealth in 1998.

Some important changes in the American economy are reflected in the list of the richest 20 people. Many of these people are now from fields like computers, entertainment, and retailing, which have grown rapidly in recent years. The ranks of the very rich used to include more people from oil and heavy manufacturing, but these industries aren't as important as they once were.

The list of tycoons in Table 15.3 is just as interesting for who it doesn't include, as for who it does include. H. Ross Perot isn't on the list, and neither is Ted Turner, although it is fair to say that these gentlemen will still be able to live comfortably.

Also, no one in the top 20 is from a family that made its money more than one generation ago. Most of the people at the top are *self-made* billionaires. Many of the families that got rich long ago (such as the Rockefellers, Fords, and duPonts) are still rich, but inheritance may be slightly less important than it used to be. Inheritance is the main source of wealth for only about 80 of the 400 richest Americans. If you want to become super-rich, you're more likely to do it if you start up your own computer or entertainment firm, instead of waiting around for an inheritance from your long-lost uncle.

Table 15.3 The 20 Richest Americans in 1998

Name	Residence	Estimated Net Worth	Primary Source Of Wealth
1. William Gates III	Bellevue, Washington	$58 billion	Microsoft Corporation
2. Warren E. Buffett	Omaha, Nebraska	$29 billion	Stock-market investing
3. Paul G. Allen	Mercer Island, WA	$22 billion	Microsoft Corporation
4. Michael Dell	Austin, Texas	$13 billion	Dell Computers
5. Steven Ballmer	Bellevue, Washington	$12 billion	Microsoft Corporation
6. Alice L. Walton	Rogers, Arkansas	$11 billion	
7. Helen Walton	Bentonville, Arkansas	$11 billion	Heirs to the
8. Jim C. Walton	Bentonville, Arkansas	$11 billion	Wal-Mart retail fortune
9. John T. Walton	Durango, Colorado	$11 billion	
10. S. Robson Walton	Bentonville, Arkansas	$11 billion	
11. John Werner Kluge	Charlottesville, VA	$9.8 billion	Metromedia Corp.
12. Barbara Cox Anthony	Honolulu, Hawaii	$7.1 billion	Heirs to fortune in
13. Anne Cox Chambers	Atlanta, Georgia	$7.1 billion	publishing and television
14. Gordon Moore	Woodside, California	$7 billion	Intel Corporation
15. Sumner M. Redstone	Newton Centre, MA	$6.4 billion	Viacom, Inc.
17. Ronald O. Perelman	New York, New York	$6 billion	Leveraged buyouts
18. Rupert Murdoch	New York, New York	$5.6 billion	Publishing, television
19. Jay Pritzker	Chicago, Illinois	$5.2 billion	Real estate, manufactures
20. Robert Pritzker	Chicago, Illinois	$5.2 billion	

Source: *Forbes*, October 12, 1998.

family is classified as being poor. If your family's income is above the poverty line, then no one in the family is officially counted as poor.

Changes in the Poverty Rate Over Time

In 1959, about 39.5 million Americans fell below the poverty line. This worked out to about 22.4 percent of the population. But wages grew rapidly during the 1960s, and unemployment was low. These factors helped to pull many people out of poverty. Moreover, the late 1960s and early 1970s saw an expansion of various government programs that increased the incomes of some of the poor. Social Security expanded, and this helped to create a large reduction in the poverty rate among elderly Americans. The official poverty rate fell to its all-time low of 11.1 percent in 1973.

In the 1970s, 1980s, and early 1990s, the wages of the people at the bottom of the wage distribution did not fare as well. Because of these and other forces, the poverty rate rose. As recently as 1993, the poverty rate stood at 15.1 percent of the American population. However, the strong economic growth of the middle and late 1990s brought the poverty rate down again. In 1998, the poverty rate was 12.7 percent.

Differences in the Poverty Rate for Different Groups

The information in the preceding paragraph deals with the poverty rate *for the United States as a whole.* However, different groups within the U.S. have very different poverty rates.

Differences by Region. Table 15.4 shows that poverty is much more common in some regions of the country than in others. Because the poverty numbers for any particular State can bounce around from year, we report the average for each State for 1996–1998. In those years, the poverty rate in the District of Columbia stood at 22.7 percent, and the poverty rate was 22.4 percent in New Mexico. These rates were much higher than in New Hampshire, with a rate of 8.4 percent, or Utah, with a rate of 8.5 percent. Generally speaking, the highest concentrations of poverty are in the South and Southwest. Some of the States with the highest poverty rates are in a band that stretches from Arizona and New Mexico to Arkansas and Mississippi. The lowest poverty rates are in New England, in the middle-Atlantic region, and in the Midwest.

Differences by Race. There are also large differences in poverty rates among the different demographic groups of the United States population. Some of these differences are shown in Table 15.5. For one thing, race plays an important role. In 1998, non-Hispanic whites had a poverty rate of 8.2 percent, whereas blacks had a rate that was about three times as high, at 26.1 percent. (On a more positive note, however, this is the lowest that the poverty rate has ever been for blacks.) The poverty rate for Hispanics was 25.6 percent.

Differences by Age. Table 15.5 also shows that there are big differences in poverty rates by age. The rate for young people (below the age of 18) was 18.9 percent in 1998, which is substantially higher than the rate for the rest of the population.

The poverty rates for different age groups have changed dramatically over the years. Forty years ago, the elderly were much more likely to be in poverty. However, the 1970s brought big increases in spending on the elderly through the Social Security programs. As a result, the poverty rate for older Americans fell sharply from the late 1960s to the middle 1980s. Unfortunately, the poverty rates for the rest of the population went up during the same period.

Table 15.4 Poverty Rates by State, Averages for 1996–1998

State	Percentage of Population In Poverty	State	Percentage of Population In Poverty
Alabama	14.7%	Montana	16.4
Alaska	8.8	Nebraska	10.8
Arizona	18.1	Nevada	9.9
Arkansas	17.2	New Hampshire	8.4
California	16.3	New Jersey	9.0
Colorado	9.3	New Mexico	22.4
Connecticut	9.9	New York	16.6
Delaware	9.5	North Carolina	12.5
Dist. of Columbia	22.7	North Dakota	13.2
Florida	13.9	Ohio	11.6
Georgia	14.3	Oklahoma	14.8
Hawaii	12.3	Oregon	12.8
Idaho	13.2	Pennsylvania	11.3
Illinois	11.1	Rhode Island	11.8
Indiana	8.6	South Carolina	13.3
Iowa	9.4	South Dakota	13.0
Kansas	10.1	Tennessee	14.5
Kentucky	15.5	Texas	16.1
Louisiana	18.6	Utah	8.5
Maine	10.6	Vermont	10.6
Maryland	8.6	Virginia	11.3
Massachusetts	10.3	Washington	10.0
Michigan	10.8	West Virginia	17.6
Minnesota	9.9	Wisconsin	8.6
Mississippi	18.3	Wyoming	12.0
Missouri	10.4		
		UNITED STATES AVERAGE	13.2

Table 15.5 Poverty Rates for Different Demographic Groups, 1998

Group	Percent In Poverty
Entire Population	12.7%
Non-Hispanic Whites	8.2
Blacks	26.1
Hispanics	25.6
Aged under 18	18.9
Aged 18–64	10.5
Aged 65 and over	10.5
Female-headed families	29.9
Married-couple families	5.3

Differences by Family Structure. One of the biggest changes in American society in the last generation has been the increase in the number of female-headed families. These families have always had relatively high poverty rates. Consequently, the rise in the number of female-headed families is one reason why poverty rates have increased. From 1970 to 1992, the number of poor people in female-headed families went up by about six million. This is sometimes called the *"feminization of poverty"*.

Problems with the Poverty Statistics

When it calculates the official poverty rate, the government uses some problematic assumptions.

In-Kind Income. One of the biggest problems with the official definition of poverty is that it only counts *cash* income. But many low-income people receive *"in-kind"* assistance (that is, assistance that doesn't come in the form of cash). Millions of low-income families receive in-kind income such as food stamps, Medicaid, Medicare, or subsidized housing, but the government does not count these forms of assistance when it decides whether a family is below the poverty line.

By ignoring in-kind income, the official poverty rate would tend to *overstate* the true amount of poverty. Some estimates suggest that the poverty rate would fall to less than 10 percent, if we were to include income in-kind. In other words, there may be several million Americans who are officially counted as poor, but who aren't *really* poor because of their in-kind income.

We need to keep in mind that the official poverty numbers *do* include cash transfers from the government, such as Social Security, unemployment benefits, and cash welfare payments. If it weren't for these payments, the poverty rate would be much higher. About 15 million Americans are kept out of poverty by cash transfers.

Under-reporting. The official poverty rate is based on a survey in which people are asked about their incomes. But it appears that many people don't report their full incomes on the survey, either because they want to hide income from illegal sources, or because they've forgotten about some of their income. Since the official poverty rate doesn't adjust for under-reporting, it would once again tend to *overstate* the true amount of poverty.

Overstating the Rate of Inflation. The poverty-line income is adjusted each year, to account for inflation. In principle, this is a good idea. However, the adjustment is done on the basis of the Consumer Price Index (CPI). For a variety of reasons, the CPI tends to overstate the true rate of inflation. An influential commission, headed by Stanford's Michael Boskin, concluded that the CPI may overstate inflation by as much as 1.1 percentage points per year. As a result, the poverty-line income is increased by more than is really necessary. This means that a standard of living that was above the poverty line in the past might be judged to be below the poverty line now. Therefore, there is a tendency for the CPI to lead to an overstatement of the poverty rate.

Income Mobility. Consider the Jackson family, who have never been in poverty. This year, however, Mr. Jackson is laid off from his job for four months. During that time, the Jacksons draw upon their savings, so that they consume just as much as they did when Mr. Jackson was working. They stay in the same apartment, and they eat the same food as before. Their lifestyle is unchanged. According to the official statistics, the Jacksons are poor this year, because their income falls below the poverty line this year. But are the Jacksons really poor?

As a result of under-reporting and income mobility, the *spending* of some families will be more than the poverty level, even though their *income* is below the poverty line. In fact, many low-income families spend twice as much as their income. For the 20 percent of the population with the lowest incomes, the share of *spending* is nearly twice as great as the share of *income*. This once again suggests that the official poverty rate may *overstate* the true amount of poverty.

Missing Persons. Each of the above points suggests that the official numbers *overstate* the number of Americans who are really poor.

However, one important factor works in the opposite direction. The Census Bureau's survey does a poor job of finding homeless people. By undercounting these people, the official statistics will tend to *understate* the true extent of poverty.

On balance, it appears that the official poverty statistics overstate the "true" poverty rate. Even if we were to adjust the official statistics in all of these ways, however, we would still find that more than 20 million Americans are in poverty, and many more are not far above the poverty line. The war on poverty isn't over. In the next few sections, we will take a look at some of the policies that have been used to fight poverty, and we'll think about how these policies could be improved.

As we said a few paragraphs ago, the poverty statistics are influenced by homelessness. The homeless population is interesting and important for other reasons, as well. We discuss homelessness in *Real Economics for Real People 15.2.*

Reality Check: Interim Review Questions

IR15-6. In calculating the official poverty statistics for households, the government ignores in-kind income (such as food stamps). Does this lead the official poverty rate to be biased? If so, is the official rate an overstatement or an understatement of the "true" rate?

IR15-7. In which region of the country does poverty tend to be highest?

IR15-8. Is poverty among the elderly higher or lower than poverty among the young?

Real Economics for Real People 15.2: The Problem of Homelessness

The poverty of the homeless appears to be even more desperate than the poverty of others. This may explain the fact that homelessness has received more attention in recent years.

For obvious reasons, it's very hard to get a good count of the homeless population. It's easy for the Census Bureau to miss people who are living in abandoned cars. Nevertheless, government agencies and private organizations have tried to count the homeless. The best estimates are that somewhere between 200,000 and 600,000 Americans are homeless at any one time. These numbers range from less than one-tenth of one percent of the American population, up to about one-quarter of one percent of the population.

However, the homeless population changes over time. Some homeless people find homes, while some people lose their homes and become homeless. Even though only a few hundred thousand people are homeless at any one time, it's possible that a few million may be homeless at one time or another, in any given year.

Why are these people without shelter? There are many reasons, but here is a partial list:

- Mental illness. In 1955, the public mental hospitals in the United States had 559,000 patients. However, thousands of mental patients were released in the 1960s. By 1978, only 150,000 patients were still in mental hospitals.

The movement toward releasing mental patients was based on good intentions. The idea was that the mentally ill could receive better treatment if they were in community-based treatment centers. Unfortunately, these centers were often funded poorly, and were not always able to provide the necessary care. As a result, many people with a history of mental problems ended up on the streets.

- Drug and alcohol abuse. Some studies report that as many as 70 percent of the homeless are abusers of alcohol or other drugs. People with serious substance-abuse problems often find it difficult to hold a job. In addition, the small amounts of money that they do have may be drained away by drugs.

When mental illness combines with drug addiction, the results can be especially frightening. One well-publicized case is Larry Hogue, the "wild man of 96th street". Mr. Hogue is addicted to crack cocaine. When he takes crack, he becomes psychotic, and terrorizes his neighborhood in New York City. He has been hospitalized for psychiatric care on more than 40 occasions. Each time, however, he returns to the streets.

- Low wages, high unemployment, and declining transfers. During the 1980s, wages fell for low-skill workers (especially for high-school dropouts), and unemployment rose. We would expect this to increase homelessness, unless incomes were supplemented by govern-ment transfer payments. But more than 80 percent of homeless people are men, and non-elderly men are the least likely to receive transfer payments, since they aren't eligible for some welfare programs.

- Lack of low-income housing. Urban renewal projects often mean that housing units are replaced by office buildings. These projects led to the destruction of more than a million rental units across the country during the 1970s and 1980s. In addition, the housing aid budget for the Federal Department of Housing and Urban Development fell during the 1980s. This forced the government to reduce its support for low-income rental units.

It should be clear that homelessness has many causes. Because of this, any serious attack on homelessness will need to address many causes at once. More housing projects may help, but they can't be the entire solution. It's probably best not to think of homelessness as merely a housing problem. If homelessness is to be reduced very much, it will be necessary to deal directly with the problems of untreated mental illness, untreated substance abuse, and low earnings.

POLICIES TO REDUCE POVERTY

Transfer payments are payments to people who do not provide any services in return. Many transfer payments are specifically targeted at low-income people. Even when transfer payments aren't aimed directly at the poor, they still may reduce poverty.

Governments in the United States spend more than a trillion dollars every year on transfers, which is a lot of money. Table 15.6 shows where some of the money goes. The table shows the estimated expenditures on various Federal-government programs, for 1998. This is not an absolutely complete list of all transfer-payment programs. (For example, the table excludes a number of Federal programs for Veterans. Also, Table 15.6 only includes Federal programs, and it is important to note that State and local governments spent about $235 billion on transfer-payment programs in 1998.) However, Table 15.6 does include all of the most important programs at the Federal level.

One thing stands out when we look at Table

Table 15.6 Federal Government Expenditures on Selected Transfer Payment Programs, 1996

Programs for the Elderly

Social Security	$328.9 billion
Medicare	193.7 billion
Total for these Programs	*$522.6 billion*

Programs for Non-Elderly Workers Who Are Out of Work

Disability Insurance	$48.4 billion
Unemployment Compensation	19.6 billion
Total for these Programs	*$68.0 billion*

Programs for Those with Low Incomes

Medicaid	$99.6 billion
Supplemental Security Income for aged and disabled poor	26.0 billion
Food Stamps	24.9 billion
Earned Income Tax Credit	23.2 billion
Temporary Assistance to Needy Families	18.6 billion
Housing programs	17.4 billion
Child Nutrition Programs	8.0 billion
Women, Infants, and Children Nutrition Program	3.9 billion
Low-income Home Energy Assistance	1.2 billion
Total for these Programs	*$222.8 billion*

Source: *Budget of the United States Government, Fiscal Year 2000.*

15.6. The Federal government spends much more on programs for elderly people (regardless of whether they are poor) than on programs targeted at the poor. The *Social Security* retirement program in the United States is the largest domestic spending program in the world, with well over $300 billion per year in spending. The rapidly growing *Medicare* program provides the elderly with an additional $200 billion per year for medical expenses. By contrast, transfer programs for the non-elderly poor are far less generous. Therefore, it's no wonder that transfer-payment programs do far more to reduce the poverty rate for the elderly than for the rest of the population.

Effects of Transfer Programs: The Equality/Efficiency Tradeoff

In our chapter on labor supply, we saw that transfer payments cause people to work less.

This means that, when $1000 is given to a poor person, the person's income will go up by *less* than $1000, because the person will work less.

Let's say that the government collects $1000 of taxes from Aaron (who has a high income), and pays the money to Zack (who has a low income). As a result of this government grant, Zack works less. In addition, low-income workers like Zack often face extremely high tax rates, which would also cause a reduction in work. If Zack's earnings in the labor market go down by $333, then his income has only gone up by ($1000 − $333) = $667, even though Aaron's income went down by the full $1000.

In other words, Aaron's loss is (1000/667) = 1.5 times as much as Zachary's gain. The true cost of the transfer is 1.5 times as great as the amount by which the poor person's income was increased. Economists have estimated that the loss to those who pay for transfer payments may be substantially greater than the gains for those who receive the transfer payments.

The Future of the Fight Against Poverty

How can we change American society, in order to reduce the rate of poverty? This has been a hot topic for years, and it will continue to be a hot topic in the future. Because poverty has many causes, there is no one change that will magically cure all of our problems. In the next few paragraphs, we outline some important ways of keeping the poverty rate down. Some of these involve government policies, but some also include changes in people's attitudes and behavior.

Sound Macroeconomic Policies. Low unemployment is one of the best anti-poverty programs. The poverty rate always rises during a recession, and falls during an economic expansion. No matter what transfer payments are used, it will be easier to rely on jobs to reduce poverty (rather than on unemployment benefits).

Responsible Parenting. By the early 1990s, over one million children per year were being born out of wedlock in the United States. Illegitimate births now account for about 30 percent of all births. The poverty rates for female-headed households are very high, which means that the increase in out-of-wedlock births is a sure prescription for poverty.

In order to discourage illegitimacy, some State governments have established new rules, under which a woman won't get any additional welfare payments if she has an additional child while on welfare. It's too early to say how much effect these changes will have. However, by themselves, these rules probably will not be enough to fix the problem. Throughout history, the greatest discouragement to illegitimate births was the disapproval

of others in the community. It appears that the social stigma associated with out-of-wedlock motherhood has been greatly reduced. If illegitimacy is greeted with social approval, the policies of the government may not make much difference.

The last few paragraphs have focused on the behavior of mothers. But, of course, fathers bear just as much responsibility. One big problem is that of the "Deadbeat Dads"—fathers who skip out on their child-support payments. In recent years, the Federal government and many State governments have tried (with some success) to increase their enforcement of the child-support laws. Still, millions of fathers are delinquent in their payments. One of the problems is that the court system is a clumsy place in which to handle child support. In the future, we can expect that child-support payments will increasingly be taken care of as an automatic payroll deduction.

Encouragement of Work. If well-paying jobs are available, most people will choose to work. Education and training are the key to getting people into good jobs.

But what about the people with the least skills, for whom good jobs are hard to find? In trying to help these people out of poverty, American governments give them cash, food stamps, Medicaid, and subsidized housing. All of these will reduce labor supply. In addition, if the poor do earn any money of their own, the earnings are taxed at very high rates. These high tax rates will also reduce labor supply. It should be no surprise that many poor people don't work very much.

And yet, the political debate is often full of talk about "lazy welfare chiselers". Having given the poor a set of severe disincentives for working, it's ironic that the rest of the population seems to be upset that the poor do not work more.

From the perspective of economics, it would make more sense to provide the poor with better work incentives. Instead of giving them cash and *taxing* them at high rates, it would work better to *subsidize the wages* of the poor. In the United States, the largest attempt to do this is the **Earned Income Tax Credit** (EITC). The EITC increases the wages for people in families with very low incomes. However, the EITC gets phased out for lower-middle-income families. Thus, the EITC will provide work *incentives* for some workers, but work *disincentives* for others. The EITC appears to increase work by some workers, but it decreases work for others. Overall, these increases and decreases probably come close to balancing out.

Thus, the EITC is no magical cure-all. But at least it's better than most other transfer payment programs.

Finding Better Ways to Provide for Retirement. The good news is that Social Security and other transfer payments lift millions of elderly Americans out of poverty. The bad news is that, *without* these transfers, more than half of the elderly population would be below the poverty line. This suggests that the poverty rate would continue to fall, if ordinary citizens would do more to save for their *own* retirements.

Today's policy debates include proposals to strengthen the incentives for retirement saving. These proposals include expanded tax credits for saving, as well as fundamental changes in the Social Security program. We'll talk more about some of the possibilities in the next chapter. But we must keep in mind that it isn't just up to the government. Whatever the government policies may be, individual families bear most of the responsibility for saving. In order to increase the saving rate by a lot, it will take more than sound government policies: It will take a cultural change toward more patience, more planning, and a greater ability to delay gratification.

Regardless of the level of saving, it is also true that our Social Security expenditures are not targeted very precisely. Hundreds of billions of dollars are paid every year to the affluent elderly. If we were to take the same amount of money, and aim it more precisely at those who are elderly and *poor,* we would get a much greater reduction in the poverty rate.

Real Economics for Real People 15.3, on p.362, takes a closer look at the Food Stamps program, which is one of the most important transfer programs for the non-elderly.

ECONOMICS AND YOU: WELFARE REFORM

The Aid to Families with Dependent Children program (AFDC) was created in the 1930s. It provided a Federal guarantee for female-headed households. The level of benefits varied widely from State to State, but families could not be denied benefits, as long as they met certain requirements.

In the 1960s, participation in the AFDC program soared, from less than 2 percent of the population to more than 5 percent. There was a widespread perception that the program was encouraging women to have children out of wedlock, and that it was discouraging work. Many taxpayers feared that AFDC was creat-ing a permanent "underclass", consisting of people with little incentive to work, and every incentive to remain dependent on government assistance. These concerns led to much political pressure for welfare reform. In the early 1990s, the Federal government granted "waivers" to many of the States. These welfare waivers allowed the States to experiment with different rules for the AFDC program. Many of the waivers allowed States to require AFDC recipients to work or go to school, in order to continue to receive benefits.

This movement culminated in the passage of a new Federal law in August, 1996. The

Real Economics for Real People 15.3:
The Black Market in Food Stamps

The *Food Stamps* program is a big one: In 1996, food stamps were received by about 27 million low-income Americans, or about 10 percent of the population, and the Federal government spent about $27 billion per year on the program. Over the years, this big program has developed some big problems.

The people who receive food stamps are only supposed to be able to redeem them for certain foods. Liquor, tobacco, and nonfood items are supposedly illegal. However, food stamps are circulated so widely that they have become a sort of second currency. In one case, a buyer in New Jersey used $30,000 in food stamps toward the purchase of a home.

But another type of fraud is even more widespread. In many cases, retail grocery stores buy the food stamps for cash, at less than face value. Then, the retailers redeem the stamps from the government at full face value. It is estimated that the government loses $1 billion per year to this type of fraud.

How can a retailer buy food stamps at less than face value? In other words, how can a store buy a $10 food-stamps coupon for only $7? It must be that the food stamps aren't worth their full face value to the person who received them.

Most low-income households are happy to use food stamps up to a point. However, eventually, the family may say "We've bought enough food this month, but the kids need new shoes." If the family can't use the food stamps to buy shoes, it may prefer to sell the stamps for cash, even if it doesn't receive the full face value of the stamps.

More than 200,000 retailers are authorized to accept food stamps. A few have been sent to jail for fraud. However, because of the large numbers involved, it isn't easy to track down fraud in the food-stamps program. The Department of Agriculture (which administers the program) is now cooperating with the Internal Revenue Service, in an attempt to improve law enforcement. The Agriculture Department also hopes that it can cut down on fraud by using a new electronic system, which would reduce the need for paper stamps.

Of course, none of these enforcement measures would be necessary if the low-income people were given cash, instead of food stamps. So why does the government give people food stamps, instead of cash? The reason is that there is a desire to keep the low-income population from using transfer payment dollars to buy liquor or cigarettes or movie tickets. For better or worse, however, it appears that this effort to restrict the choices of low-income people is not highly successful.

Finally, we should mention one other difficulty with the food-stamps program. In order to use food stamps, it is necessary to hand the stamps to the grocery clerk. It's hard to do this in secret. As a result, the person who uses food stamps must publicly reveal his or her poverty. This is embarrassing to many people. According to one study, only about 59 percent of the eligible people were actually participating in the food-stamps program. In other words, something like 18 million Americans do not participate in the program, even though they are legally entitled to do so. In some cases, these people may simply not know about the program. in other cases, however, the stigma may keep people from using food stamps.

Personal Responsibility and Work Opportunity Reconciliation Act (PRWORA) removed the Federal guarantee of benefits, and replaced it with a series of block grants to the States. The total amount of the block grants was smaller than the amount that had previously been provided by the Federal government, so that it is expected that overall spending will be reduced. PRWORA also required that, in most cases, poor adults should be required to find a job within two years of receiving aid. The law also established a five-year limit on aid coming from Federal block grants. Another important provision of the new law was a set of requirements for unmarried teenaged mothers. Those below the age of 18 are now usually required to live with an adult and attend school, if they are to receive benefits.

When PRWORA was passed, some analysts suggested that the new law would have catastrophic results, pushing a million children into poverty. At least for now, however, those dire predictions have not come true. The welfare rolls were reduced dramatically in the second half of the 1990s. From 1994 to 1999, the total number of welfare recipients fell from about 12 million to about 7 million. In spite of the reduced number of people receiving benefits, the poverty rate has continued to fall. Recent research indicates that welfare households have had *increased* incomes, on average. However, the increased income has not come mainly from increased earnings for mothers. Instead, other members of the household have increased their earnings. In many cases, these other household members are the boyfriends of welfare recipients.

It appears that welfare waivers and PRWORA have helped to reduce the number of people on welfare. However, it is important to remember that these changes were made during a time of strong growth in the overall economy. Jobs are plentiful and unemployment is down. Consequently, much of the improvement is due to the strong economy, rather than to the welfare reforms. The real test of the welfare reforms will occur when a recession throws large numbers of people out of work.

Chapter Summary

1. The Lorenz Curve shows the amount of income that is received by each portion of the population. If income were distributed completely equally, the Lorenz Curve would be an upward-sloping, straight line. In reality, however, income is distributed unequally, so that the slope of the Lorenz Curve increases as we move to the right.

2. The Gini Ratio is the best-known measure of inequality. If income were distributed completely equally, the Gini Ratio would be zero. If income were distributed extremely unequally, the Ratio would approach one. For the United States, the Gini Ratio is about 0.45. The developed countries of Europe tend to have lower Ginis than does the U.S. (that is, these countries are *more equal*), while the poorer countries of Asia, Africa, and Latin American tend to have higher Ginis (that is, they are *more unequal*).

3. Part of the inequality that we observe is due to age differences. The Gini Ratio for *lifetime* income is substantially lower than the Gini Ratio for *annual* income.

4. The income distribution in the United States has become more unequal since the 1970s. A major force behind this change is that the wage premium received by workers with a college education has gone up sharply, due to changes in the supply and demand for different kinds of labor. The decline of trade unions has also contributed to the increase in inequality.

5. Wealth is distributed much more unequally than income. The Gini Ratio for wealth is about 0.8 or 0.85.

6. The official definition of poverty depends on family size, and it is adjusted over time to account for inflation. The poverty rate fell dramatically until about 1973, when it reached 11.1 percent. During much of the period from the early 1970s to the early 1990s, the economy grew relatively slowly, and poverty rates were higher. However, as a result of the robust growth of the economy in the late 1990s, the poverty rate fell to 12.7% by 1998.

7. Different groups within the population have different poverty rates. Poverty rates tend to be highest in the South and Southwest. Poverty is more prevalent among blacks and Hispanics than among whites. Poverty rates for the elderly have fallen a great deal since the 1960s, so that the poverty rate among the elderly is now lower than average, and much less than the rate for young people. Female-headed families have high poverty rates, as do families with large numbers of children.

8. If we are to keep the poverty rate low in the future, it will be necessary to address a number of problems. First, it will be important to keep unemployment low. Second, we will need a productive, well-educated population, in order to get well-paying jobs. Third, it will be important to reverse the trend toward out-of-wedlock births and the growth of single-parent families. Fourth, we will need to improve our system of child-support payments. Fifth, instead of taxing the poor at high rates, it would be better to provide them with work incentives. This is currently done through the Earned Income Tax Credit. Sixth, poverty rates among the elderly can be reduced further if people will save more while they are young. Seventh, billions of dollars in transfer payments go to those who are not poor. If these dollars were to be concentrated on the poor, it might be possible to achieve further reductions in the poverty rate.

Key Terms

Lorenz Curve

Line of Equality

Gini Ratio, or Gini Coefficient, or Gini Index

Wealth

Poverty

Feminization of Poverty

In-Kind Income

Transfer Payments

Social Security

Medicare

Earned Income Tax Credit

Food Stamps

Questions and Problems

QP15-1. Lorenzo's income is $100, Melissa's is $200, Nancy's is $300, and Oliver's is $400. Draw the Lorenz curve for the incomes of these four people.

QP15-2. Calculate the Gini Ratio for the Lorenz curve in the previous question. HINT: The area between the Lorenz Curve and the Line of Equality can be calculated by adding together the areas of several rectangles and triangles. The area of a rectangle is the base times the height. The area of a triangle is one-half times the base times the height.

QP15-3. We have seen that wealth is distributed very unequally. The Federal estate tax can be seen as an attempt to reduce this inequality. In fact, however, rich people can usually avoid paying very much estate tax, if they plan ahead. Should the estate tax be made stronger or weaker? Should its rates be higher or lower, or should they stay the same? If the estate tax rates are

raised, do you think that people will choose to leave smaller estates?

QP15-4. One reason why the estate tax is so easy to avoid is that it is only collected once for every person, at the end of life. In an attempt to avoid this problem, some of the European countries have a small tax on wealth every year. What are the positives and negatives associated with this type of tax?

QP15-5. If you were the ruler of the world, and if you could choose any distribution of income, how much inequality would you choose? Would you want a Gini Ratio of about 0.4 or so (like we have in the United States now), or would you prefer 0.3, or 0.2, or 0.5? What about a Gini Ratio of 0.0? If the Gini Ratio were to be reduced to a very low level, it would be necessary to have much higher tax rates than we have now. What effects do you think that these higher tax rates would have on the economy?

QP15-6. Birth rates have risen in the last few years. Because of this, what do you think will happen to the wage rates of new college graduates, 20 years from now?

QP15-7. Briefly list and discuss the most important causes of income inequality. How have each of these causes changed in the last few decades?

QP15-8. Beethoven, Mozart, and Tchaikowsky, as well as many other famous musicians, were supported in their work by very rich people. The same goes for famous artists, such as Michelangelo and Leonardo. If the distribution of income had been dramatically more equal, there might not have been anyone rich enough to support artists such as these. Does this imply that society ought not to pursue equality too far?

QP15-9. Should society strive to provide equal *opportunity*, or equal *incomes*? Which would be associated with a higher Gini Ratio?

QP15-10. What are the pluses and minuses associated with the Food Stamp program? Would it be better to give cash to the people who currently receive food stamps?

Would it be better to give cash to the people who currently live in subsidized low-income housing? What about those who currently receive subsidized medical care through the Medicare and Medicaid programs?

Chapter 16

Public Goods, Government Spending, and Taxation

ECONOMICS AND YOU:
WILL SOCIAL SECURITY BE THERE WHEN YOU RETIRE?

The Old Age and Survivors Insurance system, better known as Social Security, was established in 1935. At first, the system was modest in size. Since then, however, it has grown into the largest program of government-provided cash payments in the history of the world. In Chapter 15, we saw that the Social Security system was paying out well over $300 billion per year by 1998.

In spite of the fact that the Social Security program is very popular, it does face a number of problems. The biggest problem is that the system will probably run out of money in the 2030s, unless the law is changed. Over the long run, the scheduled tax rates aren't high enough to pay for the benefits that have been promised by law. According to the latest projections, people born after the late 1960s will not be eligible to collect full benefits from Social Security until after it goes broke, unless changes are made in the program.

One part of the problem is that the "Baby Boom" generation (consisting of Americans born between 1946 and 1964) will start to retire in 2008. This will cause a rapid increase in the number of retired people. When there are

more retirees, the financial resources of the Social Security system will be stretched. However, the funding problems will continue even after the Baby Boomers are gone. This is because life expectancies are projected to continue to increase. Longer lifespans mean longer retirements, and this puts a strain on the Social Security system.

If Social Security were to run out of funds, it would be a major political disaster. Consequently, it's likely that some changes will eventually be made in the law. But which changes should be made, and who will make the decisions? These questions are somewhat different from many of the questions that we have asked in earlier chapters. In most of this book, we have concentrated on the decisions of individual households and business firms. But Social Security is a government program, and decisions regarding this system are made by elected officials and bureaucrats, rather than by households and firms.

In this chapter, the focus is on government spending, and on the taxes that are used to finance that spending. You will begin by learning about the reasons for the existence of government programs. Then, there is a discussion of the actual trends in various categories of government spending. Later in the chapter, you will read about taxes. You will learn to think about the effects of taxes on the efficiency of the private market economy, and you will also learn about how taxes affect the distribution of income. At the end of this chapter, we will return to the question of Social Security's future.

WHY DO WE NEED A GOVERNMENT?

Throughout this book, we have emphasized the virtues of the private market economy. Private markets often move quickly to deliver goods and services. When the markets are competitive, consumers can attain maximum satisfaction.

If private markets are so wonderful, then who needs a government? For one thing, governments are needed to assure that the private economy will function smoothly. Private producers and consumers rely on contracts, and it's necessary to have a system of laws and courts, so contracts can be enforced.

Beyond the need for a legal system, however, there are some important situations in which it may be necessary to rely on governments. First of all, there is a role for government in providing "public goods", which are consumed by many people at the same time. Secondly, the private market economy may give rise to a distribution of income that many people consider unacceptable. Thus, there may be a role for government in using taxes and transfer payments to affect the distribution of income. The purpose of this section is to discuss public goods and income distribution in detail.

Public Goods

Earlier in this book, you have studied imperfect competition, which is an important type of *market failure*. In this chapter, you will study another type of market failure, known as *public goods*. We discuss the characteristics of a public good below. Whenever there is a market failure, it's possible that a government may be able to intervene, in order to improve the workings of the market. (However, there is no guarantee that government programs will always improve the situation, especially if the programs are designed poorly, or if they are associated with political corruption.)

What would happen if BoomBoom Corporation were to put on a fireworks show on the Fourth of July? In order to cover its costs, the company would have to charge admission. But this presents a problem: Fireworks explode high in the sky, which means that they can be seen over a wide area. If BoomBoom Corp. were to send up the fireworks over the local stadium, and charge admission to enter the stadium, who would pay? Lots of people would probably decide to sit outside the stadium. In this way, they can enjoy the fireworks without having to pay.

Because of this problem, it's very difficult for any private company to make money by putting on a fireworks show. There are some exceptions, but most fireworks shows are sponsored by governments.

Nonrival Consumption. The fireworks show illustrates some important characteristics of public goods. First of all, the fireworks show can be enjoyed by many people at the same time. In other words, when I enjoy the show, it doesn't decrease your enjoyment of the same show. If many people can enjoy a good at the same time, consumption of the good is *nonrival*.

Nonrival consumption does not apply in the case of a *private good*. One example of a private good is a pair of socks. If I wear a particular pair of socks, there is no way that anyone else can wear that same pair of socks at the same time. For a private good like a pair of socks, we say that consumption is *rival*.

Costly Exclusion and the Free-Rider Problem. Another feature of the fireworks show is that it is hard to exclude people from enjoying the show, even if they do not pay. In a case like this, we say that consumption is characterized by *costly exclusion*, or *nonexcludability*. This is an extremely important problem. If private producers aren't able to collect money from the people who enjoy a good or service, then the private producers won't be able to stay in business. If private producers can't exclude those who don't pay, then private markets are certain to fail. When nonexcludable goods are produced at all, it will be necessary for governments to do the producing.

Costly exclusion leads to another problem for public goods. If people know that they can see the fireworks show (even if they don't pay), then they don't have any incentive to reveal whether they really want to see the show. Let's say that private producers are unable to put on a fireworks show in the town of Jonesville, USA, because of the problem of costly exclusion. As a result, the City Council is thinking of putting on a fireworks show. The Council asks residents whether they would be willing to pay higher taxes, in order to support a show. Many residents of Jonesville may say that they aren't willing to pay (even when they really are willing to pay), because they believe that someone else will eventually foot the bill. This is called the *free-rider problem*. For a nonexcludable public good, people have an incentive to be "free riders", by understating their true preferences for the public good. As a result, it will be hard to determine the amount of public good that would be best for society.

More Examples of Public Goods. Defense against nuclear attack is a classic example of a public good. If the Defense Department is able to protect you from nuclear attack, it must also be able to protect everyone within many miles of you. Therefore, missile defense is nonrival. At the same time, missile defense is also nonexcludable. It's impossible to protect Joe Jones (who paid his taxes) without also protecting Sam Smith (even though Sam didn't pay his taxes). Missile defense is a "pure" public good, because it is completely nonrival and nonexcludable.

At the other extreme are the pure private goods, such as socks. Pure private goods are completely rival and excludable. In between, there are goods that are somewhat public, but not as much so as national defense. For example, for a fireworks show, it's difficult to exclude those who do not pay, but it may not be absolutely impossible to do so. The same goes for parks, lakes, and other recreational facilities. Police protection, fire protection, and vaccination programs all have a substantial degree of nonrivalry and nonexcludability, but not as much as national defense.

Higher education has fairly low costs of exclusion, since it's hard to receive a college degree unless you enroll, and it's hard to enroll unless you pay. However, higher education is partly nonrival, since an education may provide some benefits for the entire society, and not just for the individual student.

These examples show that many goods are neither pure private goods nor pure public goods. For the pure private goods, it's best to use private markets. For the pure public goods, such as national defense, it will be necessary to rely on government. The in-between goods will have to be taken on a case-by-case basis. For example, in most States, governments pay for virtually all of the expenses of elementary and secondary education. Presumably, this is because of the belief that a large part of the benefits from a basic education are enjoyed by society as a whole, and not just by the individual. (In other words, there is a big element of "publicness" to elementary and secondary education.) However, governments pay for a smaller portion of the costs of college education. This is probably because of the belief that the individual captures a much larger part of the benefits of higher education. (In other words, higher education is less of a public good than is elementary education, even though both types of education have a degree of publicness.)

The "Demand" for Public Goods

In an earlier chapter, it was seen that the market demand curve for a private good is derived by adding the individual demand curves together. In a competitive market, every consumer faces the same price, but different consumers may choose different quantities. In graphical terms, the individual demand curves are added horizontally, in order to get the market demand curve.

Because pure public goods are characterized by nonrival consumption, it is necessary to use a different technique to evaluate the "demand" for public goods. In the case of a pure public good, every consumer receives the same quantity. However, different consumers may be willing to pay different amounts of money for the public goods that they receive.

Figure 16.1 shows the "willingness-to-pay" curves of Attila and Bartholomew, regarding the quantities of nuclear missiles. These are marked as WTP_A for Attila, and WTP_B for Bartholomew. For each individual, the willingness-to-pay curve for a public good shows the maximum amount that he is willing to pay for one additional missile, depending on the number of missiles that are already in place. Basically, these individual willingness-to-pay curves give the same information that would be given by the demand curve for a private good.

However, the method of adding the individual curves together is different for public goods than it was for private goods. For

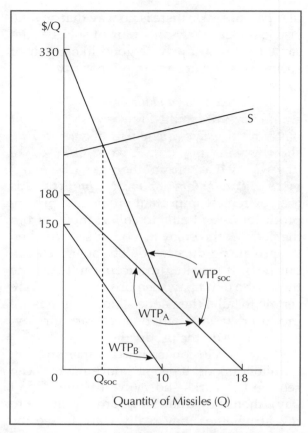

Figure 16.1 The Willingness-to-Pay Curve, or "Demand" Curve, for a Pure Public Good

Missile defense is a pure public good. Attila's willingness-to-pay curve (or demand curve) for missiles is WTP_A. Bartholomew's willingness-to-pay curve is WTP_B. We add them vertically to get WTP_{soc}, which is the willingness-to-pay curve for the entire two-person society. The optimal number of missiles is found by locating the intersection of WTP_{soc} with the supply curve, S.

private goods, everyone pays the same price. Therefore, the procedure is to pick a price, and add all of the individual demands horizontally. For pure public goods, on the other hand, everyone receives the same quantity. The procedure is to pick a quantity, and add all of the individual willingness-to-pay curves vertically. It is said that society's willingness-to-pay curve is drawn by *vertical summation* of the individual willingness-to-pay curves.

In Figure 16.1, society's willingness-to-pay curve is WTP_{soc}. When there are more than 10 missiles, Bartholomew isn't willing to pay anything for any more missiles. Therefore, when there are more than 10 missiles, the willingness-to-pay curve for this two-person society (WTP_{soc}) is exactly the same as Attila's willingness to pay (WTP_a). When the quantity of missiles is less than 10, WTP_{soc} is drawn by adding WTP_a and WTP_b vertically. For example, when the quantity of missiles falls all the way to zero, Attila is willing to pay $180 for a missile, and Bartholomew is willing to pay $150. Adding these two together, we get a total willingness to pay of $330.

It is possible, *in theory*, to identify the optimal level of a public good. The optimal quantity of a public good is found at the intersection of the social willingness-to-pay curve with the supply curve. In Figure 16.1, the supply curve is S, and the socially optimal quantity of missiles is Q_{soc}.

However, there is one other important difference between the demand for private goods and the "demand" for public goods. Demands are revealed very well in private markets. As a result, private markets tend to reach equilibrium quickly and efficiently. Unfortunately, it's different for public goods. In the "market" for public goods, the free-rider problem means that people have an incentive to conceal their true preferences. Thus, *in practice*, it will be very difficult for society to figure out what Q_{soc} should be.

Since people don't have an incentive to reveal their true preferences for public goods, there is no mechanism that will quickly lead society to the optimal level of a public good. Instead, society has to rely on the political process. In the search for the correct level of a public good, society has to rely on politicians, bureaucrats, lobbyists, and other such folks. There is no guarantee that the political process will find the optimal level of a public good. Depending on a number of factors, the political system might choose too much of a public good, or too little.

Income Distribution

Even if there were no public goods, and even if there were no market failures of any kind, the government might still have an important role to play. This is because there's no guarantee that private markets will produce a distribution of income that is considered "fair". Markets reward people on the basis of the resources that they own: Highly skilled people tend to earn higher wages and salaries, and wealthy people tend to earn more interest, dividends, royalties, and so on. Since markets don't account for fairness, it would be an accident if the market economy were to provide a "fair" distribution of income.

As was mentioned in Chapter 15, most countries use taxes and transfer payments, in an attempt to equalize the distribution of income. In the United States, governments spend more than one trillion dollars ($1,000,000,000,000) on transfer-payment programs every year. These include Social Security, Medicare, Medicaid, Food Stamps, welfare programs, and many other programs. Some of these transfer payments go to very affluent people, but most of them go to lower-income people. On average, transfer payments do reduce the inequality in the income distribution.

Once again, the amount of spending on transfers is decided upon by governments, and not by private markets. Most people won't give up their incomes voluntarily. As a result, governments are in charge of paying transfer payments, and collecting the taxes that are needed to finance them.

through the government? What about child-care services? What about retirement pensions for government workers?

TRENDS IN GOVERNMENT SPENDING

The previous section describes some of the reasons why it might be desirable to have a government. However, in order to understand government fully, it's necessary to know about the *actual* spending of governments. How many dollars do governments really spend? Which government programs have grown, and which have shrunk? Without an understanding of the actual spending levels, any discussion of government spending will be left in a theoretical vacuum.

In this section, we will describe some of the trends in government spending in the United States. We begin with the Federal government, and we then move on to the State and local governments. Finally, there is a brief comparison between the spending levels in the United States and the spending levels in some other countries.

Federal Government Spending

In 1999, the Federal government in the United States spent about $1.7 trillion. (That's $1,700,000,000,000.) This works out to about 19 percent of gross domestic product (GDP).

The Federal government's share of output has not always been so large. Back in 1799, the Federal government spent only about 1.4 percent of national income. Even as late as 1929, the Federal share of GDP was only about three percent. In the 1930s, however, the government increased its spending on domestic programs, in an effort to ease the pain of the Great Depression. Then, Federal spending really soared during the Second World War. At the height of the war, in 1944, Federal spending was about 44 percent of GDP! Federal spend-ing decreased after the war, but it never fell back to the levels of the 1920s.

In the half-century since World War II, the Federal government's share has risen gradually. During most years in the 1950s, about 18 percent of GDP went to Federal spending. This fraction rose to about 22 or 23 percent in the 1980s and early 1990s, before falling back somewhat in the late 1990s.

The Growth of Transfer Payments and Interest Payments. Although the overall level of Federal spending has increased in the last few decades, some programs have grown much more rapidly than others. As a result, it is said that the "composition" of Federal spending has changed. Figure 16.2 shows some of the changes in the composition of Federal spending from 1959 to 1999. The big story is the rapid increase in transfer payments, such as Social Security, Medicare, Medicaid, Food Stamps, unemployment compensation, and so on. In the late 1990s, about $800 billion per year were being spent on the three largest programs, Social Security, Medicare, and Medicaid.

The other large increase was in the interest payments on the national debt. The Federal government increased its debt in every year from 1969 to 1997, and this led to an increase in interest payments. Figure 16.2 shows the increase in the relative importance of interest payments. By 1997, net interest payments had grown to about $244 billion. After that, the level of interest payments decreased, because the Federal government was actually reducing its debt.

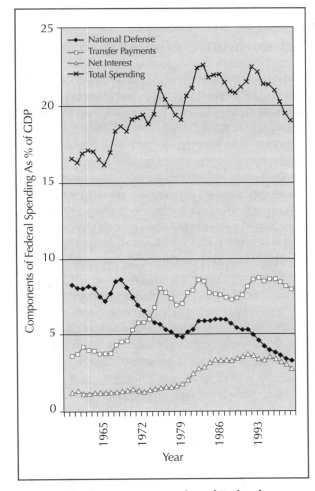

**Figure 16.2 Categories of Federal
Spending, 1959–1999**

From the 1960s to the early 1990s, Federal spending rose from about 17 percent of GDP to about 22 percent of GDP. In the late 1990s, the proportion of GDP devoted to Federal spending has fallen. Relative to GDP, defense spending has decreased fairly steadily throughout the period, while transfer payments and interest payments have risen.

The Relative Decline of Defense Spending. While transfer payments and interest on the national debt were increasing rapidly, defense spending was becoming relatively less important. After correcting for inflation, the defense

budget was almost exactly the same size in 1998 as it had been in 1960. Figure 16.2 shows that defense's share of GDP has fallen from nearly 10 percent to about three percent during this period.

In the last three paragraphs, we have described the trends in transfer payments, interest expense, and defense spending by the Federal government. In recent years, transfers, interest, and defense have accounted for nearly 90 percent of Federal spending.

Of course, the government does other things, as well. The Federal government regulates food and drugs, and it operates embassies around the world, and the National Park Service, and the Federal Bureau of Investigation (FBI), and the National Aeronautics and Space Administration (NASA), the National Weather Service, the Census Bureau, and many other agencies. In fact, these agencies provide some very important public goods. However, the amounts of money spent on these other categories are relatively small. Even if these other activities were to be reduced dramatically, the effect on the overall budget wouldn't be very great. One of the most remarkable changes of recent years has been that the Federal government is now balancing its budget, after three decades of deficits. We discuss this new environment in *Real Economics for Real People 16.1.*

Spending of State and Local Governments

In the previous section, we saw that Federal government spending had grown to about $1.7 trillion by the late 1990s. At the same time, State and local governments were spending a total of about $1 trillion. Thus, the total spending of State and local governments is very substantial, although it is somewhat less than the total spending of the Federal government.

The Federal government spends most of its money on transfer payments, interest, and

Real Economics for Real People 16.1:
The Challenge of a World without Deficits

After the huge deficits of the Second World War, the Federal government's deficits were very small for a generation. In fact, in several years during the 1950s and 1960s, the government ran a surplus, which means that taxes and other receipts were *greater* than spending. However, beginning in 1969, there was a period of three decades during which the Federal government ran a deficit in every single year. Moreover, as a proportion of GDP, the deficits were larger than anything that had ever occurred before, except during times of war. The deficit climbed to 4.2 percent of GDP in 1976. In 1983, the deficit reached 6 percent of GDP, which was an all-time record for peacetime. Even as recently as 1992, the deficit was 4.7 percent of GDP.

There are many reasons for these large budget deficits. One is that the economy grew more slowly in the 1970s and 1980s than it had in earlier decades. Serious recessions rocked the economy in 1974–75, and in 1982, and a smaller recession occurred in 1991. When the economy is shrinking, or growing slowly, it isn't possible to collect as much tax revenue. Another cause of the deficits is a political tug-of-war. The Democratic Party tends to favor higher levels of both spending and taxes, while the Republican Party tends to favor lower levels of both spending and taxes. Neither party is really in favor of deficits. However, Democratic lawmakers were generally willing to tolerate deficits, rather than reduce spending dramatically. And Republican lawmakers were generally willing to tolerate deficits, rather than approve major tax increases.

In the 1990s, these conditions began to change. Tax increases were passed in 1990 and 1993, and some spending reductions were made, as well. More importantly, after the 1991 recession, the economy achieved a long period of steady growth. A growing economy means that more tax revenues are coming in. The rapid growth of revenues was sufficient to bring the deficits to an end by 1998.

Politicians of all stripes are announcing their goals for how to "spend" the surpluses. There are several possibilities. (1) Spending can be increased. President Clinton has expressed a preference for using most of the surplus money for a variety of spending priorities. Social Security and Medicare are at the top of the list. (2) Taxes can be reduced. President Clinton has advocated a small tax cut, and Texas Governor George W. Bush has advocated a more substantial tax cut. (3) If spending is increased enough, and/or if taxes are reduced enough, there won't be any surpluses. However, if the spending increases and tax decreases are kept in check, the surpluses may continue. If this occurs, then the national debt will continue to fall. (The national debt is the sum of all of the deficits that have occurred over the years. In 1999, the Federal debt held by the public was about $3.6 trillion.) During his campaign for the Presidency in 2000, Arizona Senator John McCain advocated a plan that would eliminate the entire Federal debt in about 15 years.

The political debate has concentrated almost exclusively on the three choices described in the previous paragraph. However, there is a fourth possibility (even though political leaders don't like to talk about it). The fourth possibility is that the rapid economic growth of the 1990s will not sustain itself. If there is a recession, or a prolonged period of slower growth, then tax revenues won't increase as rapidly as has been projected. This could bring deficits back in a hurry. In formulating our plans to spend the surpluses, it's good to remember that the surpluses may not occur at all.

But what if the economy does continue to grow? What would be the best plan for spending the surpluses? In fact, there is no single "correct" answer. Reasonable people can reach different conclusions about whether to increase spending, or cut taxes, or reduce the national debt. Still, it is appropriate to make a few comments. The first comment has to do with the proposals to spend more on Social Security and Medicare. Back in 1983, Congress passed a number of changes to the Social Security program. At that time, it was said that the new laws would guarantee the solvency of the system, but that rosy prediction has not come true. This suggests that merely spending more and more money on Social Security may not be the ultimate solution to the problem. A number of prominent economists have suggested that a better solution would be to put some tax revenues into individual accounts. In this way, people could accumulate more wealth to finance their own retirements, rather than relying so heavily on transfer payments. We will return to these proposals at the end of this chapter.

The second comment has to do with proposals to retire the national debt. Figure 16.3, on p. 376, shows that the publicly held Federal debt was more than 100 percent of GDP at the end of the Second World War. The national debt did grow in the next generation, but it grew much more slowly than the economy as a whole. By the late 1960s, the debt was less than 30 percent of GDP. Thus, it is very important to realize that we can reduce the debt burden, as a percentage of GDP, even without running surpluses!

Figure 16.3 also shows what happened to the national debt as a result of the deficits of the 1970s, 1980s, and 1990s. During this period, the ratio of debt to gross domestic product rose to about 50 percent. However, the deficits shrank, and eventually disappeared, in the middle and late 1990s. As a result, the debt-to-GDP ratio has fallen substantially in recent years. Although no one really likes the national debt, it does not represent a crushing burden. As a proportion of GDP, the debt was much higher in 1945 than it has been recently. And yet, the economy did just fine in the late 1940s, in spite of the debt.

Many economists would be happy to see further reductions in the national debt. However, there isn't really much reason to think of it as an emergency. We can survive with some debt. If (1) we merely balance the Federal budget, and if (2) the economy continues to grow, then the national debt will continue to shrink as a proportion of GDP.

defense, but State and local governments tend to spend on different activities. The biggest category of State and local spending is education, which consumes more than 30 percent of the total. Highways, hospitals, police departments, fire departments, and income support for the poor are also important spending categories for the State and local governments.

International Comparisons of Government Spending

If we add together the spending of all governments in the United States (including Federal, State, and local), the total is substantially more than $2.5 trillion per year. This works out to about 30 percent of GDP. This is far more than the percentage spent by govern-

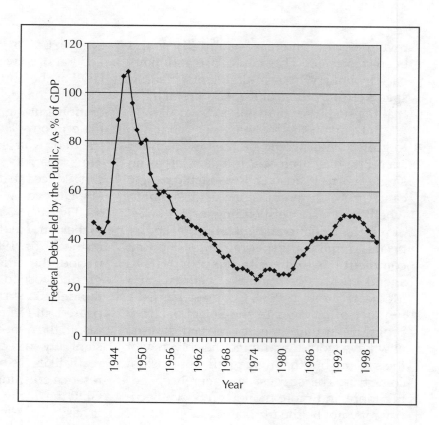

Figure 16.3 Federal Government Debt As a Percentage of GDP, 1939–2000

The ratio of Federal debt to GDP rose dramatically during the Second World War. For the next 30 years, the Federal debt increased more slowly than GDP, so that the debt-to-GDP ratio fell substantially. From the middle 1970s to the middle 1990s, the economy grew slowly and debt grew rapidly, so that the debt-to-GDP ratio increased. Finally, in the late 1990s, the ratio again began to shrink.

ments in the U.S. before the 1920s. However, the percentage for the United States is lower than that of some European countries. France, Germany, Sweden, and the United Kingdom devote more than 40 percent of GDP to government spending.

Until now, most of this chapter has been devoted to the spending programs of governments. These programs are important, but they aren't the whole story. If a government wants to spend money, it will have to find some way to pay its bills. We'll spend most of

the rest of the chapter on the economics of taxes, which are the most important method of financing government programs.

Reality Check: Interim Review Questions

IR16-2. Describe the differences between Federal government spending programs and the spending programs of State and local governments.

IR16-3. What are the three largest Federal transfer payment programs?

HOW DO GOVERNMENTS PAY FOR THEIR ACTIVITIES?

Since government programs cost money, it's necessary for governments to pay for their activities. Over the centuries, governments have tried many methods of financing. These include the following:

- Confiscation. What would you do if a hungry soldier came to your house, pointed a machine gun at you, and demanded food? You would probably decide to feed him, even if he didn't offer to give money in return. When governments acquire resources without paying for them, it is said that the governments "confiscate" the resources. Although confiscation does sometimes occur, especially in wartime, it makes up a very small part of government finance in most countries.

- Inflation. Hundreds of years ago, most money was in the form of coins. It was common for kings to clip or shave some of the gold or silver from around the edges of the coins. The kings would then melt down this gold or silver, and cast it into new coins. Today, most countries engage in a modern version of coin clipping, by issuing paper money at a rate that is faster than the growth rate of the economy. In either case, we get inflation: The value of the currency will go down, and the prices of goods will rise. In recent years, the rate of inflation in the United States has been about two percent per year. However, inflation sometimes reaches much higher levels than this. For example, Brazil's inflation rate was about 7000 percent per year in the middle of 1994.

- Bonds. Governments finance part of their activities by borrowing, which means that they issue bonds. It's common for governments to borrow heavily in wartime. For example, in 1943 (during the Second World War), borrowing by the Federal government amounted to more than 31 percent of GDP! From 1970 to the middle 1990s, the Federal government borrowed an average of about 3.3 percent of GDP per year.

- Taxes. Most governments finance most of their activities with taxes. In the United States, governments use a wide variety of taxes, including personal income taxes, corporation income taxes, payroll taxes, sales taxes, property taxes, and taxes on estates, inheritances, and gifts.

Since taxes are the most important source of revenue, we will concentrate on them in the rest of this chapter. We begin by describing the characteristics of a "good" tax system. We then move on to look at the actual effects of the tax system in the United States. Finally, we will discuss some important current controversies in tax policy.

Characteristics of A Good Tax System

In order to judge whether our current tax system does a good job, it's necessary to define the goals that a tax system is supposed to achieve. Ideally, the tax system should achieve several different goals. These goals are discussed in the next few paragraphs.

Raising Revenue. If governments didn't spend any money, there would be no need for taxes at all. Therefore, the first important goal for any tax system is to raise tax revenue. Consequently, a tax on toothpicks is not likely to be a very successful part of the tax system—the toothpick market is too small to yield very much tax revenue, even if high tax rates are used. In the United States, and in many other countries, most taxes fall on earnings in the labor market. This is partly because labor taxes can raise a lot of revenue.

Economic Efficiency. Every tax affects the behavior of households and/or firms. For example, the personal income tax creates an incentive for people to work less. Another example is the corporation income tax, which creates an incentive for people to invest in non-corporate businesses, rather than in corporations. In order to reduce their taxes, people change their behavior in many ways: They work less, and they save less, and they change their buying patterns.

When a tax leads to changes in behavior, we say that it is a *distortionary tax*. Distortionary taxes tend to mess up the workings of

– 377 –

the economy. Economists say that distortionary taxes create *inefficiency*. Thus, another important goal for the tax system is to minimize inefficiency. Later in this chapter, you will learn how to measure some of the inefficiencies caused by the tax system.

Ease of Compliance and Administration. Every year, American families spend about two billion hours (that's 2,000,000,000 hours) in keeping records, filling out tax forms, and so on. Employees of businesses also spend several billion hours every year, in complying with the business tax laws. There is a real opportunity cost to this activity, since people could have done something else with their time. When the private sector has to spend real resources in order to obey the tax law, we say that the tax system creates *compliance costs*. The Internal Revenue Service and the various State and local revenue agencies also spend real resources on getting the tax system to run smoothly. We refer to these costs as the *administrative costs* of the tax system. Another important goal for a tax system is to minimize the costs of compliance and administration.

Fairness. Another goal for the tax system is to distribute the tax burden "fairly". This may sound like a simple goal, but it isn't. The problem is that different people may have very different views about fairness. The next few paragraphs define some ways of thinking about fairness. However, it won't be possible to prove that one set of opinions about fairness is right, or that some other set of opinions is wrong.

Horizontal Equity. All else equal, it's probably desirable for the tax system to treat similar people in similar ways. If two families live in similar houses, and if they have similar incomes, and so on, then it would probably be good if they were to have similar tax payments. When a tax system treats similar people in a similar manner, the tax system is characterized by *horizontal equity*.

In order to understand horizontal equity, it may help to know of some situations in which the tax system is *not* horizontally equitable. One example is the way in which the income tax treats people according to their marital status. In the United States, there are separate tax schedules for married couples who file a joint tax return, and for married couples who file separate returns, and for single people. Because of these complications, the income tax is said to be "not neutral with respect to marital status". Some couples receive a *marriage bonus*, which means that the couple's total tax payments would be lower if they were married than if they were unmarried. On the other hand, some couples face a *marriage penalty*, which means that the couple's total tax payments would be lower if they were unmarried. These marriage bonuses and marriage penalties strike many people as being a violation of the principle of horizontal equity.

Here is another example: Virtually all homes in the United States are subject to a property tax. However, in several States, a home is only assessed to its correct market value when it is sold. Since some families stay in the same house for many years, the property tax assessments can be very far off. This is especially true in times of inflation. Even though two houses may have the same market value, they can be assessed very differently for the property tax. As a result of this, it's possible for very similar houses to be liable for very different amounts of property tax. When similar houses are taxed very differently, many people would say that we have another case of horizontal inequity.

Vertical Equity. Whereas horizontal equity involves treating *similar* people in a *similar* way, *vertical equity* involves treating *different* people in *different* ways. Vertical equity deals with the desire to allocate the tax burden in accordance with "ability to pay". This is interpreted as meaning that people with higher incomes should bear a larger tax burden than people with lower incomes.

At this point, it's important to define some terms that are often used to describe the degree of vertical equity of a tax system. A *proportional tax* is one that makes everyone pay the same percentage of income in tax. For example, if Arnold has $10,000 of income and pays $1000 in tax, he pays ten percent of his income in tax. If Alice has $20,000 of income and pays $2000 in tax, then she also pays ten percent of her income in tax. Since both people pay the same percentage, the tax is proportional.

A *progressive tax* is one that makes people with higher incomes pay a *higher* percentage of income in tax. To continue with the example from the previous paragraph, let's say once again that Arnold has $10,000 of income, and pays $1000 in tax, for a tax rate of ten percent. If Alice has $20,000 of income and pays $3000 in tax, then she pays 15 percent of her income in tax. Since the percentage of income paid in tax is rising when income rises, this is a progressive tax.

A *regressive tax* is one that allows people with higher incomes to pay a *lower* percentage of income in tax. If Alice has $20,000 of income and pays $1800 in tax, then she pays only nine percent of her income in tax, which is less than the rate of ten percent paid by Arnold. The percentage of income paid in tax is falling when income rises, so that this is a regressive tax.

Notice that a regressive tax does not necessarily mean that higher-income people pay a lower *total amount* of tax. (In the preceding paragraph, Alice has more income than Arnold has, and she pays $800 more tax than Arnold pays.) Instead, a regressive tax only means that higher-income people pay a lower *percentage* of income in tax. (Alice pays nine percent of her income, whereas Arnold pays ten percent.)

It's important to emphasize that reasonable people can disagree about the degree of progressivity that the best tax system might have. If person A prefers a progressive tax system, while person B prefers a proportional system, neither of them can prove that the other is wrong.

Conflicts Among the Goals

So far, you have read about four goals for the tax system. All else equal, it would be good for the tax system to:

- raise revenue,
- create a minimal amount of economic inefficiency,
- create a minimal amount of administrative and compliance cost, and
- distribute the tax burden "fairly".

One other goal that is sometimes discussed is macroeconomic stabilization. For example, tax policy might be used in an effort to keep the overall rates of inflation and unemployment under control. Even though macroeconomic stabilization is important, this chapter is focused on *microeconomic* issues, instead.

Unfortunately, there is no single tax that is best at achieving every goal, because the goals conflict with each other. One important conflict among the goals is the *equity-efficiency tradeoff*: Progressive taxes are often inefficient, while proportional and regressive taxes are often more efficient. For example, the personal income tax plays a very important role when it comes to promoting progressivity, but it also causes a lot of inefficiency. Also, the payroll tax is very efficient, but it is regressive over the upper range of incomes.

Because of the conflicts among goals, it won't be possible to identify the "perfect" tax system. The best that can be done is to learn more about the inefficiencies of the various taxes, as well as their costs of administration and compliance, and their effects on the distribution of income. Then, each person can decide what kind of tax system he or she would prefer, based on his or her own beliefs about the relative importance of the various goals.

Reality Check: Interim Review Question

IR16-4. Most people fill out a form when they begin to work at a new job. After the form is filled out, payment of the payroll tax is automatic, and the employee never has to do any more paperwork to pay the payroll tax. On the other hand, many taxpayers spend dozens of hours every year in filling out forms and keeping records for the individual income tax. On the basis of these facts, we can say that the payroll tax is better than the income tax in terms of one of the characteristics of a good tax system (efficiency, administration, compliance, horizontal equity, or vertical equity). Which one?

TRENDS IN TAX REVENUES

You have begun to learn how to think about taxes. Later in the chapter, you will learn more about how to analyze the effects of taxes, using supply/demand diagrams. However, so far, nothing has been said about the actual structure of the tax system. Which taxes are big, and which are little? Which have grown most rapidly, and which have grown slowly or not at all? This section provides answers to some of these questions.

Federal Taxes

By 1998, the Federal government was collecting about $1.75 trillion (i.e., $1,750,000,000,000), in the form of taxes and other receipts. This was about 19 percent of GDP. Figure 16.4 shows some of the trends in Federal tax revenues as a proportion of GDP, from 1959 to 1998. The overall total of Federal receipts does not show much of a trend. There are some fluctuations from year to year, of course. However, for the most part, the ratio of Federal taxes to GDP has stayed within a remarkably narrow range during the last several decades. The ratio was in the range of 17 percent to 19 percent of GDP in 33 of the 40 years from 1959 to 1998.

The Federal Individual Income Tax. In the 1890s, the Supreme Court ruled that an income tax was unconstitutional. As a result, the United States didn't get a permanent *individual income tax* until the Sixteenth Amendment to the Constitution, in 1913. As the name suggests, the income tax applies to many types of income, including wages and salaries, dividends, interest, rents, and royalties. In its early years, the income tax only collected a relatively small amount of revenue. However, the income tax was expanded greatly during the Second World War, and it has been the largest source of Federal revenue ever since.

Figure 16.4 shows that the individual income tax has collected between eight and ten percent of GDP in nearly every year for the last several decades. Year in and year out, the income tax is responsible for more than 40 percent of the revenues collected by the Federal government. By 1999, this tax generated nearly $880 billion in tax revenue.

Payroll Taxes. Many of the Federal government's Social Insurance programs (such as Social Security and Medicare) are paid for by a *payroll tax*, which was instituted in 1937. The payroll tax is only applied to wages and salaries. As shown in Figure 16.4, the payroll tax and the other Social Insurance taxes have been the fastest-growing source of Federal revenue for most of the last few decades.

Most wages and salaries are subject to a flat rate of payroll tax. The payroll tax rate has

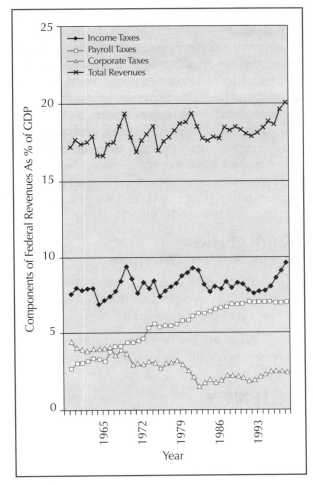

Figure 16.4 Categories of Federal Revenues, 1959–1998

For most of the last 40 years, the Federal government has taken in between 17 percent and 19 percent of GDP. Throughout this period, the individual income tax has been the most important revenue source. The payroll tax grew rapidly, especially in the 1960s and 1970s, and it is now the second-most-important revenue source. At the same time, the relative importance of the corporation income tax decreased.

increased dramatically, from two percent in 1937 to 15.3 percent today. By 1999, the payroll tax and other Social Insurance taxes were collecting more than $610 billion for the Federal government. This comes to about 33 percent of Federal revenues.

The Corporate Tax and the Excise Taxes. The individual income tax has brought in a fairly constant share of Federal tax revenues, and that the payroll tax has brought an increasing share. This means that some other taxes must have become relatively less important. The two big revenue sources that have declined are the corporation income tax and the family of Federal excise taxes. The decline of the corporation tax can be seen in Figure 16.4.

The *corporation income tax* was instituted in 1909. The corporation tax applies to the profits of corporations, although the legal definition of corporate profits is extremely complicated. The corporate tax grew rapidly during World War II. However, its share of Federal revenues declined fairly steadily from 1952 to 1986. There are many reasons for the decline, but one of the biggest is that Congress enacted a number of generous deductions and credits over the years. In 1986, an attempt was made to increase the revenues from the corporate tax. This attempt was only moderately successful, however, because interest payments remained deductible from the corporate tax. As a result, many corporations increased their use of debt, which allowed them to deduct more interest payments.

The Federal government also levies a number of *excise taxes* on the sale of specific commodities. As recently as 1963, there were excise taxes on playing cards, musical instruments, appliances, cameras, film, luggage, and dozens of other items. However, most of the smaller excise taxes have been repealed. Today, the major remaining excise taxes are on alcoholic beverages, tobacco products, gasoline and other fuels, telephone calls, and airline tickets. Even for some of the excise taxes that do remain in effect, there has been a drop in the relative amounts of revenue that are raised. This is because some of them are levied in such a way that their revenues are eroded by inflation.

In 1999, the individual income tax accounted for about 48 percent of Federal revenues, the payroll tax and other Social Insurance taxes were responsible for about 33 percent, the corporation income tax brought in about 10 percent, and the various excise taxes accounted for about 3.9 percent. The remaining 4.4 percent of the total came from tariffs on imports, taxes on the estates of people who have died, and other miscellaneous charges.

State and Local Taxes

In 1998, State and local governments in the United States raised about $1.07 trillion from their own sources. (They also received nearly $210 billion in grants from the Federal government.) For State governments, the biggest revenue sources are individual income taxes and *general retail sales taxes*. **General retail sales taxes** are usually levied on sales of clothing, hardware, and many other goods. Sales of most services (such as the services provided by lawyers, doctors, and accountants) are usually *not* covered by the sales taxes. In many States, food isn't taxed, either. For local governments, property taxes are the largest sources of revenue. Overall, about half of the State and local revenues come from income taxes, sales taxes, or property taxes.

Many States also have corporation income taxes. Alaska, Oklahoma, Texas, and other oil-producing States get a lot of revenue from "severance taxes" on oil. Finally, State and local governments also get revenue from an immense variety of smaller charges, such as professional license fees, parking fines, etc.

Reality Check:
Interim Review Questions

IR16-5. Describe the differences between the Federal tax system and the tax systems of State and local governments.

IR16-6. What are the two largest sources of tax revenue for the Federal government?

THE EFFECTS OF TAXES ON EFFICIENCY AND DISTRIBUTION

In the previous section, you learned about a number of different taxes, including individual income taxes, corporation income taxes, payroll taxes, general sales taxes, excise taxes, and property taxes. The tax-revenue system in the United States certainly has a tremendous amount of variety. Which of these taxes work well, and which don't? In order to move toward an answer to that question, this section develops some ways of thinking about the economic effects of taxes.

The best way to analyze a tax is to look at its effects on supply and demand in the marketplace. In this section, supply/demand diagrams are used to study the economic effects of taxes. You will learn to identify the revenue generated by the tax, as well as the efficiency loss that the tax generates. In addition, you will learn to think about how the burden of the tax is divided among buyers and sellers.

The Effects of a Sales Tax or Excise Tax

The simplest tax to understand is a commodity tax. You have probably had direct experience with commodity taxes, such as general retail sales taxes or excise taxes. General retail sales taxes are used in 45 of the 50 States. Excise taxes on alcoholic beverages, tobacco products, and gasoline are levied by the Federal government, and by each of the 50 States and the District of Columbia.

The No-Tax Equilibrium. When we use supply/demand diagrams to study the effects of a tax, we always start by looking at the market equilibrium that would occur if there were no tax. Then, we look at the market equilibrium that would occur after the tax is imposed, and we compare the two equilibria. (This is the same technique that we used in Chapter 5, when we studied the effects of a tariff, which is a tax on imports.) Figure 16.5 shows the effects of a sales tax on bicycles. The supply curve is horizontal in this case, which means that supply is perfectly elastic. In the absence of tax, the supply curve is S_{net}. It is called "S_{net}", to indicate that this supply curve is net of taxes. In other words, taxes are not included in the net-of-tax supply curve, S_{net}.

When there are no taxes, the market equilibrium is determined by the intersection of the demand curve, D, with the net-of-tax supply curve, S_{net}. In Figure 16.5, the no-tax quantity is Q_0, and the no-tax price is P_0. Without any taxes, the buyers' price is the same as the sellers' price. The buyers pay a price of P_0 per bicycle, and the sellers receive the same P_0 per bicycle.

The Equilibrium with a Tax. Now, the government imposes a tax on bicycle sales. (Let's assume that the tax law is obeyed, and that

people don't evade their taxes.) Because of the tax, it's now necessary to draw a new, gross-of-tax supply curve, S_{gross}.

In most of the examples in this book, there is only one supply curve. Now, however, there are two supply curves. The original supply curve, S_{net}, tells about the prices that are actually received by sellers. The new supply curve, S_{gross}, tells about the prices that are paid by buyers, when there is a tax. The difference between the two supply curves is the tax per unit: At any quantity, S_{gross} is equal to S_{net} plus the tax per unit. In Figure 16.5, the vertical distance between S_{gross} and S_{net} is the tax per unit.

With a tax, the price paid by the buyers will be greater than the price received by the sellers. The gross-of-tax supply curve, S_{gross}, shows the prices that buyers have to pay, *including* taxes. From the buyer's point of view, this is what really counts. If you're shopping for a bicycle, and you have to pay $210, you don't really care whether the entire $210 goes to the seller, or whether the seller

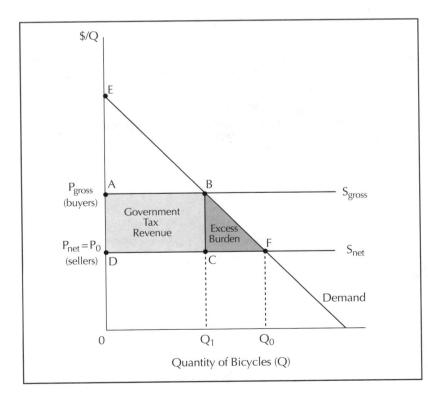

Figure 16.5 The Economic Effects of a Commodity Tax

In the absence of a tax, the market equilibrium is determined by the intersection of the supply curve, S_{net}, and the demand curve, D. The equilibrium quantity is Q_0, and the equilibrium price is P_0. When a tax is imposed, there is a new gross-of-tax supply curve, S_{gross}. The equilibrium quantity falls to Q_1. In the case shown here, with perfectly elastic supply, the sellers' price does not change. However, the buyers' price rises to P_{gross}. The government gains revenue of ABCD, but the consumer loses consumer surplus of ABFD. As a result, the excess burden is BFC.

– 383 –

gets $200 and the government gets $10 of tax revenue. Buyers care about the total amount they have to pay, including all taxes.

The new equilibrium is given by the intersection of the demand curve, D, with the new, gross-of-tax supply curve, S_{gross}. The new equilibrium quantity is Q_1.

In most of the examples in this book, the intersection of the supply and demand curves gives exactly one equilibrium price. However, when there is a tax, there are *two* equilibrium prices. The gross-of-tax price is the price paid by the buyers. In Figure 16.5, the gross-of-tax price is P_{gross}. The net-of-tax price is the price received by the sellers, which is P_{net} in Figure 16.5.

Before the tax was imposed, the sellers received P_0. After the tax is in place, the sellers receive P_{net}, which is exactly the same as P_0. Therefore, for the case shown in Figure 16.5, the tax doesn't change the price received by the sellers. The seller's price is unchanged because the supply curve is perfectly elastic. With perfectly elastic supply, the sellers must receive P_0, or they won't produce any bicycles. Later in this chapter, we will see what happens when the supply curve is not perfectly elastic.

The Government's Tax Revenue. In order to calculate the total amount of tax revenue received by the government, we multiply the amount of tax per bicycle by the number of bicycles sold. The amount of tax per bicycle is ($P_{gross} - P_{net}$), or AD in Figure 16.5. The number of bicycles sold is Q_1. So, the government's tax revenue is the area of the rectangle ABCD. If the tax were $10 per bicycle, and if one million bicycles were sold in a year, then the government's revenue would be ($10)(1 million) = $10 million.

The Excess Burden of the Tax. The public sector has gained revenue of ABCD, but the private sector has been made worse off by the tax. It would be good to know the size of the

private sector's loss, so that it can be compared with the public sector's gain. To measure the private sector's loss, we use the concept of consumer surplus, which was introduced in Chapter 7.

Consumer surplus is the excess of willingness to pay (given by the demand curve) over the amount actually paid (given by the price). Before the tax is imposed, the buyers of bicycles have consumer surplus of EFD in Figure 16.5. However, the tax raises the buyer's price to P_{gross}. Because of this, consumers decide to buy only Q_1 bicycles, and they get less consumer surplus from each bicycle that they do buy. Buyers are made worse off by the tax, as seen by the fact that consumer surplus falls to EBA.

The loss for the buyers of bicycles is the difference between the consumer surplus that they had before the tax and the consumer surplus that remains after the tax. In Figure 16.5, the consumers' loss is the area ABFD. This is the maximum amount that consumers would be willing to pay, for the privilege of having the tax on bicycles removed.

So, the government revenue is ABCD, and the consumers' loss is ABFD. The consumers' loss is greater than the government's gain. The difference is called the *excess burden* of the tax, and is shown by the area of the triangle BFC. The excess burden is sometimes also called the *deadweight loss* or *welfare cost* of the tax.

Excess burden is the best measure of the inefficiency of a tax. If efficiency is your goal, then it would be best to use the taxes that generate the smallest amount of excess burden. Later in this chapter, you will see some estimates of the excess burdens for different taxes.

It's important to understand one thing before going on. Just because taxes have excess burden, it is *not* necessarily wrong to have tax-financed government spending. After all, some government programs have great potential to improve the workings of the economy. However, excess burden *does* mean that it's important to be careful. It's important to avoid government programs that are of little value, and it's important to avoid relying on taxes that generate unusually large amounts of excess burden.

Who Really Pays the Tax? When we think about who bears the burden of the tax, we are studying something that is called *tax incidence*. It is possible to distinguish between two concepts of tax incidence. *Statutory incidence* is determined by the statutes of the law. Thus, if the law says that retail sellers are required to make sales-tax payments to the State Treasury, the "statutory incidence" falls on the retail sellers. However, just because the seller writes a check to the government, it doesn't necessarily follow that the seller *really* bears the burden of the tax. The true *economic incidence* of a tax falls on those who *really* pay. The economic incidence is determined by the elasticities of supply and demand. In Figure 16.5, the buyers are the ones who truly bear the burden of the tax on bicycles. The buyers lose a portion of their consumer surplus, whereas the sellers don't lose anything. (With a perfectly elastic supply curve, the sellers don't have any producer surplus to begin with, so they have none to lose.)

Figure 16.5 shows that the true *economic* incidence of a tax can be different from the statutory incidence. In this case, 100 percent of the economic burden of the tax is borne by buyers of bicycles, even though the law says that the retail seller is ultimately responsible for writing a check to the government.

Revenue and Excess Burden with Different Elasticities. Figure 16.5 illustrates many of the most important concepts regarding the economic analysis of taxes. However, Figure 16.5 only deals with one special case, in which the supply curve is perfectly elastic, and the demand curve slopes downward in a particular way. How will the revenue, excess burden, and incidence be changed when different elasticities are used?

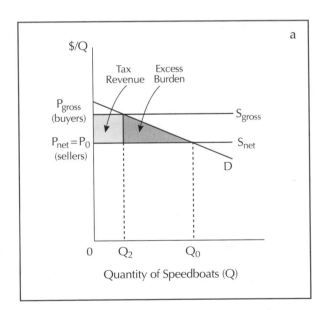
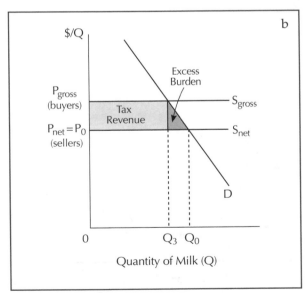

Figure 16.6 The Elasticity of Demand and the Economic Effects of a Commodity Tax

In panel (a), the demand for speedboats is fairly elastic. As a result, the tax only collects a small amount of revenue, but it generates a large amount of excess burden. In panel (b), the demand for milk is fairly inelastic. The tax on milk collects a lot of revenue, with only a small excess burden.

To begin our study of the effects of taxes with different elasticities, consider Figure 16.6, on p. 385, which is very similar to Figure 16.5. In each case, the supply curve is perfectly elastic, the initial price is P_0, and the initial quantity is Q_0. Each case also looks at the same size of tax. The difference is that panel (a) of Figure 16.6 considers the market for speedboats, which has a very elastic demand curve. On the other hand, panel (b) of Figure 16.6 shows the market for milk, which has very inelastic demand.

Panel (a) of Figure 16.6 shows what would happen if demand were very elastic: The tax would reduce the quantity of speedboats to Q_2, which is a very large reduction. As a result, the tax doesn't raise much revenue, and the excess burden is very large. If efficiency is your goal, this is a bad situation: When a tax creates lots of excess burden, but doesn't raise very much revenue, it isn't a very good tax.

From the point of view of efficiency, panel (b) of Figure 16.6 presents a better picture. With very inelastic demand, the tax causes only a small change in the quantity of milk. This means that the tax on milk raises a lot of revenue, but does not create much excess burden.

The message is this: If a government wants to raise revenue in an efficient manner, it should put higher taxes on the commodities that are relatively more inelastic. However, this may create a major tension between equity and efficiency. According to the examples in Figure 16.6, efficiency considerations would mean that the tax rate should be higher on milk than on boats. Many people would be troubled by a tax system like this, because of concerns about fairness.

Tax Incidence with Different Elasticities. In either panel of Figure 16.6, buyers bear the entire burden of the tax. When supply is perfectly elastic, there is no way for sellers to bear any of the burden. What would happen if the supply curve were upward sloping? Figure

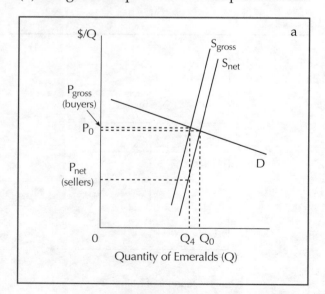 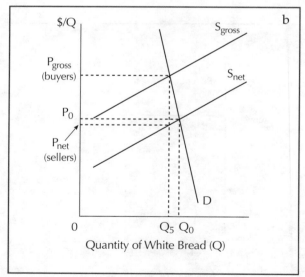

Figure 16.7 Tax Incidence and the Elasticities of Supply and Demand

In panel (a), the supply of emeralds is inelastic, but demand is elastic. As a result, a tax does not raise the buyers' price very far, but the sellers' price falls by a great deal. The sellers bear most of the burden of the tax. In panel (b), the supply of white bread is elastic, but demand is inelastic. A tax raises the buyers' price by a lot, but the sellers' price only falls by a small amount. The buyers bear most of the burden of the tax. In each case, the more inelastic side of the market bears most of the burden of the tax.

16.7 shows that *the more inelastic side of the market will bear most of the burden of the tax.*

Panel (a) of Figure 16.7 shows the market for gem-quality emeralds, in which supply is very inelastic and demand is fairly elastic. In this situation, a tax would cause a big decrease in the sellers' price, P_{net}, but only a small increase in the buyers' price, P_{gross}. Thus, the sellers would bear most of the burden of a tax on emeralds. Conversely, panel (b) of Figure 16.7 shows the market for white bread, in which supply is elastic and demand is inelas-

tic. In this case, a tax would only cause a small decrease in the sellers' price, P_{net}, but it would cause a large increase in the buyers' price, P_{gross}. This means that the buyers would bear most of the burden of a tax on white bread.

If buyers are relatively more inelastic, they will bear most of the burden. If sellers are relatively more inelastic, they will bear most of the burden. These examples show that the more inelastic side of the market will bear most of the burden of the tax. These ideas are

---

Real Economics for Real People 16.2: Who Really Pays the Payroll Tax?

Earlier in this chapter, we saw that the payroll tax is the second-largest source of revenue for the Federal government. The payroll tax is levied at a flat rate of 7.65 percent on the worker and 7.65 percent on the employer, for a total rate of 15.3 percent. Thus, the statutory incidence of the payroll tax is half on the employer and half on the employee.

It would certainly be possible to raise the same amount of revenue, while changing the way in which the tax is divided between employers and workers. If the total tax rate is 15.3 percent, then the government could raise the same amount of revenue by putting the entire 15.3 percent on the workers, or by putting it all on the employers. The government could also raise the same amount of revenue by putting 10 percent on the employers and 5.3 percent on the employees, or by using any other combination.

Occasionally, there are proposals to change the way in which the payroll tax is divided between employers and workers. One such proposal involves putting the entire 15.3 percent on the employer. The people who make this type of proposal tend to make the argument that putting more of the

tax on employers would be an advantage to the workers.

However, for better or worse, it really won't make any difference. The same effects should occur as long as the total tax rate is 15.3 percent, regardless of how much of the statutory burden goes on the employer and how much goes on the employee. The true economic incidence of taxes isn't determined by whether the government says that the employer or the worker is responsible for paying the tax. The true economic incidence is determined by the elasticities of supply and demand.

In the labor market, the workers are the suppliers of labor, and the firms are the demanders of labor. If supply is more inelastic than demand, then the workers will bear most of the burden. If demand is more inelastic than supply, then the firms will bear most of the burden. In fact, most of the evidence suggests that labor supply is more inelastic than labor demand. Consequently, the workers bear most of the burden of the payroll tax. This would still be true, even if the laws were changed to eliminate the portion of the payroll tax that is officially the responsibility of the worker.

used in *Real Economics for Real People 16.2*, which looks at the incidence of the payroll tax.

What Have We Learned About the Effects of the Tax System?

In the last few pages, you have seen some of the ways in which economic reasoning can be used to understand the effects of taxes. Over the years, economists have used these ideas to come up with estimates of the effects of the tax system.

One consistent result is that the overall tax system in the United States is nearly proportional, even though the pieces of the tax system may not be proportional. Economic studies indicate that income taxes are somewhat progressive, for two reasons. First, income taxes have *personal exemptions*. The personal exemptions allow for every person to have a certain amount of income that is not subject to tax. The exemptions are especially important for the poor. Second, the Federal income tax (like some of the State income taxes) has *graduated marginal tax rates*, which means that the tax rate that is applied to an additional dollar of taxable income is higher, for people who have higher taxable incomes.

On the other hand, sales taxes are somewhat regressive. This is because sales taxes do not apply to saving, and higher-income people tend to save a higher proportion of their incomes.

The payroll tax is progressive at lower income levels, because it doesn't apply to transfer payments. The payroll tax is then about proportional over much of the income range. Finally, the payroll tax is regressive at high incomes, for two reasons. First of all, the full payroll tax of 15.3 percent is only collected on earnings below a ceiling. (In 1999, the ceiling was $72,600.) Second, the payroll tax doesn't apply to dividends, interest, rents, royalties, or capital gains, all of which are concentrated at the upper income levels. If we add up the effects of income taxes, sales taxes, and all the other sources of revenue, we get a system that takes about the same percentage of income from everyone. For example, one famous study found that the total burden of all taxes was between 28 percent and 30 percent for four-fifths of the U.S. population.

Another important result is that the tax system generates a large amount of excess burden. One study found that the United States tax system generates an overall excess burden that is probably more than 10 percent of tax revenues, and may be as great as 24 percent of tax revenues. If this estimate is correct, it means that the efficiency losses from distortionary taxes may be as much as several hundred billion dollars per year. In many studies, economists have found that different amounts of excess burden are created by different parts of the tax system. For example, the payroll tax leads to relatively little excess burden, because labor supply is not very elastic. On the other hand, corporate taxes and personal income taxes create a much larger deadweight loss than is created by the payroll tax. This implies that the overall excess burden of the tax system could be reduced, by reducing the corporate tax and increasing the payroll tax.

CURRENT TAX POLICY ISSUES

Tax policy is extremely controversial, because nobody enjoys paying taxes. The political fighting over tax policies has been especially fierce in the 1980s and 1990s, because Congress and the White House have usually been controlled by different political parties. In this section, you will read about some of the big recent controversies in tax policy. We begin with proposals to "flatten" the schedule of marginal tax rates in the individual income tax. Later, we look at some issues in the taxation of capital income, including the corporation income tax and the taxes on "capital gains".

A "Flat Tax"

The United States, like many other countries, has a system of graduated marginal income tax rates. In 1999, the first dollar of your taxable income is taxed at a rate of 15 percent. For a married couple, the marginal tax rate increases to 28 percent when the couple's taxable income rises to $39,000. At higher incomes, the marginal tax rates continue to rise, until they reach 39.6 percent for couples with incomes over $256,500.

These tax rates are actually *low* by historical standards. In 1944 and 1945, the top marginal tax rate was 94 percent. As recently as 1981, the top marginal rate was 70 percent. During the 1980s, the highest marginal rate was dropped a great deal, until it reached 33 percent, which was the lowest that it had been since the Second World War.

Studies by economists have found that the excess burden of the income tax tends to increase very rapidly as the marginal rates increase. Thus, if your goal is to maximize economic efficiency, you would want a relatively flat tax-rate schedule, without much graduation in the tax rates. However, if your goal is to have a very progressive tax system, you would want to have graduated rates. Once again, there is an equity-efficiency tradeoff. Since different people have different views about the relative importance of equity and efficiency, the income tax rate schedule is a constant source of disagreement.

In the 1980s, the idea of a *flat tax* got a lot of attention from economists and others. Under a *flat tax*, all taxable income would be taxed at a single rate. Former California Governor Jerry Brown advocated a flat tax during his bid for the 1992 Democratic Presidential nomination. During the 1996 and 2000 Presidential campaigns, several Republican candidates made flat-tax proposals. Steve Forbes centered his Presidential campaign around a flat-tax proposal.

Virtually all of the flat-tax proposals would give up some vertical equity, in exchange for some efficiency. However, many of the proposals would do much more than merely flatten the tax rates. Because there are big differences in the other aspects of the proposals, it's difficult to make general statements that would tell the truth about all of the plans. Still, the next few paragraphs describe some of the issues.

How Much Revenue Would Flat Taxes Collect? Some of the flat-tax proposals are designed to raise the same amount of revenue as today's income tax. However, some of the plans would collect less revenue. If the amount of revenue collected from the income tax is reduced, then one of the following things must happen: Either government spending must be cut, or some other tax must be raised, or the budget deficit must go up.

What Would Happen to the Deductions and Exemptions? If you want to carry the idea of the flat tax to its logical conclusion, you would tax every single dollar of income at exactly the same rate. However, none of the popular proposals would go that far. Today's income tax has a personal exemption of $2750 per person. The personal exemption is not taxable. Thus, if the Williams family has an income that is less than the total of their personal exemptions, they don't pay any tax at all. It could be said that the income tax rate is actually zero at very low incomes. None of the popular flat-tax proposals would eliminate the personal exemptions, and some proposals would increase the exemptions by a great deal. This means that the flat-tax proposals really have *two* tax rates, instead of just one. Under these proposals, the first marginal tax rate is zero, and the other marginal tax rate is usually something like 17 percent or 19 percent.

Beyond the personal exemptions, there are hundreds of other tax breaks. For example, when your employer pays health-insurance premiums for you, or contributes to your pension fund, the income tax doesn't apply. This is an example of an *exclusion*, under which a particular type of income is excluded from the tax base. If you pay interest on your home mortgage, you get to subtract the interest payments from your taxable income. This is called a *deduction*. A *deduction* allows the taxpayer to reduce his or her taxable income, by spending money on a particular type of activity. Table 16.1 shows some of the most important deductions and exclusions, along with estimates of how much tax revenue is lost as a result.

Table 16.1 shows that the income tax system loses a tremendous amount of revenue because of all of the special tax breaks. If you were to add up the revenue losses shown in Table 16.1, along with all of the other revenue losses that aren't shown, you would get a total revenue loss of something like $500 billion per year.

These revenue losses have a major effect on the tax rates. If Congress were to eliminate the deductions, exclusions, and exemptions, it would be possible to raise the same amount of revenue that is raised now, but with lower tax rates. If you want to raise today's amount of tax revenue from a flat tax, but don't change any of the deductions, exclusions, and exemptions, you would need a tax rate of about 23 percent. However, if all of the deductions, exclusions, and exemptions were removed, a flat tax rate of about 12 percent would do the job. A system with fewer tax breaks and lower tax rates would be a more efficient system.

Of course, there are problems with removing the tax breaks. Consider the mortgage interest deduction, for example. Many people have responded to this deduction by getting big mortgages. If the tax deduction were to be removed suddenly, it would probably cause bankruptcies for some people with large mortgages, and it would cause home prices to fall. The price decreases could be large in some regions of the country. All of this could put an enormous strain on the financial system. Consequently, if we were to remove the mortgage interest deduction, it would be wise to consider phasing in the change over a long period of time, such as 15 or 20 years.

In this section, we have seen that the debate about a flat tax isn't just about the flatness or steepness of the tax rate schedule. The

---

Table 16.1 Some Important Deductions and Exclusions in the Federal Individual Income Tax

Provision of the Tax Law	Estimated Revenue Loss in 2000
Exclusion of employer-paid pension contributions	$84.4 billion
Exclusion of employer-paid health insurance	77.7 billion
Deduction for mortgage interest	55.1 billion
Deduction for State-and-local income taxes	37.0 billion
Deduction for contributions to charities	25.9 billion
Exclusion of interest on State and local debt	25.1 billion
Deduction for State and local property taxes	19.5 billion

Source: Office of Management and Budget, *Budget of the United States Government, Fiscal Year 2000, Analytical Perspectives.*

flat-tax debate is really about four important questions:

- How flat should the income tax rates be?

- How much revenue should be raised by the income tax?

- How many deductions, exclusions, and exemptions should there be?

Real Economics for Real People 16.3:
What's All the Fuss About Capital Gains Taxes?

A *capital gain* is an increase in the value of a capital asset, such as a home or a share of stock. If you buy a share of stock at a price of $50, and if the price then increases to $60, you have a capital gain of $(60 − 50) = $10. Similarly, if you buy a house for $100,000, and its price goes up to $110,000, you have a capital gain of $(110,000 − 100,000) = $10,000.

Capital gains are only subject to tax when the asset is actually sold. Thus, if you hang on to your corporate stock for many years, you won't pay any capital gains tax, even if the price of the stock goes up a long way. In addition, if you hold the stock until you die, and bequeath it to your children, the capital gain is forgiven completely. This gives a powerful incentive for investors to avoid taxes by holding on to their stocks, even if the stocks aren't performing very well. The incentive to hold on to stocks in order to avoid taxes is called the *lock-in effect*.

Another important feature of the capital-gains tax is that gains are not indexed for inflation. If your stock goes up by 20 percent during a period of years when the overall price level also goes up by 20 percent, then you haven't really increased your purchasing power at all. Nevertheless, if you sell the asset, you will have to pay taxes on the entire nominal "gain". This creates problems, both for equity and for efficiency. To many people, it seems unfair for the government to inflate prices, and then to tax people on the resulting paper gains.

Controversy has swirled around the capital-gains tax for years. Most capital gains are received by people with high incomes. As a result, if you believe in a strongly progressive tax, you may want to keep the tax rate on capital gains fairly high. On the other hand, the lock-in effect probably does a lot of damage to the efficiency of the stock market. If you are very worried about this type of efficiency issue, you will probably want to keep the tax rate on capital gains lower.

For most of the history of the income tax, this debate has been resolved in favor of those who want a special, lower tax rate for capital gains. Since 1986, however, the top tax rate on capital gains has been 28 percent, which is not extremely different from the top tax rate on other income.

Sometimes, people argue in favor of lowering the tax rates on capital gains, because of a belief that lower rates will bring about a large increase in the rate of economic growth. This is unlikely to occur, however. For several reasons, much of the capital stock is already not subject to capital gains taxes. One reason is that very wealthy stockholders may hang on to much of their stock portfolios until they die. If they do, there is no capital gains tax at all. Also, it is believed that many taxpayers get away with not paying their capital-gains taxes. Thus, even if the tax rate were cut in half, from 28 percent to 14 percent, it would still only give a modest boost to the overall rate of return on corporate stocks. This might lead to some additional saving and investment, but the amounts are likely to be small. Consequently, the effect on the overall rate of economic growth would also be small.

Sometimes, the proposals for lower tax rates on capital gains are justified on the basis of claims that they will raise more revenue. In order for this to occur, there would have to be a large increase in the number of stock sales, in response to the tax cut. In the short run, there might be a burst of sales.

Over the long haul, however, the increase in sales is unlikely to be large enough to bring about any major increase in tax revenue.

It appears that many of the arguments that are given in favor of reducing the capital gains tax rate are fairly weak. A reduced tax rate on capital gains would have some effects, but they are unlikely to be exceptionally large. However, there is a more fundamental question: Should there be any tax on capital gains at all? Nearby, in the section on corporate taxation, you will read about a proposal that would involve complete elimination of the tax on capital gains.

- If the tax system is to be changed, should the changes be phased in quickly or slowly?

It's likely that the debate over these issues will continue for years to come. The results of the debate will tell us a lot about the efficiency and equity of the tax system in the future.

Real Economics for Real People 16.3 discusses the capital-gains tax, which is another hotly debated tax-policy issue.

Must Corporate Income Be Taxed Twice?

In several countries, including the United States, corporations have to pay a tax that is separate from the individual income tax. If a corporate firm wants to pay dividends to its stockholders, it must first pay the corporate tax. Then, the stockholders have to pay individual income tax when they receive the dividends. This is called the **double taxation of corporate income.**

Some people try to justify the double taxation of corporate income on the basis of their belief that "business needs to pay its fair share of taxes". This argument can be misleading. After all, businesses don't really pay taxes: The ultimate burden of a tax can only be borne by people. A tax that is levied on a corporation can only be borne by consumers (as a result of higher prices), by workers (as a result of lower wages), by stockholders (as a result of lower share prices or lower dividends), or by other owners of capital. In fact, economic studies of the incidence of the corporation tax indicate that all of these groups are likely to bear at least some of the burden of the tax.

Corporations have to pay the corporate tax, but non-corporate firms don't have to pay a tax of this type. Therefore, the tax system favors the non-corporate sector of the economy, relative to the corporate sector. The economy ends up with less than the optimal amount of corporate output, and more than the optimal amount of non-corporate output.

Another problem with the corporate tax is that it allows a deduction for interest payments. Thus, the corporate tax creates an incentive for corporations to go into debt: If a corporation goes into debt, it will pay interest on the debt, and the interest payments will allow the firm to reduce its taxes.

In short, the corporate tax creates a large number of distortions. Some estimates suggest that the corporate tax creates more excess burden per dollar of revenue than does any other tax. With the goal of getting around this problem, economists have suggested several proposals for *"corporate tax integration"*. The idea of corporate tax integration is to coordinate the corporate income tax with the individual income tax, in order to solve the problem of double taxation.

Perhaps the best of the proposals for corporate tax integration is called a "Comprehensive Business Income Tax", or CBIT. This tax would apply equally to all businesses, regardless of whether they are incorporated. In this way, it would remove the distortion between corporate and non-corporate firms. In addition, the CBIT would not allow a deduction for interest. Therefore, it would no longer give an advantage to firms that take on a lot of debt.

Finally, the CBIT would only tax business income once. The individual income tax would not apply to business income, such as dividends, interest, rents, and so on. These incomes will already have been taxed once by the CBIT. Therefore, any attempt to tax them again under the individual income tax would lead to double taxation.

Some economists have estimated that the excess burden of the corporate tax is one-third of revenues, or even more. If a Comprehensive Business Income Tax were enacted, it would reduce the excess burden very substantially. Moreover, by eliminating the double taxation of corporate income, the CBIT would remove one important source of unfairness in the tax system.

ECONOMICS AND YOU: WILL SOCIAL SECURITY BE THERE WHEN YOU RETIRE?

At the beginning of this chapter, we saw that the Social Security system will run out of money in the 2030s, unless some changes are made. No one can predict with certainty the changes that will be made, but here are some of the possibilities:

- Raising the retirement age. In fact, the age at which you are eligible for full benefits was already raised, back in 1983. For people born before 1937, it's possible to collect full benefits at age 65. This retirement age is now scheduled to be increased gradually. People who are born after 1960 will have to wait until the age of 67 before they can collect full benefits. Whenever the retirement age is raised, there is a reduction in the amount of benefits that must be paid out. If the age for full benefits were raised to 69, the Social Security system would probably be able to survive in the long run.

- Raising taxes. As was mentioned earlier in this chapter, the payroll tax rate is now 15.3 percent. Most of the revenues are used to pay for Social Security, and the rest go for Medicare and the Disability Insurance program. If we were to leave benefits unchanged, we would have to rely exclusively on taxes in order to finance the system. This would make it necessary for the payroll tax rate to rise to about 25 percent by 2040.

- More fundamental changes. Today's Social Security system is a *pay-as-you-go retirement system*. This means that the system doesn't really do any saving. Instead, it merely taxes those who are working today, and uses the money to pay transfer payments to those who are retired today. Since the money is not invested, future generations won't do as well with Social Security as they would have done if the same amount of money had been invested in the stock market or in other investments.

Some economists have suggested that the basic character of the system should be changed. Instead of a pay-as-you-go system, the government could sponsor a system of required saving. To accomplish the transition to the new system without causing a great deal of harm to any one generation, it would be necessary to phase in the new system gradually, over a period of several decades. Since such a long transition period will be required, the best time to start is now.

One thing is certain: If any of these changes is to be made, it will be made by government officials, rather than by the private market. For better or worse, the key players will be politicians, bureaucrats, and voters. Can the political system rise to the challenge? The answer to this question will be one of the most important developments of the 21st century.

In the meantime, what can you do? The most important thing to remember is that Social Security benefits won't be enough to provide a very comfortable retirement. (Today, the average Social Security beneficiary receives less than $10,000 per year. If you want to know more about the benefits that you can expect, you can contact your local Social Security office.)

By themselves, Social Security benefits won't do much more than keep you out of poverty. If you want to have a comfortable retirement, you will have to do some saving of your own. The nature of compound interest is such that a dollar saved today will provide much more retirement income than a dollar saved ten years from now. Therefore, the earlier you start to save, the better.

Chapter Summary

1. Public goods are nonrival, which means that they can be enjoyed by many people at the same time. In addition, public goods are characterized by costly exclusion, which means that it is difficult to deny the public good to those who do not pay. Costly exclusion leads to the free-rider problem: People do not have an incentive to reveal their preferences for public goods.

2. Public goods are an example of market failure. Private markets will typically be unable to provide public goods, which means that government may have a role in providing them. The other important justification for government spending is that the private market economy may not produce a distribution of income that people consider fair. Government may be able to use taxes and transfer payments to make the distribution of income more equal.

3. Federal government spending has taken up an increasingly large proportion of GDP. In recent years, total Federal spending has been about 19 percent of GDP. Since 1960, transfer payments have been the fastest-growing component of Federal spending. Interest payments on the national debt have also risen, while the share of defense spending has declined. State and local governments spend about 13 percent of GDP. Education gets the largest share of State and local spending.

4. Ideally, a good tax system will raise revenue without causing a lot of inefficiency. A good tax system would also have low costs of administration and compliance, and it would be "fair". This means that the tax system would be horizontally equitable, that is, similar people would be treated similarly. A good tax system would

also be vertically equitable, although people disagree about the correct degree of vertical equity. Often, these goals are in conflict with each other. As a result, there is no perfect, ideal tax system.

5. In recent years, the Federal government has raised about 19 percent of GDP in tax revenue. Since World War II, the individual income tax has been the largest source of Federal revenue. The payroll tax is now the second-largest source of Federal revenue. The corporation income tax and the excise taxes have become relatively less important. For the State and local governments, the largest sources of revenue are individual income taxes, general retail sales taxes, and property taxes.

6. A tax raises revenue for the government, but it also makes consumers worse off. Usually, the losses for the private sector are greater than the revenue for the government. The difference between the private sector's loss and the government's revenue is the excess burden, or deadweight loss, of the tax. All else equal, excess burdens are greater when the taxed markets are more elastic.

7. The study of tax incidence is concerned with determining who really bears the burden of a tax. Using supply/demand diagrams, it can be shown that the more inelastic side of the market will bear most of the burden of a tax. The true economic incidence does not depend on whether the law says that buyers or sellers are ultimately responsible for paying the tax. The true economic incidence depends only on the elasticities of supply and demand.

8. One recent controversy deals with whether the individual income tax should have graduated marginal tax rates. Some have advocated a "flat tax", under which all taxable income would be taxed at the

same rate. Many economists are in favor of broadening the tax base, by removing some exclusions and deductions. This would make it possible to raise the same amount of tax revenue, while reducing the tax rates.

9. The United States tax system has a tax on corporation income, and a separate individual income tax. This leads to the double taxation of corporate income, which causes substantial excess burdens. Some economists have proposed a Comprehensive Business Income Tax, under which all business income (including corporate and non-corporate income) would be taxed once. There would then not be any need to tax business income in the individual income tax.

Key Terms

Market Failure

Public Goods

Nonrival Consumption

Private Goods

Costly Exclusion, or Nonexcludability

Free-Rider Problem

Distortionary Tax

Inefficiency

Compliance Costs

Administrative Costs

Horizontal Equity

Marriage Bonus

Marriage Penalty

Vertical Equity

Proportional Tax

Progressive Tax

Regressive Tax

Equity-Efficiency Tradeoff

Individual Income Tax

Payroll Tax

Corporation Income Tax

Excise Tax

General Retail Sales Tax

Excess Burden, or Deadweight Loss, or Welfare Cost

Tax Incidence

Statutory Incidence

Economic Incidence

Personal Exemption

Graduated Marginal Tax Rates

Flat Tax

Exclusion

Deduction

Capital Gain

Lock-in Effect

Double Taxation of Corporate Income

Corporate Tax Integration

Pay-as-you-go Retirement System

Key Figure

The key figure for this chapter is Figure 16.5. It uses a supply/demand diagram to show how a commodity tax can be viewed as creating a new, gross-of-tax supply curve. The new equilibrium is determined by the intersection of the gross-of-tax supply curve with the demand curve. Once the new equilibrium quantity and prices are known, it is possible to calculate the government's tax revenue and the excess burden.

Questions and Problems

QP16-1. The largest sources of Federal tax revenues are the individual income tax, the payroll tax, and the corporation tax. Which of these scores best in terms of administrative costs, compliance costs, and excess burden?

QP16-2. If you consider the Federal individual income tax, the payroll tax, and a general retail sales tax, which is most progressive?

QP16-3. David has income of $10,000, and he pays a tax of $2000. Amy has income of $100,000, and she also pays a tax of $2000. Is this tax regressive, or proportional, or progressive?

QP16-4. How would your answer to question (3) change, if at all, if Amy's tax were $1000? What if Amy's tax were $20,000? What if it were $40,000?

QP16-5. Discuss the appropriate role of government in providing the following: National defense, cosmetic surgery, income-maintenance payments for poor people, streets and sewers, elementary education, higher education.

QP16-6. Both Samuel and Samantha have the same willingness-to-pay curve (demand curve) for glomblats, which are a pure public good. For each of them, the willingness-to-pay curve is given by WTP = $(10 − Q)$, where Q is the quantity of glomblats.

a. Graph the willingness-to-pay curve for glomblats, for Sam or Samantha.
b. Graph the social willingness-to-pay curve for glomblats, for Sam and Samantha taken together.
c. The supply curve for glomblats is perfectly elastic. The equation for the supply curve is S = $10, which indicates that it is possible to produce any number of glomblats, at a cost of $10 each. What is the socially optimal number of glomblats?

QP16-7. A kind of compact-disc player has a perfectly elastic net-of-tax supply curve: $P_{net} = \$100$. A kind of non-glare picture frame has exactly the same supply curve: $P_{net} = \$100$. A 10-percent commodity tax is imposed in both markets. The elasticity of demand for compact-disc players is 1.0, and the elasticity of demand for non-glare picture frames is 2.0. In which market will the tax create relatively more revenue, and relatively less excess burden?

QP16-8. The net-of-tax supply curve for a kind of blue jeans is perfectly elastic: $P_{net} = \$30$. The demand curve slopes downward, and is given by Q = 100 − P.

a. If there is no tax on this type of blue jeans, what are the equilibrium price and quantity?
b. Now, suppose that a tax of $20 per pair of blue jeans is levied. What happens to the buyers' price, the sellers' price, and the equilibrium quantity?
c. How much tax revenue does the government collect from this tax? How much excess burden is generated? (Remember that the area of a rectangle is equal to the height of the rectangle, multiplied by the base of the rectangle. The area of a triangle is equal to one-half times the base of the triangle times the height of the triangle.)

QP16-9. In the market for gumdrops, the demand is inelastic and the supply is elastic. In the market for grapefruit, the demand is elastic and the supply is inelastic. Assume that a tax of the same size is levied in each of these markets. In which case would most of the burden be borne by buyers, and in which case would most of the burden be borne by sellers?

QP16-10. If you were an adviser to the President, would you advocate a flat income tax? Why or why not? If you are not in favor of a flat tax, do you think that the present income tax has about the correct amount of progressivity? Would you prefer a tax that is more progressive, or less progressive, or about the same? Why?

Chapter 17

The Environment and the Economy

ECONOMICS AND YOU:
WHAT CAN *YOU* DO ABOUT GLOBAL WARMING?

In July of 1995, a blistering heat wave gripped the Midwest, and more than 700 people died in Chicago alone. It's possible that this scorching heat was just an isolated, temporary event. But it's also possible that it could be part of a broad trend toward a hotter Earth. In the last 15 years or so, many scientists have warned that we may be entering a period of global warming, caused by the emission of "greenhouse gases" into the atmosphere. The most important of the greenhouse gases is carbon dioxide, which is released when we burn oil, coal, or other fossil fuels.

According to some predictions, the increased amounts of greenhouse gases could raise average air temperatures by 2.7 degrees Fahrenheit (1.5 degrees Celsius) or even more. This might be good for farmers in Alaska, Russia, and other cold climates, but it could cause big problems for agriculture in regions that are already hot and dry. In addition, the warmer air would lead to warmer water in the oceans, and this could increase the number of hurricanes. The polar ice caps would begin to melt, and this could raise the sea level by more than two feet. This would mean trouble for low-lying areas in Louisiana, Bangladesh, and elsewhere.

Of course, we're not at all certain about whether the earth will heat up so much. The science of climatology is still very new, and computer models of climate are highly controversial.

But let's say that we can put the uncertainty aside. What if we were absolutely convinced that global warming is occurring, and that it will cause catastrophic changes. What would *you* do about it?

In order to slow the process of global warming, it will be necessary to reduce the amount of carbon dioxide that gets spewed into the air. So, you could stop driving your car. And you could move into a tent, so that you wouldn't use any energy to heat or air condition your "home". But even if you were to take these extreme actions, you would only reduce the total amount of carbon dioxide going into the air by a fraction of one-millionth of one percent.

Clearly, no single person can do very much to solve the problem of global warming. A problem like global warming can only be addressed if we take *collective* action. People and governments will need to work together.

In this chapter, we will learn the economic approach to thinking about air pollution, water pollution, and other environmental problems. With this knowledge in hand, we'll begin to think about policies for reducing pollution.

.

THE ECONOMICS OF POLLUTION

Environmental problems occur as a result of a huge variety of human activities, and the dimensions of the problems can be staggering.

Every day, pollutants are sprayed into the air by cars, factories, and homes. In the United States in 1997, about *5.5 billion tons* of carbon dioxide went into the air. (That's about 20 tons for every person in the country.) The carbon dioxide was joined by about 87.5 million tons of carbon monoxide, along with 20 million tons of sulfur dioxide and an additional 24 million tons of nitrogen oxides. In and around the waters of the United States, there were more than 8600 oil spills in 1997. Nationwide, there were nearly 1300 high-priority hazardous waste sites.

Meanwhile, Americans generated about 217 million tons of solid waste, such as paper, yard waste, plastic, metal, and glass. (That's almost a ton per person.) Most of the solid waste went into landfill.

Some people believe that these levels of pollution are leading us down the road to an environmental catastrophe. Others aren't so pessimistic. But nearly everyone agrees that environmental damage is a cause for concern. In this section, we will develop the economic way of thinking about these concerns.

Externalities: The Strange Case of the Missing Market

SmokeBelch, Inc., is a steel producer. In the process of making steel, the firm also pollutes the air. If we look carefully at the decisions made by SmokeBelch, we can begin to understand the economics of environmental pollution.

Labor is one of SmokeBelch's most important inputs. Since SmokeBelch has to pay a wage to its workers, the firm has an incentive to employ the workers efficiently, and to avoid wasting their labor. SmokeBelch also uses coal and electricity. Since the firm has to pay for its coal and electricity, it has an incentive to avoid wasting them. The firm will be better off if it uses coal and electricity wisely.

In each of the cases above, SmokeBelch has an incentive to use scarce resources wisely, because it has to pay for them.

But SmokeBelch also uses one scarce resource for which it does not pay. When the firm spews gunk out of its smokestack, it uses clean air. *Since SmokeBelch doesn't have to pay for the clean air that it uses, it has no reason to conserve clean air. Instead, the firm has every incentive to waste clean air, by sending untreated pollutants into the air.*

Thus, the problem of air pollution can be seen as a problem of a *missing market*. The markets for labor, coal, electricity, and so on, tend to work efficiently. But clean air is wasted, because *there is no market for clean air.*

Market Failure

In this book, we've often talked about the virtues of the private market economy. Competitive markets tend to deliver goods and services very efficiently. Under certain conditions, the private market economy can produce the best outcome for society. But the market system can only do its job when markets exist! Unfortunately, there's no market for clean air, or for clean water, or for quiet streets. Because these markets are missing, the economy tends to be too polluted, too noisy, too crowded. Therefore, we say that pollution is an example of a *market failure*—a situation in which the private market economy will *not* tend to produce the best outcome for society.

Economists have a name for the problems of pollution, noise, and congestion that occur as a result of missing markets: We call them *externalities*. An *externality* occurs when the actions of one person or firm have an effect on another person or firm, and the effect is not directly accounted for by the price system. We use the word "externality", because we are talking about effects that are *external* to the price system.

To understand externalities more fully, let's consider the difference between air pollution and the purchase of a toothbrush at a drugstore. When Paula buys a toothbrush for $2.99, the market does an excellent job. We know that this purchase makes Paula better off. After all, she has the option of *not* paying $2.99. Since she *does* pay $2.99, we know that the toothbrush is worth at least that much to her.

Similarly, the store that sells the toothbrush is better off, or they wouldn't be selling that item. The buyer and the seller are both made better off by the transaction. The market helps both parties to improve their situation voluntarily. We say that the market *internalizes* everything that is important about the transaction.

Unfortunately, this happy outcome doesn't occur in the case of air pollution. When SmokeBelch, Inc., spews pollution into the air, it causes a number of problems for Paula. Her eyes sting, and she gets lots of sinus infections. If she breathes polluted air for many years, she might eventually get emphysema. The grimy air also forces Paula to wash her windows much more often that she otherwise would.

It's clear that Paula has been made worse off by the air pollution. However, she doesn't receive any payment from SmokeBelch, in order to compensate her for her losses. Thus, *the damage done by air pollution is external to the system of markets and prices*. If the market system is left alone, it won't function properly when there is a pollution externality.

The Difference Between Private Costs and Social Costs

Figure 17.1 shows one way of looking at the economic effects of a pollution externality. In the market for steel, there is a downward-sloping demand curve (D), which represents

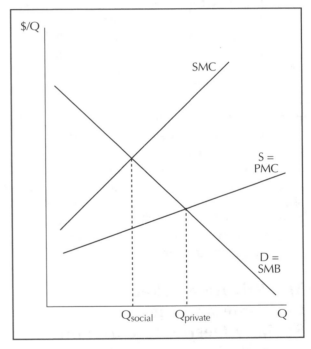

Figure 17.1 The Private Market Quantity and the Socially-Optimal Quantity In a Market with an Externality

The demand curve (D) represents the social marginal benefit (SMB) of steel consumption. The supply curve (S) reflects the private marginal costs (PMC) of steel production. However, because of the pollution externality, the true social marginal costs (SMC) are higher. The quantity supplied equals the quantity demanded at $Q_{private}$, which is the private market equilibrium. However, the socially optimal quantity is found at Q_{social}, where the social marginal benefit equals the social marginal cost.

the true social marginal benefits (SMB) of consuming steel. In other words, the demand curve shows all of the benefits of consuming steel, for the entire society.

Figure 17.1 also has an upward-sloping supply curve (S). The supply curve comes from the marginal costs that the steel companies actually have to pay for. Thus, the supply curve depends on the wage rates of workers, the price of coal, the price of electricity, and so on.

The supply curve represents the *private marginal cost (PMC)* of producing steel. But the supply curve leaves out the damage done by pollution: It ignores the poor health suffered by people and animals as a result of breathing the smoke that's belched into the air. The supply curve also ignores the damage to crops and forests from air pollution, and it ignores the fact that fish may die when pollution falls into lakes and streams. Thus, the supply curve doesn't account for all of the costs that *society* incurs when steel is produced.

Because of the pollution, the true *social marginal cost (SMC)* of producing steel is greater than the private marginal cost. This is shown in Figure 17.1: The SMC curve is higher than the PMC curve. The vertical distance between the two curves is the marginal damage (MD) from the air pollution.

The Private-Market Outcome and the Socially Desirable Outcome

What will happen if the private market is left to its own devices? As usual, the private market will find an equilibrium at the quantity where the supply curve crosses the demand curve. This is shown by $Q_{private}$ in Figure 17.1.

If there were no externality, $Q_{private}$ would be the best quantity for society. However, because of the externality, the private market will *not* achieve the best outcome for society. The only way to achieve the best outcome for society is to pay attention to *all* of the costs and benefits. In this case with an externality, the private market for steel takes all of the *benefits* into account, but it ignores some of the social *costs* of producing steel (such as dirty windows, sick lungs, and dead fish).

The quantity of steel that's best for society is Q_{social} in Figure 17.1. At Q_{social}, the *social* marginal benefit of steel production is equal to the *social* marginal cost. Q_{social} is less than $Q_{private}$, which tells us that the private market will produce too much steel. Private markets will tend to produce too much of any good that is associated with a negative externality.

Just about every industrial process involves some pollution. We generate pollution when we make clothes or furniture or medicine. Automobiles create pollution, and so do buses and trains.

Figure 17.1 shows that *the optimal amount of pollution is not zero.* In the figure, even at Q_{social}, the SMC curve is still above the PMC curve. (The vertical distance between the two curves is the amount of extra pollution damage that comes from making one extra unit of steel.) This implies that a world with no pollution is *not* our goal. Instead, our goal is to strike the *correct balance* between the true social marginal costs and social marginal benefits of the goods that we produce and consume. We may find ways to *reduce* the amount of pollution, but it's nearly impossible to cut pollution to zero. A world with no pollution would be a world of incredible poverty.

Here's another way to look at it: If we were to reduce output below Q_{social}, we would have a cleaner world, but we would *not* be better off. Less output does mean less pollution, but it also reduces the amount of goods that can be consumed. When we go below the socially optimal quantity, the pain of giving up those goods is greater than the gain from reducing pollution and the other costs of production. (In other words, when we get below Q_{social}, the social marginal benefit is greater than the social marginal cost.)

Society's Loss from the Pollution Externality

If we don't do anything to fix the externality, we will end up at $Q_{private}$ instead of Q_{social}. What difference does it make? How much worse off will we be, because of the externality?

We can answer this question by looking at Figure 17.2. When we produce more than the optimal quantity, Q_{social}, we produce units for which the social marginal cost (SMC) is greater than the social marginal benefit (SMB). As a result, society is made worse off by *every* unit of output from Q_{social} to $Q_{private}$. Thus, for each unit of output from Q_{social} to $Q_{private}$, the loss is the difference between SMC and SMB. In order to calculate the total loss to society, we add up these losses for all units from Q_{social} to $Q_{private}$. We see from Figure 17.2 that society's total loss is the shaded triangle, BAD.

For a large country like the United States, this social loss is likely to run to the hundreds of billions of dollars per year, unless action is taken to reduce pollution.

Reality Check: Interim Review Questions

IR17-1. We have often emphasized the advantages of private markets. However, pollution externalities are an example of a situation where private markets fail. Can you name another situation in which private markets do not give desirable results?

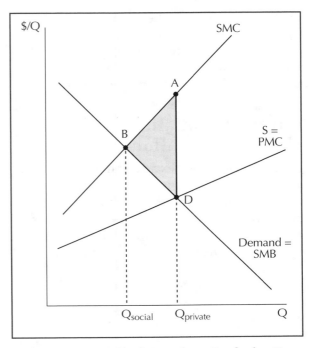

Figure 17.2 Society's Loss from Producing Too Much Output In a Market with an Externality

The socially optimal quantity is Q_{social}. If we produce a quantity that is greater than Q_{social}, the social marginal costs of each additional unit will be greater than the social marginal benefits. This means that society is made worse off by each unit above Q_{social}. If we add up the losses from all units of output between Q_{social} and $Q_{private}$, we get the total of society's loss. This loss is shown graphically by the area of the triangle BAD.

IR17-2. If it were somehow possible to establish a market in clean air, would you expect that we could solve the externality problem?

POLICY APPROACHES TO CONTROLLING POLLUTION

At the start of this chapter, we suggested that collective action will be needed for attacking problems like global warming. This means that governments will be involved. But the economist's instinct is to look for voluntary, private solutions, before turning to government. After all, private markets can do an excellent job of delivering goods and services. Isn't there some way that private actions can solve the problem of externalities?

In the next few paragraphs, we'll see that private solutions may be successful some of the time. However, if the conditions aren't just right, the private market won't do a good job of controlling pollution. Therefore, later in this section, we will also look at government policies that can help to control pollution.

Private Negotiations: The Coase Solution

Judy and Bill live next door to each other in an apartment building. They would get along well, except for one thing. Every night, Bill bakes his own pizza. He puts 27 cloves of garlic into the sauce, and he uses extra-ripe Limburger cheese, lots of anchovies, and sauerkraut. Judy is overwhelmed by the smell.

The situation faced by Judy and Bill is a classic case of an externality. Bill makes Judy worse off, but he doesn't pay her to compensate her for the loss.

Property Right Goes to "Polluter". It's possible that private negotiation could solve the problem. In order to understand this, let's start out by assuming that Bill has the legal right to use the air however he wants. Then, if Judy wants him to bake fewer pizzas, she would have to pay him a bribe. What would happen if Judy were to offer to pay $5 for every day that Bill doesn't bake one of his pizzas? If it's worth more than $5 to Bill to eat pizza (instead of waffles or hot dogs), then he would continue to bake the pizzas. However, if it's worth less than $5 to him to have pizza, he would accept Judy's bribe, and eat something else.

Let's assume that the first pizza in a given week is worth $6.50 to Bill. Since he gets more value from baking the pizza ($6.50) than from accepting Judy's bribe ($5.00), he will go ahead and bake at least one pizza per week.

If Bill is like most people, he has a downward-sloping demand curve for his special pizzas. As it turns out, the second pizza in a week is worth only $5.50. Even though the second pizza has less value for him than does the

first pizza, he will still bake the second one, because its value ($5.50) is greater than Judy's bribe ($5.00).

The third pizza in a week is worth $4.50 to Bill, the fourth is worth $3.50, and so on. For these pizzas, the value of Judy's bribe is greater than the value of the pizza, so he will choose to take the money and not bake a pizza. If the numbers given here are really a good description of Bill's demand curve, he will bake two pizzas per week, and he will accept Judy's bribe on the other five days.

If Judy and Bill can negotiate freely, they should be able to choose the "efficient" payment from her to him. In other words, they should be able to choose the payment that will exactly balance her discomfort with his benefit.

Property Right Goes to "Pollutee". Now, let's assume that Judy has the right to breathe fresh air. In this case, if Bill wants to bake pizzas, he will have to bribe *her*. What if Bill were to offer to pay $5 to Judy for every pizza that he bakes? He will only offer such a bribe if it's worth more than $5 to him to eat pizza (instead of waffles or hot dogs). If Bill's demand curve for pizzas is still the same as it was in the previous section, he would once again bake two pizzas per week.

As before, if Judy and Bill can negotiate freely, they should be able to choose the efficient payment.

The Coase Theorem

We have just stated a remarkable result. If people can negotiate freely, then they should be able to achieve the efficient outcome, regardless of who has the property right to the air! This amazing result is called the *Coase Theorem*, after Ronald H. Coase, who developed the idea in 1960. Coase says that it doesn't matter who gets the property rights— the only important thing is that the property rights must be defined *clearly*.

The Limits of Private Negotiation

There are many examples of private arrangements to protect the environment. For example, some rivers in England and Scotland have been owned privately for 800 years. This has given the owners a strong incentive to preserve the rivers, and they have succeeded in preventing over-fishing and in controlling pollution. In Maine, gangs of lobster fishermen have divided the waters into a set of informal territories. In this way, they create something that is similar to a system of private ownership. In order to enforce the territories, the lobster fishermen cut the lines to the lobster traps of those who would violate the agreements. As a result, the fishermen prevent the over-harvesting of lobster.

In most cases, when externalities are solved through private actions, only a small number of people are involved in the negotiations. But many of our environmental problems involve thousands, or even millions, of people. When an electric power plant sends soot into the air, it can hurt millions of people who live downwind. If we were to use private negotiations to solve the externality problem in a case like this, it will be necessary to have hundreds of costly meetings, and to hire lawyers, mediators, and other middlemen. Costs such as these are called *transaction costs*. In a case involving thousands or millions of people, the transaction costs of internalizing the externality may be very large. It's extremely difficult to get millions of people together to negotiate.

The private solution also has another limitation, which has to do with the *distributional* effects of the outcomes. In one case, Judy pays $5 to Bill, five times per week. In the other case, Bill pays $5 to Judy, twice per week. It's true that Bill ends up baking two pizzas per week in each case, but there's a big difference between Bill paying Judy and Judy paying Bill.

Private negotiation can solve many externality problems, but it can't solve them all. If we are to solve some of the more complex environmental problems, it will be hard to avoid relying on governments.

Controlling Industrial Pollution Through Regulations

If governments want to clean up the environment, they can choose among several policy options. For the most part, the United States government has chosen to rely on regulations. The regulatory approach to pollution control is sometimes called a *command-and-control approach*. The government dictates the details of the pollution-control effort. Unfortunately, this leaves little room for private businesses to develop innovative ways of fighting pollution.

The air-quality standards for industries are set by the Environmental Protection Agency (EPA), which was created by Congress in 1970. One of the most striking things about the EPA standards is that they are very *inflexible*. Here are some important aspects of this inflexibility:

- The law requires the EPA to set the standards *without considering what it might cost to meet the standards*.

- The law prohibits changing the degree of pollution control when the weather changes. Thus, industrial polluters must meet the same emissions standards, regardless of whether it's sunny or rainy, windy or calm.

- On paper, at least, the law applies uniformly throughout the country. This means that the EPA isn't allowed to consider the number of people who are exposed to pollution. With a few exceptions, the EPA isn't allowed to tailor its rules to suit different local situations.

Thus, the EPA simply *can't* balance the marginal costs and marginal benefits of pollution controls, unless it wants to break the law. Throughout this book, we've seen that efficiency is enhanced if we can set the marginal benefits of some activity equal to its marginal costs. Therefore, we expect that the EPA's regulations will *not* be efficient.

In fact, since 1974, the EPA has actually dictated the specific pollution-control devices that must be used by some firms. The problem with this is that it removes the incentive for firms to invent new and better technologies.

Because of the law's inflexibility, the regulatory approach to pollution control has been very inefficient. That is, we have spent a lot more money than we need to have spent, to achieve the amount of pollution control that we have achieved. Still, in many ways, the environment in the United States is cleaner today than it was in 1970. For example, sulfur dioxide emissions into the air were reduced by 17 percent from 1979 to 1988, even though the economy grew by about one-fourth during that period. Over the same period, carbon dioxide pollution fell by 25 percent. The most spectacular success involved reducing the amount of lead in the air. Because of the switch to unleaded gasoline, the emissions of lead were cut from about 221 million tons in 1970 to about 4 million tons in 1997. That's a decrease of more than 98 percent!

The Inefficiency of the Regulatory Approach

If all sources of pollution could be cleaned up for about the same cost, then the command-and-control approach would not be very inefficient. However, the fact is that different sources of pollution can have very different costs of pollution control. For example, one study in St. Louis found that it cost only $4 for a paper-products factory to reduce particulate air pollution by a ton, but it cost *$600* for a brewery to do the same thing.

The regulatory, command-and-control approach to pollution control ignores these cost differences. Regulators just command all firms to achieve the same standard. Let's say that the paper-products factory and the brewery are each required to reduce pollution by one ton. If this happens, then the total amount of pollution would fall by two tons, and the total cost would be $(4 + 600) = $604.

But it's possible to get the same amount of pollution abatement for a much lower cost. Instead of forcing each plant to cut its emissions by *one* ton, what if we could get the paper-products plant to reduce its emissions by *two* tons, while the brewery doesn't cut its emissions at all? In this case, the total amount of pollution would still fall by two tons, just as under the regulatory approach. But the total cost of pollution abatement would be only $(4 + 4) = $8.

Thus, if we could somehow get more of the pollution control to be done by the plant with lower costs for pollution control, we could remove two tons of pollution for $8, instead of $604. That comes to about a 98-percent savings.

How can we get more of the pollution control to be done by the firms for which pollution control is cheapest? The answer lies in *market-oriented approaches to pollution control*, which we discuss below.

Market-Oriented Approaches to Controlling Industrial Pollution

Even though it may be impossible to create an actual market in clean air, market-oriented policies are designed to create something like a market. The idea is to require polluters to pay a financial price when they pollute, because pollution uses our scarce environmental resources.

Pigouvian Taxes. One example of a market-oriented pollution-control strategy occurs when a tax is used to control pollution. A tax that is designed to correct a pollution externality is sometimes called a *Pigouvian tax*, after the British economist Arthur Cecil Pigou.

For the sake of simplicity, let's say that there are only two sources of pollution in the world—the paper-products plant (where pollution control costs $4 per ton) and the brewery (where pollution control costs $600 per ton). What would happen if a Pigouvian tax were levied on air pollution, at a tax rate of $20 per ton? The brewery's managers would then face a choice of whether to clean up some of the air pollution. If the brewery were to clean up one ton of pollution, it would reduce its taxes by $20, but it would also have to pay abatement costs of $600. Therefore, the brewery would lose ($600–$20) = $580 by cleaning up even one ton of pollution. The brewery managers would choose not to clean up.

It's a different story for the paper plant, however. If the paper plant cleans up one ton of pollution, its taxes will fall by $20, but it only has to pay $4 for pollution abatement. Therefore, if the paper plant were to reduce pollution by one ton, it would increase the firm's profit by $(20–4) = $16. If the managers of the power plant are smart, they will choose to clean up at least one ton of pollution. In fact, the paper plant may clean up far more than just one ton of pollution. If the cost of removing a second ton is also $4, then the firm will once again benefit from cleaning up. The paper plant will continue to reduce pollution, as long as its cost of abatement is less than the tax.

This example illustrates two big advantages of Pigouvian taxes, compared with the regulatory approach. First, Pigouvian taxes create incentives for most of the pollution abatement to be done by the firms with the lowest cleanup costs. This is exactly what we need for efficiency. Second, under the regulatory approach to pollution control, there's no incentive for any firm to clean up *more* than the standard. With a pollution tax, however, a firm may reduce pollution far more than it would under the regulatory standard. The firm will continue to reduce pollution, as long as it makes money by doing so.

We've often seen that private markets can deliver goods and services efficiently. Taxes on pollution are efficient because they copy the workings of the market. A Pigouvian tax gives a sort of "price for pollution" to firms, just as other markets also convey information by using prices. A Pigouvian tax also lets the firms make their own decisions, just as firms in other markets make their own decisions. On the other hand, with the command-and-control approach, the government dictates that all firms must meet a fixed standard, regardless of cost.

Marketable Licenses. Unfortunately, it's hard to tell whether a particular Pigouvian tax will reduce pollution by a lot or a little. This is because it's hard to predict what technologies will be used in the clean-up process. Unless the government can predict exactly how firms will respond to the tax, it won't be able to predict how much pollution will be eliminated. Fortunately, there is a different market-oriented strategy that helps to avoid this uncertainty.

Let's say that 2000 tons of gunk are currently being dumped into the air every year. Furthermore, let's say that we decide that the optimal level of gunk emissions is only 1000 tons per year. Now, what would happen if the government were to issue 1000 licenses, each of which gives permission to spew one ton of gunk into the air? If the government can make sure that no one pollutes without having a license, then it can predict with certainty that only 1000 tons of gunk would go into the air. If this license scheme is to be effective, it is important that producers be able to buy and sell the licenses. Therefore, this type of market-oriented mechanism for pollution control is known as a ***marketable-license system***.

If the clean-up technology is inexpensive, then many firms will choose to clean up, rather than buy a license. As a result, the demand for licenses will be small, and the market price of licenses will be low.

On the other hand, if it's relatively expensive to clean up, many firms will decide to buy the licenses, rather than clean up. The demand for licenses will then be strong, and the market price of licenses will be higher.

Pigouvian taxes set the *price* of pollution, and allow firms to adjust the *quantity* of pollution. But marketable licenses set the *quantity* of pollution, and allow the *price* to adjust. Since we're probably more interested in controlling the quantity of pollution, it's worth considering the marketable-license idea.

Pigouvian taxes can raise revenue for the government, and so can marketable licenses. This revenue-raising potential is another big advantage of market-oriented methods for fighting pollution. If a market-oriented method raises revenue, it allows us to reduce our reliance on other taxes (such as income taxes and sales taxes). In Chapter 16, we saw that these other taxes can do a lot of damage to the economy. If we can reduce the damaging taxes, and replace them with market-oriented methods of reducing pollution (which actually improve the economy), we'll be better off.

The Gains from Using a Market-Oriented Strategy. We've shown that we could clean up the environment more cheaply by using a market-oriented strategy to pollution control. But we also want to know whether the savings would be big enough to make much difference.

As it turns out, the savings are probably enormous. One study of sulfur dioxide pollution in Arizona, Colorado, New Mexico, and Utah found that the command-and-control approach costs *4.25 times as much* as an efficient method of cleaning up. In a study of nitrogen dioxide in Chicago, the command-and-control approach was found to be more than *14 times as costly* as the efficient approach. It was also found that the command-and-control approach was *22 times as expensive* as the

efficient approach, for controlling particulate pollution in Philadelphia and the Lower Delaware River Valley.

Our environmental laws also require pollution controls to be constant over time. In other words, firms aren't allowed to use different technologies, depending on the weather conditions. It has been estimated that constant abatement may be *five times as costly* as a strategy in which abatement can be adjusted, depending on the weather forecast.

Overall, a market-oriented strategy would probably allow us to achieve the same amount of environmental quality, while spending at least *one-third less* on pollution control. As we saw in the previous paragraphs, some estimates suggest that the savings might even be a lot more than that.

Since the nation currently spends nearly $200 *billion* per year on pollution abatement, a savings of one-third would be no small matter. We could achieve today's level of environmental quality for $60 billion less every year! Alternatively, we could spend the same amount that we spend now, and we could have a much cleaner environment.

Reality Check: Interim Review Questions

IR17-3. Consider two situations: (a) Your neighbor bothers you by playing his polka records late at night, and (b) Air pollution from electric power plants causes "acid rain" over a large portion of the eastern United States and Canada. Which of these is most likely to be solved through private negotiation?

IR17-4. So far, we have discussed four approaches to pollution control—private negotiation, government regulations, Pigouvian taxes, and marketable licenses. Which of these has the potential to raise revenue for the government?

The Politics and Economics of Pollution Control

If we could get an environment that's just as clean as the one that we have today, and if we could pay $60 billion less for it, then why don't we do it? Why would society *choose* to pay an extra $60 billion every year?

For much of the last 30 years, the environmental debate has been dominated by two groups of people. On one side have been environmentalists, who are sometimes suspicious of market-oriented incentives. On the other side have been business groups, who are sometimes reluctant to have any pollution control at all. The tide is turning, however, as more and more people are *both* eager for a clean environment, *and* eager to do the cleaning as cheaply as possible.

In fact, when the Clean Air Act was amended in 1990, the Federal government took its first big steps toward using market-oriented strategies to clean up industrial pollution. Essentially, the new law sets up a system of marketable licenses. Now, many firms are trading pollution credits for sulfur dioxide, carbon dioxide, and other pollutants. If a firm wants the right to emit pollutants, it will have to pay. It appears that environmental policy is slowly heading in the right direction.

It's important to understand that government must still be involved, regardless of how we decide to fight pollution. If we use Pigouvian taxes, some government agency must collect the taxes. If we use a system of marketable licenses, some government agency must issue the licenses and collect the license fees. More importantly, a government agency must monitor the firms, to make sure that they aren't illegally polluting more than they say they're polluting.

Thus, when we talk about the problems of regulation, we don't mean that the Environmental Protection Agency must be abolished. Instead, if we are to overcome the problems of regulation by adopting market-oriented mechanisms for pollution control, there are two options: Either the EPA must stay on (with a different role), or some other government agency must run the environmental programs.

CURRENT ENVIRONMENTAL PROBLEMS

So far in this chapter, we have looked mostly at the pollution caused by industry. In this section, we look at several other important environmental issues. We begin with the air pollution caused by automobiles. Later, we will look at garbage and recycling, toxic waste and hazardous substances, and endangered species.

Two themes will emerge from our studies. First, it's very common to run into trouble by not taking *incentives* and *human behavior* into account. We have already seen that a market-oriented approach to fighting industrial pollution has some big advantages. The market-oriented approaches are more effective, because they give relatively greater incentives for people to behave in ways that are beneficial to society. If we use command-and-control approaches, we usually provide less of these incentives. This applies in practically every area of environmental economics.

The second theme is that there is much *uncertainty* about the relationship between the environment and the economy. It would be nice if we could learn about the precise effects of economic activities on the environment. It would also be nice if we could place a precise value on a beautiful, clean environment. Unfortunately, we just don't have that kind of precise knowledge. As a result, it's often difficult to develop the correct environmental policies, because we simply don't have as much information as we would like to have. The most we can hope for is to get *close* to the optimal set of policies.

Controlling Air Pollution from Automobiles

Industrial pollution is sometimes called ***stationary-source pollution***, because it comes from sources that don't move. On the other hand, the air pollution from automobiles is sometimes called ***mobile-source pollution***.

At this time, we don't have a cheap technology to measure the amounts of carbon dioxide and other pollutants coming from the tailpipe of each and every automobile. This means that it isn't yet cost-effective to impose a Pigouvian tax directly on the pollution that comes from cars. At some point in the future, it may be possible to monitor the pollution of every car. For now, however, we have to find other policies for controlling automobile pollution.

There are three basic ways to reduce pollution from cars:

- We can build cars that get more miles per gallon;

- We can use cleaner fuels, or cleaner-burning engines;

- We can drive fewer miles.

We will look at each of these strategies in turn.

More Miles Per Gallon. America's efforts to reduce auto pollution have mostly been directed at building cars that would get more miles per gallon. The Federal government has long required the auto companies to meet a standard for *Corporate Average Fuel-Economy* (known as CAFE). By 1994, the standard was 27.5 miles per gallon for cars, and 20.6 miles per gallon for trucks.

The CAFE standards probably *have* helped to reduce the amount of gasoline burned in the U.S. However, the standards are clearly a command-and-control technique. Thus, they are likely to be inefficient. Moreover, the improved fuel-efficiency of cars and trucks was not enough to offset an increase in the number of miles driven. From 1970 to 1996, the number of miles driven by Americans more than doubled, to about 2.5 trillion miles per year. As a result, cars burned about 147 billion gallons of fuel in 1996, which was an increase of nearly 60 percent since 1970.

The American automobile companies are trying to develop a super-efficient car that might get as much as 80 miles per gallon. But it will be years before such a car is available, if it ever is.

Cleaner Fuels and Cleaner Engines. The Clean Air Act Amendments of 1990 also required service stations in some of the dirtiest metropolitan areas to sell "re-formulated gasoline". The new fuel generates about 20 percent less pollution, but it costs about five to ten cents more per gallon.

Many of the cars built before 1982 are much less efficient at burning gasoline than are the more recent models. These older cars are only about a quarter of the nation's automobile fleet, but they create more than half of the exhaust emissions. In an attempt to clean up the "clunkers", the Environmental Protection Agency ordered an inspection and maintenance program for the 83 dirtiest metropolitan areas. Every other year, the owners of vehicles in these areas have to line up for an inspection. If their cars flunk the test, they will be liable for repairs of up to $450.

One innovative idea is to pay people to take their old cars off the road. More than 8000 old cars were scrapped in a pilot program in California. It's estimated that this program reduced pollution by 13 million pounds per year.

Driving Fewer Miles. Americans have long had a love affair with the automobile. The number of miles driven continues to increase, year after year. All else equal, however, it's obvious that we will pollute less if we drive less. With the Clean Air Act amendments of 1990, Congress attempted to discourage driving in certain areas. Unfortunately, this law stuck with the old command-and-control methods in its approach to automobile pollution.

In 1995, a new set of rules began to apply to commuters in the 10 metropolitan areas with the dirtiest air, which include Los Angeles, Milwaukee, Philadelphia, and San Diego. Under the new law, an employer in these areas will have to develop plans to reduce the number of workers who drive to work alone, *if* the employer has 100 or more workers.

The process begins with each area determining the average number of people per car during the rush hour. Houston was found to have 1.17 people per car (which means that most people drive alone). New York City's average was 6.25 people per car, because of its heavy use of subways and buses. Then, each area is required to increase this ratio by 25 percent: Houston is supposed to increase to 1.47 people per car, and New York is supposed to increase to 7.81 people per car.

This command-and-control method has some serious problems. First, it seems strange to require the same percentage change for each of the ten areas. New York already has the highest ratio of commuters per car in the country, and yet it is expected to increase by the same percentage as are all of the other cities. Second, commuting only accounts for one-third of the total miles driven. Non-commute driving is completely unaffected by the law.

Third, the law applies only to businesses with 100 or more employees, even though 88 percent of all workers are employed in smaller establishments. The 100-worker rule can lead to some bizarre incentives. One employer in Houston with 101 employees has promised to lay off two workers, so that the rules would not apply.

In short, this program of "employer trip reduction" will probably have a very small effect on air pollution, but it may lead to major problems for some firms and workers. In some cases, the new law caused such an uproar that its implementation has been delayed.

If we really want to clean up automobile pollution effectively, we would rely on market-oriented methods. The most obvious method would involve increasing the tax on gasoline, so that the price of gasoline would increase. (The price of gasoline is only about one-fourth as high in the United States as it is in Europe.)

A higher price of gasoline would cause drivers to demand more fuel-efficient cars, and it would gradually lead to changes in driving habits. If we were to increase the gasoline tax, we could also reduce our reliance on other types of tax. For better or worse, however, the political opposition to increased gasoline taxes seems very powerful.

Real Economics for Real People 17.1, on p. 412, discusses the problems that accompanied a scheme for reducing automobile pollution in Mexico City.

Garbage and Recycling

Americans generate hundreds of millions of tons of garbage every year. This has the potential to be a mountain of an externality problem.

For many years, the most common way of dealing with the garbage has been to bury it in landfill sites. But in the late 1980s, many communities began to fear that they would run out of landfill space. As a result, communities increasingly began to turn to *recycling programs*, in which newspapers, bottles, and cans are collected by by city employees. The number of cities with curbside collection programs skyrocketed from about 600 in 1989 to about 4000 in 1992, to nearly 9000 in 1996.

The Economics of Recycling. Recycling programs have been fairly successful in reducing the amount of garbage that goes to landfill. However, they haven't been a big *financial* success. The reason is simple: Recycling programs

Real Economics for Real People 17.1:
The Pitfalls of Regulating Air Pollution in Mexico City

Mexico City has some of the dirtiest air in the world. The pollution comes from many sources, but one of the worst offenders is the automobile: The streets are clogged with millions of cars. In an attempt to reduce the number of cars on the streets, the Mexican government adopted a "Day-Without-a-Car" program.

Under the Day-Without-a-Car program, every car in Mexico City was assigned one day of the week on which it couldn't be driven legally. The illegal day of the week depended on the car's license plate number.

The government officials who designed this program had good intentions. They probably hoped that people would join carpools, or ride the bus. If this had happened, there would have been less pollution from cars. But people responded to the regulations in a way that the government officials had not anticipated: Many families decided to buy a second car. (Of course, they had to be careful to buy a car that could be driven on the day when their first car couldn't be driven.) As a result, there may have been an *increase* in the number of miles traveled. Families could now have two cars on the road at the same time.

It's expensive to buy a second car, especially in a relatively poor country like Mexico. Therefore, it isn't surprising that many people bought old used cars. These older cars often caused more pollution than the cars that were in use before the Day-Without-a-Car Program began. Because of this, the driving that was being done in Mexico City became dirtier, on average.

It appears that the Day-Without-a-Car Program increased the number of miles driven, and it also increased the average amount of pollution per mile. If the goal was to reduce air pollution, the program has to be called a spectacular failure.

There is a lesson to be learned from the sad experience of the Day-Without-a-Car Program. It failed because it was designed without understanding the ways in which people would respond. If we are to design successful policies for fighting pollution, we need to think carefully about how consumers and producers will change their behavior in response to the policies. The regulatory approach often fails because it doesn't use market incentives. If the Mexican officials had used the price system, they probably would have been more successful. For example, if they had increased the tax on gasoline, people would have had a clearer incentive to drive less.

lead to rightward shifts in the supply curves of scrap paper, glass, tin, and so on. As we saw in Chapter 4, when the supply curve shifts to the right, the price goes down.

The size of the price decrease will depend on the elasticity of demand. There is evidence that the demand for recyclable products may be very inelastic, which means that prices have fallen *sharply*. For example, Seattle was able to sell its recyclable waste paper for $25 per ton in 1988. By 1993, however, the paper couldn't be sold for a positive price. Instead, it was necessary to pay $25 per ton, in order to get someone to haul the stuff away.

The problem of falling prices doesn't necessarily mean that we should abandon recycling. However, it does mean that local governments will need to be very careful when they estimate the effect of recycling on their budgets.

Solid-Waste Policies for the Future. What should we do about all of our garbage? One alternative is to continue to bury it underground. More landfill sites have opened in the last few years, so that the landfill situation doesn't seem to be quite as serious as it seemed during the 1980s.

Still, if we look farther into the future, we can see a world in which solid-waste disposal becomes a bigger and bigger problem. How will we respond? The answer will depend on how much it's worth to us to control the amount of garbage that goes into landfill. This will involve judgments about benefits and costs. What is the value of avoiding the ugliness of more and more trash dumps? What is the value of avoiding the possibility of groundwater contamination? These questions aren't easy to answer, because we don't have a market to give us a dollar value for environmental protection.

Let's suppose that we look at the benefits and costs, and that we decide to do more to reduce the amount of garbage that goes to landfills. What policies would be best? It appears that *charging by the garbage bag will not do very much* to reduce the amount of garbage

that must be disposed of. (See *Real Economics for Real People 17.2.) Curbside recycling programs appear to be much more effective* in reducing the amount of garbage that goes to landfill.

Of course, we should remember that curbside recycling leads to falling prices, which means that it doesn't necessarily provide a way to balance the budgets of local governments. Here's another problem with curbside recycling: To participate in a curbside recycling program, a household must sort through its recyclable materials. It takes time and effort to recycle, and yet the household doesn't have any direct financial incentive to do so. An even more effective alternative is to have a deposit-and-return program. Under a *deposit-and-return program*, consumers pay a deposit fee up front, when they buy an item (such as a soft-drink can) that could generate solid waste. Then, if the item is returned, the consumer's deposit is refunded. With a deposit-and-return program, consumers have a real incentive to make sure that recyclable materials do get recycled.

Deposit-and-return programs have been adopted in California, Connecticut, Iowa,

---

Real Economics for Real People 17.2: The Seattle Stomp

Seattle is widely acknowledged to be the nation's leader in recycling: Over 40 percent of the city's garbage is recycled. As part of its effort to reduce the amount of garbage that goes to landfill, Seattle also charges its residents for every garbage bag collected. It's believed that over 2000 other cities and towns do the same thing.

How would you respond, if you had to pay for every bag of garbage that's hauled away? For one thing, you would probably engage in the "Seattle Stomp". This means that you would stomp down your garbage, in order to cram as much as possible into a

small number of bags. After all, you have to pay according to the number of *bags* that are collected, not according to the amount of *garbage* that is collected.

It appears that some people also avoid paying for garbage collection by dumping their garbage illegally. When Charlottesville, Virginia, started charging residents by the bag, local businesses began to find that their Dumpsters were full of unidentified garbage. For better or worse, it appears that a pay-per-bag system might not work very well, because people might not substantially reduce the amount of garbage that they generate.

Maine, Massachusetts, Michigan, New York, and Vermont. In these States, the deposit-and-return programs have mostly been restricted to aluminum cans and glass bottles. However, it should be possible to apply deposit-and-return programs to all sorts of recyclable materials.

Toxic Waste and Hazardous Substances

Beach sand is made of crystalline silica. When cancer researchers blasted laboratory rats with crystalline silica, they used doses that were 100 times greater than any worker would be exposed to. Some of the rats got cancer. On this basis, crystalline silica is now classified as a cancer-causing agent by the Occupational Safety and Health Administration.

Since 1980, government agencies have written thousands of regulations to restrict the use of certain chemicals, because the chemicals were shown to cause cancer in rats or mice. In many cases, there is simply no evidence that the chemicals are a threat to people.

America's efforts to deal with toxic waste and hazardous substances have encountered some serious problems. One of the biggest problems is that much of our attention has been focused on substances that we probably shouldn't have worried about at all (such as beach sand). Here is another example: In 1985, Congress passed a law that led governments to spend more than $15 *billion* to remove asbestos insulation from public buildings. Five years later, the EPA announced that the program had been a mistake: Ripping out the insulation releases asbestos fibers into the air. Except in rare cases, we now know that we are better off to leave the asbestos alone.

Superfund: Expensive Cleanups and High Legal Fees. The second major problem with our toxic waste laws and regulations is that they often don't consider costs and benefits. If we ignore costs and benefits, it's not surpris-

ing that we would sometimes make decisions that seem silly.

For example, the EPA has insisted on making toxic waste sites so clean that a child could eat half a teaspoon of dirt from the site each month, for 70 years, and still not get cancer. Many observers believe that these "dirt-eating rules" are much more strict than they need to be. It seems especially odd to invoke the dirt-eating rules for sites that aren't going to be used for residential development. In some cases, the cleanup costs are estimated to have run to over $10 million per acre, even for sites that pose very little health risk. One estimate is that more than $7 *billion* has been spent to comply with rules such as these.

Another problem with America's approach to toxic waste and hazardous materials is that it has encouraged an astonishing number of lawsuits. The "Superfund" law, passed in 1980, was designed to deal with some of the most badly polluted toxic waste sites. But Superfund was primarily a "litigation-based" law, and the lawsuits brought about by Superfund can be very expensive. This is because it's hard to establish the cause of contamination, especially when the contamination was created decades ago. One study looked at four large insurance companies that are involved in Superfund cases. Of the money spent by these companies, 79 percent went to legal fees, 9 percent went to administration, and only 12 percent went to covering liabilities for environmental cleanup.

We've seen that some problems show up again and again when we try to deal with externalities. First, it's often hard to make precise calculations of the damage done by externalities. Second, we have often used ineffective methods of dealing with externality problems. These problems are especially severe in our dealings with toxic wastes and hazardous substances. If we are to improve our policies in the future, we will need:

- more scientific research into the true risks associated with chemicals, and

- a much greater effort to assess the true costs and benefits of various policies.

Endangered Species

What do the Arkansas Fatmucket, the Colorado Squawfish, the Florida Scrub Jay, and the Iowa Pleistocene Snail all have in common? They are all on the list of endangered species, which was begun with passage of the Endangered Species Act of 1973. Most of the species covered by the Endangered Species Act are not very well known. A few, such as the Spotted Owl, have attracted a lot of attention.

It is difficult to make sound policy regarding endangered species. For one thing, we have only a small amount of information about the *costs* of protecting the endangered species. (One estimate suggested that the cost of the "recovery plan" for the Atlantic Green Turtle might be nearly $100 million, but this estimate is controversial.)

We have even less information about the *benefits* of protecting endangered species. Just exactly how much is it worth to society to protect the Socorro Isopod? There are two distinct views of the benefits of species protection. In one view, we think of the loss of other species as a warning sign: If some other species are in trouble, it's a signal that all is not well with the environment, which may have implications for *people*. According to this view, the biggest reason to protect other species is to protect ourselves. Another view is that, because people are the dominant species on the planet, we have a moral, ethical obligation to protect other species. The second of these views would certainly suggest that species protection is extremely important, while the first view would allow more tradeoffs. In this book, it simply isn't possible to decide what is the "correct" view. It's safe to say that species protection will continue to be an extremely controversial subject, because different people can have very different ideas about the value of protecting other species.

One thing does seem clear. The growth in the size of the human population has put pressure on many species. Two thousand years ago, there were only about 250 million people on this planet. By the year 1900, there were about 1.6 *billion*, and there were about 6 *billion* by 1999. By the year 2025, the world's population has been projected to rise to as much as 8 billion, or even more. The species *Homo sapiens* is definitely not on the endangered list.

In *Real Economics for Real People 17.3*, we discuss the plight of the African elephant. After you read the box, you will see that there are things that can be done to protect endangered species, regardless of the size of the human population. However, virtually all of our environmental problems are made more severe by the growth in the number of people. Unless people control their numbers, the outlook is probably fairly bleak for many species. Fortunately, the world's population growth rate is slowing down.

ECONOMICS AND YOU: SHOULD WE FIGHT GLOBAL WARMING? IF SO, HOW?

We began this chapter by discussing the threat of global warming, caused by the build-up of "greenhouse gases" in the upper atmosphere. The first question to ask is whether a large amount of warming will actually occur. It would be good to give a precise answer, but, unfortunately, the correct answer is "maybe".

Over the years, temperatures have fluctuated a great deal. After all, the earth has had periodic ice ages. The last major ice age (which ended about 11,000 years ago) once spread a thick sheet of ice over almost all of what is now Canada, New England, the Middle Atlantic States, and the Great Lakes States.

Average temperatures did increase by a little less than one degree Fahrenheit from 1880 to 1940. However, this increase can't be blamed on greenhouse gases, since most of the build-up of those gases has occurred more recently. Worldwide average temperatures actually *fell* from 1940 to 1970, but they have risen since then. In 1995, the International Panel on Climate Change (a group of 1500 climate experts from 60 nations) issued a report suggesting that global warming is a very real threat. But there is controversy about the size of the threat.

Because of the scientific uncertainty about global warming, there is no "correct" answer about what policies we should undertake. If you are very averse to risk, you'll want to take strong action to reduce greenhouse gases, even though there is uncertainty about the effects of the gases. If you are more willing to take your chances, you might prefer a wait-and-see attitude: During the next 10 years or so, we can study the climate much more closely. If we find that global warming is going to be a really big thing, we can take action.

If a strong effort were to be made to control carbon dioxide and the other greenhouse gases, how would we do it? For one thing, trees act as a "carbon sink". That is, trees actually absorb carbon from the atmosphere. Therefore, efforts should be made to encourage the planting of trees, and to discourage the elimination of forests. Brazil's Amazon region is one of the most heavily forested regions on earth, but the forests are being cut down at an alarming rate. One promising possibility is that the Amazon may become one of the world's foremost fruit-exporting regions. Fruits with exotic names such as acerola, camu camu, and cupuacu can be grown in the Amazon, and some of these fruits are loaded with vitamin C. If the markets for these fruits can be developed, the Amazon region will eventually be a vast fruit basket, and a carbon sink, too.

However, if we want to reduce our emissions of carbon into the atmosphere, we will have to find a way to burn less of the fossil fuels, such as oil, gas, and coal. Throughout this chapter, we've emphasized that command-and-control methods do not work as well as market-oriented methods of controlling pollution. Thus, if we try to reduce the consumption of fossil fuels, we would want to use a market-oriented mechanism, such as a carbon tax. A carbon tax would be placed on the various fossil fuels, in proportion to their carbon content.

What kind of carbon tax would be necessary, in order to stabilize the amount of carbon dioxide in the atmosphere? In all likelihood, it would take a very large tax, on the order of $100 per ton of carbon. A tax of this size would have profound effects. It would certainly raise a lot of revenue—per-haps as much as $200 billion per year in the United States alone. Unless other taxes were cut, it would be hard for the economy to swallow a tax of this magnitude without a reduction in the rate of economic growth.

Coal has a higher carbon content than do oil or natural gas. Consequently, the carbon tax rate on coal would be higher than the rate on oil or gas. This would have a big effect on coal-producing regions. Since China has some of the world's largest reserves of coal, we would expect the Chinese government to be less than enthusiastic about carbon tax proposals. What would happen if all of the world were to adopt a carbon tax, except China? In all likelihood, the Chinese economy would then grow much more rapidly than the other economies in the world. This suggests that international cooperation will be one of the thorniest issues that we face in designing a worldwide carbon tax.

What can you do? Plant a tree. Drive a fuel-efficient car. Don't keep your home or apartment too warm in winter, or too cool in summer. But the actions of isolated individuals are likely to have only a modest effect. The problem of global warming is ultimately a public, collective problem. Success or failure will ride on our ability to reach collective decisions, through national governments and international cooperation.

Chapter Summary

1. Externalities occur when the actions of one person or firm have an effect on another person or firm, and the effect is not directly accounted for by the price system. Externalities include air pollution, water pollution, congestion, noise, solid waste, and toxic waste.

2. There is no market for clean air, or for clean water, or for peace and quiet. Thus, externalities arise in cases where there is a missing market. Externalities are an example of market failure.

3. When the production of a good involves a negative externality, such as air pollution, the true social marginal cost of production is greater than the private marginal cost of pollution. Because of this, the private market will produce a quantity that is greater than the socially-optimal quantity.

4. One way to overcome pollution externalities is through private negotiation. The Coase Theorem states that private negotiations will lead to the same efficient outcome, regardless of whether property rights are held by the "polluter" or the "pollutee". The most important thing is that the property rights be defined clearly.

5. Many modern externality problems have an effect on thousands of people. In cases like these, it will be difficult to solve the problem through private negotiation, because the transaction costs of doing so are high. As a result, there is a role for government in the fight against pollution.

6. For the most part, governments in the United States have tried to deal with pollution by using regulations. This approach has had some successes, because many pollutants have been reduced substantially since 1970. However, this approach is much more costly than necessary, because it ignores the differences in the cost of pollution abatement for different sources of pollution.

7. Economists argue that "market-oriented" methods of reducing pollution will be much more cost-effective than regulations. Market-oriented policies include Pigouvian taxes and marketable licenses. The advantage of these policies is that they cause most of the cleanup to be done by the firms with the lowest cost of cleaning up.

8. The Federal government has tried to reduce the amount of automobile pollution. Its main policy tool has been Corporate Average Fuel Economy standards, which have forced producers to increase the fuel efficiency of their cars and trucks. The government has also mandated that drivers in some areas use "reformulated gasoline". These regulatory policies are limited in their effectiveness, because the number of miles driven has doubled since 1970. If we were to attempt to control the growth in the number of miles driven, an increase in the gasoline tax would be one of the best choices.

9. In order to reduce the amount of garbage that gets buried or burned, governments have started a number of programs. Curbside recycling programs are effective at reducing garbage, and so are the "deposit-and-return" programs that encourage people to return their bottles and cans for recycling. Some communities have begun to charge residents for every bag of garbage. The effectiveness of this policy has been questioned, because people tend to stuff each garbage bag until it is very full (without actually reducing the total amount of garbage). Some people also respond by dumping their waste illegally.

10. Many of the controversies in environmental economics have arisen because we aren't certain about how to value the benefits and costs of cleaning up. In the case of toxic waste dumps, there is disagreement about how safe we need to be. Our regulations have insisted on leaving the toxic waste sites extremely clean, which may have made the cleanup unnecessarily expensive. In the case of endangered species, it is very difficult to put a value on animal species. In the case of global warming, there is serious disagreement among scientists about how high we can expect temperatures to climb. As a result, there is uncertainty about whether to adopt policies that would control the emission of greenhouse gases.

Key Words

Missing Market

Market Failure

Externalities

Coase Theorem

Transaction Costs

Market-Oriented Approaches to Pollution Control

Pigouvian Taxes

Marketable Licenses

Recycling Programs

Common-Property-Resource Problem

Carbon Tax

Questions and Problems

QP17-1. We have emphasized the advantages of market-oriented methods, compared to command-and-control techniques. However, command-and-control techniques might be more appropriate during a very serious environmental emergency. What do you think would be the best policies for dealing with a "killer smog", or a meltdown at a nuclear power plant?

QP17-2. What is the Coase Theorem? Is it relevant to environmental problems?

QP17-3. The highway between Middletown and Centerville is badly congested from 6 a.m. to 9 a.m., and again from 4 p.m. to 7 p.m. (At other times, traffic flows freely on the highway.) When the highway is congested, each additional car creates a negative externality. This is because each additional car slows down all of the other cars. It has been suggested that a Pigouvian tax, in the form of a toll, could be used to encourage more efficient use of the highway.

a. If it doesn't cost anything to collect the toll, what would be the optimal toll at 8 a.m.? What would be the optimal toll at midnight?

b. How would your answer to (a) change, if we recognize that it is costly to collect the tolls?

c. Let's consider two ways of collecting tolls. With the first method, every car stops at a toll booth, in order to complete a cash transaction. With the second method (which has just begun to be used in recent years), every car would be equipped with a bar-coded device, which could be read by an optical scanner. Each car owner would be sent a bill at the end of the month, reflecting the number of times his or her car had travelled the highway. What are the pluses and minuses of using these two methods of collecting tolls?

QP17-4. There are two bridges across the river between Bigtown and Giant City. A toll is collected on one of the bridges, in an effort to deal with the externality of congestion.

However, no toll is collected on the other bridge. At rush hour, traffic flows smoothly on the bridge with the toll, but there are severe traffic jams on the bridge with no toll.

A member of the planning commission proposes that $50 million should be spent to widen the bridge with no toll, in order to deal with the problem of traffic congestion. Can you think of any alternative policies that might be more effective?

QP17-5. The demand curve for gizmos is given by P = $(10–Q). The supply curve is perfectly elastic, and is given by P = $3. Unfortunately, the production of gizmos involves industrial pollution. The marginal damage associated with this pollution is $4 for each additional gizmo. Thus, the true social marginal cost associated with the production of gizmos is $(3+4) = $7.

a. What is the equilibrium quantity that would be produced by the private market?
b. What is the socially-optimal quantity?
c. What is the dollar value of the benefit from correcting the externality? (In order to get the correct answer, you will need to calculate the area of a triangle. See Figure 17.2 for an example.)
d. How would your answer to (b) change if the marginal damage associated with this pollution were actually $7 for each additional gizmo. In this case, the true social marginal cost associated with the production of gizmos would be $(3+7) = $10.

QP17-6. When there is no market for clean air, the firm's opportunity cost of pollution is zero. However, when marketable licenses are used to establish a market for clean air, the firm has a positive opportunity cost for pollution. What does this imply about the firm's incentives to develop new technologies for cleaning up pollution?

QP17-7. Suppose that we desire to reduce water pollution. Discuss the strengths and weaknesses of the following four approaches to achieving this goal:

a. Private negotiation.
b. Regulations mandating that all sources of pollution should meet some fixed standard.
c. Pigouvian taxes.
d. Marketable licenses to pollute.

QP17-8. There are two industries in Environmuck. Each spews a noxious substance called "gunk" into the air. The cost of reducing gunk emissions by one unit is $10 in industry A, and $1 in industry B.

a. It has been decided that gunk emissions must be reduced by 30 units. One way to do this is to require each industry to clean up 15 units of pollution. What would be the total cost of cleaning up 30 units in this way?
b. Another way of cleaning up 30 units of gunk would be for industry B to do all of the cleaning. What is the total cost of cleaning up 30 units in this way?

Index

output effect, 308, 330

own-price elasticity of demand, 112–113, 115–118, 121, 123–124, 129–131, 232

P

patent, 224–226, 236, 243, 248, 250

pay-as-you-go retirement system, 393, 396

payoffs, 266–269

payroll tax, 379–382, 387–388, 393, 395–397

percentage, 12–13, 31, 92, 111–113, 118, 129, 131, 154, 178, 216, 232, 255, 275, 321, 336, 347, 352, 355–356, 375–376, 379, 388, 411

perfect price discrimination, 246–247, 251–252

perfectly elastic, 116, 129, 194, 212, 214, 218, 383–386, 397, 420

perfectly inelastic, 119, 129, 312, 334

personal exemptions, 388–389

Pigouvian tax, 406–407, 410, 419

poverty, 316, 345, 352, 354–365, 394, 402

Present discounted value, 335–339, 343

price ceiling, 76, 80–83, 85, 88–90, 104, 130

price discrimination, 227, 245–247, 250–252, 290–291, 295–297

price elasticity of demand, 110, 112–116, 119, 121, 123, 129–131

price elasticity of supply, 126, 129, 131

price floor, 76, 78–80, 83, 88–89, 123, 131

price makers, 224, 250

price-control law, 76, 78, 83, 88

price-taking firm, 193–194, 199, 219

Prisoner's Dilemma, 267–269, 274–275

product differentiation, 253, 257–260, 262–265, 273–274

production-possibilities frontier, 27–35, 39–40, 96–97

progressive tax, 379, 389, 391, 396

proportion, 12–13, 32–34, 112, 178, 185, 321–322, 330, 347, 350, 373–375, 380, 388, 395, 417

proportional tax, 379, 396

public economics, 2, 10

public goods, 367–371, 373, 395–396

Q

quantity demanded, 42–46, 58–61, 63–64, 66, 68, 71, 73–74, 77–78, 80–81, 84, 90, 110–113, 115–119, 121–123, 129–131, 141, 149, 157, 229, 232, 252, 401

quantity of output, 164–166, 168, 170–174, 178, 185, 187, 198–199, 201, 203, 209, 234, 236, 252

quantity supplied, 53–55, 58–61, 63–64, 66–68, 71, 73–74, 77–78, 80–81, 86, 89–90, 102, 126, 129, 208–209, 218, 238, 401

R

rational, 137, 147, 156, 186

reciprocal, 13, 30

recycling programs, 74–75, 411, 413, 418–419

regressive tax, 379, 396

regulatory lag, 280, 298

rent-control laws, 80–81

rents, 302, 333, 343, 380, 388, 393

returns to scale, 177–180, 185–186

Robinson-Patman Act, 291, 295, 297–298

Rule of 72, 336, 343

Rule of Reason, 292, 294, 298–299

S

shared monopoly, 266, 268, 272

Sherman Act, 289–292, 294, 297–299

short run, 122, 164, 176–177, 185–186, 197, 208–209, 261, 309, 334, 343, 392

short-run shut-down decision, 206, 219

short-run supply curve, 208–209, 218–219

shortage, 60–61, 63–65, 68–69, 73, 80–81, 84–86, 89–90, 340–341, 343

single-price monopoly, 227, 250, 252

slope of a line, 15–16, 135

Social Security, 4, 94, 352, 354, 356, 359, 361, 365, 367–368, 371–372, 374–375, 380, 393–394

Standard Oil Case, 290, 298–299

stationary-source pollution, 410

statutory incidence, 385, 387, 396

strategies, 118, 128, 192, 266, 409–410

structures, 31, 39, 190–193, 239, 253, 275, 283, 302

T

U

V

W

X

Z